Crime and Punishment in America

Crime and Punishment in America

Editor: Judith F. Buncher

Assistant Editor: Mark Henry Lazerson

Facts On File

119 West 57th Street, New York, N.Y. 10019

Crime and Punishment in America

Published by Facts on File, Inc.,
119 West 57th Street, New York, N.Y. 10019.

Library of Congress Cataloging in Publication Data
Main entry under title:

Crime and punishment in America.

   Bibliography: p.
   Includes index.
   1. Criminal justice, Administration of--United
States. 2. Crime and criminals--United States.
3. Punishment--United States. I. Buncher,
Judith F. II. Lazerson, Mark Henry. III. Facts
on File, inc., New York.
HV8138.C684   364'.973   78-50359
ISBN 0-87196-355-8

9 8 7 6 5 4 3 2
PRINTED IN THE UNITED STATES OF AMERICA

Contents

THE ENIGMA OF CRIME   7

YOUTH AND THE LAW
   Delinquent Youth: In need of treatment or punishment?   39
   Drug Abuse: Should it be criminal?   59

THE CRIMINAL PROCESS
   The Bill of Rights: Protecting criminals or our liberties?   89
   Crowded Courts: Any room for justice?   119
   Lawyers: Justice only for the rich?   143

SENTENCING
   The Federal Criminal Code: Advance or retreat?   161
   Mandatory Sentences: Punishing the crime or the criminal?   179
   Capital Punishment: Is it cruel or unusual?   205
   Alternative Sentences: Is true restitution possible?   247

THE PENAL SYSTEM
   Behind the Prison Walls: Is there any law or order?   259
   Rehabilitation and Parole: Reform or reinforcement?   277

The Enigma of Crime

Crime is a reflection of society's values. In the Soviet Union selling items for a profit, so-called economic crimes, is harshly punished. Denmark, a society that rarely imprisons criminals, uniformly imprisons its drunken drivers. The United States during Prohibition made alcohol the target of a massive police war. In some primitive communal societies even murder is not considered a serious crime, but merely a dispute between two feuding parties; whereas the pollution of a river, effecting the entire community, represents an attack on the social order.[1]

When Americans consider crime, few think of the 14,000 workers killed annually in work accidents or the 2.2 million permanently or temporarily disabled as a result of accidents and occupational disease each year.[2] Though few younger Americans think of marijuana use as a heinous crime, the sale of marijuana is a serious felony in nearly every state. While police are commonly respected as a symbol of security and safety, the Kerner Commission found that many blacks fear them as perpetrators of police brutality.[3] Crime is not as easily categorized as we would like it to be.

Neither are criminals easily demarcated from the rest of society. Criminal behavior is often viewed as limited to certain social classes and ethnic groups. But crime projections predict that 40% of all male children will be arrested at least once during their lifetimes for non-traffic offenses.[4] An even larger percentage, who do not define themselves as criminal, will commit crimes and not be arrested. A study of 1700 New Yorkers, none of whom had an arrest record, revealed that 91% had committed one felony or serious misdemeanor.[5] The group was weighted toward the upper-income bracket and was assured of anonymity. Sixty-four percent of the men and 27% of the women had commited at least one felony for which they could have served state prison terms.

These results correspond with the estimates that few offenders are actually apprehended. The great disparity between those who commit crimes and those who are arrested may partially explain why minority members are over-represented among those arrested and convicted for crimes. Police, in the absence of hard evidence, often form hunches as to which persons are guilty of crimes. Numerous studies have shown that police are more likely to target suspects fitting the stereotyped criminal prototype; often they are blacks.[6] Professor Donald Taft, a criminologist, wrote in 1956:

> "Negroes are more likely to be suspected of crime than are whites. They are also more likely to be arrested. If the perpetrator of a crime is known to be a Negro the police may arrest all Negroes who were near the scene—a procedure they would rarely dare to follow with whites."[7]

While certain prejudicial screening techniques and discretionary judgments of police officers and prosecutors might explain who gets arrested and prosecuted, they do not explain why crime occurs in the first place. Putting to the side the problems of white collar crime, which according to the President's Commission on Law Enforcement and the Administration of Justice, probably cause economic losses "far greater than those caused by the three index crimes against property," the question why crimes of violence and personal theft are so common still lingers.[8] The Federal Bureau of Investigation's statistics report a 1976 crime rate 76.2% above that of 1967.

Observers who take the long view would reject the claim that the crime rate is accelerating. Norval Morris and Gordon Hawkins, after having reviewed crime statistics for the last 100 years, wrote that "Rates of murder, non-negligent homicide, rape and assault have all appreciably declined."[9] If the crime statistics of the last decades of the 1800's, should be eyed warily so should the contemporary ones. Between 1960 and 1961, major crimes increased in Chicago by 83%, chiefly because of a new police chief who changed reporting techniques.[10] Inflation of prices, according to one observer, accounts for more than 50% of the increase in the property crime index; the F.B.I. only reports those thefts involving more than $50.[11] On the other hand, many crimes go unreported. The President's Commission on the Causes and Prevention of Violence stated that for each rape reported there are three and one-half unreported, and for each reported robbery, one and a half unreported.[12]

Even if one searches only the official statistics there are glaring contradictions. The Law Enforcement Assistance Administration's statistics in 1974 and 1975 revealed no significant increase in crime; the Uniform Crime Report, released by the F.B.I., reported 16.7% increase in 1974, and 8.9% in 1975.[13]

Public perception of crime, though perhaps unduly influenced by media images, might prove to be a better indicator of the severity of crime. A recent Gallup Poll reports that fear of crime has dropped for the first time in ten years.[14] Still, the pervasiveness of fear is startling. Forty-five percent feel "unsafe within a mile" of their homes and 15% feel unsafe within their homes. Furthermore, the reduction in fear is not uniform throughout the country: it is mostly centered in urban areas that have suffered 10 years of spiraling crime rates. Americans in rural areas and small towns, on the other hand, registered a belief that crime has increased in their neighborhoods. This perception is reflected in F.B.I. statistics for crime in rural areas; a 107.8% increase between 1967 and 1976. It appears that as developers transform rolling pasture land into surburban sprawl, and family farms into shopping malls, the social controls of rural areas begin to fade. Exactly what elements of social life affect crime are not really known. Despite massive expenditures for law enforcement, only a paltry amount is spent on researching the causes of crime.

Some, rejecting social reasons as the root cause of crime, have pointed to biology. Cesare Lombroso, a nineteenth century Italian criminologist, located the criminals by their physiognomy: "In general all criminals have long, large, projecting ears, abundant hair, thin beard, large cheekbones."[15] A more contemporary variant of Lombroso's biological premise is that men with XYY chromosomes are more prone to commit crimes. A study completed in Denmark concluded that while a disproportionate number of XYY chromosome males are among convicted criminals it "may reflect a higher detection rate than a higher rate of commission."[16] Psychological bases for criminality provide the rational kernel for most prison rehabilitation programs. Freud popularized the notion that "guilt was the motor force of crime."[17] Karl Menninger has pointed to child abuse as a cause of crime.[18] However, a recently released book authored by two psychiatrists, argues that empirical research demonstrates no correlation between abuse and violent crime.[19]

Thomas S. Szasz, a psychiatrist, has actively challenged the abnormal offender theory.

"The thesis that the criminal is a sick individual in need of treatment is false. Indeed, it is hardly more than a refurbishing, with new terms, of the main ideas and techniques of the inquisitorial process. . . . [the deviant] is first discredited as a self-responsible human being, and then subjected to humiliating punishment, defined and disguised as treatment."[20]

If biological and psychological relationships are discarded, we are left with social ones. Statistics show a definite correlation between increases in unemployment and prison populations.[21] Prison administrators even base their future housing requirements on unemployment projections.[22] The unemployment connection may help explain the disproportionate numbers of blacks and youth who are arrested, both groups having unemployment rates two to three times the national average. But unemployment is only partially satisfactory as an explanation. Most poor people do not commit crimes while many wealthy ones do.

Causal relationships between drinking and homicides have been established. Marvin Wolfgang's famous Philadelphia studies link alcohol consumption to two-thirds of all murders.[23] However, another popularly held theory, depicting narcotics addiction as a prime cause of crime, is weakened by the observation that many apprehended drug addicts have criminal records predating their addiction.[24] In addition, statistics indicating that drug users are more likely to be apprehended than other offenders explain the high proportion of addicts among those arrested.[25]

The use of guns has been cited as another factor in the crime explosion, but the true relationship remains unclear. An evaluation of Massachusetts' new mandatory gun sentencing law—requiring a minimum of a one-year jail term upon conviction for gun possession—produced inconclusive results: Gun law violators are now five times more likely to be imprisoned than under the former law; murder and assault rates have dropped, but the number of armed robberies has remained constant.

LEAA

The Law Enforcement Assistance Administration (LEAA) was established in 1968 to provide some innovative solutions to the perplexing problems of crime. This was to be accomplished through the expenditure of federal funds for crime control and prevention. Ten years and $6 billion later, the Federal Bureau of Investigation's national serious crime index (including rape, murder, and robbery among others) has risen by 75%.

Now the U.S. Justice Department, responsible for administering the LEAA, reportedly favors its dismantling. Officials cite LEAA's allegedly extravagant waste, over-bureaucratization and emphasis on exotic police equipment to reduce crime. Congress, however, opposes eliminating the LEAA for fear that the $600 million the federal government annually provides states and localities for crime projects would disappear. According to the terms of a likely compromise, most of the LEAA funds would be allocated by the Treasury Department in the form of state revenue-sharing. The money would have to be earmarked for crime categories that the LEAA considered of national importance and not for supplanting normal budget items. The only independent role to be retained by LEAA would be the funding of research proposals, which if successful would be assumed by the states.

The LEAA is in many ways a casualty of the era and spirit in which it was conceived. A decade of racial violence, particularly severe in the nation's urban ghettoes, provoked a cry for law and order. The LEAA responded with greater expenditures of funds for traditional enforcement methods rather than addressing itself to a fundamental reexamination of an archaic criminal justice system. Though Congress recognized that successful crime control involved the courts, the prisons, the rehabilitative programs, research, and the entire community—as well as the cop on the beat—most LEAA dollars went toward providing hardware for the police.

Notes

1. Related to Jessica Mitford by Professor Laura Nader, an anthropologist, in Jessica Mitford, *Kind and Usual Punishment* (New York: Alfred A. Knopf, 1973) p. 71.
2. Jeanne M. Stellman & Susan M. Daum, *Work Is Dangerous to Your Health* (New York: Vintage, 1973) p. 3.
3. *Report of the National Advisory Commission on Civil Disorders* (New York: Bantam Books, 1968) p. 302.
4. *Crimes of Violence,* A Staff Report Submitted to the President's Commission on the Causes and Prevention of Violence (Washington, D.C.: Gov't Printing Office, 1969) p. 56.
5. James Wallerstein and C. J. Wylie, "Our Law-Abiding Law-Breakers," in *Probation* (1947), quoted in *Struggle for Justice,* A Report on Crime and Punishment in America, Prepared for the American Friends Service Committee (New York: Hill & Wang, 1971). p. 107.
6. Jerome H. Skolnick, *Justice Without Trial* (New York: John Wiley, 1966) pp. 80–90.
7. Donald Taft, *Criminology,* 3rd ed. (New York: Macmillan, 1956), quoted in Harry Barnes & Negley Teeters, *New Horizons in Criminology,* 3rd ed. (Englewood Cliffs, N.J.: Prentice-Hall, 1959) p. 54.
8. "Crime and Victims in a Free Society," in *Crime and Delinquency,* ed. by Carl A. Bersani (London: Macmillan, 1967) p. 8.
9. Norval Morris & Gordon Hawkins, *The Honest Politician's Guide to Crime Control* (Chicago: University of Chicago Press, 1970) p. 56.
10. Mitford, *supra,* p. 61.
11. Albert D. Biderman: "Social Indicators and Goals," in *Social Indicators,* ed. by Raymond A. Bauer (Cambridge, Mass.: M.I.T. Press, 1966) p. 125.
12. *Crimes of Violence, supra,* p. 19.
13. 63 *American Bar Association Journal* 914 (1977).
14. *The New York Times,* December 18, 1977 p. 45.
15. Marvin E. Wolfgang, "Cesare Lombrose," in *Pioneers in Criminology,* ed. by (London: Stevens & Sons, 1960) pp. 168–225.
16. Virginia Adams, "Causes of Crimes, Maybe," *The New York Times,* December 18, 1977, p. 8.
17. Ernest Jones, *The Life and Work of Sigmund Freud* (New York: Anchor, 1963) p. 334.
18. Karl Menninger, *The Crime of Punishment* (New York: Viking Compass ed., 1969).
19. Samuel Yochelson & Stanton Samenow, *The Criminal Personality,* (New York: Jason Aronson, 1977).
20. Thomas S. Szasz, *Law, Liberty and Psychiatry* (New York: Macmillan, 1963) p. 108.
21. *N.E.P.A. News,* February, 1976 p. 16, quoted in Richard Quinney, *Class, State and Crime* (New York: David McKay, 1977) p. 135.
22. Rob Wilson, "U.S. Prison Population Again Hits New High," *Corrections Magazine,* March, 1977, p. 3.
23. Marvin E. Wolfgang, "A Sociological Analysis of Criminal Homicide," in *The Death Penalty in America,* ed. by Hugo Bedau (Garden City, N.Y.: Anchor, 1967) pp. 74–89.
24. Robert Shellow, "Drug Abuse and Crime: Fact or Fancy," 5 *Contemporary Drug Problems* 131 (1976).
25. *Ibid.*
26. James A. Beha, "And Nobody Can Get You Out," 57 *Boston University Law Review* 96–146; 289–333 (1977).

THE COMMERCIAL APPEAL
Memphis, Tenn., October 2, 1977
'The Criminal Mind'

SOME TRADITIONAL ideas about criminal behavior have been challenged by a recent Rand Corp. study, which suggested, among other things, that early identification and long imprisonment of habitual criminals would do more to protect society from them than rehabilitation, deterrence or prevention.

The study found, for instance, that:

• Such socio-economic factors as broken homes, poverty and criminal behavior by brothers or sisters don't explain the development of a hard-core criminal.

• Criminal behavior declines with age, while the chances for arrest and imprisonment increase.

• Professional criminals don't follow a common pattern of development from their juvenile to adult years, such as increasing their skills, profits and specialization in crime. In fact, diversity in personality and conduct is the more dominant theme

• Along the same line, hardened criminals are more apt to commit crimes alone than with others, do relatively little planning for the crimes they commit, and aren't as influenced by the risks of arrest as they are by the money to be gained in deciding whether to commit a crime.

• They also, in general, don't think anything could have prevented them from starting criminal careers or from returning to crime after release from prison.

These and other findings were presented by the Rand team as suggestions for further study, not as the basis for generalizations about habitual felons or for policy decisions about how to deal with them. The study involved only 49 inmates of a medium-security prison in California.

But, in the context of society's growing concern about hard-core criminality and the "criminal mind" — and that term is an oversimplification — the possible implications of the Rand study deserve wide consideration and, as the researchers urged, further investigative work.

What implications, for instance, should be drawn from the fact that some people probably will become criminals and continue criminal careers regardless of what's done to them short of "incapacitation"? The most common public reaction would be, "Lock them up and throw away the key." But, as the study pointed out, the prior record of a defendant, especially a young one, often doesn't provide sufficient information to determine habitual criminality. Even if it did, serious constitutional questions would be involved in meting out long-term imprisonment on the basis of such a finding for crimes that otherwise wouldn't warrant that punishment.

FOR YEARS criminologists have theorized that rehabilitation would return convicted criminals to society as useful citizens at a much lower cost than extensive imprisonment. That's still a major goal. Experiments in rehabilitation should be continued, especially those that keep youthful offenders out of prison "universities of crime."

But much more knowledge is needed about ways to achieve rehabilitation, deterrence and prevention, about the making of the criminal in all his "diversity," and about how society can protect itself from those who can't or who refuse to honor its laws and values. The Rand study makes an important if preliminary contribution to that need.

The Birmingham News
Birmingham, Ala., May 29, 1977
What Makes A Criminal?

The question of what makes a criminal tick has been one of the consuming passions of our society for many years.

In the absence of an answer to an important question, people very often seize upon the most likely hypothesis and operate upon it as though it were solid fact.

The hypothesis which has been almost unquestioned doctrine is that criminal behavior is a form of mental illness. The causes of the illness has been attributed to parental rejection, socioeconomic deprivation, guilt feelings and so on.

Now comes the result of a seven-year research project, conducted by Dr. Stanton E. Samenow and the late Dr. Samuel Yochelson, which suggests that the prevailing hypothesis is bunk.

According to Samenow, criminal behavior is not a mental illness; giving people education, jobs or money will not reverse criminal behavior.

After working with criminals committed to a mental hospital as insane, Samenow said he discovered that the subjects were not insane at all but simply knew how to play psychiatric games: The criminals told the psychiatrists what the doctors expected to hear.

The criminals, Samenow said, "rejected their parents, schools and society long before the institutions rejected them. They had made a series of choices early in life that had nothing to do with family, neighborhood, race or socioeconomic factors."

According to Samenow, he and Yochelson were able to identify 53 separate thinking patterns that each of their hardcore criminal subjects had in common. A few of these qualities include lying, anger, pride, sentimentality, intolerance of fear and procrastination. Although many people have some of these characteristics, criminals have them to an extreme, the researcher said.

Although this research may not provide us with a pat answer about the genesis of criminal behavior, it should help us get rid of a mistaken view which can only lead to counterproductive strategies.

When all the answers are in, the basis of criminal behavior may not be as mysterious as some would have us believe. Individuals tend to repeat that form of behavior which for them succeeds. If the child gets what he wants by breaking the law and is not punished consistently for his criminal acts, he may draw the conclusion that only suckers obey the law.

The real weakness in our society is the parent who fails to teach a child to distinguish between right and wrong at the earliest age. And that can only be done by the consistent application of loving discipline. Very often when a young offender comes before a court with the first charge against him in the adult criminal justice system, he is the veteran of countless transgressions from early childhood on. The prisons are filled with hardened criminals who had long records as juvenile offenders.

If society could just get many parents to care about the behavior of their children, we would come a long way toward preventing crime. That is assuming, of course, that the parents don't have criminal attitudes themselves.

Finally, this society needs more parents who will take the time and attention not only to punish bad behavior on the part of their children but to reward with praise that behavior which is good for them, good for the family and good for society. The green light as well as the stop sign is needed if children are to have the healthy attitude that they can reach their goals in life through constructive efforts.

Even though the influence of the home is important, however, the individual should always be held accountable for his behavior. One famous criminal, or so the story goes, was asked why he robbed banks. He replied, "Because that's where the money is."

Unfettered by the restraints which most of us acquire at an early age, the criminal may well think in just as direct a pattern of thought. And if those restraints are absent in an adult, the chances of successfully imposing them upon him through some rehabilitation program are not very great.

The Virginian-Pilot
Norfolk, Va., April 15, 1977
The Criminal Burden

For bulk and volume, the 507-page "Goals for Virginia's Criminal Justice System" is less blueprint than mail-order catalog. The authors apparently meant it that way, as a wish-book of commodities for coping with criminality. The choices are almost stupefying, yet the quality of the goods is appealing.

The report, nearly two years in the making, reflects the efforts of three task forces (on courts, police, and corrections) working under a joint committee of the Virginia Council on Criminal Justice and the State Crime Commission. The work was funded by the Federal Law Enforcement Assistance Administration and the State. As a localized refinement of work done by the National Advisory Commission on Criminal Justice Standards and Goals and by the American Bar Association, it is intended to be a resource tool for legislators, law enforcers, courts, and corrections agencies. Whether any of its mass of suggestions is ever put to use will depend on the response of local governments, the governor and the General Assembly.

Some of the study's proposals have failed in the Legislature previously—establishment of judicial nominating commissions and creation of regional jails, to name two—but merit reconsideration. Others may be doomed from the start; the aim of speeding jury trials by leaving all questioning of prospective jurors to the judges may not sit well with the lawyers who dominate the Legislature. Others recognize trends that haven't yet caught on in Virginia: better-paid but college-educated policemen, and greater police use of women, minorities, and civilian personnel. Minor court reforms suggested, including formalizing of plea-bargaining procedures and familiarization of judges with penal institutions, deserve study.

The underlying theme of the report appears to be the development of means for correcting wrongdoers without necessarily filling Virginia's jails and prisons with them. In a time when a prison system that isn't as bad as it has been is gradually improving under massive infusions of tax dollars, alternatives of the sorts presented are worth sober consideration.

Where appropriate, the study suggests, minor offenders could be diverted into noncriminal community programs in lieu of prosecution. Summonses rather than arrests in many misdemeanor cases might ease the crush on local jails. In like vein, more use could be made of nonbail release and bondsmen could be eliminated by letting defendants post token bonds directly with the court.

In treating with felons, the study urges heavier use of probation and parole, substituting community classification teams for the prison system's reception-diagnostic centers, and getting the "maximum appropriate use" out of alternatives to incarceration. While admitting that community-based facilities have proved no more rehabilitative than warehouse prisons, the study poses a choice between building more prisons "at fantastic cost" or developing community programs, utilizing agencies of employment, education, and social welfare, to retrieve salvageable felons. What that plan has going for it is that imprisonment doesn't work any better and costs more.

The study is heavy with bibliography and reflects a high order of scholarship. Visionary as some of its proposals might appear, it is not a work to be lightly regarded so long as crime remains the Number One public worry. In time the shrinkage of the oversized troublesome class of younger males, already in process, and better economic conditions should do more than tough laws and tax money can to diminish threats against civil order. But that day lies in the unforeseeable future. For now, the study may be a helpful guide for speeding its arrival.

The Topeka Daily Capital
Topeka, Kans., April 14, 1977
We plead not guilty

Turkish criminologists are blaming America and other Western nations for the rising crime rate in their country.

For America and the West we plead "Not guilty."

There are criminals in all nations. The very news item which mentions the Turkish suspicions of American movies and television shows, also pays its respects to the Turkish highwayman "a part of Turkish tradition and folklore."

He seems a much more logical criminal model for erring Turkish youths than American gangsters and western bad men.

Surely Turkish children learn about the Arabian Nights tales and Ali Baba's encounter with the "Forty Thieves" long before they ever see gangster movies or TV shows. Istanbul is much closer to the site of Arabian Nights tales than to New York. Besides, our Ironside, Kojak and Mod Squad always get their man.

Every nation has its bad men. Every nation has its tempting spots where there is plenty of cash to tempt them.

Turks should concentrate on bringing up their young people to know right from wrong, and on catching and punishing criminals as a deterrent against crime.

That's what America must do. We have no more business blaming Turkish highwaymen for our crime than Turkey has faulting our TV.

THE LINCOLN STAR
Lincoln, Neb., May 23, 1977
U.S. wears corruption crown

A Swiss public opinion research institute reports that citizens of Switzerland regard the United States and Italy as the two most corrupt countries in the world. Given historic mixed feelings about America, and recent lamentable events, that conclusion does not come as a great shock.

The polling organization, "Scope," asked Swiss citizens to name the nation with the highest level of corruption, according to a recent Sunday supplement story Of those polled, 38% chose the U.S. while 21% said Italy. The young and the unemployed viewed the U.S. as most dishonest while the old and wealthy chose Italy.

Those findings are not surprising.
Ambivalent feelings about the U.S. among those abroad go back as far as the beginning of our short history: the hope of the oppressed yet the bane of the oppressed; moral in official posture yet often hypocritical, immoral and amoral in action; violent yet worth the risk; loved as a people yet hated as individuals (or vice versa). It is not arrogant to suggest that these attitudes are often formed out of envy or disappointment and that exists to this day.

But recently this nation has done much to encourage those who think ill of us: Vietnam — no matter what good intentions we claimed at the outset — the political scandals epitomized by Watergate; the international shenanigans of our multinationals and the CIA relating to the affairs of other governments and the deplorable business ethics exhibited by some of our biggest corporations dealing in international trade.

We have given people cause to believe the worst — and they will, especially when our historic behavior has pushed expectations skyward.

Possibly the worst part of it all is that many Americans tend to excuse much of the conduct by claiming that it is standard — that everybody does it.

But not everybody is rated most corrupt.

The Salt Lake Tribune
Salt Lake City, Utah, January 31, 1977
Crime Causes Still Baffle

From his reading of some 2,500 reports on inmates at Utah State Prison, Thomas R. Harrison, a member of the State Board of Pardons, has decided that "we are approaching this (crime control) from the wrong end." Mr. Harrison is on target.

Crime, he told the Children's Service Society of Utah, starts in early childhood as the result of bad home situations "where children have not been taught the values that make life in a complex society possible."

Crime control, the board member implied, should begin at the source, not with the product.

Mr. Harrison was casting his vote with one of several long-held theories on the origin of criminal activity and how it can be curbed. His statement that 90 percent of the 2,500 inmate reports reflected poor home conditions in early childhood is easy to believe.

But there are hitches which flaw the cause-and-effect theory. Critics are quick to note that while a high percentage of convicted criminals come from depressed areas and deprived homes, there are many more people who grow up under similar circumstances and do not become criminals. Also, crime is increasingly rampant in relatively affluent neighborhoods.

This suggests that the challenge is not so much one of mending broken homes and pumping money into economically depressed areas as it is finding a way of identifying early those individuals predisposed to criminality and discovering what motivates them

A major obstacle to this approach is paucity of knowledge. Why, for instance, does one boy in a family go bad, when two others do not? Why do people who seem to have everyghing cheat and steal to get more? Why will one human kill while another will not?

Mr. Harrison's observation that society is approaching crime control from the wrong end is indeed valid. But the search for fundamental causes, we suspect, will lead past the dreary conditions he blames and into channels of the human psyche as yet barely plumbed.

Roanoke Times & World-News
Roanoke, Va., March 13, 1977
Crime Cause Unknown Anywhere

On the theory that misery loves company, perhaps some comfort can be taken from a scholarly study of world-wide crime. Crime is rising in all countries, even in three which for a while seemed more immune: Japan, West Germany and Israel. So report Sir Leon Radzinowicz, a fellow of Trinity College in Cambridge, England, and Joan King, senior assistant in research at a British Institute of Criminology. (*The Growth of Crime, the International Experience*, Basic Books, New York, $11.95).

These scholars also aren't very sure what to do about it—a finding we think is refreshing. An affliction in the field are the assumptions, arrived at without sufficient evidence, that psychiatrists can cure the criminal; or that crime would drop sharply if society could just be re-arranged to eliminate poverty. The latter view was spread on this page March 3 in an article by David L. Bazelon, chief judge of the U.S. Court of Appeals in Washington. The more careful judgment of these British scholars is:

So far there has been no sign of reversal, even stabilization, in the trends of crime. For the time being we have to live with it and try to contain it. For all its imperfections, the criminal law is designed not merely as a buttress for the privileges of the powerful but as a shield for the elemental human liberties of the poor and weak against the assaults of the strong and the treacherous. In that context the rigour of the law must be seen as an expression of social concern. There is a place for severity of sentence in response to deliberate and callous crime.

Sir Leon and Joan King, of course, do not advocate deliberate inhumanity in the treatment of criminals; their book has several eloquent paragraphs on that point. The sum total of their advice seems to be this: Society should do what it can do—arrest, try and punish—punish humanely but punish.

Applied to Virginia, their advice would urge that the state not be distracted by efforts purporting to "cure" that of which the cause is unknown. A swift and fair criminal justice system, and an array of safe and capacious prisons—these are the certain requirements. Virginia has far enough to go on that prescription before turning to unproved and expensive notions. This international study is further proof of an intriguing thesis: When it comes to crime and punishment, the very top scholars agree with the average man in the street. The confusion comes in between.

The Des Moines Register
Des Moines, Iowa, February 20, 1977
Even in the country

It seems time to mark the unfortunate passing of another tradition in rural America. A survey in Ohio has found that country dwellers have just about stopped leaving their doors unlocked.

Sadly but not surprisingly, farmers and others who live on the land have found that crime is no longer a big-city evil. Even sadder is the realization that friendliness and trust, for so long the hallmarks of country life, are to an increasing number of people a temptation.

The number of rural crimes per 100,000 population reported to the FBI increased about 29 per cent between 1970 and 1974, compared with a 16 per cent corresponding increase for crimes in metropolitan areas during the period.

Rural crimes in Iowa continue to increase, too. The latest figures show an approximate three per cent rise in eight major crimes in 1975 in rural counties. The increase for 1974 (about 25 per cent) was more dramatic, but apparently created in part by markedly better reporting.

Vandalism is not measured by the national or Iowa figures. The Ohio survey indicates (and farmers can verify) that vandalism is the most prevalent criminal action in the country. Probably it is vandalism — committed often but not always by teenagers (about 60 per cent of those arrested for rural vandalism in Ohio in 1973 were under 18) — that directly touches most rural residents.

Regardless of the statistics, it is the locking of doors that tells us when country dwellers have had all they can take. It is an understandable reaction, but we can't help lamenting that it has happened.

The Honolulu Advertiser
Honolulu, Ha., May 19, 1977
What to do about crime?

Civic leader Herbert Cornuelle's talk to the 200 Club's annual luncheon honoring Honolulu police reflected the citizen's concern over crime in American communities, including ours.

He noted the growing number of crimes, the relatively far fewer prosecutions and still fewer jailings. He said that while crime is often laid to poverty and ignorance, only 11 per cent of all families now live below the poverty line compared to 50 per cent in 1920—and that even though education and psychiatric care have increased, the crime rates have increased even more.

FOR HONOLULU last year, Cornuelle quoted and commented on these statistics from the police department:

"For 94,397 actual offenses committed in 1976, there were 5,568 adult convictions and 4,353 juvenile convictions, a total of 9,921 convictions.

"There were 268 adults sent to jail; I don't know how many juveniles went to jail" because of the secrecy of records. "9,921 convictions is 10.5 per cent of the actual offenses; 268 is 0.3 per cent of the actual offenses. Fifty-three per cent of the people arrested in Honolulu between January and December 1976 were repeaters."

Nationwide "two-thirds of all crime is committed by repeaters."

His conclusion: "crime pays."

AS TO WHAT can be done about crime, Cornuelle observed that many liberals are joining conservatives in the view that rehabilitation has largely failed, has had virtually no effect on recidivism.

He offered what he termed as five "modest proposals":

● Reclassify some crimes and reduce case loads of the courts. Hawaii has "made a fine start" on this with the new penal code. Concentrate on fewer crimes—on robberies, rapes, the possession of weapons, assault with injuries and repeat offenses of non-violent crimes.

● Provide "swift, sure justice with milder, more certain punishment for more of us." He favors "statutory minimum sentences (no plea bargaining below the minimum); limited paroles; even-handed justice for both rich and poor, advantaged and disadvantaged.

● Recognize that rehabilitation is voluntary, that it must stem from personal commitment and is "not connected with the term of incarceration." Look at the record and "don't expect the process to produce what it has never produced."

● Expand the present law which provides government insurance to a formal restitution program—victim compensation—and use the 1975 Hawaii amendment regarding restitution or reparations for the victim. Fourteen states now have such programs.

● Strive for more public and citizen involvement in the whole process of dealing with crime and delinquency. Less isolation, less insulation for the process. Monitor and preview and analyze what is happening in Hawaii. The ventilation and open discussion will surely be helpful.

CORNUELLE WAS venting the frustration that so many feel, while simultaneously seeking constructive movement. His thoughtful proposals deserve consideration and public discussion by authorities and laymen alike.

If the focus of the criminal justice system was on major, violent crime; if "certainty of punishment (was accepted as) a stronger deterrent than the severity of punishment;" if rich and poor were treated alike; if rehabilitation was viewed as helpful only to those prisoners who genuinely want it; and if society was especially protected from the repeater who commits most of the crimes (see example just below) — if those become norms, than the system might indeed work more effectively and regain much of the citizen respect it has lost.

Amsterdam News
New York, N.Y., April 16, 1977
It's Not Easy

The New York Times, in its issue of Sunday, April 10, devoted roughly 60 column inches of its hard hitting news columns to a story on crime, the highlight of which was the fact that while every other neighborhood in New York City experienced sharp increases in crime last year, the crime index in Harlem and the South Bronx showed a decided drop.

Having made that statement, the Times reporter proceeded to dig deeply through 60 inches of column space, but not once did he pinpoint the reason why there has been a drop in the crime index in Harlem and the South Bronx.

We think the reporter did a good job of objective reporting, except for one oversight.

But we do not intend to let that oversight slip past.

On the contrary, we are proud to state that the reason the crime index in Harlem and the South Bronx dropped sharply during 1976 was due to the anti-crime war launched at the beginning of the year by the New York Amsterdam News.

We did it with the full cooperation and support of Police Commissioner Codd, the commanding officers and policemen of Manhattan North and all the precincts in Harlem and the South Bronx and the supportive efforts of the Citizens Against Crime in Harlem (CASH) headed by Arthur Barnes of the Urban Coalition and last, but certainly not least, the fair minded and hard working citizens of Harlem and the South Bronx who read the Amsterdam News each week and listens to what it has to say.

We don't like to get into that "We told you so" bit, nor do we like the idea of patting ourselves on the back, but neither are we the type to shrink from credit when credit is due us.

For it is not easy to call on a father, whose son is a drug pusher, to turn his son into the police. But the Amsterdam News did just that and we headlined the fact when some fathers turned their sons in to police.

We called out for an "attitudinal change" among our readers and we explained that when we asked for this attitudinal change, we meant that citizens of our community would no longer look the other way when the law was being violated.

We asked that they stop and identify law breakers and point them out to policemen. And we are proud to say that many of our readers have done just that.

It is not easy to be in the middle of the ghetto and write a front page editorial which says to policemen, both white and Black, that you are the law, and although each day you encounter some of our readers who are lawbreakers, we stand behind you as long as you enforce the law.

It is not easy to do that in a front page editorial in the ghetto. But the Amsterdam News did it and every policeman on his beat in Harlem and the South Bronx knows where the Amsterdam News stands.

It is not easy to be in the ghetto and know that a 12-year old boy who has never had more than $10 of his own in his life is now making $250 a day serving as a courier for dope pushers, and then have that young boy busted.

It is not easy to do this, but the Amsterdam News has done it.

It is not easy to see a misfit policeman who is a disgrace to his Blue uniform, beat a Black youth senseless without cause and then announce to your Black reading public that, although you condemn the acts of that one misguided policeman, you still stand squarely behind law and order and the other men in Blue.

That is not easy to do in the ghetto, but the Amsterdam News has done it.

Finally, it is not easy to do all these things and then have one of the city's most influential newspapers ignore all that you have done, and still continue to do the job in your community that you know has to be done.

That is not easy.

But the Amsterdam News has never sought the easier wrong when the harder right has been available.

It is not easy, but we will continue to go on as we have been going, with the firm conviction that though we may never be given full credit for what we are doing, the crime rate index in our community will continue to go down.

THE BLADE
Toledo, Ohio, January 20, 1977
Downtown Crime In Perspective

THE familiar old bugaboo that downtown Toledo is unsafe to visit because of a supposed high incidence of crime has been neatly punctured by Leslie Barr, president of the Greater Toledo Corp. Skeptical of the current method of reporting crime in the downtown area, he cites persuasive evidence to show that the picture is distorted and that downtown actually is not the high-risk area it is commonly assumed to be.

Statistics can be, and often are, misleading. And the Toledo-Lucas County Criminal Justice Regional Planning Unit, which compiles and releases annual crime rates for the city, admits that the GTC president is right and that its own figures do not represent the true situation. While these show the downtown rate to be the highest by far in the city, they are based on a small permanent downtown population — only about 700 at last count. This automatically inflates the crime rate when the number of actual offenses is compared to the number of residents.

What is ignored, as Mr. Barr properly points out, are the 18,000 workers and more than 2,000 shoppers and other visitors who daily populate the downtown sector. If these were taken into account, the perceived risk of being victimized by criminals would be drastically reduced, at least during the daytime hours, and would be comparable to the least crime-ridden areas of the community. On that basis, GTC studies indicate that virtually all offenses decreased downtown from 1973 to 1975 while they increased elsewhere in the city.

Similarly, there is justification for questioning the unrealistically broad geographical area defined by the RPU as the central business district, the outer fringes of which might more logically be reported separately or included with other districts.

The public's image of downtown as a high-crime sector is, as the GTC report notes, "inextricably linked to the economy of downtown Toledo and can have a substantial impact on the area." This report has performed a public service in helping to dispel some of the myth surrounding crime in the district and to put it in better perspective.

HERALD-JOURNAL
Syracuse, N.Y., March 22, 1977
Deterrence possible

In the "Courses by Newspaper" report printed March 20 in The Herald-American Opinion section, Ernest van den Haag, a psychoanalyst, pointed out:

"One reason the crime rate is currently rising is that so few offenders are punished — less than one per cent of all crimes lead to prison terms — that crime does pay for many people."

In one experiment, van den Haag says the threat of punishment was made believable. Consequently, cheating among participating college students dropped 66 per cent compared with the norm. By contrast, moral exhortation did nothing.

In a statistical analysis of murders over a 35-year span, a University of Chicago professor concluded that "one more execution per year . . . would have probably deterred an average of seven or eight murders per year."

Eighteen thousand die yearly, the identified victims of murder.

* * *

Van den Haag adds this distressing set of facts:

"Between 1960 and 1970, the crime rate (per 100,000 people) rose 144 per cent; the arrest rate did not keep pace; it rose only 31 per cent. And while 117 persons were imprisoned per 100,000 inhabitants in 1960, only 96 were in 1970."

The social scientist who teaches at New York University and the New School for Social Research concluded:

"The decline in punishment occurred in the face of accumulating scientific evidence which shows that swift, certain and reasonably severe punishment can significantly reduce crime rates."

He asks:

"Why, despite rising crime rates, are convictions hard to obtain? Why are courts lenient, despite the fact that 50 per cent of all violent crimes are committed by persons out on probation, parole or bail? One reason is that we have long accepted the generous idea that offenders are misguided or sick and could — and, therefore, should — be rehabilitated rather than punished.

"But no effective ways of rehabilitating offenders have been discovered, either in this country or any other."

* * *

He presents a depressing message. No wonder the General Accounting Office found the U.S. Department of Justice doesn't know really what organized crime is and hasn't, consequently, put together a strategy to fight organized crime after spending more than $80 million in the last 10 years.

With those two sets of conclusions, what is an ordinary community like the Town of Camillus, the City of Syracuse or Onondaga County to expect in the control of the every day variety of street crime — muggings, break-ins, hold-ups?

THE INDIANAPOLIS STAR
Indianapolis, Ind., March 29, 1977
On Poverty And Crime

It is just as illogical to say, simply because some poor people commit crimes, that "poverty causes crime" as it is to say "wealth causes crime" because some rich people swindle, embezzle, accept bribes or evade tax payments. The majority of people, rich and poor, are law-abiding.

This fact has led June Brown Carner, a Detroit News columnist, to ask the public to look into a new proposition. She says, "As the theory that poverty causes crime is being weakened, we should consider the reverse possibility — that crime can cause poverty."

She asserts that crime can and does keep people in poverty by decreasing the legitimate ways to make money. In high-crime areas, she points out, young boys have trouble delivering newspapers because punks beat and rob them. Also, young people in such areas don't have many opportunities for work at national chain stores because they are reluctant to open new outlets there. Further, the price of food in high-crime areas is generally higher than in other locations to compensate for the costs the food stores face in more shoplifting, employe theft and armed robberies.

Miss Garner also points out that selling goods door-to-door which long was one traditional way of young people getting started in life, hardly exists in high-crime sections because most salesmen won't venture where dope is prevalent. Also, most residents in such areas fear to open their doors to strangers, which door-to-door sellers usually are.

"Crime is like a vice that squeezes economic opportunity from an area. It leaves a community drained and helpless."

Miss Garner concludes that no matter how many anti-poverty programs the government begins there will be little success unless there is personal safety in the area involved. "The safety of the people in high-crime areas must be among our top priorities." That's true in Indianapolis as well as in Detroit.

Miss Garner has done good service in asking whether "poverty causes crime" is putting the cart before the horse. There appears to be a better case for holding that crime can cause poverty.

The Kansas City Times
Kansas City, Mo., April 15, 1977
What Price Responsibility?

And the Lord said unto Cain, Where is Abel thy brother? And he said I know not: Am I my brother's keeper?- Genesis 4:9

That scripture verse has become the source of great philosophical debate over the centuries. It is a fine line one walks in deciding whether to take on the implied responsibility of caring for mankind or to shun responsibility for fear of being tagged an intruder.

Such fear of intrusion may be the source of high crime rates in some neighborhoods while the willingness of one to watch after another's brother could be the source of keeping crime low in other areas. In the context of the scripture Cain was not charged with being a bodyguard or watching the household of his brother, Abel. But the inference is clear.

Police for a long time have insisted that neighborhood watches could combat crimes against persons and property. For example, if strangers back a truck up to your neighbor's house while the owners are away then the police should be notified. If the movers produce a valid work order then your neighbors should be glad, not offended, that someone cared enough to investigate.

Screams on the street, gunshots or other disturbances out of the ordinary should not be dismissed and ignored.

In response to a high rate of crimes against persons and property the city is considering the establishment of a reward fund to be used by the Kansas City Police Department in gathering information on violence in the inner city. It is not a pleasant task to ponder what price to place on responsibility and how desperate a situation must be before remuneration is granted.

The purpose of the proposed reward fund is not to cultivate a livelihood for neighborhood busybodies. It is a means of gathering information with the hope of increasing the chances of catching criminals and bringing them to trial.

Beyond the financial incentive, and realizing the natural inclination of people to shun involvement in any scrape with the law, is the somewhat distasteful matter of paying persons to do what is right. But there remains the reality that if man really were his brother's keeper, there would be no need for police . . . or firearms . . . or double-steel door locks . . .

FORT WORTH STAR-TELEGRAM
Fort Worth, Tex., July 11, 1977

It's time to block crime

Citizens of Fort Worth, you're about to get the chance you've been waiting for—the chance to do something about crime.

Crime Blockers, a new program spawned by the Fort Worth Crime Resistance Task Force, gets under way at 7:30 p.m. Tuesday.

In meetings at three high schools—Paschal, Eastern Hills and North Side—persons who want to participate in Crime Blockers will be enlisted. They will be contacted later by a liaison officer to schedule block meetings, at which an effort will be made to sign up all residents of the neighborhood to help in the anti-crime effort.

The Crime Blockers will learn to spot suspicious activities on their streets and report them to team policing units assigned to their neighborhoods.

Mayor Hugh Parmer and Police Chief A. J. Brown announced the new program along with Dr. Paul Stevens, chairman of the crime resistance task force.

Thus, the city government and the police department are firmly committed to the effort.

Four police officers will be assigned to help full time with the effort for its first 45 days.

The success of the program, however, depends primarily on the enthusiasm and dedication with which ordinary citizens respond to this new opportunity to do something about crime.

How about it, people of Fort Worth? Are you ready to block crime?

Then turn out Tuesday night—and in the block meetings to follow—and sign up to be Crime Blockers.

EVENING EXPRESS
Portland, Me., November 5, 1977

VIGILANTES

It's Not Solution

When vandalism, break-ins and other such criminal activities invade a community, local citizens are understandably upset and anxious to combat the problem.

But if those citizens seek a remedy by taking the law into their own hands, the trouble can only be compounded.

Such is potentially the case in Orrington, Maine where a group of volunteers has been patrolling the streets in an effort to halt a wave of lawlessness plaguing the town.

The trouble is some of the volunteers may be a bit too enthusiastic in their efforts to combat crime.

The Penobscot County sheriff complains that some members of the citizen-patrols are close to engaging in vigilante operations rather than merely assisting area law enforcement officers.

The sheriff characterizes these people as "bounty hunters" and he wants them to leave law enforcement up to the professionals.

We agree. Certainly there is a need for citizen involvement in the prevention of crime at the neighborhood level. All citizens should be on the lookout for criminal activity.

But when they see something amiss, the next step is decidedly not to step in and deal directly with offenders. The next step is to notify the authorities.

Anything beyond that takes the law-abiding citizen himself outside of the law.

CASPER STAR-TRIBUNE
Casper, Wyo., April 29, 1977

Fighting crime at home

With crime, as with disease, prevention is better than the cure.

The Casper Police Department, working with local Kiwanis Clubs, has started its "Operation Identification." The department will loan any citizen an electric engraver and a personal serial number to put on all belongings. Included in the kit for citizens are stickers for cars and homes, courtesy Kiwanis, warning, "Stop Thief."

Protecting your valuables costs nothing but a little time — time that can be paid off many times over if the goods are taken, then recovered. Police annually are forced to unload recovered property that cannot be returned to its owners because of lack of proper, positive identification.

And in Casper, theft is the major crime, according to the department's 1976 report. In other towns where the program has been tried, the results have shown that those who engraved and announced it with the stickers were victimized by thieves far less often.

The effort is obviously a step forward in law enforcement for Casper. Citizen appreciation should go to both local Kiwanis clubs. They have generously pledged some $1,500 for equipment and supplies to support the program.

Casper Police Crime Prevention Officer Glenn Crabb will appear on the platform for the next month encouraging the use of the free equipment and supplies, and trying to boost a "Neighborhood Alert" program.

In principle, we like the looks of this program too. What's better than citizens tending to their own property and their neighbors? The old "grass roots" bit, that takes something back into the hands of the citizens.

But the program also has its dangers. Somehow, the idea of block watch groups and suspicion for every stranger who wanders down the street smells a bit of a vigilante if not fascist system. Such a system, if not checked, could effectively trap us inside our homes, afraid to leave for fear of being suspect. A walk at night, into different residential blocks, with or without the family dog, or even aimless biking, might be deterred. It would be a shame. Casper is not, or even remotely near, being out of control as unfortunately many urban cities are and that's what we like about the West.

We are not saying that vigilante rule will occur in Casper. We expect only that the Casper Police Department will not overreact to calls on those who enjoy midnight ambles through the neighborhood, or calls from those residents who suspect everyone of foul play.

Simply — be cautious with our rights, night and day.

The Topeka Daily Capital
Topeka, Kans., June 5, 1977

Preventing crime in rural areas

Crime prevention and detection in rural areas, especially out in the solid farm country of Kansas, is a difficult and frustrating task, with usually understaffed sheriff's departments trying their best to cover hundreds of square miles of isolated homes and communities.

Robbers and thieves occasionally make treks into the country to pick up what they consider easy plums. They rifle homes when the owners are away shopping or working in a distant field; or they steal expensive farm equipment after first disabling the homeowner.

The chances of a sheriff's patrol car cruising by and catching a crook in the act are slim.

So rural law enforcement has come up with a program to help solve the problem: stamped, coded identification on farm machinery, tools and other property. It is similar to projects undertaken in many cities, where residents may have their name or Social Security number engraved on such property as stereos, appliances and other belongings.

The main difference is that the farm identification program would include a computerized list of code numbers, fed into a nationwide system. A farmer would mark each of his items in a specific place known only to himself and the police. Each farmer would have his own number, indicating the state, county and farmer's initial.

Then if a policeman spots a piece of farm machinery he suspects may be stolen, all he has to do is check the identification number on the computer cross-reference.

There is even a provision to mark stored grain with the numbers printed on confetti, which is blown away when the grain is being cleaned for processing.

It promises to be a successful program. But it will work only if rural residents take part in the effort.

The Evening Bulletin

Philadelphia, Pa.,
November 6, 1977

Varied views on 'town watch'

The "town watch" or neighborhood block association in your community probably has brought a lot of people together, knocked down some unfortunate barriers between residents and, in general, made everyone feel safer in their homes and on the streets.

That's what we're told by the people who organized a thousand city blocks in Philadelphia and a growing number of blocks in suburban towns.

So what do you do when a college professor comes along and does a study that says, as far as crime prevention, your town watch and block associations aren't worth the paper last month's community announcements were printed on?

For one thing, you don't pack up your CBs or stop watching your neighbor's house. And then you step back and take a closer look at just what Professor Ezra S. Krendel of the University of Pennsylvania's Wharton School said in his report.

The study was based on interviews with 2,076 persons living in 22 Philadelphia police districts. Few of the people had heard of block groups or town watch groups, which patrol the streets and alert police if they spot a crime or something suspicious.

What can be deduced is that there are plenty of people in our region who have not been exposed to these community action programs. And why not? There are 29,000 Philadelphia blocks that have not been organized, compared to the 1,000 that have.

But to criticize these citizen groups solely on grounds of their low-profile as surrogate police is really to miss a large part of their valuable role in our communities. People may come to their first block meeting out of a concern for rising neighborhood crime. But they also may meet many neighbors for the first time. They'll exchange phone numbers with the latest talk on the street, and they'll probably come away feeling better about the place where they live.

Professor Krendel's study was done to gauge the effectiveness of federal money spent on these community projects. Nearly $2 million has been spent in Philadelphia. Any assessment should weigh the overall contributions made to neighborhoods by "town watch" units and their members.

The Detroit News

Detroit, Mich., May 31, 1977

More police a deterrent to crime

"Once burned, twice shy" is the folk wisdom behind Mayor Young's decision to increase the police force by 14 percent. We couldn't be happier about it.

The city is recruiting 700 police officers to bring Detroit's force to 5,700 — its highest strength — by midsummer.

The mayor is not just avoiding his mistake of last summer. He is challenging criminals in general and gangs in particular. He is warning them that city streets must be free of fear and terror.

Although a bleak financial situation forced Young to lay off 972 officers last summer, the results were disastrous: youth gang rampages in the neighborhoods and the Cobo Hall violence in August.

Wisely, the 700 new officers will be assigned to the streets.

While it is impossible to put police on every street corner, street visibility is a proven deterrent to crime. Increased foot patrols downtown have helped cut downtown crime 50 percent.

The mayor also promises not to neglect the neighborhoods in his crash training program, vowing "equal police protection throughout the city."

Young is giving fair warning to thugs and hoodlums that city streets belong to the people.

Pittsburgh Post-Gazette

Pittsburgh, Pa., February 11, 1977

If Police Desire Cooperation . . .

THERE is general agreement among professionals and lay persons alike in the criminal justice system that the neighborhoods must help fight crime, that there simply can never be enough policemen to do the job by themselves.

That underlines the discouraging element of the delayed release of a state Justice Department report on a 1974 search for killers of a Pittsburgh police officer. State Asst. Atty. Gen. Michael Louik, head of the state's Community Advocate's office here, charged that city and police officials had the report a year and a half ago and have made no plans to avoid similar potentially dangerous racial confrontations since. He cited the police handling of a disturbance at all-black Baxter Middle School in Homewood last October as an example.

In both cases police came into confrontation with community residents not directly involved in the original event.

Without attempting to sort out the rights and wrongs of those controversial affairs, it is discouraging if the police have not established procedures to obviate such dynamite-laden situations in the future, procedures which to succeed would require linkages of understanding with the community. If police are to have the cooperation of level-headed people in neighborhoods to avoid dangerous flareups, they must build an atmosphere in which trust can grow. It isn't enough to complain that loudmouths sometimes dominate community groups. There are plenty of law-abiding citizens with whom contact can be made in more tranquil times.

An atmosphere of trust is hard to accomplish if citizens, whether in black or white neighborhoods, feel the police are ignoring reports calling for improvements in procedures. That only fuels feelings of frustration caused by the police trial board system, an in-house arrangement which seldom does anything but exonerate officers charged with misconduct.

The police department does have community relations officers, but the involvement of the police with the community must go up and down the chain of command, too.

Some years ago community action groups vis-a-vis the police usually were hostile, a platform for charges of "police brutality" and the like. But neighborhoods, both black and white, are coming to realize that fighting the police just for fighting's sake is no way to curb crime. Now community groups, whether formed just to combat crime or for multiple purposes, realize they need to work with the police.

That requires a two-way relationship, one in which the police are willing to understand community feelings as well as to ask the community to understand the problems of the police. And the police must show themselves willing to improve procedures that have deeply angered community feelings and be willing to let the communities know they have acted.

Only in that way can trust be built between neighborhoods and police so they can work together to curb crime.

DAILY NEWS
New York, N.Y., April 16, 1977
GET THE 'ANIMALS!'

We heartily applaud the Transit Authority for at last redeploying its policemen from turnstiles and change booths, and posting 105 additional cops down to the subway platforms and trains, where they will be protecting lives and property.

The order, from Harold Fisher, acting Metropolitan Transportation Authority boss, came none too soon. The straphanger was rapidly becoming an endangered urban species.

Just in the past six weeks, subway crime has ballooned 39%, compared to the same period last year.

Harold Fisher

Added proof of the near-anarchic conditions—if any were needed—came on Thursday. Two subway rats—"animals," Fisher calls them—mugged a 70-year-old Bolivian diplomat in a midtown IND station at 9:40 a.m.

We also heartily second the appeal by Fisher and Mayor Beame for cops and firemen to ride subways and buses in uniform as a crime deterrent. Their presence would greatly reassure the other passengers.

Public transportation is critically important to New York. We must rescue it from the "animals."

THE TENNESSEAN
Nashville, Tenn., April 1, 1977
Blowing Whistle On Crime

JOINING hands with the Metro Police Department is the best means of protection available to the Nashville community.

The department recognized this and made "Join Hands With the Badge" the slogan for a pilot program in East Nashville last fall.

As part of the project, police officers educated residents in an East Nashville neighborhood about the best ways to secure their property. And people have been encouraged to look out for one another's property because joining hands with each other is an integral aspect of community protection.

That program is having its successes, such as the increasing number of persons using a special crime call number. It is not spectacular, but it makes the community safer.

And now, the Metropolitan Police Ladies Auxiliary is making important elements of this project available to the community as a whole.

Members of the auxiliary are setting up exhibits at shopping centers around Nashville and distributing leaflets detailing methods of crime prevention and property protection, such as those used in the East Nashville project.

There will be an exhibit at Harding Mall tomorrow, and others at Rivergate Mall on April 8 and at Old Town Village on April 16.

Joining hands with the badge is the best way to blow the whistle on crime in the community.

AKRON BEACON JOURNAL
Akron, Ohio, October 30, 1977
Helping seniors fight crime

ALL TOO often senior citizens are victims of crimes that might have been prevented if the victims had known how to outsmart those intent on breaking laws.

And if it were not for the fear some senior citizens have of reporting something suspicious or alerting police to a crime in progress, more criminals might be caught on the spot.

The Akron Police Department has devised a comprehensive program that officers hope will address both these problems and free many senior citizens who are now, as Sgt. Hugh Bennett put it, "prisoners of fear." Sgt. Bennett is helping direct the effort.

The program has several key elements: crime prevention clinics; a study by police of crime statistics to determine in which areas of the city the elderly are most vulnerable; an awards program for those who give police tips that lead to arrests; an attempt to organize neighborhood groups to combat crime by working with the police, and identification numbers for senior citizens.

The numbers are available for use by those who fear having their names on a police report when they tell the police about a crime.

The police have set a goal of reducing crimes against senior citizens by 25 percent in two years.

More than 1,600 senior citizens signed up for the new program at locations throughout the city last weekend. Police now plan to visit senior citizen centers, churches, Akron Metropolitan Housing Authority apartment buildings and other places where seniors congregate to enlist more participants.

Anyone 55 or older is eligible. It is a unique opportunity for seniors to take the initiative in the fight against crime.

St. Louis Globe-Democrat
St. Louis, Mo., February 17, 1977
Fighting Crime Made Easier

The average citizen can play a vital role in helping to solve crime. Many law enforcement officials admit police can't do the job alone. They gratefully acknowledge that citizens who alert police about suspicious activities and provide other information are rendering a valuable assistance in the never-ending fight on crime.

The Crime Blocker program in St. Louis County recently brought home this fact in a big way. January was a record month for the number of telephone calls with information from individuals participating in the program.

Sometimes one such call can go a long way. That's all it took to provide the information needed to solve an arson last New Year's Eve at Jury Elementary School in the north county. Damage at the school exceeded $21,000.

The tip also paid a handsome bonus as investigating detectives arrested five suspects that led to cleaning up 47 other arson cases in the area. Information from three callers also resulted in arrests in other cases.

January, 1977, is but one of the proud chapters in the county's Crime Blocker program that was inaugurated two years ago. Spurred by this fine performance the county's Bureau of Police Community Relations is urging other citizens to join the program in an effort to make life safer and happier for everyone but the criminals.

Post-Tribune
Gary, Ind., January 31, 1977
Combination of factors key to crime solution

It usually takes a combination of factors to clear up a crime — such, for instance, as luck, coolness, determination, quickness and perseverance.

All of those factors worked together last week in reaching a possible solution of a particularly nasty and annoying crime which had been plaguing women of the area. That was the case of the man who called women telling them to burn off their hair as a means of helping save their husbands who had been rushed to the hospital and of avoiding a similar fate for themselves.

The luck came in the husband of the woman called being beside her when she answered the phone so she knew he was in no hospital. The coolness involved her holding the caller on the line while her husband went next door to call the Indiana Bell Telephone Co. The quickness came in his fast call and the phone company's rapid tapping in of the line and quick calling of the police. The determination came in the telephone company's developing of techniques and in the police following up to catch the man even though he had left the pay phone booth, and the perseverance showed there, too.

We don't know what may happen to the culprit even if his alleged confession of this and other calls holds up. Anyone must obviously be sick to be involved in such an affair. Confinement for mental illness rather than criminal intent seems the more likely development.

But we take our hats off to all those involved in the roundup.

And we sincerely hope that clears up that sort of thing around here for years to come.

FBI REPORTS LESS THAN 1% RISE IN SERIOUS CRIME RATE IN 1976

The Federal Bureau of Investigation Sept. 27, 1977 reported that the rate of serious crime had risen 0.4% in 1976 over the 1975 figure, the smallest increase in four years. According to the bureau, 11,304,800 serious crimes were reported in 1976. The 1976 rate represented a 3.9% decrease in violent crimes. However, that was offset by a 4.9% increase in larceny-theft. Murder decreased 8.4%; robbery, 9.6%; burglary, 5%, and motor vehicle theft, 4.3%. Increases included rape, 1.1%, and aggravated assault, 1.3%. The number of serious crimes per 100,000 population decreased 0.3%. The overall 1976 crime rate was 37% above that of 1972 and 76.2% above that of 1967.

THE ARIZONA REPUBLIC
Phoenix, Ariz., November 13, 1977

THE CRIME wave is subsiding.

From 1960 through 1975, the number of serious crimes rose 232 per cent. Last year, the crime rate was down 4 per cent, the first decline in 16 years; in Phoenix, it was down 6 per cent.

Criminologists say it will be down again next year and the year after that. They expect the decline to continue for years to come.

That's not because the police are any more efficient or the courts any more severe, they say. It's simply a reflection of the fact that, as a nation, we are getting older.

Most crimes, including murder and mayhem, are committed by those between 14 and 21. In 1960, they comprised 15 per cent of the population. By 1975, because of the baby boom that followed World War II, they were 21 per cent. Now the percentage has started to decline. It's expected to drop to 17 per cent in the mid-Eighties. And, if the experts are right, the crime rate will drop with it.

Youngsters are attracted to crime for a variety of reasons. Not the least of them is a perverted appetite for excitement, adventure and violence, which fades as they grow older.

Says Prof. James Q. Wilson of Harvard: "The babies born in the baby boom of the early Fifties are starting to age. Some of the men who helped produce the crime wave of the Sixties are getting too old for that nonsense."

The relationship between youth and crime would appear to indicate that our whole system of justice is upside down.

The fact is, say the criminologists, the youngsters are the ones we have to fear. Half the crimes of violence committed in this country are committed by kids under 18.

Logic seems to dictate that we should throw the book at the kids, and keep them locked up until they reach the age when they are less prone to violence.

There is little chance that the laws will ever be changed to make this possible. Americans have become too permeated with the philosophy of Father Flanagan, who said: "There's no such thing as a bad boy."

They probably will continue to believe this even though the statistics show the country is full of bad boys.

THE TENNESSEAN
Nashville, Tenn., October 9, 1977

CRIME reports this year are generally more encouraging than they have been in some time.

There has been a 14.3% reduction in serious crimes in Nashville for the first eight months of this year compared to the same period last year, according to Metro police reports.

Serious crime for all the nation increased very slightly in 1976 over 1975, according to a recent FBI report. This was the first time in four years there had not been a substantial rise in the nation.

The national increase was only 0.4% and this was due to a rise in population, according to the FBI figures. The number of serious crimes per 100,000 population was down by 0.3%.

There was a 3.9% decrease in violent crimes, but a 4.9% increase in larceny caused the rate of serious crimes to show the slight increase.

Larcenies in Nashville the first eight months of the year were down 26.6% and robberies were off 7%. This helped to account for the 14.3% reduction in serious crimes despite increases in other serious crimes.

A 30.4% increase in rapes was the most alarming trend in the local figures for the first eight months of the year. Aggravated assaults also were up 13.7%, auto thefts 8%, homicides 2.2% and burglaries only 1.1%.

While the general trend is downward, it is obvious that there are certain areas in which the rate of increase is unacceptable.

The decline in "serious" crime cannot be too gratifying as long as the serious crime of rape continues to increase and women feel threatened in their homes or on the streets.

Considerable progress has been made against rape in recent years, but it is clear that more needs to be done.

In spite of the increases of a few crimes, there is much to be pleased about in the statistics. However, the public should not be satisfied until the rate of serious crimes shows a steady decline.

THE KANSAS CITY STAR
Kansas City, Mo., October 3, 1977

Crime and the threat of crime is one of the most distressing problems of contemporary society. Americans are quite rightfully concerned about efforts to combat it.

What are the trends, the causes, who are the principal victims and who is committing the violations? And what is the disposition of the cases—are those who are arrested found guilty and if so do they serve prison sentences?

It may come as a surprise to many Americans but it is impossible to get a comprehensive, complete picture of this nation's criminal activities. By far the most widely publicized statistics are provided annually and quarterly by the FBI. These are based, however, on reports to the bureau from state and local law enforcement agencies. Only seven categories are included, murder, assault, rape, burglary, robbery, motor vehicle theft and larceny.

Other crimes, white-collar offenses among them, are not covered.

This fragmented approach has its critics, especially those who feel a serious effort against crime cannot be waged until the nature and scope of the problem are known. A presidential commission as long as 10 years ago noted that statistics were compiled by a "system that was less than adequate in the days of the horse and buggy."

The Department of Justice is considering the establishment of a special bureau to compile and analyze figures on crime. The statistics, designed to reflect the broad spectrum and details of the criminal dilemma, would be available to the public and the government. Presumably these facts could be the basis for mustering a well-directed assault on crime. Certainly more information would be useful if a full-fledged campaign is to be waged.

FORT WORTH STAR-TELEGRAM
Fort Worth, Tex., October 14, 1977

Statistics can sometimes give a distorted view of a situation.

But even allowing for anticipated distortion the recently released FBI crime statistics for Fort Worth give one the shudders.

Those figures say that for the first six months of this year reported offenses in this city increased by 16 per cent over the corresponding period a year ago.

And while this statistical increase was occurring in Fort Worth overall national crime statisics reflected a 7 per cent decrease in reported offenses.

Although that bare comparison is startling, city police officials say it does not constitute as much of a cause for alarm as it appears to at first glimpse.

They point out that last January Fort Worth began using the same crime reporting guidelines in general use by major cities across the nation. Because of that change, much of the increase is basically statistical.

Crime in Fort Worth, says Police Chief A. J. Brown, has not soared that severely. It's just that it was reported inaccurately under the old system.

Still Brown says he expects this city to end the year with a 25 per cent increase in the crime rate. And that's alarming no matter how you allow for statistical distortion.

Consider the FBI statistics for Fort Worth: murders, up from 33 to 57; rape, up from 80 to 97; aggravated assault, up from 252 to 556; burglary, up from 3,970 to 5,563 and larceny theft, up from 9,019 to 9,173.

All of that can't be merely statistical increase. If it is, the level of criminal activity in Fort Worth over the years must have been considerably higher than most citizens of this city realized.

But, like the police chief said, none of this should be interpreted as an indication that Fort Worth is not a safe place to live. It is one of the safest. Many of the cities that are reporting crime rate decreases this year already had much higher levels of crime than Fort Worth and still have.

However, the statistics should not be dismissed as inconsequential. The citizens of this community should be alarmed by them, as long as that alarm does not translate into panic or a fatalistic acceptance of crime.

What those perhaps distorted statistics should arouse is a determination in every law-abiding member of this community to protect himself against crime and to cooperate with his neighbors, fellow citizens and law enforcement officials in combatting it.

TULSA WORLD
Tulsa, Okla., October 13, 1977

AT FIRST glance, the FBI's new crime statistics show reason for hope.

Reports of serious crime, the agency announced, fell seven per cent during the first six months of 1977, when compared with the same period of 1976.

But the cruel joker in this is that violent offenses against persons — as opposed to crimes against property — remained at the same high level as 1976. And in two of the most common and brutal types of crime — rape and aggravated assault — there were alarming increases. The number of rapes reported was up 8 per cent. Assault reports rose 4 per cent.

Attorney General Griffin B. Bell called the overall statistics "encouraging evidence that the surge of crime in recent years is ebbing."

"However," Mr. Bell added, "the number of violent crimes — those against persons — remained high. We must persist in our efforts to develop more effective deterrents to all crimes."

The Attorney General may be overly optimistic. It is hard to find too much encouragement in figures which show the country is still the most violent of all advanced industrial democracies and that in two important categories, it continues to grow even more violent.

OKLAHOMA CITY TIMES
Oklahoma City, Okla., October 13, 1977

THE crime picture is a fluid one right now, and the latest official figures don't help it to jell any. Is it getting worse or is it getting better? Should we build more prisons, or fewer?

The confusion wasn't relieved any by Wednesday's reports simultaneously telling of a 7 per cent drop in the nation's crime rate in the first half of this year and of a staggering 115 per cent rise in Oklahoma City's homicide rate in the same period.

While figures may not lie, they have to be examined carefully as to their exact application before valid conclusions can be drawn. An increase seems greater, expressed as a percentage, if it stems from a low base. But in this case the total rose from 13 in 1976 to 28 in 1977 for the same period.

The Oklahoma City homicide picture is bound to look even worse for the second half of the year. Police investigated a record total of 13 killings in August alone. And a 150 per cent rise in homicide reports was indicated for September, compared with the same month in 1976. Police fully expect the year-end picture to be pretty grim locally.

Yet, the city's over-all crime index—the total of all kinds of crime—decreased 21 per cent in the first half of 1977. Other cities of like population registered a composite 11 per cent decline.

Even the 7 per cent national drop reported by the FBI has to be taken with a grain of salt. For one thing, the six-month period is too short to justify a conclusion that the country is finally winning the war on crime.

For another, the decline contains some mixed blessings. Murder was down 2 per cent and robbery, 5 per cent. But rape soared 8 per cent and assaults climbed 4 per cent.

Furthermore, while the big cities generally thought of as "crime-ridden" reported lower crime rates, some smaller Sun Belt communities saw a rise in crime. Partially this is explained by last winter's severe weather, which kept criminals and victims alike off the streets in the North but had lesser effect in the South.

Nevertheless, figures can show certain trends, or beginnings of trends. Violent crime declined in the United States last year for the first time in 16 years. Some criminologists linked this to a 39 per cent rise in the prison population over the last four years. They perceived a "lock-'em-up" attitude by judges and parole boards responding to a public clamor stirred up by soaring crime rates.

Inasmuch as most crime is committed by repeaters, putting chronic offenders in prison automatically causes crime rates to drop.

This has created another problem—overcrowded prisons. Several states, including Oklahoma, are under federal court orders to reduce their prison populations to eliminate overcrowding. They have also rushed to erect new prisons to help comply with the orders and to accommodate the expected influx of additional prisoners.

But now some criminologists are predicting crime will continue to decline in the coming years. An improved economy and more public interest in crime-prevention programs are cited as factors.

Most important, however, is a maturing of the population. Most crimes, records show, are committed by teen-agers. As the products of the 1950s' baby boom pass into adulthood, fewer of them will be getting into trouble. Some authorities see a continuing drop into the 1980s.

Will the burning public issue of the future be what to do with empty prison cells?

WORCESTER TELEGRAM.
Worcester, Mass., October 14, 1977

The latest FBI Uniform Crime Reports strongly support the theory that the crime wave has crested and has started to recede. It now looks as if the crime peak was reached in 1973-74. It flattened out in 1975. Now it definitely is on the wane.

According to the new figures — which cover the first six months of this year — serious crime totals are seven per cent below what they were last year for the same six months. This decline follows a six per cent drop in the last three months of last year. So, for at least nine months, the trend has been sharply down.

Some of the declines have been dramatic. Boston reported almost 6,500 fewer crimes in the first half of 1977 than in the first half of 1976. Worcester's crime index total is down from 7,403 to 6,398 for the same periods. New York City's totals are down by 20,000, despite 5,000 fewer police in uniform than in 1975. The big reduction in police power was forced by New York's financial squeeze, but the dire predictions about increased crime did not come true at all.

As penologists and criminologissts study the latest figures, they will try to figure out just why crime is on the wane. Crime prevention activities in various cities deserve some credit. Some good was probably done by some of the various programs funded by the federal Law Enforcement As-sistance Administration. Stiffer sentencing by judges may have played a part.

But the big reason, according to most experts, is demographic. There just are not as many teen-age males on the streets to commit crimes as there were five years ago.

Crime is primarily a youthful enterprise. Eighty-five of every 100 persons arrested for burglary or auto theft are under 25. The drop in the birthrate ovet the past 10 years is beginning to be felt in the ranks of the teenagers. By 1990, according to the statisticians, the number of Americans aged 14 to 25 will decline from 45 million in 1975 to less than 38 million.

Although some may question this theory, it is a fact that, from 1960 to 1975, the years of a big bulge in the teen population, crime went up by 232 per cent. Now that the 1960s baby bust is being felt, crime is off correspondingly.

That may disappoint some theorists who thought they had the answer to crime and how to handle it. It suggests that a certain number of people — expecially young people — in any community are going to commit crime no matter what.

But for the rest of us ordinary folks, it is encouraging to know that our streets and homes are becoming at least a bit safer, whatever the reason.

THE MILWAUKEE JOURNAL
Milwaukee, Wisc., October 21, 1977

The latest FBI crime figures are unlikely to send folks to the hardware store for a new dead bolt lock. The news is heartening, if inconclusive: After more than a decade of record shattering crime years, reported serious crimes decreased 7% in the first half of 1977. Locally, the decrease appeared to be even more dramatic.

In the past, there has been nothing like a new set of FBI stats to arouse fears. Whether the anxiety was always justified is hard to say. There are faults in reporting methods. The figures are only as good as each police department that compiles them; statistics represent not all crime, but that which is reported; they focus on street crime — involving physical violence and theft — and ignore suite crime, the more costly white collar version of felonious conduct.

As for the new report, it remains to be seen whether the lower reported crime rates constitute a trend or a respite similar to the misleading dip in rates in 1972.

If crime actually has declined this year, there are several possible explanations. The proportion of Americans that constitutes the statistically proven highest crime category — youth — is leveling off after whopping increases throughout the 1960s and smaller increases in the early 1970s. More sophisticated security devices have made crime more difficult to commit, and improved law enforcement has made prosecution more successful. In addition, more convicted criminals are behind bars now than ever before, rendering them incapable of committing new crimes.

However, before anyone can confidently predict permanent reductions in street crime, much more has to be accomplished. We need better ways to identify and help criminals — particularly young ones — who can be rehabilitated. We need more professionalism in our criminal justice system. Most of all, we need to concentrate on some of the causes of crime, such as unemployment and conditions of unequal opportunity.

The Seattle Times
Seattle, Wash., October 13, 1977

NOBODY pretends that the Federal Bureau of Investigation's uniform crime reports present a totally accurate picture of serious crime in the United States.

There obviously are flaws and variances in the reporting techniques of the law-enforcement agencies, large and small, from which the bureau prepares its national index. One can only guess at the number of serious crimes that yet go unreported.

Still, there is no substitute for the F.B.I.'s yardstick, and if it is cause for coast-to-coast handwringing when a serious-crime increase is shown, then surely there is good reason for satisfaction in the reports made public yesterday. These show a decrease of 7 per cent in the first six months of 1977, as compared with the first half of 1976.

(Seattle's crime-index total dropped from 19,503 in the first half of 1976 to 18,646 in the comparable period of this year.)

The Wall Street Journal noted recently that a disproportionate number of serious crimes are committed by young people, especially teen-aged males. In coming years there will be fewer of those people around.

Also, there has been a notable decrease in lenient treatment by the courts of hard-core offenders — a practice seen by F.B.I. Director Clarence M. Kelley as a major impediment to progress in the war on crime.

But what is most encouraging, the decline in serious crimes also reflects increased citizen interest in crime prevention. Many cities have cut law violations with formal crime-prevention programs. The Wall Street Journal took note, for instance, of the installation by Seattle police of 75 hidden electronic cameras in selected business places to photograph robberies in progress — a program that cut commercial robberies in this city by 50 per cent since June, 1976.

"By practicing simple crime-resistance measures," Kelley observed in connection with yesterday's report, "citizens in all walks of life can constructively lessen the opportunities for crime in every part of our nation."

The highly publicized federal programs of recent years may have helped, but the key factor in what has been some turning of the tide in the anti-crime war is the increased alertness of the ordinary citizen.

Wisconsin State Journal
Madison, Wisc., October 5, 1977

Some experts are predicting that the crime rate will reverse itself and head down in coming years.

The reason? Some criminologists and police contend that the population is getting older and that maturing populations have less crime.

"The babies born in the baby boom of the early '50s are starting to age," says James Q. Wilson, a well-known criminologist at Harvard University. "Some of the young men who helped produce the crime wave of the '60s are getting too old for that nonsense."

The Wall Street Journal, which recently did a study on the subject, found Prof. James A. Fox, a criminal justice professor at Boston's Northeastern University, agreeing. "We're definitely past the peak," he said.

The statistics seem to bear them out.

Although police statistics are not always the most accurate, the number of violent crimes reported to police — homicide, rape, robbery and aggravated assault — fell 4 percent last year. Property-related crimes — burglary, larceny-theft and auto-theft — stayed about even with 1975 which is heartening because it was the first time these crimes hadn't risen substantially since 1972.

This year, the trend continues. The FBI reports that the seven serious offenses dropped 9 percent during the first quarter of 1977 — the steepest drop since 1958.

The theory that crime is directly related to population age was advanced by the Rand Corp., the California-based think-tank.

Rand researchers found that it probably does more good to impose long prison sentences on young offenders than on habitual offenders when they are older.

"The greatest effect in crime prevented would come from imprisoning the younger, more active offenders, since offense rates appear to decline substantially with age," they said.

Although rehabilitative research should surely continue, evidence seems to be mounting against disillusioning ourselves about the redemptive powers of prisons.

As Professor Wilson has written:

"We know that confining criminals prevents them from harming society, and we have grounds for suspecting that some would-be criminals can be deterred by this confinement of others...Wicked people exist. Nothing avails except to set them apart from innocent people."

Oregon Journal

Portland, Ore., October 11, 1977

It should come as no surprise that statistics show a rise in criminal activities in Portland's suburbs.

Population has been growing steadily upward in towns such as Beaverton, Gresham, Hillsboro and Oregon City, and with population increases, crime increases are certain to follow, even though annually the jump is erratic from county to county in the metro area.

While in absolute numbers, serious crimes are increasing most in Washington County, police officials there believe the rate of increase is actually dropping.

In other words, proportionate to its continuing rise in population, Washington County is looking at a slower growth rate in criminal activity, even though the number of crimes is going up.

While this may sound like playing with numbers, bar graphs and charts, the statistical side of police work has its place. Although sometimes it merely confirms the obvious — criminals are shifting to the suburbs where the action is — the numbers game also shows something else.

The great American suburban dream is spawning many of the problems its dreamers sought to avoid, and crime born of unfulfilled expectations, particularly among suburban youth, is one of those problems.

If anything, it is more likely a resident of the suburbs is going to be hit by crime than a city resident, even though one of the motives for moving to the suburbs is because it's more crime-free than the city.

These are the pressures facing suburban towns, where police forces which had once to deal only with traffic problems now find themselves worrying with the same intensity as any inner city department.

San Jose Mercury

San Jose, Calif., October 14, 1977

San Joseans can take justifiable pride in the fact that serious crime is on the decrease here, according to the Federal Bureau of Investigation.

During the first six months of 1977, serious crime in San Jose was down 12.7 per cent from the same period a year ago. This compares to a nationwide decline of only 7 per cent and drops of 5.6 per cent and 3.8 per cent in San Francisco and Oakland respectively.

There is, however, serious crime and other serious crime. Robbery, burglary and assault may be down, but murder is up in San Jose, and—at least in the last half of the year so far—so is rape and attempted rape. These are facts that should temper municipal pride somewhat.

It is welcome news that the City Council has authorized the hiring of 15 security guards to augment San Jose State University's 13-man campus police force. That action, coupled with intensifed police patrols in the university area, is a proper response to the eight rapes or attempted rapes of women students since July.

San Joseans will have more reason for self-congratulation when all categories of crime, and especially crimes against persons, show a consistent statistical decline.

The Cincinnati Post

Cincinnati, Ohio, January 21, 1977

As reported in our news columns earlier, violent crime in Cincinnati declined 6.85 per cent in 1976, compared to 1975. That is good news indeed.

Burglaries of homes and businesses were down 17 per cent, auto thefts down 16, robberies down 12. Manslaughter and murder were down also, while rape and larceny remained about the same. Only aggravated assaults went up significantly, by 7 per cent.

Of course, the reporting of crimes is an inexact science. Many crimes are not reported to police, out of fear of reprisal or a hopeless sense of what's-the-use. But Sgt. Milton Dills, head of the Crime Prevention Bureau, is right when he said crime figures are a good indicator of year-to-year trends.

Why did crime go down as much in the Queen City last year? That's hard to say with precision. Chief Leistler cited "superior police performance, changing social and economic conditions and awareness by citizens of their personal responsibility for crime prevention."

We can agree with—and endorse—that too.

The Crime Prevention Bureau, Robbery Squad and Community Relations Bureau have spent many hours advising householders and businessmen on how to prevent burglaries. Financial institutions have tightened their security methods and improved their crime-reporting techniques.

Owners of Citizens Band radios have learned better to guard their sets. And Detroit has helped lower auto thefts just by mounting the ignition on the steering wheel, instead of the dashboard. Murders, on the other hand, usually involve family members and close friends (!)—and hand guns.

The drop in crime last year—when the police force underwent layoffs because of city budget cuts—added to the evidence elsewhere (New York City, for example) that police manpower alone doesn't affect crime ups and downs. Rather, the crime index is a function of a broad range of factors including poverty, economic conditions, unemployment levels, social conditions, citizens' attitudes, and the effectiveness of police, courts and corrections.

So while we're glad the crime rate went down last year, the trend is neither necessarily permanent nor self-sustaining. Remember, there were 31,363 serious crimes reported in our city last year. That is 86 a day. Or one for every 14 of our citizens. That's much too much, and we've got to do more than we're doing now to bring it down.

The Burlington Free Press

Burlington, Vt., November 21, 1977

VIOLENT CRIME in Vermont has been rising at an alarming rate in the past decade.

While statistics may be cold comfort to those who have been victimized by criminals, state and local officials should use them as incentives to step up their efforts to curb the incidence of violent crime.

Figures compiled by the attorney general's office show that the state's violent crime rate has outstripped national and regional increases from 1965 to 1976. While the national rate increased 7.5 percent annually and New England's 12.6 percent, the state's rate rose 18 percent a year during that period.

Although the state's crime rate is still lower than the rest of the nation, the gap is steadily narrowing. Only 12 years ago, the national crime rate was 8.7 times that of Vermont; by last year, the national rate was but 3.8 times more than the state's.

The figures no doubt reflect a drastic increase in the state's population and an increase in urbanization. Inadequate police protection also must be blamed, particularly in communities where the size of the police departments has not kept pace with mushrooming growth.

In many cities and towns, undermanned and under-equipped police departments simply are unable to provide adequate protection for the citizenry. Several communities in Chittenden County have failed to respond to the need for more police protection even though it is obvious that departments are overburdened.

Police training programs also should be expanded to expose all officers to the latest investigative techniques. Every patrolman should at least be acquainted with the rudiments of criminal investigation.

The rising crime rate should concern all Vermonters and they must be willing to face up to the hard decisions that must be made if the trend is to be reversed. Adequate police protection can only be purchased at the price of higher taxes.

Unless the people are willing to make a financial commitment to improve and expand their police departments, the crime rate in the state may soar even higher than it is now.

1975-76 statistics

Here are the statistics on reported serious crimes in the City of Cincinnati during 1975 and 1976 and the per cent of increase or decrease:

Crime	1975	1976	% Change
Murders	64	56	− 12.50
Manslaughters	32	17	− 46.87
Forcible rapes	261	263	+ .76
Aggravated assaults	1508	1617	+ 7.22
Robberies	1745	1525	− 12.60
Burglaries	10,378	8543	− 17.68
Larcenies	17,471	17,492	+ .12
Auto thefts	2212	1850	− 16.36
Total	33,671	31,363	− 6.85

Yearly statistics

These are statistics on total reported serious crimes .

Year	Total
1955	7031
1960	9242
1965	15,526
1970	28,862
1971	33,870
1972	31,899
1973	32,428
1974	30,822
1975	33,671
1976	31,363

The Detroit News
Detroit, Mich., October 4, 1977

Crime statistics, much like palm readings, are always subject to various interpretations. The ways of looking at murder rates, like looking at a broken heart-line, are numerous and, at best, only marginally representative.

It is not surprising, therefore, that the Federal Bureau of Investigation's murder rate for the city of Detroit does not jibe with local police counts. The FBI says it has risen slightly, while the police statistics show a whopping 33 percent decrease.

No matter which side we view the crime rates from, we find little solace. At best, the results leave a homicide rate of well over 600 murders per year. Almost two a day. Almost one every 12 hours. And the state in general, thanks in large part to Detroit, still ranks third in per capita violent crimes. Michigan is ranked seventh in population.

Even if the comparisons are made by the same department using the same statistical tools, Detroit does poorly. The FBI's national comparison of major cities showed Detroit to rank third, behind New York and Chicago, in murder rates.

We would readily accept the opportunity to congratulate Mayor Coleman Young and Police Chief William Hart on the decrease in crime, if we could be sure there was one. But if there was the drop that Detroit police claim, it would still only be a decrease from terrible to awful.

We cannot be sure of how the crime rate is faring, so there will be no blessings from us this time. What with the recruiting scandal, the alleged corruption of the police force, the apparent lack of serious interdepartmental discipline and, of course, the fact that this is an election year, we are just a bit suspicious of the police figures.

We will reserve our praise, if no one objects, until more convincing numbers crop up.

The Houston Post
Houston, Tex., October 2, 1977

Until five years ago, the FBI's Uniform Crime Report, tabulating crimes reported by state and local law enforcement agencies, was the pre-eminent source of information on national lawlessness. In most respects it still is. But in 1972 the Law Enforcement Assistance Administration, a branch of the Justice Department, began financing a Census Bureau survey on crime victims. Census personnel interviewed members of 60,000 households and nearly 40,000 businesses every six months to determine if they had experienced various types of crime.

The most startling finding of the survey was the high volume of crime that went unreported—two to five times the amount reported to police. In 1975, for example, the FBI tallied 11,256,600 serious crimes. But the Census Bureau estimated, on the basis of its survey, that 40,483,000 crimes had been committed that year, nearly four times the number compiled by the FBI from police reports. The LEAA-sponsored survey also challenged FBI estimates of a substantial increase in crime between 1974 and 1975. The census survey indicated that there had been little if any percentage increase in violent crimes and most crimes against property if population growth is considered.

The Census Bureau survey was hailed as "a whole new dimension" in developing a national crime profile. Yet the Justice Department is suspending it. The reason: The National Academy of Sciences assessed the survey, at the LEAA's request, and concluded that it contained what acting LEAA administrator James M. H. Gregg calls "serious methodological problems." That is, there were questionable procedures in gathering or evaluating data, or both.

It is not clear to what extent these problems might have affected the reliability of the survey, but Gregg expressed guarded optimism that it would be resumed once they had been worked out. But the survey's continuation may also be threatened by a tight budget. The project costs $6.5 million a year, not a high price to pay for reliable information that would provide a cross check on the FBI's Uniform Crime Report. The survey also had another dimension, one as important as its statistics-gathering function.

The LEAA-sponsored survey, flawed through it may be, has given us valuable new insight into the national crime picture. It has also given us an example of the wide range of crime-related data that could—and should—be developed. Atty. Gen Griffin Bell has proposed the creation of a central Bureau of Criminal Justice Statistics for this purpose. It would combine the work of 17 federal agencies now compiling information on various aspects of the criminal justice system. In addition to raw figures, we need to know more about the circumstances of lawbreaking, its effects on society and society's response. The Justice Department should not let the crime-victim survey become a victim of tight budgets or neglect.

The Times-Picayune
New Orleans, La., February 15, 1977

Crime is one of the most serious problems in this country, and one would think that crime statistics would be accurate and readily available. Not so, says a Justice Department official. "There really is not in this country a fairly good idea of what crime exists," says Ronald L. Gainer.

The outspoken director of the Justice Department's Office of Policy and Planning is not alone in deploring this situation. In fact, some people have proposed that an independent national agency under the Justice Department be created to collect and analyze a wide range of facts about crime, criminals and victims.

Critics of present reporting methods point out that the FBI and the Law Enforcement Assistance Administration (LEAA) collect and report their data in slightly different ways, making correlation of the two statistical sets difficult. The LEAA's poll of citizens to determine how many have been victims of crime fills a gap in the FBI figures but does not reveal who committed the crimes or whether they were arrested or convicted.

Also, the FBI statistics are gleaned from individual police department reports, which may themselves be inaccurate. And the crimes reported are typically street crimes, leaving to the imagination extortion, tax evasion and a wide range of white—collar crimes.

Critics are correct in their demand for more complete and accurate crime statistics. This is far more than a matter of mere curiosity. Enforcement officials must know accurately what crimes are being committed where, by whom and against whom in order to properly deploy their limited resources to protect the public.

However, the critics are on the wrong track with the separate data-gathering agency concept. The last thing this nation needs is another bureaucracy. When this matter is placed before Atty. Gen. Griffin Bell in the next few weeks, he should undertake to standardize and coordinate data and reporting systems of the FBI and the LEAA. If the two agencies need to throw a wider net to get more information, so be it; but this should not require the invention of a new agency.

The Salt Lake Tribune
Salt Lake City, Utah, May 27, 1977

Too much crime in America goes unreported.

If this point wasn't clear before, it certainly should be now from the report this week from the U.S. Census Bureau.

For instance, the Federal Bureau of Investigation reported that during 1975 11,256,600 serious crimes were committed.

By contrast, the Census Bureau survey shows 40,483,000 persons, households, and businesses were victimized that year.

Another big difference is that this week's survey shows crime began leveling off in 1975, almost a year earlier than FBI statistics show.

This finding challenges the conventional view that the nation experienced an unremitting rise in crime between 1974 and 1975. But the significance goes even deeper than that.

Unlike the FBI figures, the Census Bureau found a decline in the rate of robberies against upper-income families and a decrease in the rate for all crimes of violence against males 20 to 24 years old.

What's the reason for such differences? While the FBI gathers data only on crimes that victims report, the Census Bureau bases its survey on two personal interviews a year with a representative national sample of about 60,000 households and 15,000 commercial firms.

Though this enables the Census Bureau to turn up many crimes that have never been reported to lawmen, even its more extensive figures are far from complete. The Census Bureau survey includes only those crimes that victims can and will tell interviewers about. This obviously precludes murders. It also leaves out several types of crimes the FBI includes, and limits interviews to victims who are at least 12 years old.

Until the full extent of crime in America is more accurately known, authorities must necessarily grope in the dark when it comes to determining how many lawmen a given community needs and toward what violations their efforts are best directed.

Clearly, this nation's lawmen and statisticians need to mount a joint effort aimed at producing a better system for reporting crime.

HOUSE JUDICIARY PANEL SHELVES BILL BANNING 'CONCEALABLE' GUNS

The House Judiciary Committee March 2 voted 17–16 to recommit to subcommittee for further consideration a bill that would have banned the sale or manufacture of new "concealable" handguns. Weapons considered "concealable" are pistols less than 8-1/2 inches in length, and revolvers less than 5-3/4 inches long, or with a barrel under 4 inches. Rep. Robert F. Drinan (D, Mass.) said March 2 that the recommittal vote which followed a weekend of intensive lobbying by the National Rifle Association "kills gun control legislation for this session."

On Feb. 24 the committee had voted 18–14 to strengthen a relatively weak gun control bill by incorporating the ban on small handguns—said by its sponsor, Rep. Martin A. Russo (D, Ill.), to apply to about 70% of the handguns currently available in the U.S. Russo argued that the measure would outlaw the guns criminals preferred, while still allowing homeowners to lawfully buy guns for their protection.

The motion to recommit to subcommittee was made by Rep. Thomas F. Railsback (R, Ill.). He said he was not opposed to "reasonable gun control," but that he objected to using size as the sole criterion for banning guns. The Administration and some legislators, citing the use of cheap "Saturday night specials" by criminals, had urged that price should be a criterion in a ban on handguns. Committee chairman Peter W. Rodino (D, N.J.), said March 2 he was "disappointed" with the vote to recommit. He added that Railsback "convinces me of his sincerity," but that changes in the bill could have been offered as amendments on the House floor. NRA lobbyist Richard Corrigan March 2 greeted the recommittal vote as a "great victory" for constitutional rights, terming the bill a "horrible piece of legislation ... diabolically contrived to limit access to firearms." Harlan Carter, also an NRA lobbyist, the same day said: "Gun control is a cop-out. It has no relevancy to crime in this country."

A federal study, in which 7,815 handguns taken by police over a 32-month period were traced, was described Feb. 17 by the Director of the Bureau of Alcohol, Tobacco and Firearms, Rex D. Lee, as furnishing previously unavailable statistical support for gun control. The study found that "Saturday night specials" were used in 45% of street crimes involving guns, because they were cheap and readily concealable. The study also revealed that only 6% of the guns had been reported as stolen to the FBI. Lee noted that 71% of the guns had barrels not more than 3 inches in length.

THE SACRAMENTO BEE

Sacramento, Calif., March 5, 1976

The gun lobby has done it again. It displayed its power just when there was a glimmer of a chance for action this year to cut down on the guns of street crime — the Saturday night special.

The House Judiciary Committee, as ever before, rejected a measure to create a national gun registration program. But last week, for the very first time, it gave approval by an 18-14 margin to a proposal to outlaw the sale, manufacture and importation of the cheap, easily concealed pistols which are a major menace in America.

It was a short-lived victory for advocates of gun control. Progun forces proceeded to buttonhole Judiciary members over the weekend, with the result the bill was returned to subcommittee, and probable death, by a 17-16 vote.

The turnabout is all the more incredible in view of the fact the bill would not impose a total ban. It would apply only to new guns. It would not, mind you, affect private ownership and sale of existing pistols, regardless of size or quality.

Who would be directly affected by ridding the nation of the deadly nuisance of the Saturday night special? Only the criminal — and his victim. According to a nationwide federal study, the small pistol was used in 45 per cent of street crimes in which a gun was involved. In states and cities with strict laws, the vast majority of handguns used in crimes were purchased out of state. In New York City, which has a rigid gun statute, 95 per cent of 2,048 handguns seized after being used in crimes were purchased outside New York State.

The Judiciary Committee would not even clear another bill which did not mention the Saturday night special. The measure called for mandatory sentences for criminals who use guns and such other provisions as a waiting period for sales and police checks of gun purchases.

The simple fact of the matter, as one member observed, is that a number of congressmen, regardless of public opinion, are opposed to effective firearms legislation or, we might add, any gun controls. How many more killings must there be before the lawmakers face up to the vicious trafficking in handguns and stand up to the gun lobby?

Herald American

Syracuse, N.Y., March 4, 1976

The National Rifle Association's most recent success — the burying of the latest gun control bill by the House Judiciary Committee — brings to mind a question that has yet to be answered.

Why does the NRA focus its efforts on fighting laws that would take guns out of the hands of those who shouldn't have them?

Sportsmen and target shooters who have a lawful purpose for owning guns would not be hurt by such legislation.

Instead of opposing responsible gun controls at every turn, the NRA should take the position that restricting the use of guns, hand guns in particular, is to the advantage of the law-abiding gun-collector, target-shooter or hunter.

Despite statements to the contrary, guns — in the wrong hands — DO kill.

Portland Press Herald

Portland, Me., March 6, 1976

Another Congress apparently will live out its time and pass into history without enacting any gun legislation.

The most recent version of a measure to control handguns was sent back to a subcommittee where, in all probability, it will be interred. By a vote of 17 to 16, with Rep. William S. Cohen among the majority, the House Judiciary Committee sent the bill back to the subcommittee for revisions. It presumably will be revised right into oblivion.

The Committee did not give its Subcommittee on Crime specific instructions as to what should be revised, but the feature of the bill which has attracted much heat is the provision which called for a ban on the manufacture and sale of about 70 per cent of the handguns produced in this country. The important feature of the bill was fixed by the dimensions set on gun frame length.

And so another victory can be chalked up to the potent National Rifle Association and the gun lobby. It hardly seems possible that this newest defeat for handgun legislation is not reflecting the power and influence of the gun lobby. A week earlier the Judiciary Committee approved the measure by a vote of 18 to 14. But after a weekend, ample time for intensive lobbying, the committee had a change of heart.

Rep. John Conyers Jr., the Michigan Democrat who has guided the gun control matter through nearly a year of hearings and bill writing and rewriting, said "the simple fact of the matter is that a number of congressmen regardless of public opinion, are opposed to effective firearms legislation."

A number of congressmen also would seem to be apprehensive about going on the record on this issue. The action of the Judiciary Committee kept the bill from the floor and spared many representatives the ordeal of being counted on the sensitive subject.

An earlier bill did not contain the ban on small guns, which Conyers himself opposed, but provided for mandatory sentences for criminals, a waiting period for gun purchases, restrictions on multiple sales, etc. Who is to say the stiff ban was not added with the hope that it would make the whole package unacceptable?

For some time, polls have indicated a public desire for stricter gun control. Unfortunately, those people are not organized. The gun lobby is.

THE DALLAS TIMES HERALD

Dallas, Tex., March 7, 1976

THE U.S. HOUSE Judiciary Committee has flipflopped in its voting on proposed legislation to control the proliferation of certain classes of dangerous handguns in our society.

Committee members voted 17 to 16 to return one of the strongest control bills to subcommittee, making it a virtual hopeless cause for this congressional session.

President Ford has asked in his crime proposals for a national ban on the manufacture and sale of cheap handguns commonly known as "Saturday Night Specials."

The Judiciary Committee originally drafted a plan to ban short-barreled handguns. It was a proposal with considerable merit since it allowed the continued use of longer-barrel handguns for sport and for self protection in the home or business. Too, the legislation would have increased the waiting time for acquiring handguns from dealers.

However, the pro-gun lobby is so blindly opposed to any gun regulation that pressure against Congress became intense enough to stifle legislation in committee.

The full Congress should be given the opportunity to speak for the American people on this national issue. Rep. Peter Rodino, D-N.J., chairman of the Judiciary Committee, should get handgun control legislation out of his committee.

The role of cheap, easily concealable handguns in the growing violence and criminality of American society has been overwhelmingly documented. Congress must move to take stern action against the manufacture and sale of certain handguns and the users of any gun in the commission of a crime.

THE STATES-ITEM

New Orleans, La., March 15, 1976

Election year politics have sidetracked what appeared for a time to be a successful effort to stop the assembly-line production of cheap handguns in this country.

The two assassination attempts on President Ford last year had given impetus to the proposal to ban both the manufacture and sale of small, cheap handguns which are easily concealed.

Atty. Gen. Edward H. Levi had proposed such restrictions on the "Saturday night specials," but when the showdown came the administration did not push the measure. Meanwhile, the well organized and well financed national gun lobby did its usually effective job of opposing the legislation, and the House Judiciary Committee voted 17 to 16 to return the measure to subcommittee. That action effectively killed the gun-control effort for this year.

Meanwhile, the handgun mayhem continues across the country unabated. At least Congress and the President have publicly recognized the problem. That in itself is progress, indicating that sooner or later such a ban will be enacted.

Post-Tribune

Gary, Ind., March 4, 1976

In practice, as perhaps differentiated from in theory, "democracy" must face up to the reality of pressure politics.

That seems a logical conclusion to draw from House Judiciary Committee action last Tuesday and its labeling by Harlan Carter, chief lobbyist for the National Rifle Association, as "democracy in action."

What the full committee did was to send back to the subcommittee which drew it a bill which would have prohibited the manufacture, importation and sale of so-called concealable handguns; set higher license fees for gun dealers and imposed a 28-day waiting period before a handgun sale could be completed.

The signal is clear. The majority of the parent committee either wants the bill weakened or is afraid to say it doesn't. The majority of the National Rifle Association doubtless wants the bill sidetracked, too. We doubt if that is true of the majority of the country with its mounting fear of crime.

But the desires of the national majority can sometimes be brushed aside by the desires of a sizeable minority who are much more ready to express their objections at the ballot box.

That definitely is an example of power "in action."

Whether it can properly be labeled "democracy" may again become a moot point.

THE MILWAUKEE JOURNAL

Milwaukee, Wisc., March 5, 1976

The House Judiciary Committee knuckled under to pressure from the National Rifle Association and sent proposed gun controls back to a subcommitteee, effectively killing the legislation for this session. That is more than regrettable. It is a deplorable disregard for the safety and lives of Americans at all levels.

The bill was an extremely cautious effort to limit access to the kinds of cheap and easily concealed handguns that are used in 45% of street crime—and not by responsible sportsmen. Despite that, the bill failed by one vote to survive the NRA onslaught. One committee member called the effort "one of the most blatantly crass lobbying campaigns ever." Others claimed that opponents misrepresented what the bill would do.

Maybe so. But committee members cannot so easily absolve themselves for failing to stand against that pressure. They first allowed this private interest to gut the gun control bill, and then to gut the committee.

THE ROANOKE TIMES
Roanoke, Va., March 10, 1976

Few tears need be shed over the death of the latest gun control bill in Congress. Despite some redeeming features—in particular a mandatory delay on firearms purchases, plus a required police check on would-be gun buyers—it is questionable whether the measure would have set workable standards on the small guns it sought to ban.

The bill would have prohibited the manufacture, sale or importation of "concealable" pistols, which it defined as weapons less than 8½ inches long with frames shorter than 5¾ inches. That kind of guidelines would lead to a numbers game which the gun-makers would surely win. Inches don't kill people; guns kill people. It is not always realistic to try outlawing a particular type of gun; what the law should do is make it more difficult for the under-age, unqualified or dangerous person to get hold of one.

What is notable about the latest failure is the gun lobby's tactics. Week before last the House Judiciary Committee voted 18-14 to send the bill to the floor. The anti-gun control forces, chief among them the National Rifle Association, swung into action, the NRA blitzing its members with mailgrams to contact Judiciary Committee members.

They did. And the following week, enough members had changed their stand to recommit the bill, 17-16. "Democracy in action," said the NRA's chief lobbyist; "your basic orchestrated campaign," said a congressional aide. Politicians know that the gun lobby speaks for a minority, but an impassioned one, whose vote can turn upon this one issue; people who favor gun control (in a national majority according to the polls) are less committed and less organized.

This is not to say that the pro-controllers should be as committed. A legislator's duties require attention to many different issues; he should not be elected, or defeated, solely for how he stands on gun control. But the least the gun control forces must do is become better organized, better able to make their sentiments felt by members of Congress and state legislatures. For better or for worse, intensive, last-minute lobbying determines the fate of many a piece of legislation.

Arkansas Gazette.
Little Rock, Ark., March 10, 1976

For a while there, it seemed that the House of Representatives might stand up against the almighty pistol — actually do something to stem the flood of "Saturday night specials" which are killing Americans faster all the time. True, it was almost unbelievable that anything would be done in an election year. But the House Judiciary Committee took an amazing turn the other day and voted — for the first time — to approve a measure banning the sale, manufacture and importation of cheap, easily concealable handguns.

This extraordinary decision, by an 18 to 14 vote, represented a fine mustering of courage which, unfortunately, melted like paraffin in the heat that followed. Of course the widespread infatuation with instruments of death in this country has stalled such action previously, even in non-election years. Though most Americans want handgun controls, the minority which doesn't is highly vocal, politically mobilized, and has the most effective lobby in Washington. It will hear nothing of curbing even the vicious little pocket weapons that are the chief instruments of our swelling street crime, for fear that this would lead someday to control of deer rifles, shotguns and the like — an irrational apprehension. But in any case, the gun lobby has shown its awesome power again; the Judiciary Committee beat a craven retreat and sent the measure back to a subcommittee by a new vote of 17 to 16.

And in all likelihood, that kills any hope of effective pistol control in this Congress. Seldom had Capitol Hill seen such concentrated pressure, as gun defenders pulled all the stops in what Representative John Seiberling of Ohio called "one of the most blatantly crass lobbying campaigns ever." This sensible measure had the capability of cutting down by 70 per cent the flow of new pistols into the U.S. marketplace, and now we expect the flow will accelerate right along with the homicide rate.

But this need not be so. The bill isn't dead, only buried for the present, and it still could be passed if enough citizens would bother to get on their congressmen's backs. Legislators fear an aroused bloc much more than unexpressed majority opinion, and people who have no desire to live in what is increasingly an armed camp ought to sound off.

Many favor mandatory prison sentences for all gun-committed crimes, and this might be an effective part of a crime-reduction program. In fact it is part of the Judiciary Committee's bill. But pistols themselves have a momentum all their own in the psychology of violence — especially the famous "Saturday night special," that ubiquitous gat not much larger than a man's hand which takes such a harrowing toll of Americans every day. This is the "belly gun," designed only for use against people, and it has no place in our society. But we Americans continue to set new killing records with it which are not even approached anywhere else in the world, multiplying annually into the thousands.

No other weapon has the compact efficiency, the appeal to muggers who stalk the streets of evening, and the alleys and parking lots, in ever greater numbers. The powerful psychological appeal extends as well, sadly enough, to millions of other citizens who treasure the little pocket cannon as a matchless symbol of personal power, and who also vote, as congressmen know all too well.

And really, this bill which the committee shied away from is mild medicine — certainly no panacea. It would prohibit the importation, sale or manufacture of any handgun with a frame of less than 5.75 inches or an over-all length of less than 8.5 inches. Prevention of concealment is its purpose, and it would not affect the possession of any existing pistols, which run into untold tens of millions.

But if this would not reduce the already staggering inventory of pistols among us, at least it would slow down the proliferation of new ones, in the category that kills the most people. It would be a first step toward protective sanity in a society which even finds it necessary, more and more, to remove cheap pistols off children at school.

THE SPRINGFIELD UNION
Springfield, Mass., March 5, 1976

The gun lobby scored another setback Tuesday for hopes of federal legislation to outlaw the concealable handgun — a lethal and commonly used weapon of murder, robbery and assault in this nation.

In the last week of February the House Judiciary Committee approved a ban on that weapon, otherwise known as the "Saturday night special." The approval settled the last major difference between House and Senate proposals.

At that stage the House and Senate versions and a Ford administration measure all contained provisions for banning the concealable handgun, mandatory sentencing for crimes involving firearms, restrictions on multiple handgun purchases, and illegal firearms traffic.

Then the gun lobby, with the National Rifle Association in the driver's seat, shifted into high gear. The prime target apparently was the proposed ban on the manufacture and sale of concealable handguns.

The mails and phone lines to House Judiciary Committee members and congressional offices became jammed with protests, many of which contained "distorted and misleading information," according to Rep. Martin Russo, D-Ill., who authored the ban amendment.

In pressuring the judiciary committee to send the bill back to a subcommittee — in effect killing it for the year — the industry - supported NRA and its supporters revived the script of 1972, when a proposed ban on "Saturday night specials" died in a House subcommittee.

Gun control proponents say there was insufficient public interest, apparently, to turn the tide in favor of the measure. Congress, in other words, was swayed by the strength of the gun lobby rather than by the key role of the concealable handgun in major crime.

By that standard, the only stimulant to public interest, and thus the success of a significant control measure, will be crime and violence on an even larger scale. That's a likely prospect, with the handgun ban defeated; but it's a ridiculous price to pay.

St. Petersburg Times

St. Peterburg, Fla., March 7, 1976

What is alleged by some to be a constitutional right to risk getting shot by a friend, spouse, neighbor or stranger has just been upheld.

Not by the Supreme Court, but by the Judiciary Committee of the U.S. House of Representatives. On a 17 to 16 vote it decided this week against even limiting the multiple purchase of handguns.

It sent back to subcommittee, for burial alongside other gun control efforts of recent years, a compromised small-bore bill to bar the manufacture and sale of small, cheap, easily concealable pistols. And no more than one handgun of any kind could have been purchased by one person per month.

Small pistols are the weapons most used and misused not only by thugs but by honest citizens who envision themselves shooting it out with a burglar but are more likely to end up — and that's if they're lucky — plugging themselves i the foot.

THE SUBCOMMITTEE for weeks had worked hard on this bill, inspired by last September's assassination attempts against President Ford. But the gun lobby had worked even harder. Committee members now seem to agree that gun control can be pronounced dead in the 49th Congress.

There is no telling how many more needless death pronouncements, of a more personal nature, will have to be issued before Congress finally concludes that the only real function of handguns is the killing of people. And that nobody really needs them but the police.

DAYTON DAILY NEWS

Dayton, Ohio, March 4, 1976

The dedicated few have done it again. Killed — an appropriate word — handgun control for another year. The congressmen who caved in under the gun lobby's pressures know that it can mobilize a relative handful of voters into a powerful force that can decide a close election.

So they gave in again — despite repeated polls that show the overwhelming majority of Americans favor sensible laws to regulate sale of the handguns which are killing us by the thousands, most of the time in personal arguments that have nothing to do with "protecting" ourselves from criminals.

The gun lobby is truly a phenomenon. Financed by the firearms manufacturers, bolstered by skillful propaganda in gun magazines (supported in large part by gun ads, natch), and peopled by sincere folks who have been convinced that their deadly toys protect them from criminals and from subversives seizing the government.

Everybody has fantasies, but the facts are that handguns in the home are virtually useless as "protection," and more often end up killing a spouse than a burglar. And is anybody actually serious about defending their block against the U.S. or Russian military with pistols, rifles and shotguns?

The latest victim of the gun lobby's deadly barrage was a bill to ban the manufacture and sale of handguns that are easily concealed — the kind crooks like best. It would have left alone the larger versions that are used for legitimate purposes such as target shooting.

So to pacify a group that will tolerate no serious regulation of guns, the rest of us will continue to be potential victims for street punks who buy concealable guns from pawn shops or steal them from our night tables. It is, in the true meaning of the word, insane.

Newsday

Garden City, N.Y., March 4, 1976

The House Judiciary Committee hasn't sent a gun control bill to the House floor since 1968, the year Robert Kennedy and Martin Luther King were assassinated. This year, after two handguns were aimed at President Ford, the committee did come close: At one point it voted 18-14 to approve a mild bill that would have prohibited the manufacture, importation or sale of small, easily concealed handguns. But that was before the National Rifle Association mobilized its battalions for a lobbying blitz. When the smoke cleared, the vote was 17-16 to send the bill back to subcommittee, where it will almost certainly perish.

If Congress won't clamp down on firearms that kill thousands of Americans every year, how can you expect it to worry about arms exports that now add about $12 billion annually to the credit side of the nation's balance of payments? Well, the United States has been selling so many weapons abroad that the Pentagon sometimes has to get in line to acquire the hardware it wants; that's certainly some kind of risk to national security. A greater risk is the possibility that the United States itself could be drawn into a war begun by two countries equipped with American arms.

The United States has spent years trying to control its own arms race with the Soviet Union. Why does it have a different policy for the rest of the world?

OREGON Journal

AN INDEPENDENT NEWSPAPER

Portland, Ore., March 6, 1976

Proponents of legislation which would have helped to slow the spread of cheap, easily concealable handguns — the so-called "Saturday night specials" used by many criminals — are getting closer to success; but for the time being, another defeat must be marked up.

The House Judiciary Committee recently voted 17 to 16 to send a gun control measure back to the crime subcommittee.

The bill's supporters complained of intense lobbying against the bill by the National Rifle Association, and Rep. John Seiberling, D-Ohio, said, "This was one of the most blatantly crass lobbying campaigns ever."

The measure was intended to ban the sale and manufacture of new handguns but would not have affected some 40 million handguns already in circulation.

Also, the bill would have provided a mandatory sentence for anyone using a firearm in the commission of a felony and higher license fees and stricter licensing procedures for gun dealers. It would have limited any person to only one handgun purchase a month.

In addition, the bill would have made the sale of a gun to a person known by the seller to have a criminal record a felony and would have required a 21-day waiting period for anyone wishing to buy a handgun.

Such a bill would not wipe out murders, nor would it, with 40 million handguns in circulation, wipe out armed robbery.

But it would be a start in the campaign to stop the senseless shootings with the Saturday night specials.

About the only arguments mustered by the opponents were that the bill would have banned some models used by sportsmen and made acquisition of a gun for self-protection more difficult.

Possession of a handgun for self-protection is pretty much a fallacy because, almost invariably, the assailant or robber has the drop on you and the usual result of reaching for your gun is to get yourself shot.

The basic reason for opposition is the desire of gunmakers to continue making and selling guns, plus the fanatical desire of some to put the love of a pistol in the same class with love of mother, the flag and God.

Fanatics and lovers of money are not easily changed, but it is to be hoped that some day the gun-loving hysteria abates sufficiently so that some sensible controls can be established.

The Philadelphia Inquirer

Philadelphia, Pa., March 7, 1976

A bill to ban the manufacture and sale of concealable handguns, about 70 percent of the handguns made in this country, missed being sent to the House floor by one vote. The Judiciary Committee voted, 17-16, to return it to subcommittee for "revisions."

"This is not meant to sound the death knell for reasonable gun control legislation," said Illinois Republican Rep. Thomas F. Railsback, who made the motion to recommit.

That, however, will almost certainly be the consequence. Proponents of gun control legislation, including committee Chairman Peter W. Rodino Jr. of New Jersey, doubt that anything better, or anything at all, can be brought out of committee and approved this election year.

Shelving the bill will also, of course, sound the death knell for how many thousands of Americans this year and in years to come? No one can be sure, but we do know that in an average year 10,000 Americans are slaughtered by handguns.

A lobbyist for the National Rifle Association, which went all-out to defeat the legislation, described its defeat as a "great victory" for constitutional rights.

Tell that to the families of the thousands of Americans who are killed by handguns annually.

The NRA has indeed scored a "great victory" for which citizens will pay with their lives.

THE LOUISVILLE TIMES

Louisville, Ky., March 9, 1976

In accordance with long-standing tradition, Congress has surrendered again this year to the gun lobby. As a result, hopes for injecting some measure of sanity into our national handgun control policy have all but evaporated, at least until the next session convenes in 1977.

The House Judiciary Committee had actually gone so far as to approve a measure that would have banned the manufacture and sale of concealable handguns, or about 70 per cent of those sold in this country every year. Needless to say, this is also the type of firearm that is frequently used to commit murders and armed robberies, and to settle family fights.

The proposed legislation also included some other worthwhile provisions. For instance, it would have required a three-week waiting period between the purchase and delivery of a handgun. The sale of large numbers of guns to a single customer would have been forbidden. Federal restrictions on dealers would have been tightened up.

The end result would have been to make the type of handguns that are designed specifically for homicide less easily available, and to put some obstacles in the path of gunrunners who transport weapons from rural states to metropolitan areas.

In what has become a well-rehearsed Washington ritual, however, the fanatics of the National Rifle Association and other groups bombarded congressmen with letters opposing this entirely reasonable effort to banish from the marketplace the firearms that figure in 300,000 violent crimes every year. Rep. John Seiberling of Ohio called it "the most blatant lobbying campaign I have ever seen."

As a result the bill was sent back to a subcommittee for revision, which was equivalent to pumping it full of slugs from a .44 Magnum.

The Senate has also been considering handgun legislation, but decided not to act unless a gun-control bill cleared the House for the first time since 1968. Even though two attempts have recently been made on the life of President Ford, the chances of any action have therefore dropped to zero.

If there is a silver lining in this sorry situation, it is that some members of Congress finally appear to recognize that effective handgun control involves more than simply banning the so-called Saturday night special.

Most gun bills during the past few years have been aimed at these cheap, poorly constructed, small-caliber arms. The theory has been that the specials figure in most street crime, since they are within the financial reach of all but our poorest citizens. Some congressmen also hoped, naively as it turned out, that the gun groups would be less determined in their opposition to a measure that banned only low-quality firearms.

Experience has shown, however, that the expensive, large-caliber handguns turned out by the American arms industry are not purchased exclusively by sportsmen and other law-abiding citizens. Indeed, they are more apt to be used for criminal purposes than cheap guns in some cities. Not only that, but most models are just as easily concealed and twice as deadly.

The Judiciary Committee was on the right track, then, when it decided to make concealability, rather than caliber or quality of construction, the standard for determining which guns represent a menace to a civilized society.

Handgun control will of necessity be a gradual process. There are at least 40 million pistols and revolvers, the vast majority of which have no legitimate sporting purpose, in private hands now, and another two or three million are added to the supply every year. Even if all sales were stopped tomorrow, there would be enough deadly weapons in circulation to arm street-corner gunslingers for a generation.

But a start has to be made, and the first step has to be a law that has not been shot full of loopholes by the gun lobby's toadies in Congress.

A few optimists in Washington predict that the lack of action this year will actually have the effect of building up pressure for even stricter controls in the next session. That could be, but only if the majority that wants to prevent city streets from turning into shooting galleries can finally match the gun lobby's output of mail.

TULSA DAILY WORLD

Tulsa, Okla., March 4, 1976

ANOTHER move to outlaw the so-called "Saturday Night Special" pistol has been killed in the House Judiciary Committee. The bill would have banned certain short-barreled, easily-concealed weapons that are usually found by police after someone has been shot to death in a Saturday night bar room or street brawl.

The 17-16 vote by which the measure was buried in Congress is being hailed or condemned—depending on your viewpoint— as a victory for the "gun lobby." Certainly, in the short range view, it is another success story for the National Rifle Association and other groups representing gun owners and the arms industry. Another gun control bill has been stopped.

In the long run, though, this kind of "victory" may return to haunt hunters, collectors and others who own and enjoy guns for legitimate and useful purposes. Those who insist on an all-or-nothing approach to gun ownership may very well find themselves with nothing. This will almost certainly be the case if sportsmen and other law-abiding firearms users don't start making some sharp distinctions between their own interests and those of street thugs who rely on the cheap, hideaway pistol as a normal tool of their trade.

We are talking about the type of short-range gun that has absolutely no useful, lawful purpose. If someone suggested using a "Saturday Night Special" for hunting, collecting or serious target shooting, the editors of "Rifleman," the NRA magazine, would double up in laughter. Yet they feel obliged to defend the "rights" of people to own and carry these on the same grounds that they defend the use of guns for hunting and other beneficial purposes.

It's time to point out some differences. One of these days an increasingly urbanized public will get a bellyful of pistol crimes and demand and get some real controls. When the time comes, legitimate gun owners may wish they had separated their own case from that of the "Saturday Night Special" crowd.

The Boston Globe

Boston, Mass., March 1, 1976

Playing with guns is a big sport in Congress. Almost anybody can participate — lobbyists, representatives, senators, members of the Justice Department, even Presidents.

The object of the game is to make it look as though you are committed to the cause of gun control while you are actually delaying or sidetracking it. One of the oldest and most successful ploys concerns the Saturday Night Special. It has been particularly popular this year.

The Saturday Night Special defies definition. That doesn't faze those who say they want to outlaw it. They go right ahead defining it over and over again and each definition is at odds with the last.

Sometimes the SNS is described as a tiny weapon with a barrel as long as a pencil stub. Sometimes it is as big as a long, skinny target pistol. Sometimes its value is taken into consideration and sometimes the material it is made of is part of the formula.

But one thing is sure. If weapons of a certain size are banned this year, the manufacturers will be making them just a fraction of an inch larger next year. Sure, retooling might be expensive but 1,714,983 handguns were manufactured in this country for non-military use in fiscal 1974. That's big business.

Rep. Martin A. Russo (D-Ill.) has tried to stiffen the Administration's current SNS bill by broadening the definition. His amendment (which barely passed in the House Judiciary Committee) would ban the manufacture and sale of all "concealable" handguns — revolvers less than four and three-quarters inches long and pistols less than eight and a half inches long.

Undoubtedly Rep. Russo wants to see a good gun law passed, but even if his amendment went through intact it would not make much difference. Size, type, cost, concealability, don't mean much. Lynette "Squeaky" Fromme tried to shoot President Ford with a .45 caliber pistol, the cannon of handguns, which she had easily hidden in her handbag.

Here in Massachusetts People vs. Handguns and other civic groups have been working for a ban on all handguns for everybody except the police and the military. That's the only way.

ARKANSAS DEMOCRAT
Little Rock, Ark., March 12, 1976

House backers of gun-control tried a new line of attack against handguns last week, but lost anyway, probably ending any hopes of legislation for the session. It is just as well; for the legislators dropped their effort to ban the cheap handgun called the Saturday Night Special and proposed banning the manufacture, importation sale or possession of three-quarters of all new handguns.

Size, not nomenclature, was the specification in the proposed ban. "Concealability" was the selling point. But the lawmakers themselves were charged with concealment. The new specs took in the SNS, all right, but a lot more besides. The ban would have fallen on any pistol shorter than eight-and-a-half inches. The National Rifle Organization pointed out the consequences, and the Judiciary Committee decided by a margin of only one vote to recommit the bill to its subcommittee on crime.

The campaign against the Saturday Night Special lost from this attempt at overkill. Gun enthusiasts don't hold much of a brief for the SNS. Most would be content to see its assembly and sale banned in this country. If the legislators had stuck to their original line against the SNS, they might have won. But they got too "cute" with definitions, though the ban would have applied only to new handguns.

As for the 40 million old ones in circulation, the legislative odds against their being registered or outlawed are practically insurmountable. The House has refused to touch gun legislation since 1968.

The chairman of the Judiciary subcommittee says that in spite of the defeat he will try one more time for a bill this session. But he refuses even to tell friends of gun-control what he has in mind, which instantly suggests another cute definition of ban-worthy handguns similar to the one just tried and rejected. The committee would do better to stop these end runs and revert to its forthright campaign against the Saturday Night Special. It is the only campaign it can hope to win or should win.

Wisconsin ⬩ State Journal
Madison, Wisc., March 16, 1976

It may be either poetic justice or irony but the National Rifle Assn. is considering moving its headquarters out of Washington partly because of gun-related crimes against its employees.

The NRA, major voice of the powerful gun lobby, is not about to soften its stand against gun control, however.

"There's been no evidence presented by anyone that strong gun control will deter crime," insists Thomas A. Hodges, the NRA's director of public affairs.

He may be right. There has never been strong gun control in this country and if the NRA has its way there never will be. But when even the NRA is afraid to walk the streets in the nation's capitol, maybe it would be worth a try.

The head of the FBI, most major city police chief's and task forces which have studied the problem have all advocated gun control. Public opinion polls show the majority of Americasns favor it.

It is needed and should be enacted.

THE ANN ARBOR NEWS
Ann Arbor, Mich., March 16, 1976

THE National Rifle Association has announced that it may move its headquarters out of Washington, D.C. to, it is rumored, Denver. There's not much news in that, except for the reason cited by the NRA for the move.

It seems the NRA is seeking a "safer and more compatible environment" for its national staff, following the shootings of two employes. The NRA, of course, is the nation's most powerful opponent of gun control legislation.

If it leaves "crime-ridden" Washington for other parts, the NRA will appear to be following the example of thousands of other citizens who have fled central cities because they thought their lives were in danger. And one reason why their lives were in danger was because of the thriving traffic in handguns.

But the NRA still has its blinders on in that respect. Instead of doing something to dry up the flood of guns in Americans' possession, the NRA proposes mandatory jail sentences as a crime control measure. Mandatory sentences for some crimes committed with a gun do have some merit, but the NRA position is a persistent refusal to see the proliferation of handguns in this country as the number one menace.

Pittsburgh Post-Gazette
Pittsburgh, Pa., March 30, 1976

GUN CONTROL advocates are getting much wry satisfaction out of the news that the National Rifle Association is contemplating moving its headquarters out of Washington, D.C., partly because of gun-related crimes against its employes there.

The NRA is the highly effective lobby organization which has been able to defeat congressional efforts at bringing sanity to our chaotic gun policy. With its usual ability to bring from around the country an instantaneous deluge of mail and calls raining down on senators and congressmen, the NRA just a few weeks ago was able once again to block a modest bill, perhaps killing any hope this session for any restrictions on the alarming spread of firearms.

Of its Washington move an NRA spokesman insisted, "There's been no evidence presented by anyone that strong gun control will deter crime." This turns a blind eye to the low rate of deaths from gun-related homicides or accidents in Europe, whose countries historically have had tight controls on weapons, as compared to the United States. It confuses the understandable desire of sportsmen to have weapons with the growing evidence that society must find some way to keep track of, if not curb, the deadly proliferation of weapons such as handguns.

In 1971, the last year for which comparable figures were available, seven persons were murdered with handguns in England and Wales, compared to 8,991 in the U.S. Even in "frontier" countries like Australia and Canada, the firearms homicide rate is one-tenth that of the U.S.

It's perhaps too much to expect the NRA to see the obvious lesson in its move out of Washington. But others, including congressmen constantly harried by NRA lobbying fire, should not miss it.

New York Post
New York, N.Y., March 16, 1976

Many an inhabitant of Washington, D. C., has been the terrified target of violent crime by gunmen; a sense of vulnerability threatens many others. In fact, one particularly prominent resident seems to have decided it is right in front of the bull's-eye: the National Rifle Association.

In the past year or so, one NRA staff man has been fatally shot and several others have been assaulted or robbed. For this and some other reasons—such as increased operating costs, officials say—the NRA, aggressive leader in the Congressional campaign against gun control legislation, is contemplating a move from Washington to someplace "safer," probably Colorado Springs, Colorado.

According to president Merrill W. Wright, the NRA is looking for new neighbors "who understand the gun and what it stands for." And an organization spokesman says the Colorado location will put the NRA conveniently close to land it owns in northern New Mexico, which it plans to transform into "a showcase of conservation."

No doubt such a shift of NRA headquarters would relieve some of the members of Congress who have been regularly subjected to its lobbying against tougher handgun laws.

The NRA is well-financed and ably organized. Its members include some of this country's most prominent public officials and private leaders. It might lend its energy to the reasoned regulation of a national traffic in illegal arms that imperils millions.

Unhappily, the gun merchants who so heavily sponsor the lobby might lose interest in its "sporting" mission. But it would be a noble experiment.

STUDIES SCORE LEAA'S INEFFICACY; JUDICIARY PANELS VOTE REFUNDING

Despite four reports criticizing as ineffective the eight-year old Law Enforcement Assistance Administration, the Senate and House Judiciary Committees have recommended that it be refunded. The LEAA was created in 1968 to assist state and local governments in reducing crime, and has spent more than $4 billion on its various projects.

The House Judiciary Committee May 12 reported out of committee a bill providing for one year's funding at the present level of $880 million. The Senate Judiciary Committee May 13 passed a bill approving a five-year extension totalling $5.4 billion, but added an amendment requiring the LEAA to evaluate its programs "to determine whether [they] are likely to contribute to the improvement of law enforcement and criminal justice and the reduction and prevention of crime and juvenile delinquency and whether [they] have achieved the goals stated in the original plan and application."

The most recent report on the LEAA is expected to be published July 1 by the Center for National Security Studies. A draft copy was obtained by the Associated Press. Written by Sarah Carey, the report states that "the nation is in no better position today than it was when the Omnibus Crime Control and Safe Streets Act of 1968 was enacted." Recommending that the LEAA be abolished, Carey found "crime has increased and no solutions to the crime problem are on the horizon."

The General Accounting Office released a report May 28 scoring the LEAA's administration, a view shared by the Twentieth Century Fund and the Mitre studies. The Twentieth Century Fund published *Law Enforcement: The Federal Role* earlier this year, which recommended that the LEAA be continued, but only with Congress' "more rigorous oversight." The study concluded "there is substantial evidence that LEAA, as currently structured and administered, has generally failed to carry out the mission Congress gave it."

The Mitre report was commissioned by the LEAA itself for $2.4 million, and was released March 2. Analyzing the high impact program which spent $160 million in eight cities, the Mitre study said that violent crime had considerably worsened in the eight cities, but added that the increase might have been greater if the program had not been begun. The eight cities were Atlanta, Baltimore, Cleveland, Dallas, Denver, Newark, St. Louis, and Portland, Ore.

LEAA Administrator Richard W. Velde March 17 told the Senate Subcommittee on Criminal Laws and Procedures that the agency's purpose was generally misunderstood. "...Crime control in this country is a prime responsibility of state and local government and ... the federal role should be a limited one, limited to financial assistance, technical assistance, research and evaluation. But no agency, whether it be LEAA or the FBI or whatever, has been seriously considered to assume the responsibility for crime control at the state and local level."

The Oregonian

Portland, Ore., May 13, 1976

"Law and Disorder IV," the draft of an independent study released this week, recommends dismantling the federal Law Enforcement Assistance Administration because the agency "is unclear as to its mission, and what it has attempted, it has done poorly." The editors have not seen the entire study, only a 43-page chapter that deals in detail with the Portland Impact anti-crime program and wire service summaries of the rest. But the agency certainly does not deserve the execution block based on what the evaluators had to say about LEAA-funded programs here.

There are some generalized criticisms of Portland-area anti-crime program spending, but a close reading of the report shows that the independent analysts were impressed with planning, execution and evaluation of anti-crime spending strategies — with the notable exception of the CRISS computer program. In short, the chapter on Portland does not support the contention that what LEAA has done has been done poorly. (There are local officials who do believe the case can be made, but it certainly was not done in this evaluation.)

Much should be done to improve LEAA, which was born out of a naive government notion that a complex social phenomenon, such as crime, can be controlled simply by throwing money at it. Further, LEAA, a creature of the Nixon-Agnew administration, was bedeviled by revolving-door leadership changes that accompanied Watergate. The agency has been as unstable as some of the inner cities on which it has lavished most of its $4.4 billion of funding.

However, that does not mean it should be abandoned. The money that has been spent so far on Impact and other projects has produced numerous programs that have helped to stem crime and have been cost-effective. They should be grafted onto police agendas on a local-option basis, where suitable.

Even LEAA programs that cannot be judged successful are not total losses: They constitute a table of contents of what not to do in the police and corrections fields, and should save billions of dollars of fruitless, duplicative experimentation in the future.

"Law and Disorder IV" does make a contribution in pointing to conceptual and procedural snafus in national LEAA operations — interference with local programs for national political reasons rather than crime-related reasons and the unresolved problem of tension between the decentralization strategy of the New Federalism and a growing national sense of what will work, what won't, and what the priority targets should be, for example.

LEAA does need a thorough overhaul, but to send it to the junk yard now, before it has completed a useful life, would amount to abandoning the only national agency that is committed to welding all the separate criminal justice operations — enforcement, prevention, corrections — into a cooperative, effective system, probably the best chance to control crime.

A quote from the Portland chapter of the study underlines the point. The analysts noted that Portland police, compared with those in other cities, were not particularly aggressive in seeking a large share of Impact's $20 million local grant:

"Police we interviewed in Portland confirmed this, stating: 'You can't fight crime with just one segment of the criminal justice system. We are kidding ourselves if we think that making a lot of arrests in itself will reduce crime.'"

It is an enlightened view, and decapitating LEAA would not contribute to the all-fronts fight against crime that it implies is required.

HOUSTON CHRONICLE

Houston, Tex., May 11, 1976

In Washington, programs aren't launched in a tentative manner. No one dares to say: "We don't know what to do about this problem, but we are going to give it our best try." Instead, crusades a r e proclaimed against one great social problem after another. And instead of pie in the sky, there is more likely to be pie in the face.

The Law Enforcement Assistance Administration has fallen victim to this process. It is being tripped up by its own publicity releases.

Studies conducted by LEAA and by independent groups find that t h e agency isn't reaching its stated goals.

Four years ago, a "high-impact anti-crime" project was announced, heralded as an "across-the-board attack on street crimes and burglaries" in eight cities. After $160 million has been spent, the results are poor at best. The LEAA's own study shows crime worsened in the target cities.

LEAA's money hasn't stopped burglaries or made the streets safe. That is expecting too much. The problem is too broad. But LEAA funds have helped. Court processes h a v e b e e n improved. Police have better c o m munications and get better training. A lot of myths about fighting crime—such as "high-impact" attacks—have been dissipated.

These new studies mean that LEAA should learn from its mistakes. Programs should be carefully selected from now on, and should not repeat past errors. And LEAA should settle for modest goals and not proclaim crusades. Crime is one of the great national concerns, and because programs don't live up to their advance publicity, that is no reason to give up the fight.

The Providence Journal

Providence, R.I., May 12, 1976

Crime in the streets was a hot political issue back in 1968. Violence had erupted in a number of large cities and the civil rights movement was at its zenith. The congressional response, stirred by public outcry, was enactment of the Omnibus Crime Control and Safe Streets Act.

Under the act, the Law Enforcement Assistance Administration (LEAA) was created as a catalyst for strengthening the criminal justice system and feeding federal dollars into the state and local pipeline. Few quarreled with the concept at the time. In general, Americans were convinced something had to be done in a big way to control what seemed an epidemic of crime.

Some $4.5 billion and seven years later, congressional authorization is up for renewal. The question becomes whether Washington should continue to pump dollars into a diverse and costly endeavor, the results of which at this point are anything but encouraging. The fact is that the crime rate continues to climb. What the country has to show for its huge investment is a somewhat better equipped police force viewed collectively and a vast bureaucracy that consumes a large share of available resources in tangling and untangling red tape.

Two independent studies recently completed have come down hard on LEAA and the block grant program. One to be published by the Center for National Security Studies urges that the program be abolished. "Crime has increased and no solutions to the crime problem are on the horizon . . . LEAA's performance in the High Impact program was an irresponsible, ill-conceived and politically-motivated effort to 'throw money at a social program.'"

Corroborating these findings, consultants hired by LEAA for $2.4 million to assess its concentrated anti-crime effort in eight large cities found last March that crime had worsened considerably in the target cities.

The prestigious Twentieth Century Fund this week added its voice to the criticism with a task force report and recommendations that make a great deal of sense. The task force, headed by former Gov. A. Linwood Holton of Virginia, would extend the life of LEAA only if it is thoroughly restructured and transformed, doing away with the regional bureaucracy. It would assign half the funds available as special revenue sharing with no strings attached other than compliance with civil rights laws. And it would reconstitute the agency's Washington headquarters as a vehicle for research, evaluation and demonstration projects. Congress, the task force believes, should exercise vigorous oversight over the agency.

The Ford administration has proposed extending LEAA for five years with an annual budget of $1.5 billion. Given the disappointing results to date and the strong likelihood that renewed authority and funding without altering the approach would be throwing good money after bad, we believe Congress should come up with some fresh thinking and an extension bill for one or two years.

One recommendation of the Twentieth Century Fund report above all others we strongly endorse. It is that there be "a basic clarification of the agency's legislative mandate, eliminating the false promise of crime reduction and clearly establishing that LEAA's primary purpose is to enable the states and local units of government to improve the effectiveness of their police, courts, and corrections agencies in dealing with crime."

THE   SUN

Baltimore, Md., May 18, 1976

Police Commissioner Donald Pomerleau says a federal grant helped him reduce the crime rate in the city. Sara Carey of the Center for National Security Studies says it didn't. But they agree that the Law Enforcement Assistance Administration, the federal agency which provided the funds, is poorly run, wasteful and ought to be abolished. Studies by the Twentieth Century Fund and the General Accounting Office came to similar conclusions. LEAA was set up in 1968 to "prevent" crime. For several years most of the funds LEAA disbursed were for police equipment. In the past few years there has been a welcome shift in emphasis from guns to courts and corrections, but not yet enough of a shift. One thing America has learned in its war against crime in the past two decades is that the police alone can not prevent crime. The whole justice system has a role.

LEAA has had its successes. In many cities police, court and corrections officials are working together for the first time looking for a co-ordinated way to make the system work better. LEAA has failed miserably to reduce crime nationwide, but it never should have been expected that a single agency could achieve that goal. Mr. Pomerleau and many other close observers of LEAA favor shifting some if not all the money LEAA now spends to revenue sharing.

Since LEAA legislation expires this year, a decision to let the agency die and put the money in the revenue sharing pot would be simple, but we would not like to see LEAA die—yet. That would make it more difficult for state and local officials to pursue the coordinated, long term approach the problem of crime demands. LEAA deserves a chance to straighten itself out. Legislation to extend the agency, with some reforms, is pending in Congress now. If the agency were to have its life extended for a short period of time—say two years—Congress could exercise the sort of thorough oversight it has not performed so far. If it should determine the concept of a federal anti-crime effort is unworkable, even with reforms, then the decision should be made to disband LEAA and give the money involved directly to the governments which have traditionally dealt with crime and criminals.

The Washington Star

Washington, D.C., May 15, 1976

The anti-Washington clamor that is the big gun in most campaign arsenals is largely fustian. But there is specificity to substantiate the horror stories: For instance, the Law Enforcement Assistance Administration and the flaccid performance in both House and Senate recently in considering more money for the Justice Department unit.

The Senate Judiciary Committee decided the other day by an 11-1 vote to continue funding LEAA for another five years at a comfy level of $1.1 billion annually. On the House side, the Judiciary Committee, by an equally lopsided vote, 29-1 there, allowed LEAA to be funded for only one additional year, for $880 million. Differences in the two bills, if passed by the respective houses, then would have to be resolved in conference.

But that is not the point. Agreement by the two Judiciary Committees to let the Law Enforcement Assistance Administration hang around came despite fairly wide agreement that no one could say whether the $4 billion funneled into the agency since 1968 has had any effect whatsoever in combatting crime. Brilliant! When in doubt about a federal program, give it more money.

Senator Birch Bayh, the only dissenting vote over there, said bluntly: "If we were the board of directors of a corporation, responsible to the stockholders for $4 billion, they'd change the board of directors pretty quickly." Any similarity, of course, between Congress and a functioning corporate entity is accidental.

The Law Enforcement Assistance Administration has generated, in our view, some thoughtful initiatives. It also has been prey to gimcrackish anti-crime projects in which the glittering allure of technology has overwhelmed common sense.

The question for Congress one of these days must be whether LEAA can continue to justify its high-dollar existence. Both House and Senate committees nimbly avoided that hard determination.

We won't attempt to extend this example too far through the federal maze. What is worrisome is that the handling of the LEAA budget request does not appear to be unusual. Senator Bayh's board-of-directors observation ought to be more widely absorbed on Capitol Hill.

THE ATLANTA CONSTITUTION

Atlanta, Ga., May 19, 1976

The Law Enforcement Assistance Administration (LEAA), which has not always been acclaimed nationally for its good works, has poured $19 million into Atlanta to prevent and combat crime in a far-reaching three-year model project. As far as we can tell, most of the money has been well spent.

Now Atlanta is threatened with losing the LEAA funding. LEAA chief Richard Velde has told Mayor Maynard Jackson: "We have met our initial commitment to Atlanta. From the beginning, we all agreed the program would end in three years."

Unless Congress approves more "high crime impact" money for LEAA, Atlanta apparently will be left out. The federal funds which run out this summer are for, among other things, 300 police positions.

Public Safety Commissioner Eaves has said he will try to save those positions by combining some operations and taking some economy measures in the Bureau of Police Services. Nevertheless it has been estimated that $1.5 million must be squeezed out of the already sagging city budget if the presently federally funded anti-crime programs are to be continued next year without LEAA money.

It is too bad the city may lose some of these programs and manpower. With the help of LEAA funding, the city has made significant progress in reducing crime, according to figures supplied by the Bureau of Police Services.

Hopefully, some of the federal funds will be restored by Congress so that the city may continue to reduce crime and the perception of crime here.

THE COMMERCIAL APPEAL

Memphis, Tenn., May 15, 1976

WITH ONLY ONE negative vote the Senate Judiciary Committee has approved a $5.4-billion authorization to continue the Law Enforcement Assistance Administration for another five years.

The action, taken without benefit of full hearings or debate, walked right over two citizens' reports made in the past week which were highly critical of LEAA.

One study, the fourth in a series on LEAA directed by Washington attorney Sarah C. Carey under the auspices of the nonprofit Center for National Security Studies, concluded that "the LEAA program should be abolished."

The second study, made by a task force for the independent Twentieth Century Fund of New York, recommended that the crime-fighting federal agency be kept in being only if it is thoroughly restructured and transformed. LEAA's regional bureaucracy should be "dismantled" and half the federal appropriation for criminal justice should be distributed directly from Washington to state and local governments in revenue-sharing grants, the task force said.

AT THE HEART of both studies is the fact that LEAA, created by Congress in 1968 as part of the Omnibus Crime and Safe Streets Act, has not reduced crime.

Born as the Lyndon Johnson administration's response to the rising crime rate of the 1960s, LEAA set out to fight crime at the local and state level with infusions of federal dollars. In seven years it has spent $4.5 billion.

Crime rates -- especially violent crime — have continued to soar.

LEAA is not to blame. But it is time to stop and take a hard look at its programs. If the present approach is ineffective, it is wrong to pour more billions into programs that are not producing. On top of that is the need to insure that LEAA funds will not be used for political purposes, as the studies show they have in some cases over the past seven years.

SAYS THE TWENTIETH Century Fund task force report: "Congress has never conducted a thorough investigation of LEAA. And no reliable inventory now describes with accuracy the nature, far less the degree of success or failure, of the 105,000 grants LEAA has funded to date."

That failure can be laid right on the laps of the judiciary committees of both the House and Senate. Members seem more interested in getting money for their states or districts than in following up on effectiveness of grants for research and experimental programs.

Lawyer Sarah Carey's Nader-type watch over LEAA has been a lonely vigil. But the Twentieth Century Fund task force brings up some big guns. The study was presided over by former Virginia Gov. Linwood Holton, and task force members included James Ahern, director of the Insurance Crime Prevention Institute; Michael Armstrong, former counsel for the Knapp Commission investigation of New York police corruption; Hubert Locke, associate dean of the University of Washington; Cecil Poole, former deputy U.S. attorney in San Francisco; William D. Ruckelshaus, former deputy U.S. attorney general, and Quinn Tamm, former head of the International Association of Chiefs of Police, among others.

One of that task force's recommendations is that Congress direct crime-fighting funds into less-restricted state and local programs, and that there be more comprehensive planning and less showy hardware.

The haste with which LEAA is getting a new five-year lease on life, at a cost of billions of dollars, is not good politics or good judgment. Congress needs to ask more questions and learn more answers.

FORT WORTH STAR-TELEGRAM

Fort Worth, Tex., May 11, 1976

Here's a prescription for curing this nation's festering crime problem.

Money. Lots of money. Millions, even billions, in green legal tender. Spread it over the afflicted areas in a heavy paste.

This is what's known as the LEAA (Law Enforcement Assistance Administration) prescription. It's a simple cure. It doesn't require much diagnostic ability or concern about how the salve is applied or when signs of recovery should occur.

A very simple prescription. There is one problem. It doesn't work. So says a study soon to be published by the Center for National Security Studies. The study takes the position that the LEAA has been a waste of money and should be abolished.

"Crime has increased and no solutions to the crime problem are on the horizon.

The nation is in no better position today than it was when the Omnibus Crime Control and Safe Streets Act of 1968 (which created the LEAA) was enacted," says the report.

Thus far the LEAA has thrown about $4.4 billion at the national crime problem. Of that amount $160 million was spent in Dallas, Atlanta, Baltimore, Cleveland, Denver, Newark, St. Louis and Portland, Ore. for a concentrated assault on crime in those urban settings.

The study sharply criticizes that high impact program, concluding that its objectives were fuzzy, its guiding ideas not well thought out and that it "did not produce significant results in regard to crime."

The LEAA has itself paid a consulting firm $2.4 million to tell it essentially the same thing, adding to the waste of the taxpayers' dollars.

And, after all this money has been spent, LEAA officials now freely admit that they don't know what can be done to curb crime.

Well, it is pretty obvious that throwing money at it isn't enough. It is just as obvious, however, that some more money will have to be spent for whatever form the next concentrated prescription against crime takes.

But let's hope the application of that prescription will be preceded by more research and planning than have previous LEAA approaches.

It could well be that any prescription to be really effective would have to penetrate deeper than the mere symptoms of the malady, the bare criminal acts.

That medicine would have to be a mixture concocted to do its work within the context of the social and economic problems that contribute to so much of the nation's crime.

In many instances it would have to be an agent of change.

The Dispatch

Columbus, Ohio, May 12, 1976

TWO NEW STUDIES of the federal Law Enforcement Assistance Administration are critical of the program which has dispensed $4.5 billion with the objective of reducing crime.

They call forceful attention to the fact that crime has risen regardless of the large amount of money spent.

ON THE OTHER hand, the studies do not find the funds granted to state and local law enforcement agencies have been a total waste.

Some of the modern equipment and additional manpower the money provided has assured more successful apprehension of criminals.

Both the Twentieth Century Fund and the Center for National Security Studies believe federal law enforcement assistance funds, henceforth, should be distributed as federal revenue sharing grants.

ESSENTIALLY what these two private study groups are saying is LEAA after seven years has come up with no more crime prevention solutions than anybody else.

One unhappy reminder of that fact, among others, is the new burst in the crime of arson.

As the two critical reports were unveiled, one suspect conflagration burned 30 families out of their homes in Cleveland. Another killed six persons in a Chicago fire suspected to have been set.

UNLIKE the Center for National Security Studies, the Twentieth Century Fund study group does not recommend LEAA be abolished.

It suggests the agency be restructured and given the role of examining what local and state law agencies are doing to improve the criminal justice system, publicize effective programs and offer incentives for their emulation.

No other agency performs this role and on a trial basis such an idea may have merit.

THE NATION, somehow, must continue the effort to find workable means to curtail violent street crime and strengthen criminal justice everywhere. The evidence continues to mount that LEAA, as presently conceived and with $7.5 billion over five more years, as proposed, may no longer suffice.

The answers obviously lie more closely at home. Money alone is not the solution.

The Standard-Times

New Bedford, Mass., May 24, 1976

The 20th-Century Fund has just aired a report that amounts to a grim assessment of the Law Enforcement Assistance Administration's eight-year crusade to bring scientific solutions to the nation's mushrooming problems with crime.

Summing up LEAA's efforts and noting the $4.5-billion spent to further them, the report concludes that "all the manifest ills of the criminal justice system still persist."

Neither our homes, our property, nor the streets are safe. Crime rates are up nearly everywhere. The courts are overcrowded, jails are overcrowded. Sentencing and parole procedures are uncoordinated and generally unsatisfactory.

That was true when LEAA was launched in 1968. It is true today. Despite the money and efforts expended, we do not know any more about the root causes of crime than we did then.

With this in mind, President Ford proposes cutting $102-million in 1977 from the 1976 LEAA budget of $810-million. A House subcommittee suggests cutting the total to $600-million.

Under the Ford proposal, Massachusetts' LEAA allocation would be cut from $15.7-million to $11.9-million. The House subcommittee proposal, if approved, would cut the Bay State grant to $8.5-million.

This is not to suggest throwing out the entire concept of a coordinated, well-financed attack on crime, organized and otherwise, particularly in light of the grim increase in crime statistics.

And there certainly is no question that LEAA funds have been put to good uses. The Archibald Cox Committee on Judicial Needs and the attorney general's violent crime unit are two examples that come to mind.

But results — or lack of them — demand a re-examination of LEAA, using the 20th-Century fund report's findings and recommendations as a starting-point.

For instance, the report recommends that the regional LEAA bureaucracies be "dismantled" and that half the federal funds for criminal justice be given directly to state and local governments in the form of revenue-sharing grants.

Of the remaining money, half would be earmarked for state and local experimental and "demonstration" programs, with the balance to pay for federal-level evaluation and experimental work.

The recommended approach certainly is worth looking into. Somehow, we have to come closer to an anticrime program that lives up to LEAA's original promise.

HERALD-JOURNAL

Syracuse, N.Y., May 15, 1976

Congress could strike a blow for the taxpayer: Eliminate the federal Law Enforcement Assistance Administration.

The private Center for National Security Studies rates the agency as having accomplished next to nothing with its $4.4 billions over the last few years.

We'd interpose an exception. The LEAA has helped police and sheriff departments upgrade their patrol and communications equipment as we've seen here in Syracuse and Onondaga County.

But the rating agency reported:

"Not only has the LEAA failed to halt the rising crime rates, but LEAA administrators haven't yet determined the steps or procedures that can be taken to achieve that goal."

We should expect more for $4.4 billions than a confused agency in Washington and updated equipment in Syracuse, Onondaga County and like communities

Statistics provided by police agencies every quarter demonstrate the LEAA hasn't lived up to its high sounding charter.

Therefore, eliminate it.

OKLAHOMA CITY TIMES

Oklahoma City, Okla., May 11, 1976

CRITICISM of the government's crime-fighting program as an ill-conceived effort to throw money at social problems has a familiar ring. This has been a long-standing complaint of people fed up with costly liberal nostrums for the nation's ills.

The target of the latest blast is the Law Enforcement Assistance Administration, created under the Omnibus crime Control and Safe Streets Act of 1968. In the seven years of its operation the LEAA has spent $4.5 billion. But crime rates—especially violent crime—have continued to rise, except for an unexplained respite in 1972.

Last year, reported crimes rose 18 per cent, the biggest increase in the 50 years the Federal Bureau of Investigation has been keeping statistics. Yet there is no apparent improvement in the criminal justice system: Jails and prisons are still crowded, the courts are overloaded, prosecutors' offices are generally underfunded and debate rages over sentencing and parole procedures.

The Center for National Security Studies, in its appraisal of the LEAA, says no solutions to the crime problem are on the horizon. It declares that the LEAA has accomplished little despite all the money spent and recommends that it be abolished. It would convert the agency into a "high level, scholarly research resource." Its mission: examine the causes of criminal behavior, ways of protecting society from that behavior and means of reducing the incidence of such behavior.

Congress has before it an administration proposal to refund the agency for another five years at an estimated cost of $6.8 billion.

The center's report recommends that, if Congress chooses to abolish the program, some of the money allocated to communities under the LEAA's block program be included in general revenue sharing. If the program is continued, it states, the current state planning apparatus should be dismantled and each state be allowed to select its own conduit for funding.

Critics of the LEAA take a dim view of what they consider to be its emphasis on showy but unnecessary "hardware" to fight crime rather than getting at the root causes of the problem.

The agency has provided such items as walkie-talkies, communications and information equipment, more comfortable shoes for policemen, a riot-control program, a Dale Carnegie course for policemen, electronic surveillance equipment and a wristwatch that sends beeps when its wearer is in trouble.

But it has also funded a computerized scheduling system for harried prosecutors, a public defender service, a volunteer probation-counselor program, antifraud divisions, juvenile diversion programs and community-based corrections facilities.

Likely, many small-town police forces would question whether the additional equipment they received through LEAA grants has been a waste of money. Probably they could point to improved communications, both internally and with other departments, for example.

Citizens, while lauding the report's condemnation of the unnecessary spending of federal funds, might wonder if what is proposed is simply more study of the problem without action. They might also question the absence of any push for "certainty of punishment" as a crime deterrent —a concept more and more experts in the field are supporting.

THE ARIZONA REPUBLIC
Phoenix, Ariz., May 13, 1976

The facts conclusively prove otherwise. Yet, somehow, the delusion that we can solve our social problems simply by throwing money at them manages to persist.

Seven years ago, Congress created the Law Enforcement Assistance Administration to help the cities and states fight crime. LEAA has been throwing money at the problem ever since. Its budget has grown from $60 million to $886 million. In all, the agency has spent $4.5 billion.

LEAA has supplied the State of Louisiana with an armored personnel carrier called "Big Bertha" and funded such programs as SWAT (Special Weapons and Tactics) in Los Angeles, STRESS (Stop the Robberies, Ensure Safe Streets) in Detroit, SCAT (Special Crime Attack Team) and ESCORT (Eliminate Street Crimes on Residential Thoroughfares) in Denver.

It has given $239,700 to Loyola University to assess the need for a loose-leaf encyclopedia on law enforcement.

It has provided walkie-talkies and communications and information equipment and more comfortable shoes to policemen across the nation, a Dale Carnegie course for policemen in Kentucky, and a riot-control program for the State of Maine.

Despite this, year by year, with the exception of 1972 when there was a slight downturn, crime has continued to increase.

Money obviously is not the answer to crime. Yet, President Ford has asked Congress to extend the life of LEAA for another five years at a cost of $6.8 billion.

The President's request is all the more baffling in the light of two recent studies of the LEAA, one by the Center for National Security Studies in Washington, the other by a task force of the Twentieth Century Fund in New York.

Both studies reach the same conclusion: LEAA has been a waste of money. It has not had any visible effect on crime. All it has done is generate Himalayas of red tape and driven police departments crazy doing paperwork.

Both studies are particularly critical of the High Impact Anti-Crime Program, LEAA's most expensive and ambitious effort. The agency poured $160 million into eight cities — Atlanta, Baltimore, Cleveland, Dallas, Denver, Newark, Portland and St. Louis — with the announced goal of reducing rape, homicide, robbery, assault and burglary by 5 per cent in two years and by 20 per cent in five.

The result: Zilch. Crime in all eight cities increased.

The Center for National Securities Studies advocates the outright abolition of the LEAA; the Twentieth Century Fund says that it should either be abolished or else transformed from an agency that ladles out money to one that conducts research, program evaluation and demonstration programs in the field of criminal justice.

The fund's suggestion may be worth trying. Certainly, there's no excuse for continuing to spend money on the LEAA as now constituted.

THE ROANOKE TIMES
Roanoke, Va., May 18, 1976

Jimmy Carter says that if he's elected president, he'd do away with hundreds of federal bureaus, and some people would like him to be specific about it. Lo, here's a high-level candidate for abolition: the Law Enforcement Assistance Administration (LEAA).

The Center for National Security Studies, a private, non-profit research group, has commissioned a series of studies highly critical of LEAA. The agency was created under the Omnibus Crime Control and Safe Streets Act of 1968, and has disbursed $4.4 billion in grants to communities of all sizes across the nation to help them fight crime.

Most of that money, the Center concludes, was wasted. "The nation is in no better position today than it was (in 1968) . . . Crime has increased and no solutions to the crime problem are on the horizon." Having taken a close look at crime-lessening projects in eight large cities, the Center says that "LEAA's performance . . . was an irresponsible, ill-conceived, and politically motivated effort to 'throw money at a social program.' Many of the cities had no idea how to effectively spend (their share of $160 million) in such a short period of time and complained bitterly about LEAA's lack of assistance." The group says the agency should be abolished and, in its place, the government should fund research into the causes of crime and how to protect society.

Well, the country has had a gracious plenty of federally financed studies; even when their findings seem sound, they are usually ignored. But LEAA's cost-effectiveness certainly is suspect. If the agency should not be eliminated, the monies it has lavished on local law enforcement could at least be trimmed back considerably to experimental, pilot-type programs to help determine what, if anything, will reduce crime.

Such budget-cutting may be politically difficult. A lot of police departments, large and small, would like to retain access to funds that finance crime-fighting gimmicks and accessories of doubtful utility. Some people who object to government money being thrown at social problems have no qualms about cash being heaved at law enforcers. But there are definite limits to what the feds can do about crime, which is primarily a state and local responsibility. LEAA's activities have been mostly charade.

Richmond Times-Dispatch
Richmond, Va., May 21, 1976

The people in the federal government seem to believe that any problem can be solved by setting up a new bureaucracy to spend billions of dollars on it. While this approach seldom succeeds, many Americans were willing, almost in desperation, to see it tried in the war on crime.

So in 1968 Congress established the Law Enforcement Assistance Administration (LEAA) to fight crime largely through making grants to states and localities intended to strengthen the law enforcement and justice systems. In seven years LEAA has spent $4.5 billion of the taxpayers' money.

Alas, many critics feel that there is no evidence that the program has had any significant success in reducing crime. Now two separate studies by private groups call for abolition of the LEAA in its present form on the grounds that it is not doing the job for which it was created.

A Twentieth Century Fund task force, headed by former Virginia Gov. Linwood Holton, points out that the legislation creating LEAA required each state to establish a state planning agency to draw up an annual plan for use of federal funds within its jurisdiction. LEAA, the report says, "has encumbered the planning process with red tape...The printed guidelines for state plans are 200 pages long. The agency has spent hundreds of thousands of man-hours and millions of dollars in bureaucratic hairsplitting with 55 state and territorial planning agencies over the adequacy of the plans."

LEAA's failure, the report says, "suggests that it may be impossible to devise an administrative structure that can effectively police thousands of agencies and projects without infringing on states' rights, misconstruing local priorities, invading civil liberties, or maintaining a vast, expensive, and ultimately counterproductive staff."

In another report, this one of a study directed by Sarah C. Carey, a Washington lawyer, the Center for National Security Studies takes a look at LEAA's "high impact" program under which $160 million was channeled to eight cities to fight crime.

"LEAA's performance in the 'high impact' program was an irresponsible, ill-conceived and politically motivated effort to 'throw money at a social program'," the report declares. "Many of the cities had no idea how to effectively spend such a high level of funding in such a short period of time and complained bitterly about LEAA's lack of assistance."

Both of the reports recommend dismantling the LEAA bureaucracy and making any federal anti-crime grants available to the states and localities on a revenue sharing basis without federal designation as to exactly which projects can be financed.

Most of the LEAA money has been spent for police and related activities—that is, to aid in catching criminals. This is important, of course, but the fact is that, under present conditions, apprehending violators of the law is of limited value. For a variety of reasons, many apparently guilty criminals are not convicted, and even if convicted they often are back on the streets on probation or parole in relatively short time.

There is one good reason for not putting more criminals behind bars for long periods of time: There simply is nowhere to put them.

In Virginia, for example, the present rated capacity of the adult penal institutions is 5,893. The present inmate population is about 6,400. Furthermore, local jails hold nearly 2,300 convicted felons and misdemeanants who should be in state institutions. Under present building plans, by mid-1978 the rated capacity of state penal institutions will be 8,235. *If those 8,235 beds were available today, they would still not take care of prisoners for whom the state is now responsible.* And by mid-1978, the beds then available will be far short of taking care of the 12,500 prisoners estimated to be in the penal system by that time. The figures indicate that the state must step up its building plans, as costly as it may be to do so.

The expenditure of $4.5 billion by the LEAA certainly has not been without some benefits; certain state and local programs in Virginia, as in other states, have been improved through the federal grants. And any criticism of those who have administered the LEAA must be tempered by the knowledge that if they have been floundering in carrying out their part of the anti-crime war, they have plenty of company. A decade ago the conventional wisdom in this whole field was that prisons would soon be outmoded (except for a few hardcore vicious criminals) because the vast majority of law violators would be kept on probation or parole or under supervision in community-based rehabilitative programs. In just a few years there has been a complete turn-around in thinking on this subject, and now virtually everyone agrees that incarceration is necessary for large numbers of criminals.

The search for effective weapons for use in the war on crime must continue, but with the realization that tax dollars indiscriminately spent aren't such a weapon.

The Courier-Journal

Louisville, Ky., May 12, 1976

IF A SUNSET LAW were in operation for federal agencies, a prime candidate for having its mandate lapse would be the Law Enforcement Assistance Administration. Even at its inception in 1968, at the height of the public concern for law and order, there were doubts whether this agency was anything more than a cosmetic approach to the problems of crime. Now, as an independent study has confirmed, that is just what it was, to the tune of $4.4 billion.

The study, prepared for the nonprofit Center for National Security Studies, is laced with pungent criticisms of the way the LEAA went about coping with the crime wave. Money was handed out indiscriminately, yet cities found themselves burdened with red tape whenever they moved a step. In particular, the report attacks the High Impact Program, launched in 1972, as "an irresponsible, ill-conceived and politically motivated effort to 'throw money at a social program.'" The eight target cities actually experienced an increase in violent crime during the period.

None of this is really news. Other critics of the LEAA have been saying similar things for years. Some of the money has been spent wisely. But undermanned and ill-trained police forces using LEAA funds to buy armored cars and anti-riot gear, for instance, were criticized during the early years for extravagant spending on items hardly likely to reduce burglaries, rapes and muggings. Yet this latest report, fourth in a series on the agency, also has useful recommendations to offer.

One is that more reliable methods of reporting and collating crime statistics should be developed. If workable ways are to be found to reduce crime rates, they must be based on accurate facts and figures, not on myths or fantasies. Yet, for years, crime statistics have been subject to the whims of local politicians and police chiefs more anxious to make their own records look good than to present a realistic picture of what is happening.

Secondly, money should be spent on top-level research into the causes of crime and ways to protect society instead of being dumped into the cities in a hodge-podge of uncontrolled experiments. Some hypotheses would have to be tested out in the cities. But expenditures of funds should be geared to scientific analysis of a particular situation rather than to the police chief's urge for sophisticated hardware or a judge's desire to improve his image.

Finally, and most urgently, the LEAA should be abolished as quickly as possible, before it can waste any more billions of dollars. Since it has spread so much gravy around during its eight years, the agency doubtless has acquired a powerful constituency that would fight any attempt to kill it. But the extravagance has been so great and the results so minimal that politicians should leap at the chance to accomplish a dramatic trimming of the federal budget by letting the sun set on the LEAA.

St. Petersburg Times

St. Petersburg, Fla., May 11, 1976

Richard Kleindienst is credited with suggesting "law and order" as the theme of Barry Goldwater's presidential campaign in 1964. Lyndon Johnson asked Congress for the Law Enforcement Assistance Act of 1968 to give federal financing to local police projects. John Mitchell made law and order a theme of Richard Nixon's campaigns in 1968 and 1972. Nixon embraced the concept of LEAA and had Spiro T. Agnew personally launch its most ambitious program, an unsuccessful effort to reduce crime in eight major cities.

IN THE 12 YEARS since, Kleindienst, Mitchell, Nixon and Agnew have had their own encounters with the law. $4.4-billion later, LEAA also is in trouble. An independent study of the agency concludes that it should be abolished: "LEAA is unclear as to its mission, and what it has attempted it has done poorly . . . The nation is in no better position today than it was" in 1968.

Many of the individual LEAA grants have been worthwhile. Police communications equipment has been upgraded. Law enforcement training and planning have improved. Excellent programs to enlist community volunteers in anti-crime efforts have been started. Grants the police like best have gone for crime labs, computers and helicopters.

But LEAA also has set new standards for waste and mismanagement.

LEAA spent $2.3-million on research for an economical police car only to recommend a standard compact sedan costing $10,000. It spent $422,073 in California to buy mini-bikes, which it called "outreach tools," for a youth project. It paid out $67,000 for three Army tanks for the Birmingham, Ala., police department. It spent $117,000 in planning funds to pay college tuition costs for sons of high-ranking police officers, including the son of the Alabama public safety director and the son of one of Gov. George Wallace's bodyguards. LEAA paid a Washington writer $99,330 to write its annual reports.

The worst mismanagement of LEAA funds in Florida came during the administration of former governor Claude R. Kirk Jr. Six days before the first primary election in 1970 in which Kirk was seeking re-election, he personally issued 10 "Owl Eye" night vision devices costing $7,500 each to 10 police departments. It turned out the owl eyes had been bought on credit without proper authorization. The state auditor reported that the agency under Kirk spent $476,000 without complying with the law.

ALL OF THESE details give added authority to the conclusions of the study.

The question is what is Congress going to do about it when the agency's authorization expires July 1. Like other federal grant programs, LEAA has created its own constituency of law enforcement officers who want the money to keep coming.

Instead of listening to those with a vested interest, Congress should examine the performance and efficiency of LEAA on its own merits. From the evidence at hand, it should follow the recommendation of this week's study and let the LEAA die at the end of this fiscal year.

The Hartford Courant

Hartford, Conn., May 13, 1976

During the late 1960s, federal politicians were placed under great pressure to do something about "crime in the streets." That was, and still is, primarily a state and local responsibility. Nevertheless, Congress created the "Omnibus Crime Control and Safe Streets Act of 1968."

A major creation of that act is the Law Enforcement Assistance Administration, which has spent $4.5 billion, and continues to spend nearly $1 billion a year, for the stated purpose of aiding local law enforcement efforts. Despite that good intent, however, and despite the 1968 act's self-serving title, the streets have become more dangerous. LEAA has failed in its purpose, and its legal mandate, up for renewal this year, should be allowed to expire.

By significant coincidence, two major independent studies of the LEAA have both just concluded it should not be continued, at least not in its present form. One report comes from the Center for National Security Studies; the other from the Twentieth Century Fund.

Both also suggest that the money now devoted to LEAA programs be concentrated in two major areas: Federal research and evaluation of new anti-crime ideas, and direct revenue-sharing aid to local governments.

Rising crime statistics alone are testimony to LEAA's expensive ineffectiveness. This is the agency that armed small-town police forces with exotic weapons they probably will never have occasion to use. LEAA was also behind the "Berlin wall" scheme to confine Hartford's crime within its high-crime area.

Not all LEAA programs have been as ill-conceived but its overall record is still one of an expensive failure. The research and revenue-sharing proposals should be considered as constructive alternatives, but there is doubt that even these would prove to be worth their cost.

And whatever is to be done must be done by Congress, which at the moment is proceeding in the wrong direction. One of the major study-group criticisms of LEAA is that local officials have been overburdened with guidelines to be followed and mandatory programs to be executed. The current atmosphere in Congress is to add even more guidelines and programs.

Congress should instead take the rare step of letting LEAA expire when its time is up. A not-so-small bonus would be to save nearly $1 billion a year.

LEAA RESTRUCTURING SUGGESTED; ALL REGIONAL OFFICES TO BE SHUT

Attorney General Griffin B. Bell June 30, 1977 released a report by a Justice Department special committee urging a restructuring of the Law Enforcement Assistance Administration (LEAA). The report is to be circulated to Congress, governors, state attorneys general and other state and local officials for comment. The LEAA is chiefly responsible for providing states with federal crime-fighting aid. Almost $6 billion has been spent on LEAA programs since 1969. Bell frequently has criticized the agency for spending too much time and money on bureaucratic red tape.

Among other things, the study group recommended that the LEAA put more emphasis on research and funnel money more directly to the states. The agency was also urged to loosen the requirements of the detailed spending plans that states had to submit in order to receive federal funds. Only one person on the seven-member committee recommended a dismantling of the LEAA. Paul A. Nejelski, a deputy assistant attorney general, estimated such a move would save about $700 million a year. The money, he suggested, could be better spent in other programs.

All 10 of the LEAA's regional offices would be closed in September, Deputy Attorney General Peter F. Flaherty announced June 20. The move, he said, was "an essential step to streamlining LEAA's delivery" of federal anti-crime funds. He stressed that the action was not related to the LEAA reorganization study then underway. Set to close were the offices in: New York, Boston, Denver, Dallas, Seattle, Kansas City, Kan., Chicago, Philadelphia, Atlanta and San Francisco. The closings would eliminate 200 of the 335 jobs held by LEAA employes in the regional offices. The remaining employes would be transferred to Washington or to the four regional audit offices, in Atlanta, Chicago, Denver and Sacramento. Flaherty estimated that the job eliminations would result in an annual saving of $3 million.

President Carter August 2 signed a $7.7-billion appropriations bill which allocated $2.3-billion for the Justice Department in Fiscal 1978. Included in the Justice Department total were $529 million for the Federal Bureau of Investigation; $182 million for the Drug Enforcement Administration; $266 million for the Immigration and Naturalization Service; $308 million for the federal prison system and $647 million for the LEAA.

The Washington Post
Times Herald

Washington, D.C., April 13, 1977

ATTORNEY GENERAL BELL'S decision to conduct a full scale review of the organization and operations of the Law Enforcement Assistance Administration is well founded. LEAA has been the target of heavy criticism almost from the day it was created in 1968. Some of the criticism is justified and some is not. But the time has come for a careful study of where LEAA is going.

LEAA was created out of a sense of despair over the rising crime rate and in the hope that throwing federal dollars at law enforcement would somehow bring the crime problem under control. A good many dollars have been thrown—about $6 billion—although that is just a drop compared to what state and local governments spent in the same period. And not all of them were aimed well. In its early years, LEAA spent far too much of its resources on police forces, particularly on equipping them. More recently, it has spread itself too thin; it has more than 50,000 programs under way and sometimes gives the impression of being out of administrative control. Add to that the politicking and log-rolling that inevitably accompany a half-billion-dollars-a-year grant budget and it is easy to understand why Mr. Bell wants a thorough review.

Despite its problems, LEAA has had considerable success. Its existence has forced states to start coordinating their law enforcement programs and has forced politicians to deal in the realities, rather than the rhetoric, of crime control. It has financed many programs that would not otherwise have gotten off the planning boards. And a majority of its projects have proved their worth to local officials who have continued them after federal money ran out.

At the root of many of LEAA's problems is federalism. Law enforcement and crime control are local problems, and the federal government has no direct role in the way they are handled. Thus, there is a strong argument that any federal money used to bolster these activities should go to the states without strings attached. Yet the purpose of LEAA is to stimulate new approaches and to foster better programs. To do that, strings need to be attached if only to stop local governments from substituting federal funds for locally raised funds to pay for the same old programs. And, as LEAA has grown older, more and more strings have been attached to the money it hands out, thus complicating administration and creating bureaucratic snarls.

That is one of the problems to which the Attorney General's study group should direct itself. Have state and local governments become sufficiently sophisticated now about crime control problems to use federal funds wisely with much less federal supervision? There are others. Is there a better way than LEAA has devised to channel money to promising projects? Is the country getting its money's worth out of the $750 million LEAA spends annually? And, above all, is there still a need for federal support of programs that are so totally local in nature? These questions deserve the kind of thorough inquiry the Attorney General has ordered.

THE BLADE

Toledo, Ohio, July 5, 1977

PRESIDENT Carter has vowed to reorganize several federal bureaucracies and the Law Enforcement Assistance Agency is high on the list. We cannot think of a better place to start.

Amid lots of law-and-order hoopla, LEAA was formed in 1968 to come up with innovative ideas to help states and cities fight crime. Since then the agency has spent $6 billion and, judging from the booming rate of violent crime throughout the nation, has failed miserably on its basic assignment — so much so that the question arises whether the agency is worth continuing at all.

LEAA's main accomplishments have been to create mountains of red tape and to spend a disproportionate amount of its money supplying police units with computers, fancy communications gear, or other gadgetry. This overgenerous funneling of funds to police has been at the expense of two other branches of law enforcement — the courts and the corrections systems. Toledo, of course, did get a $1.5 million contribution toward its new municipal courts building, but only after a long, hard struggle.

Although logic dictates that LEAA could well be disbanded without being missed by most Americans, that is unlikely to happen since the agency still has strong backing on Capitol Hill. It is a rare politician who will vote against anything that maintains the posture of crime fighting, ineffective though it may be.

The best that can be hoped for — assuming that this agency will be continued — is that LEAA will be restructured to make it less of a bureaucratic dud than it is. The Carter administration has this in mind, according to Deputy Attorney General Peter Flaherty. He told the U.S. Conference of Mayors recently that the agency "has failed to establish proper priorities for its programs," and added, "We are not satisfied with LEAA's record."

Attorney General Griffin Bell, a former federal judge, is said to favor loosening the strings Washington now attaches to LEAA allocations. That might be a good move, especially if it results in less money going to provide lawmen at local levels across the country with expensive paraphernalia rather than meaningful training that conceivably could help lower the crime rate.

The Houston Post

Houston, Tex., July 10, 1977

Atty. Gen. Griffin Bell thinks the nation may be able to do without the Law Enforcement Assistance Administration (LEAA). He has not yet decided to recommend that the controversial agency be abolished. But he has said on more than one occasion that he is considering it, most recently in outlining proposals to reorganize the Justice Department. Before he makes a final decision, however, Bell says he wants to hear from the public.

The history of the LEAA offers a classic study in the difficulty of abolishing, or even altering, a bureaucracy once it becomes entrenched. The agency was created in 1968 to help state and local justice systems reverse the spiraling rise in crime. Since then it has spent more than $4.5 billion in support of more effective law enforcement. Yet the crime rate continues to climb. The law authorizing the LEAA expired last year, but Congress voted to extend it another three years and approved the expenditure of another $2.5 billion by the agency over that period.

The LEAA was given a new lease on life despite several reports critical of its performance. Some of these recommended that it be terminated or drastically altered. One study by the Twentieth Century Fund proposed that the agency be extended only if it were restructured and the "false promise" to reduce crime was removed from its mandate.

Bell has suggested that if the LEAA is abolished, some of its functions should be retained and incorporated into other Justice Department agencies. He cited its research work as an example of the activities he feels have contributed to a better understanding of the crime problem. The strongest resistance to abolition of the LEAA has come from police and other criminal justice officials whose agencies have benefitted from millions in federal grants it has dispensed. But Bell has proposed that, if the agency is shut down, crime-fighting funds could be distributed through the revenue-sharing program. Under such an arrangement, state and local governments would no longer have to submit plans to Washington detailing how the money was to be spent.

It would be unfair to blame the LEAA for failing to reverse the spiraling crime rate or not to give it credit for doing some valuable work. But the three-year extension Congress voted for the agency last year was predicated in part on the assumption that the agency's performance would be evaluated and changes made to improve its effectiveness. There is little evidence that this is happening. Perhaps it is too soon to make a judgment, but if more isn't done to change the LEAA's generally negative public image, we should salvage those parts of it that have demonstrably contributed to the fight against crime and jettison the rest.

THE CINCINNATI ENQUIRER

Cincinnati, Ohio, March 4, 1977

GRANTED THE RECORD of the Law Enforcement Assistance Administration (LEAA) is spotty, at best. Crime zooms despite the $4.5 billion the agency has spent since its creation in 1968.

But as Carter administration staffers determine precisely the role to be played by the agency, they might well consider LEAA simply may have been a slow learner. For there are signs of hopeful new life in the agency, that it may at last be gripping the root causes of the crime spiral.

For example, the agency has committed $8.5 million to 18 cities—including Columbus, Indianapolis and Louisville—to help them clear the streets of career criminals. The grants were aimed at beefing up prosecutorial staffs, focusing specialists on repeat offenders who have no business being anywhere but in prison. Many law-enforcement experts are convinced the only way to cut violent crimes—murders, holdups and the like—is to get the career criminals in jail and keep them there.

A Federal Bureau of Investigation (FBI) study shows at least 250,000 persons in the active pursuit of crime. City and state police agencies will need every aid to get and keep them off the streets. Obviously, federal funds, accompanied by the expertise LEAA officials muster from their experience, cannot do it all. But with a rifling, on-target approach, as opposed to the broad grant-allotments that may have cut its effectiveness, LEAA might yet measure up to the hopes of its originators.

Moreover, there's no way to prove the crime rate would not have been even higher without LEAA. This much is certain: The agency has galvanized thinking at local, regional and state levels about how to move co-operatively against crime. It has been the unwavering catalyst of regionalizing attacks on narcotics—as in the Cincinnati-Hamilton County area.

Critics charge LEAA with being nothing more than a spigot of funds for new police equipment—shiny radio systems and the like. But the agency has also financed instruction at University of Cincinnati and Xavier University to improve police fitness for the myriad emotional and psychological situations they encounter. And it has been the repository of annual state anticrime reports that rank as the best index, perhaps, on what's happening in law enforcement from local level up.

The agency may indeed need changes in its operations. New legislation may be required, for example, to give it a sharper focus, to modify any necessity it may feel to parcel out funds just to make sure every locality, however small and relatively crime-free, gets a share. But perhaps LEAA, charged with one of the highest-priority missions, deserves another chance.

AKRON BEACON JOURNAL
Akron, Ohio, April 18, 1977

BACK IN 1968, when Lyndon B. Johnson was urging lawmakers to enact his Safe Streets and Crime Control Act, he told Congress, "This year America must decisively capture the initiative in the battle against crime."

Nine years and nearly $6 billion in federal taxes later, the initiative indeed has been captured, but the villain remains on the loose. Crime still has its hands clasped tightly around the throat of American life

The chief weapon in the Johnson program was the Law Enforcement Assistance Administration (LEAA), which channels federal tax funds back to the states for research and support of local crimefighting projects. LEAA will have distributed nearly $753 million in the year ending Sept. 30. That's nearly one-third of the overall Justice Department budget.

But while the money was changing hands from the taxpayers to Washington back to state capitals and then back to local police and law enforcement agencies. crime continued to flourish. Was the money going down a rathole?

Atty. Gen. Griffin B. Bell is now asking the same question. The word in Washington is that he has ordered a study to determine whether LEAA should be drastically revised or abolished. He repeatedly has complained about the agency's past.

It certainly makes one wonder about the usefulness of Washington's anticrime effort when there's cheering over 1976 statistics showing that for the first time since 1972 the FBI's crime index didn't rise. Mind you, it didn't drop, either. It just stayed level. That's considered by many law enforcement officers a victory of sorts.

Despite the leveling off of violent crime nationally, New York City experienced an all-time record number of reported felonies and serious crimes: 658,147. That's about one crime for every 12 residents, not even counting misdemeanors and unreported felonies.

A University of Pennsylvania study completed last December projected a continued leveling trend in violent crime in the late 1970s and early 1980s. But it based its predictions not on the impact of the LEAA programs, but rather a decrease in the proportion of the population in the most crime-prone age group of 14 to 21.

A big chunk of the LEAA funds has gone to purchase hardware and gadgetry of questionable value in combating crime. Other grants have been used to finance foolish studies, such as why inmates want to escape from prison and why there's more crime in neighborhoods where people move in and out a lot.

With the LEAA's undistinguished record, it strikes us as a crime to allow it to continue to exist in its current form.

The Evening Bulletin
Philadelphia, Pa., April 27, 1977

Attorney General Griffin Bell wants a searching evaluation made of the Law Enforcement Assistance Administration (LEAA). He wonders whether we really need the agency.

The way LEAA has been operating, there really doesn't seem to be question but that we could quite easily do without it.

LEAA was set up ten years ago, at the height of the "make our streets safe" furor, to reduce crime by improving the criminal justice system. The criminal justice system is in need of sweeping improvement, but LEAA has failed to achieve this. What LEAA has done is spend about $6 billion for a seemingly endless number of studies and surveys that appear to have done little or nothing beyond creating jobs for a great many lawyers, criminologists, sociologists and psychologists.

LEAA also spent a great deal of money to finance routine police work and buy such basic police equipment as patrol cars and radio equipment. There was a financial saving for the localities involved in these latter projects, but LEAA was to come up with innovative police methods, not serve as a revenue sharing device for police departments.

LEAA ought to have its basic mission restated in very simple terms. Our courts don't do the job they are supposed to. Our penal institutions don't, either. And our police clearly cannot keep pace with changing crime techniques. So there is a great deal that LEAA can do, but hasn't. The trouble may be that the states, in exerting their control over LEAA spending distort the agency's mission. Or this distortion may come at the local level, since law enforcement and crime control have long been regarded as local problems.

If Attorney General Bell and his study group cannot get LEAA on the track it should be on, it would be better to scrap LEAA and save the $750 million it spends each year.

The Salt Lake Tribune
Salt Lake City, Utah, July 12, 1977

In the last few years the federal Law Enforcement Assistance Administration (LEAA) has been fighting for its life as well as fighting crime. The two battles are closely related.

LEAA was created in 1968 as a response to rising national crime rates. It was supposed to help local governments improve their crime-fighting techniques and to distribute federal money to them for that purpose.

Anti-crime plans and programs were produced in abundance. And some $6 billion was expended. But neither the money nor the programs seemed to have any effect on crime which continued to increase. LEAA was increasingly labeled a failure but Congress refused to scrap an agency which provided so much federal money to local government. Besides, it was noted with a good deal of truth, LEAA had not been created as a sure-fire means of reducing crime.

In addition to its inability to show spectacular crime-curbing results, LEAA has been criticized for being wasteful and overly bureaucratic and for spending too much money on exotic police hardware and for needless studies.

So unpopular has LEAA become that the Justice Department is reported to want to remove the agency from its jurisdiction if it cannot be abolished altogether. Ten regional offices are scheduled to close in September and other reductions are under consideration.

There is a line in a Robert W. Service poem about a "race of men who don't fit in" and LEAA can be described as a government agency that never fit in. Since crime fighting in the United States is predominantly a local affair, a federal agency, even one willing to give large sums of money away, is doomed to the role of prying outsider.

It was much the same at the federal level. LEAA was conceived as an innovator but it was placed under the wing of the Justice Department which is moored to tradition.

In addition, LEAA faced the difficult, often unpleasant, task of inducing local governments to change longstanding policies and practices and to try new, supposedly better methods, many of which became a local tax burden when the federal funding ran out.

There is not much doubt that LEAA succeeded in injecting new concepts and shattering old ones that hobbled the country's criminal justice system. But there is considerable question that the job was worth $6 billion and whether it should be continued, at least in the present mold.

LEAA is ripe for a full-dress reappraisal in light of a decade of experience and changed conditions.

THE INDIANAPOLIS NEWS
Indianapolis, Ind., July 8, 1977

Where may soaring crime rates best be controlled? At the Federal level, with uniformity and a great deal of money? Or at the community level, where crime most actively affects citizens?

"There isn't a criminal element out there large enough or powerful enough or sinister enough to stand up against an aroused community," said Police Chief James P. Damos of University City, Missouri, last week, while addressing the first meeting of the new National Crime Prevention Association. Crime can be effectively controlled at the community level. And it looks as though President Carter and the Justice Department agree with that assessment.

In the past, American presidents have spent billions futilely trying to control crime from the Federal level. Special programs, new equipment, high powered consultants — all were tried in an attempt to stop crime that grew like fast-spreading cancer. Federal money was wasted on layers of bureaucracy and salaries for those paid to administer anti-crime grants. A case in point is the Law Enforcement Assistance Administration.

The LEAA, born in 1968, provides block grants to fund projects initiated at the local level. Layer after layer of bureaucracy and paperwork have swamped the good ideas. The Carter administration and Atty. Gen. Griffin B. Bell have decided to close down the agency's 10 regional offices in September of this year, eliminating one-fourth of the LEAA's 850 jobs. And yet, by Bell's estimate, that move will eliminate only one of five layers of planning bureaucracy in the agency. In fact, the Justice Department would like to abolish the LEAA altogether, and institute revenue sharing earmarked for special projects and administered by the Treasury Department.

Since the government has such a dismal record in helping to retard rising crime rates, perhaps it is time to quit counting on effective help from the Federal level. The News' recent series on juvenile justice showed that crime is a very local, very personal experience. Mayer Maloney's stories and interviews illustrated how crime can victimize you or your neighbors, and how it inevitably costs you money in taxes for correctional institutions.

Crime is an outgrowth and a reflection of local conditions. It mirrors the teen-age unemployment, the decaying streets, the impersonality and anonymity of your town, your street, your life.

Local programs can be very effective. Indianapolis' own Concerned Neighbors' Crime Watch has been credited as a powerful factor in reducing crime in this community month after month since its inception. Such programs are extremely important in fighting the massive increases in crime this country has seen.

Only concerned citizens and concerned local law-enforcement agencies can give the proper care and attention to a problem that affects them so directly and so violently.

THE TENNESSEAN
Nashville, Tenn., June 24, 1977

THERE are some significant signs that the Law Enforcement Assistance Administration may be facing the beginning of its end.

The Justice Department has announced plans to close 10 regional offices stretching from New York to San Francisco. The closings may eliminate about 200 jobs from the agency that oversees anti-crime grants to the states.

While the Justice Department denied that the closings were a step toward loosening LEAA control over crime fighting grants, that step, along with some remarks by Attorney General Griffin Bell, do not bode well for the agency.

In an interview with the Associated Press, Mr. Bell indicated he is considering abolishing most or all of the Justice Department agencies that pass out federal crime-fighting money.

The LEAA in its present role probably wouldn't be missed. It has been under fire since its beginning for allegedly wasting money on poorly conceived and ineffective projects.

At least two independent studies have concluded that the LEAA has accomplished little in fighting crime, and both indicated the program might be ended.

One study, by the Twentieth Century Fund task force on the LEAA, noted that the agency's expenditure of $4.5 billion over a seven-year period improved the criminal justice system only slightly and had no noticeable effect on crime rates.

Another study, directed for the Center for National Security Studies, examined the LEAA "high impact" program under which $160 million was channeled to eight cities in the U.S. It said:

"LEAA's performance in the high impact program was an irresponsible, ill-conceived and politically-motivated program to 'throw money at a social problem.'"

LEAA money has gone for a good many frills for law enforcement, including such things as a Dale Carnegie course for policemen.

If the agency is to be kept, it should be restructured and given a role change. It could be a research and program evaluation body that could help law enforcement agencies improve their own programs.

One of the studies urged that the regional bureaucracy be dismantled and it can be assumed that the closing of 10 regional offices is a step in that direction.

The increase of crime is a matter of concern from the community to the national level and there should be no flagging of effort in trying to deal with the problem. But the LEAA efforts haven't seemed to work very well and that is why the handwriting is on the wall.

Rocky Mountain News
Denver, Colo., November 29, 1977

THANKS TO A PROGRAM being funded by the Law Enforcement Assistance Administration, at least several thousand potential crimes will not be committed during at least the next several years.

The program is an effort to crack down on "career criminals" by assisting local prosecutors to identify repeat offenders as they are arrested for new crimes, to speed such cases through the courts and to obtain stiff prison sentences.

Begun in 22 cities in May 1975, the program resulted in the identification of 5,107 career criminals through Aug. 1, 1977. More than 4,700 of them were convicted of a variety of crimes, mostly serious, and were given prison sentences averaging 14.3 years.

At the time of their latest arrest, about half of these career criminals were free on bond or were on probation or parole for previous offenses. Indeed, the 5,107 criminals had a total of 30,000 prior convictions.

James Gregg, acting administrator of the agency, calls the program "one of LEAA's most worthwhile undertakings." We agree.

So effective has the approach been, in fact, that many cities and counties are financing their own programs with their own money.

More and more people involved in the justice system are coming around to the belief that there is such a thing as the career criminal and that there really isn't a great deal that can be done to rehabilitate him. Some studies have indicated that merely growing older is the surest cure for criminal tendencies.

It follows then that the best thing both for society and for the repeat offender is to keep him out of circulation as long as possible.

The nation's war on crime finally may have found the enemy.

Delinquent Youth: In need of treatment or punishment?

Juvenile delinquency appears to be the motor force behind the crime explosion. Though juveniles under 18 represent only 30% of the population they commit approximately 50% of all serious property crimes and 25% of all violent crimes.[1] Furthermore, between 25% to 66% of those in adult correctional centers have had juvenile delinquency records.[2] While demographers foresee a decline in the proportion of juveniles to the total population, the problem of juvenile crime and its consequences will remain severe.

A prominent feature of the criminal justice is its differentiated approach to juvenile crime. A child found guilty by a court of a criminal act is not adjudged a criminal but a juvenile delinquent who is not to be sentenced but treated according to his specific needs. The origins of this philosophy date back to the Quaker-inspired House of Refuge reform movement of the early 1800's.[3] The reformers were appalled by the practice of sentencing children to long prison terms and placing them in jails with hardened criminals. Houses of Refuge spread throughout the country as alternatives to prisons for children. The goal of the houses was to provide moral regeneration to children; religion and education were stressed as an aid in rehabilitation. Still, life was harsh in the Houses, solitary confinement and beatings common occurrences. Thomas Eddy, a founding father of the movement, explained the moral underpinnings for the child's regimen: "Misery is ordained to be the companion and the punishment of vice."[4] Because of the stiff discipline some judges were known to order less hardened delinquents to adult prisons where the sentences were shorter and life less severe.[5]

The Chicago Reform Movement followed the Houses of Refuge movement. It differed from its predecessor in stressing the importance of family life in molding the character of wayward youth. The passage of the first juvenile court statute by the Illinois state legislature in 1899 is attributed to its influence. The establishment of juvenile courts has since spread to every state in the country.

In principle the juvenile court system espoused the theories of the early child reform movement: the court process should be neither punitive nor adversary, and the child should be made to feel that he is the object of the state's care and solicitude.[6] The court and the judge were cast as the child's substitute parent (*parens patriae*).

The non-adversary approach, the informal atmosphere and the precedent of the early criminal courts' treatment of children created a situation where the constitutional rights accorded to adults were not applied to children in the juvenile court. The United States Supreme Court first recognized this problem in the mid-1960's.

"There is evidence that the child receives the worst of both worlds: that he gets neither the protections accorded to adults nor the solicitious care and regenerative treatment postulated for children."[7]

In 1967, the Supreme Court's ruling in the case of *In re Gault*[8] revolutionized juvenile court procedure. The Court found that Gerald Gault, a minor convicted of making indecent telephone calls, had been denied his constitutional right to due process. The Court's ruling accorded juvenile defendants the right to confront their accusers through cross-examination, to information about the bases of the charges, to free legal counsel, to an impartial hearing and to protection against self-incrimination. The court's opinion also clearly stated the inadequacies of the juvenile justice system as it then existed:

"The rhetoric of the juvenile court movement has developed without any close correspondence to the realities of court and institutional routines."[9]

While Gault eliminated some of the procedural inequities between delinquency and criminal trials, many differences remained unchallenged. By reaffirming the guardian role of the juvenile courts over children, the Gault decision did not compel juvenile court procedure to meet the same constitutional demands as a criminal trial. (Subsequently, in *McKeiver V. Pennsylvania*, the Court ruled that jury trials in juvenile delinquency cases were not essential to comport with due process requirements.)[10]

Inasmuch as constitutional abuses of children's rights are less likely under the Gault mandate, many critics of the juvenile court system would like to see further equalization of adult and juvenile processes. One target has been the informal adjudication of delinquency charges by a probation officer prior to having the case sent before a judge. The goal of this pre-trial process is to screen out baseless charges and avoid stigmatizing a child with an arrest record if the offense is minor. In New York, an estimated 50% of the complaints lodged against juveniles are dismissed in pre-trial adjudications.[11] Other disputed practices have been the sealing of the criminal records of juveniles, the requirement that newspapers respect the anonymity of minors and the indeterminate sentence.

Indeterminate sentences remain the linchpin of the juvenile treatment process. Actually, the indeterminate sentence has a maximum period, usually three-to-six years for children. Because juveniles convicted of criminal acts are considered to be in need of individual rehabilitation as opposed to punishment, the argument follows that only a trained child therapist is qualified to determine when confinement should end. Gerald Gault [see above] had been sentenced to up to six years for making indecent telephone calls. If he had been an adult, he would have received no more than two months. On the other hand, children convicted of serious crimes may be incarcerated for very short periods, if at all, depending upon their perceived need for treatment. In New York, only a minute fraction of those convicted are placed under strict confinement.[12]

The treatment issue has become the new battleground in the juvenile delinquency field. If a child is being institutionalized solely for treatment and not for punishment, it is argued that he should be released if the treatment is not working.[13] The high recidivism rate among juvenile offenders seems to be proof of the failure of rehabilitation strategies. Some, like psychiatrist Thomas S. Szasz, attribute the failure of the treatment approach to its basic assumption that delinquent children are mentally unbalanced.[14] Szasz feels otherwise: children who commit anti-social acts are not necessarily abnormal and non-punitive concepts of treatment only inhibit a child from taking full responsibility for his unacceptable behavior.

If juvenile programs remain unsuccessful, should not youths be imprisoned for the same reasons that adults are—retribution, condemnation, deterrence and the protection of the community? The outcome of debate on this subject will probably be an amalgam of several treatment approaches, resulting in greater emphasis on rehabilitative theory but avoiding an exclusive preoccupation with it.

Notes

1. F.B.I. Uniform Crime Reports, 1974 pp. 186–187.
2. Barbara Wootton, *Social Science and Social Pathology* (London: G. Allen & Unwin, 1959) p. 136.
3. Anthony M. Platt, *The Child Savers: The Emergence of the Juvenile Court in Chicago* (Chicago: University of Chicago Press, 1968).
4. Quoted in David Schneider, *The History of Public Welfare in New York State 1609–1866* (Chicago: University of Chicago Press, 1938–41) p. 317.
5. Sanford Fox, "Juvenile Justice Reform: An Historical Perspective," 22 *Stanford Law Review* 1187, 1215 (1968).
6. Julien W. Mack, "Juvenile Courts," 23 Harvard Law Review 104, 120 (1909–1910).
7. *Kent v. United States,* 383 U.S. 541, 546 (1966).
8. *In re Gault,* 387 U.S. 1 (1967).
9. Stanton Wheeler & Leonard Cottroll, *Juvenile Delinquency: Its Prevention and Control* (New York: Russell Sage Foundation, 1966) p. 35. Quoted in *In re Gault,* 387 U.S. 30.
10. *Mckeiver v. Pennsylvania,* 403 U.S. 528 (1971).
11. Notes, "Ungovernability: The Unjustifiable Jurisdiction," 83 *Yale Law Journal* 1383, 1395 (1974).
12. Internal memorandum of the Legal Aid Society of New York, Juvenile Rights Division, from Janis Morton of October 7, 1977, p. 2. The memorandum, based on a survey of 2409 juvenile delinquency cases in the five boroughs of New York City, revealed that only 2.4% of all petitions closed in a six-month period resulted in strict confinement and another 7.3% in general placement.
13. Anna Louise Simpson, "Rehabilitation as the Justification of a Separate Juvenile Justice System," 64 *California Law Review* 984, 996–999 (1976).
14. Thomas S. Szasz, *Law, Liberty and Psychiatry* (New York: Macmillan, 1963).

SCHOOL CRIME'S 'CRISIS PROPORTIONS' REPORTED BY SENATE SUBCOMMITTEE

Violence and vandalism in the nation's schools cost over $500 million annually, a Senate subcommittee reported April 9. In an 18-month study of the public schools between 1970 and 1973, the Judiciary Subcommittee to Investigate Juvenile Delinquency found that more than 100 murders were committed annually. By 1973, at least 70,000 serious assaults against teachers were reported each year.

In the 1970–73 period, assaults on teachers increased 77.4%; on students 85.3%; robberies 36.7%; rapes and attempted rapes 40.1%; and homicides 18%. The New York City school system spent more than $1.25 million to replace 248,000 windows in one year. The report warned that increasing crime and an "unprecedented wave of wanton destruction and vandalism" were reaching "crisis proportions which seriously threaten the ability of our educational system to carry out its primary function" of teaching.

Sen. Birch Bayh (D, Ind.), the subcommittee's chairman, who began hearings April 16 on this problem announced his intention to introduce a bill that would provide grants to states to help make schools safer. (Similar safe-school bills had been introduced in the previous two Congresses but had failed to pass, although funding for the National Institution of Education to report on such legislation by 1976 was approved in 1974.)

Witnesses testifying before Bayh's subcommittee offered a number of reasons for escalating school violence and vandalism. James Harris, president of the National Education Association, suggested that major causes were alienation from and depersonalization of school systems, outmoded discipline practices, racial hostility and "increased use of violence in the society." Owen B. Kiernan, executive secretary of the National Association of Secondary School Principals, added to that list: breakdown of the family and family control, street crime spilling into the schools and "subgroup solidarity, with no allegiance to the larger society [and] contempt for the value of personal and public property." Albert Shanker, president of the American Federation of Teachers, cited the ineffectiveness of the courts in dealing with juvenile offenders. Even when the courts found a student dangerous to himself and those around him, Shanker said, they were often powerless to act because there were no special schools or institutional facilities available.

The Washington Star
and Daily News

Washington, D.C., April 14, 1975

Violence in the schools has reached suc alarming proportions that a Senate subcommittee chairman, Birch Bayh, has likened a repo on the subject to "a casualty list from a wa zone or a vice squad annual report." Unfortunately, the subcommittee seems unlikely come up with anything more helpful than th usual congressional tactic of trying to smother problem with money.

The report from Bayh's Judiciary subcommittee on juvenile delinquency is truly staggering The committee, drawing on a study made 1973, conservatively estimated that schoo vandalism is costing taxpayers a half billion do lars a year, which equals the amount spent na tionwide on school textbooks in 1972.

But even worse is the growing incidence violence against persons in the schools. Hu dreds of thousands of students are assaulte every year, the report said, and 100 of the were murdered in 1973 in the 757 school district surveyed. The subcommittee estimates that 70 000 teachers are physically assaulted annually Each year the problem gets worse. The subcom mittee said that between 1970 and 1973, assault on teachers increased 77.4 percent; robberies students and teachers increased 36.7 percent rapes and attempted rapes 40.1 percent; hom cides 18.1 percent. The number of weapon confiscated from students increased 54.4 pe cent.

How can we read such statistics and call our selves a civilized society? A more apt descrip tion is that we have become a knuckleheade society so overtaken with the misguided notio that everyone should be allowed to do his or he "thing" that we have produced a school syster near anarchy. Schools are, as Bayh remarked "too often . . . an environment dominated b fear, chaos, destruction and violence."

Bayh said he will introduce legislation to pro vide financial aid "to reduce delinquency an crime in and against our public schools." W submit that money is not the answer. The ar swer is for parents to find enough guts to tak back the school system. Until they demand tha discipline be enforced, it is not going to be.

School violence didn't just spring up over night. It has grown as discipline has been re placed by permissiveness. Dress and persona grooming codes were allowed to go by th boards; smoking regulations were all but abol ished; grades were made to come easier; clas cutting was blinked at or made to seem a lark swearing and abusive language were tolerated It was a natural progression to drugs vandalism and physical violence. Students hav been given so many inches, is it any wonde they have taken a mile?

But don't blame it all on the teachers an administrators, although they can share in it Blame it on the parents who gave encourage ment, acquiesced or looked the other way whe all this was coming about — who allowed per missiveness and lax discipline to permeate no only the schools but the home and society i general.

Sure, money can buy more police. But is tha what Americans want for their schools? Do the want schools in which security forces have t patrol the halls? What kind of learning environ ment is that?

It doesn't take money to know that crime an violence are not going to disappear from th schools until parents wake up to what they hav done to their children and allowed to be done i their schools — and find the courage to do some thing about it.

THE PLAIN DEALER

Cleveland, Ohio, April 14, 1975

When violence is increasing everywhere, it would be foolish to expect school buildings to be oases of order.

So it is no surprise, though it is disturbing nevertheless, to hear from Sen. Birch Bayh, D-Ind., that violence in the schools took at least 100 lives last year and that vandalism cost school systems a half billion dollars.

Cleveland and its suburbs have had pupils shot and stabbed in school or on school grounds, and vandalism is a major problem here. When a community organization last month studied three schools, many of the youngsters questioned reported that knives and guns are carried to school even by the youngest pupils.

The National Institute of Education is now conducting a wider study, in which Cleveland is included, of school crime and its prevention.

Legislation proposed by Sen. Bayh would give a school district that needed such help money for educational programs to combat juvenile delinquency. An equal amount, with certain restrictions, could be used by the district to support security programs.

Somewhat parallel legislation has been introduced in the House by Rep. Edward R. Roybal, D-Calif.

It must be kept in mind, however, that what is happening in the schools reflects a social climate that accepts violence even if it does not condone it and that glorifies brutality when it is called entertainment.

Certainly students should be able to attend schools where they are safe, and we can endorse efforts at any level to insure a safe school environment. But both Congress and local school officials should be wary about expecting the schools to take on and solve juvenile delinquency. The primary responsibility belongs to parents and to the community in general.

This may be another instance in which the schools are being encouraged monetarily to take on a responsibility that is not strictly an educational task.

CHICAGO Daily Defender

Chicago, Ill., April 21, 1975

There is much reasonable substance in the statement submitted by Acting Superintendent James F. Redmond to the Senate Judiciary subcommittee on juvenile delinquency. He said that much harm is done to educational programs when classroom windows are shattered, teaching materials destroyed or stolen, and schools damaged by fire and other acts of vandalism.

This description is meticulously correct. The emphasis is on harm done to school buildings. Though the money spent to repair them represents an enormous drain on school funds, there are other problems that impede far more seriously the educational process. The physical security of teachers, who are often beaten, shot and intimidated by unruly pupils, is far more an impediment to good teaching than anything that could happen to a school building. You can replace broken windows and stolen teaching materials, but you can't very well replace teacher-confidence and ability to teach once he is intimidated and threatened.

A total of 359 bomb threats were received by Chicago public schools in the last two school years. Dr. Redmond believes that an increase in allocation of federal funds to schools in areas with high crime rates would check violence and vandalism through utilization of more electronic alarms and more security officers.

We question the validity of that assumption. A deep-seated social wrong is not likely to be uprooted by surveillance—personal or electronic. At best, the results obtained would be temporary. What is sorely needed is a law making parents responsible for overt acts and violence committed by their school children.

Unruly pupils come from homes where discipline is an unknown quantity. When negligent parents find out that they will go to jail and pay a heavy fine for criminal offenses committed in the public schools by their children, it will be a horse of a different color.

Chicago Tribune

Chicago, Ill., April 22, 1975

There are at least two dimensions to the picture of violence and vandalism in the nation's schools. One is represented by figures and statistics released by the Senate Judiciary subcommittee on juvenile delinquency, and it is horrifying enough. It shows things like an 85 per cent increase in assaults on students between 1970 and 1973, a total bill for vandalism alone in excess of $500 million annually, more than 100 murders and 70,000 assaults on teachers committed in the schools each year.

The other dimension is what these numbers represent: an atmosphere of fear, violence, criminality, and near-anarchy in which millions of American school children must live and try to learn. It is hardly surprising if they do not learn very well. In the schools and districts that contribute most to these figures, the important subject is not geography or math; it is survival.

In testimony before the subcommittee this week, a spokesman for Chicago public schools — Deputy Superintendent Manford Byrd, sitting in for Acting Supt. James F. Redmond — drew the distinction between the losses that are measurable in numbers and those that are not.

"No one," said Mr. Byrd, "has measured the immediate and long-term effects on the education of children resulting from the climate of fear. . . . Many hours of education are lost because of false fire alarms and bomb threats. Much harm is done to educational programs when classroom windows are shattered, teaching materials destroyed or stolen, and schools damaged by fire and other acts of vandalism. When students and teachers are fearful of going to school — terrified by assaults and other acts of personal violence — a healthy environment for learning is lost. . . . The children lose and society loses, now and in the future."

Chicago's answers to these problems — which Mr. Byrd recommended to the senators — center on tighter security measures: picture identification cards for high school students, more security personnel, "silent alarm" systems connected with police stations, security teams including principals, teachers, staff, parents, and students.

Measures like these may "help to stabilize" the situation, in Mr. Bryd's words. Solving it is a different and much harder question. It will involve dealing with social conditions which produce violence. It is as tho great numbers of young people had concluded that the only way to prove their own existence is to destroy something.

And here, perhaps, is the missing third dimension in the problem of school violence.

According to the psychologists, destructive "acting out" is a way of expressing an unrecognized need. If so, we had better find out what "need" is being expressed by the surge of mindless violence in our schools. The answer when found may be a surprise.

It may well be that the need these children feel is not for more freedom, but for clearer guidance on how to use it — for rules backed up by real discipline, for school systems [and parents] who say "No" and mean it. Perhaps they are not, after all, rebels without a cause.

THE DAILY HERALD

Biloxi, Miss., April 23, 1975

In saner times than these, the introduction of the Juvenile Delinquency in Schools Act of 1975 in Congress last week would have brought an uproar reverberating throughout the 50 states. It went, instead, little noticed.

The report preceding the introduction paints a shocking picture of violence and vandalism in the schools. Its implications are frightening. Even the title of the Senate Subcommittee on Juvenile Delinquency report sounds like a lurid expose in a second rate tabloid: Our Nation's School—A Report Card: 'A' in School Violence and Vandalism.

Statistics quoted show that last year, the cost of vandalism and violence in schools was $590 million. In the last three years, more lives of boys and girls were lost in the schools than were lost in the first three years of America's involvement in Vietnam.

Surveying 757 public elementary and secondary school districts across the country, the subcommittee found approximately 70,000 serious physical assaults on teachers each year, and hundreds of thousands of assaults on students, including more than 100 students murdered in 1973 in the districts surveyed.

In one school district in one year, 250 weapons were confiscated; extortion, drug and prostitution rings were found in many of the school districts.

The present extent of the situation is one factor; another is that the survey demonstrates a continuing and dramatic increase during the three years covered. The following percentages of increases were experienced: assaults on teachers, up 77.4 per cent; assaults on students, up 85.3 per cent; robber-

ies of students and teachers, up 36.7 per cent; rapes and attempted rapes, up 40.1 per cent; homicides in the schools, up 18.5 per cent; number of weapons confiscated from students, up 54.4 per cent.

Apart from the cost, apart from the crime catalogue, students are finding an environment dominated by fear, chaos, destruction and violence instead of the quiet atmosphere of instruction, enrichment and encouragement. Teachers are engaged in dangerous and frustrating attempts to secure personal safety for themselves and their students.

The excessive portrayal of violence on television long ago captured the attention of parents concerned that its influence was unhealthy for their children. Their protests have brought abatement.

The schools exert a far more pervasive influence on the development of youngsters, determining whether a student becomes a contributing, useful member of society, or begins a life of frustration, failure and crime.

Two of the purposes of Senate Bill 1440, the Juvenile Delinquency in the Schools Act of 1975, are to curb delinquency, violence and vandalism in public schools and to protect the right of every student to due process and the right to receive an education in a school environment free of disruption and fear of personal harm.

As Congress concerns itself with this Act and deliberates its passage, parents would do well to familiarize themselves with its provisions and lend their support.

Young minds and young bodies are national resources too valuable to waste in blackboard jungles.

THE DALLAS TIMES HERALD

Dallas, Tex., April 21, 1975

THE ISSUE: *Violence in the schools.*

VIOLENCE IN the schools is not a myth. It is a shocking reality of today's society.

More than 100 students were murdered in 1973 on and near the premises of schools, according to a U.S. Senate subcommittee's report on violence in the nation's educational system.

The report further said there are about 70,000 serious assaults a year on teachers and hundreds of thousands of assaults on students.

Concern about this serious growth of violence was focused last week in the Senate as some of the nation's educators and educational groups pleaded for more help from Congress.

No ready, simple solution is in sight. But there is an urgent call for more funding to provide security systems in the public schools and to have special facilities for disruptive and violence-proned students.

The cause of this upsurge of student violence is manyfold, but one great factor is the decline of parental supervision over children and the decline of community support for discipline in the public schools.

Society no longer holds parents responsible for the conduct of their children. And discipline too often gets defined as uniform dress codes rather than respect for teachers.

The public schools face a particularly difficult problem in that demands are placed upon them which private schools do not have to meet.

Private schools do not face the same problems for one simple reason. They can just expel the unruly and enroll only the best behaved students. To expel the public schools have to go through due process, hearings and even trials. They must enroll all who apply. Even if public schools do expell students, the problems are just put out into the streets.

More funds for security will help some school districts. Reducing the size of some schools would make the student populations more manageable, hiring more specially trained teachers and counselors might help, and building special facilities for problem students could help too.

But even more important is creating more respect for teachers and the educational system. Parents should join with teachers in stemming the violent tide.

Communities should find ways to hold parents more responsible for the conduct of their children.

If we dare let this violence grow in the schools, we will undermine one of the basic needs of our civilization—a good educational system.

TULSA DAILY WORLD

Tulsa, Okla., April 21, 1975

THE NATIONAL Education Association told a Senate subcommittee last week that 64,000 teachers were assaulted by students during the first half of the 1973-74 school year.

The Senators also learned from the NEA spokesman, JAMES A. HARRIS, that school robberies increased 117 per cent from 1970 to 1973; assault and battery on school grounds rose 58 per cent; sex offenses were up 62 per cent and drug-related problems, 81 per cent.

In spite of all this, HARRIS made it perfectly clear that NEA does not yet take the problem seriously enough to offer any new or drastic solutions.

HARRIS' principal proposal was the creation of a new Federal agency. His major criticism was directed at Local school boards and school administrators who have tried to protect their students and teachers by expelling the violent hoodlums.

HARRIS asserted that school boards and State officials have a mandatory responsibility to provide free public education for all children instead of excluding some from schools. (Believe it or not, that is the exact language used in an NEA press release.)

That makes sense. But until such programs are developed and the money is found to pay for them, teachers and students are still entitled to protection from robbery, assault and violent threats.

No number of new Federal bureaus or "guidelines" or "special programs" can have any real effect on the problem until the hoodlums are culled out of the regular classrooms. That has to be the first step.

One must sympathize with the teen-ager or sub-teen youngster whose deprived background and lack of family care may have made him violent and dangerous. Certainly, such children need special help and plenty of it. But to suggest that they must not be expelled from classes after they have become a threat to life and safety is pure bunk.

THE ARIZONA REPUBLIC
Phoenix, Ariz., April 16, 1975

The problem has been with us for years, but until recently it was like the weather. Everybody talked about it but nobody did anything.

Now, at last, communities across the nation are beginning to crack down on violence in the schools.

It's become a crime wave. In school after school, in affluent suburbs as well as slums, a Junior Mafia has taken over, terrorizing principals, teachers a n d pupils alike.

The Godfather would be proud of them.

Last year, says the National Association of School Security Directors, they committed 8,568 rapes a n d other sex offenses, 11,160 armed robberies, 256,000 b u r-glaries a n d 189,332 "major assaults."

Nobody can even begin to estimate how many windows they smashed, how many classrooms they destroyed. Anyway, for them, that's "kid stuff."

Crime in the schools is growing at a much greater rate than crime in the streets.

According to a recent Senate report, between 1970 and 1973, assaults on teachers increased 77.4 per cent; assaults on pupils, 85.3 per cent; robberies of teachers and pupils, 36.7 per cent; rapes and attempted rapes, 40.1 per cent; number of weapons taken from students, 54.4 per cent.

Obviously, the crackdown now under way is long overdue.

The schools are attempting to cope with the problem in a variety of ways.

In San Francisco, any student found with a weapon, even a first-grader with a Cub Scout knife, is subject to automatic suspension.

Houston, Tex., and Monticello, Ark., have given teachers a free hand to use wooden paddles on troublesome students.

New York City has set aside $10 million for school guards and security equipment, including equipment that enables a teacher to summon the guards when she's in trouble.

Elsewhere, schools are putting in closed-circuit television and electronic sensors that can smell out weapons.

North Carolina has passed a law making it a crime for a student to fight, attempt to provoke a fight, or ignore an order to leave a school building. An offender can get 6 months in jail.

Detroit is permitting armed police to patrol in and around the schools.

Unfortunately, a recent Supreme Court decision is going to make it more difficult for the schools to deal with troublemakers. The court ruled that children suspended from school have the right to due process and to sue for damages. The possibility of being hit with a suit is bound to give a good many teachers pause.

Another problem is that many states have laws that permit a youngster under 16 literally to get away with murder and rape, to say nothing of lesser crimes. New York has found that scores of youngsters willfully committed murder because they knew they would be treated merely as juvenile delinquents.

It's time such laws were changed.

The Dispatch
Columbus, Ohio, April 21, 1975

ALARMING DATA before a U.S. Senate subcommittee on judicial matters serve to compliment the wisdom of the Columbus Board of Education in planning a "traditional school" here.

The subcommittee has been told that vandalism in the nation's public schools cost an estimated $594.1 million last year, about the same amount as was spent on school textbooks.

THE STARTLING report, presented by the National Association of School Security Directors, also revealed that schools were the sites for 270,000 burglaries, 204,-000 assaults, 12,000 armed robberies and 9,000 forcible rapes.

Such statistics indicate that in too many instances public school atmosphere is approaching the point of anarchy.

Who is to blame? Surely, school administrators share responsibility for this development. However, there is an element in society which necessarily must be saddled with most of the blame.

THAT ELEMENT is the same which is pooh-poohing the "traditional school" concept.

It is the parent who insists a child must be free to do his own thing, who acquiesces to lax discipline not only in the home but in society as a whole and who screams to high heaven when discipline is mentioned in the school.

Among the announced concepts for the forthcoming "traditional school" is strict discipline. The parent who adheres to the permissive philosophy will not permit his child to be subjected to such atmosphere. Instead, he will send his child into the blackboard jungle where jungle law prevails.

OF COURSE, there will be demands that government furnish more money to pay for more security forces in the public schools.

But what responsible American parent actually wants his child to acquire an education under the barrel of a policeman's gun?

Money will not stop the robbers and rapists in the classroom.

WHAT WILL stop it will be the parent with courage enough and responsibility enough to discipline his own child in his own home before he enters the classroom.

Herald News
Fall River, Mass., April 16, 1975

Vandalism in the schools is now a national problem, which costs the country millions of dollars annually. As much is now spent repairing the damage done by vandals in our schools as is spent on textbooks. The total bill comes to about $500 million a year. This staggering sum is consumed for no reason except to pay for the malicious mischief of young people.

For there is no question but that virtually all of the vandalism in schools is committed by young people with grudges of one kind or another against the educational system. A certain amount of this is probably inevitable; it has always existed and presumably always will, unless human nature changes.

But the dimensions of the problem have now become so large that they can no longer be ignored. The amount of money involved is huge in the aggregate, but equally important is the interruption to normal classroom procedures as a result of damage done. Society as a whole has an immense stake in education; it has a right to demand that countermeasures be taken to curb vandalism.

The most obvious is to enforce existing laws so that some vandals are punished for their crimes. The deterrent of fear is more likely to be effective than any other. It is too infrequently employed these days.

Vandals are difficult to catch, but occasionally they are arrested, tried and convicted. The trouble is that the penalties crimes of this kind should entail are too often diluted or waived to the point where the vandals feel they have not really been punished at all.

Let the punishment fit the crimes, and the number of times schools are vandalized will drop.

THE ATLANTA CONSTITUTION
Atlanta, Ga., April 15, 1975

Crime in schools, as crime everywhere, can never be completely erased. But neither can it be tolerated.

A recent U.S. government survey of 500 school districts, including Atlanta's, showed that many thousands of crimes are committed annually in the schools, including murder, assaults on students and teachers, rapes, burglaries, extortion, and prostitution.

In Atlanta between 1971 and 1973, there were six homicides in the city's schools, 53 rapes or attempted rapes, 281 assaults upon either students or teachers and 1,046 burglaries or larcencies.

Atlanta detectives assigned to the schools report that all crimes, but particularly burglary and larcenies, have dropped considerably in the past year and a half, due to increased patrolling and the addition of burglary alarms.

The decline is good, but school officials and police should continue to concentrate strongly on reducing crime in school as much as absolutely possible. That is easier said than done, of course, but it has to be done in some way.

For those of us who grew up in an older time, crime in school meant playing hookey and buying beer from the old grocer who didn't ask about age. But it is much more serious than that now, and reflects the spread of crime throughout our society.

One way not to correct the situation is to pretend there is no crime in schools or it. try to ignore There's plenty of it and, kids being kids, many victims of crimes probably never report them to their parents or school officials.

The major step toward correcting crime in schools is the same as correcting it everywhere: When the criminals (and that's what they are, whether 15 or 40) are caught and found guilty, the penalty should be swift and severe.

When that happens, the old axiom about crime does not pay will begin to have some truth to it.

The Burlington Free Press
Burlington, Vt., April 23, 1975

VIOLENCE IN THE public schools of the United States is disrupting classrooms, causing fear for the safety of both teachers and pupils and costing taxpayers millions of dollars, according to reports from across the nation.

The National Association of School Security Directors reports 8,568 rapes and other sex offenses, 11,160 armed robberies, 256,000 burglaries, and 189,332 "major assaults" in schools of the nation in 1974. It is estimated that only about one of 20 such "incidents" in the schools is reported to the police. The cost to the taxpayers is estimated at above $600 million a year.

U.S. News & World Report, in a special report in the issue of April 14, outlines what is happening in the schools and some of the things being done to improve the situation.

The North Carolina Legislature has passed a law making it a crime for students to fight, to provoke violence by gestures or words, or to ignore an order to leave the building, in fact to do anything which "disrupts, disturbs or interferes with the teaching of students in any public or private educational institution." The maximum penalty: Six months in jail and a $500 fine.

In San Francisco, a new policy requires automatic suspension of any youngster carrying a weapon — even a first-grader with a Cub Scout knife. This is to counteract an increasing number of armed attacks in the schools. Uniformed hall guards, discontinued because of lack of funds, were rehired when disorders multiplied.

Chicago is spending nearly $3 million on school security this year after an elementary-school pupil shot a principal to death and 1,300 verbal and physical assaults on teachers were reported last year.

New York City's school board is planning to spend $10 million on school guards, special aides and security equipment, including pocket-size "panic buttons" that enable teachers to signal the central office when in trouble with violence they cannot handle alone.

It is reported that other security systems have been installed in thousands of schools, including closed-circuit television and electric sensors. A proposed Safe Schools Act now pending in Congress would provide up to $200 million to buy more such systems.

But the question is whether such efforts will be successful unless there is greater cooperation from parents and the majority of young people in the schools who realize that what is happening threatens to seriously interfere with their opportunities for education.

* * *

SOME NEW APPROACHES to the problem are said to be meeting with success. One of these is to segregate trouble-makers in special classes taught by teachers trained to handle them. It is recognized that not all teachers can adjust to meet these special needs.

At New Rochelle High School, outside New York City, disruptive youths attend evening classes, along with students who are taking extra courses and jobholders who work during the day. The atmosphere in these night classes seems to have a restraining effect on disruption efforts.

At San Francisco's "crime-plagued" Balboa High School, students organized themselves a few months ago, after a wave of purse-snatching and violence by teenagers. A group called Students for a Safer Community committed themselves to turn in disrupters and has won widespread community support. The city's human relations commission voted $1,000 for the effort.

While there may be dangers in promoting efforts of young people to police themselves, it is encouraging that they recognize the need for it. When faced with chaotic conditions which adults seem unable to handle alone, youngsters may give valuable cooperation in solving the problem. — E.F. Crane

THE BLADE
Toledo, Ohio, April 23, 1975

ESTIMATES given to a Senate panel that school vandalism and related crimes are costing the nation's school districts upward of a half-billion dollars annually are shocking enough, if true. But what the figure says about the lack of guidance and discipline in the home is even more disturbing.

As one yardstick, the cost was reported to equal the total amount of money spent on textbooks in every school in the country in 1972. Sen. Birch Bayh, chairman of a judiciary subcommittee, likened a report on the situation to "a casualty list from a war zone or a vice squad annual report," noting that 70,000 teachers and hundreds of thousands of students are victims of assault each year.

Although the situation in Toledo is not as bad as in some larger cities, and even allowing for a certain degree of overdramatization, there clearly is a need to cope with burglary losses estimated by the National Association of School Security Directors at $243-million annually, vandalism at $100-million, and fire losses at $109 million.

While school districts can take certain steps to try to minimize the problem, there is obviously a limit to what they can accomplish. The Toledo district has, in fact, made considerable progress along this line, having reduced the damage total from a previous yearly average of about $350,000 to an estimated $135,000. It did so by instituting certain security measures, such as brightly lighting all school buildings at night, installing an effective alarm system, using a new type of unbreakable window, assigning aids in schools to help keep order, and making parents liable, whenever possible, for damages done by juveniles.

Senator Bayh says he will introduce legislation to provide financial assistance for schools to reduce delinquency and crime. But no matter how much federal money is poured into such efforts, assuming it can be found at all, schools can conduct only a holding operation. They cannot alter undesirable attitudes and values that are established in the home during a child's formative years.

Today's more permissive social milieu is unquestionably a major factor in all this, but parents still retain the primary responsibility. Until more of them discharge their obligation more adequately, school budgets will have to allow for crime losses.

THE ANN ARBOR NEWS
Ann Arbor, Mich., April 19, 1975

RIGHT NOW, it's anybody's guess what is responsible for the staggering amount of violence and vandalism in public schools, as detailed in a Senate report last week.

Sen. Birch Bayh of Indiana, chairman of the Judiciary Committee's subcommittee to investigate juvenile delinquency, says he doesn't know what should be done, but he thinks the federal governemnt ought to step in.

Perhaps it's time to resurrect the special commission on the causes of violence. Maybe, however, we don't have to look any farther than society itself.

If one accepts the notion that the schools mirror society, then one may postulate that the school-age person sees violence approved in his society in the reality of war and the presentation of violence as justifiable and exciting on television and in movies.

One child development expert is quoted as saying that the school environment now breeds violence. What is needed is more respect for the individual needs of students.

Is that a vote of confidence for more types of alternative schools, such as Ann Arbor's Roberto Clemente center? We don't know. Surely there's something to be said for spotting the violence-prone ahead of time, but the schools and society itself are very weak in isolating anti-social behavior before it manifests itself.

* * *

EMERSON POWRIE, the school district's deputy superintendent for administration, says that Ann Arbor schools' levels of vandalism and violence are down. Assaults have declined or stayed about the same over the last two years.

The whole idea of posting officers in the corridors is repugnant to the traditional educational setting, but security in the schools is one of the things the Bayh subcommittee mentioned as something to consider on a larger scale.

The surge in school crime needs to be dramatized still further, and Sen. Bayh intends to hold public hearings on the problem. The taxpayer may be apathetic at times about crime in the streets because it seems so impersonal, but crime in the classroom is something else. When schools are crime bastions, then things are really bad.

THE RICHMOND NEWS LEADER

Richmond, Va., April 25, 1975

Every parent and every citizen who believes in quality public education will be appalled by the recent report of the Senate Subcommittee on Juvenile Delinquency. That report documents the turmoil and violence that now afflicts almost every public school in the nation.

The subcommittee found that in 1973 about 70,000 teachers were physically assaulted, 100 students were murdered, and $500 million worth of damage was caused by vandals. The cost of vandalism alone would have covered the cost of all textbooks purchased for public school systems in 1972. The subcommittee found that school violence cut across all lines — racial, ethnic, economic, rural, city, and suburban. The report is peppered with references to arson, drug traffic, prostitution, extortion, rape, robbery, and gang wars.

The report substantiates a trend of the past decade that has turned many schools into custodial facilities, where principals, teachers, and students fear for their lives. The miracle is that any child expecting a productive education learns anything at all. The breakdown in school discipline has resulted in millions of dollars being channeled into security forces: New York City will spend $10 million on security measures, and Chicago now is spending $3 million.

The need to provide security protection through armed guards, closed-circuit television, walkie-talkies, and other measures is robbing school systems of money that otherwise could be devoted to education. In many communities, the price of vandalism could build a new school every year. Some teachers and principals now carry guns for self-protection.

What has caused this brutalization of public school education in a country committed to the ideal that every child deserves an education? There is no single answer. Some child psychologists blame television violence. Others blame a depersonalization of the school system. Still others blame a lack of discipline at home. Recent Supreme Court decisions curbing the disciplinary authority of school officials probably have been contributing factors, as well as the popular theory among some ideologues that schools can be used as sociological workshops. A student at a rural Missouri school wracked by violence also offered a clue. "When people get bored, there's trouble," he said.

The subcommittee currently is holding hearings in an effort to gather suggestions for reversing the trend of increasing violence in the schools. Subcommittee members will hear proposals for innovative curricula that will be no improvement over similar proposals that have been made since the Soviets launched Sputnik I in 1957. Witnesses will suggest that the federal government give cities and communities more money to spend for security purposes. These proposals would treat the symptoms, not the cause, of America's blackboard jungles.

A more likely approach might lie in an examination of child labor laws that keep restless teen-agers from acquiring jobs. No one would urge outright repeal of these laws, nor a return to sweat-shop labor. But teen-agers today have the highest unemployment rate in the labor market, and revisions in child labor laws and a special exemption from the federal minimum wage would improve their job opportunities.

Another step could be taken to restore disciplinary authority to school officials, who often find it impossible to suspend or to expel trouble-makers. A climate of permissiveness gives students cause to think that no one cares what they do; strict rules of discipline would set limits on their behavior — limits that they need and want. Lower student-teacher ratios would help to create personal relationships and individual responsibility. Alternatives to curricula, such as early apprenticeships or on-the-job training, also could help.

But Congress perceives every problem only as another reason to appropriate cash. Money alone for more security guards will not reduce school violence. Instead, Congress ought to look at the records of several schools that have been established to meet parents' demands for patterned, disciplined academic climates. These schools have long waiting lists, and students attending them respond well when they know what a school administration expects from them. They don't burn their schools down, they learn in them. And they don't rape their teachers.

Unhappily, the prospects are good that another subcommittee report some years hence will reflect the same dismaying rise in school violence as this one does. Student "rights" have become sacred, and the balance of authority has been seriously breached. Perhaps it is too late for the public schools; it may be that the only hope for effective education rests in private schools — as is the case in Great Britain.

In the public schools, it may not be long before teachers have to teach behind bullet-proof glass, and armed guards have to ride shotgun with principals. Then the only education public school students will get will be in surviving a system that is supposed to serve them.

THE INDIANAPOLIS STAR

Indianapolis, Ind., April 23, 1975

A report on violence in the nation's schools, estimating 70,000 serious physical attacks on teachers each year, hundreds of thousands of attacks on pupils and a $500 million loss to vandalism has been issued by Senator Birch Bayh (D-Ind.).

Bayh is chairman of the Senate's juvenile delinquency subcommittee. which is holding hearings to try to measure the size of the problem and determine what to do about it.

"From our experience, we know there is no easy, quick solution," Bayh said. But he did introduce legislation to provide Federal funds to school systems for special education programs and security plans, following the usual liberal pattern of seeking to beat problems to death with moneybags.

The subcommittee's survey painted a gory, scary picture.

It showed that between 1970 and 1973 assaults on schoolteachers rose 77.4 per cent, assaults on pupils 85.3 per cent, robberies of teachers and pupils 36.7 per cent, rapes and attempted assaults 40.1 per cent, homicides 18.5 per cent and number of weapons taken from pupils 54.4 per cent.

Bayh said that thousands of teachers who have "dedicated their lives to their careers now have to be concerned too often about preserving their own lives."

He ruminated: "Too often, youngsters arriving at our public schools today are not finding the quiet atmosphere of instruction, enrichment and encouragement but instead an environment dominated by fear, chaos, destruction and violence."

And Bayh and his Senate colleagues wonder why. Has it by chance occurred to them that the disruption, erosion, rot and growing malignancy of conditions in American schools coincide with the intrusion of the long, meddlesome and clumsy arms of the Federal government into the school systems?

Massive, coercive scrambling of pupils and teachers from school to school and district to district by court o r d e r, the forcible diminishing of neighborhood influence and local administration, the weakening of discipline, morale, respect and order through court rulings on hair and dress styles, publications, codes of conduct and punishment policies, the subordination of education to social engineering and school "welfare" programs all have played their part in the disintegration process.

Let us hope that Bayh and the committee get down into the harsh realities of the situation and talk to teachers, parents and administrators who have seen the corruption grow from the seedling stage to the present plague and whose warnings, when sounded, were ignored by the fanatical "innovators" responsible for the mess.

Let us hope they learn that schools, like other local institutions, cannot be ruled from Washington and that the way to undo the damage is to remove the cause — myopic, gratuitious and impertinent Federal power.

Detroit Free Press
Detroit, Mich., March 11, 1977

Perplexing System Called Juvenile Justice...

THE JUVENILE JUSTICE system in the state of Michigan is akin to a rubber band being pulled, vigorously, in several directions.

Asked to carry more quasi-judicial responsibilities than any other justice-related entity in the state, it struggles—often muddles—through such dual and sometimes conflicting tasks as providing counseling and rehabilitation, operating correctional institutions, guarding the public from juvenile offenders, and protecting neglected and abused children from those who have harmed them. It attempts to do this with a system in which juvenile judges and the state Department of Social Services are jointly responsible for what happens to a youngster's life, even though they might not agree on what should be done.

It is a system whose courts have been operating since 1967 under due process rules and procedures that were attached like a barnacle to the rusty hulk of an outmoded juvenile code.

As readers who have followed the series of articles on this page for the past four days have noted, the system of juvenile justice comes at its tasks with a different attitude than the adult courts and justice institutions.

...Changes Must Be Made

THE JUVENILE justice system was set up originally to offer benevolence and guidance to youngsters who came in contact with it.

The court was in subtle ways to function as an extension of the traditionally idealized home. Children who were not obedient to their parents could—and still can—find themselves sitting before a judge. Children who needed for some reason to be removed from their homes, either because of delinquency or because of abuse, were to be provided care "as nearly as possible equivalent to the care which should have been given" by the parents.

While U.S. Supreme Court rulings have made it clear that due process is to be part of Juvenile Court, the protectionism and paternalism that lingers is evident, for example, in the fact that social workers—not judges—in many counties decide where a youngster will go after his contact with the court.

It would be hard to argue that many of the children—particularly the younger ones—who come before Juvenile Court do not require shelter under that protective attitude. It would be equally hard to argue that Juvenile Court is not, in many instances, very effective in dealing with youngsters who have or cause problems.

But it is not hard to argue that in two situations, the system has either greatly overreacted or vastly underreacted.

It has been too harsh on status offenders—that group of youngsters who have committed "crimes" such as being disobedient, or running away, that would not be crimes if they were adults. Status offenders can still be locked up in Michigan.

It has been too lenient on many violent young felons. Although it is now the policy of the state Department of Social Services to place such offenders in a locked-up setting, juvenile judges still do not have the power to commit them to a state institution for a certain length of time.

Juvenile Justice In Michigan

One of the two main partners in the juvenile justice network, the Department of Social Services (DSS), is overextended. In Wayne County, for example, there is a high client to caseworker ratio that is probably one of the main reasons for an exceedingly rapid worker turnover rate.

Recent scandals in DSS-operated institutions clearly indicate that more control over them and better inspection of them is necessary.

There is awareness, now, that changes must be made. A gigantic study of juvenile justice services is being made by a special commission due to report to the Legislature by July. Reports from task forces within that commission indicate that the final report will include literally hundreds of specific recommendations.

The Legislature will—and must—spend long hours assimilating and taking action on that material. Over the coming months, the Free Press will explore many of those recommendations.

Today a selected group of suggestions, which we view as being of the most immediate concern, follows.

...Some Immediate Needs

TWO PROPOSED new juvenile codes before the Legislature both include some provisions that appear sensible and that would improve juvenile justice in the state.

One, written by a group headed by Rep. Mark Clodfelter, D-Flint, breaks important new ground on due process for juveniles, and eliminates court jurisdiction over status offenders (such as truants and runaways). The other, introduced by Rep. Dennis Cawthorne, R-Muskegon, permits juvenile judges to sentence young offenders directly to a secure institution for up to one year, and differentiates between youngsters who commit minor and serious offenses.

Although the lobbying is already intense from backers of both bills, what is really needed now is a third, compromise piece of legislation that picks out the best of both, and combines them into one.

The legislative leadership should not try to rush a new juvenile code through. It would be to the benefit of everyone in this state if those who consider themselves youth advocates and those who consider themselves Juvenile Court or law enforcement advocates could stop straining against one another and write a bill that would satisfy both.

As indicated above, such a bill should include among its major provisions:
• At least the same due process rights for

It is essential that everyone understand that the extension of complete due process to juveniles benefits society at least as much as the juvenile.

For one thing, studies have shown that youngsters granted due process rights feel they have been treated more fairly and have more respect for the justice system than those who have not. That becomes important in relation to their committing further offenses.

More important, stringent enforcement of due process in Juvenile Court would eliminate many of the lingering effects of an outmoded informal system that grew out of a philosophy that juveniles, even fairly mature teen-agers, were not really responsible for their actions.
• The acknowledgment that the extension of rights to juveniles also implies the extension of responsibilities, at least where older juveniles are concerned.

We believe judges should have the ability to sentence serious offenders over 15 to a secure state institution for a set length of time up to one year. Those youngsters under 15 and those who commit minor offenses should not be included in that provision.
• The decriminalization of status offenses. Neither runaways nor truants, any more than youngsters who "habitually idle away" their time, should be processed through the Juvenile Courts.

It is imperative, however, that an alternative program funded by the state be set up to offer help to such youngsters, and be operating at the time decriminalization takes effect.

In addition to the badly needed new juvenile code, there are other improvements in the juvenile justice system that deserve close and rather immediate attention.
• There should be outside regulation and inspection of institutions operated by the Department of Social Services. Current self-policing methods are unacceptable.
• In Wayne County, funds must be found to meet the staffing needs of Juvenile Court and the juvenile prosecutors.
• The Legislature should move ahead with the appropriation of funds to construct additional youth detention facilities.

Detroit Free Press
Detroit, Mich., April 3, 1977

Juvenile Justice Needs Complete Due Process

ONE OF THE MOST important principles that should guide the Legislature as it continues its study of proposed changes in the juvenile justice system is that of extending complete due process to juveniles.

Although Michigan's Juvenile Courts operate under a set of state Supreme Court rules that have straightened up procedures immeasurably since 1967, there are still too many lingering traces of the hoary doctrine of "parens patriae."

"Parens patriae" is a doctrine with some of its origins in old English common law that held that a child was really just the property of the parent (or the parental substitute, the court), who could do as he wished with the child. Part of it can also be traced to a reformist movement of about a century ago that believed

Juvenile Justice In Michigan

that a child needed kindness and guidance from Juvenile Court, not punishment for criminal acts.

The doctrine came to mean that there was nearly boundless freedom for a judge to do with a child as he would, but only if he was acting "in the best interests" of the child (and thus the best interests of society).

It mattered little that the "kindliness" of the judge often took the form of tearing the child apart from his home and sending him to an institution where he could be locked up, sometimes for years, for such "crimes" as truancy.

The doctrine has been fairly discredited by the U.S. Supreme Court, but lingering traces are not difficult to find locally.

The most apparent remnant is the state policy of allowing a social worker, not a judge, to determine in many instances what is to be the sentence for a juvenile crime.

Others include:

• The practice of allowing a parent to waive an attorney for a youngster because the parents do not want to bother with the cost.

• The "informality" of Juvenile Court hearings, which is supposed to make the youngsters feel relaxed (but can be used to give the judge more leeway than he would have in adult court).

• The secret, closed-door nature of both juvenile hearings and Juvenile Court records that is supposed to protect the youngster, but also keeps the court free from outside scrutiny.

Juvenile Court can be improved. And it will be when complete due process comes to the court proceedings. There will always be a need for a great deal of discretion on the part of a Juvenile Court judge in determining the outcome of a case; the lives of thousands of different children at different states of maturity are involved.

But with full due process in place, it will be easier for the judge to separate those youngsters who do need help from those who need to repay society for their untoward acts. Everyone—especially the locked-out taxpayers—will benefit.

Detroit Free Press
Detroit, Mich., October 8, 1977

Juvenile Justice Reform Must Not Be Dropped

THE WORST THING that could happen in the state's juvenile justice system would not be, as some people believe, to remove truants, runaways and incorrigibles from court authority.

The worst thing would be for no changes at all to be made in the system.

And there is always an outside chance that, with public opinion sharply divided over the controversial "status offender" issue (as such offenses are called), the Legislature, in its infinite capacity for messing up, might let the whole thing die.

It has happened before. The current Juvenile Justice Services Commission, which has been working for the past 18 months on a comprehensive plan for improving the ragged organizational structure that passes for a juvenile justice system in the state, is only the latest in a long list of study groups that have expectantly issued reports calling for reforms, and then stood by to watch nothing happen.

Change *is* necessary.

There is, for example, a great degree of variation in what a juvenile court does from one part of the state to another.

While some only hold court, and depend on the county jail or the state Department of Social Services to provide physically for the needs of youngsters who come before them, others rule over vast complexes.

There are some juvenile courts in Michigan that not only hear and dispose of cases, but operate the facilities to which an errant or troubled youngster may be sent.

That clearly results in a conflict of interest. It can, for example, become advantageous to the court to keep the facility full, even if borderline cases must be locked up. As Judge Luke Quinn, of Genessee County Juvenile Court, has put it: "The potential for abuse is simply too great."

The current Juvenile Justice Services Commission report, now undergoing final editing in Lansing, recommends a major change in that judicial-executive overlap.

Juvenile courts would be permitted only to operate temporary pre-trial detention facilities.

The bulk of the service delivery would be supplied through a local Office of Youth Services, which would include a local implementing board, similar to the currently operating local mental health boards. A state agency strictly devoted to children and youth would also be established.

Although the commission has adamantly, wrongly, and naively insisted that such an agency must be a full-fledged department, the basis for that reorganization is sound.

Similarly, recommendations guaranteeing full due process for juveniles accused of felonies, requiring on-the-record reviews of dispositions, and abolishing the dual-wardship system wherein either the Department of Social Services or the court may maintain the jurisdiction over a child are based on solid grounds.

There are also good and compelling reasons for removing status offenses from the juvenile code, even if the issue has been clouded by emotional responses.

To quote Judge Quinn again: "All the commission is saying is don't put children with problems into the same machine as rapists and murderers."

But whether truants and runaways are completely removed from Juvenile Court, or are sent through the court only as a last resort, or continue to be, as they often are now, rubberstamped through an overloaded system may not prove to be as ultimately important as restructuring an outmoded and often overly paternalistic system.

That is why it is important that this latest report not be allowed to dangle until it dies, as others have done.

That is why it is encouraging that an ad hoc committee on juvenile code revision has been formed in the House.

And that is why legislators and knowledgeable citizens must not let the deep emotions that surround the status offender issue keep them from coming to thoughtful conclusions, and responsible actions, on the overall revision of the Juvenile Code.

THE PLAIN DEALER

Cleveland, Ohio, March 27, 1977

Ensuring juvenile justice

The Omnibus Juvenile Justice Reform Act introduced in the Ohio House and Senate this week is billed as a comprehensive piece of legislation to cure the ills of the juvenile justice system in Ohio. And it appears to closely fill the need.

The bill's aim is not necessarily to improve upon the performance of the state's juvenile court judges as they deal with young people in their courtrooms, despite the Ohio Association of Juvenile Court Judges taking its "bill of rights" as an affront.

The section of the proposed legislation dealing with rights, which has been labeled the "Juvenile Bill of Rights," is only a very small portion of the 140-page measure. If some juvenile court judges are violating the rights of youngsters in their courtrooms, the bill would provide a stronger guarantee that the juveniles' rights would be observed.

A much more widespread and pressing problem is the need for the system to distinguish more clearly between minor offenders, like runaways and truants, and juvenile delinquents who are committing criminal acts.

Not only are there currently youngsters in both categories being detained in the same institutions — in which the minor offender learns about crime — but there are 56 counties in Ohio with no local or regional centers for the detention of any juveniles.

In such areas, youngsters who are detained are often locked in the local jail or drunk tank. The proposed law is designed to move the state from juvenile detention centers where youngsters exit with a better knowledge of crime or find themselves locked up with adult offenders.

The proposed legislation introduces a new authority to the courts to help counsel families of problem youngsters as well as counsel youngsters

toying with crime who might be guided away from a criminal path. Such intervention will use existing social agencies in areas where they are available and create new programs for other areas.

All in all, the bill, an outgrowth of the state attorney general's task force on juvenile justice, is being called the most comprehensive piece of legislation on the juvenile justice system in Ohio in 50 years.

While it might not be the panacea that will completely cure all the ills of the juvenile justice system in the state, it should go a long way toward treatment of many of the symptoms.

The Detroit News

Detroit, Mich., March 28, 1977

Tougher juvenile code urged to combat crime

The ravages of old age are sad: declining physical and economic power and social undesirability. To those sorrows, older people in cities are now being paralyzed by fear of crime.

Most of the fear is being generated by teenagers and youth gangs who have discovered the elderly are the easiest prey.

The problem has become so bad that the New York assembly has just passed a bill mandating jail terms for violent crimes against people more than 62 years old.

What should be done in Michigan?

The Legislature must revise the juvenile code which has been on the books since 1939.

We have little "wisdom" about what specific changes should be made. But the facts about juvenile crime are grim.

Youth between 10 and 17 make up 16 percent of the population, yet account for 45 percent of people arrested for serious crimes annually.

Detroit Mayor Young, never known as a social hard-liner, has pleaded in Lansing for more power for juvenile judges and tougher juvenile sentencing.

We have agreed with Judge James Lincoln of Wayne County Juvenile Court that the law should be changed to prevent juvenile felons from being released by the Department of Social Services when they should be jailed.

Apparently a bipartisan grouping in the House

agrees that the law gives social workers too much power.

But a knottier problem is status offenders — truants, runaways and "incorrigibles."

Rep. Mark Clodfelter, D-Flint, would take status offenders from juvenile jurisdiction, arguing that "kids are being treated as offenders for what is a social problem."

Yet Rep. Dennis Cawthorne, R-Muskegon, has a bill that would reduce but not eliminate court involvement in status offenders.

We agree with Cawthorne that the state needs some mechanism to deal with status offenders.

Why not a "family court" for handling status offenders?

Although we are hesitant to propose another layer in the judicial bureaucracy, some alternative must be devised if status offenders are removed from juvenile court jurisdiction.

Although there are party jealousies about who should get credit for laws, we have reason to hope that Democrats and Republicans will mesh efforts to produce a better juvenile code.

Here are some suggestions:

• Keep in mind Clodfelter's stress on due process for juveniles. No matter how serious our crime problems, we should never tear up the Constitution.

• Strip the secrecy from juvenile courts, opening

records and ending juvenile immunity to official review. The notion that youths should not be "stigmatized" by juvenile offenses in their adult lives makes no sense when juveniles are clearly establishing a career in crime.

• Build more juvenile facilities. As Judge Lincoln says, more important than any bill that emerges from the Legislature is "the need for more detention facilities."

More juvenile facilities raise the same problem as that of getting tough on adult crime: Is the state willing to pay the price? (It costs about $18,000 a year to keep a youngster at the W. J. Maxey Training School near Brighton.)

As for proposals by both Cawthorne and the Clodfelter subcommittee to raise the age of juvenile jurisdiction from 17 to 18, that would be folly. Yet we question Judge Lincoln's suggestion that the jurisdiction age be lowered to 16.

(A five-year study sponsored by the American Bar Association and the Judicial Administration concluded that juveniles aged 16 and 17 who commit violent crimes should be tried in adult courts.)

As Clodfelter concedes, there are "good points in all bills" on code revision before the Legislature.

The encouraging thing is that juvenile code revision has a strong possibility of passage this year.

The Virginian-Pilot
Norfolk, Va., February 28, 1977
A New Juvenile Code

Increased reliance on public institutions for domestic crisis-solving evident in the years since World War II has bred problems while attacking them. People expect schools to watch over all children between the ages of 6 and 18, and the police and courts to tend to those unfortunates who fall between the cracks.

Regrettably, juvenile law isn't calibrated to distinguish high spirits from rebellion, arrogance from menace, pranks from crime. Detention—a polite way of saying jail—is a consequence that awaits runaways, truants, problem children, incorrigibles. The misbehavior of such "status offenders" contributes substantially to the statistics on juvenile crime, though their misdeeds may be criminal only by a stretch of statutory imagination. How many status offenders are tracked into true criminal careers as a result of the law's inflexibility is conjectural, but a potential is implied by the staggering fact that fully 32 per cent of the children in the custody of state institutions last year were status offenders.

The problem of criminal treatment of status offenders is recognized in proposed legislation passed by the Virginia House of Delegates and awaiting State Senate action. The first revision of the State's juvenile code since the 1950s would channel status offenders away from lockups and into corrective services intended to alleviate their conflicts with society. Meanwhile, further differentiating between unruly kids and bad ones, more stringent treatment would be in store for those who do commit crimes. Penalties would be stiffened. The rights to counsel and to appeal from juvenile to Circuit court for jury trial would be provided.

Overhaul of juvenile laws to keep pace with changing times is desirable from time to time. The proposal in the legislative works reflects a thoughtful approach. This has not been a stellar session of the General Assembly but some good could be salvaged by the passage of a more humane juvenile code.

The Des Moines Register
Des Moines, Iowa, March 20, 1977
Justice for juveniles

Remember the session-long legislative fight last year over the criminal code? This year we have an encore: the juvenile justice code. Two articles on this page show the breadth of the quarrel.

The proposed revision has many good features. It contains needed reforms — such as requiring hearings within 48 hours if a child is placed in detention or shelter care; providing for appointment of an attorney at the initial interview if the child wants one; defining child abuse to include sexual abuse; and prohibiting the sentencing of a child for longer than an adult could get for the same offense.

It also has many weaknesses. It would, in effect, place a three-year statute of limitations on murder if the murderer were nearly 18. It mistakenly invalidates drinking-age laws by defining a delinquent act as one that would be a crime if committed by an adult. It proposes an untried concept for helping a child and his family if no crime has been committed but the family has problems.

The major objection of many juvenile justice professionals is that it would remove incorrigible, wayward youngsters from the "child in need of assistance" category. They say that parents need the ultimate power of the state to make their offspring behave.

Currently, children in need of assistance are those who are neglected, abused, wayward, incorrigible or whose mental or physical health is endangered. The court can give them counseling, send them to a foster home or a private institution. It cannot send them to the state training schools, as it could a delinquent.

Proponents of the change contend that the current law is vague, and that if a child is "incorrigible" or "wayward," it's a family problem, not just a child's problem. So they created the "family in need of assistance" category. The juvenile court could intervene only upon request of the parents or child. (Now anyone with knowledge of the facts can bring in the court.)

Under the proposed law, the court could order counseling, but would have to obtain the child's consent for removal from the home or for placing him on probation. The contempt power is all that the court could use to enforce the counseling order. If the child, as Gary Ventling suggests in his article, refused counseling, the judge could only order him jailed or put in a juvenile detention center. Perhaps this would not happen often, but jail is no help.

Iowa would be the first state to adopt such an approach to handling wayward youngsters. The family provision is recommended by the U.S. Law Enforcement Assistance Administration, but has never been tried.

It sounds promising in theory, but we are concerned about the consequences Ventling predicts. The Legislature should consider trying to authorize the concept in one or two jurisdictions and subjecting it to careful evaluation. In any case, no such drastic change as this, or some of the proposed changes in juvenile court procedure, should be approved without provision for monitoring and evaluation. If the fears of the critics prove justified, the law could be modified.

The Des Moines Register
Des Moines, Iowa, March 27, 1977
Juvenile justice

Our Mar. 20 editorial, "Justice for Juveniles," said the proposed revision of the juvenile code has many good features and many weaknesses. Backers of the proposed code dispute several of our findings of shortcomings.

We said the measure would place a three-year statute of limitations on murder if the murderer were nearly 18. We are persuaded that the bill would not have this effect, though there is enough ambiguity in the language to have caused a clarifying amendment to be drafted. Clarifying this section would be a good idea.

We said that the bill would invalidate drinking-age laws. We should have said that the measure would prevent juvenile-drinking offenses from being taken to juvenile court, where they are handled in some counties, but it was incorrect to say that the laws against juvenile drinking would be voided.

A major issue in dispute is whether juveniles who have broken no law but are merely difficult to handle — so-called status offenders — should be brought into court involuntarily and be subjected to being removed from their homes. Under present law, a wayward or incorrigible youngster can be ordered by the court to a group home or other facility.

The emphasis in the proposed revision is on the voluntary seeking and accepting of help. The wayward youngster in a family seeking help could be ordered by juvenile court to obtain counseling or other services, but he could not be ordered from the home. The stress is on employing the least drastic means of dealing with youngsters to keep families intact.

If a youngster violated a court order to obtain counseling, he could be punished for contempt of court. This could involve jailing him or placing him in a juvenile detention center — the same punishment available now to juvenile court judges when wayward youngsters disobey court orders. A juvenile who disobeyed a court order to obtain counseling also presumably could be adjudged delinquent and be dealt with by being placed in a group home or other facility. But the hope is that coercive measures would not be needed.

The approach to status offenders generally taken by the bill has been endorsed by such groups as the National Council on Crime and Delinquency, the National Juvenile Law Center and the Juvenile Standards Project of the American Bar Association. No state has yet adopted such a reform, though successful pilot projects have been undertaken.

We suggested that the Iowa Legislature consider trying to authorize such a pilot study. Iowa's Constitution requires that laws have general application, so status offenders could not be treated differently under the law in different counties, but a lot could be done to vary the treatment of juveniles without changing the law. In any case, adoption of the proposed reform should be accompanied by careful evaluation.

Sentinel Star
Orlando, Fla., February 3, 1977

A Delinquent Is A Delinquent Is . . .

THE LAW Enforcement Assistance Administration has spent $1.9 million of our money to learn what it could have found out by asking any wayward child or any cop — that youngsters as a rule are nudged into crime by their own peers rather than by adults.

That startling conclusion was arrived at by the Illinois Institute for Juvenile Research with funding by the LEAA. Said Joseph Puntil, co-director of the project: "In most cases kids reporting delinquency are nearly as likely to be white as black, just about as likely to be a girl as a boy, as likely to live anywhere in the state as in highly urbanized Chicago, and just as likely to come from an intact home as a broken home."

The LEAA report is preliminary and a more complete one is due in September, no doubt after more taxpayer dollars are consumed. If any money is left, we'd like to suggest the next project: Find out why bureaucrats spend substantial sums chasing facts that either are irrelevant, obvious or available for the asking at no cost.

Chicago Daily News
Chicago, Ill., January 26, 1977

Crime and Illinois youth

At first glance, the report on juvenile behavior in Illinois is a shocker. Fully a third of the state's teen-agers have at some time committed what is called a "serious" offense; half admit they have done some shoplifting; 40 per cent say they have kept items they knew had been stolen.

The report arises from a still-incomplete six-year study funded by the federal Law Enforcement Assistance Administration at a cost of nearly $2 million. Employes of the Illinois Department of Mental Health interviewed 3,180 teen-agers in all parts of the state, including urban, suburban and rural areas. The principal conclusions are that "delinquency" is almost a part of growing up in Illinois, and that "peer group" influence is the most important factor in juvenile behavior — far beyond the influence of parents, who generally knew nothing of their children's transgressions.

There is no doubt that violent crime by youths has increased in recent years, and the horror tales of murders and armed robberies by youngsters barely old enough to hold a gun provide ample testimony. But the researchers have taken a long leap from that problem when they extend their findings to smear a whole generation of teen-agers.

We suspect there are few adults who could examine their own youth and fail to find something they blush to remember, whether it be filching a pack of gum (shoplifting), taking candy from a younger child (robbery or extortion) or such exhilarating pastimes in rural areas as dumping over an outhouse on Halloween (vandalism). Naturally, most kids did (and do) such things because their friends were doing it, not because their parents sanctioned it, but we can't recall ever hearing the excuse "I did it because of peer-group pressure."

Breaking the rules — and getting punished for it — has always been a part of growing up. Which is another way of saying that almost everybody bears a youthful stigma of "delinquency" as it is now defined, and about all that is new is that it is taking $2 million in tax money to write a report about it.

This is not to say that violent crime among youths can be lightly dismissed. Far from it. That trend must be reversed somehow, and if the researchers can tell us how to do it, more power to them. But we suggest they concentrate their efforts in that area, rather than raising their hands in horror about peer-group influences and the obvious and eternal fact that parents don't always know what their children are up to.

And if they must deal in statistics, let them point out that two-thirds of the teen-agers interviewed came through looking pretty good. Maybe finding that out is worth the $2 million, after all.

TULSA WORLD
Tulsa, Okla., January 25, 1977

On Peers And Crime

HAS YOUR child ever committed an offense punishable by a jail sentence?

No, you say. Better think again. A six-year study of juveniles in Illinois reports that 80 per cent of the parents of youthful offenders didn't know of their children's offense.

That's only one of several worrisome statistics the study brought out, including the fact that nearly a third of all juveniles have committed a serious crime.

Thirteen per cent admitted taking part in a robbery; 40 per cent to keeping stolen property, and 50 per cent admitted shoplifting.

The statistics are of course frightening, but the chief cause of the problems is even more so.

The investigators found that "peer group" pressure determines whether a specific youth will become delinquent.

In other words the role of parents in controlling their children is much less than friends of their own age.

Parents and institutions do have an influence on their children the study showed but the very complicated process of forming peer attitudes is the "place where they work it out—whether to steal or not to steal."

Perhaps parents can do little to shield their children from crime but they can work harder during the children's formative years to instill worthwhile values and work with community institutions to subtly influence youngsters.

It is a problem that all of society —but particularly parents—ought to be worrying about. Because when crime becomes the "in" thing in teen groups, everyone is in for trouble.

Chicago Tribune
Chicago, Ill., January 25, 1977

Parents, teens, and crime

Traditional middle class values "good" parents try to use in raising their offspring may not be enough to keep those children from committing delinquent acts as adolescents. That's the sobering warning implicit in the six year study of delinquency in Illinois reported originally in a four-part series in The Tribune in May, 1975, and released again from Washington Sunday by the Law Enforcement Assistance Administration.

Adolescent delinquency is found to be much higher than official statistics show. As many as one-third of all Illinois teen-agers have committed a felony, the report says. It also shatters many stereotypes about what teen-age delinquents are really like, finding that almost as many girls as boys commit serious crimes and that many delinquents come from affluent suburbs and small towns, and from supposedly "good," intact families with caring parents.

It's the adolescent peer group — not parents — which holds the primary influence over teen-agers, the study concludes. And it's the peer group — not the parents — which determines whether a youngster will commit a serious crime or become involved in delinquent behavior. [The family, however, does play a major role in whether a boy or girl who commits a delinquent act is shuttled into the juvenile correction system and is counted as a crime statistic, however.]

Parents make a serious mistake by underestimating peer group influences, the research says. They assume that teen-agers will automatically be influenced by the values the parents have tried to instill, discounting what powerful influences school, peers, and the social climate in general exert on young people at the stage in their development when they are growing away from parental control. "Too many parents still prefer to think of adolescents as Penrods or Andy Hardys, when they live in a world vastly different from that," one researcher commented.

But it is at least as mistaken, it seems to us, to minimize the role of parents. We can't simply blame the peer group and accept delinquent behavior as being so common it's a "normal" part of growing up, as some sociologists and psychologists suggest. Peer group attitudes in themselves arise in part from a child's earlier upbringing. Nor can parents assume that because they are law-abiding and have tried to teach their teen-agers to be so, too, this will offset their offspring against powerful peer pressures to behave otherwise.

Parents will have to rethink the amount of supervision they give their teen-age children. They will have to exert more control on the friends their children choose and monitor their activities more closely. They will have to work harder at improving the social and moral climate of schools and of society. It's a tough order. But there is no alternative, except massive delinquency.

The Idaho STATESMAN
Boise, Idaho, March 26, 1977

Why Print Juveniles' Names?

The names of two young men charged with first-degree murder in the death of a Boise man are being published today.

The names were released in open court despite an appeal pending before the Idaho Supreme Court asking that the youths be tried as juveniles. The decision to print the names requires explanation.

We fully support the concept of anonymity for juvenile offenders involved in minor crimes, but in the case at hand the crime is not minor, and in the eyes of the court the young men are no longer juveniles.

We have long known the names of the young men, and long believed they should be brought to trial in adult court.

While the youths must be considered not guilty unless it is proved otherwise, the severity of the crime with which they are charged, plus criminal records that include convictions for kidnaping and rape, suggest the youths no longer deserve the protection of either the juvenile court system or its provision for anonymity.

In this case, the need to protect and inform the public must come first.

THE DAILY OKLAHOMAN
Oklahoma City, Okla., March 22, 1977

More Light on Juvenile Crime

FOR the past several decades most American newspapers, including The Oklahoman and Times, have voluntarily restricted the publication of news stories involving juvenile offenders.

This policy reflected the opinion of judges, law enforcement officials and social scientists that youths who get into trouble, especially first offenders, should not be scarred for life by publicity.

In particular, most editors have refrained from printing the names, ages and addresses of youngsters who run afoul of the law, except in the case of serious felonies. It was felt that public exposure of their misdeeds would only hamper their rehabilitation.

Indeed, the prevailing theory of handling young offenders with compassion resulted in the adoption by most states of laws that mandated special protective treatment for persons under the age of legal adulthood, usually 18.

Those codes generally provided for strict secrecy in juvenile court proceedings, except when a youth was ordered to stand trial as an adult for committing one of the more serious or violent crimes. Oklahoma's law in this respect is fairly typical.

In recent years, however, the shocking growth in the amount of serious crime being committed by persons under 18 has forced a rethinking of our juvenile justice system. In the process many authorities are seriously questioning the wisdom of shrouding the problem in secrecy.

That trend is currently manifested in New York state, where the cutoff age is 16 for treating juveniles like adult criminals in court. Bills also are pending in that state to allow fingerprinting and photographing of juveniles and to open juvenile records to law enforcement agencies.

Here in Oklahoma, the issue recently received national attention in the case of an 11-year-old boy who fatally shot a railroad employee. Although a gag order against the news media by Special Dist. Judge Charles Halley was ruled unconstitutional by the U.S. Supreme Court, the problem of how to handle crime stories involving juveniles is a continuing one for editors.

Having carefully considered all the arguments, this newspaper has concluded that a policy of shedding more light on the true nature of juvenile crime will serve the public interest better than secrecy.

Accordingly, The Oklahoman and Times will print the names, ages and addresses of all juveniles aged 14 and older who are involved in felonies if the information is made available to reporters. Non-felony offenders will not be identified.

In the case of capital crimes, however, offenders will be identified regardless of their age if the information can be obtained.

This policy has been adopted in the conviction that overly protective treatment of juvenile criminals hasn't worked as intended. Juvenile crime has reached monstrous proportions in our society, and those who rob, steal, burglarize, assault and murder should not escape exposure simply because of an arbitrary age limit that is at variance with reality.

The Burlington Free Press
Burlington, Vt., March 16, 1977

Efforts To Curb Juvenile Crime

PUBLIC EXPOSURE would be used as a weapon in combatting juvenile crime under a proposal which has been made to the Vermont House Judiciary Committee by Chittenden County State's Atty. Francis X. Murray.

Because so many juvenile offenders flaunt their ages before police and other law enforcement authorities with the knowledge that their youth provides an escape from punishment for their crimes, Murray believes the threat of publicity for children under 16 who have committed serious crimes will do much to dissuade them from future criminal activity.

"I believe that public exposure of serious problems serves to deter future offenses by informing juvenile offenders that the community is dealing quickly and effectively with the problem," he said.

His proposal is an alternative to one by Atty. Gen. M. Jerome Diamond who has asked for legislation to allow prosecutors the option of bringing charges against children under 16 in adult courts with the understanding that they would not be sent to adult medium or maximum security jails.

Murray would take other steps to prevent juvenile crime, including the creation of a mini-jail at Weeks School in Vergennes to detain youthful criminals who now can simply walk away from the institution, a fixed sentence for youngsters who are sent to Weeks for serious crimes and release of their names to victims to permit suits for personal or property damage.

Murray told the committee there are 10 youngsters in Chittenden County between 14 and 16 who "insist on running away" from Weeks. They have committed 300 burglaries in the county. A mini-jail would be used to prevent their escape.

Under present law, a youngster under 16 who is convicted of a serious crime can only be detained at Weeks School until he reaches 18. The fixed sentence would extend the term if the offender was considered dangerous.

Though victims of juvenile crimes can sue the parents of offenders for a maximum of $250 for personal or property damage, state law prevents them from finding out who committed the crime, he said.

Murray's proposal certainly deserves serious consideration by the committee as a sensible attempt to deal with the problems of juvenile crime. If juveniles realize they will be held accountable by the public for serious crimes, they might indeed have second thoughts about embarking on such ventures.

Press Herald

Portland, Me., February 3, 1977

Revealing Names

District Court Judge Julian Turner has charted a good course in disclosing the names of juveniles who repeatedly break the law.

No one, including the judge, knows what this policy will accomplish. But no one ever would know unless some judge tried it.

Maine law provides that names of juveniles in criminal proceedings be kept secret unless released by a judge. Judge Turner does not identify every youth who comes before him, only those who appear frequently.

The Judge, who presides at Houlton and Presque Isle, says he has received favorable comment from all over the country even though some parents are less than happy to be identified and to have their children identified.

One of the early considerations of a commission studying juvenile law was that juveniles be tried in open court when charged with felonies. That approach has merit but Judge Turner's policy goes further in that it applies to those who may not commit felonies but who are frequently in court for lesser offenses.

The principle of protecting the identity of a juvenile offender evolves from the desire to permit the youth to straighten out, to respond to rehabilitation if that is indicated. The purpose is to avoid fixing a label of criminal upon a youth who may never again violate a law.

The principle, for the most part, is defensible. When the crime involves the taking of a human life, aggravated assault, armed robbery, or that sort of thing, the principle is open to challenge.

When a youth's repeated conduct indicates that he is not changing his ways or responding to rehabilitation, he sacrifices the protection of secrecy. The community has a right to know because it is the victim and it is paying the cost of attempted rehabilitation or punishment.

Given that knowledge, Judge Turner hopes the community may be able to exert pressure which will deter criminal activity by juveniles. We share that hope. From the reaction to Judge Turner's experiment, apparently many others do too.

As Judge Turner pointed out, the old approach to juvenile crime wasn't accomplishing much. It was time to try something else. He's to be commended for being willing to try.

THE BLADE

Toledo, Ohio, November 16, 1977

Misguided Juvenile Court Debate

A BREWING controversy in Ohio over the handling of such juvenile offenders as runaways and truants is a debate that misses the basic point. The question at issue is whether juvenile courts should have jurisdiction over these so-called status offenders — minors whose infractions would not be crimes if committed by adults. But about that there should be no argument: The courts should have a role.

Oddly enough, the dispute — which is not confined to Ohio — arises from broad agreement that youngsters involved in these cases should not be incarcerated with other juvenile offenders, as has been past practice. Truancy, chronic misbehavior, and running away from home often are symptoms of other problems which usually can and should more properly be dealt with by other agencies and in other ways than detention.

The argument has developed because some advocates of this view believe the only way to avoid incarceration is to bar juvenile courts from any jurisdiction over status offenders. It is a glaring example of the pendulum swinging too far in the opposite direction. And the basic point that is missed in this debate is that the very presence of the court — if only in the background — can be the catalyst that makes the alternate approaches work. The fact that the court has ultimate authority to step in if necessary sometimes is the only factor that can prompt a youngster, family, and agency to cooperate in trying to resolve the problem.

What complicates the issue is that Congress has passed legislation which makes federal aid for juvenile justice improvement virtually dependent on acceptance by the states of the view that courts should be excluded. It is a particularly onerous case of making federal assistance tantamount to blackmail.

Nearly a dozen states have refused to accept the aid rather than go along. Some states that have adopted the policy of no court involvement with status offenders are having second thoughts because youngsters are thumbing their noses at other agencies and authorities which have no way to bring them under control.

The Ohio task force considering whether this state should participate in the federal program is split on the court issue. It should not be. Yielding the right to deal with all juvenile violators — including status offenders — in the most effective way that Ohio can devise is not worth the bribe-like aid dangled by the Federal Government.

The Cleveland Press

Cleveland, Ohio, November 8, 1977

Next mayor must deal with juvenile crime

For several weeks members of The Press editorial board interviewed candidates for Cleveland Council.

A standard question for the candidates was: "What particular problems do you have in your ward?"

An astonishingly large number listed juvenile crime as a persistent and paramount concern.

This observation was mentioned most often, but not exclusively, by those in inner city neighborhoods.

If the candidate was already in Council, he would say, yes, there is a juvenile crime problem, but we are doing something about it.

If a candidate was a challenger, he would say that nothing, or virtually nothing, was being done about it.

These refrains, with minor variations, recurred a disturbing number of times. And the comments came from concerned men and women who had walked the wards, knocked on doors and listened to what folks in the neighborhoods had to say.

Often some kind of drug was involved. Youngsters would be sniffing glue or were turned on by the latest chemical craze — known as angel dust or PCP.

Mostly, it seems, curfew laws are being ignored — not enforced. Youngsters, bent on mischief or worse, are roaming the streets at all hours — singly, in pairs or in gangs.

The most pitiful stories came from neighborhoods where young toughs were preying on old folks. People too old or infirm to defend themselves lock themselves in at night, afraid to venture out; some are too fearful even to go out in the daytime.

Often, we were told, juveniles are running wild within the shadow of the local district police headquarters.

Neighborhood folks who know which hooligans are responsible for vandalism and arson were told to keep quiet or they would be the next victims. And they kept quiet.

A few years back the controversial movie "A Clockwork Orange," adapted from Anthony Burgess' novel, depicted a society in the future in which vicious young toughs ran wild and the authorities were helpless.

It is not the future we are worried about but the here and now.

Whether Dennis Kucinich or Edward Feighan is the next mayor, this is a problem he will have to deal with.

Tax abatement and the future of the Muny Light Plant are not the most pressing urban problems to an aged couple fearful for their safety in their own neighborhood.

A society that often is accused of worshiping youth cannot look the other way when a small, but menacing, minority of those young people are running wild.

The Evening Bulletin
Philadelphia, Pa., June 21, 1977

Girls and boys and justice

The nation's juvenile criminal justice system is guilty of sex discrimination. That is the conclusion of a study released by the Female Offenders Resource Center, an affiliate of the American Bar Association.

With juvenile curfew laws becoming common in our area, the findings are of more than academic interest.

Specifically, the researchers found that girls who run away, disobey their parents or are sexually active at an early age are more likely to be referred to juvenile courts than boys who do the same thing. Also, girls are more likely to be detained by authorities than are boys, even though the boys' offenses tend to be more serious. Further, once the girls are incarcerated, fewer vocational and educational programs are available to them.

Underlying these inequities is an outmoded, sexist attitude—a double standard, if you will. Many of the offenses for which girls are detained—"incorrigibility," for instance—involve sexual activity. The kind of sexual behavior that has been tolerated or even expected in boys has been punished in girls.

Of course, it is patently unfair for courts to place girls in detention centers for behavior that would go unpunished in boys. Judges, attorneys and probation officers should look carefully at the assumptions that may be underlying their treatment of girls referred to the courts.

Beyond that is a more overt problem. Meaningful rehabilitation programs for girls—like those for adult women offenders— have been woefully lacking. One reason is that women have been a distinct minority in the correctional system. (The FBI says that girls represented about 22 per cent of the juveniles arrested nationwide in 1975.)

Certainly each person deserves equal treatment in the criminal justice system. Girls as well as boys need a chance to further their education or to learn a useful vocation. Juvenile offenders should not be the throwaways of our society, and girls should not be the throwaways of the juvenile justice system.

Some of the people who work with juvenile offenders in Pennsylvania and New Jersey confirm that most of the problems presented in the ABA study do indeed exist in these states in one degree or another. Here and elsewhere the double standard in juvenile justice must be eliminated.

THE MILWAUKEE JOURNAL
Milwaukee, Wisc., March 30, 1977

That Kid With a Gun in Your Ribs

Young people under 18 commit nearly half of this country's serious crimes — murder, rape, armed robbery and arson. Why?

Many villains are cited — lenient courts, women's lib, available handguns, poverty, the family breakdown. None by itself is an adequate explanation. Yet perhaps, if we look deeper, we can glimpse the outline of a pattern, the hint of a national characteristic. Could it be that many of our children are becoming brutal at least partly because we as a people have become so self-indulgent?

Traditionally, Americans have been acquisitive. We are fiercely capitalistic. We often cannibalize family life and the inner person to get ahead. The pressure to achieve leads to cutting corners on the social amenities. We devote ourselves less to being friendly than to developing "contacts."

Yes, this restless, perpetual dissatisfaction built the frontier; but unbridled, it can destroy our humanity. Its particularly dangerous manifestation in our age is the mania for unrestrained self-fulfillment. Young people are overwhelmed by cultural signals saying that, above all else, they should express themselves freely and fully. We are supposed to work satisfyingly hard on our jobs, houses, bank accounts, physiques, hairdos — but always, of course, with stamina left to swing. This compulsion to "do your own thing," to get attention by achieving in your own way, is sending many adults into emotional tailspins. Is it any wonder that children feel insecure?

Says Dr. David Abrahamsen, the psychoanalyst: "The American Dream is, in part, responsible for a great deal of crime and violence. People feel that America owes them not only a living but a good living, and they take short cuts to get what they feel is owing to them. . . . Frustration is the wet nurse to violence."

What can be done? At least two things seem necessary. First, we adults should — by what we do as well as what we say — engender in young people a view of life that is simultaneously less self-centered and more realistic. Second, we should take pains to assure that youngsters can pursue reasonable expectations.

A place to begin? Try youth employment. It's not unreasonable to want a job. Yet the jobless rate between ages 16 and 24 is more than 2½ times the rate for older people. This summer will be worse.

High teenage unemployment has been addressed by President Carter with a $1.5 billion, 18 month proposal that would expand the Job Corps — a residential training program for seriously disadvantaged youths — and create three new programs for the jobless young. Carter wants to give the labor secretary $450 million for job innovation. He also wants to get urban youth working on rural conservation programs, 1930s style, through a National Youth Conservation Corps. This would provide meaningful work without taking jobs from adults. Although the training benefits might be only short range, Carter's programs would be a start.

In Milwaukee, federal funds last summer paid about 100 high school seniors who painted houses for the elderly and handicapped. That excellent program will continue this summer, but will not be nearly enough. How many frustrated young people, lacking a chance to fulfill a reasonable expectation, will then turn in frustration to crime?

The Kansas City Times
Kansas City, Mo., April 8, 1977

Many juvenile delinquents are beset with more than behavioral problems. Reading is a notable example. The average youth who is incarcerated is at the fourth-grade level in reading. That is considered functionally illiterate. Some of them have difficulty understanding job applications, road signs, directions on food packages and newspapers. This gap in education is a serious impediment for those who want to attempt to rehabilitate themselves.

Employment and schooling, considered basic to self-improvement programs, simply are not in reach of individuals who must grapple with reading. Former offenders are expected to obtain jobs, which often require training. Without the ability to get work, the juvenile can be tempted to resort to crime. The result can be, and often is, a hardened criminal. That means the public must pay the bill for the prison time and lose a tax-paying citizen.

This reading deficiency is being attacked. The Law Enforcement Assistance Administration is sponsoring a program called Reading Efficiency and Delinquency (READ). The early indications are encouraging. An examination of 2,500 READ students at selected correctional institutions showed a jump in mental age from 11 years, 10 months, to 12 years, five months, in a 4-month period. Usually an increase of this scale requires about triple that time.

This intensive approach at 148 institutions holds promise. If it turns out to be a solid educational innovation, the READ venture could play an integral part in curbing crime that endangers all of society.

The Dallas Morning News
Dallas, Tex., October 31, 1977
Face Reality About Juveniles

Many myths are being dispelled from the public's opinion of the criminal justice system. An important one remains: Kids are kids.

In truth some kids—teen-agers—are becoming vicious criminals. But even if caught, they aren't treated as serious threats to society.

Time magazine recently recounted a series of horror stories involving kids too young to be prosecuted under statutes applicable to adults. Indeed, in the new tong wars in San Francisco's Chinatown, reports have it that 14-year-olds are being used as hit men. The reason? If caught, they get lighter penalties than their older confederates. Some get no penalties at all.

Indeed, in recent years, fully 30 percent of the major crimes in Dallas have been committed by criminals under 17 years of age.

Yet our juvenile justice system continues to treat offenders as though they were involved in harmless pranks. Even the Legislature refused to pass a bill this year that would have allowed the media to publicize the names of youths accused of heinous or multiple crimes.

Studies also have revealed that young offenders develop their criminal skills at an early age.

Society must correct its attitude toward youthful criminals; it is in danger of being eaten alive by its young.

The Standard-Times
New Bedford, Mass., May 17, 1977
Youth and crime

Once upon a time, the American tradition taught that the nation's hope for the future lay in its youth; as a people, we have always believed that and it has become customary for one generation to invest heavily in the next, even if it required sacrifice to do so. Obviously, there is still truth to the premise, yet it comes as something of a shock to hear from demographers that America's future is brightening perceptibly because the country's youthful population will shrink dramatically over the next few years.

The statistics are sobering. According to federal reports for 1975, young people 14 through 24 accounted for 51 per cent of all criminal arrests. They were responsible for 76 per cent of all arrests for auto theft, 72 per cent of all burglaries, 71 per cent of all robberies, 56 per cent of all forcible rapes, and 44 per cent of all murders. They also accounted for a disproportionate share of the nation's unemployment, traffic accidents, unwanted pregnancies, illegitimate children, and venereal disease. And as a group, they made up only 20.9 per cent of the population.

Furthermore, the latest Harris Survey concludes that sixty-eight per cent of the public nationwide believes that crimes by teen-agers have been increasing in the past year.

The demographers, assuming that the rate of juvenile delinquency, crime, and unemployment will remain constant, nevertheless predict a brighter future because in thirteen years the group of Americans aged 14 through 24 will drop by several million and be fourteen per cent smaller than it was in 1975.

Thus, because the effects of a "baby boom" that peaked in the '50s are gradually being phased out by the passage of time, we can apparently look forward to a better, safer, and more economically stable society.

The bothersome factors here, of course, involve both cause and cure of this national problem. If it simply "goes away" because youth grows up and fewer youths succeed to the role of antisocial behavior, the suggestion is that we will be sufficiently relieved as to let the matter drop — without knowing why the crime of the '60s was the worst we ever had, or what to do about this wretched phenomenon if it ever recurs.

Does sheer weight of numbers and the resultant competition for goods, services, space, and opportunity in a society such as ours guarantee a rise in youth crime? Were parents in this age of relative affluence poorer parents? Did objection to war and disenchantment with government trigger a broad rejection of customs and morals, especially by the young? Did inflation widen savagely the gap between the haves and have-nots? If most crime was committed by young people neither poor nor black — and there is this suggestion — what was the motive?

Somehow, at some point — and not necessarily by means of a costly government study — we need to address ourselves to these questions. We need to because it is as distressing to assume that we cannot have an orderly society without periodically reducing our youth population as it is to concede that we cannot have a flourishing economy without an occasional war.

DAILY NEWS
New York, N.Y., April 1, 1977
PUT SAFETY FIRST

Reading scores may be dropping, but violent crime is rising in our city schools, and at a shocking rate.

Statistics obtained by The News show that since September serious crimes against teachers and students have jumped 12% over last year.

It's disgraceful. School authorities should intensify efforts to obtain federal funds to hire and train more school guards. They should also sit down with police officials, the mayor's office, the teachers' union and concerned citizens' groups to hammer out a hard-nosed safety program, and fast.

The Seattle Times
Seattle, Wash., January 31, 1977
School crime down

INCIDENTS of crime in the Seattle schools decreased by 9.1 per cent during the 1975-76 school year. How much of the decline can be attributed to a change in student behavior and how much to the improved network of alarm systems in the school is uncertain.

But it has been demonstrated here that a combination of the two can work within public facilities.

At the same time, school officials must be concerned over the increases in property damage and narcotics offenses of 16.1 per cent and 21.7 per cent, respectively.

These offenses represent major costs to the public, in terms of both money and student health.

The fact that the improvement in the Seattle schools comes at a time when school violence nationally is on an upswing is a credit to the students, faculty and administration of the schools and to the city as a whole.

The News American
Baltimore, Md., February 27, 1977
Teenage Criminals

ONE OF modern society's most pressing problems is the need of more protection against the spread of violent crimes being committed by young hoodlums who have the protection of outmoded juvenile delinquency laws.

In recent years, in many states, much study has been given and some action taken toward updating such laws. By and large, however, they continue to be used as a shield by a proliferating class of vicious, street-wise teeners.

Just because they are below a certain age, usually 16, these young but savage predators automatically are excused from the penalties normally imposed for their crimes. Instead, when caught, they are treated as mere offenders. Their identities are kept secret along with details of the usually lenient treatment received.

The frightening new class of young outlaws now roaming the nation's cities, often directed by older gang leaders, are by no means the kind of children that the juvenile delinquency system was designed to help. They are nothing but hardened criminals and should be treated as such.

They commit virtually every crime in the book, from burglary to brutal muggings of the elderly — even rape and murder. Giving them the kid glove treatment simply because of their age is nothing short of self-defeating.

The problem obviously is as perplexing as it is pressing. Differentiating between degrees of criminality and responsibility would baffle a Solomon, but certainly some drastic changes in the present system are mandatory for the good of society as a whole.

One starting point would be to give the full penalty of the law to young people guilty of repeatedly committing violent crimes. Another would be to lower the present juvenile delinquency age cut-off by several years — to 16, say, instead of 18.

It has been accepted that young people mature more rapidly in responsibility these days, as evidenced when the voting age was lowered to 18.

Some of them, as police reports indisputably prove, have been maturing even more rapidly in brazen criminality.

The Wichita Beacon
Wichita, Kans., March 30, 1977
Juvenile justice

Somewhere between the severely hard-line approach to juvenile offenders in Sedgwick County and the ineffective coddling of them is a workable middle ground that the district court's juvenile department should seek.

The original aim of the juvenile justice system — the individual rehabilitation of each offender — appears outmoded in today's society.

Adolescents are a much different breed than they were at the turn of the century and finding a "cure" for each young offender is a difficult if not impossible task.

Yet the search continues for ways to make the juvenile justice system work more effectively. In some communities there has been a shift away from helping "disturbed" juveniles and toward protecting the victimized citizenry.

This reflects a "get tough" policy which often is characterized by attempts to deal with youthful perpetrators of violent crime as adults.

An educator and psychologist, Ernest van den Haag, perhaps summed up the feeling of many adults when he wrote in his book Punishing Criminals: "The victim of a 15-year-old is as much mugged as the victim of a 21-year-old mugger, the victim of a 14-year-old murderer or rapist is as dead or as raped as the victim of an older one. The need for social defense or protection is the same."

After a four-year study of the juvenile justice system, the Joint Commission on Juvenile Standards, made up of prominent psychiatrists, sociologists, penologists, educators, lawyers and judges, has approved a comprehensive set of recommendations for improving the system. Eventually the recommendations will be offered as models for new state legislation.

Specifically, the commission has proposed an end to "indeterminate" sentencing of juvenile criminals — a procedure that slowly is losing appeal among criminologists and penologists and has been criticized for being unfair and ineffective.

Present juvenile sentencing procedures would be overhauled to provide defined and strict sentencing for the most serious juvenile offenders.

Non-criminal behavior — the so-called "status offenses" like incorrigibility, immoral conduct and truancy — would be removed from the jurisdiction of the juvenile court altogether and would be handled by social agencies instead.

The Dispatch
Columbus, Ohio, November 15, 1977
Confining Young Criminals

AN INTERESTING study, subject to challenge, contends prisons are not a training school for criminals but that professional criminals learn their skills earlier.

As a result, the Rand Corp. researchers indicate fewer serious crimes would be committed if young, hardened criminals were given longer prison terms.

The analysts state juvenile crime records should be given more weight by judges in determining the sentence of an offender. Too often these records are not admissable evidence.

The study researchers go on to say many of the "intensive (hardened) criminals" committed serious crimes prior to the age of 13 and thus legal restrictions ought to be lifted on juvenile records to reveal background essential to a jurist.

Criminals mellow as they grow older, the report says. However, an older person often receives a severe sentence on his past record and not on the crime for which he is being sentenced nor on his future potential as a criminal.

The report, indicating criminal activity diminishes with age, points out the studied criminals committed an average of 38 serious crimes per year as juveniles, 18 per year as young adults and seven each year in the mature adult period.

Perhaps the lone hopeful note in the report relates to prisoner job training to enable a convict to adjust upon release. But even this says he merely commits fewer crimes.

For most, the report says bluntly, crime was the occupation of choice. Thus, it concludes prison provides the lone protection to society from habitual offenders.

The report is tough. It says rehabilitation has failed because prisoners in most instances reject it.

Financed by federal grants, the study will be pursued and no doubt debated. But it follows the trend in legislatures and courtrooms to remove the habitual criminal from the streets.

But it flies in the face of those who hold young criminals are most subject to rehabilitation.

The Philadelphia Inquirer
Philadelphia, Pa., March 27, 1977
Wrong ways to fight crime

Crime and the fear of crime are problems that will not be solved by lashing out at the wrong targets.

That is what is happening in Philadelphia City Council with a bill that would punish parents for offenses by their children.

It also is happening in New York State where a proposal in the legislature would impose different penalties for the same offense depending on whether the victim was over or under 60 years of age.

Both proposals are well-meaning but misguided attempts to "do something" about crime. But they would do nothing to alleviate crime and probably would make it worse.

The bill in City Council, originally proposed by Harry Jannotti but subsequently amended by the Law and Government Committee, would subject parents to liability of up to $1,000 per incident for personal injuries or property losses resulting from crimes committed by their children under 18.

It also would increase from $5 to $25 and from $100 to $300 the minimum and maximum fines for parents of children under 18 on the streets after 10:30 p.m. (midnight Friday and Saturday) unaccompanied by parents or not having some "legitimate business" such as going to and from a job. Failure to pay the fine could result in a jail sentence up to 10 days.

The fact is that some children would like nothing better than to have their parents punished. Moreover, it is an injustice to assume that parents of all juvenile lawbreakers are negligent and irresponsible. Many parents who do their best and set a good example, nonetheless are unable to keep their children from running afoul of the law.

In New York, the legislature is seeking to reduce the deplorable increase in crimes of violence against the elderly by arbitrarily imposing penalties if the victim is 60 or older (62 under a proposed amendment to the bill. Such a law, if it ever were enacted and upheld in the courts, would discriminate against victims 59 or younger—if it had any effect at all.

Such efforts to fight crime have a superficial appeal but they are counter-productive and distract attention from the need for effective improvements in criminal justice and correctional systems.

Richmond Times-Dispatch

Richmond, Va., April 23, 1977

Apathy and Crime

Gangs of youths, directed by adult criminals, are making life so miserable for about a dozen small manufacturing plants in one area of New York that the owners say they may be forced to move out of the city.

The plants are being burglarized time after time by young hoodlums who are so brazen as to threaten plant officials face-to-face and to admit that they are involved in the crimes. The young criminals have no fear of getting caught, or of being successfully prosecuted if they are caught. One businessman describes the situation as "living hell."

Those plants are located in the Queens Borough, but crime knows no boundaries. A doctor, in a letter to a New York newspaper, tells how his car, parked on a busy street not more than 100 yards from the world-famous Bloomingdale's department store in Manhattan, was broken into one recent evening in plain view of hundreds of shoppers and other passers-by. The window was smashed, the trunk opened, the spare tire carefully unscrewed and removed, and the doctor's medical bag stolen.

"Obviously, the police cannot be everywhere, but then what is the solution?" the doctor asks. "Where is it safe to walk? Where is it safe to sit? What park can we go into? Where will it all end? Someone or some group will have to lead an aroused citizenry into a new solution. The alternative is to abandon the city to the hoodlums."

Because of its size and other factors, New York has more crime than many other communities, but no place is immune. Indeed, one of the problems seems to be that criminal activity has become so widespread that much of the public apathetically accepts it as inevitable and feels little can be done to combat it.

Sooner or later — and it better not be much later — law-abiding society must declare war on crime, not a war conducted by vigilantes or using other extralegal methods, but one utilizing the full resources of law enforcement, the judiciary and the corrections system.

The Evening Gazette

Worcester, Mass., April 20, 1977

Turning Youth Gangs Around

Sorely needed these days is an "energy policy" dealing with the misdirected power generated by youth gangs or groups.

Last week news reports were circulated widely of teenage gangs, perhaps as many as 225 of them involving 8,000 members, burglarizing, looting and shaking down owners of factories in the Queens borough of New York City.

Over the weekend, group savagery destroyed the common peace of the nearby community of Franklin. Injuries to police officers, including one serious injury, and arrests of several youths resulted from a wild and dangerous brawl.

In Queens the spark that ignites the power show is believed to be adult direction; in Franklin the volatile situation was fanned by alcohol consumption and restlessness following disciplinary attempts.

But, in both instances, the collective running amok is a serious matter and must be dealt with by the community-at-large. Town officials, victims, police, parents and the youths themselves must participate in establishing a policy that can turn these destructive forces to more constructive ends.

In small towns or the big city, there must be a way to channel youth energy into beneficial endeavors instead of crippling crimes.

Long Island Press

Jamaica, N.Y., January 28, 1977

Shock treatment that works

"It ain't glamorous in here the way it is pictured in the old Bogart and Cagney movies. It is like hell."

That's what a man serving a life term in New Jersey's maximum security prison shouted at a group of teen-agers the other day.

The youngsters had been in trouble with the law, and were seeing for themselves what prison life is like.

For more than an hour, seven convicts told them in brutal, explicit terms of the terror, misery and humiliation of prison life, and of the unhappiness they had caused their families. When they finished, the youngsters were taken on a tour by prison guards, and told just what to expect from them.

The session was part of a program begun last August by inmates at Rahway State Prison. It's shock treatment — and apparently brutally effective.

About 300 teen-agers have been exposed to it. Only four have been arrested again.

Does anyone know of a better way to convince youngsters that breaking the law is the first toward a life of horror?

Los Angeles Times

Los Angeles, Calif., January 30, 1977

'It Is Like Hell'

Since last August a novel program has been under way in New Jersey to expose juvenile-law offenders to the harsh and often brutal realities of prison life. The program was conceived and is run by the Lifers Group—inmates who, as the name they have chosen makes clear, are serving life sentences. Its aim is to deter the juveniles from running afoul of the law in the future. Early indications are that the approach is effective.

The basic idea behind what is called Juvenile Awareness, Project Help, is probably as old as civilization itself: to allow some to profit from the folly of others.

The inmates who participate in the program speak with the voice of bitter experience. They do not preach, they do not repeat the maxims that the young offenders have heard so often before. They simply describe, in the language of the street and with the passion of believers, the hellishness and hopelessness of prison life.

A New York Times reporter who witnessed one such encounter at the maximum-security Rahway State Prison describes the juveniles as visibly shaken by what they saw and heard, the prisoners emotionally drained by the ordeal of expressing what they live through daily.

Prison is being buried alive, with no hope of getting out, the youths were told. It is having to worry constantly about getting a knife in the back, it is having to defend yourself against homosexual assaults, it is fighting for everything you get and having to fight to keep it. It means having to adapt to a social system unlike any ever experienced before. It is a life of terror and humiliation and deprivation. "It is like hell."

Not all prisons have the unrelieved grimness of Rahway. But in all states there are prisons for the hard cases, the major offenders, where life as it goes on at Rahway is paralleled.

Does brief exposure to that life influence the juveniles involved? In the six months that the program has been under way, 300 youths have visited Rahway. Only four are known to have subsequently been arrested for new crimes. That statistic, while not conclusive, is at least suggestive. Other states might profit from the New Jersey experiment.

Drug Abuse:
Should it be criminal?

American society continues to vacillate in its approach to controlling the use of narcotic drugs. Since 1914, with the passage of the Harrison Act outlawing heroin and other hard drugs, criminal enforcement and penal sanctions have been the preferred methods.[2] Ironically, in the 1920s when prohibitionist fewer swept the land, heroin maintenance programs existed in New York, Shreveport, La. and other U.S. cities.[2] The failure of the first criminal sanctions to stem the rising tide of narcotics use only resulted in more of the same: more expenditures for criminal enforcement and even longer prison sentences.

New York State's present law, with its mandatory prison sentences (often from 15 years to life) might represent the ultimate in drug deterrence through draconian punishment. The law, which went into effect on September 1, 1973, was hailed by its creator, then-Governor Nelson Rockefeller, as the "toughest anti-drug program in the nation."[3] The law not only provided for stiffer sentences, but concurrently funnelled millions of dollars into the courts for new judges, prosecutors, public defenders and other personnel to handle the expected crush of new cases. Direct police enforcement also received new infusions of money.

Scattered reports of the law's impact, first reported in the press, were echoed in a costly study funded by the Law Enforcement Assistance Administration of the four-year-old drug law: the mandatory sentencing law neither reduced drug-related crime nor resulted in more prison sentences for second-offenders.[4]

The backlog of drug cases in the courts remained undiminished despite massive increases in money and personnel. The mandatory sentencing rule resulted in a large increase in trials because of the absence of plea-bargaining. To compensate for the long prison terms, prosecutors who took issue with the new law substituted lighter charges for heavier ones. Judges became more sensitive to search and seizure motions urging suppression of evidence, and juries were less likely to convict. In the streets, the number of arrests did not rise appreciably, and the failure of the law to differentiate between large and small narcotic dealers reduced efforts to break up major drug rings.

The New York drug law's problems might be ascribed less to its execution and application than to its basic premise: that drug use can be halted through criminal sanctions. The use of such penalties is particularly put to the test with the sale of heroin, where the risks of arrest are balanced against potentially enormous financial profits. Several sociologists argue that no matter how great the deterrence, there is no evidence that it will significantly effect drug use.[5] Instead, such stringent measures could conceivably defeat their own purpose: A study of 1,800 convicted marijuana users revealed that, if anything, severe penalties and a perceived certainty of arrest increased marijuana use.[6]

The hypothesis that defining too many acts as "criminal" debilitates law enforcement in general and undermines drug deterrence schemes in particular has been used to promote the reform of marijuana laws.[7] Observers attribute New York's impetus to decriminalize possession of small amounts of marijuana to the harshness of the 1973 drug law.[8] President Carter has endorsed legislation that would amend the federal marijuana prohibition enacted in 1937. Marijuana use would still be discouraged, but it would be a misdemeanor, subject to small fines in a manner similar to traffic violations. The influential American Bar and American Medical Associations have also joined the movement for decriminalization.

Even some strongly hostile to marijuana use have encouraged a reduction of penalties. Dr. Robert L. DuPont, director of the National Institute on Drug Abuse, is one:

> "There is now a very broad consensus in the U.S. that marijuana use should be discouraged and that the government's role is to discourage marijuana use. But . . . most people agree that it does not make sense to put people in prison for the possession of small amounts of marijuana."[9]

The numbers exposing themselves to arrest are large: 37 million Americans have used marijuana at least once, while eight percent of adults and 12% of youth are regular users.[10]

Marijuana is now the nation's third most frequently used drug after tobacco and alcohol. Dr. Peter G. Bourne, President Carter's Special Assistant for Mental Health and Drug Abuse, holds that the preponderance of the evidence shows marijuana not to be physically addictive.[11] Nor does infrequent or moderate use pose an immediate or substantial health hazard to the individual. However, he cautions that the effect of long-term use are unknown and more research is necessary.

Limited results are available on Oregon's early decriminalization in 1973.[12] During the first two years of the new law, usage did not increase substantially. It did increase in the third year to about the average level of consumption in the other western states. This increase is attributed not to the diminution of penalties, but to a discernible shift in medical opinion on the health consequences associated with smoking marijuana. Surveys in six other states that have revised their marijuana laws produced similar results: use increased slightly because of a perceived change in the moral, social and medical acceptability of marijuana. Apparently, the threat of prosecution had not inhibited marijuana use.[13]

Liberalized marijuana laws in individual states and the prevailing attitude elsewhere that police tend to disregard marijuana law violators have produced a generation of Americans seemingly indifferent to the progress of federal decriminalization. Still, it should be noted that in 1976, 441,000 people were arrested for marijuana offenses, just below the 1974 record of 445,600.[14]

Notes

1. *President's Commission on Law Enforcement & Administration of Justice: The Challenge of Crime in a Free Society* (Washington, D.C.: Gov't Printing Office, 1967) p. 222.
2. David Musto, *American Disease: Origins of Narcotic Control* (New Haven: Yale University Press, 1973) pp. 121–209. Drug maintenance clinics continued to exist after the passage of the Harrison Act because of delayed enforcement and judicial disagreement as to the scope of the Act. In *Nigro v. United States,* 276 U.S. 332 (1928), the Supreme Court conclusively interpreted the law as prohibiting narcotic maintenance by physicians.
3. *The New York Times,* September 1, 1977 p. 1.
4. *Nation's Toughest Drug Law: Evaluating N.Y.'s Drug Law* (New York: Association of the Bar of the City of New York, 1977).
5. Norman Zinberg & John Robertson, *Drugs and the Public,* (New York: Simon & Schuster, 1972).
6. Patricia Erikson, "Deterrence and Deviance," 67 *Journal of Criminal Law & Criminology* 222 (1976).
7. For a general discussion of this principle see Sanford Kadish, "The Crisis of Overcriminalization," 374 *Annals* 157 (1957).
8. *The New York Times,* January 29, 1975 pp. 1, 32.
9. Chuck Fager, "Pot Happy," *In These Times,* January 4, 1978 p. 24.
10. *Marijuana: A Study of State Policies and Penalties,* prepared by Peat, Marwick, Mitchell & Co. for the National Governors Conference. (Washington, D.C.: Hall of the States, 1977) pp. 6–7.
11. *Ibid.,* p. 8.
12. *Ibid.,* pp. 33–36.
13. *Ibid.*
14. Chuck Fager, *supra.*

N.Y. GOVERNOR ASKS LIFE SENTENCES FOR DRUG PUSHERS, VIOLENT ADDICTS

New York Gov. Nelson A. Rockefeller (R) asked the state legislature Jan. 3 to enact laws making the penalty "for all illegal trafficking in hard drugs" and "for all violent crimes committed by person under the influence of hard drugs" a mandatory life prison sentence. Rockefeller made the request in his 15th annual State of the State message, saying the time had come to take "bold and decisive steps" to deal with the narcotics menace. (The state had spent $1 billion for narcotics addiction prevention and rehabilitation in recent years, much of it in New York City, which was estimated to have an addict population in excess of 100,000, without any apparent reduction of the addiction rate) The governor asked the legislature to bar plea bargaining, probation, parole and suspended sentence in narcotics cases. He proposed making youthful narcotics offenders subject to the same penalties faced by adults, with the exception of possible parole after 15 years imprisonment. Rockefeller also suggested $1,000 bounties to informants of narcotics dealers, an expansion of the New York City Narcotics Court, and broader discretionary authority of the State Addiction Control Commission in dealing with addicts.

New York Post

New York, N.Y., January 4, 1973

At the outset of his impassioned remarks on drug addiction yesterday—during his State of the State address—Governor Rockefeller conceded: "We have achieved very little permanent rehabilitation—and we have found no cure." It would be a misfortune, however, if the public believed that he offered any sure remedy in his latest proposals, deeply as many will endorse the high priority he gave the problem.

For notwithstanding the Governor's understandable concern about the narcotics-crime curse and the Legislature's approving reception of his proposal that "pushers" be given immutable life sentences, there are no simple answers contained in his frankly "drastic" program.

The big pusher deserves neither mercy nor apologia; in a very real sense, he is a killer. At one time or another, however, many addicts sell drugs in some quantity. There are possibly some 300,000 addicts here alone. How many is the state really prepared to arrest and maintain in prisons for decades? What prisons? At what costs? (The state prison census is less than a tenth of 300,000).

There are other grim considerations. The Governor proposes a milder, 15-year term for teen-age pushers. Assuming the life sentence threat has some deterrent effect, some of these youths, subject to lighter penalties, would presumably be increasingly engaged in heavier selling. Some may be arrested and jailed. Will they emerge, reformed and rehabilitated, after 15 years in this state's prisons? These are questions not quickly resolved by rhetoric.

The governor was on much firmer ground with other legislative proposals. Having committed himself earlier to protection of the state's liberalized abortion law, he is also moving to restore some of the harsh cuts in welfare and Medicaid funding he demanded two years ago. That may make a difference to some ravaged families, even taking into account the effects of inflation in the meantime.

Mr. Rockefeller's interests in court reform, no-fault insurance, gun control, consumer protection and administrative modifications in government—his descriptions of the latter seemed occasionally to entail more bureaucracy than promised "simplifications"—are all generally progressive and welcome; they can form the basis for some sound measures. His rededication to civil rights was a timely rebuttal to those who signal retreat.

But his assertion that "society has no alternative" to his drug-law proposals is a cry of desperation rather than a solution; it could also prove diversionary. A great many patient people, professionals and private citizens alike, have been laboring over the years on addiction treatment and prevention and their industry deserves considerably more financial reward and support than "society" has so far seen fit to provide. There is an obvious case to be made for heavier drug-selling penalties for the highest-ranking adult importers and wholesalers. The gravest problem in dealing with them, however, is that they so often and so mysteriously elude any apprehension while 15-year-olds without the right connections are being caught and jailed.

Newsday

Garden City, N.Y., January 7, 1973

To close off "all avenues of escape" for drug pushers, Governor Rockefeller would impose mandatory life prison terms for anyone convicted of selling heroin, amphetamines, LSD, hashish or "other dangerous drugs." He proposes to "forbid acceptance of a plea to a lesser charge, forbid probation, forbid parole and forbid suspension of sentence." The same lifetime penalty would also apply to those convicted of violent crimes while under the influence of drugs.

We don't for one moment downgrade the enormity and severity of the state's drug problem, nor do we argue the priority Rockefeller quite rightly gave the issue in his State of the State message last week. But in our opinion his proposals fail to stand up to the tests of past experience in law enforcement or present knowledge of drug traffic.

Did the death penalty stop homicides? Do long jail sentences rehabilitate offenders? Robert McKay, dean of the New York University law school and chairman of the commission that investigated the Attica riot, says of the governor's proposal: "It is completely counter to everything the civilized world has been working for. The notion of populating our jails with people with no hope of release ever is terribly destructive."

The governor makes no distinction between a first offender and a commercial drug trafficker. He makes no distinction between a user who pushes to support his own habit and a big-time wholesaler of drugs. He makes no distinction between selling a buddy an ounce of hashish and marketing pounds of heroin.

The most disturbing aspect of the governor's proposal is that he seems to believe that harsh new penalties would serve as a substitute for the treatment and rehabilitation programs the state now sponsors. That would be fatal, in our view. It's true that the state's drug programs have been only marginally successful, but the state is largely responsible for that. State programs have been turned on and shut off as often as a beer tap at a fraternity party. Emphasis has swung back and forth from education to treatment to rehabilitation, causing serious problems in programs that were just beginning to work.

But this is a time to learn from our mistakes, not a time to give up hope, as the governor has apparently done. After spending $1 billion on drug programs, says the governor, "we have achieved very little permanent rehabilitation—and we have found no cure." We haven't found a cure for cancer yet either, but nobody is suggesting we stop trying.

Long Island Press

Jamaica, N.Y., January 9, 1973

Gov. Rockefeller's frustration over failure to solve the problems of drug addiction is understandable.

The state has spent more than $1 billion in education, therapy, commitment and rehabilitation programs, with disappointing results. While some addicts have been led away from drugs to a more meaningful life, the problem continues to grow, and, with it, crime and fear.

The governor thus concludes that there are only two alternatives—to continue as we have been doing "with little real hope of changing the present trend," or to take stern measures. He opts for the latter.

Mr. Rockefeller's program, spelled out in generalized recommendations in his State of the State message last week, includes life prison sentences for all pushers—without chance for plea bargaining, probation, parole or suspended sentance—the same for addicts who commit violent crimes, and the removal of youth offender protection for pushers in their late teens. The governor also would offer a $1,000 cash bounty for information leading to the conviction of drug pushers.

The desire to get drug pushers off the streets is laudatory. Nobody will dispute that they are a menace to society. But the governor's program leaves something to be desired, in concept, in scope and in its severity.

It fails to differentiate the big-time drug dealers and the addict pusher who sells narcotics to maintain his own supply. The big profiteers certainly deserve long jail sentences, but the existing laws already make that possible—if they can be caught.

Addict pushers are another matter, and a life sentence with no chance of parole seems extreme. These men and women need treatment and rehabilitation, not a lifetime behind bars. The fear of such punishment will not deter addicts from crime, either.

The fears voiced by Appellate Division Presiding Justices Samuel Rabin and Harold A. Stevens—that the governor's program would tie the courts into a hopeless knot—also must be considered. They say plea bargaining is a necessary evil, and warned that mandatory life sentences might lead to more acquittals, because the more severe the penalty, the more juries are reluctant to convict.

Both agree—and so do we—that the thrust "should be against Mr. Big." Justice Stevens also suggested experimenting with the English system of having the state distribute heroin to addicts, to take the profit out of drug pushing.

Gov. Rockefeller's plan will be spelled out in more detail when bills to implement it are introduced into the Legislature. We hope he modifies it before the bills are prepared.

DAILY NEWS

New York, N.Y., January 4, 1973

—ran through the State of the State message Gov. Nelson A. Rockefeller delivered yesterday to the Legislature.

Nowhere was it more evident than in the governor's

Gov. Rockefeller

call for harsh measures to curb the drug traffic, which he rightly called the "number one concern of the American people."

If the governor has his way, narcotics pushers and addicts who turn to violent crime will be jugged for keeps the first time they are convicted.

Rockefeller's proposal leaves no loopholes for tenderness or misguided mercy in dealing with pushers. No guilty-plea bargaining with cut-rate sentences; no parole—except for what are now called "youthful offenders." These latter would, under Rockefeller's plan, be handled as adults henceforth and made to serve 15 years before they could be considered for release.

Merciless as they are, the governor's recommendations will evoke a chorus of approving cheers from the vast majority of New Yorkers.

Drug pushers are the scum of humanity and the scourge of society; cold-hearted vermin who are pitiless themselves and deserve to be treated without pity.

The drug traffic thrives because it promises immense profits and, as things now stand, little risk of severe punishment for operators who take a fall.

A one-strike-and-you're-out law, we think, would cause hordes of pushers to go out of business rather than chance a lifetime in the clink. It's certainly worth a try.

WORCESTER TELEGRAM.

Worcester, Mass., January 7, 1973

Gov. Nelson Rockefeller's proposal to crack down on convicted drug pushers with mandatory life sentences is a counsel of desperation.

Nothing else has worked, the governor told the New York state legislature, so now it is time for laws to give pushers life sentences with no chance of parole. He also demands no suspended sentences, no plea-bargaining, a 100 per cent tax on the assets of convicted drug dealers, and $1,000 rewards to persons giving information leading to conviction of drug pushers.

Given the desperate drug situation in places like New York City, it is small wonder that officials are proposing drastic solutions. But would these proposals really be solutions? It seems unlikely.

In the first place, a mandatory life sentence with no parole would tend to make juries even more reluctant to convict than they are now. The result might be fewer pushers in jail rather than more.

Second, the governor makes a common mistake in drawing a hard and fast line between "pushers" and "users." All the studies on the drug problem show that most users of hard drugs sell or give drugs to their acquaintances, at least occasionally. Some do it to support their habit. Many of these addicted persons are not pushers in the usual sense of being parasites getting rich on the misery of others. Rather, they share the misery of the drug culture.

Make no mistake about it: Those persons convicted of exploiting others by selling hard drugs deserve to have the book thrown at them. But it is our opinion that most convicted pushers suffer severe punishments now — 5, 10 or 20 years, in many cases.

It may be that some of these punishments should be increased. But it may also be that some persons brought in on drug charges should be treated in different ways. Gov. Rockefeller's proposals do not take that into account.

THE LINCOLN STAR

Lincoln, Neb., January 8, 1973

The philosophy of controlling the drug problem has turned full circle in New York, where the drug-connected crime rate is far above the national average.

Feeling that the emphasis on rehabilitating the user has failed to turn the tide against drug addiction, Gov. Nelson Rockefeller wants to renew the emphasis on harsh punishment for the provider.

The four-term governor proposed to the New York Legislature last week that mandatory life imprisonment sentences be meted out to anyone convicted of selling heroin or other hard drugs. The laws called for by the governor would not allow pleas to reduced charges, suspended sentences or parole. In other words, a life sentence would be just that — a sentence for life.

As appropriate as is the governor's concern for the drug problem, his proposed methods to deal with it raise some questions.

The argument isn't that there should not be stiff penalties for drug trafficking, but a mandatory life sentence also runs contrary to the accepted penal philosophy that the potential for rehabilitation of each individual should be sought out. And aside from all that, it is unlikely that the prospect of life in prison will deter pushers to the extent that the drug problem will be wiped out. Greed drives men to madness and the potential profit in the illegal drug trade is an undeniable temptress.

As long as there is a poppy seed there will be heroin and as long as people can't live with themselves there will be drug addiction — whether it is by heroin, alcohol or pills. It is a problem of such magnitude that it perhaps defies solution. Going overboard in calling for harsh, if not unconstitutional, punishment will not help solve the problem in the long run.

The New York Times

New York, N.Y., January 9, 1973

While hardly any penalty can be considered too severe for big-time peddlers of hard narcotics, Governor Rockefeller's proposed crackdown on the addiction problem as outlined in his State of the State message is little better than a politically attuned harangue that threatens to make a bad situation worse.

It has all the appeal of simplicity—mandatory life terms for offenders—but it also has all the faults. It fails to distinguish between those Mr. Rockefeller calls the "master minds" of drug trafficking and those who may only occasionally use drugs. Although the Governor included hashish on his list of dangerous drugs, that is a form of marijuana and not a narcotic at all. A Presidential commission and others have recently urged the decriminalization of marijuana. Yet, the Governor demands a life term for occasional users of hashish, without even hope of parole.

The drug problem in this state is real. It has a demonstrated relationship to crime. The public's interest in its solution is understandably keen. That makes it doubly imperative for legislators to insist on measures that offer realistic promise of success.

* * *

A life sentence can already be imposed under existing laws for big-drug dealers. The real question is why prosecutors have failed to demand such penalties and why courts have refused to impose them.

As the Joint Legislative Committee on Crime recently pointed out, the whole criminal justice system needs vast improvement. The committee also pointed out that Governor Rockefeller is responsible for the orderly working of this system. After a detailed examination of recent narcotics cases, the committee issued a report saying that "there is less risk and more profit in dealing in heroin in New York City than in the ordinary crime of larceny." The report concluded: "The Governor is constitutionally charged with the responsibility of seeing to it that the narcotics laws are faithfully executed. Until now, that responsibility has been shirked with disastrous consequences."

Governor Rockefeller is calling for new laws with harsher penalties for dealing in drugs while the old ones already on the books lack effective enforcement. The committee's study found that a scandalously small number of narcotics dealers are arrested, a smaller number brought to trial and a still smaller number convicted. Those who are convicted receive only 2.5 per cent of the maximum penalty available to law-enforcement officials. Where has Governor Rockefeller been? Why didn't he follow up this Joint Legislative Committee investigation?

* * *

The Governor's failure has been even broader in the anti-addiction struggle. He admits that "very little" has been achieved despite the expenditure of $1 billion on various aspects of the narcotics problem, including prevention and rehabilitation. One reason for this failure has been his administration's neglect to audit programs and require records. The state has simply been shoveling out money to virtually all takers in the anti-addiction field.

Even so, in spite of inexcusably sloppy administration, there has been at least a small degree of accomplishment. Some rehabilitation programs do seem to be moving addicts from lives of crime into productive pursuits. Addicts in this city's methadone maintenance program and in several of the drug-free programs are beginning to show encouraging progress, remaining free of crime, taking jobs, maintaining stable family relationships. Crime statistics tend to provide some confirmation for this development. Criminals in the city's prison system offer other corroborating evidence. While more than 50 per cent used to require detoxification from drug habits, only 30 per cent do so now.

A call to expand the slow work of addiction prevention and rehabilitation would probably have got Governor Rockefeller few headlines. A dedication to making the criminal justice system work might even have been a greater confession of past failure. Bring every addict into care? Get them jobs? There is little here for the politician, and the Governor in his most recent State of the State message shows that he remains a prisoner of politicians' passions.

©1973 by The New York Times Company. Reprinted by permission.

New York, N.Y., January 10, 1973

The fault with Governor Rockefeller's indiscriminate lock-'em-up-for-life response to the challenge posed by drug pushers and addicts lies not solely in its unworkability. The bitter irony is that it would replace a currently effective program that holds some promise of success.

Discouraging though it has often been, the state's experience with the drug problem, especially in recent months, does raise hope that addicts can in fact be rehabilitated. It suggests that some methods of rehabilitation offer improved chances of success and that many addicts accept adequate care when offered. Yet Governor Rockefeller seems willing to toss in the towel of rehabilitation just as real progress seems to be under way.

By the most recent estimate, there are about 100,000 hard-core heroin addicts in New York City. About half of them, or some 50,000, are receiving some form of treatment. An increasing number of addicts is being successfully rehabilitated and thrust into the job market. This being so, the first priority of Governor Rockefeller and the State Legislature ought to be to get every addict in some effective form of care. Long waiting lists for entry into established methadone programs have largely been eliminated by expanding this form of treatment; but further expansion is clearly in order.

Those in charge of treatment programs should not wait for addicts to come knocking on the door seeking admission. There ought to be a community-based recruitment program with ex-addicts and community leaders actively moving about the streets, bringing known addicts into programs. This is being done in Illinois. It should be done in New York.

Addicts must be sought out in prisons, where they require detoxification, in the courts, in the hospitals, in the schools. While it makes no sense simply to round up addicts and confine them, it is on the contrary sound public policy to require addicts to submit to effective treatment programs. Heroin addiction takes on some of the characteristics of an epidemic in urban slum areas, as users become pushers and contaminate whole neighborhoods. Known users represent a menace to society; they ought to be segregated and rehabilitated.

Any effective rehabilitation program should include job training and job placement. To return ex-addicts to the streets without prospect of productive employment is to risk reversion to the drug culture. Unemployment now runs as high as 60 per cent among this especially vulnerable social group. The state needs to set up programs offering businesses incentives and support in the employment of ex-addicts.

This is not to say that there should be no crackdown on drug traffickers. A responsible law enforcement effort that carefully distinguishes among kinds of traffickers and kinds of drugs is clearly needed. Improved law enforcement is an essential element in a comprehensive attack on the drug problem. The state's criminal justice system, which has responded to this problem with disgraceful inadequacy, requires careful review and reform. Harsh penalties already available in the law, including life imprisonment, ought to be imposed in appropriate cases.

But the Governor's simplistic, lock-'em-up-for-life-for-everyone proposal is a gross disservice, making adoption of a responsible program less likely than ever.

©1973 by The New York Times Company. Reprinted by permission.

BUFFALO EVENING NEWS

Buffalo, N.Y., January 12, 1973

Unless he has deliberately decorated them with a lot of unwanted extremism in order to have something to give away during the legislative bargaining process, Gov. Rockefeller's proposals for tougher narcotics laws read like some kind of tasteless bad joke. In fact, the bills themselves appear to be so much tougher in so many respects than even his annual message indicated that they seem almost a caricature of the lock-'em-up-for-life approach.

Thus, it turns out that the governor is not merely proposing a mandatory life sentence for all hard-drug sellers—with no possibility of either plea-bargaining or parole—but his bills would now even change the definition of hard drugs to embrace amphetamines, LSD and hashish along with heroin, cocaine, opium and morphine.

And an actual sale would not even have to be proved, in order to invoke the mandatory life sentence; the Rockefeller bill would treat possession of more than a pound of any of the expanded list of banned items the same as a sale. Not only that, but conspiracy to sell hard drugs would likewise be the same as an actual sale, punishable by the same unbargainable, irreducible life sentence.

And for addicts who commit "violent crimes" while "under the influence" of drugs, the same array of surprises lurks in the "new Rocky's" new proposals for mandatory life sentences. Here, the full harshness of the law is not reserved for addict-pushers, but applies also to addicts driven to crime to feed their habit.

The toughening gimmicks in this package of mandatory-life bills lurk in the definition of when a crime is "violent" and of when it was committed "under the influence." Among crimes elevated to life-sentence offenses under these bills are not just muggings, vicious assaults and killings, but a whole range of such crimes as robbery (where no physical injury occurred) and first-degree burglary (where a dwelling was entered at night with a weapon). The irreducible life sentence would apply in such cases if the drug was found in the defendant's bloodstream at the time of the crime—or within 48 hours afterward unless he could prove he took it after the crime was committed and not beforehand.

Getting tough on drug pushers and on addicts turned violent by narcotics is one thing. But coming from a governor who until now has generally put his emphasis on the rehabilitative approach, this package seems so utterly extreme—and so pregnant with invitations to serious miscarriages of justice—that it is almost self-discrediting on its face.

If we're going to mandate life penalties for pushers of hard-drugs, then surely we should be MORE cautious, rather than less so, over how we define both hard drugs and pushing.

And if we're going to lock up for life anyone who commits a violent crime under the influence of drugs, then we should be super-careful about what crimes we define as violent and what proof of "influence" we require. But in all these cases, the Rockefeller bills would seem to throw caution aside and cast so wide a net that they conceivably could catch numerous innocent victims of circumstances as well as first-offending users driven by drugs to commit an offense not now defined as violent.

St. Louis Globe-Democrat
St. Louis, Mo., January 5, 1973

New York State has the worst drug problem in the nation despite the expenditure of more than $1 billion in state funds on rehabilitation and cures. Yet, Gov. Nelson Rockefeller admitted, "We have found no cure." Dope addiction, he said, continues to spread a "reign of terror."

Rockefeller, yesterday's bleeding-heart to some, has yielded to the exigencies of today's situation and called for some tough measures. There is simply no way convicted drug pushers would return to the street under Rocky's proposal — they would be imprisoned for life, with no parole or plea bargaining permissible.

The same fate would befall addicts who commit violent crime. None of this baloney about "he did it because his second-cousin-once-removed kicked him when he was age 4" — the convicted pusher or violent addict goes directly to jail without passing "go." No suspension of sentence or parole.

Drastic? Rockefeller thinks so, but it's not as drastic as the death sentence, which is what merciless pushers should get.

Said the four-term governor: "I am completely convinced, after trying everything else, that nothing else will do. The hard-drug pusher destroys life just as surely and far more cooly than a cold-blooded killer. He threatens our society as a whole, whether he engages in large scale traffic or small time operation."

The only exception to the Rockefeller proposal we would make for Missouri is to differentiate between child and adult drug pushers, and to provide lesser penalties than life to pushers who are proven addicts themselves. These persons should still receive long prison terms — without parole, copping pleas, suspension of sentence, etc.

As Rockefeller proposes for New York, laws must be changed to make pushing drugs a uniform first degree felony with uniform penalties.

New York has been through all the proposals of the sociologists, social workers, psychiatrists, and do-gooders, and undertook unparalleled state programs in addition to those financed by federal funds. The programs haven't worked. The latest proposal, if implemented, can't fail to remove every convicted pusher from the streets forever.

Los Angeles Times
Los Angeles, Calif., January 7, 1973

Gov. Nelson A. Rockefeller is angry and frustrated about the narcotics problem in New York and his mood, shared by many, has prompted him to propose a desperate measure for control. Rockefeller wants a law requiring mandatory sentences of life imprisonment for all convicted hard-drug pushers. The law would forbid acceptance of a plea to a lesser charge and would forbid probation, parole or suspension of sentence. The penalty would mean what it says: a convicted drug seller would be put behind bars for the rest of his life.

The New York Civil Liberties Union was appalled. A black doctor who has worked with addicts for five years welcomed it, saying, "I'm not a civil libertarian any more when it comes to the destruction of lives." A state supreme court justice said he thought that big drug dealers ought to be given life sentences, though he worried about applying the law to young people on the fringes of the narcotics trade. A law school dean expressed concern that the concept of rehabilitation was being discarded.

Behind the Rockefeller proposal is the fact that the narcotics problem in New York has reached huge and frightening proportions, and that all efforts to reduce it have failed.

Rockefeller's idea is not, of course, any solution. The narcotics traffic exists even in the face of strict laws because there are immense profits in it, profits shared not just by big suppliers and small pushers but by corrupt law enforcement officials, as recent revelations in New York City have shown again. The harsh and immutable punishment Rockefeller wants for drug selling might edge some pushers into less risky pursuits, though undoubtedly there would be others ready to take their places. Its deterrent effect can easily be oversold. Probably its main appeal is emotional: the threat to put away for good those persons who simply by the nature of their crimes deserve to be outlawed from society.

But that won't stop the narcotics traffic. Fewer pushers or not, the addicts will still be there, and the costly and often brutal crimes they commit to support their habits will go on. And that, for most people, is the real heart of the matter: it is not the wrecked lives of addicts or the profits of the narcotics business that most concern them, but the terrible climate of personal insecurity created by tens of thousands of addicts in a constant and frantic search for money to buy drugs.

That aspect of the narcotics problem seems likely to remain so long as addicts have to spend great amounts of money in the illegal drug market to satisfy their needs. Some time ago we suggested that the way to defeat the illicit narcotics trade might be through government-sponsored heroin-maintenance clinics, where addicts could obtain without charge the drugs they need, where the profit would be taken out of narcotics. We recognize that it is a morally disturbing proposal. But the threat to society posed by narcotics-related crime is even more frightening.

Heroin-maintenance clinics are still only an idea; the narcotics problem is an actuality. Rockefeller wants a tougher law enforcement approach, and though his idea is flawed in its specifics we think it is right in principle. Moreover, that principle can be applied through existing laws.

Many drug cases now are disposed of through plea-bargaining—allowing a defendant to plead guilty to a lesser charge so that the state can be spared the cost of a jury trial. The frequent results of this practice are probation or minimal jail terms, and a quick return to the streets of unrehabilitated narcotics criminals. It is, on its face, a bad practice, and the arguments for it—that it saves the state money and reduces court congestion—are insignificant alongside the social harm done by narcotics criminals.

There is, as we noted, no guarantee that tougher sentences would deter narcotics pushers. But at least they would lessen the problem of persons who are proven menaces to human well-being.

THE MILWAUKEE JOURNAL
Milwaukee, Wis., January 13, 1973

Declaring all else has largely failed in the battle against drug addiction, New York Gov. Rockefeller now takes an extremist stance that other governors might be tempted to imitate. He urges mandatory life imprisonment of all sellers of hard drugs and all who commit a violent crime while under the influence of drugs. There would be no plea bargaining, no probation, no parole.

The severity of the drug plague, particularly in New York City, cannot be doubted. And surely the cold blooded professional peddler of addiction doesn't deserve mercy. Nevertheless, Rockefeller's far-out remedy is unconvincing. Grossly indiscriminate, it draws no distinction between amateurs and hardened pros, between the college student who sells a pep pill to his roommate and the big time operator who deals in heroin by the pound. It denies judges and juries all flexibility in sentencing, and allows the offender not the smallest hope of release through rehabilitation — not ever.

The impact of Rockefeller's proposal on the overloaded criminal justice system could be staggering. There are perhaps as many as 300,000 heroin addicts in New York City. The majority at some time probably sell the drug. Thus perhaps 100,000 or more are potential candidates for life terms. But even if the current rate of arrest is not exceeded, about 10,000 persons would be tried each year. Without plea bargaining, this alone would require scores of added judges. And if only half the defendants were convicted, prisons in several years would overflow with lifers — each costing about $6,000 a year to maintain.

Meanwhile, Rockefeller exaggerates the shortcomings of drug treatment programs. Despite erratic funding and other difficulties, there are signs of headway. Also, there are techniques that remain to be tested. For example, careful experimentation with heroin dispensing clinics, based on the British model, might reveal a way to displace underworld trafficking and eliminate an addict's need to rob or push to support his compulsion.

Of course, law enforcement must also be stressed. But New York and other states already have tough drug laws that hit especially hard at peddlers. Too often, though, the laws are poorly enforced, sometimes because of official corruption. This laxity should be corrected before talking of wildly escalating penalties.

Chicago Tribune

Chicago, Ill., January 13, 1973

With respect to hard drugs, Atty. Gen. Kleindienst recently urged more attention to rehabilitation, while the get-tough policy is advocated by New York's Gov. Nelson Rockefeller, a man with impeccable liberal credentials. And while their proposals seem contradictory, there is room for both.

Having tried what he describes as "every possible approach" to stop addiction and rehabilitate the addict, Gov. Rockefeller has now proposed that those who sell hard drugs or commit violent crimes while under their influence be given mandatory life sentences upon conviction without the possibility of parole, suspended sentences, or plea bargaining.

Despite massive efforts—New York State alone has spent $1 billion for education, therapy, and rehabilitation—the number of hard drug users continues to increase. Nor do all the laws on the books seem to deter pushers of these drugs. Thru harsh laws uniformly applied they must be taught that the penalties for the sale of narcotics and dangerous drugs are bigger than the potential profit.

At the same time, peaceful users, when denied the source of their illicit drugs, must be rehabilitated so they may lead useful lives in the community.

As with many such situations, there is no clearcut line separating pushers from addicts. Is a young man who buys cocaine and gives it to his friends to be considered a pusher? Or the heroin user who induces his girl friend to use the drug? There are some users who sell drugs to support their habit. How should they be treated?

It has been pointed out many times that our drug laws, federal, state, and local, have contributed to the problem by making the illegal sale of narcotics and dangerous drugs profitable. Great Britain has tried to go in the other direction by making morphine-base drugs available to users at low cost thru doctors while, at the same time, significantly increasing the penalties for the illegal sale of the narcotics. The result has been a measurable reduction in the number of new addicts and fewer drug-related crimes.

The penalties meted out for selling drugs and for drug-related crimes must be harsh enough to serve as a deterrent to others. And, as Mr. Kleindienst has recommended, we must provide more and better facilities for the rehabilitation of those who are addicted to the hard drugs. Only then can we successfully begin to eradicate the drug menace.

The Christian Science Monitor

Boston, Mass., January 5, 1973

Perhaps no governor of any state has fought harder to set aside tax dollars for a meaningful drug control program than has Nelson A. Rockefeller. In the past several years, with his active encouragement, New York has spent a billion dollars to get the monkey off its back — and failed. Thus it is with some sympathy that we express strongest reservations to the Governor's extreme new tough line against drug pushers.

The Governor has called for mandatory life sentences, with no possibility of pardon, parole, probation or suspension of sentence, and no plea bargaining. In face of the continuing drug traffic, with its terrible toll in wasted lives and increasing crime, we can understand why the Governor feels he must act with such vigor against the professional drug pusher. Our first reservation arises at this point. We would expect that the people of New York, and the Legislature, would want to make a distinction which the Governor fails to make, between the professional pusher and the nonprofessional.

The man who engages in drug smuggling and distributing purely for profit, and often within the context of syndicated crime, is on the par with a murderer — even a mass murderer. He rates the severest judicial treatment. But there is a distinction between the professional and the addict on the street corner who "pushes" a sale in order to pay for his habit, or the college kid who sells a packet of hashish to a classmate on a one-time basis.

This distinction is first a matter of moral judgment, but it also has its practical side. New York City alone is estimated to have more than 50,000 addicts. With the sorry state of affairs in that state's overburdened courts and prisons, how are thousands of new life-sentence prisoners going to be handled?

And what of the concept of rehabilitation? Is society to categorize this one type of criminal as being forever beyond redemption?

Governor Rockefeller certainly is aware that the drug problem has many roots and many branches. The desperate poverty of the core city slums in New York, Buffalo, Rochester, and other cities across the state; decrepit housing; overcrowded and tension-wrought schools; the very jails to which he would consign convicted pushers; and, last but certainly not least, the police who are charged with rounding up the pushers — and who, as headlines of recent weeks have revealed, have in their midst fellow officers not averse to expropriating and selling tens of millions of dollars worth of drugs seized from pushers.

Certainly the drug traffic is a huge social problem. Certainly it requires some tough action to stop it. But that toughness has to be aimed at every weak spot in the social fabric, at the conditions which cause young people to turn to drugs in the first place. And at the well-organized syndicates which import, manufacture, and distribute the stuff.

Governor Rockefeller is right in his desire to bring the drug addiction juggernaut to a halt. But that effort cannot be so narrowly conceived. His proposal is now in the hands of the Legislature. It will serve its purpose if that body uses it as a springboard to a broader attack on the drug problem, thus maintaining New York's well-deserved reputation as a pioneer in this shadowed area of American life.

THE RICHMOND NEWS LEADER

Richmond, Va., January 10, 1973

In his annual "State of the State" message, Governor Nelson Rockefeller shook up New York legislators the other day by offering the toughest anti-drug proposals in recent memory. Saying that "all the laws we now have on the books won't work to deter the pusher of drugs," Rockefeller recommended life sentences — without plea-bargaining, without probation, without parole — for "all illegal drug trafficking in hard drugs. . . ." Pushers in their late 'teens, to be denied "youthful offender" status, would be subject to the same penalties, as would be drug addicts who committed crimes of violence. All in all, said the Governor, "these are drastic measures. But, I am thoroughly convinced, after trying everything else, that nothing less will do."

The words had to be spoken, and it is appropriate that the Governor of New York, the Governor of the State which harbors the nation's largest addict population, said them first. As the situation in New York terrifyingly reflects, the easy-going approach to drug-pushing and to drug abuse has been scandously ineffective to the point that — as Governor Rockefeller said in his speech — "we face the risk of undermining our will as a people, and the ultimate destruction of our society as a whole."

But not everyone seems as worried as Mr. Rockefeller. With predictable speed, the New York Civil Liberties Union condemned the Governor's plan as a "frightening leap towards the imposition of a total police state." Other exponents of law-with-license quickly voiced similar complaints, with that peculiar liberal penchant for defending unworkable principle far past the onset of provable failure: One suspects that if the drive for prison reform ended with convicts guarding jailers, the professional "civil libertarians" somehow would find cause for cheer.

Not that Governor Rockefeller's ideas do not need work: They do, if the suggested laws are not to produce new mischief. As one legislator hypothesized, an accused pusher might shoot a State's witness and get a better deal as a murderer — New York law allows plea-bargaining and parole in murder cases. Or less dramatically, the new laws, unless carefully written, could fall with merciless regularity on only the small-time pill-pushers, while the major death-dealers remained beyond reach.

Yet such are the problems that legislators are paid to work out. Once Governor Rockefeller submits the specific bills in his program, the New York lawmakers will have ample time to turn a well-directed initiative into a series of enforceable and effective statutes. As the Governor correctly stated, "either we can go on as we have been, with little real hope of changing the present trend; or we (can) take (the) stern measures that . . . common sense demands. This has to stop. This . . . is . . . going . . . to . . . stop."

WINSTON-SALEM JOURNAL
Winston-Salem, N.C., January 10, 1973

AS FAR as hard drugs are concerned, New York City is probably the "tightest" port in the world. The municipal narcotics division alone, with its teams of investigators and technicians, is large enough to police a city the size of Winston-Salem.

And the men and women who make up this force are exceptions to the popular notion that state law-enforcers are more competent than local lawmen, while federal agents are the best of all. The U.S. Bureau of Narcotics and Dangerous Drugs, though a much improved force, admits that it still has much to learn from the New York City units.

But all that these federal and municipal agencies can hope to do is reduce the flow of hard drugs into the city. New York is a sieve for illicit heroin and other narcotics; and it will remain a sieve so long as a merchant seaman can toss a pouch of heroin and a signal buoy overboard in the Lower Bay. It will be a sieve so long as drug-toting foreign diplomats can sidestep customs inspection, so long as commercial aircraft arrive from Chicago and Montreal and Paris at the rate of one every 12 seconds. And the city's drug problem is the nation's as well.

This partly explains Gov. Nelson Rockefeller's tough new proposals to combat drug pushers and drug addiction. To some, it may seem unreasonable (if not unconstitutional) to throw even a convicted heroin pusher into prison for life — literally for the remainder of his life. To others, it seems even more unreasonable to do the same thing to persons convicted of violent crimes while using drugs. After all, they argue, a person murdered by a "clean" assailant is just as dead as one murdered by a hyped-up addict.

But these proposals were shaped by the problem, not by a governor or a police commissioner trying to play storm trooper.

In a city and state where some residents pay as much as $3,000 a year for private police guards and for bright sodium-vapor street lights that officials refuse to purchase with tax money, in a climate of fear made worse by the paradox of more drug-induced violence and fewer dollars to invest in law enforcement, the greatest threat to civil liberties is not a "get-tough" policy against pushers and addicts. The greatest threat lies in what desperate citizens will do for themselves when law enforcement is ineffective — the vigilante movements, the hiring of private security forces, the fencing in of neighborhoods and buildings, the blind support of anyone who waves a clenched fist at crime.

Something has to be done to stop the violence. If state and municipal authorities are not willing or able to move against lawless elements effectively, then our violent past offers a number of alternatives. And the fact that some of these alternatives have already been adopted by crime-ridden neighborhoods should be of greater concern to civil libertarians than the fate of a convicted dope pusher.

"I've been a civil libertarian all of my life," said one black New Yorker involved in rehabilitating drug addicts, "but not when it comes to the destruction of innocent lives. I want these (drug) pushers dead or in prison for life. It doesn't matter which, not anymore."

It is this sort of despair that the Rockefeller proposals seek to allay. We hope the proposals are enacted and we hope they work.

Herald News
Fall River, Mass., January 9, 1973

The Massachusetts legislature might well consider a proposal by New York Gov. Nelson Rockefeller to aid in solving the horrendous drug problem.

He has proposed that all convicted pushers of hard narcotics be given mandatory life sentences with no possibility of parole or pardon. Legislative members are reported to be reacting favorably, albeit a few want to see the proposal in bill form because the governor advocates increasing all sentences involving drug traffickers.

This is the only type of punishment which is going to end the narcotics scourge and we are sure that the police of Greater Fall River agree upon that.

Only such tough attitudes here as well as in New York will curb the drug problem spread that has led to the burglary and killing waves which have struck this and all other areas of the nation.

The sooner such a law is enacted the better. It will end plea-bargaining in the courts. It will imprison the killers. It will save lives.

The Standard-Times
New Bedford, Mass., January 9, 1973

New York Governor Nelson Rockefeller's proposal for a no-mercy war on the narcotics traffic, including mandatory life sentences for hard drug pushers, was made in his annual State of the State address to the legislature.

It could well serve as the heart of a State of the Union address: Nothing —war, racial strife, poverty, welfare, crime, pollution — offers a threat to this nation comparable to that of drug sale, use and addiction. Indeed, drugs are a contributing evil in all these problems, crime in particular.

There has been, however, a curious inability to come to grips with the drug threat, a reluctance to declare, as did Governor Rockefeller, that the time has come to acknowledge the problem is worsening despite money and effort for education, rehabilitation and treatment.

"Lots of wonderful young people have died, and hundreds of thousands more have been and are being crippled for life," said the governor. "Addiction has kept on growing. A rising percentage of our high school and college students, from every background and economic level, have become involved, whether as victims or pushers or both.

"The crime, the muggings, the robberies, the murders associated with addiction continue to spread a reign of terror. Whole neighborhoods have been as effectively destroyed by addicts as by an invading army. We face the risk of undermining our will as a people — and the ultimate destruction of our society as a whole."

No other threat to the people or the nation can be so described. And yet the national effort to enforce Prohibition was greater than the drive against drugs today; federal laws against kidnaping and hijacking are stiffer than against the drug criminal; and more money is spent on refining auto exhausts than in repelling the drug invasion.

Governor Rockefeller is right: Common sense demands a change, not by lessening the education and treatment program, but by increasing the deterrence. And he went the whole way in asking for laws that would jail for life —forbidding pleas to a lesser charge, probation, parole and suspension of sentence — for illegal trafficking in hard drugs and for violent crime committed under the influence of hard drugs.

A year or two ago, when there was a tendency to extend permissiveness about marijuana to include any drug use, Rockefeller's stringent proposals would have brought an outcry from "modern penologists," sociologists and many liberals. Some have, indeed, protested about the "injustice" to a "22-year-old youngster" who might "experiment" with cocaine by giving it to his friends, and incur a life sentence.

But bitter experience has brought others to share the governor's thinking. A black physician who heads a rehabilitation center in New York City commented that he was "not a civil libertarian any more when it comes to the destruction of lives. I hate to sound so conservative, man, but this is from five years in the field."

Will the ultimate in punishment deter? The question has not been satisfactorily answered when crime of the moment, like murder or rape, is involved. But hard-drug pushing is a purposeful business of weighed liabilities and assets. The prospects of risking a life behind bars surely should discourage the neophyte, like the "22-year-older," and would make it much more difficult for the professional to operate.

Governor Rockefeller has rendered a notable service by "telling it like it is." The humanitarian approach to the drug problem is not, of itself, a solution. There is not time to chance further experiment. The drug traffic is hugely profitable, its effects hugely degrading. Punishment must be tailored for the crime of engaging in it.

TOUGHEST DRUG LAW IN NATION COMES INTO FORCE IN NEW YORK

The most stringent narcotics abuse law in the nation came into force Sept. 1 in New York State. The New York law provided minimum prison sentences for both the sellers and possessors of drugs and limits the use of plea bargaining in narcotics cases. The new law was expected to increase the caseload of the state's court system and further crowd its prisons. Gov. Nelson A. Rockefeller (R) was authorized under the new law to name 100 additional judges to help handle the increase.

The state legislature had enacted the tough drug law at the governor's urging following repeated failures of state, federal and private programs to dampen the narcotics problem through efforts centered upon education, treatment and rehabilitation of addicts and potential addicts.

THE WALL STREET JOURNAL.
New York, N.Y., September 11, 1973

Since New York's tough new drug law has been in effect for barely over a week, it's obviously far too early to tell whether its harsh sentencing policies will reduce the drug problem. Yet whatever modifications may eventually prove necessary, the law is a welcome sign of seriousness about the drug problem.

The law, passed at the urging of Governor Rockefeller, requires judges to sentence anyone convicted of selling heroin or other narcotics to life imprisonment, subject to parole after a minimum term. It drastically limits "plea bargaining," the practice under which the state will drop serious charges if the accused pleads guilty to lesser offenses. The law also provides stiff terms for sale or possession of other drugs—for example, mandatory imprisonment for one to 15 years for a second offense of possessing one ounce of marijuana. Also, a $1,000 reward is established for turning in a drug pusher.

Naturally, a chorus of denunciation is currently being heard. Some find the law "repressive." The New York Civil Liberties Union is seeking ways to test its constitutionality. Some anti-drug workers suggest it's not needed because new methadone programs and a street shortage of heroin have already dented the drug problem. People worry about the teenagers caught experimenting with marijuana. Governor Rockefeller's critics say the only reason for the law is to further his presidential ambitions.

The New York City administration and even police officials have opposed the law. They contend the elimination of plea bargaining means that many more cases will require full-fledged trials, and that even the 100 new judgeships created in conjunction with the law will not be enough to keep up with the load. Judges resent the law's strict limits on their discretion.

These complaints would be easier to sympathize with were it not for the statistics on enforcement of the previous drug law. They show that in New York City only 2% of those arrested on drug felonies were sent to prison, and that within this 2% only 2.5% were given the maximum term. In other words, Governor Rockefeller's law is intended to reverse a total collapse in enforcement. In that situation Draconian measures are scarcely surprising, and for that matter, scarcely inappropriate.

The reasons for the lax enforcement of drug laws are not difficult to find. Chiefly they consist of too many people, including too many judges, believing that society is to blame for the drug problem, that the addict is sick and to be pitied, that law enforcement is suspect in general. There is of course some truth in most of this, but it is scarcely all there is to be said about the drug problem. We would think it far more important to recognize, for example, that the problem is a terrible curse on many innocent people, especially poor people in urban slums.

Given the cultural milieu in which the new law will operate, indeed, we think it entirely premature to worry that it will send too many people to jail. We would think it at least as likely that it will fail in something close to the opposite sense. To wit, that the current law enforcement system cannot be forced to carry out such a law, that ways will be found around its mandatory features, and that the previous pattern of non-enforcement will remain little changed.

If the time should come when the new law sends addicts to jail in throngs, that will be the time to relax some of its harshness. If a system of mandatory treatment would be made to work, for example, it would be both far more humane and far less costly than mandatory jail sentences. But the key to this ideal is making the treatment truly mandatory. Those who skip out must be found and jailed, not only in theory but in fact. In short, you come back to the same point: The first problem is getting the law enforced.

So while Governor Rockefeller's law is far from the one we would choose in an ideal world, in today's world there is a good deal of sense behind it. The mandatory sentencing is a forthright attack on the central problem of non-enforcement, and the show of seriousness may in itself help to change the attitudes that have hampered enforcement. We would hope eventually to move on to something better, but in our view that will happen not if the new law fails but if it succeeds.

THE ARIZONA REPUBLIC
Phoenix, Ariz., August 28, 1973

New York's boyish, happy-go-lucky mayor, John Lindsay, tried without success to make Gotham seem like Fun City. The image-making failed, just as his personal veneering failed to win a presidential nomination.

The fault was in the facts. New York is not fun.

It is a jungle from which 13,000 businesses fled between 1965 and 1970 (under the Lindsay administration), and in which one out of seven inhabitants is on welfare.

But leaving much more of a pall over New York City is its drug problem, one which has been suffused with various forms of permissiveness and official winking while sociologists poured out upwards of $1 billion in coddling care for a d d i c t s, pushers and first-timers.

The consequences h a v e been disastrous. K i d s are recruited openly on the streets by pushers. Muggers and bandits have turned streets into havens of horror as they rob to pay for habits. Even the welfare department found itself providing dole for 32,000 addicts.

The black community has been the most terror-stricken.

This week, New York Gov. Nelson Rockefeller — responding to demands from top to bottom — rolled out a tough new drug law which would require mandatory 15-year jail terms for possession or sale of hard drugs (heroin, cocaine or opium).

That is to say, there will be no plea bargaining, no probation, no early parole.

"The p e o p l e are frightened," said one of the state's drug control officials.

Some penal officials fear the strictness of the law will overload prisons and jails and create new riot conditions. Some police fear that mandatory jail terms will remove their ability to bargain with defendants for n a m e s of higher-ups in the drug rackets.

The special irony in the New York crackdown is that it pioneered some of today's universally accepted treatment projects — programs, however, which seem to have backfired.

Mandatory jail terms face judicial testing, obviously.

But the spirit in which it is being pressed in behalf of the citizens of that state indicates that coddling drug abuse has had poor rewards and a frightened public is in the mood to remove the threat from the streets.

DAILY ☆ NEWS

New York, N.Y., September 4, 1973

A TOUGH, NEW ANTIDRUG LAW

Gov. Rockefeller

—is now in effect. Pushed through the Legislature by Gov. Rockefeller, it imposes stiff minimum sentences for possession or sale of dangerous narcotics. Heroin pushers, selling as little as one-eighth of an ounce, can be convicted and imprisoned for from one year to life.

Despite the law's stern penalties, the judges will have some flexibility. In cases of mere possession, plea bargaining could allow shorter sentences and parole. But all other convictions or guilty pleas for second offenses or sale of any amount of narcotics would carry at least a one-year sentence.

Drug dealers, liable for 15 years to life if caught and convicted, could have sentences reduced, but all will serve time. This is the big change in this new statute.

The parole board, too, will be able to grant parole, but only after the minimum mandatory sentence has been served. So, much of the future success of the law in curbing this slimy trade still depends on how severe the judges are in sentencing, and how determined the parole board is to make it work.

There will be 16 new—

COURT OF CLAIMS JUDGES

—sitting on narcotics cases in New York City by the end of this month. They will first take a two-week crash course in the intricacies of the statute at Fordham University. So will new Supreme Court justices named to handle narcotics cases.

Critics of the law predict that courts will be loaded with narco trials. They well may be. But new judges and more court facilities will be provided. By the end of 1974 there should be a total of 100 new judges to handle them.

We hope that the new and old judges and the parole board get this message:

When the governor held town meetings throughout the state last winter, voters told him in unmistakable words they wanted a tough drug law. Now they want it strictly enforced. They are determined to get rid of the pushers and peddlers and cut down the crime that goes with addiction.

The Afro ⊕ American

Baltimore, Md., September 15, 1973

Gov. Nelson Rockefeller, who still wants to be president of the United States, already is claiming that New York's tough new anti-drug law is getting the job done.

It's much too early to tell.

One thing, whether for political reasons or otherwise, Gov. Rockefeller is attempting to do something about the problem. He is insisting his approach is one of toughness mixed with compassion.

Rockefeller is adding a large number of judges to help with the expected increased court loads. He also wants to see every man, woman or child hooked on narcotics given proper treatment. At the same time, he says his tough program is needed to cut off the flood of drugs in the community.

Pushers and others caught with large sums of drugs could find themselves in jail for life. They easily are likely to find themselves unable to get out of jail without a lifetime probation, meaning their hands would be pretty tightly tied.

Dope in the community has become a nasty problem. Police seem not to be able to solve it, to some degree because many of them have their hands out for payoffs.

To the average citizen the prevalence of dope means their families are threatened on every turn. Children could become victims, addicts steal and kill and the costs to taxpayers and property owners are mushrooming.

If Gov. Rockefeller's new law shows any progress in curbing the problem, maybe some of its questionable aspects can be compromised should they prove infringements on civil and human rights.

If nothing else, the New York law may provide some new directions on which tactics might best be used to curb the drug menace.

The San Diego Union

San Diego, Calif., September 1, 1973

Narcotics traffic probably has taken a greater toll in New York City than anywhere in America. It is the major factor behind a shameful crime rate. It helps perpetuate a huge welfare burden. With an addict population estimated as high as 300,000, New York provides a grim example of how drugs can change the character of an entire city.

Finally, New York is striking back at its drug problem in a way that promises to have an immediate and telling effect. A tough new set of penalties for narcotics violations will take effect today under laws passed by the New York Legislature at the prompting of Gov. Nelson Rockefeller.

A person convicted of selling an ounce or more of heroin, for instance, will face a mandatory life sentence with a requirement that a minimum of 15 years be served in prison before he becomes eligible for parole. Possession of hard drugs also will bring stiffer sentences. New York now will have the most rigorous drug laws of any state in the nation.

A promising aspect of this crackdown is that it is supported by officials of most addict treatment centers in the city. They believe the impact on the availability of drugs will help force addicts into treatment programs and persuade them to stay. Police, of course, hope to see less of the plea bargaining, quick parole and other compromises which have blunted the effect of their law enforcement efforts.

This example may be profitable to lawmakers and judges in other states and cities which in varying degrees face the same problem as New York.

Boston Herald American

Combining the best features of the Herald Traveler and Record American

Boston, Mass., August 31, 1973

New York has a tough drug law. But it will have a much tougher one in effect Sept. 1, a law whose purpose is to get addicts and pushers off the streets with long prison terms so that a new effort can be made to control narcotics use.

There have been many objections to the harsh law and there are many questions about how it will work. But it was passed after medical treatment, rehabilitation efforts, social programs and considerable tolerance failed. Drug use continues to be rampant and Gov. Nelson Rockefeller and the legislature are determined to stamp it out.

The key feature of the new law is that it sets up long-term penalties, some as long as life, for possessing and peddling hard narcotics. Sentences are mandatory and it has been made quite clear that countless addicts and pushers will soon be in jail.

Some of the questions are obvious. Where are all the prisoners going to be put? What will happen to a prison population when it is joined by several hundred addicts hardly in control of themselves and willing to make any desperate move to get the only thing of value to them, another fix? Are there sufficient courts and judges to try the numerous cases that are foreseen, at least temporarily? And perhaps most important of all, will the new law be a "cop killer," as it has been termed, because it will force addicts and pushers to shoot it out and take their chances on escaping rather than to submit and face certain incarceration?

One drug user interviewed said there was no reason not to shoot it out because the penalty for killing a policeman is no worse than that for handling drugs.

But despite the questions, the law is a stern approach to a problem that too long has eluded solution. There is precedent for hard drug laws. Japan has a very harsh code and practically no drug use. Turkey, where much of the poppy crop for the world's heroin is grown, has little drug use of its own, and it has an extremely harsh law.

There is some doubt about the constitutionality of the law, but that will be tested. Meanwhile a brand new approach is being taken, one that gives police the tools to lock up the pushers and addicts, to clear the streets of them — the goal of all the drug programs — and give young people an environment far more free of narcotics use.

The harsh method is worthy of a try. Surely it can't do worse than those of the past. Other states will be watching the experiment with interest. And they just may learn something about how to handle their own drug problems.

Victoria Times

Victoria, B.C., September 17, 1973

In passing what amounts to some of the toughest hard drug legislation in North America, New York state is saying that drugs are a criminal problem which have little to do with social conditions, personal weakness or the age in which we live. If the new laws result in fewer heroin, cocaine and morphine addicts, they are likely to be emulated in other parts of the continent.

Sale or possession of hard drugs can now result in life imprisonment in New York State, and those few who manage to receive parole will have to report to local authorities for the rest of their lives. On the other side of the law such harsh penalties produce desperate criminals who might be prepared to kill rather than spend a lifetime behind bars.

In recent months a few studies point to a levelling off of drug use in British Columbia. But in New York City the problem appears to be endemic. Even 30 years ago during the Second World War, parts of Harlem were off limits to U.S. troops because of the availability of drugs and vice. And as late as 1969 passersbys were being offered drugs a few blocks north of 125th Street and Columbus circle, near Columbia University and on the Harlem border.

It is interesting to note that in the sixties high ghetto drug use was said to be caused by the people having little hope and wanting an escape, no matter how transient or unreal. An addict faced with life imprisonment will have even less hope. But if the laws radically reduce hard drug use they will have served their purpose and saved countless people as well. People and laws being what they are, the jails will fill up immediately, but the drugs will remain as long as the ghetto.

The Standard-Times

New Bedford, Mass., September 11, 1973

Traffic in drugs, as in most other commodities, involves three classes of people — suppliers, sellers, and buyers. Eliminate one class, and the whole enterprise will collapse. In recent years, the federal government has concentrated on cutting off supplies of dangerous drugs, principally heroin, smuggled into this country from abroad. A number of local governments, as well as private efforts, have introduced methadone-maintenance programs to stabilize or reduce the number of heroin users.

Now, effective last Saturday, New York State has launched all-out war on the sellers — or pushers — of hard drugs. Under legislation that is nationally pattern-setting, drug traffickers face (1) mandatory minimum prison sentences; (2) a limited form of plea-bargaining; and (3) a system of "mandatory life sentences" that would permit parole but require lifetime supervision of the parolee.

These provisions are tough, although almost permissive when judged against Gov. Rockefeller's original legislative requests, which called for mandatory life sentences for drug pushers.

National Review summed up the rationale of the governor's program: "The measures favored by conventional 'enlightened' opinion have not worked. If we have to wait for the elimination of 'poverty' and 'injustice' —alleged causes of addiction — we will wait a long time. Education in the harmful effect of drugs, and publicity campaigns to the same end, appear to have zero effect. Methadone and other treatments have had a negligible impact. Ditto, stepped-up investigative effort by the police to uncover the source of drugs."

Many would disagree with this approach, including Gov. Cahill of neighboring New Jersey. He believes that ". . . the solution to the drug problem is multifaceted. It cannot be confined simply to legal redress in court. It (has) to encompass an educational approach, a health program and rehabilitation system as well as a stepped-up law-enforcement program."

Harper's magazine takes an almost fatalistic view: "The beginning of wisdom about the drug-crime axis is the recognition that drug users want to use drugs, and that as long as they do, there will be people willing and eager to sell to them. The cry to punish is a politician's ploy that satisfies our need for instant gratification. It does nothing to push our leaders into helping us create a more satisfying society."

After signing the antidrug legislation last May, Rockefeller denounced the "strange alliance of vested establishment interests, political opportunists and misguided soft-liners who joined forces and tried unsuccessfully to stop this program."

Those who were against the Rockefeller crackdown were, significantly, not groups generally thought of as among the bleeding-hearts. Asked to name them, the New York governor said, "Well, the Judicial Conference opposed it, the District Attorneys Association opposed it, and there were police officials here opposing it."

The answer to this is that law-enforcement officials involved said they fear the new antidrug program will overtax the courts and the jury system and further swell the already bloated prison population. And limitations on plea-bargaining, it is maintained, will cripple police efforts to recruit informers by permitting arrested pushers to plead guilty to lesser offenses.

Does New York State have the answer to the drug problem with its new law? Many closely involved with that problem would seem to think otherwise, and thus the nation will watch the situation with greatest interest.

The Evening Bulletin

Philadelphia, Pa., September 7, 1973

New York Governor Nelson Rockefeller, launching the first full-scale, no-holds-barred offensive in President Nixon's oft-declared war on drugs, says his state's tough new antidrug law will work if police, prosecutors and judges cooperate in enforcing it.

Opinion in and out of the state is divided on this, however.

For one thing, even with the 100 new judges Mr. Rockefeller is authorized to appoint, there is widespread concern about bogging down already overcrowded courts. The feeling is that addicts and pushers faced with long mandatory jail sentences will insist on jury trials, and take advantage of every avenue of appeal open to them.

Another fear is that jails and prisons will quickly become crowded with persons who need rehabilitation more than punishment.

Also that the bans against plea-bargaining will deprive police of a means for getting information against high-level distributors.

More than one critic has also pointed out an inherent danger to police. The penalty for pushing narcotics is the same — life in prison — as that for killing a law enforcement officer.

Under the new law, New York will require judges to impose the life sentence for selling any amount of narcotics, and also certain amounts of other dangerous drugs.

Possession of even a limited amount of LSD, for another example, could bring life. And sale of any amount of marijuana could result in up to 15 years in prison.

Mr. Rockefeller says he has turned to tougher penalties against drug users and pushers because he feels the recent emphasis in this country on rehabilitating addicts is not working.

"I got to feel maybe we've got to focus on the public that is being mugged, mobbed, robbed, murdered, raped and so forth," he said.

One result of New York's law could be to run high-level pushers out of that state and into New Jersey and Pennsylvania. It is something officials here will need to watch closely.

New York, however, unquestionably has the worst narcotics problem in the U.S. — an estimated 100,000 addicts. If the tougher approach is warranted anywhere, that is the place to try.

The Virginian-Pilot

Norfolk, Va., June 24, 1977

Report From the Crusades

The spirit of whisky Prohibition's colossal failure seemed to hover over the deliberations of the New York Committee on Drug Law Evaluation. Stamping out perceived evil in human conduct, the committee unsurprisingly rediscovered, is futility compounded by heightened disrespect for authority.

The group, funded by nearly $1 million in Federal grants, reported this week on its study of New York State's harsh 1973 drug law, pushed to adoption by then Governor Nelson Rockefeller. Its conclusion, all the more depressing for being predictable, was that the law, with its emphasis on mandatory prison for repeat offenders, had had no effect whatever in discouraging drug use or drug-related crime. Heroin addiction in New York City was as widespread as it was before the law was passed, drug-related property crimes had increased sharply between 1973 and 1975, and the risk of prison for second offenders was appreciably lower than it had been under an older, more lenient law. Small wonder, therefore, that drug traffickers consider the law a slight hazard to their profitable business.

The committee put the onus of the law's inadequacy on the criminal justice system. Even though the legislature created 31 judgeships to deal specifically with drug offenses, fewer cases were disposed of after the law's inception than before. That finding jibed with earlier evidence that convictions are more elusive under mandatory sentencing, and plea-bargaining for lighter treatment more prevalent.

How New Yorkers respond to the apparent bankruptcy of the tough policy against illegal drug merchants is their concern. But the depressing report is symbolic of the general inability, over much of this century, of Federal or state governments to curb the illicit sale and use of narcotics, principally heroin, through a series of crusades. Stiffer laws and more law enforcement have been invoked in the delusion that repression can permanently reduce or eliminate the supply of illegal drugs and dissuade their users. The disappointments have greatly exceeded the expectations.

Americans have been seeking an answer to drug abuse since a surge of opiate addiction after the Civil War. A high rate of addiction at the turn of the century was greatly diminished by laws removing opiates from patent medicines, but a more or less constant hard core of addicts has persisted. From a modern low of about 20,000 known or suspected addicts 30 years ago the number rose to 50,000 in 1953, when a tough Federal law to discourage drug trafficking was passed, to an estimated 560,000 to 750,000 users in 1975, the year President Ford embraced mandatory sentencing of drug dealers.

Attempts to interrupt the supply from foreign sources have been disappointing, understandably so in view of the country's long coastlines, extended international borders, and many remote air strips, all conducive to smuggling. Nor have diplomatic efforts proved fruitful. Turkey only briefly abolished the growing of opium poppies, from which heroin is derived, in response to polite American bribery. Mexico is getting meager results from its American-backed war against domestic poppy growers. Furthermore, the Burma-Laos-Thailand "Golden Triangle" which produces three-fourths of the world's opium for heroin is for any practical purpose beyond the reach of American authority.

Discouraging addicts is a profitless exercise and "cure" programs generally have proved flops. Moreover, as outcasts users turn to street crime to support expensive habits, at a high toll in cash and lost merchandise and in police, court, and penal efforts to cope with a problem more medical and social than criminal.

If drug traffic is unstoppable (as it must be when the illegal profits are so tempting) and junkies incurable, a solution other than legal militancy should merit consideration. England, for one, has managed to control addiction, while avoiding the crime and public anguish suffered in this country, by carefully regulated maintenance of its few habitual users through licensed physicians. In this country methadone maintenance of heroin addicts has had some success despite its drawbacks (including the preference of many junkies for heroin).

No matter that he may have chosen his affliction, the drug addict, like the alcoholic (or the diabetic or the arthritic, for that matter) suffers from a complaint that can be kept in control through medical maintenance at a fraction of the illicit cost, at the same time diverting him to productive rather than criminal capacity. The availability of inexpensive, legal narcotics would do for the pusher what Repeal did for the bootlegger. The question is whether the American people and their lawmakers, conditioned by decades of clamorous warfare against illegal drugs, are ready to concede a social Vietnam.

The Washington Post

Times Herald

Washington, D.C., July 3, 1977

How Not to Fight the Drug War

"THE TRUTH IS, we have a leniency problem," one New Yorker wrote in a recent letter to The New York Times. "Attacking the causes of crime will have no short-term effect. So, let's get tough." The sentiment is widespread and understandable. In our view, it is also shortsighted. Substandard social conditions and the failings of the criminal justice system do have the effect of encouraging some people—especially young people—to become criminals. Merely "getting tough" with criminals without regard for some of these related aspects of the crime problem is likely to be a futile exercise. In no area of law enforcement is this more apparent than in attempts to reduce illegal drug activity. And the classic example of the failure of a one-dimensional effort to deal with the drug problem is the New York State Drug Law of 1973.

Four years ago, then-Gov. Nelson Rockefeller, with considerable fanfare, supported and signed legislation that he said would substantially reduce illegal drug activity in the state. The controversial measure almost completely eliminated judicial discretion from the sentencing process and established harsh, mandatory penalties—ranging from one year to life in prison—for those convicted of using drugs, selling drugs or committing a drug-related crime. The law raised them from misdemeanor to felony status the sale and possession of several drugs, including some that are non-addictive. And it barred plea-bargaining for persons arrested for any but the least serious violations. Gov. Rockefeller brushed aside criticisms from judges, bar associations, police and civil libertarians that the law was draconian and/or unworkable.

Recently the Joint Committee on New York Drug Law Evaluation released its three-year study of the Rockefeller law's impact. The report's conclusion: Despite the $76 million spent to provide new judges, other court personnel and court facilities to handle the increased case load, the law did not reduce either illegal drug use or drug-related crime; illegal drug activity flourished in New York City and throughout the state at about the same levels as in nearby cities and states without such a law.

The report states that the existing congestion in the New York City courts and the increased time taken up by the trials of persons indicted under the 1973 law worked to lessen its deterrent effect. Even in one upstate county where there was no court backlog, illegal drug activity during the three-year study period continued unchecked. This would seem to support the view that the legislation's basic flaw was that it dealt too narrowly with sentencing, while ignoring the necessity of addressing the entire criminal justice system.

The unwritten conclusion of this report is that the Rockefeller statute was a bad law—one drafted in anger and frustration and with a greater interest in gaining immediate political credit than in fashioning an effective battle plan in the war on drugs. The written conclusion, which makes good sense to us, is that illicit drug use "is deeply rooted in broader social maladies" and is "part of a wider complex of problems. . . . It is implausible that social problems as basic as these can be effectively solved [only] by the criminal law."

Honolulu Star-Bulletin
Honolulu, Hawaii, June 29, 1977

Better Performance by Courts Needed

In the battle against crime, there is one more disconcerting report.

New York's stiff 1973 drug law with its mandatory long-term sentences, including life imprisonment, hasn't done a thing to reduce either drug use or drug-related crime.

This is the finding of a committee of prominent lawyers and law-enforcement officials convened to evaluate the law.

Nor was the failure due to lack of effort at the judicial level: New York state added 31 new judges to deal with drug cases, yet disposed of fewer cases in a two-year period under the new law than in a comparable period under the old law.

The Committee on Drug Law Evaluation reached a conclusion that many others are coming to share — that criminal deterrence "must rest upon swift and sure enforcement and a dramatic increase in the odds that violators will in fact be punished".

In New York, the committee found that despite the 1973 law's requirement for mandatory imprisonment for repeat offenders, the risk of imprisonment for a second-felony offender was lower after the 1973 law revision than before. Since the risk of arrest for drug law offenders did not increase under the law, the committee said, "drug traffickers were not likely to see the new law as a serious threat".

The New York problem finds counterparts in many jurisdictions, including Hawaii. Two months ago in a Law Day speech, business leader Herbert C. Cornuelle cited statistics for Honolulu in 1976 that show 94,397 offenses committed and only 9,921 convictions.

Of the 5,568 adult offenders convicted, only 268 were sent to jail.

Cornuelle cited the case of one offender arrested 34 times between 1971 and 1977 on charges involving burglary, theft, bank robbery and promoting dangerous drugs, among other things. With the exception of three simultaneous six-month jail sentences that kept him out of circulation briefly in 1974, the offender mostly got probation or had the charges dropped.

"Crime pays," Cornuelle concluded, echoing a sentiment being voiced nationwide.

Laws alone aren't the answer to our crime problem. The New York experience underlines that.

Further, there is a feeling that extremely harsh mandatory sentences also may cause judges and juries to hesitate to convict.

It would be ideal, of course, if the police could solve more crimes and make more arrests, but it is obvious that most of our law-breakers do wind up under arrest, though not necessarily for more than a portion of their offenses. More than half of the people arrested are repeat offenders. Many of these are the people who — like the 34-arrest veteran cited above — have found out that crime really can pay.

If we can't solve our problem with legislation, and if we can't reasonably expect too many more arrests out of the police, where can we look?

One obvious answer is the courts. Can't we reasonably ask the judiciary for swifter and surer justice?

The jail sentences for the 34-arrest offender mentioned above didn't come until nearly three years after his crimes. That is too long.

Without becoming a police state, we can insist on faster court procedures — faster disposition of motions, fewer continuances, a reasonably quick decision once a charge is placed.

Some lawyers see the courtroom as a game room where victory is more important than justice. So be it. But that is not the way a crime-burdened public sees it. And no judge on the bench should ever allow the law to become simply a game played at the expense of the community.

It may be that our best early hope of making a dent in the crime rates, of producing "swift and sure enforcement and a dramatic increase in the odds that violators will in fact be punished" lies with the courts.

The Hartford Courant
Hartford, Conn., June 27, 1977

Laws Are Not Enough

Some Americans believe that more stringent laws, swift enforcement and mandatory sentences can deter a crime. The courts have been blamed for being too lenient and too late with too little punishment.

A study just published by the Bar Association of the City of New York finds, in effect, that the blame must be shared by society in general.

The Bar review covered the first three years of New York State's tough anti-drug law, passed in 1973, which set mandatory minimum sentences for convicted narcotics sellers and buyers, put limits on plea bargaining, and established lifetime supervision of parolees.

More judges were assigned to handle the heavier case loads and, for a time, New York officials believed the heroin traffic was "drying up."

It may have been true briefly, but three years after passage, the law's effects were nil. The illegal use of soft drugs other than heroin had grown, and heroin use in New York City was as prevalent as in 1973. The beefed-up courts, the added narcotics raids and the rigid sentencing did nothing to deter the drug traffic.

What, then, would make a difference? The Bar Association's report points to some basic reasons for drug abuse: family break-ups, unemployment, low income, poor education, poverty, loss of hope, and lack of support from agencies supposed to help the helpless.

Before the law was a year old, it was obvious that wherever there was a market for drugs, sellers were present to provide the product.

Drug abuse, then, is a symptom of deeper ills. It is not possible to cure a sickness unless its cause is recognized and addressed.

HERALD-JOURNAL
Syracuse, N.Y., June 26, 1977

Expensive failure

Recall the multi-million dollar drug attack mounted by the State of New York in 1973 under the generalship of Gov. Rockefeller?

Previously, we had spent millions in a crash effort also promoted by Rockefeller to help drug offenders by establishing small, minimum-security treatment centers. The state pushed ahead so fast motels were converted into clinics.

Rockefeller decided to do more than treat the human wrecks left by the money makers.

Stiff new laws requiring judges to sentence offenders to prison were put on the books. Thirty-one new judges were appointed in New York City and 18 were added upstate to handle the extra business.

Rockefeller, in waging a statewide campaign for the laws, identified them as the No. 1 weapon against crime.

A committee of attorneys and law enforcement officials funded with nearly a million dollars, nine-tenths from the Justice Department's Law Enforcement Administration, has checked the results. It discovered:

Fewer drug cases were handled by the courts between 1974 and June, 1976, than during the same time period under previous laws.

Of the $76 million spent on judges, prosecutors, defense lawyers, and support staff, only $32 million went directly to enforcement.

Heroin consumption was as widespread in New York City as when the law was passsed.

Serious property damage and loss linked to heroin users increased between 1973 and 1975 not only in New York but in nearby states with milder laws.

Second-felony offenders ran less risk of imprisonment, despite the mandates of the law, than before 1973 and thus, "drug traffickers were not likely to see the law as a serious threat."

(By the end of 1976, 2,208 persons had been given the maximum sentence, lifetime in prison.)

The committee's conclusions should attract the intense interest of each member of the State Legislature. The committee said:

"The key lesson to be drawn from the experience of 1973 drug law is that passing a new law is not enough. What criminal statutes say matters a great deal, but the efficiency, morale and capacity of the criminal justice system is even more of a factor in determining whether the law is effectively implemented."

Effectiveness, as we all know and as the committee underscores, depends on "swift and sure enforcement and a dramatic increase in the odds that violators will in fact be punished."

Neither happened in 1973, 1974, 1975 or 1976.

The committee explained:

"Until New York's criminal justice process is reformed so that it can do its work with reasonable speed and reasonable certainty, the legislation does not in reality have serious policy options to choose from. Without implementation there is no policy; there are only words."

After all of the legal words, the spending of $76 million, the addition of 49 judges, the drug traffic rolls on with the millionaire merchants seldom touched.

What's ahead?

This is an assignment our legislators should ponder starting with insuring that funds designated for enforcement are spent on enforcement.

Pittsburgh Post-Gazette
Pittsburgh, Pa., July 7, 1977
A 'Pot' Lesson from New York

THREE years ago, when this newspaper editorially urged that marijuana be legalized, the myth of "reefer madness" was alive and well in a large part of the American consciousness. Today, when the word "madness" surfaces in a discussion of marijuana it is as likely to refer to the outdated criminal sanctions for marijuana use as to the imagined effects of the substance on a user's psyche.

The short of it is that middle-class America increasingly believes that it is wrong to imprison otherwise law-abiding persons for indulging in a pastime that may be less harmful than heavy cigarette smoking.

Translating that contemporary view into law, however, has proved to be a difficult task. New York's state legislature recently approved a rather timid marijuana decriminalization bill only after a cliffhanger-filled parliamentary drama in which the lame and the convalescing among the legislators had to be carried into the chamber to assure passage.

However traumatically, New York did achieve decriminalization. Pennsylvania, on the other hand, retains on its statute books relatively Draconian sanctions for marijuana use and sale which, contrary to complacent popular belief, are enforced. According to a recent annual crime report of the State Police, marijuana arrests accounted for 8,751— or 77 per cent—of all drug arrests.

An overdue first step towards remedying this injustice can be made if the General Assembly approves—or, better yet, improves upon—a marijuana decriminalization bill introduced by state Rep. Joseph Rhodes of East Liberty. Like the New York law which passed with a pathetically bare majority, the Rhodes bill is far from perfect. While it does reduce possession of a small amount of marijuana from a criminal offense to a civil one, punishable by a $50 fine, it defines "small amount" as 30 grams. It is not clear to us that a person possessing one gram or even 10 grams more than that has crossed the line separating evildoers from good citizens.

A more glaring defect is the failure of the bill to modify penalties for the sale of marijuana. As we have observed frequently, it defies both logic and justice to punish the sale of a substance the possession of which is not a crime. And to that logical objection can be added a more practical one: Contrary to the "pusher" mythology, no sharp moral boundary line separates users of marijuana from sellers. Under present law, which the Rhodes bill does not seek to amend, a person who casually sells a small amount of marijuana to a friend or roommate could still find himself in prison, and branded as a criminal.

We recognize the political reality that reform of marijuana laws may have to be accomplished on a piecemeal basis. The Rhodes bill undoubtedly represents an improvement over the out-dated present law. Our hope is that when the parlimentary dust clears the legislature will have eliminated penalties not only for the use but also for the sale of marijuana.

THE ANN ARBOR NEWS
Ann Arbor, Mich., June 24, 1977
Law Isn't Enough

EVERYONE except the parasites who live off drug smuggling and peddling can be expected to favor legislation Sen. Sam Nunn, D-Ga., is advocating.

The question is whether Nunn's determination to suppress the narcotics business is really shared widely enough to make any difference if his proposals do become law.

Nunn wants minimum prison sentences and no possibility of parole for convicted drug peddlers: three years for first convictions, 10 for repeaters, and higher minimums if the sales were to minors.

★ ★ ★

UNFORTUNATELY, it isn't as if no one has tried.

Four years ago, New York began requiring minimum sentences for hard drug offenses, including life sentences for dealers high up in the drug rackets. And more than 2,000 life sentences have been imposed on drug law violators.

On the same day that Sen. Nunn was urging a similar federal effort, a federal study of New York's effort was released. Its findings make very unpleasant reading.

There has been no decline in heroin use in New York City. Use levels there are similar to those in major cities in other eastern states.

Although $76 million has been spent on enforcement efforts, more than half was spent on court staffs, not for police work. There has been no increase in the risk of arrest and imprisonment for repeat offenders of drug laws.

What the federal study basically contends is that neither public opinion, nor determination of law enforcement officials, has been strong enough to make New York's tough drug law effective.

"The key lesson," the study declares, "is that passing a new law is not enough. What criminal statutes say matters a great deal, but the efficiency, morale and capacity of the criminal justice system is even more of a factor in determining whether the law is effectively implemented."

Well, that doesn't mean the nation overall wouldn't do better than New York has, so far, if some or all of Nunn's get-tough approach is tried. The study is, however, a harsh reminder that too many are making too much off the drug rackets to make mere enactment of a new law, by itself, mean anything.

THE PLAIN DEALER
Cleveland, Ohio, June 27, 1977
Toughest drug law fails

New York's drug law, the toughest in the country, is a failure. It did not reduce drug use, addiction or crime.

Its threat of severe mandatory prison terms — even life terms — did not cut down the use of heroin. It did not stave off an increase in thievery associated with heroin. It made no difference to drug users or drug pushers.

That was the finding by a lawyers' and citizens' committee study which cost almost $1 million and took three years. It should sober all Americans who think stiffer penalties will halt crime.

"Passing a new law is not enough," said the study's summing up. "The efficiency, morale and capacity of the criminal justice system is even more of a factor."

New York not only passed the tough drug law but also hired 31 new judges and other court and prosecutorial staff in its drug war, in which then-Gov. Nelson A. Rockefeller was a leader.

But the no-plea-bargaining, harsh prison term features still did not work.

"The depressing bottom line is that ... the disposition of cases remained just what it was before," concluded Bayless Manning, former Clevelander, who was vice chairman of the Committee on Drug Law Enforcement which did the study.

Two of the worst results were that offenders' stays in prison were longer, and thus cost society more, and that juries were more reluctant to convict because penalties were sure to be so severe.

PRESIDENT ASKS TOUGHER STAND AGAINST HARD-DRUG TRAFFICKERS

President Ford called April 27 for an "aggressive" program against drug abuse. In a special message to Congress, the President viewed drug abuse as "a clear and present threat to the health and future of our nation." The President urged Congress to enact minimum mandatory prison sentences and to authorize preventive detention for "high-level" hard-drug traffickers. He recommended sentences of at least three years for a first offense, six years for a second offense and six years for selling to a minor. Legislation also was requested by the President to:

■ Let judges deny bail for drug-traffic defendants with previous felony drug convictions, or if they were on parole, were nonresident aliens, were fugitives or were arrested while in possession of a false passport.

■ Allow the Customs Service to search for cash being "smuggled out of the country" for possible use in purchasing drugs.

■ Raise to $10,000 from $2,500 the value of property, such as boats, that could be seized by administrative action, if the property was used in drug-smuggling.

■ Require masters of small privately owned boats to report to the Customs Service immediately upon arrival in the U.S. instead of within 24 hours as had been provided.

In addition, the President announced these administrative actions related to drugs:

■ Appointment of two new Cabinet committees, one focusing on law enforcement, the other on drug abuse prevention, treatment and rehabilitation.

■ Development of a tax-enforcement program against high-level drug traffickers.

■ Intensification of diplomatic efforts to obtain international cooperation on the drug problem.

HOUSTON CHRONICLE
Houston, Tex., May 1, 1976

The tide appears to be turning against drug traffickers, and that is good news for everybody, since drug abuse is a menace to every community in America.

President Ford has asked Congress to legislate mandatory prison sentences for convicted traffickers in heroin and similar drugs, and he has asked that certain defendants be denied bail. There is a great deal of public sympathy for President Ford's hard line.

The President also has announced he will create two new cabinet committees to deal with the problem, one to deal with law enforcement and the other with drug abuse prevention, treatment and rehabilitation, and has called for domestic and foreign agencies to cooperate in cracking down on narcotics traffic.

Cities across the country have launched vigorous antidrug campaigns, some successful and some not.

Even the Supreme Court has ruled that government agents can supply suspected drug dealers with heroin, then arrest the suspects after they attempt to sell the drug back to undercover agents.

Foreign cooperation is steadily improving, and perhaps one of the chief reasons for this is that other nations are finding to their dismay that the drug problem isn't strictly an American problem. For instance, Mexico has stepped up its antidrug campaign and has launched a program to detroy the poppy fields that had become a rich source for heroin traffic in the United States.

As President Ford said, drug abuse is "a clear and present threat to the health and future of our nation." The vicious web has spread across the country, and even partial eradication won't be easy. But the problem is getting the emphasis it deserves. That is a good sign.

The Washington Star
Washington, D.C., May 5, 1976

Little progress can be made in slowing down the drug traffic until the traffickers are taken off the streets and the business is made less profitable. President Ford, in a message to Congress, has proposed an attack on both fronts.

Mandatory minimum sentences for pushers of heroin and other narcotic drugs are the heart of Mr. Ford's plan. He proposes a minimum sentence of three years on a first conviction and six years for subsequent offenses or for selling to a minor

This is not the first time mandatory sentences have been suggested by Mr. Ford and others, including members of Congress. Yet Congress has been more inclined to talk than act. It is time to let drug traffickers or potential traffickers know that conviction will result in certain and substantial punishment. A Justice Department study shows that one of every four persons convicted of trafficking in heroin receives no prison sentence and that one of every three sent to prison stays less than three years.

The President also asked for legislation to allow judges to deny bail to persons arrested for trafficking in heroin or other dangerous drugs if they have previously been convicted of a felony, are free on parole, are fugitives, have phony passports or are non-resident aliens. The Justice Department study is ample evidence of the need for this; it shows that nearly half the persons arrested for drug trafficking commit new offenses while out on bail. The White House said other studies show that one-fourth of bail jumpers in drug cases are aliens.

To remove some of the profit from the illicit drug traffic, Mr. Ford is directing the Treasury and Justice Department to develop a plan to enforce the tax laws against high-level drug dealers who now escape paying income taxes on their enormous profits from criminal activities. Why this isn't being done already is a mystery, but we're happy to see that action is contemplated.

Mr. Ford also wants Congress to allow Customs agents to search persons suspected of smuggling money out of the United States — profits from the sale of drugs that were smuggled into the country — much of which is used buy more drugs to smuggle in and a good deal of which is transferred to secret bank accounts abroad.

The horrors of the illegal drug trade ought to be known to everyone by now. Mr. Ford cited a few of the statistics: 5,000 American deaths every year from misuse of drugs; one-half of all street crime — robberies, muggings, burglaries — committed by drug addicts to support their habits; a $17 billion-a-year cost to the nation related to drug abuse.

The public is tired of coddling drug traffickers, tired of letting these merchants of death pile up fortunes on the broken minds and bodies of addicts. The time for talking is long past; it's time for a crackdown.

THE DALLAS TIMES HERALD

Dallas, Tex., May 5, 1976

DRUG ABUSE kills 5,000 Americans a year and costs the nation $17 billion, President Ford said in asking Congress for tough new penalties against major heroin dealers.

Despite the well-known tragedies of drug abuse, traffickers in narcotics have been getting off with slaps on the wrists. A study of 3,925 federal drug convictions during the 1975 fiscal year showed that 1,286 defendants were placed on probation and another 838 received sentences of less than three years.

The President is asking Congress to require mandatory minimum prison sentences for persons convicted of trafficking in heroin, morphine and opium. A first offense would draw a sentence of at least three years, with a minimum six-year sentence for sales to anyone under 21. Additional convictions would also carry a minimum six-year sentence.

Legislation was also requested to deny bail if a defendant arrested for drug dealing has been previously convicted of a drug felony.

It is obvious that existing penalties are having little effect in curbing the drug traffic. Drug use is increasing and the first need for stronger action is against the criminal drug trafficker.

We hope the Congress moves promptly to enact the stronger penalties against drug dealers. Those who sell narcotics belong in jail, not on the streets where they can continue their criminal careers while on probation.

THE DAILY OKLAHOMAN

Oklahoma City, Okla., May 3, 1976

IN his message to Congress on the problems of drug abuse, President Ford said that in simple dollar terms, drug abuse costs this country up to $17 billion per year. But he pointed out that the dollar cost is only a shadow of the real cost in human suffering, crime, and other effects.

More than 5,000 Americans die each year from the improper use of drugs, according to government statistics. That is probably a gross understatement of the cost in lives. Many overdoses are not reported as such. And the misuse of prescription drugs itself is an abuse that often leads to death.

Law enforcement officials estimate that as much as half of all so-called street crimes—robberies, muggings, and burglaries, are committed by drug addicts who must have money to support their expensive habit. Those who sell to them demand and get exorbitant prices for their illegal wares, and as the addict becomes more and more dependent on the drug, its cost per dose goes up as the heartless merchants of death prey on the victim's craving. The doses must be evermore frequent, too, so that the daily requirement for cash—there is no credit card for buying drugs on the street—rises in a constant curve.

There is a legend, widely believed by those who are not fully informed on the problem, that drugs are misused only by the very young. But any narcotics officer can attest that the problem affects adults — housewives and professors and lawyers —as often as it does students and dropouts.

The government is engaged in a serious war on drug abuse today. The battle cost the nation $100 million in 1969 to operate federal programs alone. By 1974, that bill had risen to $750 million. But even that figure is incomplete. It is also rising.

An important aspect of this battle is its international component. Drugs move across national borders by various paths, almost all illegal, in various stages of processing. In some of the countries which grow opium poppies as a cash crop, there was resentment of the efforts of the United States and other destination nations to halt the illicit commerce. Much diplomatic work resulted in reductions in this traffic, but it still continues.

The medical communities of this and other nations joined in research on the cure of addiction and in studies of the physiological effects of drugs. The phamaceutical firms have contributed both knowledge and research. They require legal sources of some of the same plants which provide raw materials to the illicit market. Their expensive and elaborate processing plants concentrate on the purity of the product supplied the medical professions. In contrast, the illegal product is often contaminated, and the instruments by which drugs are injected into the bodies of addicts are often crude or dirty. The risk is enormous.

All of these efforts, including the increased penalties for illegal trafficking in drugs recommended by the President, are helping to bring this problem under control. But the final responsibility lies closer to home.

Education is the only real answer. No individual, of any age, will enter the drug scene if fully informed of the dangers inherent in abuse. Parents, family physicians, school officials, and churches all share in the responsibility for making the most effective effort open to us today— credible and factual information on these dangers.

As in so many other great problems of our age, the final answer lies with the individual citizen, whether adult or adolescent. There is no substitute for individual responsibility.

Long Island Press

Jamaica, N.Y., May 2, 1976

As President Ford has reminded Congress, America's efforts to reduce the appalling traffic in hard drugs have failed. In human terms, as Mr. Ford says, "drug abuse has become a national tragedy."

More than 5,000 Americans die annually from illegal use of drugs, and no one knows how many thousands survive but lead shattered lives — and shatter the lives of those close to them as well. There are enough, sadly, to contribute to another grim statistic: About half of all street crimes are drug related.

That's appalling, and so is the cost to the nation in terms of dollars — estimated by Mr. Ford at $17 billion a year.

The President wants "the merchants of death who profit from the misery and suffering of others" to get not just a full measure of national revulsion, but a full — though fair — measure of criminal justice. So do we.

Mr. Ford says Congress should enact an "aggressive new program" that will include minimum mandatory sentences. He suggests mandatory terms of at least three years in prison for first offenders, six years for a second offense, plus six years for selling to a minor.

The President wants judges to be able to deny bail for defendants previously convicted of a drug felony, or if they are on parole, are nonresident aliens, fugitives, or were attested while in possession of a false passport.

Unquestionably, lawmakers should require stiff penalties for drug peddlers, the courts should impose them, and bail should be made more difficult for repeaters. We have tried a softer approach in recent years with much stress on rehabilitation. Unfortunately, it hasn't worked.

But a harder approach can be too hard, as New York has learned. The tough punishment meted out for users as well as sellers in the law passed during the Rockefeller administration, while well intentioned, hasn't worked either. Its harshness, in fact, has discouraged juries from convicting accused dealers as well as buyers, particularly first offenders.

As Mr. Ford says, the aim should be not to impose vindictive punishment, "but to protect society from those who prey upon it, and to deter others who might be tempted to sell drugs."

The President's request that the Senate approve a treaty for more international controls should be honored. Immediately helpful is his order to the Treasury Department to join the fight on drugs. "We know that many of the biggest drug dealers do not pay taxes on the enormous profits they make on this criminal activity," he told Congress.

That's a weapon that worked well in the 1920s aand 1930s against mobsters who had friends in police stations, the courts and legislative halls. Al Capone, the Chicago gangster didn't go to prison for murder or other violent crimes. He was jailed for a common white collar crime: Income tax evasion.

Congress must do its part by giving careful attention to the President's recommendations. The criminal justice system must get all the tools it needs, and the police and courts must use them unsparingly. But they must be constitutional tools, that abuse no one, if they are to work properly.

The Seattle Times

Seattle, Wash., April 28, 1976

THE traffic in illegal narcotics doesn't get as much attention as it once did. Drug abuse is no longer the centerpiece of a widespread, much-publicized counter-culture movement. But the problem is as big as it ever was.

President Ford yesterday called drug abuse a "national tragedy." He noted that 5,000 Americans die each year from improper use of drugs, and that law-enforcement officials estimate "as much as one half of all street crime — robberies, muggings, burglaries — is committed by drug addicts to support their habits."

It ought to be plain, then, that Mr. Ford was not just raking over old coals when he told Congress yesterday it is necessary to take stronger action against drug traffickers.

(The United States Supreme Court yesterday struck a blow for more effective narcotics-law enforcement, ruling that a defendant may be convicted of selling drugs illegally even though government agents supplied him with the contraband and bought it from him. The court found that the defendant in the case at issue was "predisposed" to commit the crime, and that the agents' conduct was fair.)

Borrowing a page, perhaps, from Vice President Rockefeller's tough stance on drug abuse when he was governor of New York, Mr. Ford called for stronger penalties for the illegal traders, whom he called "merchants of death."

The President will send Congress legislation this week that would require mandatory minimum sentences of at least three years for a first conviction of trafficking in heroin or other narcotic drugs.

Mandatory minimums of at least six years would be required for subsequent offenses or for selling to a minor.

The President called on Congress to ratify an existing treaty for international control of synthetic drugs, saying delay has become an embarrassment to the United States and is making it difficult to get other countries to tighten controls on narcotics.

Some of the foreign governments that have been most eager to cooperate have a point, too, when they complain about permissive attitudes in American courts undercutting law-enforcement efforts.

Those permissive attitudes are the main reason, obviously, for the mandatory minimum terms Mr. Ford seeks.

THE INDIANAPOLIS NEWS

Indianapolis, Ind., May 6, 1976

Among the drugs that are frequently abused, heroin is known as a killer. It is also one of the more addictive drugs.

In light of heroin's characteristics and the dangers associated with its use, it is disturbing to learn that one of four persons convicted of selling heroin receives no prison sentence and that one of every three convicted is sentenced to a prison term of less than three years.

This fact was revealed recently by President Ford who noted that given the lenient parole policies "even those who received longer sentences rarely served more than a few years."

Heroin traffickers, according to Ford, are eligible for parole after serving one-third of their sentence.

Society cannot eradicate any practice if the practice is rewarded rather than punished. Criminals, like anyone else, are capable of weighing benefits against costs in deciding on a course of action.

We think the President is making the right move in asking Congress to establish mandatory prison terms for heroin traffickers and sellers of similar narcotic drugs. Ford is asking for a prison term of no less than three years for a first offense and for subsequent conviction — or for selling to a minor — no less than six years behind bars.

He is also asking for legislation to make bail more difficult for accused heroin sellers. The President proposes to deny bail to anyone arrested for selling dangerous drugs if the suspect has a previous conviction on a drug felony, is free on parole at the time of his arrest, or is a fugitive.

Denying bail to a criminal suspect is a drastic step. A suspect, however strong the suspicions of police or incriminating the circumstances of his arrest, is technically innocent. However, we believe the conditions Ford has outlined are reasonable and would result in the denial of bail only in those circumstances where the probability of the suspect's jumping bail or of danger to the community is high.

Not all of Ford's proposals for dealing with the heroin problem are as meritorious as these two and the Congress would be wise not to rubber stamp Ford's entire legislative package. But these two measures — more restrictive bail criteria and more severe punishment — go directly to the heart of the problem, that selling heroin offers high reward and few risks.

That situation must be reversed.

The Cleveland Press

Cleveland, Ohio, May 7, 1976

It's beginning to look as though our much-heralded "victories" over drug abuse have been less significant than we thought.

Three years ago it appeared that the number of heroin addicts had dropped sharply and drug abuse was on the decline in this country.

Now we're told the situation is worse than ever and isn't likely to improve until we crack down harder on dope peddlers.

President Ford asked Congress the other day to impose mandatory sentences for the sale of heroin or other hard drugs. He went on to say that bail should be denied to drug pushers who've been convicted of similar crimes in the past.

Both of these proposals have merit — especially as they apply to the old pros of the drug business who go from conviction to conviction without spending much time in jail.

Stiffer terms for pushers would be more effective if the nation were doing a better job of treating addicts, preferably with the heroin substitute called methadone.

In some cities there's a waiting list for treatment, despite the fact that untreated addicts commit as many as half of our street crimes to raise money for illicit drugs.

Every addict who needs help should be able to get it, even if it requires a sharp increase in federal aid to local drug treatment centers, some of which are on the brink of financial collapse.

THE CHRISTIAN SCIENCE MONITOR

Boston, Mass., April 29, 1976

Imagine a world with heroin in the role of alcohol and tobacco today. That long-range possibility is one of the grim reasons behind President Ford's welcome call for sterner legal measures against the "national tragedy" of drug abuse — and for the community and home influence without which such measures will mean little.

Mr. Ford's message to Congress on drugs comes after his top drug specialist's comments earlier this month on a United States heroin "epidemic" that has revived after a downturn a few years ago. It is part of a world problem, added Robert L. DuPont, director of the National Institute of Drug Abuse. And he compared the move toward such drugs today with the early stages of the spread of liquor and smoking.

"What happened in the 16th century with the introduction of tobacco into the world and what happened with the introduction of distilled spirits in the 17th century is the kind of global drug-use phenomenon that we're seeing now with other drugs," he said. Though marijuana is "on the cutting edge" of this change, the parallel could extend to heroin, cocaine, barbiturates, and amphetamines.

It is an ominous prospect, and not only the U.S. needs to work against the present activities that could help to bring it to pass. Mexican and U.S. agents, for example, are already cooperating against the illegal drug traffic. But last year 90 percent of the heroin coming into the U.S. was derived from opium poppies grown in Mexico. To stop the illegal raising of such poppies would be a major step forward.

The Ford message happened to arrive at the same time as other indications of a toughened American mood toward drug abuse:

• A controversial Supreme Court decision that appeared to give police new leeway in supplying drugs to suspects or otherwise setting up illegal sales of contraband for the sake of seeking arrests and convictions. The majority of five ruled that government involvement in the crime would not bar conviction if the defendant was "predisposed" to commit it. The three dissenters argued: "That the accused is 'predisposed' cannot possibly justify the action of government officials in purposefully creating the crime."

• A report by the Inspector General of the Army citing violations of regulations and ethical standards in Army drug experiments on thousands over a 20-year period.

• Recommendations in this week's Senate intelligence committee report to prevent further drug abuses by the Central Intelligence Agency and the military. One helpful step would be to bring the CIA and other intelligence agencies under the jurisdiction of the National Commission for the Protection of Human Subjects of Biomedical and Behavioral Research.

Certainly the government has to set an example of renouncing improper use of drugs if it is to play its part in relation to the President's call for a national antidrug climate. After announcing the formation of two new Cabinet committees to deal with drugs and recommending such measures as mandatory sentences for drug traffickers, Mr. Ford reached the heart of his message not just for Congress but for every American:

"All of this will be of little use, however, unless the American people rally and fight the scourge of drug abuse within their own communities and their own families. We cannot provide all the answers to young people in search of themselves, but we can provide a loving and caring home; we can provide good counsel; and we can provide good communities in which to live."

The Houston Post

Houston, Tex., May 8, 1976

President Ford has opened a hard-nosed offensive against hard-drug abuse by citing figures that lend urgency to his call for tougher laws against drug traffickers and more effective programs of prevention and treatment. In a special message to Congress outlining his new anti-drug campaign, Mr. Ford stressed the human and economic price the nation pays for drug abuse—5,000 deaths and $17 billion a year. He noted law enforcement officials' estimates that as much as half of all street crime, such as burglaries and robberies, is committed by addicts.

To curb this "staggering" toll, the President says he will ask Congress to authorize mandatory minimum sentences and preventive detention for high-level dealers in hard drugs. As justification for this tough stance on drug offenders, Mr. Ford cited Justice Department statistics showing that one out of four persons convicted of dealing in heroin received no prison sentence and one out of three received a sentence of less than three years.

Mr. Ford also wants federal judges authorized to deny bail to persons charged with drug trafficking if they have been convicted of previous felony drug crimes, or if they are parolees, non-resident aliens, fugitives, have been convicted of being a fugitive, or have been arrested with a false passport. In addition, he will ask that the Customs Service be empowered to search for cash being smuggled out of the country for possible use in buying drugs. And he is seeking a $10,-000 ceiling on the value of property that can be seized by administrative action if it is used in drug smuggling. He says the present $2,500 limit is unrealistically low. Any seizures of property over that amount require court action.

The President will further ask that operators of boats, including pleasure craft, be required to report immediately to customs upon docking in this country. Present law gives them 24 hours to report, which, Mr. Ford says, is ample time to remove contraband.

The President is matching his requests to Congress with executive initiatives of his own. He has established two Cabinet-level committees—one on drug law enforcement, headed by the attorney general, and the other on drug-abuse prevention, treatment and rehabilitation, headed by the secretary of Health, Education and Welfare. He has also ordered closer cooperation between the Treasury Department and the Internal Revenue Service in a tax-enforcement crackdown on big dealers in illicit narcotics, and has pledged continued U.S. cooperation with other countries to dry up the international drug traffic.

Mr. Ford's proposals and actions add up to an intelligently balanced program of drug-abuse control with the emphasis where it belongs — putting the big dealers in hard drugs out of business. Congress should waste no time in acting on the President's requests for new laws to curb the devastating effect of illicit drugs on our society.

THE CINCINNATI ENQUIRER

Cincinnati, Ohio, May 13, 1976

PRESIDENT FORD has put his finger on a principle cause of the toll in lives and property drug abuse takes in America: Despite increases in the arrests made, only one out of every four persons convicted of trafficking in heroin receives a prison sentence. Of those convicted, one out of three receives a sentence of less than three years. Since convicted traffickers are eligible for parole after serving a third of the sentence, those who do receive longer sentences rarely serve more than a few years.

This is too light a price for the professional drug trafficker to pay for the 5000 lives that are lost to drug abuse and the $17 billion drug abuse costs the American people each year.

But it will not be enough to demand more certain punishment for offenders, as President Ford has asked in his message to Congress on drug abuse.

Once arrested, drug traffickers are quick to post bond and return to the street. In 1974, according to one sample survey, 48% of those arrested for trafficking in narcotics were implicated in post-arrest drug trafficking while out on bail.

"Other studies," the President has told Congress, "show that approximately one-fourth of all bail jumpers in drug cases are aliens who were caught smuggling drugs into the country."

This problem has become particulary acute. Leftist Mexican guerrillas are trading U.S.-bound heroin for guns in brisk trading along the 2000-mile U. S. border with Mexico. As a result, Mexico is producing 90% of the heroin consumed in our country. The Drug Enforcement Administration says these arms "are reaching not only narcotic organizations, but, more threateningly, extremely active terrorist groups and revolutionary organizations, in particular Communist-front groups and organizations."

The President's plan to deal with this multifaceted problem is a good one. It combines mandatory prison sentences of at least three years for a first offense and six years for subsequent offenses, or for selling narcotics to a minor, with the denial of bail to traffickers previously convicted free on parole. Nonresident aliens or fugitives would also be denied bail. It would permit those suspected of smuggling money out of the United States to be searched.

Cash and personal property found in possession of a narcotics violator could be confiscated. Boats, vehicles and aircraft valued at up to $10,000 could be seized by administrative action, thus avoiding court delays. Small, private boats arriving in the United States would have to report to customs immediately, not 24 hours later as presently required.

Two new Cabinet committees, one to deal with law enforcement and the other to work on drug-abuse prevention, treatment and rehabilitation, will be established by administrative action. Intensified diplomatic efforts will attempt to cope with the global nature of this problem.

The President's proposals to Congress to enact the legislation it must to assure swift, sure, certain punishment for drug traffickers are good ones and Congress would do well to enact them quickly. Together with the administrative and diplomatic inititatives the President himself will undertake, this program should go a long way in solving a complex problem that affects every American.

CARTER ADMINISTRATION SUGGESTS DECRIMINALIZATION OF MARIJUANA

Decriminalization of marijuana—punishing the possession of small amounts by civil fines rather than jail sentences—was suggested by the Carter Administration March 14. In the first of three-day hearings before the House Select Committee on Narcotics Abuse and Control, Dr. Peter Bourne outlined the Administration's plan. Dr. Bourne, the director-designate of the Office of Drug Abuse, stressed that legalization of marijuana would be "totally inappropriate."

Reading from a prepared statement, Dr. Bourne said that President Carter was "deeply concerned about the problem of drug abuse," and wished to discourage the use of all drugs, alcohol, and tobacco. Dr. Bourne said, "We will continue to discourage marijuana use, but we feel criminal penalties that brand otherwise law-abiding people for life are neither an effective nor an appropriate deterrent."

The Carter Administration estimates that as many as 11 million Americans may be using marijuana on a weekly basis, and 35 million have tried using it. Possession of marijuana may be punishable by a one-year prison sentence and a $5,000 fine for the first offense, with doubled penalties for a second offense, under the current federal law.

THE BLADE

Toledo, Ohio, March 18, 1977

IN endorsing the removal of federal criminal penalties for possession of small amounts of marijuana, the Carter administration is pursuing the same sensible course urged by former President Ford's drug-abuse advisers two years ago: to bring the federal law into conformity with modern realities.

The Justice Department, the Drug Enforcement Agency, and Dr. Peter G. Bourne of the Office of Drug Abuse Policy agree that the harsh penalty of up to a year in jail or a fine of up to $5,000 is not justified.

Dr. Bourne is joined by scores of others — including many judges, legislators, and prosecutors — who hold that an individual's choice to use marijuana should not lead to his being treated as a criminal. Severe penalties, Dr. Bourne said, "have resulted in otherwise law-abiding young people spending time in prison and incurring permanent damage to their careers and their ability to enter professions."

The Administration is not attempting to impose its views on individual states, but Dr. Bourne made the pointed observation t h a t decriminalization "seems to have been an effective and appropriate approach" in the eight states that so far have dropped criminal penalties for simple possession.

Ohio, among them, adopted its lenient statute 15 months ago. Subsequently, all eight states have reported that there has been no noticeable change in the number of casual users.

The precise physiological effects of marijuana use still are the subject of medical research and some controversy. But some of the wild notions recited as recently as a decade ago that marijuana use leads to insanity and violence have been laid to rest. Education has replaced ignorance belatedly because the number of Americans using marijuana has never been higher than it has become in the last few years. Dr. Bourne reports that as many as 35 million Americans have tried marijuana and that perhaps 11 million are now using it at least weekly.

As in the case of Prohibition, laws against marijuana have succeeded only in creating cynicism about the law and the gratuitous harassment to which users are subsequently subjected. Legislation that would decriminalize simple possession but would provide for a civil fine of up to $100 is receiving active consideration in Congress. Its passage would remove a stigma that should encourage still more states to do at least as much.

Democrat Chronicle

Rochester, N.Y., March 22, 1977

DECRIMINALIZATION of marijuana possession is an idea whose time is surely coming.

In this general area, the prison sentences imposed by Orleans County Judge Hamilton Doherty on two recent offenders are probably doing more than anything else to create a climate of public acceptance of change in the law.

On the national level, Mr. Carter has become the first president to go on public record as favoring the kind of law that would make possession of small amounts of pot a civil offense punishable by a fine, rather than a crime punishable by jail.

The President's Administration has told the Congressional inquiry now going on that it believes jailing people for marijuana use causes much more damage than the drug itself.

"We believe," says special presidential assistant Dr. Peter G. Bourne, "that the mechanism for discouragement of drug abuse should not be more damaging to the individual than the drugs themselves."

That's been our position on this issue for some time; the impact that jail can have on families is pointed up by a letter on this page today.

SEN. JAVITS put the situation in a nutshell when he told the House Select Committee on Narcotics Abuse and Control that if marijuana remains a criminal offense, "I would suggest a criminal penalty for the drinking of alcohol and smoking of cigarets and taking of some pills."

And like it or not, we had best face the fact that marijuana smoking is moving from a gesture of social protest to an accepted part of the lifestyle of millions of Americans.

Quite apart from the harshness of the penalty, putting all those people in jail for that kind of offense would be like trying to reverse the flow of water over Niagara Falls. It can't be done.

And nothing, incidentally, could be more symptomatic of the change in public outlook than the news that 800 members of the traditionally conservative state PTA were in Albany the other day buttonholing legislators and urging them to support decriminalization.

"The PTA," according to a spokeswoman, "believes that young people who use marijuana are guilty of violating the law, but they are not criminals."

Almost as if in response to that appeal, Sen. H. Douglas Barclay of Pulaski, chairman of the code committee, has now introduced into the State Senate, where reform efforts have been killed in the past, a bill to remove criminal penalties for the possession of small amounts of pot.

That's a significant step, an overdue one. Pot offenders just don't belong in jail.

AKRON BEACON JOURNAL
Akron, Ohio, March 24, 1977

ONE DAY soon, assuming that conclusive scientific evidence is developed showing that it does not significantly harm the body, marijuana smoking may be legal in this country. What's more, state and federal governments may be taxing sales, much as they now tax cigarets and alcohol.

However, as long as marijuana remains illegal, it makes a lot more sense to us to concentrate law enforcement efforts on sellers rather than users.

For one thing, the number of marijuana users has become so large that it is nearly as futile to go after them as it was to discourage the consumption of alcohol during Prohibition. The National Institute on Drug Abuse estimates there are 13 million regular pot smokers in the country — about eight to nine percent of all adults. During 1976, the institute surveyed 17,000 high school seniors across the country and found that 53 percent had tried marijuana, while three out of 10 were users at graduation.

Ohio's new drug law, enacted in 1975, gave a major new emphasis to enforcement priorities by effectively decriminalizing the possession of small amounts of pot, while imposing minimum mandatory prison sentences on those who sell drugs. The law reduced the punishment for possession of up to 100 grams (about 3.5 ounces or 80 joints) to a $100 fine, with no jail time and no criminal record. Previously, conviction on a charge of possessing marijuana — any amount — could have netted the offender a prison term of up to a year and a fine up to $1,000.

Now, Congress also is examining more lenient marijuana legislation. Currently, the federal penalty for possessing an ounce or less of pot is up to a year in jail or a fine of up to $5,000. Bills pending in the House and Senate would reduce the penalty to a maximum $100 fine, with no jail time.

Congress should adopt the change.

Some may argue that reducing penalties for pot smoking will only encourage more people to try it. However, that is not what was found in a study conducted for the National Governors Conference under a grant from the Law Enforcement Assistance Administration. The survey determined that neither marijuana usage nor the number of smokers increased in Ohio and seven other states directly as a result of their more lenient marijuana laws.

Under the new Ohio law, the Ohio Bureau of Criminal Identification has shifted its emphasis from sellers of marijuana to sellers of hard drugs. A spokesman said about 60 percent of the money available to undercover agents now is used to purchase cocaine and other hard drugs and only about 40 percent to buy marijuana. Previously, the percentages were reversed.

The change is encouraging. All law enforcement agencies need to get maximum impact from the limited funds and manpower available to them.

It generally was much easier — almost like shooting fish in a barrel — and produced just as large headlines for police to concentrate in the past on marijuana offenses than more serious ones involving dangerous narcotics. But that strategy was a bust in terms of protecting society from the growing number of drug dependents who resorted to violence to feed their hard drug habits.

We do not advocate complete legalization of marijuana at this point. Like others, we still await the results of some important scientific research. In the meantime, though, we believe users should not bear the stigma of a criminal record for minor offenses. Save the prisons and the big fines for the sellers.

The Idaho STATESMAN
Boise, Idaho, March 20, 1977

The White House wants to make the most of a good idea. It wants the rest of the nation to follow examples set by the seven states that have decriminalized possession of small amounts of marijuana.

There is a distinct difference between decriminalizing marijuana use and legalizing it. Legalization would mean total condonement. Anyone of legal age would be able to walk into the grocery store and pick up a pack of Rocky Mountain Highs.

Decriminalization would simply change possession from a criminal offense to a civil offense, with civil penalties similar to those levied for traffic violations. The idea is not to condone use of marijuana — the White House still plans to discourage it — but to make the penalties commensurate with the act. It is a travesty for an otherwise law-abiding citizen to go to jail and obtain a criminal record simply for smoking a marijuana cigarette.

Many well-intentioned but misguided people oppose lesser penalties for marijuana possession on the basis of myths that were prevalent before the drug was as widely used or as thoroughly researched as it is today. A federal study found marijuana is not physically addictive and "in infrequent or moderate use probably does not pose an immediate substantial health hazard to the individual." The study also found marijuana use has not increased in the seven states that have decriminalized it.

Some who view marijuana smoking as anathema condone the use of alcohol. Yet the body of evidence shows alcohol has caused far more problems in terms of illness and human suffering. Some researchers consider tobacco more harmful than marijuana.

This is not to say marijuana is without drawbacks. Some users become passive and emotionally dependent on it. Like alcohol, marijuana can cause traffic accidents. But it is not the monstrous drug it was once thought to be.

People convicted of possessing fewer than three ounces of marijuana in Idaho are subject to penalties of up to a year in prison and a $1,000 fine. Those with more than three ounces can go to jail for five years and be fined up to $15,000. Either way, they end up with criminal records.

People are doing time in the Idaho State Penitentiary for marijuana possession right now. They are living proof that the penalty is worse than the offense.

THE STATES-ITEM
New Orleans, La., March 17, 1977

President Jimmy Carter is on the right track in calling for decriminalization of penalties for possession of marijuana in small amounts.

The Carter Administration has asked Congress to act on liberalization of the law on possession. Dr. Peter Bourne, head of the Office of Drug Abuse Policy, told the House Committee on Narcotics that the administration will continue to discourage marijuana use but, "we feel criminal penalties that brand otherwise law-abiding people for life are neither an effective nor an appropriate deterrent."

The Carter Administration proposes to remove criminal penalties for possession of small quantities of marijuana for the owner's personal use. There would be a civil fine, but no criminal record. Dealing in the drug would continue to carry stiff penalties.

Criminal penalties for possession of a small quantity of marijuana are harsh and unrealistic. State Atty. Gen. William Guste told Louisiana legislators in 1976 that 30 million Americans use or have used marijuana and that the laws are ignored. State Sen. Anthony Guarisco observed that, "If you jailed everyone who has used marijuana, you'd have to build a fence around the state to make a prison."

Sometimes, the arrest for possession does much more harm than the drug possibly could. This is especially true in the case of young first offenders. Although they may never have another serious brush with the law they go through life with a criminal record.

Although the Louisiana Legislature turned down a marijuana decriminalization measure during last year's session, several other states have acted to make possession a misdemeanor. The states include Oregon, Alaska, Maine, Colorado, California, Ohio, South Dakota, and Minnesota.

Use of marijuana should not be encouraged, just as use of alcohol should not be encouraged. Reducing the penalty for the possession of small amounts of marijuana to a reasonable fine would discourage use without branding the user a criminal.

Roanoke Times & World-News

Roanoke, Va., March 20, 1977

Jimmy Carter's administration is throwing its weight behind the push to end criminal penalties for personal use (not pushing) of marijuana.

This does not signal a collapse of American legal and moral standards. All it would mean is that the person apprehended with a small amount of marijuana would not, if prosecuted, be branded a criminal and perhaps sent to prison. He or she could, instead, be charged with a civil offense and fined.

That would be enlightened. Not because marijuana is good or its use praiseworthy. But the weed has not been demonstrated to be any more of an evil than, say, alcohol when used moderately; nor is its use necessarily a steppingstone to hard drugs. It makes little more sense to imprison teen-aged pot-smokers than to lock them up for puffing cigarettes or sneaking a can of beer.

In defense of decriminalization, it has been routinely said that too much police time and resources are devoted to small-scale pot busts. We doubt that's nearly so true any more. Surrounded by more serious crime, police tend more and more to wink at marijuana use, as they do at jaywalking. Public opinion doesn't support heavy-handed crackdowns on social grass-smokers. There are millions of users of all ages and recent surveys by the federal Drug Abuse Institute show 86 per cent of the American public endorses decriminalization.

Congress nearly always lags well behind public opinion, so it's not at all certain the legislators will follow the Carter lead at this time. Change could come, though, before Mr. Carter's first term is up. To favor decriminalization of personal marijuana possession is not to favor either crime or sin. It's just common sense.

THE LINCOLN STAR

Lincoln, Neb., March 17, 1977

The Carter administration's proposal to abolish federal penalties for possession of small amounts of marijuana will certainly not inhibit the pot controversy. And the proposal, coming on the heels of pardon for Vietnam war draft resisters, will give credence to the argument that the new gang in Washington is permissive.

The arguments in favor of the administration's position are sound, however, and backed by figures pointing up certain absurdities in anti-marijuana attitudes.

The administration is saying simply that it will try to discourage use of marijuana, and will leave to the states their own penalties for possession, but that it can see little justification for keeping a law on the books which is rare-ly enforced and for imposing stringent penalties for the use of what has become a popular drug. Thirteen million Americans are said to use it regularly, not as many as use alcohol, which is more dangerous, but a significant number nevertheless.

Said the chairman of a congressional committee now studying the question of drug abuse: "It (marijuana) is a complex and controversial issue on which vast numbers of Americans do not agree." But the extensive use of marijuana requires that the issue be faced, he said.

The Carter administration deserves credit for facing the issue realistically, regardless of which way the winds of public opinion are blowing.

The Miami Herald

Miami, Fla., March 16, 1977

MARIJUANA is potentially harmful to some users and its use should be discouraged by public policy, but criminal penalties are not the way.

That's the gist of a recommendation to Congress by the Carter administration. It is based on findings of considerable research conducted over the last several years under the auspices of the federal government and the National Institute of Mental Health.

Removing criminal penalties for possession of small amounts of marijuana would not legalize it, but possession would be classed as a civil offense, like most minor traffic-law violations.

Surveys indicating regular use of marijuana by an estimated 13 million Americans and occasional experimentation by countless others indicate that criminal sanctions have failed to discourage use.

Such penalties have, however, adversely affected the lives of many young Americans who got caught breaking the laws against marijuana — laws often enforced quite selectively.

Now that scientific research indicates the effects of marijuana are probably no more harmful to individuals or society than the effects of alcohol, these penalties seem worse than the offense they were intended to discourage.

We hope, therefore, that Congress and the individual states will respond by making pragmatic reforms in laws governing marijuana use so that the criminal justice system may concentrate its resources on discouraging offenses with more serious social consequences.

The Evening Bulletin

Philadelphia, Pa., March 17, 1977

Under current federal law, the maximum penalty for possession of a single marijuana cigaret is one year in prison and $5,000 fine. But in actual practice this draconian law is not enforced, nor is it likely to be.

By seeking to decriminalize the possession of small amounts of marijuana, the Carter Administration would change the law to conform more closely with reality today, in terms of the use of the drug and law enforcement. Such a change would make the law more equitable for individuals and assist authorities and courts to uphold the statutes.

Decriminalization of marijuana in this context should not be considered an endorsement of it. Many questions remain to be answered about its uses. While not physiologically addictive like tobacco, it can be psychologically addictive. It may not be as harmful to the human body as alcohol, but it can be just as incapacitating. But most of all, we just do not know enough about either its immediate or long term effects.

The Carter Administration's proposal does not even remove all penalties for using marijuana. In fact, the Administration is endorsing a bill that would impose a civil fine of up to $100. Criminal penalties for the sale or distribution of marijuana would remain.

What the proposal would do, however, is to remove the existing excessive criminal penalties for using the drug and the blot a criminal conviction can put on a person's record for life.

A similar change in state laws also would be appropriate even though the Carter Administration did not advocate it. Both Pennsylvania and New Jersey punish possession of marijuana with jail terms and stiff fines. However, many district attorneys and police departments admit that they do not actively enforce local laws.

Given what is known and unknown about marijuana's use and effects, decriminalizing its use at the federal and state level seems a reasonable, not a radical, step.

OREGON Journal
AN INDEPENDENT NEWSPAPER

Portland, Ore., March 18, 1977

In actions by eight states, including Oregon, to decriminalize possession of small amounts of marijuana, the drug has not been given a clean bill of health.

The same can be said of President Carter's endorsement of this "middle way" treatment of the problem.

The President, presumably influenced by the position of Dr. Peter G. Bourne, director-designate of the Office of Drug Abuse Policy, has given his support to decriminalization, preferring that it be done by the states. While he has not proposed federal legislation, he has endorsed a bill introduced by Sens. Alan Cranston, D-Calif., and Jacob Javits, R.-N.Y., which is similar to the Oregon law.

Present federal law calls for harsh penalties for simple possession of small amounts, but this phase of the law has never been enforced.

Under the Cranston-Javits bill, trafficking in marijuana, even in small amounts, would continue to be a criminal offense, subject to heavy penalties, as it is in Oregon.

With decriminalization, simple possession of small amounts continues to be a violation subject to penalty, but not a crime.

The case for the "middle way" approach rests on two basic facts:

1. Marijuana, while less of a problem than alcohol abuse, is harmful, particularly with prolonged use, which should be discouraged.

2. Excessive penalties for use or possession of small amounts are counterproductive. Usually they are not enforced or, if they are, they can destroy the lives of essentially good kids.

There is little sentiment among drug experts or the public for legalizing marijuana.

Opinion has been fairly well divided on the decriminalization route, but the trend is in that direction.

The News and Courier

Charleston, W.Va., March 17, 1977

The Carter administration's proposal for decriminalizing possession of pot ignores warnings sounded only last week by the National Institute on Drug Abuse in its annual report to Congress.

Use of marijuana, the institute cautioned, has passed the fad stage. It is on its way to becoming a national habit. But it is unsafe. What's known about its short-term effects and what's not known about its long-term effects make marijuana a dangerous candidate for acceptance as a social custom.

Acceptance as a social custom is, however, a predictable consequence of decriminalization. Removal of the fear of prosecution — equating possession of pot with a parking meter violation — will encourage greater involvement in trafficking and use. The more users there are, the more the public will be inclined to tolerate or accept the practice ("...everybody does it. It's O.K.").

The idea that marijuana is safe has gained popular support, the director of the Institute on Drug Abuse told Congress, but it is not endorsed by the research community. In the short run, marijuana is a known intoxicant. More users will mean more safety hazards, such as more auto drivers under its influence. No one knows for sure what are the long-run effects of marijuana on body and mind. Continued study, Congress was told, is essential to detect any serious health risks before usage becomes even more widespread.

Decriminalization is a move in the opposite direction just when all the signs urge going slow.

OKLAHOMA CITY TIMES

Oklahoma City, Okla., March 16, 1977

THE latest proposal for decriminalization of marijuana is no more palatable for being the official position of the Carter administration than are the pronouncements of various study groups.

The administration would remove criminal penalties for possession of small quantities of marijuana for the owner's personal use. It would provide for a civil fine, which would not result in a criminal record.

The incongruity of the proposal is striking. If possession of small amounts of marijuana is no longer to be considered wrong, thus not deserving punishment, why the civil fine?

Dr. Peter Bourne, President Carter's personal friend and his choice to head the Office of Drug Abuse Policy, told a congressional committee the administration will continue to discourage marijuana use. Criminal penalties that brand "otherwise law-abiding" people for life are not effective or appropriate as a deterrent, he said.

If the government still wants to discourage use of marijuana, it must be convinced the drug is harmful at least to some degree. A Domestic Council Task Force report in September, 1975, said pot holds the "least potential" to harm the individual and society. Yet the government officially continues to chase and prosecute marijuana smugglers.

Bourne's contention notwithstanding, the threat of a criminal record is probably the very thing that has kept even more people from being involved with marijuana.

Many advocates of decriminalization claim marijuana is no worse a drug than nicotine or alcohol, and these are not banned. Again, government policy is ambivalent. One branch of government subsidizes the tobacco crop while another tries to discourage use of tobacco by warning of its hazard to health.

If the Domestic Council report reflects official policy, the government seems to draw the line between marijuana, on the one hand, and alcohol and nicotine, because the latter are "legally obtainable and socially acceptable." Even the advocates of decriminalization of pot are divided; some are sufficiently concerned about its long-term effects that they don't urge legalization.

Indeed, scientific evidence is now showing the dangers of marijuana use. Dr. Hardin B. Jones, physiologist at the University of California at Berkeley, terms marijuana 100 times more damaging to the body than alcohol or tobacco cigarettes. The active ingredient, THC, accumulates in the body and may cause irreversible brain damage as marijuana use extends beyond three years.

Tobacco, like marijuana, is harmful to the body. But, unlike it, tobacco doesn't alter thought processes in a way that might present a threat to others—such as in automobile traffic.

And, even if marijuana were no worse than alcohol as a drug, does society really want to create a whole new liquor-type syndrome? Abuse of alcohol—in the form of alcoholism and drunken driving—is bad enough, but because of its "social acceptability," outlawing it is impractical. Prohibition proved that.

The same argument is made in behalf of marijuana because of its widespread use. But why make matters worse and open the door to a whole new bundle of problems when scientific evidence indicates marijuana is medically damaging?

The San Diego Union

San Diego, Calif., March 21, 1977

Dr. Peter Bourne, taking over as head of the federal Office of Drug Abuse, wants Congress to eliminate criminal penalties for marijuana use. At the same time, Dr. Bourne says his boss, President Carter, wants federal policy to be aimed at discouraging drug abuse.

The idea that laws against the use of a particular drug can be relaxed without encouraging the use of that drug is hard to buy. This has been one of the main objections to the decriminalization of marijuana use — a step already taken by California and seven other states and under consideration by the legislatures of 35 others.

Rewriting federal law to make possession of small amounts of marijuana subject to a civil fine rather than a jail term would be largely a symbolic act. Ninety-nine per cent of the arrests for marijuana possession occur under state laws. The federal government concerns itself mostly with traffic in the drug.

That is part of the ambiguity which is overtaking the subject of marijuana in our society. On the one hand, the law continues to come down hard on those who smuggle marijuana into the country and sell it, while settling for a slap on the wrist — if there is any prosecution at all — for those caught using it or presumably intending to.

Either marijuana is dangerous or it isn't. Dr. Robert L. Dupont, director of the National Institute on Drug Abuse, has just issued an annual review of the research on that question and decries once again the hasty presumption that smoking pot is safe simply because scientists cannot produce definitive findings that say otherwise.

Indeed, Dr. Dupont has added a new dimension to the worries about marijuana use. With signs that pot-smoking has become more than a fad or a gesture of protest, and may be turning into an "enduring cultural pattern" in our society, he raises the issue of what this means to the traffic accident rate.

Police already face the fact that about half our traffic fatalities involve drivers intoxicated by alcohol. Now a study in one city shows that an additional 16 per cent of drivers in fatal auto accidents were high on marijuana. We seem to be compounding an already baffling problem of drugs and public safety.

A survey conducted for the California Health and Welfare Department shows that 14 per cent of the state's adults consider themselves marijuana users — an increase since the laws were relaxed here and a figure higher than what is considered a national average. It is hard to avoid the conclusion that there is a connection between the willingness of people to intoxicate themselves with marijuana and the attitude which the law takes toward what they're doing.

Dr. Bourne is bothered by the stigma of criminal charges brought against "otherwise law-abiding people" who are arrested for smoking pot. Perhaps President Carter is bothered by that, too. But there is a lot more to bothered about in the implications for the health and safety of Americans, and the moral quality of our society, if the federal government throws in the towel on this issue.

THE INDIANAPOLIS STAR

Indianapolis, Ind., March 20, 1977

Decriminalization of marijuana possession, which the Carter administration has proposed to Congress, involves a thicket of thorny questions.

Marijuana has joined such common drugs as alcohol, caffeine and tobacco as part of the national lifestyle, according to "Marijuana and Health," the annual report made to Congress by the Department of Health, Education and Welfare.

HEW's report says some 36 million Americans have experimented with marijuana and 10 per cent of the population uses the drug regularly. This is more than 20 million people. It obviously would take many large new prisons to hold them all.

The idea of removing criminal penalties for possession of certain amounts of marijuana is for such reasons highly appealing to a large number of people.

Here the questions begin. How much marijuana would it be legal to possess? An ounce, a kilo? More? What about dealing? Should marijuana traffic be decriminalized? Should it be controlled, as with alcoholic beverages, in all phases of manufacture, processing, packaging, shipping, wholesaling and retailing? Should marijuana be licensed and taxed, as alcohol is?

Should its use by minors — who are ardent experimenters with pot as an underground drug — be prohibited? Should special criminal penalties be attached to selling or giving pot to minors?

Would decriminalization apply only to marijuana in its unrefined form, or would it also apply to its more powerful products, such as hashish and cannibis extract?

Would persons intoxicated by marijuana be subject to arrest for driving motor vehicles? Dr. Robert L. DuPont, director of HEW's National Institute on Drug Abuse, said a few days ago that his greatest concern over widespread marijuana use "is its potential effect on automobile accidents in this country."

"Intoxication itself is the most unequivocable effect of marijuana on health," Dr. DuPont said. It is undeniably the province of law to deal with the intoxicated person who becomes a public menace, no matter what the agent of intoxication.

The HEW report said that many widely publicized studies which supposedly showed marijuana use causes chromosome damage, brain damage, impairment of endocrine functioning and impairment of the body's system of defense against disease were inconclusive or unresolved.

But the report did stress that marijuana causes loss of psychomotor co-ordination, as does alcohol, and possible lung damage after heavy, long-term use.

Dr. Peter Bourne, President Carter's choice to head the Office of Drug Abuse Policy, said the administration will keep on discouraging marijuana use, but that "we feel criminal penalties that brand otherwise law-abiding people for life are neither an effective nor an appropriate deterrent."

It is true that present law is not very effective. But care is needed to avoid changing it in such a way as to create a whole new legion of hazards to health, safety and even life.

The Detroit News

Detroit, Mich., March 16, 1977

Since doctors continue to disagree sharply as to the effects of "pot" on the mind and body, the American public must be puzzled and dismayed by the Carter administration's request that Congress decriminalize marijuana.

The administration wants to remove criminal penalties for possession of small amounts of marijuana for personal use. Such possession would draw a civil fine but result in no criminal record. This action would certainly remove the inhibitions of many persons who until now have kept away from pot because of a possible criminal penalty.

We share the administration's distaste for imposing criminal penalties which brand young men and women for life. But we feel an even greater concern about encouraging further use of drugs by a society which already has 27 million users of marijuana, heroin and cocaine. Drugs

ruin more lives than felony records do.

Down through the years medical research has built a powerful case against pot. A group of British scientists conducted tests which suggested that pot-smoking may cause serious brain damage. Two Philadelphia psychiatrists noted that the pot smoker often loses his ability to resolve his problems and gets "hung up" in another world.

Other studies suggest that pot smokers risk decreasing their fertility; that the main active ingredients of pot may accumulate in the brain and in the body's fatty tissues; that pot tends to blunt the emotions and rob the smoker of motivation.

Those who favor removing penalties for the use of marijuana cite other studies which, they say, disprove all these findings. Those advocates only succeed in illustrating the division of scientific

opinion on this topic and the lack of conclusive findings. Without conclusive findings, it is folly to take action that will encourage use of marijuana.

Marijuana must be regarded as potentially harmful in itself. Not only that. The evidence suggests that, whatever marijuana's immediate effect on the user, it tends to serve as a stepping stone to experimentation with harder and more dangerous drugs.

In short, the Carter administration proposes to open a Pandora's box of potential new evils in the field of drug addiction, already one of the nation's most serious health and social problems. Giving legal relief to possessors of small quantities of pot is not nearly as important as keeping the lid shut on that box.

St. Louis Globe-Democrat

St. Louis, Mo., March 16, 1977

Congress should defeat President Carter's unwise proposal to abolish federal penalties for possession of small amounts of marijuana because this action could greatly increase the use of a drug which a growing number of researchers are linking with possible brain, cellular and genetic damage.

U.S. Commissioner of Customs Vernon Acree said marijuana decriminalization may cause many who feared prosecution to begin using marijuana. The amount of the drug smuggled into this country could increase, he said

The argument being put forward by the Carter Administration that criminal penalties for possession of marijuana aren't an effective deterrent is beside the point. Marijuana

has been proven to be a dangerous drug in many studies. It is against the best interests of the public to take any action that will increase the use of a substance that one researcher recently called 100 times more dangerous than alcohol.

Dr. Hardin B. Jones, professor of medical physics and physiology and assistant director of the Donner Laboratory at the University of California at Berkeley, said several months ago that marijuana "probably is the most cytotoxic (cell-poisoning) substance known."

He said that studies have shown that irreversible brain changes may be encountered as marijuana use extends beyond three years.

When marijuana is used heavily, Jones said, the average user exhibits a wide range of brain changes:

—He shifts from a self-activating, interesting person to one who is withdrawn and given to disoriented thinking.

—Thought formation tends to be less powerful, as though some of the reference thinking has gone astray.

—Attention span and ability to concentrate are reduced.

—Facial circulation is impaired. The skin is pallid; eye focus is less precise.

—Because marijuana is an hypnotic drug, the user is likely to be talked into many situations he otherwise would avoid.

—The male is deficient in hormones.

—Users are likely to have a tendency toward paranoia or schizophrenia.

—They are likely to have an increased number of broken chromosomes in the culture of their white blood cells.

—The white blood cell immune response is lowered.

There are other findings equally damaging to health but this should be enough to keep any person who values his or her health away from marijuana.

President Carter is in a position to know about these study results. So it is very bad judgment on his part to propose an action that might invite millions of young people to start smoking this extremely dangerous drug.

PRESIDENT URGES LEGISLATION TO DECRIMINALIZE MARIJUANA

President Carter endorsed legislation Aug. 2 that would impose a civil penalty instead of a criminal penalty for possession of an ounce or less of marijuana. The federal penalty currently was one year in prison, a $5,000 fine or both for possession.

"We can and should continue to discourage the use of marijuana" without "defining the smoker as a criminal," Carter said at a press briefing on his message to Congress on drug abuse. Federal laws on trafficking in marijuana "would remain in force," he said, and the states "would remain free to adopt whatever laws they wish concerning the marijuana smoker." In his message to Congress, he said the sale of marijuana should remain" a serious, federal criminal offense."

The President also called for an increase effort to curb international narcotics traffic, a study on the use of barbiturates and other widely used sedatives and a focus on drug research and drug treatment. The larger goal, he said, was "to discourage all drug abuse in America," including excessive use of alcohol and tobacco.

The Honolulu Advertiser
Honolulu, Hawaii, August 3, 1977

President Carter is probably right in urging removal of all Federal criminal penalties for the possession of small amounts of marijuana.

Too many Americans now use pot to threaten them with a potential criminal record for something that is possibly no worse for them than consuming alcohol or smoking tobacco.

BUT THERE should be no illusions this would be true progress for mankind. It is at best a pragmatic half-step toward the inevitable legalization of yet another drug. It will in some ways add to, or change the nature of, a problem already with us.

As we noted after the four murders and other violence over marijuana on Molokai in May, decriminalization is not the answer to the problem of what to do about the major marijuana-growing-and-distribution industry and organized crime involvement here and elsewhere.

In fact, by making pot less legally dangerous and more respectable, it could increase the local market and the pressure to grow more — an activity that would still be illegal, yet an even greater lure for both organized crime and small "farmers."

IF DECRIMINALIZATION seems the best of poor choices now, it seems hypocritical to suggest it is anything but a way station en route to legalization of growing and distribution.

Some see that possibility as a stimulant for a new industry already well under way illegally here. Maybe so, especially since Hawaii grows high-quality marijuana and already exports considerable amounts.

But Big Island police officials also report cultivation of peyote cactus and poppy plant (for opium or heroin) is also increasing. So we might also see some persons now producing pot switch to other truly dangerous, and more profitable, drugs.

All of which suggests the drug problem and its effects will be with us no matter what. And marijuana is a growing part of it. Like alcohol, it can provide relatively harmless pleasure (and some medical benefits) for some, and problems for others who go beyond small amounts for social use.

SO PRESIDENT Carter may have been too optimistic in saying: "We can, and should, continue to discourage the use of marijuana. But this can be done without defining the smoker as a criminal."

Still, at least he was right in noting the high social cost of drug abuse in our nation — $15 billion a year for crime, sickness and death caused by all drugs, including barbiturates and alcohol — and calling for more to be done about the total situation.

The Chattanooga Times
Chattanooga, Tenn., August 5, 1977

President Carter acted correctly Tuesday in proposing legislation that would bring a needed measure of common sense to federal laws on marijuana possession, although some would have the public believe he seeks to turn the country into a nation of potheads.

Simply put, Mr. Carter asked Congress to abolish federal criminal penalties for the possession of small amounts of marijuana; small is defined as up to one ounce.

The proposed "decriminalization" is not the same as legalization, which would permit no penalty at all. To replace the present federal penalty for possession of any amount of marijuana — a $5,000 fine and up to a year in prison — the Carter proposal urges a civil penalty, such as a fine. But it also couples that with proposals for a crackdown on international narcotics smuggling, a study on the use of barbiturates and other sedatives (an area too long ignored) and improved programs for drug research and treatment.

The proposed legislation is valuable for at least two reasons. By eliminating small time drug cases from the federal courts, that system will be able to function more efficiently. More important, it recognizes that a law that cannot be enforced is worse than no law at all.

We would need a virtual army of federal narcotics working full time to corral all those who possess an ounce or less of marijuana, an amount not commensurate with the seriousness of the offense; it is roughly analogous to imposing the death penalty for jaywalking. As Mr. Carter noted in his message to Congress, "Penalties against possession of a drug should not be more damaging to an individual than the use of the drug itself."

Mr. Carter is not proposing anything radically new. Numerous states, including North Carolina, have decriminalized the law on possessing a small amount of marijuana, and the last time we looked, Tar Heels weren't completely zonked out on grass.

There are almost as many theories on the effects of using marijuana as there are researchers, which is why Mr. Carter says efforts must continue to discourage use of the drug. But that can be done, it seems to us, without dumping the full force of a draconian federal law on the heads of violators.

The Virginian-Pilot

Norfolk, Va., August 4, 1977

In asking Congress to end the criminal penalties for possessing up to an ounce of marijuana, President Carter is asking only that the Federal laws conform to current practice.

Marijuana possession is not a Federal offense, normally speaking. Federal prosecutors are not interested in jailing the casual smoker.

Peter B. Bensinger, administrator of the Drug Enforcement Administration, said the Carter proposal amounts to Presidential recognition of the state of things. "There's not a Federal prosecutor in the United States today who would prosecute a case of possessing an ounce or less or marijuana."

That does not mean that Mr. Carter or the Feds would encourage the pot smoker. "We can, and should, continue to discourage the use of marijuana," the President said in his message to Congress. "But this can be done without defining the smoker as a criminal."

Mr. Carter wants the civil penalties for possession to be retained. But that is only symbolic. Indeed, his message was mostly symbolic, since the enforcement — or nonenforcement — of the laws on marijuana is almost entirely a matter of state and local authority. The President set an example for the states in commending the decriminalizing of marijuana.

He's right. The average pot smoker is not a criminal. If not a juvenile, he is likely to be under 30. Blue jeans, pot, and rock are the boundaries of the generation gap in the United States. The National Institute of Drug Abuse in a survey of 17,000 high school seniors last year discovered more than half had tried marijuana and roughly one-third were regular users. Millions of Americans smoke marijuana. Prohibition is unworkable. Decriminalization is inevitable.

The General Assembly hardly would vote today in favor of the Virginia law making marijuana possession a criminal offense. But it is hard to get a bad statute off the books. Whoever is elected Governor in November, John Dalton or Henry Howell, ought to urge the decriminalizing of marijuana in Virginia and, in the interests of justice, should review the sentences of all those serving time for marijuana use.

Roanoke Times & World-News

Roanoke, Va., August 5, 1977

President Carter's proposal that Congress ease federal penalties for possessing small amounts of marijuana may seem far-reaching. Politically, perhaps it is. Despite recommendations by various study groups, no other president has dared suggest that simply having a marijuana cigarette ought not be considered a felony.

From the legal and practical standpoint, though, what the President proposes is not at all radical. He merely wants Congress to make the law conform with practice; federal prosecutors, their hands filled with other matters, no longer bother to prosecute cases involving possession of an ounce or less of pot.

In most states and localities, including Virginia, the prosecutorial practice is similar. It's obvious why: There are too many such instances.

The spread of illegal "recreational" drug use may be taken as a sad commentary on our society, but such actions are one way society is made to alter its laws. The main reason Prohibition couldn't last was that it lacked popular support. Marijuana laws also lose support steadily as more Americans (45 million by a recent estimate) have experimented with the drug and perhaps 11 million use it regularly.

A sane system of priorities suggests it is wrong to brand people of any age criminals for owning a small quantity of a drug that seems less harmful than alcohol and is in such widespread use. "Too much manpower," Superior Court Judge Harold Greene of the District of Columbia has said, "is wasted on arresting and trying people who have minor amounts of marijuana." There are many other crimes (such as drug-pushing and possession of addictive narcotics) that police and prosecutors can pursue with greater benefit to a community.

Legal changes still would bother some people. Dr. Robert L. DuPont, then director of the White House Special Action Office for Drug Abuse Prevention, took the position in late 1974 that prison sentences for marijuana use are wrong. But he added that he did not "want to encourage use by legalizing (decriminalizing) it."

What's wrong with this is that it makes law enforcement officially capricious. Police are expected to wink at most violations, a practice that does not foster respect for law in general; but they retain the option of using a discredited law when and against whom they choose. This kind of selectivity is not uncommon, but it is hardly in tune with a society whose government is supposed to be one of laws, not of men.

Be it noted that President Carter has not asked that marijuana use be legalized—it would remain a misdemeanor, perhaps punishable by a small fine. A staff study for the Joint Legislative Audit and Review Commission recommended a similar change in Virginia's drug laws nearly two years ago; with the prod of federal change, the state might finally get around to such common-sense action. To draw an imperfect analogy, citizens would not want a community's police busting jaywalkers at every corner while downtown stores were being robbed and the criminals getting away. Let's put drug-law enforcement matters into perspective.

The Seattle Times

Seattle, Wash., August 4, 1977

IN ONE of the symbolic touches that are now his trademark, President Carter made a personal appearance in the White House press room this week to announce his message to Congress on drug abuse.

His call for elimination of federal criminal penalties for possession of up to an ounce of marijuana was also, in essence, a symbolic action.

Only a small percentage of the annual arrests for simple marijuana possession are by federal authorities, although the present federal penalty is a fine of up to $5,000 and up to one year in prison. The vast majority of arrests fall under state and local laws.

Federal drug-control officials rightly spend more time trying to stop large-scale trafficking in marijuana. Mr. Carter emphasized that such traffic should remain a "serious, federal criminal offense."

Those who see an inherent contradiction in efforts to decriminalize the use while discouraging the sale of marijuana should realize that Mr. Carter is practicing elementary politics: The art of the possible.

The President knows, as a Gallup Poll reported in May, that 55 per cent of the American people believe marijuana is physically harmful, 59 per cent consider it addictive, and 59 per cent think it leads to use of hard drugs, such as heroin.

But Mr. Carter also knows that some 45 million Americans have tried marijuana, at least 11 million are regular users, and younger and higher-educated persons are more likely to be pro-marijuana.

Furthermore, marijuana possession has been reclassified as a misdemeanor in all 50 states, and 10 states have passed decriminalization laws.

Such laws took effect in Oregon in 1973; Alaska, Colorado and Ohio in 1975; California, Maine and Minnesota in 1976; New York, North Carolina and Mississippi in 1977. (A marijuana-decriminalization bill passed the House in the Washington Legislature this year but died in the Senate.)

The President correctly recognizes that trying to stamp out marijuana use would be as futile and costly as Prohibition's attempt to eliminate liquor consumption.

Mr. Carter is well aware that alcohol and tobacco take a far larger toll on society in terms of cost, health and life than does marijuana. Symbolic or not, the President is on the right course.

The Boston Globe

Boston, Mass., August 4, 1977

President Carter's recommendation this week that Federal criminal penalties for possession of small amounts of marijuana be abolished draws on a fast accumulating reservoir of experience in states of varying sizes and population characteristics.

The first state to remove criminal penalties for possession of small amounts of the substance — known as decriminalization — was Oregon in 1973, where critics predicted direfully that there would be a sharp increase in the use of the drug and an influx of smokers to the state.

Neither happened, as attested by state officials and confirmed by an exhaustive study done for the Law Enforcement Assistance Administration at the behest of the National Governors Conference. The Federal study covered the eight states that had then decriminalized: Oregon, Colorado, Ohio, California, Alaska, Minnesota, Maine and South Dakota. (New York State has since passed a decriminalization act.)

Mr. Carter put forward a prudent legal maxim in calling for Federal decriminalization. "Penalties against possession of a drug should not be more damaging to an individual than the use of the drug itself," he told the Congress. There is, of course, substantial disagreement on how much damage, if any, the drug does, but there is an overwhelming consensus that the current penalties at the Federal level and in 42 states, incarceration and/or stiff fines as well as the stigma of a permanent criminal record are far out of proportion to the offense.

This disproportion and the superstitions that have surrounded the marijuana debate help breed a contempt for law on the part of users, particularly young people who hardly need encouragement in a habit of disregard of their elders' warnings.

The current Federal law, for instance, is extremely punitive, providing for a fine of up to $5000 and a year in jail for possession of any amount of the substance. Mr. Carter is asking that this be scaled down to a modest fine, carrying no criminal record. He would retain criminal penalties for sale, much to the annoyance of those who argue that all legal barriers to sale, growth and possession should be dropped immediately and the substance should be put on a legal par with tobacco or alcohol.

On the local scene, the Carter proposal has had an immediate impact. State Rep. Michael F. Flaherty, co-chairman of the Legislature's Judiciary Committee, told The Globe yesterday that he believed Carter's proposal had "tipped the balance" in the committee in favor of decriminalization in Massachusetts, and he predicted it would be reported favorably to the House and Senate. It is to be hoped that the Carter recommendation will also have enough impetus to push the local bill to final passage.

St. Louis Globe-Democrat
St. Louis, Mo., August 4, 1977

President Carter has given marijuana pushers and users a tremendous boost by his request for Congress to pass legislation decriminalizing possession of marijuana up to one ounce.

His call for a crackdown on dope dealers to insure "swift, certain and severe punishment" couldn't begin to undo the damage that would be caused by decriminalizing possession of marijuana.

If Congress were to follow the President's proposal, it would mean every marijuana user in the country could carry about 20 marijuana cigarettes all the time (a package of tobacco cigarettes weighs one ounce) and be subject only to a civil fine.

It is incredible that the President of the United States would want to give this kind of encouragement to use of a drug which studies show is more harmful than alcohol.

In a recent study of some 1,900 drug abusers it was found that marijuana damages chromosomes, affects DNA, RNA and the immune response. It also was found to cause irreversible brain changes after only three years of daily usage. Three persons in six who use marijuana are likely to become addicted, according to the survey.

In view of these findings President Carter should be warning all Americans against using this dangerous drug rather than proposing legislation that will encourage this deadly habit.

What good will it do to get tough on distributors of marijuana if anyone can carry up to an ounce of the drug without fear of criminal prosecution? Pushers could simply make sure they never carry more than an ounce at a time.

And what leverage would prosecutors have to gain the testimony of users against the pushers?

This is a terrible proposal. Mr. Carter was extremely unwise to make it. The marijuana vote may be important but the health of the public should supersede this political consideration.

The Cleveland Press
Cleveland, Ohio, August 5, 1977

President Carter's latest statement on marijuana should help to restore some common sense and perspective to an argument that up to now has been conducted on a highly emotional plane.

Carter urged Congress to eliminate all criminal penalties, under federal law, for the simple possession of one ounce or less of marijuana, a euphoric drug which has been tried at one time or another by more than 45 million Americans.

"Decriminalization is not legalization," the President said. "It means only that the federal penalty for possession would be reduced and a person would receive a fine rather than a criminal penalty."

As a practical matter, no one has been arrested by the federal government for more than three years on a possession-of-marijuana charge. Nor is it likely that the law will be amended in the near future.

But the Carter statement is important because it marks the first time a president has formally endorsed the decriminalization of marijuana. Ten states, including California, Ohio, Colorado and Mississippi, already have lowered their state-imposed penalties for marijuana possession. And others are likely to do so, now that a president has endorsed the idea.

There is, by the way, no reason to assume that Carter is "soft" on drug abuse because he opposes jail terms for occasional (or even regular) marijuana smokers. The President continues to favor stiff penalties for trafficking in marijuana or any other illegal drug.

He suggested the other day, for example, that notorious heroin and hard-drug dealers be held without bail, that their assets be frozen and that their passports be taken away.

That kind of action would do much more to discourage drug pushing than spending endless amounts of time, manpower and money trying to put marijuana smokers in jail.

THE BLADE
Toledo, Ohio, August 5, 1977

PRESIDENT CARTER makes it perfectly clear that, if he had his druthers, no Americans would use marijuana. Neither, for that matter, would anybody smoke cigarettes or drink alcoholic beverages to excess. But in addressing himself to the drug problems in this country, Mr. Carter embraces the view that the effects of marijuana have been grossly exaggerated and that all federal criminal penalties for possession of an ounce or less of it should be removed. As he said in his special message to Congress, we can and should discourage its use without defining the marijuana smoker as a criminal.

Although the President leaves to the states the option of changing their statutes, his wish is clear enough. Some 45 million Americans have tried marijuana, he said, and 11 million are regular users. Until several states, including Ohio, removed criminal penalties for simple possession, users were constantly subject to police harassment; they still are in those states that maintain stiff penalties.

Rather than encouraging such dissipation of law-enforcement energies, the President is clearing the decks for an all-out assault on dealers and traffickers in hard drugs and narcotics of all kinds. In ordering Attorney General Griffin Bell to "concentrate on breaking the links between organized crime and drug traffic" and to convict and swiftly punish traffickers, Mr. Carter is taking aim at the sources of illegal drugs with a vengeance.

The Government's reported success in cutting the flow of heroin to the United States to record-low levels is an encouraging reflection of international cooperation that promises to get even more attention. Finally, it seems, the thrust against the drug traffic is being properly as well as intensively directed. De-emphasis of marijuana use should sharpen the focus on really dangerous drugs and the criminal suppliers behind the scenes.

Los Angeles Times
Los Angeles, Calif., August 4, 1977

If Congress follows President Carter's urging and removes the federal criminal sanctions for possession of small amounts of marijuana, the action will neither reduce arrests dramatically nor end federal efforts to curtail marijuana traffic.

Federal arrests for mere possession of an ounce or less—Carter's proposed standard—have been few; U.S. drug enforcement has concentrated instead on the apprehending of suspected smugglers and dealers. And Carter has pledged to crack down harder on them.

But substituting a civil fine of perhaps $100 for the present criminal penalties, which can amount to a $5,000 fine and a year in prison, should increase the chance of similar action by states, many of them in the South, whose penalties have remained excessively harsh. California already treats possession of an ounce or less as only a misdemeanor. Oregon and New York have similar laws.

Experience so far shows no significant increase in marijuana use or abuse. But it shows a reduction in the unfair treatment of marijuana users.

The Morning Union
Springfield, Mass., August 4, 1977

President Carter's proposal to "decriminalize" possession of small amounts of marijuana seems reasonable and fairly harmless, so long as it is not construed as a step toward legalization of the drug. In no way can we condone marijuana use — nor does Carter — but the President's recommendation recognizes that it is unrealistic to consider all marijuana smokers to be hard-core criminals.

As Carter has often done with controversial proposals, he has tempered his recommendation with a series of proposals aimed at discouraging all drug use in the nation. But these measures will be overshadowed by his call for an end to federal criminal penalties for possession of less than an ounce of marijuana.

Use of the drug has become so widespread that many federal and local law enforcement officials no longer actively prosecute the simple possession of small amounts. The present federal penalty for possession of any amount of marijuana — a $5,000 fine and up to a year in prison — is much too excessive.

Carter's proposal, following the lead of states like New York, Oregon and California, would make possession of less than an ounce of marijuana a civil crime, punishable by a fine. In those states which have adopted that approach to marijuana possession, the President noted, use of the drug has not significantly increased.

However, the President recommended retaining stiff criminal penalties for the sale of marijuana. We agree that a line must be drawn between the casual user and the trafficker.

There is little conclusive evidence that marijuana is completely harmless. Although it is non-addictive in the strict physical sense, many medical authorities believe that prolonged use of the drug carries potentially damaging physical and psychological effects. The same is true of excessive use of alcohol and tobacco — and Carter believes the government should also do all in its power to discourage heavy use of those substances.

DESERET NEWS
Salt Lake City, Utah, August 4, 1977

"It wasn't too many months ago that this man was talking of a new morality in this country. I pray that this isn't what he was talking about."

— *Los Angeles Police Chief Edward M. Davis, commenting on President Carter's proposal to decriminalize marijuana.*

When President Carter this week proposed fines instead of criminal penalties for possession of small amounts of marijuana for personal use, he did it in the name of "discouraging all drug abuse in America."

What nonsense. Instead, as the police chief of Los Angeles and other lawmen indicate, it could easily have just the opposite effect.

In effect, this nation's chief executive is telling America's young people that the use of marijuana is socially acceptable.

Once that message gets across, it becomes harder for young Americans who have steered clear of marijuana to keep resisting peer pressure to try the drug. Likewise, it could become easier for those already using marijuana to move on to harder drugs in pursuit of bigger thrills and because of the lure of the forbidden.

Though decriminalization of marijuana is not the same as legalization, it leads in that direction. Decriminalization means that possession and use of small amounts of the drug would become a civil, rather than a criminal, offense similar to a parking violation. Once that step is taken, it becomes harder to resist pressure to abandon even nominal fines.

The next step down this road could easily involve major commercial firms advertising and promoting the use of marijuana just as they now push the use of tobacco and alcohol. Is this really what the White House wants?

In recent years, considerable research has been done on the effects of marijuana on the human body. Some reputable scientists insist that marijuana is no more harmful than alcohol, nicotine, or caffeine. Other equally qualified researchers maintain that marijuana does serious harm to the brain, reproductive system, and other bodily functions, particularly when used over a long period of time in large doses. Whatever happened to that sensible philosophy: When in doubt, don't?

What President Carter is trying to do also smacks of ideological schizophrenia. Though possession of marijuana in small amounts would be decriminalized, stiff penalties would be retained for making and distributing the drug.

This nation cannot have an effective criminal justice system based on a philosophy that something is half legal and half illegal.

OKLAHOMA CITY TIMES
Oklahoma City, Okla., August 4, 1977

THE reasoning behind the Carter administration's push to decriminalize possession of small amounts of marijuana for personal use defies logic.

The President is asking Congress to remove the penalty for possession of up to an ounce of marijuana and substitute civil fines in federal cases. At present the penalty for first-offense possession is a $5,000 fine and possibly up to a year in prison.

Thus, a person arrested at a pot-smoking party in possession of an ounce and a half of marijuana would be adjudged a criminal. The one next to him with only an ounce of pot would not be a criminal. And, if that is the case, why the civil fine?

Carter also demanded a crackdown on dope dealers to insure "swift, certain and severe punishment." But most dope dealers also handle marijuana, and the predictable result of the Carter approach would be to improve the market for them. They would find a stimulated demand from users no longer intimidated by fear of arrest.

Backers of legal pot insist states that have lifted criminal penalties from marijuana possession have experienced no great rise in use. But both that argument and the claim that an estimated 11 million Americans already use pot regularly beg the real point.

The basic flaw in the administration plan is that it would have the United States government, in a sense, putting its stamp of approval on a substance that is demonstrably harmful to the human body. More and more scientific reports detail the accumulative effect of THC, the active ingredient of the cannabis drugs.

It is inconsistent for the government to be taking such a step at a time it is squeezing off the market, or severely limiting the use of substances like saccharin that are for the most part beneficial to life.

THE CHRISTIAN SCIENCE MONITOR
Boston, Mass., August 4, 1977

It is a sorrowful tenor of the times that President Carter should even be addressing the subject of decriminalizing marijuana. The widespread and evidently growing use of the drug — some 45 million Americans have tried it and about 11 million are said to be regular users — points to a shocking pursuit after empty materialistic pleasure which can only help to undermine the moral and spiritual fiber of American society.

The President no doubt shares this concern, as reflected in his promises "to discourage all drug abuse in America," including the excessive use of alcohol and tobacco. Yet he confronts an extremely complex and difficult legal problem. The fact is, social practice has far outstripped the ability of the law to cope with the "crime" and hence marijuana laws everywhere are being flagrantly flouted. They have thus not served as a deterrent. Moreover, the penalties can differ markedly from state to state with the result that some marijuana users are harshly punished by stiff jail sentences while others either go scot-free or receive mild fines. In Nevada and Arizona, marijuana possession can even be prosecuted as a felony.

This is why Mr. Carter seeks to abolish all federal penalties for the possession of up to one ounce of marijuana, making it a civil offense that would receive only a fine. A change in the federal law presumably would have limited practical effect since federal authorities last year were involved in fewer than 1 percent of all marijuana cases. But there is no doubt that a revised federal stand would have a strong impact on the states, where the trend already is toward decriminalization. Ten states have now moved in this direction.

We can appreciate Mr. Carter's desire to bring the law more reasonably into accord with public attitudes. It can certainly be argued that it is better to have a realistic law which can be enforced than to have an unrealistic law that is unenforceable. But the President's move nonetheless leaves us uneasy. The primary question is whether federal removal of criminal penalties for the possession of small amounts of marijuana would be but the opening wedge toward full legalization of the drug in which its sale would be regulated like alcohol. Mr. Carter surely would oppose such a move but this is precisely the strategy of such a lobbying group as the National Organization for the Reform of Marijuana Laws. Congress will have to ask itself whether it will be possible to hold the line once the federal government breaches the dike.

A second concern is the impact of such a federal reform on the trafficking in marijuana and other drugs. Once the penalties on marijuana use are eased, it is hard to imagine that traffickers would not make even greater efforts to supply the probable increased demand for the drug, even though criminal penalties for the cultivation, sale, and distribution of marijuana would remain. Organized crime, too, would likely profit from a loosening of the legal standard.

On this score, we welcome President Carter's call for a vigorous government crackdown on drug traffickers. This, certainly, is where the primary federal law-enforcement effort must be directed. The President promises to step up cooperation with other nations to stem the flow of narcotics and to intensify federal investigation of the links between organized crime and the drug traffic.

In short, President Carter, as he promised during his campaign, has now brought the subject of marijuana use to the fore. In the legal debate that is bound to ensue it is to be hoped the White House will not fail to make clear its unequivocal opposition to the drug, however benign some claim it to be. President Carter is the first chief executive to publicly favor a change in the law and it will be doubly incumbent upon him to justify the view that such a change would not lead to an even further deterioration of the nation's standards.

THE LINCOLN STAR
Lincoln, Neb., November 18, 1977
An idea whose time has come

The idea that stiff criminal penalties for individual marijuana use are unjust is not exactly new. From the fringes that attitude has evolved slowly into an idea that now enjoys mainstream sanction.

As a symbol of establishment judgment that simple marijuana use should be decriminalized, consider the joint statement issued last weekend by the American Medical Association and the American Bar Association. Neither can be considered ultra-liberal organizations in matters of manners and morals.

The ABA-AMA statement, noting President Carter's similar position on the subject, called on Congress and state legislatures across the country to eliminate criminal penalties for marijuana possession.

The penalties ofen exceed the crime, the professionals said. The penalties are unrealistic as well — they have not diminished the widespread appeal of pot use and they have caused chaos and waste in the criminal justice system. Too much of our law enforcement resources are given over to apprehending and prosecuting pot users.

If the judgment is not yet in on the effects, over a long period of time, of marijuana use, the judgment is in on the effectiveness of prohibitions; that is to say, they are not effective. Society has known for a long time of the disastrous long-term effects of alcohol use, but has realized the futility of legislating it out of existence, or even of legislating against its consumption.

Dr. Peter Bourne, President Carter's top drug and health policy adviser, observed that "the most important thing about this is that it's a very significant signal that this issue is no longer controversial. I think when you have the joint endorsement of our highest medical and legal associations, it suggests there is an acceptance of the change . . . throughout society."

The AMA-ABA statement does not signal the end of all support for criminal penalties for marijuana use, of course, but it does indicate that the mainstream of American society is ready to give its blessings to fair and realistic treatment of marijuana users.

DAYTON DAILY NEWS
Dayton, Ohio, November 17, 1977
Joint appeal

It ought to be a knockout punch to the aging myths about marijuana: The American Medical Association and the American Bar Association have issued a joint, so to speak, appeal for "reason and moderation" in state and federal marijuana laws.

By that, they mean ending the the criminal penalities for possession of small amounts of the drug. President Carter has proposed that, and the Senate is considering such a bill. Nine states, Ohio among them, already have enacted sensible reforms.

It would be most sensible just to legalize marijuana and be done with the issue. That's almost certain to happen some day. Politically, however, few legislators are willing to risk the creation of a marijuana version of Anita Bryant that legalization might incite.

At least the reforms that the administration supports would bring the law closer to social reality, the public interest, scientific knowledge. The endorsement of the AMA and ABA, two of the stodgiest outfits this side of the Veterans of San Juan Hill, should make it eaiser for lawmakers to do what, by now, is self-evidently correct.

Pittsburgh Post-Gazette
Pittsburgh, Pa., November 17, 1977
Marijuana and the Establishment

Among those who have followed the issue, there were few raised eyebrows the other day when the American Bar Association and the American Medical Association, twin pillars of "establishment" opinion, endorsed the decriminalization of marijuana. After all, opposition to imprisoning otherwise law-abiding marijuana users has been the "establishment" view at least since the 1972 report of the National Commisssion on Marijuana and Drug Abuse (the "Shafer Commission").

Unfortunately, however, there has been a dramatic lag between changes in even the "establishment" view of decriminalization and a reflection of that changed perception in the statute books. Some states, notably New York and Ohio, have repealed Draconian sanctions against the possession of small amounts of marijuana, but others, including Pennsylvania, retain on the books fines and jail terms which were enacted when marijuana was thought to be a "loco weed" that induced murderous "reefer madness."

Organizations like the AMA and the ABA—which are unlikely to be regarded as tools of the counter-culture—thus have a special role to play in lobbying for the abolition of such outdated (and indiscriminately applied) sanctions.

Such a strategy is especially needed in Pennsylvania. Pittsburgh's state Rep., Joseph Rhodes has introduced a modest—some would say too modest—decriminalization bill, HB 904. But that measure has been languishing in the House Judiciary Committee because of the skittishness of rural—and some urban—legislators who fear that many of their constituents still subscribe to the "reefer madness" mythology.

If the Pennsylvania Bar Association and the Pennsylvania Medical Society took an active, public and combative role in encouraging decriminalization, those legislators might summon the courage to proclaim publicly—and with their votes—what many of them acknowledge privately: that it is absurd—and wasteful—to make criminals out of marijuana smokers.

San Francisco Chronicle
San Francisco, Calif., November 15, 1977
Lifting A Penalty

THE AMERICAN Medical Association and the American Bar Association have gotten together, rather remarkably, to issue a statement we find of substantial significance. They've taken a look at the marijuana laws in this country and found the punishment clearly does not fit the crime. So they've asked Congress and state legislatures to repeal criminal penalties for use of marijuana.

This goes along with President Carter's call for "decriminalization" of the substance. He said penalties against possession of a drug "should not be more damaging than the drug itself." And it conforms with California's new law that reduced the penalty for possessing a single ounce from a felony to a simple misdemeanor subject to mere citation and fine. That law, in actual fact, hasn't been enforced to the letter.

The stance of the AMA and the ABA, which calls for "reason and moderation," is a sensible and realistic one. It's looking at the situation as it is. Only by this kind of thinking may some solution to the problem be achieved.

THE STATES-ITEM
New Orleans, La., November 17, 1977

Marijuana decision

A joint statement by the American Medical Association (AMA) and the American Bar Association (ABA) in favor of decriminalizing the personal use of small amounts of marijuana should encourage Congress to get on with the business of removing existing unfair penalties from the law.

Both organizations traditionally favor a conservative approach to change, yet both recognize the unfair nature of existing law pertaining to possession of small amounts of marijuana.

"We believe the time has come to liberalize laws regarding the possession of marijuana for personal use," the organizations stated in a position paper on the issue. The statement calls for reform of both federal and state laws.

"In too many states, statutes exact punishment that far exceeds the crime," the organizations concluded. "We agree with President Carter who showed a reasonable attitude in asking that the possession of insignificant amounts for personal use should not subject the user to criminal charges."

Indeed, the time has come, and both the Senate and House have under consideration legislation designed to do the job. It is time to end the inequities and the harm, especially to young first offenders, caused by the harsh laws.

The marijuana possession laws should be changed for several good reasons. To begin with, they are unenforceable. The use of small amounts of marijuana by individuals is overwhelming. Law enforcement officers spend valuable time attempting to enforce them. Their time could be better spent dealing with more serious crimes.

The lives of young people arrested for possession of small amounts of the drug can be severely damaged if the judiciary elects to carry out the letter of the law. This presents another inequity. Many judges simply refuse to apply the law.

Neither the AMA nor the ABA is condoning the use of marijuana. The organizations, like President Carter, are asking that federal and state governments enact fair laws that recognize the reality of marijuana use.

THE ARIZONA REPUBLIC
Phoenix, Ariz., November 13, 1977

The Use of Pot

THE American Bar Association is the most powerful lawyers' group in the country. The American Medical Association is the most powerful doctors' group in the country.

Early this month the ABA and the AMA jointly called for "liberalization of the federal and state marijuana laws."

President William B. Spann, Jr., of the ABA, and President John H. Budd, M.D., of the AMA issued a statement which said:

"We believe the time has come to liberalize laws regarding the possession of marijuana for personal use. In too many states statutes exact punishment that far exceeds the crime. . . we do not condone the use of marijuana. . . We do ask, however, for reason and moderation in state as well as federal laws that seek to control its use."

The lawyers and the doctors didn't come out flatly for decriminalization of the possession of small amounts of marijuana for personal use. So far as we can see, that's the only real issue involved. The ABA and the AMA were wise to steer clear of the issue.

The judiciary committee of the United States Senate has been considering the marijuana problem in its work on revision of federal criminal code. It refused to place decriminalization in S 1437, the bill which revises and codifies criminal law. The committee agreed to make possession of marijuana a crime, but possession of less than an ounce will be punishable by a fine rather than by imprisonment.

This won't please the liberals, who see nothing wrong with the use of marijuana. (Oddly, these are the same people who object to smoking cigarets or cigars in public places.) But the committee action follows the practice which prevails in most jurisdictions. Federal law-enforcement agents seldom if ever prosecute someone for owning a small amount of marijuana, and local prosecutors are following that example in many places.

Obviously, it is the pusher who should have the book thrown at him. But it doesn't make much sense to have one law which punishes the sale of the weed and another which condones its use.

There is still considerable difference of opinion as to whether marijuana does permanent damage to one's health. If it is ever proved harmless, that will be the time to decriminalize its possession, and its sale as well. For the present, we can see little gain in holding that its possession is legal but its sale is illegal.

The Kansas City Times
Kansas City, Mo., November 17, 1977

Right Stand by AMA-ABA

In a joint announcement from the American Medical Association and the American Bar Association the two professional societies have endorsed legislative efforts to decriminalize the penalties for possession of small amounts of marijuana. The impact of this announcement is twofold. One, it definitely does not recommend legalization of marijuana. Two, it could be influential in state legislatures, which currently have prohibitive criminal penalties attached to possession of even small amounts of marijuana.

The Senate Judiciary Committee has endorsed a form of decriminalization, which will be brought before the full Senate as part of the revision of the U.S. Criminal Code. The House is considering similar legislation.

The support by the two powerful and prestigious professional associations makes it easier for Congress to back decriminalization of marijuana. The thrust of this support is that current penalties often include marijuana in the catch-all of laws governing the use and possession of dangerous drugs.

Washington, D.C., offers a perfect example. The city council there recently passed a measure that would reduce the penalty for possession of less than one ounce of marijuana to a penalty similar to that for a traffic violation. At the same time it increased the penalty for sale and possession of heroin. The two were the same — a $1,000 fine and up to one year in jail — virtually a misdemeanor.

Decriminalization of marijuana is not an example of a nation gone soft on law enforcement, but demonstrates the plight of a country that is bogged down in processing petty marijuana possession cases while heroin pushers proliferate. The AMA-ABA appeal to lawmakers is a forward-thinking, supportive effort for Congress and the state legislatures.

St. Louis Globe-Democrat
St. Louis, Mo., December 7, 1977

HARMFUL EFFECTS OF POT

When the American Medical Association recently joined the American Bar Association in proposing an end to criminal penalties for using small amounts of marijuana it apparently jumped the gun.

An AMA council now has reported to the AMA house of delegates, meeting in Chicago, that recent research shows marijuana use has been linked to lung impairment in otherwise healthy persons and has caused rapid heart beat and psychiatric disturbances of various types.

"Flashbacks, the re-experiencing of the drug's intoxicating effects at a late date without further use, also have been reported by both regular and infrequent users," the council said.

It further has been shown that marijuana causes a drop in testerone levels in the blood of men, and that it could alter chromosomes and thus have a detrimental effect on the offspring of users.

But, having found this damaging new evidence, the AMA council asked the house of delegates only to modify a position it took five years ago when it advocated a policy of "discouragement" because of a "possibility of some deleterious effects on the user." The delegates, without dissent, accepted the report.

The council should have proposed that the AMA withdraw its recommendations to abolish criminal penalties on small amounts of pot for personal use. The delegates of this plan Tuesday will open the floodgates for use of this dangerous drug by giving it social acceptability and giving users the false impression that it is safe.

The idea of decriminalizing the possession of small amounts of marijuana while keeping criminal penalties on possession of large amounts of the drug has another major drawback. It assumes that only persons not connected with the sale and distribution of marijuana would take advantage of the immunity.

This is ludicrous. Pushers would immediately seize upon this loophole. They would carry only the limited amount specified as exempt from criminal prosecution. The net effect would be to make it infinitely safer for racketeers selling the drug to operate and to increase their gasoline usage.

The American Bar Association also should reassess its position in light of the new findings on marijuana.

The AMA and the ABA have an obligation to protect the health of Americans. Their proposal to decriminalize small amounts of marijuana is tantamount to helping a great many Americans to risk serious health damage because it could cause millions to think that it now is safe to use marijuana.

This is a totally irresponsible position for the AMA and ABA to take. Rather than joining in an unworthy movement to promote the wider use of this dangerous drug they should be engaged in finding ways to persuade Americans to stop using this menace to their health.

The fact that most marijuana users are relatively young makes this disservice by the AMA and ABA even more offensive. Many of these young people, in an effort to continue their pot habit, have been dismissing the research findings showing marijuana's harmful effects.

When two widely respected national professional organizations come along and say, in effect, "Yes, it's all right for you to use as much marijuana as you like," this gives pot users and potential users of the drug tremendous reinforcement of their bad judgment.

Each year brings new research showing marijuana's damaging effects. It is foolhardy in the face of this mounting evidence to enable millions more young people to get hooked on pot.

The Bill of Rights: Protecting criminals or our liberties?

The 1960's registered a series of landmark Supreme Court decisions extending fundamental due process rights to criminal defendants. Most of these rights had long been available to defendants in federal courts through the Bill of Rights. Sharp judicial conflicts marked the debate as to which sections of the Bill of Rights were guaranteed to citizens in state courts through the application of the Fourteenth Amendment. Under the late Chief Justice Earl Warren, a consensus was formed in the Court that held that the constitutional guarantees basic to due process, such as the Fourth Amendment protection against illegal search and seizure, the Fifth Amendment right against self-incrimination and the Sixth Amendment right to counsel and trial by jury should apply uniformly to start court proceedings.

The early 1970's marked a turning point in the due process activism of the Supreme Court. Chief Justice Warren retired, Warren Burger replaced him and several other justices were appointed to fill positions vacated. The advent of the Burger Court forced a halt in the Supreme Court's willingness to correct practices in state criminal proceedings through a liberal interpretation of the Fourteenth Amendment and the Bill of Rights. Though the Burger Court has yet to completely overturn the rulings of the Warren Court, it has narrowed them and carved out critical areas where they do not apply.

The exclusionary rule is a principle feature of the Warren Court that has been continually under attack. The rule promulgated first in *Mapp v. Ohio* forbids the use of any evidence in state criminal trials that was seized in violation of the Fourth Amendment search and seizure requirements.[1] The rule has no basis in the Fourth Amendment itself. Rather, the rule has been formulated by the Court to serve as a deterrent to illegal police practices. It is reasoned that if the police are unable to benefit by the fruit of their unconstitutional activity they will take pains to adhere to lawful procedures in their work.

Chief Justice Burger has long opposed the exclusionary rule on the ground that it has little or no effect on halting illegal police conduct but does allow the guilty to go free because of police bungling. The Chief Justice argues that other methods, such as administrative suits seeking monetary damages against the government for illegal searches and seizures, would be a more effective remedy to correct police impropriety.

While the Chief Justice has yet to succeed in scuttling the entire rule, he has whittled away at it by redefining the scope of illegal police conduct. In the Fourth Amendment sector, the Court has held that the financial records of an individual on file with a bank were not covered by the search and seizure requirements and therefore a search warrant was unnecessary.[2]

The exclusionary rule has also suffered in the area of confessions. In *Miranda v. Arizona*, it was required that police inform suspects in custody of their right to remain silent, of the right to counsel and to appointed counsel if they are indigent and the fact that any statement they made could be held against them.[3] If police obtain statements in violation of this rule they must be suppressed, and can not be used at trial. In the area of confessions, the exclusionary rule is of value not only in limiting police misconduct but in preventing the use of forced confessions which are inherently suspect.

The Burger Court has also redefined the rule on the law of confessions. In *Michigan v. Tucker,* the Supreme Court ruled that a defendant who had received all of the *Miranda* warnings from the police (except for his right to appointed counsel) was not permitted to suppress the testimony of an unfavorable witness.[4] The witness' existence was uncovered by the defendant's own statements which were suppressed. The majority of the Court reasoned that since the defendant had been warned of his right against self-incrimination, had not been coerced into making a statement, and the police had not acted in bad faith, exclusion of the witness' testimony would have little bearing on deterring future illegal police conduct. The import of the decision is that the strictures of the Warren Court governing police confessions were interpreted as only "prophylactic rules," a more flexible approach.

Miranda suffered further dilution in *Oregon v. Mathieson.*[5] The defendant had been called to a police station and informed that there was "incriminating evidence" against him. The suspect, a parolee, after confessing to the crime was informed of his *Miranda* rights. The Court held that the police were under no obligation to inform him of his right against self-incrimination prior to arrest because he had not been placed under arrest or in custody. The Court was of the view that the defendant's visit to the police station after he received the telephone call was a voluntary act rather than a result of any police coercion or intimidation. The majority also bypassed an examination of the parole status of the defendant: failure to appear for questioning could have caused revocation of his parole status. The police, the Court stated, are not obliged to read *Miranda* to every person they question. The dissenting justices argued that the majority's definition of "in custody," a situation necessary for triggering the *Miranda* warnings, was so restrictive that the police would be encouraged to first call a suspect to the police station, question him and only then arrest him.

However, over the strenuous dissent of Chief Justice Burger, the Supreme Court rejected an opportunity to make futher inroads into *Miranda* and the exclusionary rule in *Brewer v. Williams.*[6] Williams voluntarily surrendered to the police after having been charged with the murder of a 10-year-old girl. He was then transported in a police car to Des Moines. Before Williams departed for Des Moines the police promised the defendant's lawyer that he would not be questioned. During the course of the trip a detective in the car, addressing Williams as "Reverend," recited a religious sermon about the little girl's need for a "Christian burial." The detective was aware that Williams was both deeply religious and a recent escapee from a mental hospital. He hoped that by appealing to Williams' religious desire to see the child "properly buried" the suspect would reveal the location of the girl. Williams did lead the police to the body and the evidence was used in a trial resulting in his conviction. The Supreme Court reversed the conviction and ordered a new trial. The Court held that the defendant did not affirmatively waive his right to remain silent by leading the police to the dead girl. Rather, the police intentionally violated the attorney's express order not to question the suspect; the "Christian burial" speech was ruled a form of interrogation. Justice Thurgood Marshall used the occasion to challenge what Chief Justice Burger's minority decision described as "good work" on the part of the police:

> "[G]ood police work is something far different from catching the criminal at any price. It is equally important that the police as guardians of the law fulfill their responsibility to obey its commands scrupulously. For in the end life and liberty

can be as much endangered from illegal methods used to convict those thought to be criminals as from the actual criminals themselves"[7]

The effect on the local level of any substantive changes in the earlier Warren Court decisions is difficult to assess. Confessions have always played a minor role in crime-solving.[8] Even after *Miranda* the rate of confessions did not significantly diminish, partially because police questioning is inherently intimidating.[9] The Supreme Court's restrictions on search and seizure were frequently obstructed by police who lied about the circumstances of the arrest.[10] Trial courts in many jurisdictions, not overly sensitive to the rights of defendants, often gave the Supreme Court's decisions a narrow interpretation.[11] An unexpected twist, however, has been the growing trend of state appellate courts to expand defendant's rights by relying on independent state grounds, usually state constitutions or statutes.[12] Supreme Court rulings only mandate minimum constitutional standards; states may set more expansive ones.

Bail

The purpose of bail is to keep an accused out of prison until a trial has found him guilty. In this way those falsely accused of crimes will not unduly suffer imprisonment. The U.S. Constitution in the Eighth Amendment protects against excessive bail. Most state constitutions guarantee bail in all but capital cases.

The right to bail has been seriously compromised by the large numbers of defendants who lack the means to provide bail money. The problem is compounded by crowded trial court calendars which frequently require an individual to languish in prison a year or more before coming to trial. The consequences of this are obvious: deprivation of freedom for one still presumed innocent; loss of job or income; disruption of family and personal life; and difficulty in finding witnesses and preparing for trial. Periods in pre-trial detention also seem to have a direct correlation to success at trial: those unable to make bail are more likely to be found guilty than those charged with the same crimes who made bail, and more likely to be sentenced to prison terms than those released on bail.[13]

To remedy this situation, many states have paroled defendants on their own recognizance and dispensed with bail money. Being paroled on one's own recognizance requires that the individual have ties to the community such as a family, a job, a residence, etc. Such ties are an indication that the defendant will return to court for trial. Even with the special release programs judges remain hesitant to bail defendants accused of more serious crimes without an actual cash bond.

Historically the court's only concern in setting bail conditions was that the defendant appear for his trial. Now judges consider the weight of the evidence and the probability that the defendant will commit other crimes while at liberty. A study in the District of Columbia revealed that 7.5% of released defendants were alleged to have committed crimes while at liberty.[14] Society's interest in preventing the release of those likely to commit crimes prior to trial must be balanced against the realization that at present no sophisticated methods exist to predict who will commit future crimes. At the least, elaborate court procedures would have to be established to carefully review the record of each defendant. The result might well lead to even more congested courts: the cause of the bail crisis in the first place.

Grand Juries

The grand jury has been a feature of Anglo-Saxon jurisprudence since the twelfth century. Its symbolic role as an impediment to governmental abuse has its historical antecedents in the grand jury's opposition to the political persecutions of the Stuart dynasty in seventeenth century England. The secretive nature of grand jury functions is also rooted in this period when jurors were targets of the king's wrath.

After the American Revolution the right to be indicted by a grand jury was incorporated into the Fifth Amendment of the Constitution. The founding fathers believed that a person should not be placed in jeopardy of a felony prosecution unless a body of citizens finds it probable that he committed the offense charged. Many states also followed suit by constitutionally requiring an indictment by grand jury for any felony charge. However, in *Hurtado v. California,* the Supreme Court held that a grand jury indictment in state criminal court was not necessary for due process of law under the Fourteenth Amendment.[15]

Hurtado encouraged a number of states to either eliminate indictment by grand jury or circumvent it. Some critics viewed this as a not undesirable result. The independent role of the grand jury in preventing prosecutors from arbitrarily indicting citizens for serious crimes had largely disappeared by the twentieth century. England, the birthplace of the grand jury, had abolished it in 1933, finding it obsolete.

The grand jury's power to initiate and conduct its own independent investigation is so rarely invoked that when it does the term "run-away grand jury" is used. The grand jury has become little more than a tool of prosecutors in obtaining criminal indictments.[16] Indictments by a grand jury are supposed to be grounded on a quantum of evidence sufficient to prove a *prima facie* case at trial.[17] However, the prosecutor's practice of only presenting facts favorable to the state's position has prevented grand juries from obtaining a complete picture of the entire episode. In many states witnesses under investigation have no right to testify before a grand jury. Nor are prosecutors under any obligation to reveal exculpatory evidence, that is, evidence favorable to the target of the grand jury investigation. Neither in state nor federal grand juries do witnesses have the right to have their counsel present.

Another criticism of the grand jury system is that the members of the grand jury are not representative of the population at large. Grand juries generally tend to be composed of elderly, white males with high incomes.[18] The frequency of such composition is so common that the term "blue-ribbon grand jury" has been coined. The make-up of a grand jury is of critical importance in determining the outcome of its decisions. One observer concluded: "The composition of a grand jury will inevitably influence which topics the grand jurors choose to investigate and which persons they indict."[19]

In 1977, the Supreme Court overturned the conviction of a Mexican-American because the ratio of minority group members on the Texas grand jury was disproportionately lower than their ratio to the general population.[20] The Court found that a *prima facie* case of juror discrimination in the context of the Fourteenth Amendment had been demonstrated.

A movement to reform the grand jury gained impetus during the years of the Nixon Administration when the Justice Department impaneled grand juries throughout the country. Their purpose was to investigate a wide range of political and radical activities and was generally not aimed at solving any particular crimes.[21] Though the Nixon administration's use of the grand jury was of unique dimensions, the practice of conducting probes without any specific goals was not. The Supreme Court, as early as 1906, had ruled such practices not unconstitutional.[22]

The possible threats that such grand jury activity may pose to civil liberties have been enhanced by recent Supreme Court decisions that sharply curtail the protections of the Bill of Rights before grand juries.

Since 1966, the Supreme Court has recognized the right of a grand jury to use illegally obtained evidence in the pursuit of its investigation.[23] This exception to the Fourth Amendment search and seizure provision was widened considerably in *United States v. Calandra.*[24] There it was held that a witness had no right to refuse to answer grand jury questions based upon the illegal seizure of evidence. The exclusionary rule, the Court reasoned, had no application in a grand jury proceeding investigating criminal activity. Then in 1976 the Supreme Court appeared to reject a witness' right to receive *Miranda* warnings before a grand jury, even if he was the focus of a criminal investigation.[25] In that case, *United States v. Mandujano,* the witness was called before a grand jury. There he gave perjured testimony. He had not been given full *Miranda* warnings even though he was the target of a prosecutorial investigation. The Court argued that no witness had a right to lie before a grand jury and therefore exclusion of the perjured testimony was inappropriate. However, a plurality of the Court, led by Chief Justice Burger, opined that *Miranda* warnings were totally inappropriate in a grand jury: judicial inquires and custodial investigation were not constitutionally equivalent. Furthermore, *Miranda* was fashioned in part to preserve the suspect's right to counsel. But in the grand jury where a witness has no right to counsel the logic of *Miranda* fades. Any doubts about the place of *Miranda* in the grand jury were put to rest in *United States v. Washington.*[26] In *Washington* the witness did not perjure himself, but instead gave self-incriminating evidence to the grand jury which was used against him in a subsequent trial. As with Mandujano, Washington was also a target of a prosecutorial investigation and was never so informed. The Court, now in a majority opinion, rejected the claim of any suspect to be warned of his constitutional right to remain silent.

Incidents of perceived grand jury abuse and judicial diminutions of individual rights before the grand jury have engendered the introduction of a reform proposal in the 1977 session of Congress. The bill would only apply to federal grand juries. Its most salient features are: the right of a witness to be warned that he is the target of an investigation; the requirement that exculpatory material be presented to the grand jury; prohibit the government from calling witnesses who have indicated a prior intention of invoking the Fifth Amendment self-incrimination clause; permit private counsel in the grand jury room; limit the grand jury subpoena power; require the recording of the proceedings; and a return to transactional immunity.[27]

The American Bar Association is giving its strong support to the proposal. The bill is opposed by the Justice Department and various prosecutorial and law enforcement associations that claim criminal investigations would be unduly hindered by the bill's passage. Whatever the outcome, the image of the grand jury standing with the individual against the state has become a vestige of the past.

Notes

1. *Mapp v. Ohio,* 367 U.S. 643 (1961).
2. *United States v. Miller,* 425 U.S. 435 (1976).
3. *Miranda v. Arizona,* 384 U.S. 486 (1966).
4. *Michigan v. Tucker,* 417 U.S. 433 (1974).
5. *Oregon v. Mathieson,* 429 U.S. 492 (1977).
6. *Brewer v. Williams,* 430 U.S. 387 (1977).
7. *Brewer, supra,* 407.
8. "Interrogations in New Haven: The Impact of Miranda," 76 *Yale Law Journal* 1519, 1613 (1967).
9. *Ibid.*
10. For a discussion of police reaction to the exclusionary rule, see Jerome H. Skolnick, *Justice Without Trial* (New York: John Wiley & Sons, 1966) pp. 215–219.
11. For a discussion of the general problems encountered enforcing defendant's rights in the

state trial courts see Anthony G. Amsterdam, "The Supreme Court and the Rights of Suspects in Criminal Cases," 45 *New York University Law Review* 785 (1970).

12. See generally Donald E. Wilkes, Jr., "The New Federalism in Criminal Procedure: State Court Evasion of the Burger Court," 62 *Kentucky Law Journal* 421 (1974); Jerome B. Falk, Jr., "The State Constitution: A More Than Adequate Non Federal Ground," 61 *California Law Review* 273 (1973).

13. "Money Bail as a Denial of Equal Protection," (Bellamy Brief) in *Prisoners' Rights Sourcebook,* ed. by Marilyn G. Haft & Michele G. Hermann. (New York: Clark Boardman, 1973) pp. 133–162.

14. *Report of the D.C. Crime Commission Study,* quoted in *Pre-trial Release: American Bar Association Project on Minimum Standards for Criminal Justice* (New York: Institute of Judicial Administration, 1968) pp. 66–68. For a general discussion of the problems of bail and other pre-trial release programs see, Paul B. Wice, *Freedom for Sale,* (Lexington, Mass: D.C. Heath, 1974).

15. *Hurtado v. California,* 110 U.S. 156 (1884). The Fifth Amendment right to be indicted by a grand jury, along with the Seventh Amendment right to a jury trial in any civil matter where more than $20 is in dispute are the only sections of the Bill of Rights that are not applicable to the states under the Fourteenth Amendment.

16. See Robert G. Johnston, "The Grand Jury: Prosecutorial Abuse of the Indictment Process," 65 *Journal of Criminal Law and Criminology* 157, 160–61 (1974); Comment, "Federal Grand Jury Investigation of Political Dissidents," 7 *Harvard Civil Liberties Review* 432, 440 (1972).

17. *Prima facie* may be defined as evidence sufficient to establish a given fact, unless rebutted or contradicted. A *prima facie* case, however, is insufficient to prove guilt.

18. Jon Van Dyke, "The Grand Jury: Representative or Elite?" 28 *Hastings Law Review* 37 (1976).

19. *Ibid.,* p. 38.

20. *Castenada v. Partida,* 430 U.S. 482 (1977).

21. Fred J. Solowey, "Grand Jury and Post-Watergate America," 10 *Trial* 32 (1974).

22. *Hale v. Henkel,* 201 U.S. 43 (1906).

23. *United States v. Blue,* 384 U.S. 251 (1966).

24. *United States v. Calandra,* 414 U.S. 564 (1976).

25. *United States v. Mandujano,* 425 U.S. 564 (1976).

26. *United States v. Washington,* 431 U.S. 181 (1977).

27. Transactional immunity is a form of immunity that assures the witness to whom it has been given that he will not be prosecuted for any offenses to which his testimony relates. This section of the bill is a response to the Supreme Court decision of *Kastigar v. United States,* 406 U.S. 441 (1972), where it was held that witnesses were only entitled to "use immunity." "Use immunity" would only protect a witness from prosecution upon the specific facts to which he testified, not to the entire incident. Thus a prosecutor could bring criminal charges against a witness who testified under "use immunity" if independent sources exist as a basis for the prosecution.

'ILLEGAL' EVIDENCE PERMITTED, LIMITING 'EXCLUSIONARY RULE'

The Supreme Court July 6 held, 6–3, that federal courts could not set aside a state conviction on the grounds that illegally obtained evidence had been used if a defendant had a "full and fair" opportunity to raise the evidence question in state courts. The ruling marked a retreat by the high court from advocacy of the 'exclusionary rule'—a rule barring from evidence material acquired illegally by law enforcement officers. The rule had been developed by courts to deter police from deliberately violating Fourth Amendment protections against unreasonable search and seizure. The exclusionary rule had applied to federal trials since 1921 and to state trials since 1961. In 1969, the Supreme Court had held that federal courts, in reviewing state convictions, should consider challenges based on the exclusionary rule. It was this view which the present ruling reversed as "unjustified."

Prisoners had been challenging state court convictions by instituting a habeas corpus proceeding in federal court. Such a proceeding permitted a federal judge to set aside the conviction if the trial fell short of constitutional standards, i.e., if illegally obtained evidence had been used.

Justice Lewis F. Powell Jr., author of the majority opinion, argued that "application of the [exclusionary] rule...deflects the truthfinding process and often frees the guilty." He went on to note that "the disparity in particular cases between the error committed by the police officer and the windfall afforded a guilty defendant by application of the rule is contrary to the idea of proportionality that is essential to the concept of justice." In a concurring opinion, Chief Justice Warren E. Burger criticized the exclusionary rule as a "draconian, discredited device" which no longer should be employed.

Justice William J. Brennan Jr. wrote a sharply worded dissent that was joined by Justice Thurgood Marshall. Brennan maintained that use of illegally seized evidence in a trial created a "constitutional deprivation" and that it was precisely the function of federal courts to afford habeas corpus relief in such situations. The third dissenter was Justice Byron R. White. White agreed with Brennan on the role for federal courts in such cases, but observed that the exclusionary rule had become "a senseless obstacle to arriving at the truth in many criminal trials." White urged that it not be applied in cases where an officer acted in "good faith belief that his conduct comported with existing law...."

The ruling, which had the effect of upholding the California and Nebraska murder convictions of two men, came on the cases of *Stone v. Powell* and *Wolff v. Rice*.

On the same day, the court issued two other rulings strengthening the hand of law enforcement officers against challenges based on the Fourth Amendment. They were:

■ A 7–2 ruling that law officers trying to block illegal aliens could, without a warrant or specific reason, stop automobiles at permanent check points not on an international border and question occupants.

■ A 5–4 ruling that police could constitutionally search cars impounded for traffic violations, and use as evidence for unrelated charges items found in the car.

The Salt Lake Tribune
Salt Lake City, Utah, July 8, 1976

In strictly curbing state prisoners' rights to relief in federal court the Supreme Court of the United States acted to end abuse of a good thing.

There is little doubt that state prisoners took outrageous advantage of earlier court rulings which made it easy to seek redress from real or imagined wrongs by state tribunals. The number of such appeals grew to ridiculous extremes.

The Tuesday ruling substantially limits the scope of habeas corpus proceedings under which federal judges have been able to order new trials where an inmate's original trial was marked by constitutional defects. Many such actions involved claims that the individual was convicted on evidence obtained in violation of Four Amendment rights against illegal searches.

State prisoners, with plenty of time and nothing to lose, had been bringing all kinds of charges of constitutional impropriety during their state court trials. They had clearly corrupted what was and is a fundamentally sound means of correcting errors of the lower courts. The appeal option also served notice on police and other state officials that the high court would not countenance illegal police and judicial shortcuts. Actual effect in this area is hotly debated, however.

In its 6 to 3 ruling the court majority apparently sought to preserve the opportunity of appeal for ruly meritorious cases. It permitted an exception to the ban—where the defendant can show that the state did not provide an opportunity for "full and fair litigation" of Fourth Amendment, and presumably other, constitutional claims.

Depending on the attitudes of the 50 state court systems regarding unreasonable searches and seizures, probable cause and like matters, the practical effect of the high court ruling could be to severely limit the citizen's protection in these areas.

The possible negative results will be slow emerging. But state prisoners and others considering frivolous judicial action will get the message right away. Federal courts are maintained for serious business, not to help a prisoner pass time or to rule on every disagreement that comes down the pike.

THE DALLAS TIMES HERALD

Dallas, Tex., July 8, 1976

THE ISSUE: New Supreme Court decisions on the rights of criminal defendants.

THE SUPREME COURT, in a handful of decisions handed down Tuesday, has strengthened the hand of police and prosecutors in criminal cases, but has laid a heavier burden on judges in state courts.

In separate cases the justices have ruled that: 1. A prisoner who has had a fair chance in state courts to prove that he was convicted on illegally seized evidence isn't entitled to appeal to the federal courts; 2. Illegally seized evidence may be used in a federal civil case, such as a trial to determine tax liability; 3. Police making a routine inventory of an auto impounded for illegal parking may look inside a closed glove compartment without violating the owner's rights; 4. The Border Patrol doesn't need a warrant to stop a motorist and question him briefly, even if officers have no reason to suspect the presence of illegal aliens in the car.

Obviously, the decisions ease the burden of police and prosecutors, who have accused the federal courts of hamstringing justice during the past several years by releasing guilty defendants on "technicalities," such as improperly drawn search warrants or other lapses in paperwork.

It is disheartening to the public to see murderers and thieves set free for flimsy reasons. And perhaps the Supreme Court's backpedalling on defendants' rights affirmed by the court only a few years ago is necessary to rebalance the scales of Lady Justice.

However, the police and prosecutors must not construe the new decisions as a license for sloppiness or a permit to run roughshod over the rights of citizens who fall into the clutches of the law. After all, it was bad investigation and prosecution that brought about the so-called "criminal-coddling" decisions of the court in the first place. If the enforcers of the law don't maintain a little slack in the longer tether they have been given, it may be shortened again.

The decisions place a lot of confidence in the ability of state and local judges to protect the rights of citizens who come before them. These judges must be vigilant in fulfilling that responsibility.

The judicial system must be just as vigilant in protecting the rights of the victims of crime—and society at large. Justice demands that no innocent person be punished; justice also demands that no one who has committed a crime be allowed to escape punishment because of overly rigid guidelines.

The Supreme Court's latest rulings provide a needed brake to the permissive decisions of the recent past, which too often favored the criminal at the expense of the law-abiding citizen.

The Seattle Times

Seattle, Wash., July 11, 1976

THE pendulum which had swung too far in the direction of giving criminals' rights greater weight than those of law-abiding citizens during Chief Justice Earl Warren's Supreme Court tenure has been slowly moving back toward the center.

The so-called Burger court has produced several decisions in recent months narrowing the rights of criminal defendants. The latest, last week, was a ruling that a defendant may not challenge his state-court conviction in federal courts on grounds that evidence used at his trial had been obtained illegally by police.

Appeals to federal courts had become commonplace since the high court's holding in 1961 that evidence obtained in illegal searches had to be excluded from consideration in trials as a means of deterring police misconduct.

Emphasizing that it was not sanctioning the use of evidence obtained in violation of Fourth Amendment rights, the Supreme Court majority said that state appellate courts are fully capable of handling illegal-search problems and that reviews in the federal courts are unnecessary.

That finding was a practical response to the over-use of the federal appeals process.

Justice Lewis F. Powell noted that indiscriminate application of the "exclusionary rule" (the legal term describing the grounds for appeal on illegal-search issues) has generated a disrespect for the law and administration of justice.

Its use in recent years, the court said, often hes deflected the truth-finding process and has allowed guilty men to go free.

Few thoughtful Americans would quibble with the fundamental theme of the majority's finding that "the ultimate question of guilt or innocence should be the central concern in a criminal proceeding."

THE ARIZONA REPUBLIC

Phoenix, Ariz., July 7, 1976

The U.S. Supreme Court took another sharp turn back toward more realistic law-and-order guarantees yesterday with a crippling decision on the so-called "exclusionary rule."

By a vote of 6-3, the high court said that federal courts may not automatically free state prisoners on grounds that criminal evidence was seized illegally.

Since 1961, when the Supreme Court under Chief Justice Earl Warren institutionalized the "exclusionary rule," federal courts have been flooded with thousands of prisoners' petitions for release or retrial. The Warren court, in effect, ruled that evidence seized without a search warrant cannot be admitted at a trial.

The ruling has crippled police work time and again, and led to freedom for obviously guilty criminals.

For example, smugglers caught red-handed with caches of dope have been set free because courts ruled police discovered the contraband only incidentally to another arrest action.

One of the cases leading to yesterday's high court decision involved a Nebraska man whose conviction for the bombing murder of a policeman was thrown out because of a defective search warrant.

Police long have maintained that the "exclusionary rule" gives criminals the edge in court, and forces trials to concentrate on procedural matters instead of the crime and the guilt of the accused.

On that point, the high court yesterday spoke out loud and clear.

In the majority opinion written by Justice Lewis Powell, the court said that the "exclusionary rule"—which exists only in the United States — diverts justice "from the ultimate question of guilt or innocence that should be the central concern."

The Fourth Amendment still prevents police authorities from "unreasonable searches and seizures." There is nothing unreasonable about police, acting in good-faith law enforcement, discovering prima facie evidence for use in criminal trial work.

In its latest decision, the Supreme Court is departing from the liberal dogma of the high court of the 1960s, which gave criminals undue protection, while lessening society's.

FORT WORTH STAR-TELEGRAM

Fort Worth, Tex., July 9, 1976

The Supreme Court, after years of rulings that seemed bent on making it impossible to put a criminal behind bars, now appears to be taking a more rational tack.

In its latest major decision it has reduced one of the loopholes that many convicted criminals were using to get out of prison and back into their lawbreaking careers.

That loophole was a 1969 decision that allowed prisoners sentenced by state courts to appeal to federal courts on grounds that the evidence presented against them was illegally obtained.

The 1969 decision was related to one issued in 1961 requiring state courts to exclude from criminal trials any evidence obtained in violation of the constitutional guarantee against unreasonable searches and seizures.

The 1961 ruling was a sound one. But the 1969 decision had, as Justice Lewis Powell Jr. said in the new ruling, interfered with the truth finding process and often freed the guilty.

Under the new ruling, state prisoners will not be granted a second chance in federal court to argue that the evidence against them was illegally obtained if "the state has provided an opportunity for full and fair litigation" on the claim.

The dissenters to the 6-3 decision—Justices William Brennan Jr., Thurgood Marshall and Byron White—expressed fear that "the same treatment ultimately will be accorded state prisoners' claims of violations of other constitutional rights."

A concern for the protection of constitutional rights is always justified.

At the moment, however, the rights of crime's victims are the ones in most urgent need of attention. And victims' rights can be better protected when punishment for the criminal is made more certain, thus serving as a deterrent to crime.

By making it more difficult for a criminal convicted in a state court to get out through an appeal to a federal court, therefore, the new Supreme Court ruling represents a significant blow for the rights of the victim.

The Detroit News

Detroit, Mich., July 9, 1976

The U.S. Supreme Court took measured strides this week toward a more rational view of the so-called exclusionary rule, which has caused so many miscarriages of justice since 1961.

A product of the Earl Warren court, the exclusionary rule requires state courts to exclude evidence obtained by "unreasonable search and seizure," even though such evidence may decisively prove the guilt of the suspect. In short, it orders the courts to close their minds against the truth.

In a series of practical decisions, the Supreme Court this week expanded the definition of reasonable search and seizure, increased the federal government's power to use illegally-obtained evidence in court and limited the power of federal courts to set aside state court convictions that rely on such evidence.

As a result, it is now reasonable for a border patrolman, in his search for illegal aliens, to stop and question motorists at a checkpoint without running off to court each time for a warrant. If police find evidence of a crime in a car they impounded for a parking violation, that evidence may be used at the trial of the suspect. Evidence illegally seized by police and ruled inadmissible in state courts may nevertheless be used by the federal government as evidence in a civil tax proceeding.

In curtailing the right of prisoners to challenge their convictions on the grounds of illegal search and seizure, the Supreme Court said the exclusionary rule diverts attention "from the ultimate question of guilt or innocence that should be the central concern."

One of the cases on which the court ruled this week provides an outrageous example of justice diverted from its main course.

In 1970, an Omaha policeman answered an anonymous report that a woman was in danger in a vacant house. As he entered the house, a bomb exploded and killed him. Police identified the caller and sought him at the home of a known companion.

Nobody answered the door, so they got a search warrant. In the house they found 14 sticks of dynamite, caps, a battery, wire pincers and other items used in the manufacture of bombs. These findings were used in evidence at a suspect's trial, which ended in the man's conviction of first-degree murder. A federal judge overturned the conviction, asserting that there had been no sufficient statement to support the search warrant.

This absurdity, thank God, has now been corrected by a Supreme Court decision reinstating the conviction. Unfortunately, the Supreme Court failed to follow its own reasoning all the way to the logical conclusion.

First, the justices observed that the exclusionary rule directs attention away from the main business at hand. Second, they stated that indiscriminate application of the rule could generate disrespect for the law and the administration of justice. Third, with reference to the case described above, they restricted federal use of the rule to order a new trial. Fourth, however, they said the rule can still be used in trials.

We agree with Chief Justice Warren E. Burger's separate opinion stating that the exclusionary rule, which he described as a "judicially contrived doctrine," should be even more severely restricted or abandoned entirely.

This does not suggest any desire to destroy the Fourth Amendment, which protects citizens against unreasonable search and seizure. When the police violate that amendment, they should be punished for doing so; but it makes no sense to punish society by letting convicted murderers walk free on a technicality — which is still possible.

The Supreme Court has written a more reasonable interpretation of the meaning and uses of the Fourth Amendment but obviously the issue has not yet been completely and satisfactorily resolved. The mills of justice grind slowly.

St. Louis Globe-Democrat

St. Louis, Mo., July 7, 1976

The Supreme Court's decision that a defendant may not challenge his state court criminal conviction in federal courts on the grounds that police illegally obtained evidence used at his trial should close a big escape hatch for many convicted murderers and perpetrators of other violent crimes.

This decision reversed lower federal court rulings ordering new trials for murder defendants. The Supreme Court majority (the vote was 6 to 3) said that state courts are capable of resolving illegal search problems, and the review by federal courts is unnecessary.

In Tuesday's ruling, the high court closed one of the avenues used most frequently by those condemned to death for murder. Even if there was no real challenge to police evidence obtained in a search, appeals contesting the legality of these searches could delay final determination of these cases for years.

The volume of cases of this nature rose sharply after the Warren Supreme Court in 1961 held that illegal evidence must be excluded at criminal trials in order to deter police misconduct. Tuesday's decree coming close on the heels of the Supreme Court's historic ruling upholding the death penalty and sustaining capital punishment statutes in Florida, Texas and Georgia, has made it unmistakably clear that the days of the high court leaning over backward to find technicalities upon which murderers can be freed are over.

The present, more conservatively oriented Supreme Court is steering a middle course, observing the rights of the accused but not providing them with the means for long delays or frustrating attempts to bring them to justice. This is a healthy trend. It should reduce crime in the nation substantially as criminals begin to recognize they can't beat the system by appealing their cases forever.

AKRON BEACON JOURNAL

Akron, Ohio, July 9, 1976

THE U. S. SUPREME Court apparently has decided that state courts are now adequate to "police the police" in cases involving illegal arrests and searches.

The ruling seems to signal part of the growing trend by the Burger Court to ease away from the activist role staked out by the old Warren Court.

Tuesday's ruling leaves a feeling of ambivalence: On the one hand, it leaves open to question whether the state courts can be trusted to offer adequate protection under the Fourth Amendment; on the other, it is an attempt to limit the seemingly endless appeal process and help clear crowded federal dockets.

In a matter weighing constitutional protection on one side and streamlining court caseloads on the other, the balance should go to the Constitution, it seems to us. Still, the court has a way of stepping back in when constitutional abuses abound; so it might be worth seeing how the state courts rise to the challenge.

In its 6-3 ruling, the Supreme Court decided that, for the most part, federal courts won't bother with prisoners convicted in state courts with evidence that police took in arrests and searches which violated the Fourth Amendment.

The Fourth Amendment states: "The right of the the people to be secure in their persons, houses, papers and effects, against unreasonable searches and seizures, shall not be violated, and no warrants shall issue, but upon probable cause, supported by oath or affirmation, and particularly describing the place to be searched and the persons or things to be seized."

The court held that a state prisoner could win his release by going to federal court only if he could prove he had not been given a "full and fair opportunity" to make his complaint in state courts, and that his Fourth Amendment rights were violated by the use at his trial of evidence obtained in an unconstitutional search and seizure.

Justice Lewis F. Powell Jr., writing for the majority, said the court would still require that evidence obtained by illegal means be barred from use in criminal trials. But the enforcement apparently will lie almost entirely with state appellate courts from now on.

However, it is worth noting that most of the constitutional milestones in Supreme Court rulings on Fourth Amendment rights came as a result of the federal appeal process after state appeals were exhausted. One of the most important, Mapp v. Ohio (1961), involved Ohio's supreme court, which had upheld the conviction of a woman based primarily on the introduction of evidence "unlawfully seized during an unlawful search of defendant's home."

The enforcement of the Fourth Amendment is not designed to help criminals beat the system. It is to protect the constitutional rights of the rest of us by keeping the police within proper bounds.

It may be that the Burger Court now sees the ground staked out by predecessor courts as clear and adhered to by state courts. The Supreme Court still is available for complaints about violations of the Fourth Amendment. But most of the watching over this important constitutional right will now sit squarely on the shoulders of state courts. Whether those shoulders are broad enough remains to be seen.

HOUSTON CHRONICLE

Houston, Tex., July 23, 1976

Only time and experience will tell whether the U.S. Supreme Court has hit a reasonable balance in its recent rulings on "search and seizure."

During its last term, and particularly in a series of term-ending decisions, a court majority has significantly narrowed some of the constitutional protections against "unreasonable search and seizure" that were so tightly woven by the court under the late Chief Justice Earl Warren.

It has long been evident that the Warren court went too far in its rulings barring use of evidence judged to be illegally obtained by authorities. These rulings have hampered law enforcement personnel and are a principal reason for the continual outcry about the known guilty going free on technicalities.

That viewpoint is perhaps best expressed by Justice Lewis Powell, writing for the court in the most noteworthy of the recent decisions. It cut back sharply on the right of prisoners convicted in state courts to then go into federal courts and obtain their release or a new trial based on a claim that evidence used against them was obtained illegally in some way. Powell wrote:

"Application of the rule (barring use of the evidence). . .deflects the truth-finding process and often frees the guilty. The disparity in particular cases between the error committed by the police officer and the windfall afforded a guilty defendant by application of the rule is contrary to the idea of proportionality that is essential to the concept of justice."

Most of the court's search-and-seizure decisions this term — and many last term — have been along the lines of giving police and prosecutors a stronger hand. For instance, allowing the border patrol to stop cars at away-from-the-border checkpoints and briefly question occupants in a search for illegal aliens, without the necessity of a warrant or legal reason to believe the car contains illegals. And the decision which found proper the use of evidence (marijuana) obtained in a routine search of a car impounded only for a parking violation.

We believe it reasonable that law enforcement authorities not be hampered in obtaining and presenting evidence by the kind of nitpicking technicalities which have become the hallmark of the search-and-seizure dispute. That is what the Supreme Court seems to be saying and with this we agree.

At the same time we are keenly aware that there also must be strong legal restraints on deliberate or clearly improper abuses of a citizen's search-and-seizure rights by police and prosecutors.

That is what helped produce the Warren court's rulings in the first place. Authorities must not be allowed to react excessively to their perceived new freedom of action.

Police and prosecutors should keep in mind they have not now been set free to run roughshod in seeking evidence. The key aspect of the major decision cutting back federal court access in these cases is not that illegally obtained evidence is admissible in court, but that state courts have a duty to decide those questions under Supreme Court guidelines and should be allowed to with finality not subject to constant federal second-guessing.

State courts and police and prosecutors are thus put on notice they must be sensitive to this constitutional right. It is up to them to disprove the notion that true justice can only be had in the federal courts. It is a challenge local courts and authorities should gladly accept, considering their previous complaints of federal interference.

In this years-long controversy over search-and-seizure rights, honest men have been searching for a middle ground. We shall just have to see if the Supreme Court has now found it.

Arkansas Gazette.

Little Rock, Ark., July 10, 1976

Just before quitting for the summer, the Burger Court knocked a chunk off the "exclusionary rule" — a passport to freedom handed guilty criminals by the Warren Court 15 years ago. The Burger Court didn't go far enough in undoing the rule, however, and more needs to be done.

The rule worked (and still works) like this: The police bring cold proof of a crime to court, but the accused shows that, in gathering the evidence, they invaded his privacy. The judge excludes the evidence and the guilty man goes free.

Convictions immediately took a nosedive when the rule was adopted in 1961. The Warren Court justified the rule by declaring that the police had to be absolutely sure in amassing evidence not to breach the Fourth Amendment's ban on illegal search and seizure.

That sounds good; nobody wants to be broken in upon. But prosecutors and others have argued for years that there's something awfully wrong with justice when a court declares police procedure to be worse than a vicious crime itself — especially when the proof of the crime is beyond question.

Prosecutors asked the Burger Court en masse to throw out the exclusionary rule and find some other way for citizens to get redress when police wrongfully breach their privacy. The court wouldn't throw out the rule but it did declare that any defendant who fails in future to argue invasion of privacy during his trial in a state court can't get a habeas corpus to argue his case in federal court. In other words, he has his chance at his trial and doesn't get a second one.

That means, of course, that the exclusionary rule still applies and that the guilty can still go free because of police blunders in gathering evidence — failing to get a warrant, mainly. It also means that federal appeals courts can still second-guess trial courts on the question of whether they rule properly on invasions of the defendants' privacy.

The only gain for justice is that a convicted criminal who fails to argue breach of privacy at his trial can't do it later. The practical effect of the restriction, however, may be slight. Criminal lawyers will simply make certain to throw in the "privacy" argument during trial, knowing they can get a federal review later if the trial judge turns them down.

So the real problem still remains — how to take the curse off cold, convicting evidence of crime in cases of police error. Often the crime is horrible and the police error trifling, which adds to the obvious defeat of justice under the exclusionary rule.

The British look at the thing differently. If the police get the goods on a criminal, he gets what's coming to him. If the police err, then the person whose privacy has been invaded can sue. In this way, the rights of the innocent are protected but the criminal isn't able to use his privacy as a shield against punishment.

That's how it ought to be in this country. Congress is considering authorizing the right to sue under the Fourth Amendment. If such a law were adopted, then the Supreme Court might be induced to undo the evil done under the exclusionary rule. It could take the privacy shield away from the guilty (who don't deserve it) and limit its use to the innocent, who at present have no protection at all.

The Ottawa Citizen

Ottawa, Ont., July 17, 1976

The United States Supreme Court has ruled that a prisoner may not be released from jail simply on the grounds that the evidence used to convict him was illegally obtained.

This is a step back from the earlier trend established by the more liberal pre-Warren Burger court, which ruled that accused people have rights under the constitution which offer protection from illegally-obtained evidence.

While the latest ruling does not go so far as to permit the use of unconstitutionally-obtained evidence, it is nonetheless indicative of the growing resentment in the U.S. toward what has been called the revolving-door legal system.

Despite the new ruling, American law is still light-years ahead of Canada.

Illegally-obtained evidence is admissible as evidence in Canadian courts. For example, even if police conduct a search without benefit of a warrant, whatever is uncovered can still be introduced as evidence.

Even more dangerous is the writ of assistance, the instrument which permits the RCMP to enter any premises and conduct a search without establishing before a magistrate that there is a legitimate need for that search.

Canadians simply do not have the same kind of constitutional guarantees which are available to citizens of the U.S. It is high time they did.

The Boston Globe

Boston, Mass., July 12, 1976

In the session that ended last week, the US Supreme Court took a number of steps along the road toward expanded police powers — expanded powers that may add to confusion in the administration of justice rather than improve control of crime.

This is not to say that the court has been single-mindedly chipping away at all civil liberties. The same court, in the same session, improved the outlook for many Americans by banning discriminatory handling of housing subsidies, giving women greater freedom of choice in connection with abortion, sharply curtailing judicial gag rules on the press and barring racial discrimination by private schools.

But the court has, in the area of criminal justice, opened some major uncertainties. In its most spectacular ruling it has said the death penalty is not automatically cruel and unusual punishment — but it has yet to spell out the precise terms under which it would sanction that penalty. By inviting the states to deal with the problem, it has come close to implying that a man might be executed for a crime in one state but receive a lesser penalty for the same crime in another state.

The court also upheld arrests for "probable cause" without warrants, even when the police had time to obtain warrants as required by the Fourth Amendment. The decision is almost certain to prompt further summary arrests by at least some police officers.

But its most important decision, the one that threatens to produce the greatest amount of confusion, is its decision not to review in the future any state convictions based on illegally seized evidence so long as that issue had been reviewed at the state level.

The Fourth Amendment ban on unreasonable search and seizures is quite broad and had been the basis for many appeals to Federal courts. In such cases, a defendant might have been accused of one crime on evidence obtained legally. During investigation, police might have seized material they thought was evidence of some other, unrelated crime. But since that evidence had not been named in the original warrant, courts have ruled that it could not be used in new or enlarged prosecution.

The objective of this practice has been to discourage police from engaging in "fishing expeditions," accusing a person of one crime, perhaps trivial, in order to snoop around to see whether something else is going on.

The Supreme Court did not repeal the Fourth Amendment, of course. But it did throw virtually the entire burden of enforcing its provisions onto the state courts. Some states will do that job well. Last Wednesday, for example, the Massachusetts Superior Court ruled against admission of evidence in the Saxe case specifically because it had been obtained illegally.

The danger is that there will now be 50 different interpretations of the meaning of the Fourth Amendment — not tomorrow, but over time. Judges are human. State judges don't like their rulings to be overturned by Federal courts. As long as their Fourth Amendment rulings were subject to Federal review, state judges could be expected to try to be consistent with Federal precedents. Now, no longer subject to that review, individual state judges may well take a less rigorous stance on the meaning of the Fourth Amendment.

There are a number of important ingredients to justice. One of them is uniformity of application. Whatever the court's motives, it has clearly moved away from that principle. Justice, with time, will suffer accordingly.

Detroit Free Press

Detroit, Mich., July 17, 1976

ONCE AGAIN, the U.S. Supreme Court has taken a long step back from the Warren Court's landmark decisions on civil liberties. which revolutionized American jurisprudence in the 1950s and 1960s.

In a series of four rulings handed down this month, the high court sharply limited the so-called "exclusionary rule," under which evidence obtained ilelgally by police can be excluded from consideration in criminal trials.

The court held that:

• Federal courts may not grant relief to defendants convicted in state courts on the basis of illegally seized evidence.

• Police may search an impounded automobile without a warrant, even if the auto was impounded for non-investigatory reasons, and may introduce in court any evidence obtained by such a search.

• Evidence excluded from a state court because it was obtained illegally may be used by the federal government in tax liability cases.

• The U.S. Border Patrol may make random checks on motorists at permanent, "reasonably located" checkpoints on highways— even when officers have no warrant and no reasonable suspicions about the motorists they stop.

Taken as a whole, this series of decisions seriously limits the practical value of the Fourth Amendment's ban on unreasonable search and seizure. This guarantee is of little value, unless the courts back it up by rigorously excluding any tainted evidence from criminal trials.

To be sure, Tuesday's rulings do not revoke the exclusionary rule in total. But its scope will be significantly curtailed. State courts can vary widely in their application of constitutional standards; the federal court system has provided an important avenue of appeal for a defendant whose rights had been violated by police and local courts. That route of redress has now been blocked.

Equally important, a key deterrent to abuses of police power has been compromised. There is, of course, no way to guarantee complete police compliance with the requirements of the Fourth Amendment. But the knowledge that any evidence gathered by unlawful means would be valueless in court has certainly exerted a restraining influence on police at all levels. In backing away from full enforcement of the exclusionary rule, the high court is weakening the force of this restraint—at precisely the moment when abuse of police and executive power, at all levels of government, has become a major concern in America.

The exclusionary rule has been criticized over the years by prosecutors and police for being too restrictive. Indeed, in a relatively few instances, the rule has resulted in the acquittal of an obviously guilty defendant on technical grounds.

But on balance, the exclusionary rule has been an important judicial safeguard against unrestrained police power. In times of social crisis, it is always tempting to look for shortcuts; to trim a few constitutional corners in the vain hope of restoring some order to society. Such efforts rarely prove to be wise in the end; and we regret the Supreme Court's latest retreat from the sound legal perspectives of the Warren Court.

Wisconsin ▲ State Journal

Madison, Wisc.,
July 20, 1976

The U.S. Supreme Court has taken a step away from personal freedom in its decision limiting the power of federal courts to overturn state court convictions based on illegally obtained evidence.

The six to three decision lessens the scope of the Fourth Amendment protection against illegal search and seizure and the so-called "exclusionary rule," which prohibits admission of evidence seized in violation of the Fourth Amendment.

The court's reasoning was that the cost to society in requiring repeated inquiry into the legality of searches outweighs the benefits.

It's a matter of practicality and boils down to a legal philosophy that if a prisoner is guilty he should not be freed on technicalities.

Those technicalities included in the Fourth Amendment, however, must not be taken lightly.

The exclusionary rule was not established to free criminals. It was established to discourage police and prosecutors from employing illegal searches and seizures.

In other decisions involving Fourth Amendment guarantees, the court philosophy prevailed.

It ruled that it was constitutional for Border Patrol policemen to stop cars for questioning of occupants regarding citizenship without warrants or even reason to suspect the occupants other than that they think the occupants are of apparent Mexican ancestry.

Another ruling held that illegally seized evidence which had been ruled inadmissible in state criminal proceedings may be used by the federal government as evidence against the owner in a civil tax proceeding.

In still another case the court ruled that it is not unconstitutional to use in court against the owner evidence obtained in a warrantless search of an automobile impounded for parking violations.

The rulings drew bitter dissents, primarily from Justices William J. Brennan Jr. and Thurgood Marshall.

"Today's decision is the ninth this term marking the continuing evisceration of Fourth Amendment protections against unreasonable search and seizures," Brennan wrote in a dissent in the Border Patrol case.

The Fourth Amendment goes to the very heart of this nation's judicial system.

The above cases may not seem too serious on the surface, especially in the current atmosphere that the judicial pendulum has swung too far in favor of criminals to the expense of the rights of society as a whole.

But the basic constitutional protections against such government action as illegal searches must be jealously guarded even if it hampers some law enforcement activities in the short run.

Rather than weaken the protections, law enforcement techniques should be improved.

Minneapolis Tribune

Minneapolis, Minn., July 11, 1976

Last week's U.S. Supreme Court rulings on the use of illegally obtained evidence were part of a "continuing evisceration of Fourth Amendment protections against unreasonable searches and seizures," wrote Justice Brennan in a dissenting opinion. That's an overstatement; the Fourth Amendment still stands. But its scope has been narrowed, and the trend—apparent in nine rulings this term—has been for the court to erode the broad protections defined by the Warren Court.

The major ruling last week sharply limited the power of federal courts to set aside state court convictions based on illegally obtained evidence—despite a 1961 Warren Court ruling that the "exclusionary rule" barring the admission of such evidence applied to state courts. If state courts disregard the 1961 opinion and admit illegal evidence, the high court seems to be saying, federal courts have only limited power to undo the damage. In a related ruling, the court declared that evidence excluded from a state-court criminal trial because it was illegally obtained may nonetheless be used against the defendant in a federal civil suit over tax liability.

The exclusionary rule has been an effective deterrent to improper searches and seizures. If illegally obtained evidence could not be used to win a conviction, there was less temptation for prosecutors and law-enforcement agencies to disregard proper procedures—and the rights of those being searched. Now there is less of a deterrent, for there will be less chance of obtaining a remedy in a federal court if state courts fail to exclude illegal evidence. Efforts to use such evidence may even have been encouraged by Justice Powell's contention, in writing for the majority, that the "exclusionary rule . . . deflects the truth-finding process and often frees the guilty."

We sympathize with the frustration of prosecutors and the police when they lose a case on a technicality. And we agree with Powell's argument that there must be a "balancing act" between Fourth Amendment rights and society's interest in obtaining evidence for a trial. But we think that the court has tipped the balance too far towards the side of the prosecutors—and has allowed more opportunity for the use of questionable means to reach justifiable ends. Convictions may be won more easily that way, but justice is maintained best when courts scrupulously adhere to constitutional principles and procedures. And, in the long run, the interests of society will be better served by the maintenance of justice.

The Washington Post

Washington, D.C., July 11, 1976

WHEN THE Supreme Court finally adjourned for the summer a few days ago, it left behind a series of decisions that lessen substantially the protection the Fourth Amendment affords to individual privacy. A few more terms of court like this and the once highly valued constitutional guarantee against search and seizure will have gone the way of the dodo bird. Perhaps a partial list of what the Court has done in recent weeks will make the point:

—If the police impound your locked car for parking violations, they can legally open it and search both its interior and its glove compartment. The Court has not yet said the search can include a locked glove compartment or trunk, but the logic of the recent decision says it can.

—If you are standing on your porch or in the open doorway of your house, you have no greater right of privacy than you would have if you were standing in the middle of Pennsylvania Avenue.

—If the police set up a border checkpoint 65 miles away from the nearest border, they can stop every car and detain for questioning as an illegal alien anyone in any car.

—While a court cannot constitutionally order you to hand over to prosecutors your business records—cancelled checks, memos and so on—it can issue a search warrant authorizing those same prosecutors to rummage through your files for those same records.

—While it is illegal for a state court to admit in evidence at a criminal trial anything seized in violation of the Fourth Amendment, if such a court does admit it anyway, no federal court other than the Supreme Court can redress the error. Strangely enough, lower federal courts can redress similar errors involving other parts of the Bill of Rights.

—While state officials are not supposed to use illegally seized evidence in criminal trials, they can turn that evidence over to federal officials who can use it in civil trials although not in criminal ones.

Now if this recitation of what the Court has done sounds somewhat confusing, don't worry; it is. A large part of that confusion arises out of efforts of the Court's majority to avoid overruling past decisions. The majority, for instance, seems to have no stomach for overturning the exclusionary rule (which bars the use of evidence seized in violation of the Fourth Amendment and which has applied to the federal courts since 1914). So it is undermining it by cutting off federal review of state court errors. Similarly, the majority does not want to overrule flatly an 1886 decision holding that business records cannot be seized. So it has drawn a somewhat illogical distinction between the government's forcing an individual to hand over such records and its simply taking them by force itself.

Running through these decisions are two evident assumptions that suggest to us that the current majority of the Court is out of touch with reality. One is that state court judges are as zealous in their protection of federal constitutional rights as are federal judges. While we are certain that many of them are—particularly those whom the members of the Supreme Court encounter at meetings and conventions—the same cannot be said of many lower court judges. The other assumption that disturbs us is that individual citizens ought not particularly to mind being stopped, detained and/or having their belongings searched by police. Justice Powell, for instance, says in the border patrol case that being detained for questioning a few minutes "may involve some annoyance" but should not be "frightening or offensive." And Chief Justice Burger says, in the case involving a search of a locked, but impounded, car, "The expectation of privacy with respect to one's automobile is significantly less than that relating to one's home or office." We wonder how many of the Justices would find it only annoying to be detained for questioning while driving back from Mexico or to discover that the police had gone through the papers they left in the glove compartment of their car.

Richard M. Nixon promised in 1968 that he would name to the Supreme Court justices who would change what he thought was the Court's overly zealous protection of the rights of criminals. His promise is now being fulfilled—but in a way that reduces the rights of the innocent as well. The Court has now joined forces with the computer and the new electronic gadgets to threaten what little individual privacy still exists.

COURT MODIFIES 'MIRANDA' RULING ON SUSPECT'S RIGHT TO SILENCE

The Supreme Court ruled 6–2 Dec. 9 that after a suspect exercised his right to remain silent about one crime, police could still question him about another. The dissenting justices, William J. Brennan Jr. and Thurgood Marshall, argued that the ruling was a retreat from the court's decision in the *Miranda* case in 1966. In that case, the court had said that a suspect must be advised of his right to remain silent, to have a lawyer and to be told that anything he said might be used against him.

The decision reversed a Michigan Supreme Court ruling that vacated the conviction of Robert Bert Mosley for the murder of Leroy Williams in Detroit in 1971. Picked up by police in connection with a series of robberies, Mosley told police he wished to exercise his right to remain silent, and they halted their interrogation. Two hours later, other detectives, who also informed Mosley of his rights, questioned him about the Williams killing. When Mosley did not object to the questioning, the detectives disclosed he had been named by an accomplice. Mosley then made self-incriminating statements.

The Michigan court ruled the statements inadmissible, reasoning that once Mosley had exercised his right to remain silent, the police could not question him further. Justice Potter Stewart, author of the majority opinion, disagreed, however, arguing that Mosley could have cut off the questioning at any time.

THE SUN
Baltimore, Md., December 12, 1975

"Law enforcement . . . in defeating the criminal, must maintain inviolate the historic liberties of the individual. To turn back the criminal, yet, by so doing, destroy the dignity of the individual, would be a hollow victory." So wrote the late J. Edgar Hoover in 1952. The former Chief Justice, Earl Warren, cited this passage in his famous *Miranda v Arizona* opinion in 1966. That decision required police departments to warn suspects of their rights under the Fifth Amendment, as the FBI was already doing.

The Fifth Amendment guarantees that no person "shall be compelled in any criminal case to be a witness against himself. . . ." Court doctrine already held that this protection begins well before trial. The Warren court decreed in *Miranda* that a person being taken into custody must be warned before questioning that he has the right to remain silent, that anything he says may be used against him, that he has the right to an attorney during the interrogation, and that if he cannot afford an attorney, one will be provided.

Few Warren court decisions upset local law authorities as much as this one. Capable professional criminals already knew their rights. *Miranda* aided the bumblers and losers who help to improve conviction statistics. While the police forces of the nation have learned to live with *Miranda*, the hope that it might be overturned has never died. Two dissenters of 1966, Justices White and Stewart, remain on the court, and helped provide its 6-2 majority for a decision which does not overturn *Miranda* but does hem in its meaning. This is that police, having respected Richard Bert Mosley's refusal to talk about robberies, were entitled to ask him about a murder, once again informing him of his rights, and convict him on his answers.

Justice Brennan, one of the 1966 majority, wrote in a gloomy dissent that *Mosley* is "another step toward the erosion and, I suppose, ultimate overruling of *Miranda*'s enforcement of the privilege against self-incrimination." But Justice Stewart, now writing for the majority, assures that this is not the intent. The suspect still has the option to end questioning and therefore controls the timing, subject matter and duration of interrogation. "The requirement that law enforcement authorities must respect a person's exercise of that option counteracts the coercive pressures of the custodial setting."

It makes sense to take Justice Stewart at face value. The *Miranda* decision lives.

The Birmingham News
Birmingham, Ala., December 13, 1975

The two dissenting justices in the recent Supreme Court ruling on the questioning of suspects stridently protested what they viewed as an erosion of the Miranda rule, laid down in 1966.

But the recent ruling, rather than eroding the Miranda precedent, merely seems to straighten out a technical point of procedure.

What the court said was that after a suspect exercises his right not to answer questions from police about one crime, he may still be questioned, if he is willing to answer, about a different crime.

These circumstances prevailed in the case: A suspect, Richard Bert Mosley, had been picked up by police and questioned about a number of robberies. When policemen read him his rights, Mosley said he didn't want to say anything about the robberies. So the police stopped questioning him. Two hours later, the police again read Mosley his rights and began questioning him about a killing. This time, Mosley was willing to talk—and made some incriminating statements.

The above took place in Detroit. Later, the Michigan Supreme Court reversed the conviction of Mösley for the killing. The Supreme Court ruling now has overruled the Michigan high court.

In dissenting, Justice William J. Brennan Jr. said, "Today's distortion of Miranda's constitutional principles can be viewed only as yet another step toward the erosion and, I suppose, ultimate overruling of Miranda's enforcement of the privilege against self-incrimination."

It is difficult to see how Brennan arrived at that conclusion. In the Mosley case, two separate crimes were involved; Mosley was fully informed of his right to remain silent; the defense could not prove that police applied any coercion to Mosley to persuade him to talk.

The Miranda doctrine is the accused's protection against, say, the rubber hose as a means of forcing confessions or self-incriminating statements. Miranda has not been overruled, nor should it be.

It appears that in the Mosley case, defense attorneys were merely grasping at a straw of technicality in hopes of securing an acquittal despite the fact that their client had been convicted on the evidence.

The Supreme Court, in refusing to stretch Miranda to an absurd degree, should be applauded rather than deplored.

ST. LOUIS POST-DISPATCH
St. Louis, Mo., December 12, 1975

For the third time in four years the Supreme Court has nibbled away at the historic Miranda decision, which was one of former President Nixon's campaign targets. While each decision may seem to alter that decision only slightly, the cumulative effect is to diminish the citizen's right to remain silent and to demand counsel when faced by the power of the state.

The Miranda decision was delivered by the Warren court in 1966. It said in no uncertain terms that police had to inform a suspect of his constitutional right to remain silent against interrogation and to have the services of a defense attorney. What was demanded of the police was simple enough and so was the enforcement of the constitutional guarantees— the courts would not admit statements in trials of defendants who had not been apprised of their rights.

In the 1971 Harris case, a high court altered by the Nixon appointments made the first modification in Miranda. With a 5-to-4 opinion by Chief Justice Burger, the court held that the state could use incriminating statements made by a defendant before he was told of his rights, if these were useful to show that his testimony was untrue. Justice Brennan said in dissent that "the privilege against self-incrimination protects the individual from being compelled to incriminate himself in any manner." In the Harris case the individual was not protected against self-incrimination.

Then, last March, in a 6-to-2 decision given by Justice Blackmun, the court held that the prosecution could similarly use self-incriminating statements made by a defendant who had been told of his right to counsel but had not yet been afforded one. In dissent again, Justice Brennan said that "after today's decision, if an individual states that he wants an attorney, police interrogation will doubtless now be vigorously pressed to obtain statements before the attorney arrives."

The court's latest decision, a 6-to-2 opinion presented by Justice Stewart, holds that in some cases police may continue questioning suspects who have already exercised their right to remain silent. In this case a Michigan man claimed his privilege against answering questions the police posed about some robberies, but the police then proceeded to ask him about a murder and he made self-incriminating statements.

Justice Brennan, once more in dissent with Justice Marshall, concluded that police had been given further excuse for invading the Fifth Amendment. He added that the decision was "yet another step toward the erosion and, I suppose, ultimate overruling of Miranda's enforcement against self-incrimination."

Undoubtedly the court majority believed that each case required a practical interpretation of what the police might do, but the sum of the cases is a reduction of the protection that the individual should be able to expect from his Constitution. He can no longer be certain that the courts will fully uphold his rights to counsel and to silence against the police power. Mr. Nixon is gone from the White House but his legacy endures in the Supreme Court.

St. Petersburg Times
St. Petersburg, Fla., December 12, 1975

Oldtime police reporters recall how it was, only a couple of decades ago. The officer hauled in his suspect, grilled him, scared him, slapped him behind bars. If the suspect was black he likely was addressed as "boy" or maybe "nigger." And when he confessed, the case was wrapped up.

And if now and again it turned out they had got the wrong fellow, well, too bad about that; but he probably had done something else just as heinous.

The police who followed such practices weren't evil folks. They were doing their job, the way they understood it was supposed to be done. And often their conduct — let's face it — wasn't far out of line with community standards.

FORTUNATELY that era is over, although there always will be instances of abuse. Police now are better educated, better trained, more sensitive to human dignity and individual rights. Public attitudes also have changed.

More specifically, the new police standards reflect a series of eight Supreme Court decisions, dating from 1957, setting guidelines to be followed by authorities seeking information from a suspect.

The court based these rules on constitutional guarantees often ignored in the past. Due process. Speedy trial. No "unreasonable" search. No involuntary confession.

Police everywhere still grind their teeth at these legal restraints. Any veteran officer can cite chapter and verse on the case where some known criminal beat the rap because of "technicalities," as they usually are called.

THE MIRANDA RULE is the one under which they chafe most. Under this 1966 decision (in the case of a convicted rapist named Ernesto Miranda) the officer must advise the suspect he has the right not to talk; that he may ask for a lawyer; and that if he does talk what he says can be used against him in court.

Police now routinely comply with that ruling. In some places they carry the appropriate wording around on a card in their hats, to have it handy for reading.

Of course, not every defendant can be expected to understand what he is told, and many don't. But Miranda and other court rules have recast law enforcement procedures. Some police insist their hands are unfairly tied. They blame the court for rising crime rates. They say smart lawyers are using the rules to spring crooks who belong in the jail.

UNDOUBTEDLY, police work now is more difficult. Successful prosecutions may be harder to come by. Some guilty persons no doubt have got off.

But many thoughtful police officials, not as close to the street as the average officer, now agree with legal scholars that the court's landmark rulings on the rights of defendants were proper.

They recognize that the Miranda ruling (and the Bill of Rights on which it and related rulings were based) was born not out of concern for protecting the guilty; but out of the necessity to protect the innocent. So we are saddened to see the Supreme Court, under new management, now nibbling away at this legal safeguard.

In a 6-2 ruling Tuesday, the court said, yes, a defendant can exercise his right to remain silent; but that later the police can press him again, and if this time he makes a confession, the police can use it against him.

THAT WASN'T the court's first pullback from the original ruling. In a 1971 case it said a confession inadmissible as evidence under Miranda might nevertheless be used, if the accused takes the stand at his trial, to show that he is a liar.

In a dissenting opinion Justice William Brennan, a holdover from the Warren court that propounded the Miranda and related decisions, said Tuesday's action "can be viewed only as another step toward the erosion and, I suppose, ultimate overruling of Miranda's enforcement of the privilege against self-incrimination."

We hope he is wrong; we are afraid he is right. The old police reporters among us remember how it was, only a couple of decades ago.

THE COMMERCIAL APPEAL
Memphis, Tenn., December 13, 1975

IN WHAT appears to be a needed clarification of the 1966 Miranda decision, the U.S. Supreme Court has ruled that a suspect who exercises his right to remain silent concerning one crime can still be questioned by police about another.

Two of the justices dissented, claiming that the earlier protections against self-incrimination would be eroded. But the case in point convinces us that the suspect's Miranda rights were not violated.

Richard Mosley had been picked up for questioning about a series of robberies. He was read his rights, and he chose to remain silent. Later, he was again read his rights. This time he willingly answered questions about a murder. He incriminated himself when he was told an accomplice had named him.

The Michigan Supreme Court had overturned his conviction on grounds that police should not have questioned him after he had first said he wished to remain silent. But he had a chance to exercise that right before the second questioning. Whatever his reasons, he decided not to of his own accord.

Landmark decisions such as Miranda undergo a process of refinement as cases with differing sets of circumstances require adjustments in the application of the law. In 1974, for instance, the court ruled that evidence from the questioning of a suspect might still be used against him even if he did not receive the entire warning spelled out by Miranda. The majority decision said, in part, that the law "cannot realistically require that policemen investigating serious crimes make no errors whatsoever."

Tuesday's ruling seems to represent a similar injection of common sense into how Miranda should be applied. It's common in police investigations for a suspect in one case to end up implicated in another. The literal interpretation of Miranda used by the Michigan court would make it more difficult for police to effectively pursue leads and tie together the loose ends of various cases. As the court said in 1974, the realities of law-enforcement work also should be considered. This has been done without leaving suspects unprotected or putting them under undue pressure.

THE SAGINAW NEWS

Saginaw, Mich., December 18, 1975

The current "set" of the U.S. Supreme Court seems to suggest that the court may be embarked on a succession of rulings that will chip away at the landmark 1966 Miranda ruling.

If that indeed is the "set" of the court, it should take care that chipping doesn't become blasting that will tear down a pillar of constitutional rights so clearly enunciated by the Warren court 10 years ago.

There was nothing mysterious about the Miranda decision then. There is nothing mysterious about it now.

It simply affirmed the right of every individual held as a criminal suspect to protection against self-incrimination by duplicity or coercion. It said that every suspect be advised of his right to remain silent, of his right to legal counsel — and that anything he said might be held against him later in court.

Of course this immediately shifted the full burden of proof of guilt to police and prosecutors — and the agonizing was great for a long time. It has never really subsided. And now with the current wave of crime in the country, the Miranda decision is gaining new currency as an anti-popular decision.

To hear Miranda critics rail against its alleged impositions

against law and order, one would think no party has ever paid the price for guilt in a crime since the decision was handed down.

That, of course, is absurd. What Miranda really said was that everybody has the right to constitutional safeguards against illegal invasions of privacy that can lead to self-incrimination; that one doesn't forfeit those rights with an arrest. The Fifth Amendment supports the same principle. Miranda also suggested that due process meant just that; that conviction be obtained on clear arrest and advise procedures and clean evidence take before a court and a jury.

In this, the highest court set down concise guidelines and simple standards for all law enforcement agencies and all courts. No longer would there be a veritable jungle of ways to get convictions.

We have never thought that excessive or hard to grasp even as we are not without empathy for the law and the prosecutors.

There have been cases where courts have thrown out confessions and juries have subsequently dismissed criminal charges on lack of solid evidence over and above confessions. That has gnawed at many a cop and many a prosecutor.

The general feeling at that level is that Miranda has so purified the rights of the accused that it has gone beyond what is reasonable to accept. We think not. Miranda dwells upon a suspect — not an accused. And we are unwilling to blame Miranda for any breakdowns or slowdowns in the process of due process.

We're no longer sure the current Supreme Court accepts our premise. Its recent decision upholding the confession of a suspect in Detroit robbery case suggests at the least that a mini-frontal attack on Miranda could be building. That is not cause for panic. But it is cause to keep an eye on future high court decisions involving appeals on grounds similar to those connected with the Detroit case.

In that one, the robbery suspect accepted his Miranda rights. But several hours later was questioned again in connection with a murder — and confessed to a role in that after being tricked into believing another party had implicated him. The Michigan courts rigidly applied Miranda and ruled the confession inadmissable. The high court has now struck an exception. And it will shortly review another case from Iowa most similar in context.

Yale Kamisar, authority on criminal law at the University of Michigan Law School, regards the high court's decision on the Detroit case as "symbolic," the same as many others. But he also regards it as a weakening of the Miranda ruling.

Prof. Kamisar has some fear that the decision is likely to encourage lower federal and state courts to give Miranda "a very narrow and begrudging ierpretation."

We agree. If not this one, a few more like it will. Surely the high court has already ignored the admonition of the Miranda ruling against self-incrimination by deception or coercion.

As Prof. Kamisar asks, "how many times will any suspect have to assert his rights over and over again?"

The high court has tampered with Miranda. If it was not a good law in the first place, the present court should have the courage to strike it down. Chipping away at it can only end standards and reintroduce confusion at all levels of law enforcement and administration of justice.

BUFFALO EVENING NEWS

Buffalo, N.Y., December 11, 1975

When a 6-to-2 decision on a case involving police grilling of a suspect went against them in the Supreme Court this week, the dissenters saw the case as "another step toward the erosion and . . . ultimate overruling" of the landmark Miranda decision which requires police to fully inform a criminal suspect of his rights before questioning him.

Whether Miranda is on the way to being overruled in a more conservative court, we'll have to wait and see. Certainly its impact has been modified somewhat by recent decisions which supporters of the original Miranda rule would call "erosion." Forgetting Miranda in the present case, however, and just looking at the common sense, we'd have to say the majority opinion has more of it than does the dissent.

The facts are that a Michigan robbery suspect had been fully read his rights when quizzed about the robberies, and he elected to remain silent. But when other police came in, again told him his rights and asked him about a murder, he did not again object to being further questioned on that. Finally, after being told about an accomplice's confession, he made self-incriminating statements and was later convicted of the murder.

The conviction was overrruled on appeal, on the contention that police should have respected his initial decision to keep silent. But now the Supreme Court majority, calling that kind of interpretation of the Miranda rule "absurd," concludes — quite sensibly, in our opinion — that the admissibility of any statement obtained after a suspect has decided to remain silent depends on whether "his right to cut off questioning was scrupulously honored." Since he didn't exercise that right in this case, we can't see why any far-fetched rendering of the Miranda rule should void his murder conviction.

The Morning Star

Rockford, Ill., December 12, 1975

Justice will be better-served as a result of a U.S. Supreme Court ruling which tempers the landmark Miranda ruling of 1966.

In the new ruling, the court majority said that the police may question a criminal suspect on other matters even though he has chosen to remain silent as regards a specific charge.

The Miranda ruling established certain rights of an accused, such as being told he has the right to remain silent, that he has a right to be represented by a lawyer present, and that what he does say may be used as evidence against him.

Generally, the Miranda ruling has served well to protect basic rights of an accused person.

This does not mean that all of the various lower-level interpretations of the 1966 Supreme Court ruling should forever endure.

In fact, the ruling has been modified before, principally by the Omnibus Crime Bill (federal) of 1968.

The latest modification is welcome. It moves the police a step closer to being able to carry on the fight against crime without artificial restrictions.

It is interesting to note that Justice Potter Stewart, spokesman for the court's six-member majority in the new ruling, was a member of the four-member minority in the 1966 Miranda ruling of the "Warren Court," as the Supreme Court of that era has come to be known.

The Washington Star
and Daily News

Washington, D.C., December 11, 1975

The U. S. Supreme Court's 1966 decision in *Miranda v. Arizona*, which one student of constitutional law has called "the high-water mark of the due process revolution," is a key link in the judicial process known in some quarters as "handcuffing the police." It sought to raise the standard of voluntariness in "voluntary" confessions, and many critics of the decision thought the standard altogether too exalted.

The betting was, accordingly, that when President Nixon's appointees got a grasp on things at the Court the *Miranda* ruling would become an immediate casualty of counter-revolution. And that for several reasons, both crude and technical.

It was crudely claimed, and it was often true, that the *Miranda* rules allowed even confessed criminals to walk free if improperly questioned. It was more technically claimed, and again it was largely true, that the Supreme Court had "legislated" restraints on police interrogation which, given the political realities, no legislative body could conceivably have passed.

This was the drift of debate, and the betting, in the immediate aftermath of *Miranda*. But for reasons not yet clear, the furious slanging match over the decision shortly subsided. The "Miranda rules" for police questioning, if they were not extended, were not cancelled when the Warren Court majority vanished. It even began to seem that the effects of the ruling on law enforcement had been overestimated, by both the Court and its critics.

The actual and more subtle course of events in this great Fifth Amendment controversy was again evident, this week, when the Court put a new gloss on one Miranda rule. In 1966, Chief Justice Warren had written that "if the individual (i. e., a suspect) is alone and indicates in any manner that he does not wish to be interrogated, the police may not question him." A few sentences before, the Chief Justice had declared it the Court's aim to assure "a continuous opportunity" to exercise a "right of silence" so as to avoid unwitting or involuntary self-incrimination.

But what is a "continuous opportunity" to remain silent? Does it mean that once a suspect has chosen not to answer questions, the police are then bound by Miranda rules not to seek answers to questions on an altogether different matter? The Court had before it recently a Michigan case in which one Richard Mosley, after declining to answer questions about several robberies, was shortly thereafter questioned about a murder and willingly confessed to it in the presence of a detective.

Was his right to "continuous silence" violated? The Court thought not. It held this an allowable exception to the Miranda rules, presumably because the subject of the second series of questions was different. Two dissenters, Justices Brennan and Marshall, both of them participants in the original decision, call this a "distortion" of the "constitutional principles" enunciated nine years ago.

Their concern is due respect, but it seems needlessly rigid. The fact is that the rulebook for police questioning issued by the Warren Court, sound as it may be in principle, does not consist of immutable "constitutional principles." It consists, rather, of what the 1966 Supreme Court majority viewed as valid inferences from the Fifth Amendment's great and valuable privilege against self-incrimination.

The Court's concern nine years ago was to secure that privilege against subtle as well as blatant forms of coercion, and that was a worthy aim.

But the exception the Court allowed this week is reasonable. The interval between questionings may be the main consideration. If the police move with reasonable dispatch from one topic to another, it is hard to see how that violates the privilege. Prolonged detention, or a return to the same subject after a suspect chooses silence, might make a different story.

In principle, the Supreme Court is doing now no more or less than what it did back in 1966 — it is construing and embellishing a constitutional right. Perhaps, indeed, it is still "legislating" — or *unlegislating*. That the balance of presumption has tipped mildly from the side of the criminal suspect to the side of authority is not in itself cause for alarm. The right to silence remains. And that, after all, is the right that the Fifth Amendment guarantees.

THE NASHVILLE TENNESSEAN
Nashville, Tenn., December 14, 1975

THE SUPREME COURT continues to chip away at the controversial "Miranda doctrine," which protects an accused person from incriminating himself before obtaining counsel.

The court has not yet reversed the ruling, but it has been narrowed substantially, and last week it was eroded even more by a decision that after a suspect exercises his right to remain silent about one crime, police may still question him about another.

The Miranda rule held as inadmissible statements made by an accused person before the time the police had warned him that he had a right to remain silent; that he had a right to counsel, and that if he chose to speak, whatever he said could be used against him.

The 1966 ruling was hailed by many as a forward step in protecting the rights of individuals who might be accused of a crime and arrested. It drew criticism from police and prosecutors as being a barrier to police work in that it tended to prevent voluntary confession.

The Burger court seemed to feel that the ruling did, somehow, inhibit the fight against crime. In 1971 the court modified the Miranda rule by making it possible for incriminating statements made by an accused before being told of his rights admissible on cross-examination. This was in order to impeach his credibility in case the defendant chose to testify in his own defense.

Subsequently, the court carried the change a step further. In an Oregon case, a man was arrested and charged with the theft of two bicycles. Although informed of his rights, and even though he requested an opportunity to seek counsel, the arresting officer delayed his use of the telephone.

During this delay, the defendant made incriminating statements to the arresting officer which were then admitted as trial evidence.

The accused was convicted, but the Oregon supreme court later reversed the conviction on grounds that it weakened the Miranda rule.

The Supreme Court reinstated the conviction, and opened the door to the obvious: If police could delay, they could extract incriminating statements from the accused before he had counsel.

Last week, the court reversed a Michigan supreme court decision involving a man who had been picked up for questioning about a series of robberies. He told police he would remain silent and the interrogation stopped. But later, other officers questioned him about a slaying and told him he had been named by an accomplice. At that point, the accused made self-incriminating statements.

The Michigan court ruled the statements inadmissible as evidence. But the Supreme Court, by a 6 to 2 ruling, said that even if a suspect chooses to remain silent under questioning for one crime, police can question him again later about another.

Justice Potter Stewart said the suspect's Miranda rights were still preserved. But the door is again opened to the obvious. It would appear that police could arrest someone on one charge, but really be interested in another and different matter.

Justice William Brennan, who was joined in dissent by Justice Thurgood Marshall, said, "today's distortion of Miranda's constitutional principles can be viewed only as yet another step toward the erosion and, I suppose, ultimate overruling of Miranda's enforcement of the privilege against self-incrimination."

When constitutional protections are denied some, because they are bad or are judged by the public to be guilty, then it is not a tremendously large step to their denial to others, who may be neither bad nor guilty.

Justice Brennan is probably right in saying that Miranda may be ultimately overruled. But those who see such an event as a triumph over the "criminal element" ought to pause and reflect where the road leads when constitutional protections are stripped away, a layer at a time.

SUPREME COURT AFFIRMS 'MIRANDA'; MURDER CONFESSION RULED INVALID

The Supreme Court March 23 ruled that a 1968 confession of murder was invalid because it was made without advice of counsel. In a 5-4 ruling, the court rejected pleas from the prosecutors of 21 states to overrule the *Miranda* decision, which established guidelines for the questioning of suspects.

While Iowa police were driving Robert Williams, 33, between Davenport and Des Moines, they elicited his confession of murdering 10-year-old Pamela Powers. The police knew that Williams was deeply religious and a mental hospital escapee, and asked him to locate the body so that it could be given "a Christian burial." Williams' attorney had sought to be present on the 160-mile ride, but his request was denied by the police, who promised that they would not attempt to question Williams during the trip.

Justice Potter Stewart, writing the majority opinion in *Brewer v. Williams,* concluded that Williams had never intentionally waived his right to counsel when he agreed to show the police the sexually molested body of the girl. Stewart did not comment on the *Miranda* decision, saying he saw no need to review the issue, which was based on the Fifth Amendment protection against self-incrimination. Stewart held that Williams had been "deprived of a different constitutional right— the right to the assistance of counsel" granted by the Sixth and Fourteenth Amendments. Stewart cited a 1938 Supreme Court decision that the right to counsel was in force unless "intentionally relinquished."

The sharpest criticism of the decision came from Chief Justice Warren E. Burger, who took the unusual action of expressing his dissatisfaction from the bench in open court. Burger called the decision "weird" and an "error" and opined that the majority had kept the high court on the "much criticized course of punishing the public for the mistakes and misdeeds of law enforcement officers." He concluded that the decision was "happily" close, "so that only one convert is needed to bring back rationality."

Roanoke Times & World-News

Roanoke, Va., March 28, 1977

The Supreme Court, deciding 5 to 4, has given a new trial to another murderer of whose guilt there was no doubt. Most people will agree with Chief Justice Warren E. Burger that the majority opinion was "weird... once more exalting the sporting theory" of justice.

The case involved a 10-year-old girl, sexually molested, killed and her body thrown into a culvert to be nibbled by animals. The horror of the case would not obviate the necessity of pair police procedure, so the question is: What error did the police make?

The defendant was not beaten or hounded into a confession; he was warned of his legal rights, and in fact, had turned himself in on the advice of a lawyer. The lawyer told him not to answer questions; but the advice was unheeded on a ride with police from Davenport (where he turned himself in) to Des Moines (where the crime took place). During that ride a detective asked questions which led the defendant to take police to the body.

The detective made an error? Technically, it seems an error was made. But many a person will wonder just what a policeman is supposed to do in a case of this kind. The error was not of such a degree of force and general wickedness as to unconscionably deprive the defendant of his rights, including the right to a fair trial.

Suppose, however, that in a company of angels what looks here like a simple error was, in fact, a gross error—as angels might so consider. Should society be punished if the policeman makes a mistake? The high court makes it difficult to have confidence in justice and the only comforting note is the closeness of the decision. As the chief justice observed, the addition of one rational opinion to the court could make the difference.

The Washington Post

Washington, D.C., March 26, 1977

THERE IS LITTLE that is extraordinary about the Supreme Court's decision this week in the Robert Williams case other than the outburst of temper on the part of the Chief Justice. The case did involve a particularly vicious murder—the killing on Christmas Eve, 1968, of a 10-year-old girl by an escaped mental patient. And the decision was close—his conviction was overturned by a vote of 5 to 4 when a majority of the justices ruled he had been denied effective assistance of counsel. But no new legal ground was broken, and the outcome turned on how established constitutional rules should be applied to a particular set of facts. However, the Chief Justice, disagreeing with both the rules and their application, used the occasion to flay his colleagues and to assert that any organized society ought to find their decision "intolerable."

The question that gave rise to this outburst is a basic one. Why should the conviction of an obviously guilty man be set aside because the police failed to follow the rules? And the answer is also basic. Rules, by their very nature, protect the guilty as well as the innocent, and, if rights are to have any meaning, the rules that embody them must be applied in difficult as well as easy cases. The principal rule involved in this case gives suspects the right to have a lawyer present when they are questioned by police. It grew out of a long series of cases in which confessions were extracted from suspects, many of whom did not know that they had a constitutional right to refuse to answer questions. Those cases led a majority of the Court, some years ago, to establish the so-called "exclusionary doctrine," which bars from use at trial evidence seized in violation of the rules. The purpose is to discourage illegal police actions and to ensure that government, as well as private citizens, follows the rules and obeys the law.

In the case decided by the Court this week, the facts made the decision close. Robert Williams had given two detectives the information they sought during a 160-mile auto trip from Davenport to Des Moines, Iowa. The question was whether the detectives had used the period when he was without the help of a lawyer to persuade him to talk or whether he had decided to talk despite his lawyer's advice. Before the case reached the U.S. Supreme Court, the Iowa Supreme Court had split, 5 to 4, against the defendant and the Sixth Circuit Court of Appeals had split, 2 to 1 for him.

The Supreme Court also split, 5 to 4, on whether Mr. Williams had been questioned or just talked to and whether he had waived his right to counsel. That is not surprising. Cases of this kind often produce sharp divisions among the justices. What is surprising is the Chief Justice's denunciation of those who disagree with him. Indeed, he appears to be the only justice who favored the upholding of this conviction outright. The three other dissenters voted to send the case back to a lower court for a determination of whether Robert Williams had talked to the detectives voluntarily.

The Chief Justice has repeatedly made it clear that he believes the exclusionary rules are wrong and should be overturned. In fact, the court *has* overturned some of them. But Justice Powell, who has sided with the Chief Justice in some of these cases, went the other way. Having lost the vote, the Chief Justice wrote so harsh an attack on his colleagues that it provoked separate opinions from Justices Powell, Marshall and Stevens defending the majority opinion of Justice Stewart.

In our view, Justice Stewart's opinion needs no defense. It is terrible when police bungling produces a result such as that in the Williams case. But Mr. Williams is not yet free; he can be tried again. And the complaint of the Chief Justice that the result is "intolerable" seems to us to stand values on their head. What would be truly intolerable is a legal system that permitted police deliberately to violate the constitutional rights of anyone anytime they want to.

HOUSTON CHRONICLE

Houston, Tex., March 28, 1977

We are just a little surprised that anyone thought the U. S. Supreme Court was going to overturn the whole "Miranda rule."

This 1966 decision by the court under former Chief Justice Earl Warren generally requires police to warn a suspect of his rights to silence and to have an attorney present during interrogation. It is much disliked by authorities and much beloved by civil libertarians.

The court had an Iowa murder case before it which turned on this rule. Some 22 states joined the case in what was seen as an all-out attack on the controversial ruling. There were quite a few who thought the now more conservative court would just wipe out Miranda.

The court didn't. It upheld the ruling, *in these particular circumstances*, and ordered a new trial for the obviously guilty man, this time barring evidence obtained in violation of the Miranda rule. It was a narrow (5-4) and rather impassioned decision on both sides, more or less reflecting in miniature the general public feelings and passions of this controversy.

Even had the decision gone the other way, we seriously doubt it would have overturned the Miranda rule, but rather have limited its application.

This Supreme Court has foreshadowed that approach before. It should come as no surprise.

The thinking was that since the court under Chief Justice Warren Burger had been restricting use of Miranda in a number of cases, it might just ditch the entire thing.

This was the same thinking put forward last year when there was a hue and cry that the court was fixing to demolish some other Warren-court rulings. These are in the area of "unreasonable search and seizure" and generally put tight restrictions on how the police obtain evidence and use it. They are kissing cousins of the Miranda rule.

Well, the court didn't. It loosened the restrictions because the Warren court went too far. But it didn't abandon the principle.

The same thing has applied to Miranda. The court has been striving to reach some sort of middle ground between the Warren court's excesses and the excesses that caused the Warren court's rulings.

It still seems to be plugging along that route as it decides individual cases with individual circumstances. While we may not agree with the court in particular cases, it seems overall a sensible approach.

OREGON **Journal**
AN INDEPENDENT NEWSPAPER
Portland, Ore., March 26, 1977

Many citizens may disagree with the U.S. Supreme Court's recent decision that supported a previous court's ruling on the rights of an accused person in the hands of the police.

The so-called "Miranda" decision held that the accused must be informed of his right to legal counsel and to remain silent if he chooses until he has an attorney.

Ever since the Supreme Court under the late Chief Justice Earl Warren established the Miranda principle, there had been a strong effort in some quarters to get it overturned.

Their strongest hope lay in the Iowa case that went to the Supreme Court the other day. Adding to their hope was the fact that the court headed by Chief Justice Warren Burger is more conservative than the Warren court.

The case was one which certainly would inspire little public sympathy for the defendant. He had been convicted of killing a little girl on Christmas Eve eight years ago.

But police did question him without a lawyer present and, in fact, after his attorney had been assured that they would not. As a result of the 5-4 decision, he must be retried.

The point is not excessive protection for a murderer. It is rather, as Justice Thurgood Marshall noted, that there is as much danger from the state using illegal methods to convict alleged criminals as there is from the criminals themselves.

As with every right of free people in a free country, no one has it if the least among us is denied it. The Supreme Court's upholding the convicted murderer's right to counsel protects everyone's right to have a lawyer between himself and the power of the state, a power which can be and has been abused.

The opinion of the majority is in keeping with the cause of a citizen's legal rights. Burger's emotional dissent was hardly in keeping with the judicial temperament that might be expected from the chief justice.

THE SACRAMENTO BEE

Sacramento, Calif., March 29, 1977

Refusal of a U.S. Supreme Court majority to overturn the Miranda rule governing rights of criminal defendants is a significant affirmation of a landmark guideline for prosecutors and the judiciary.

The rule laid down by the Warren Court in 1966 provides that persons under arrest must be advised of their rights to remain silent, told anything they say may be used against them and that they have a right to a lawyer.

The Burger Court did not rule directly on Miranda last week in a case involving an Iowa murder conviction. In effect, the 5-4 majority upheld other Supreme Court precedents, particularly the exclusionary rule. That rule, substantially subdued in recent opinions, bars trial evidence obtained in violation of the constitutional right to counsel.

The Iowa defendant, an escaped mental patient, was tricked into confessing the brutal killing of a young girl while riding in a car with detectives and without counsel present. The Iowa attorney general argued that a degree of trickery and deceit should be permitted in police interrogation as long as it is aimed at getting at the truth.

The late Chief Justice Earl Warren himself a former district attorney and attorney general, disagreed totally with such an idea. In a 1969 interview, after stepping down from the bench, he said: "The prosecutor under our system is not paid to convict people. He's there to protect the rights of people in our community and to see that when there is a violation of the law, it is vindicated by trial and prosecution under fair judicial standards.

It is heartening that a majority of the nation's highest tribunal should stand behind this credo and the protection to the rights of accused persons provided by Miranda.

Sentinel Star

Orlando, Fla., March 26, 1977

THE SUPREME Court has said in effect that it's sticking by its dictum that law officers make sure under all circumstances, even in the most heinous crimes, that the person in their custody is questioned only in the presence of his lawyer after being advised of his rights.

Ordering a new trial for a convicted child murderer was a close and controversial decision that elicited the scathing criticism of Chief Justice Warren E. Burger. But it stands as much as if it had been unanimous, and in the broad spectrum of American justice, the 5 to 4 majority was right.

What the justices did is affirm the Miranda decision which in 1966 laid down strict constitutional guidelines to make sure suspects are warned of their rights and offered counsel before they're interrogated.

The present case in point is that of a mental hospital escapee convicted in Iowa of the 1968 sex murder of 10-year-old Pamela Powers. What troubled the court was that while Robert Williams was being driven in a police car from Davenport to Des Moines a detective, knowing of the suspect's religious background, shamed him into locating Pamela's body so that the child could have a Christian burial.

While most people would consider the detective's action reasonable, the court obviously decided the question on the belief that the smallest breach of Miranda could lead to serious erosion of the principle. Williams doesn't necessarily go free; it's just that the prosecution now must get its conviction on evidence other than the automobile confession.

Over the years the court has been wise in providing safeguards that keep accused persons from being railroaded to prison through trickery or exploitation of their ignorance of constitutional rights.

This isn't to say court actions of the past that freed obviously guilty criminals on minor technical points were justified.

There is a distinction, fine though the line often is, between technical nit-picking and the legitimate safeguarding of a defendant's rights.

The really important point is that policemen know the rules of evidence and obey them meticulously. In the Iowa case it took an emotional and unpopular decision to convey the message that Miranda still is the law of the land and that departure from that rule isn't acceptable.

ST. LOUIS POST-DISPATCH
St. Louis, Mo., March 24, 1977

The four justices who dissented in the new Supreme Court ruling upholding the Miranda decision accuse, if that is the word, the five-member majority of believing that society might be injured if the decision were overturned. That is what the majority believed and they are right.

Miranda, of course, was the famous 1966 case in which a more liberal court ruled that police had to advise a suspect of his right to counsel and to silence. Former President Nixon made a campaign issue of it, contending it supported criminals against the public. The Supreme Court that his appointments rearranged has indeed nibbled at Miranda in various ways, but its new 5-to-4 decision refuses to weaken it fundamentally.

This decision requires not freedom but another trial for a mentally disturbed Iowa suspect who told police where to find the body of a young girl he was believed to have murdered. The suspect's attorney had advised him not to make any statements; and police agreed not to question him on a ride from Davenport to Des Moines, but they questioned him anyway and extracted the information.

Justice Stewart, joined by Justices Brennan, Marshall, Powell and Stevens, held that this was a flat violation of the right to counsel guaranteed by the Sixth and Fourteenth Amendments. It was also, apparently, a deliberate violation, since the police broke their word in getting the suspect to ignore his lawyer's advice. In this case the police left the right to counsel meaningless.

In bitter dissent read in part from the bench, Chief Justice Burger held that the court was punishing the public for the mistakes of law enforcement officers. The public is not being punished, for the suspect can be tried again. What the police did was more than a mere mistake — they destroyed the purpose of a constitutional guarantee.

Beyond that, the public is being protected, for the fair trial rights guaranteed the most dubious suspect are also guaranteed to society in general. If they are denied to one they can be denied to all. In both Miranda and its new decision the Supreme Court recognizes the indivisibility of fundamental liberties.

The Des Moines Register
Des Moines, Iowa, March 27, 1977

It would be appalling if the U.S. Supreme Court ruling overturning the conviction of Robert Williams causes Williams to go free because the loss of evidence ruled inadmissible by the court weakens the case against him.

The evidence implicating Williams in the 1968 Des Moines murder of 10-year-old Pamela Powers was so strong that a jury deliberated only about 90 minutes before finding him guilty. Every effort should be made to re-try Williams.

But more appalling than the prospect of an apparently guilty person going free would be the prospect of innocent persons going to prison. The high court's 5-4 ruling that police violated Williams's right to a lawyer takes its place in a long line of cases safeguarding the rights of the accused — the innocent as well as the guilty.

Police cannot be counted on to defend zealously the rights of suspects. That is the function of defendant's counsel. As the Supreme Court majority said in the Williams case the right to a lawyer "is indispensable to the fair administration of our adversary system of criminal justice."

Williams had sought the assistance of counsel. He telephoned a Des Moines lawyer, who advised him to give himself up but not to talk to police about the case until he consulted the lawyer. Police entered into an agreement with the attorney not to question Williams during the trip bringing Williams from Davenport to Des Moines.

Despite the agreement, police admitted that they tried to get all the information they could from Williams during the trip. The information they elicited included the location of the victim's body. The high court majority said the state failed to show that Williams voluntarily had waived his right to an attorney when he made his damaging statements to police; the dissenters disagreed.

The setting for the interrogation, wrote Justice Louis Powell in a concurring opinion, "was conducive to the psychological coercion that was successfully exploited." The incriminating statements made in this case were truthful, but the annals of criminal justice are filled with examples of suspects who were brainwashed by skillful interrogators into making false confessions.

The assistance of counsel is essential to prevent such psychological coercion. In the Williams case, police denied the request of an attorney to accompany Williams to Des Moines, in addition to breaching the agreement not to question the suspect.

If the high court condoned police conduct in this case, it would be an invitation to police to deceive attorneys and to try to break down their clients. As Federal Judge William Hanson said when he ruled in 1974 that police actions in the Williams case were impermissible:

"To allow into evidence statements obtained as were the statements involved in this case might make it unethical for defense counsel to advise a client to surrender in his absence, or to ever leave a client's side after arrest."

The murder and molestation of Pamela Powers were brutal and revolting. It takes courage for justices to overturn convictions in such cases. They do so to protect the rights of all of us. Many of the most important principles of justice have been established in cases involving reprehensible characters; nice folks do not usually get charged with crime.

The best answer to a heinous crime is care and diligence in bringing the suspect to justice. We hope that care and diligence will be evident in the re-trial of Williams.

THE DALLAS TIMES HERALD
Dallas, Tex., March 25, 1977

NO CASE in recent years better illustrates the hard, mind-bending decisions to be made by courts and police officers these days in weighing the rights of law-abiding society against the rights of the individual citizen accused of crime.

No case better illustrates the danger in which criminals put even the most beautiful and innocent of us. No case better illustrates the horrors of the duty placed upon the courts and the police by the Constitution, which states not only that even the most evil ones among us are innocent until proven guilty, but that the benefit of doubt always falls on the side of the accused.

The enormity of the crime of which Robert Anthony Williams is accused shocks every nerve. He was an escapee from a mental hospital. The victim of the crime was a 10-year-old girl, who was abducted, sexually molested and then murdered.

After his surrender to the police, Williams was informed, not once but several times of his constitutional rights to remain silent and to be provided legal counsel, as required under the Supreme Court's controversial Miranda decision of 1966.

But police officers, after refusing to allow Williams' attorney to accompany them and their prisoner from one Iowa city to another, and after agreeing not to question the prisoner en route, tricked Williams into taking them to the body of the slain child.

The State of Iowa interpreted this action as good police work. But a bitterly divided Supreme Court, in a decision that the Chief Justice called "bizarre," "intolerable," "blind," "irrational" and "absurd," ruled by a majority of one that Williams had been deprived of counsel, had been tricked into self-incrimination, and is entitled to a new trial.

Twenty-one other states had filed briefs on Iowa's side in the case, hoping that the Supreme Court would reverse the Miranda decision, which is despised by police and prosecutors as a hedgehog of legal technicalities and pitfalls which allow too many criminals to go free.

Indeed, the Iowa attorney general launched an all-out attack on the Miranda doctrine, arguing that it stands as an unnecessary obstruction to what he called the search for truth, and he urged that a degree of trickery and deceit should be permitted police in their attempts to protect society.

Chief Justice Burger agreed, saying that the majority's ruling "continues the court, by the narrowest margin, on the much criticized course of punishing the public for the mistakes and misdeeds of law enforcement officers." And the emotions of the public obviously are on his side.

But whether or not we agree with its ruling, the courage of the court's majority must be acknowledged. And Justice Potter Stewart's opinion restates yet again the intention of the Constitution to defend even the cruelest and most guilty among us from just such emotion.

"The pressures on state executive and judicial officers charged with the administration of the criminal law are great," he said, "especially when the crime is murder and the victim is a small child. But it is precisely the predictability of those pressures that makes imperative a resolute loyalty to the guarantees that the Constitution extends to us all."

The justices were wise not to accept Iowa's challenge to use this case as a test of the Miranda decision. Although Chief Justice Burger is right in saying that that doctrine too often "mechanically and blindly keeps reliable evidence from juries," any attempt to redress the balance between the rights of society and the rights of the accused is best left to another day and another case — one less tainted with questions of mental competence, police deceit and primal emotion.

A new trial for Robert Anthony Williams, nine years after the horrible crime was committed, is "a bitter pill to swallow," as the disappointed Iowa attorney general said. But it is not as bitter as a major change in the criminal law, made by a passionately divided Supreme Court, on the basis of such a murky case.

The Philadelphia Inquirer
Philadelphia, Pa.,
March 25, 1977

Chief Justice Warren Burger has never been reticent about his dislike for the 1966 landmark Miranda decision, requiring police to warn suspects of their constitutional rights. He outdid himself, however, when in an apparent fit of pique he publicly castigated the court's majority for suppressing the confession of an Iowa murder suspect.

Mr. Burger's dissent was more noteworthy for its emotionalism and apparent appeal to public passion than for its logic and wisdom. Contrary to what his dissent might lead one to believe, the murder conviction was not overturned because of some "technicality," but because the Iowa police intentionally violated the suspect's fundamental right to have a lawyer present when being questioned.

The suspect, Robert Williams, was wanted for the murder of a 10-year-old girl in 1968. His lawyer urged him to surrender. When he turned himself in, the police assured his lawyers they would not question him while the lawyers were not present.

Despite the explicit agreement and the explicit constitutional right to counsel, the police questioned Williams while he was being transported — without his lawyers present — to Des Moines, Iowa, even though Williams had said he would tell "the whole story" once he got to Des Moines, where his lawyer was.

Mr. Justice Burger found the majority decision "intolerable in any society which purports to call itself an organized society." We believe that if society is to be organized and governed by the rule of law, the Supreme Court must continue to tell the police that such misconduct is prohibited by the Bill of Rights.

As Justice Thurgood Marshall wrote, "The heinous nature of the crime is no excuse, as the dissenters would have it, for condoning knowing and intentional misconduct in police transgressions of the constitutional rights of a defendant."

For several years, the Supreme Court, under Justice Burger's initiative, has been chipping away at the effects of the Miranda decision. Many thought the Williams case would be the vehicle for the court to overturn Miranda.

By a 5-4 margin, Miranda survives. The closeness of the vote, however, is cause for serious concern. As Mr. Justice Burger noted, "Only one convert is needed" to bring back what he called "rationality."

The Miranda decision made good sense when it was handed down 11 years ago and it makes good sense today.

By all accounts the police have adjusted well to the decision. There is no evidence that it has caused an increase in crime. If anything, it has resulted in police and prosecutors preparing better cases. It has helped curb improper practices by police and prosecutors, which occur, nevertheless, much too often. So long as they do, none of us are secure against abuse by the authorities.

Los Angeles Times
Los Angeles, Calif., March 25, 1977

The U.S. Supreme Court, in a sharply divided 5-4 decision, upheld the reversal of the murder conviction of an Iowa man but, more significantly, the court turned aside a request by 22 states, including California, to reverse the 1966 Miranda ruling on confessions.

The states had sought to turn the Iowa case, involving the mutilation slaying of a 10-year-old girl, into a test of the Miranda decision. The majority opinion, instead, found that the defendant's right to counsel had been violated when, in the absence of an attorney, he told police where he had buried the child's body.

In effect, the majority also reaffirmed the Warren court's 1964 exclusionary rule, which bars evidence from use at trial if the evidence is obtained in violation of the constitutional right to counsel. The man's incriminating statement was part of the evidence used to convict him.

Chief Justice Warren E. Burger, who opposes the exclusionary rule, denounced the majority opinion as weird, and another dissenting justice, Bryon R. White, called the decision "utterly senseless," and said the police did nothing wrong, let alone anything unconstitutional.

It must be granted that strict application of constitutional protections is especially difficult for the courts to apply to defendants tried for grisly crimes.

Justice Potter Stewart, writing for the majority, acknowledged that the Iowa crime was senseless, and emphasized that the pressures on judges were heavy in grisly offenses against children. But he went to the heart of the issue by emphasizing: "It is precisely the predictability of those pressures that makes imperative a resolute loyalty to the guarantees that the Constitution extends to us all."

Everyone's safety is involved in the fair and impartial enforcement of the law under the Constitution. It was this vital principle that the majority of the justices upheld Wednesday.

The Washington Star
and Daily News
Washington, D.C., March 25, 1977

The Supreme Court's uncommonly bitter disagreement over the case of *Brewer v. Williams* — a grisly case arising from the abduction and murder of a 10-year-old Iowa girl on Christmas Eve 1968 — is not, we suspect, to be explained by the legal issues, difficult as they are.

If the case involved a less grievous crime, we cannot imagine that a Chief Justice would declare the Court's decision "intolerable" or accuse his brethren of "punishing the public for the mistakes and misdeeds of law enforcement officers."

Indeed, the crime was hideous. An escaped mental patient, Robert Williams, abducted and killed the child, disposed of her body while driving from Des Moines to Davenport, and two days later decided to surrender.

The constitutional case in the Court arose from Williams' self-incriminating decision to lead two police officers to the body after he had been arrested and arraigned and was being driven by them back to Des Moines for trial. During the long ride, notwithstanding warnings from his two lawyers and from the arraigning and arresting officers, Williams "confessed," in effect, by leading the two policemen to the girl's body. He did so after one of the escorting officers, Detective Leaming, gave him "something to think about" in the form of a "Christian burial speech," knowing that the suspect had a history of mental illness and religious preoccupation.

To his credit, Detective Leaming made no attempt, afterwards, to conceal his purpose. "You were hoping to get all the information you could before Williams got back to McKnight (his lawyer), weren't you?" he was asked. "Yes sir," he said.

Was Williams, then, in view of the commitment of the police that he would not be questioned during the long ride to Des Moines, and in view of the shrewd psychological manipulations of Detective Leaming, deprived of his Sixth Amendment right to counsel? Or, alternatively, did he knowingly and legitimately "waive" that right?

On these questions — and others less central to the case — the Supreme Court produced seven opinions, some of them impassioned. Yet we find it hard to imagine that the decision of five justices to grant Williams a new trial would have set tempers aboil had the crime been less heinous, the facts being otherwise the same.

Surely, if the right to the protection of counsel was written for anyone it was written for a mentally-ill religious fanatic, accused of the most heartbreaking of crimes, whose "urge to confess" might so easily be tripped by the clever manipulation of his emotions during a long, somber, lawyerless automobile ride.

It is an understandable but impermissible attitude that we can or should compromise standards of procedural justice if the crime "confessed" to is sufficiently awful. But it is not the quality of procedural rights, it is the punishment, that we adjust to fit the crime.

Now, whether Detective Leaming's "Christian burial speech" was an interrogation, strictly speaking; whether it should be considered that the police had agreed not to question Williams during the ride; whether the waiver of a right is an issue of law or fact; whether illicitly-obtained evidence should be excluded when guilt seems otherwise so certain and society could perhaps be injured if the new trial failed to convict — all these are hard questions, on which reasonable people may differ.

But in our view, the strict accountability of law-enforcement officials, however heinous the crime, is not a value safely negotiable. "A murder case," wrote Chief Justice Burger in his strong dissent, "ought not to turn on such tenuous strands." Similarly, "the consequence of the majority's decision is extremely serious," wrote Justice White, also dissenting. "A mentally disturbed killer whose guilt is not in question may be released."

Unless, however, the quality of procedural justice is to be dependent on the severity of the suspect's crime, the latter considerations must yield. By the logic of the dissenters, carried to an improbable extreme, the commission of a crime of sufficient severity would become an occasion for summoning the vigilantes to hunt down and shoot the villain at sight.

Finally, Chief Justice Burger's impassioned exclamation that "the result reached by the Court . . . ought to be intolerable in any society which purports to call itself . . . organized" calls for a passing comment. Organization — good order — is a paramount value; so, however, is civilization — including uniform and predictable standards of official behavior. No good society can do without either, but the distinction is crucial. Russia, we may say, is in the above sense more organized than civilized; Italy, the reverse. If there is in the clash between the two an inescapable choice, this country has long since chosen to err, if it errs, on the side of civilization.

The Boston Globe

Boston. Mass., March 27, 1977

Civil libertarians are unquestionably breathing easier following the Supreme Court's rejection of a major effort to overturn the Warren Court's still-controversial Miranda decision. Nonetheless, the court's narrow 5-4 vote to reaffirm another Warren Court decision barring evidence obtained in violation of the constitutional right to counsel was a clear warning that the Warren Court's landmark rulings on criminal procedure are still very much in jeopardy.

The crime from which the case arose was a particularly brutal murder of a 10-year-old girl in Iowa on Christmas Eve in 1968. The factual situation undoubtedly contributed to the decision by 22 states to use it as a vehicle for overturning the Miranda ruling requiring criminal suspects to be notified of their rights prior to interrogation. To many, the ruling is symbolic of the Warren Court's "pro-defendant" stance, and they had hoped the Burger Court would narrow it.

However, the court sidestepped the Miranda question and instead focused on whether the defendant had been unfairly convicted because incriminating statements he made to police while he was being driven from one city to another without his lawyer present were introduced at his trial.

Writing for the majority, Justice Potter Stewart affirmed the order of a Federal appeals court that ruled the defendant was due a new trial. The right to counsel, guaranteed by the 6th and 14th Amendments, is, he wrote, "indispensable to the fair administration of our adversary system."

The majority opinion was roundly attacked by Chief Justice Burger. He said the majority was "playing the grisly game of hide and seek and once more exalting the sporting theory" of justice. "The result reached by the court," Chief Justice Burger wrote, "ought to be intolerable in any society which purports to call itself an organized society."

Few would dispute the Chief Justice's support for an "organized society." But such a society has to be governed by generally acceptable and equitably applied rules. In the United States those rules are contained in the Constitution and for more than a decade now they have been understood to bar the admission into criminal trials of incriminating statements made to police by a defendant if his attorney is not present.

Burger declared the defendant was guilty of a "savage murder." That may well be so, but if the rules of society are going to be amended to fit the crime, they are not rules at all. As Justice Thurgood Marshall wrote in a concurring opinion in the case: "The heinous nature of the crime is no excuse... for condoning, knowing and intentional police transgressions of the constitutional rights of a defendant."

The critics of the Warren Court's "pro-defendant" rulings have argued they cripple police investigations and criminal prosecutions. Yet, it is notable that in the case before the Court the defendant had already been identified as a suspect, was under arrest and had agreed to talk to police with his lawyer present.

It seems altogether reasonable to presume that the necessary evidence could have been obtained without inducing the defendant's incriminating statements, without narrowing his — and, by implication, every American's — constitutional rights.

The Charlotte Observer

Charlotte, N.C., March 27, 1977

In 1966 the U.S. Supreme Court held that a criminal suspect's confession couldn't be used to convict him unless police, before questioning, advised him of his right to have an attorney present and to remain silent.

That ruling, known as the Miranda doctrine, and others by the Earl Warren court have been widely criticized by law enforcement officials, who say they impede the search for truth.

In the years that followed, President Nixon was able to name four justices generally considered more conservative than their predecessors. Under the leadership of Chief Justice Warren Burger, the court has chipped away at some of the Warren Court rulings and has adopted the view that criminals should not be freed on mere procedural technicalities.

When the court heard arguments in an Iowa case involving the murder of a 10-year-old girl, there were widespread predictions that it would reverse the Miranda doctrine because the suspect, Robert Williams, was so obviously guilty. (Columnist James Wieghart describes the circumstances on today's Viewpoint page.)

Iowa Attorney General Richard Tucker had argued that some deceit and trickery should be permitted during interrogation in order to get at the truth. But the court held, 5-4, that in this case the police deceit and trickery was illegal and said it would not relax further its standards for admissible evidence in criminal trials.

It was a revolting crime. Since it happened eight years ago, a retrial may be impossible; a dangerous criminal may be set free. But there is no evidence to suggest that the police had to go outside the law to gain a conviction. The police trickery was a gross violation of Williams' Sixth Amendment rights. In declining to consider Miranda, the court majority emphasized those rights.

The basic issue is whether the courts will approve of illegal activity by the police in their pursuit of criminals. The court's minority would have ignored Williams' rights because he seemed so obviously guilty; the majority reaffirmed the importance of those rights.

If the majority's philosophy prevails, some criminals will inevitably go free. But if it doesn't, those "technicalities" that sometimes, tragically, protect the guilty will no longer be around to protect the innocent.

CHICAGO Daily Defender

Chicago, Ill., March 31, 1977

It was a sane and laudable decision that the Supreme Court rendered when it turned back pleas by 22 states for dilution or abandonment of the Miranda rule and other broad constitutional protections that the court under Chief Justice Earl Warren had provided for criminal defendants. The Justices, according to the Washington Post, wrote seven separate opinions. Their sometimes harsh and impassioned language suggested that the case was divisive.

The victim was a 10-year-old girl who was kidnapped on Christmas Eve, 1968, raped and suffocated. In a rare action, Chief Justice Warren Burger read aloud a 15-page dissent attacking the decision as one that "ought to be intolerable in any society which purports to call itself an organized society."

Justice Lewis F. Powell, in turn, wrote that Burger disregards and misperceives key facts bearing on the critical issue: had the accused man, former mental patient, voluntarily waived his right to counsel under the Sixth and Fourteenth Amendments?

It is clear that any abandonment of these legal principles throws into jeopardy the protective safeguard of many defendants who are often too poor to hire competent counsel or too ignorant to know what their rights are. The Miranda ruling compels an arresting officer to inform a criminal of his right to keep silent and to have counsel before making a statement. This has been a blessing particularly to black defendants.

THE COMMERCIAL APPEAL
Memphis, Tenn., March 26, 1977

THERE SEEMS to be no doubt that Robert A. Williams sexually assaulted and murdered 10-year-old Pamela Powers in Des Moines, Iowa, on Christmas Eve, 1968. He confessed to the crime. He showed police where the girl's body could be found. The proof of his guilt seems to be incontrovertible. The only doubt in the case is whether that proof was obtained legally. And because of that doubt Williams apparently will be freed.

The U.S. Supreme Court has ruled that Williams' constitutional right to counsel was violated at his murder trial by the introduction of incriminating statements he made to police when he was not accompanied by an attorney. The vote was 5 to 4.

CHIEF JUSTICE Warren E. Burger, in a rare outburst from the bench, called the decision "knee-jerk," "bizarre" and "weird." Noting the closeness of the vote, Burger said that "only one convert is needed to bring back rationality" to the court.

The facts of the case certainly called for more common sense and flexibility on the court's part.

In an apparent attempt to soften the impact of the majority decision, Justice John Paul Stevens commented that "nothing we write, no matter how well reasoned or forcefully expressed, can bring back the victim of this tragedy . . .

But the purpose of sentencing Williams to jail was not to make amends to the memory of Pamela Powers or her family. The purpose, in large part, was to give society as much protection from Williams as the law allowed. Now that protection has been withdrawn — not because it wasn't needed, but because of a technicality that has no bearing on the fact of Williams' guilt.

And how monstrous was the wrong done Williams? He was advised of his rights as required by the Supreme Court's Miranda decision. (Although 22 states tried to make Miranda an issue in the case, the court refused to do so.) He was allowed to consult with attorneys. He wasn't held incommunicado or given the third degree.

The constitutional violation that the court discovered occurred while Williams was being taken from Davenport, Iowa, where he had given himself up, to Des Moines. A clever officer played upon Williams' state of mind — he had escaped from a mental institution — by suggesting that the slain girl should have a Christian burial before her body was covered with snow. Williams agreed, and took police to a culvert by the side of a road. The victim was found there.

TO ARGUE FOR "common sense" and "flexibility" in the application of criminal laws is not to deny the importance of a suspect's constitutional rights. Law-enforcement officials should not be given free rein to get incriminating evidence any way they can in criminal investigations. The ends don't justify the means. The fact that many suspects used to be harassed — sometimes unmercifully — led to the constitutional restrictions established by the Supreme Court. But cases differ. This isn't the first time that a rigid interpretation has given freedom to the guilty. In the Williams case, the Supreme Court did, indeed, reach a "bizarre" decision.

THE ATLANTA CONSTITUTION
Atlanta, Ga., March 25, 1977

The Miranda decision was one of the most controversial of all the rulings handed down by the Warren Court. It sought to protect the rights of persons accused in criminal cases, but it has been severely criticized for making police work vastly more difficult. This week the Miranda controversy was back in the news—as troubling as ever.

The U.S. Supreme Court in a 5-4 ruling declined the request by 22 states that the Miranda ruling be overturned. At issue was an Iowa murder case in which the defendant held that his constitutional right to counsel had been violated by the use at his trial of incriminating statements he made alone to the police.

The Supreme Court refused to make the Iowa case a test of the Miranda decision and other Warren Court decisions guaranteeing the accused the right to remain silent until he has counsel and to be informed by the police of his constitutional rights. The present court held that the Iowa defendant's rights had been violated.

Chief Justice Burger, in a strongly worded dissent, called the majority decision "weird." He is not alone in the belief that the Warren Court went too far in protecting the accused—so far, in fact, that many feel criminals have an unfair advantage in the courts over the police and the law-abiding public.

Probably most Americans would agree with the basics of the Miranda and other decisions on the rights of the accused. The big problem is to avoid leaning over backwards so far that justice falls down and criminals get away with crime. The Iowa case provided a fairly clear-cut example of how this can happen.

The case involved the brutal murder of a 10-year-old girl in 1968. She was sexually molested and her body thrown into a culvert. The defendant, who turned himself in, made remarks to a detective, no lawyer being present, that led to the discovery of the child's body. These remarks by the defendant were used against him in gaining a conviction.

Quite clearly the case might not have been solved at all, the accused might have been acquitted, if the police had not acted on the accused's remarks. Chief Justice Burger has plenty of company in feeling that somehow, granted the basic rightness of the Miranda and other decisions, this kind of "justice" is wrong. It subverts justice in its concern over niggling, trivial mistakes. Surely that's not what the Constitution requires of us.

St. Louis Globe-Democrat
St. Louis, Mo., March 25, 1977

When a man who has been convicted of a brutal, cold-blooded killing stands a better chance of getting a ticket to freedom than a one-way trip to the gallows, there has to be something horrendously wrong with the law. Even worse, such a situation underscores the moral weakness of a society which not only allows but upholds these mixed-up criminal priorities.

The author of this injustice is the United States Supreme Court, which, when it isn't voiding state laws on capital punishment, busies itself with throwing out murder convictions because of legal technicalities. The end result is wholesale criminal coddling at the expense of the victims of crime.

In its latest assault on criminal justice, the court overturned the conviction of an Iowa man who had been found guilty of murder after he had led police to the mutilated body of a 10-year-old girl. At the time of the killing, the man was a fugitive from a mental hospital. The justices ruled that police had questioned the man illegally when an attorney was not present.

There was no question of the man's guilt, not even a reasonable doubt. His conviction was overthrown only on the ground that police had not played the game according to the rules established a decade ago by the Supreme Court's highly controversial Miranda decision restricting police questioning of criminal suspects. The game plan calls for fairness to the suspect at any cost, never mind the fact that the accused may have been merciless to his victim.

The Justices were sharply divided on the ruling, voting 5-4 that the Iowa man had been unfairly convicted. It is the opinion of the minority that is worth noting, because it reflects the feeling of the majority of Americans, if not the Supreme Court.

It was an emotional dissent. In an unusual move, Chief Justice Warren E. Burger read part of his dissenting opinion from the bench:

"The result reached by the court in this case ought to be intolerable in any society which purports to call itself an organized society. It continues the court, by the narrowest margin, on the much-criticized course of punishing the public for the mistakes and misdeeds of law enforcement officers."

Burger went on to call the decision bizarre, blind, irrational and absurd.

A joint dissent was filed by Justices Byron R. White, William H. Rehnquist and Harry A. Blackmun, in which they branded the ruling as utterly senseless. They said:

"The consequence of the majority's decision is, as the majority recognizes, extremely serious. A mentally disturbed killer whose guilt is not in question may be released (pending a new trial). Why? Apparently, the answer is that the majority believes that the law enforcement officers acted in a way which involves some risk of injury to society and that such conduct should be deterred."

The five Justices who formed the majority have unleashed a far greater threat to society by tightening the shackles they placed on law enforcement 10 years ago. In their strict adherence to the ground rules of the Miranda decision — unmindful of any other circumstances or the consequences of their actions — they are playing a dangerous game in which society is the loser.

The Dallas Morning News
Dallas, Tex., March 28, 1977

THE SUPREME COURT had a chance recently to modify the Miranda ruling, which forbids use of a suspect's confession unless he has an attorney present when he is questioned.

The case involved an Iowa man who was charged with kidnaping and killing a 10-year-old girl on Christmas Eve, 1968, in Des Moines. The man was arrested in Davenport, given his Miranda warning and legal counsel.

The accused said he would tell "the whole story" when he got to Des Moines. But during the 160-mile drive to that city, a detective talked to the suspect about the need to give the little girl "a Christian burial," reminding him that a snowfall predicted for that evening would make it hard to find the body.

The suspect then agreed to show officers where the body was, though his lawyers were not present.

His lawyers said that this conversation begun by the detective violated both a promise made by police not to question the suspect during the drive and Miranda and that the evidence of how the body was discovered was therefore not admissible. The Iowa court did not go along with this line of reasoning.

The suspect was convicted, but when the case was appealed to the federal courts, they threw out the conviction. Twenty-one other states joined Iowa in urging the Supreme Court to reinstate it.

By doing so, the Supreme Court could not only affirm the conviction of a brutal killer, but ease restrictions on law enforcement all over the nation.

Instead, by a 5-4 majority, the high court threw out the conviction and ordered a new trial. The majority opinion did say that at the new trial "while neither (the defendant's) incriminating statements themselves nor any testimony describing his having led the police to the victim's body can constitutionally be admitted into evidence," evidence of where the body was found and its condition might well be admitted on the theory that it would have been found in any event.

This gesture completely fails to obscure the main fact, that the high court has once again let a man who is clearly guilty of a terrible crime escape society's judgment.

As Chief Justice Warren Burger put it in his dissenting opinion, the ruling keeps the court "on the much criticized course of punishing the public for the mistakes and misdeeds of law officers."

If the detective who spoke of the need for a Christian burial for the murdered child and thus touched the conscience of the suspect was by that act, guilty of an offense then he should be tried.

But this has no bearing on the main question in the murder case: Is the accused guilty or innocent in the kidnaping and murder of the child?

As to the points of law involved here, the dissenting opinions make it clear that even the most expert do not agree. But as to the central point of justice, any rational human can see that what the court has done is revolting.

The Cleveland Press
Cleveland, Ohio, March 31, 1977

"The result reached by the court in this case ought to be intolerable in any society which purports to call itself an organized society".

These words from U.S Chief Justice Warren Burger in a scathing dissent last week were not an overstatement, as we see it, and should cause citizens to focus attention

What had the chief justice's blood pressure up was a 5-to-4 U.S Supreme Court decision overturning the conviction of an Iowa man for the sex-slaying of a 10-year-old girl in Des Moines on Christmas Eve, 1968 The majority held police had obtained evidence against the man, Robert Williams, while he was denied his constitutional right to counsel

The circumstances:

Pamela Powers had gone with her family to the YMCA in Des Moines to watch her brother compete in a wrestling tournament. Sometime during the afternoon she said she was going to the washroom. She never returned Two days later her body was found in a ditch between Des Moines and Davenport. She had been raped and suffocated.

A boy had seen Williams, an escaped mental patient, load into a car outside the YMCA a blanket with two legs sticking out. A warrant was issued and Williams surrendered in Davenport the day after Christmas

Williams had contacted lawyers in both Des Moines and Davenport before he surrendered. The evidence showed, without dispute, that five times before he got into a car with two policemen to ride back to Des Moines he had been advised both by his own counsel and by police of his right to have an attorney present during any questioning The two policemen also promised Williams' lawyers they would not question him during the ride back and they declined to let the Davenport lawyer ride along

Shortly after they left Davenport one detective said he wanted to give the prisoner something to think about — that in view of the freezing weather and several inches of snow predicted for the night, and that since they were going back by the area where the body was they could stop and locate it because the parents were entitled to a Christian burial for their little girl snatched from them on Christmas Eve The detective told Williams he did not want him to answer, just think about it.

About 100 miles on down the road, Williams started talking and ended by leading the police to the body

The core question in the case was whether Williams had intentionally and voluntarily relinquished his right to be silent and to have counsel present when he talked with police. Five justices, with Potter Stewart writing the majority decision, said he had been deprived of his constitutional right. Four said he had not

Nowhere was there any evidence of coercian, or even brow-beating And nowhere was there the slightest shred of evidence that Williams is an innocent man.

The court's minority thinks Williams probably will now go free, so difficult will it be to reconstruct a new trial nine years later and so many are the bits of evidence which under the majority's decision cannot be used The next jury, for example, cannot be told how the body was found.

The court's majority thinks that somehow Iowa authorities can bring about a retrial. But, if not and if no conviction is possible, Williams will be free. And the majority feels that will be the fault of the cops.

It is especially difficult to see how the cause of justice has been served in this case.

The Oregonian
Portland, Ore., March 24, 1977

By the narrowest of margins, 5-to-4, the U. S. Supreme Court ruled Wednesday that a convicted Iowa murderer, whose guilt was certain, should have a new trial because he was questioned without a lawyer present. The ruling affirmed the 1966 Miranda ruling restricting police questioning of criminal suspects. But, considering the circumstances in the Iowa case, the decision was outrageous.

These are the circumstances, as shown on the court record: Robert Anthony Williams, an escapee from a state mental hospital, was arrested in Davenport, Iowa, as a suspect in the murder of 10-year-old Pamela Powers of Des Moines. As he was returned by car to Des Moines, a detective suggested that he reveal the location of the girl's body so that she could have a "decent burial." Williams thereupon led the police to the mutilated body of the young victim.

That was enough to seal his guilt then and forever. He was convicted of the murder in 1968. But his appeal, based on the Miranda decision, finally found its way to the Supreme Court.

For the court's majority, Justice Potter Stewart wrote: "Whatever else it may mean, the right to counsel granted by the Sixth and 14th amendments means at least that a person is entitled to the help of a lawyer at or after the time that judicial proceedings have been initiated against him."

But the dissenters had the more convincing statements. Chief Justice Warren Burger, taking the unusual action of reading his dissent from the bench, said: "The result reached by the court in this case ought to be intolerable in any society which purports to call itself an organized society. It continues the court on the much criticized course of punishing the public for the mistakes and misdeeds of law enforcement officers." And the other dissenters joined in an opinion written by Justice Byron White calling the majority decision "utterly senseless," and adding: "The consequence of the majority's decision is, as the majority recognizes, extremely serious. A mentally disturbed killer whose guilt is not in question may be released pending a new trial."

There will be a new trial, but to what end? The convict's guilt is unquestioned, but he could still go free on the technicality.

As Justice White says, this is an "extremely serious" matter, not just in the case of Robert Anthony Williams, but in similar circumstances anywhere.

If law enforcement authorities make procedural errors, they should be called to account. But murderers should not be unleashed on the public on such technical grounds.

As Chief Justice Burger says, it "ought to be intolerable."

The Detroit News
Detroit, Mich., March 27, 1977

The U.S. Supreme Court, which in recent years has shown increasing concern for society's rights vis-a-vis those of criminals, did some backsliding last week when it practically wrote a pardon for Robert Anthony Williams, convicted murderer of a 10-year-old girl.

The story goes back to Christmas eve, 1968, when Williams became a suspect in the disappearance of the child and surrendered to police in Davenport, Iowa.

Advised of his rights and aided by a court-appointed attorney, Williams chose not to answer questions asked by the police. However, during a car ride from Davenport to Des Moines, a detective suggested that Williams reveal the location of the little girl's body so she could be given a decent burial.

Williams led police to the body. He was tried and convicted. But now the Supreme Court has overturned that conviction on grounds that the detective's questioning, however effective in nailing down the case against the murderer of a child, was illegal. As of now, Williams is presumed innocent in the eyes of the law. In case of a new trial, the vital evidence would not be permitted. He could walk free.

Such are the outrageous consequences of a pair of legal doctrines handed down by the Earl Warren court. In case after case, confessed criminals have been released because evidence against them was obtained by "illegal" questioning (the infamous Miranda doctrine) or "unreasonable search and seizure."

Last year, the Supreme Court handed down a decision curtailing the right of prisoners to challenge their convictions on grounds of illegal search and seizure, noting that the exclusionary rule diverts attention "from the ultimate question of guilt or innocence that should be the central concern."

However, in the case under discussion — the savage, proven murder of an innocent child — the Miranda principle obviously took precedence over the ultimate question of guilt or innocence.

We heartily agree with Chief Justice Warren Burger's dissenting assertion: "The result reached by the court in this case ought to be intolerable in any society which purports to call itself an organized society. It mechanically and blindly keeps reliable evidence from juries."

A decision which tells courts to close their eyes to truth is a bad decision. If law officials question an accused person illegally, the law should penalize the questioners. It should not penalize society by virtually dismissing the enormously greater crime committed by the person questioned.

Chicago Daily News
Chicago, Ill., March 25, 1977

The self-confessed murderer of a child in Iowa may go unpunished because the U.S. Supreme Court gave more weight to the tangling technicalities of the law than to basic principles of justice. In a 5-to-4 decision bitterly opposed by Chief Justice Warren E. Burger, the court ruled that Iowa police had made a slight error in handling the case, therefore the conviction was invalid and the case must be retried.

Since the conviction of Robert Williams rested mainly on his confession, and the fact that he led officers to the body of the 10-year-old girl he had raped and killed, the exclusion of this evidence could make the retrial a travesty. Justice Byron White, who dissented, said the majority was ordering a retrial "under circumstances that probably make it impossible to retry" the murderer.

The five justices who prevailed in this case based their decision on the fact that Williams' lawyer was not present when he confessed. Never mind that he had been read his "Miranda rights" and had been warned by his lawyer not to talk. While he was being taken from Davenport to Des Moines, a police officer suggested that the child (whose body had not yet been found) should have a Christian burial. Williams took the police to the body. The court majority held that this sequence infringed on the defendant's constitutional rights.

Protection of individual rights is a valid — even vital — concern. There can be no argument about that. But protecting society from murderers is surely of equal importance. And if the Supreme Court loses sight of its obligation to that score to make a fine point of law, the criminal justice system in this country is in even worse trouble than we thought.

If this decision becomes a precedent, it could put the police under even greater handicaps than they now face in dealing with killers and child molesters. A series of child murders in Michigan makes that prospect especially chilling just now.

The four dissenting justices used such terms as "bizarre," and "irrational" to describe the majority opinion — strong words for the Supreme Court. But a public unimpressed with technicalities when guilt is so clear might go even further. Where in the law does it say that the Supreme Court must overrule common sense?

Post-Tribune
Guarding Your Interests Daily

Gary, Ind., March 25, 1977

In a crime-ridden nation where the main concern of our elderly and others is centered on crime in the streets and in the home it appears we have become a society bent on self-destruction through a greater concern for the criminals than the victim.

The United States Supreme Court, in a bitter 5-4 decision, has ordered a new trial for a mentally disturbed killer whose guilt has never been questioned and who, pending a new trial, may be released. The case involved a convicted Iowa murderer who, the court says, must have a new trial because he was illegally questioned by a police officer when he did not have the assistance of an attorney.

Police officers agreed not to question the man when he was on a trip from Davenport to Des Moines. But an officer engaged the man in a conversation which led to finding the location of the murdered child's body. The officer said the information was given voluntarily.

In the much-maligned name of justice, where in the hell do we think we are going? Who is going to explain to another set of parents why this came about if this mentally disturbed man is released pending a new trial and another murder takes place?

There is no question of being fair and just if a man has yet to be proven guilty. But is it wrong when a man admits to his part in a crime by telling where he hid the body? Is he any less guilty if he provides such information without an attorney present? Or, for that matter, would he be any more guilty if he gave the same information when an attorney was present?

There seems to be a basic question before the American public: Is our sense of justice one in which a person can get out of any crime of any nature because of typing errors by clerks, misconduct of any

kind by law enforcement officers or is our justice to be a just verdict for the crime committed?

In books and on television we all have been entertained and perhaps even thrilled with the "underdog" winner when a brilliant attorney comes up with an obscure ploy that wins freedom. In real life it seems quite clear the same public is more than just fed-up with the criminals getting better treatment than the victims who also must stand the awesome tax expense of a trial on top of a trial because a slip is made that has nothing to do with actual guilt or innocence.

The decision apparently was made because the majority (of the Supreme Court) believes that the law enforcement officers acted in a way which involves some risk of injury to society and that such conduct should be deterred. Did anyone weigh that risk against the risk of turning the man loose in society?

Richmond Times-Dispatch

Richmond, Va., March 28, 1977

Last Wednesday the U. S. Supreme Court overturned the conviction — and possibly assured the freedom — of a man who murdered a 10-year-old girl.

The vote was 5-to-4. We note with surprise, and disappointment, that former Richmonder Lewis F. Powell Jr., one of the most distinguished and valuable members of the court, joined liberal members to make possible the five-man majority.

Chief Justice Burger, in a blistering dissenting opinion, also said it was "surprising" that Justice Powell "today makes the fifth vote for the court's judgment," since, Burger said, previous opinions by Justice Powell had taken a generally different view concerning the throwing out of evidence because of police errors.

As to the majority decision in general, Chief Justice Burger wrote:

The result reached by the court in this case ought to be intolerable in any society which purports to call itself an organized society. It continues the court — by the narrowest margin — on the much criticized course of punishing the public for the mistakes and misdeeds of law enforcement officers, instead of punishing the officer directly, if in fact he is guilty of wrongdoing. It mechanically and blindly keeps reliable evidence from juries whether the claimed constitutional violation involves gross police misconduct or honest human error.

Briefly, this was the case on which the court acted:

On Christmas eve of 1968 a 10-year-old girl named Pamela Powers went with her family to the YMCA in Des Moines to watch a wrestling tournament in which her brother was participating. When she failed to return from a trip to a lavatory in the building, a search was begun but she was not found.

Robert Williams, who had recently escaped from a mental hospital, was a resident of the YMCA. Soon after Pamela's disappearance, Williams was seen in the lobby carrying a large bundle wrapped in a blanket. He asked a 14-year-old boy to open the YMCA door for him and also the door of his automobile parked outside. When Williams placed the bundle in the front seat of his car, the boy "saw two legs in it and they were skinny and white." Williams drove away, and his abandoned car was found the following day in Davenport, Iowa, about 160 miles from Des Moines. A warrant was issued for his arrest.

On the day after Christmas, Williams telephoned a lawyer in Des Moines and was advised to give himself up in Davenport, which he did. Des Moines police went to Davenport, and after giving Williams the required *Miranda* warnings, put him in their car for the trip back to Des Moines.

On the trip one of the policemen made a little speech to Williams

about how bad it was that the little girl was probably lying out in the snow somewhere and was being denied a Christian burial. He said "I feel we should stop and locate" the body. He said nothing further about the matter, but after a while Williams voluntarily directed the police to the girl's body.

Williams was tried and convicted of murder, and it was the appeal from that conviction that the Supreme Court decided last Wednesday.

The five-man majority (Justices Stewart, Brennan, Marshall, Stevens and Powell) held that Williams' constitutional rights were violated because he was questioned in the absence of his attorney although he had not waived his right to counsel

The four dissenters held that Williams had voluntarily waived his right to counsel and that even if the policeman's statements should not have been made during the trip, the error was not of such a serious nature as to overturn the murder conviction. The dissenters said that since the prosecution would not be able to tell the jury in a new trial how the body was found, it probably will be impossible to retry and convict Williams.

Ten years ago, Mr. Powell and three other members of the 19-member President's Crime Commission issued a separate report in which they argued that the Supreme Court had so widened the rights of accused persons that there was serious question

"whether the scales have tilted in favor of the accused and against law enforcement and the public further than the best interest of the country permits.

"We are passing through a phase in our history of understandable, yet unprecedented, concern with the rights of accused persons," Mr. Powell and his three colleagues wrote. "This has been welcomed as long overdue in many areas. But the time has come for a like concern for the rights of citizens to be free from criminal molestation of their persons and property. In many respects, the victims of crime have been the forgotten men of our society . . ."

In his concurring opinion Wednesday, Justice Powell sought to draw a distinction between "flagrant violations by the police, on the one hand, and technical, trivial, or inadvertent violations on the other." He concluded that the statements made to Williams in the absence of his attorney constituted a flagrant violation of Williams' rights.

But we think Chief Justice Burger was on the right track when he declared that by its decision, "the court regresses to playing a grisly game of 'hide and seek,' once more exalting the sporting theory of criminal justice which has been experiencing a decline in our jurisprudence."

So Robert Williams, who everyone agrees murdered Pamela Powers, may now go free. It doesn't make sense.

The Providence Journal
Providence, R.I., October 6, 1977
Bail — a right to fair treatment

Black groups are not alone in their concern over findings of a study that, all other factors being equal, black defendants in Rhode Island courts have to put up bail twice as often as whites to obtain pretrial release. Why this apparent disparity exists was not explained in a statistical report by the public defender's office on a selective survey of bail practices in the state's District and Superior Courts. But it has triggered new inquiries that may develop a clearer picture.

The importance of this cannot be stressed too much. The ideal of equal justice for all is enshrined in the courts. Nothing could be more damaging than to convey the impression that completely fair treatment cannot be expected there. Atty. Gen. Julius C. Michaelson correctly has called for improved procedures to guard against "any appearance" of racial discrimination in the fixing of bail.

However, the exact nature of the problem must first be determined. In this respect, Presiding Justice Joseph R. Weisberger of the Superior Court himself has undertaken a "fairly intensive monitoring" of bail decisions at that level. He said he "simply cannot accept the suggestion of racial bias" among his colleagues, nor should such suggestion be assumed based on the material at hand. The head of the District Court, Chief Judge Henry E. Laliberte, wants more information than contained in the public defender's report. These are reasonable reactions.

According to the survey by the defender's office, there is a disadvantage not only for blacks, but for the poor in the way defendants are released pending trial. While these groups are less likely to be able to afford surety, it is disproportionately imposed on them instead of personal recognizance, a sort of honor system pledge to reappear. One conclusion of the report is that "Rhode Island judges administer pretrial release on the basis of scanty information."

If this is so, then further judicial review should indicate what corrective action is needed. In response to a meeting with representatives of black and civil rights groups, Attorney General Michaelson has promised to work with the courts on this. He also has proposed a joint session of all concerned to discuss the matter. These are proper and necessary steps to take in resolving it.

ST. LOUIS POST-DISPATCH
St. Louis, Mo., May 14, 1977
Pretrial Problem

Only one area of major concern has been found in St. Louis's "highly successful" pretrial release program under which suspects in criminal cases now enjoy various alternatives to having to ransom their freedom from a private bondsman. One of the alternatives is release on personal recognizance. An evaluating committee has found that the vast majority of those persons so released are appearing in court, as promised, to answer the charges against them.

The continuing problem with the program, however, is that about 30 per cent of the suspects are not seen by staff members of the pretrial program within 12 hours of their arrest, as mandated by the Missouri Supreme Court. The court acted after *Post-Dispatch* disclosures that persons too poor to afford a bondsman frequently had to wait several *days* before being considered for some form of non-bond release. All that did was to play into the hands of the professional bondsman.

Once suspects are delivered to the central police holdover downtown, about 98 per cent of them are evaluated by pretrial officers within the 12-hour period. The failure to conform to the rule — mandating interviews after arrest, not arrival downtown — grows in large measure out of bureaucratic delays occasioned by inadequate Police Department procedures. Suspects are held in district stations until shifts change or until a wagon load of them has been accumulated, which of course is convenient and even efficient for the police.

That might be acceptable if police were in the bulk commodity business, say, and were making transfers between warehouses. But the suspects are flesh and blood persons who under the law must be presumed to be innocent. They are entitled to their freedom as quickly as it can be determined that they are good risks to appear in court when scheduled.

Beyond that, as has been pointed out by Director Norman A. Carlson of the Federal Bureau of Prisons, pretrial detention is costly; it takes detainees away from their families and their jobs, and most detention facilities are unsuited for confining suspects in a safe and humane manner. District lockups and the central holdover in St. Louis may be relatively safe as places of that kind go — safer, say, than the notoriously dangerous City Jail — but they are not set up to hold suspects for extended periods of time and to use them for that purpose is hardly humane.

As Mr. Carlson says, "Those persons who are not a threat to others should be released into the community." Accordingly, the Police Board ought to see that suspects are brought downtown at once; and the pretrial office should aim to decide on whether they are good risks not merely within 12 hours but as quickly as a bondsman does when he sees cash — that is, at once.

Democrat Chronicle
Rochester, N.Y., May 18, 1977
The public needs this protection

UNDER existing state law, a suspect's juvenile record cannot be disclosed at a bail hearing.

When 19-year-old Ronald Timmons of the Bronx was arrested last fall after an 82-year-old woman had been brutally beaten and robbed of $2, the judge in the case did not know that the defendant had a long record of attacks on the elderly. Indeed, he had 67 separate court appearances as a juvenile on a variety of charges.

As a matter of law, the judge was not privy to these facts. Forced to make a decision on the basis of this one charge of beating and robbing the 82-year-old woman, he set bail at $500. Shortly after, the defendant Timmons fled, and the public, when it was acquainted with the case, was outraged.

Timmons was later arrested in Baltimore and he interrupted jury selection at his trial in Bronx Criminal Court in March to plead guilty to a seven-count indictment charging him with robbery, burglary, assault and possession of a weapon.

Last week, Timmons was sentenced to the maximum term — 8½ to 25 years in prison.

In imposing sentence, Justice Joseph P. Sullivan denounced Timmons in these terms:

"This defendant, by his past conduct, must be sentenced to the maximum period of time allowed by the law. He is a predator in the dirtiest sense of the word — preying on the helpless. We cannot continue to countenance teenage predators taking advantage of the elderly."

This was the criminal who jumped low bail and who might still be beating up the elderly had he not been recaptured by the FBI in Baltimore.

CLEARLY the judge, in setting bail, should have had Timmons' bad juvenile record available to him, and under the change in the law proposed by the State Division for Youth, he would have confidential access to it.

Peter Edelman, the division's director, has said: "We should let criminal court judges and counsel examine and utilize on a confidential basis records for serious crimes committed by youth at the ages of 14 and 15. Records are relevant."

Indeed they are, especially where violence is involved.

In his latest package of legislation affecting the state criminal justice system, Gov. Carey has proposed a bill which would require, among other things, "that judges in adult criminal courts know about and consider prior juvenile delinquency and youthful offender adjudications when deciding whether or not to release a defendant from custody prior to trial."

The judges need this help and the public deserves this protection.

Chicago Tribune

Chicago, Ill., October 11, 1977

A bail law on trial

A new anticrime law, signed by Gov. Thompson Sept. 29, was designed to end a long-lasting and frightening situation: that of the accused criminal who is arrested time after time for repeated crimes, but after each offense is released on bond pending trial. To the victims, it looks as though the courts were giving these criminals a temporary permit to commit all the crimes they can before they are finally tried for one.

The new law, sponsored by Rep. Roman Kosinski [D., Chicago] is an attempt to break this chain. It requires judges to revoke the previously set bail of a defendant when that defendant is charged with a new crime involving violence. It does this primarily by changing the earlier law to read "shall" instead of "may"; judges always had the option of revoking bail in these circumstances, but the amended law says they must do so. [The defendant jailed by such an order, however, must be brought to trial within 10 days.]

The question now is whether this law is working, or even being used. So far the results are mixed and puzzling.

On Oct. 3, Judge David J. Shields of Felony Court made the first use of the new law. He ordered a defendant jailed without bond on a charge of armed robbery, and revoked the previous bond on a similar charge. The defendant, Johnnie Walton, had been released on his own recognizance July 25 by Judge Earl Strayhorn; the judge gave the curious explanation that Walton's mental state "deteriorated" while he was in jail, so he was let out on the streets.

In the second instance, Judge Gino DiVito in Violence Court revoked a $150,000 bond previously set for Dennis Cardenas, a former convict awaiting trial for three rapes and three burglaries, after Cardenas was charged with a fourth rape. Yet Judge DiVito, instead of using the law to put Cardenas in custody pending trial, set a new bond of $200,000, leaving the disposition of this case—and the status of the law—still fuzzy.

Presumably some judges, pending a court test of the new law, are hesitant to use it on their own initiative and want the state's attorney's office to request its use. [And prosecutors themselves may be reluctant to risk an appeal that might cost them a conviction.]

The law, however, needs to be tested through appeal, and it is judges—not assistant state's attorneys—who are given the power to test it. Timidity about using the new law will solve nothing—certainly not the problem of the criminal repeater out on another pass.

The Pittsburgh Press

Pittsburgh, Pa., June 22, 1977

Bailing Out

Too many persons charged with crimes in Allegheny County are skipping bail and failing to appear for trial. Some of these are repeat felons or previous bond jumpers.

This has Common Pleas Judge Robert Dauer concerned, as well it should.

Last year, more than 8 per cent of 7,432 defendants released on bail literally "bailed out" and failed to show up in court. This year the figure has already crept up to 9 per cent.

★ ★ ★

Judge Dauer, who is a former chief city magistrate and who handles appeals on bail set by the county's 53 magistrates, wants the District Attorney's office to assign an assistant DA to the task of calling low criminal bonds to his attention.

Under the current system, usually only the defendant's attorney and a representative of the county bail agency are present when bail is set. This puts the bail agency itself in the position of an advocate for higher bail, according to Judge Dauer, and this is not proper because it is supposed to be simply an objective fact-finding agency.

★ ★ ★

The judges have favored lower bail so the poor would not be discriminated against. But it is clear to Judge Dauer, and the records substantiate his concern, that the present system is being abused by an ever-increasing number of bail-jumpers.

In fact, there have been some spectacular cases where persons accused of serious crimes have been set loose on very low bail.

District Attorney Bob Colville has not commented on Judge Dauer's recommendation. But his first assistant has — and favorably — as has the head of the area prosecutors who routinely represent the DA's office at magistrate hearings.

The system needs teeth. Judge Dauer's proposal may not be a cure-all, as he himself concedes, but there are some magistrates who repeatedly set low bail and this would be one way to stop such crime-abetting nonsense.

Detroit Free Press

Detroit, Mich., February 7, 1977

High Court Should End Bail Bondsmen System

WHILE THE Detroit Recorder's Court ponders what to do about the Goldfarb Bonding Agency, the Michigan Supreme Court is procrastinating on the best answer to the whole problem of bail bondsmen in this state: Get rid of them.

If at least four of the Supreme Court's seven justices decided to do so, the court could issue a rule that would replace bondsmen with a system that has been working well in Illinois for more than a decade and recently has been adopted elsewhere, too.

It vastly reduces the "checkbook justice" of the bail bond system without appreciably affecting whether defendants show up in court when they are supposed to. In eliminating the role of bail bond companies, it removes a potential source of corruption and a breeder of great inequity.

In Michigan courts, it is common for bail bondsmen to write some or most of the bail bonds for defendants. The usual charge is 10 percent. Thus if a judge sets a bond at $5,000, a defendant may pay a private agency $500 to post a surety bond. In theory, fewer defendants flee because bondsmen have a strong monetary interest in seeing that they show up in court on schedule.

Criminal Justice In Detroit

The Detroit Recorder's Court last year authorized 2,369 surety bonds with a value of $6,625,250. An estimated 90 percent of those bonds were written by the Goldfarb agency—a figure that demonstrates the Recorder's Court's dangerous dependence upon one bonding company.

In 1964 Illinois introduced a system that has eliminated bondsmen. It enables a defendant to deposit 10 percent of his own bond—the same amount he would have to pay a bondsman to do it—and regain all but one percent if he appears in court at the time ordered. The one percent covers costs of administration.

An alternative, seldom used, enables a defendant to post the full amount of his bond and regain the entire amount when he appears in court.

The system works. Judge Peter Bakakos, who heads the bail bond division of Cook County Circuit Court in Chicago, tells us that the frequency of defendants' appearance is "as good as or better than" it was when bonding companies were used. He says 14 to 15 percent of the defendants released under the 10 percent deposit plan fail to appear when scheduled and eight out of 10 of those appear or are caught within a year. Last year the Chicago court released 150,000 defendants under this plan.

That record compares favorably with the experience of courts that are heavily dependent upon bail bondsmen. It also tends to reduce the jail population, since some defendants who could post a 10 percent bail bondsman's fee fail to obtain a bond because they do not have collateral.

A similar system seems to be working well in Philadelphia. Kentucky recently has adopted the system and gone a step further by outlawing bondsmen. Other states, too, are moving in this direction. The American Bar Association, among other organizations, has recommended the elimination of bondsmen.

It is clear that Recorder's Court, which deals with a third of Michigan's serious criminal cases, is using an anachronistic bond system that invites trouble. Some of that trouble is suggested by the Michigan Judicial Tenure Commission's recent charges of misconduct against two Recorder's Court judges for what they did in returning about $75,000 in forfeited bonds to the Goldfarb agency.

Chief Justice Thomas G. Kavanagh and his associates on the Michigan Supreme Court have been asked to adopt the 10 percent deposit plan. By simple approval of a new rule for Michigan's courts, they can end the role of bondsmen in courts throughout the state. We hope they will move to do that without further delay.

ABA PROPOSES GRAND JURY REFORM; ATTORNEY GENERAL BELL DISAGREES

The American Bar Association Aug. 9, 1977 urged Congress and the states to adopt far-reaching proposals it had formulated to change the grand jury system. At its 99th annual convention in Chicago, the ABA's policy-making body, the House of Delegates recommended, among other points, that witnesses be allowed to have their lawyers present in the grand jury room, and that those lawyers be allowed to address the grand jury. It was also proposed that prosecutors inform witnesses who had been granted immunity that they were liable for prosecution on the basis of other evidence. Attorney General Griffin B. Bell, who had led a Justice Department team at the convention in opposition to the grand jury proposals, called the recommendation to allow attorneys in the grand jury room "a lawyers' relief act" that would "generate plenty of business" for the profession.

The Supreme Court May 23 had ruled in two cases on the rights of grand jury witnesses. In the first case, *U.S. v. Wong*, the court held, 9–0, that a person indicted for perjury on the basis of testimony before a grand jury could not have that testimony excluded as trial evidence because he had not been warned of his right to remain silent under the Fifth Amendment. In the second case, *U.S. v. Washington*, the court ruled, 7–2, that the testimony of a grand jury witness suspected of criminal activity could be used as evidence against him even though he had not been warned in advance of his testimony that he was liable for later prosecution. Justices Brennan and Marshall dissented.

Houston Chronicle
Houston, Tex., December 5, 1977

One of the benefits of the American constitutional system is the ability of the 50 states, and the central government, to profit from the experience of the individual states.

Such a learning experience appears likely over the next few years in the matter of grand juries.

The grand jury system has become a subject of controversy. Critics charge that grand juries, as now constituted, are being abused by government ("tools of the prosecution") rather than serving to protect the citizen. Various changes, including outright abolition, have been proposed.

One of the more important changes advocated is to allow witnesses to have their attorney present in the grand jury room. There are strong opinions pro and con and rational arguments that can be made on both sides.

In dealing with proposals for basic change in systems and institutions, it has always seemed prudent to us to try them out, if possible, on a smaller scale before plunging full ahead into unknown territory.

This opportunity presents itself in the question of witnesses bringing attorneys with them before the grand jury. The state of Massachusetts has passed legislation which grants witnesses that legal right.

No one really knows how this is going to work out. The experience of Massachusetts — or any other state which cares to try it — will presumably be quite instructive, regardless of what that experience is. A wise course for the nation as a whole would be to just wait and see. It is much better to act on the basis of experience than theory.

RENO EVENING GAZETTE
Reno, Nev., October 18, 1977

GRAND JURIES have become a target of so much criticism that if there is no progress in reforming their procedures, critics may succeed in abolishment.

The grand jury system can be an effective tool of justice and protector of citizens. But, it also can become a political tool of a few to harass opposition.

The subpoena powers of a grand jury are an investigative sword, but as a panel of citizens who must decide whether to issue an indictment, it can serve to protect persons from over-zealous prosecutors — willing to ruin a life based on flimsy evidence.

This nation's Founding Fathers thought enough of the grand jury system — started in Medieval England — to provide for it in the Constitution at the federal level. Most states use grand juries as well.

The problem is the sword is becoming too sharp, and the shield too thin. Widespread complaints that grand juries are abusing their power suggest that procedures are not keeping pace with the evolution of law and public sensitivity to individual rights.

Nevada has not been exempt from this tragic turn of events. The most recent example was with the Clark County Grand Jury which investigated possible child abuse in the state children's home.

The intent of that investigation is to be lauded. If such a deplorable situation exists in the home, it should be thoroughly investigated by our justice system and corrected. Appropriate indictments should follow.

This grand jury did just that — but then some.

Roger Trounday, former head of the state Department of Human Resources, testified before the grand jury as the ultimate manager responsible for the home's operations.

The jury did indict a house parent for the alleged abusive actions, but some members apparently did not think that was enough.

A news story was leaked on testimony before the jury and the jury's deliberations in which they found there was not evidence enough to indict others — including Trounday. The implication, however, was the jury had considered such an indictment against the department head, despite the fact he was far removed from the situation.

Why such an incident occurred is difficult to determine. Perhaps a member of the jury has a personal vendetta. Or, maybe one of the prosecutors is overly ambitious and the publicity would benefit future goals. Who knows?

The point is the effect such an incident has on present and future grand juries.

In the past the grand jury was a place where a citizen could testify with assurance his personal integrity would not be bantered about without good cause.

The American Bar Association has presented proposals which are designed to bring the sword and the shield into a better balance.

The need for reform is sufficiently demonstrated.

Lincoln Journal

Lincoln, Neb., June 2, 1977

A House Judiciary subcommittee is taking testimony on possible reforms in the federal grand jury system.

Initial recommendations seem constructive. If enacted, they might cure some of the more dangerous and rightly criticized procedures.

For sure, there ought to be a time limit on jailing, for contempt, those people who refuse to give evidence to a grand jury. Now, such persons can be imprisoned for as long as the particular grand jury sits. That may be two years.

Other proposals, such as allowing subpoenaed individuals to be accompanied in the closed chambers by their attorney, should be carefully examined.

Frankly, the heavy reliance upon the grand jury system by the U.S. Department of Justice always has made many citizens uneasy.

This system enlists the community to make an accusation of a crime. Such an indictment carries a greater psychological weight in society than if the indictment were the exclusive responsibility of the government's prosecutor. As it is, the grand jury normally sees and hears in secret only what the prosecutor wants it to mentally digest.

Nebraska is a state which makes very little use of grand juries, leaving criminal accusations to the discretion of elected prosecutors.

There is, however, a procedure allowing citizens to petition judges for convening of grand juries, when there is sufficient community unrest and a belief investigations are in order.

This is a reasonable public safety net arrangement, so long as citizens don't abuse it. And Nebraskans haven't.

If and when they do, however, the sorts of protections now proposed for the federal grand jury system would be well to incorporate in the state's structure.

The Charlotte Observer

Charlotte, N.C., July 11, 1977

The constitutional provision for grand juries was intended to protect citizens from repressive government, to place a shield between the prosecutor and the accused.

That function has become obscured, however. It's time for Congress and the states to tackle grand jury reform.

Hearings on one such bill for the federal judicial system before a House Judiciary subcommittee are about to end. The bill will go before the full House this fall. The Carter administration has announced its opposition to some of the bill's key provisions, contending that grand jury abuse is rare. There is evidence that it may be more common than the administration thinks.

Grand jury witnesses do not enjoy the constitutional protections they'd get in a trial. And the grand jury can become a tool of the government whose power it was meant to check. That became clear during the early '70s, when the U.S. Justice Department used grand juries to harass antiwar activists.

Among the questions Congress must answer are these:

● Should witnesses be denied the constitutional privilege against self-incrimination because a judge grants them immunity from prosecution for anything they might tell a grand jury? Under federal law, a grand jury witness can be forced to testify if the judge promises immunity.

Two Charlotte police officers faced that situation recently in a grand jury investigation of alleged illegal police wiretapping. U.S. District Judge James McMillan expressed his disagreement with the law, though he saw no alternative to enforcing it.

"Given a free choice in the matter, I would refuse (to do so)," the judge said. " . . . Locking a person up for not talking is . . . only a small degree removed from other traditional types of torture used to make men talk, such as the rack, the saw, the screw, the water treatment . . . ." We share the judge's distaste for forced testimony.

● Should witnesses be denied the presence of an attorney inside the grand jury room?

Presently, witnesses must leave their lawyers outside the hearing room. They must face questioning by the jurors and district attorney on their own, traipsing back and forth to the hallway to seek legal advice. Prosecutors argue that allowing lawyers in would delay things and cause more breaches in grand jury secrecy. We need to hear more arguments pro and con before we take a position on that issue.

● Should grand juries be allowed to seek help from independent lawyers and investigators?

Grand juries must rely for impartial legal counsel primarily on the same person who wants them to return indictments: the prosecutor. The availability of advice from an independent attorney would help prevent charges of collusion and make the grand jury system work as it's supposed to.

It's hard to say how widespread grand jury abuses may be. But the present system leaves too much room for them to occur.

Sentinel Star

Orlando, Fla., April 9, 1977

HOUSE Speaker Donald Tucker is ill advised in seeking to abolish Florida's grand jury law, which has served justice well since territorial days. He'd do well to direct his wrath toward weaknesses of the system rather than the system itself, which gives the citizen a hand in seeing that crooks are found out and tried, and that corruption in public office is called to public notice.

"Instead of being accusatorial, for which it was designed, it is now being inquisitorial," said Tucker. "Except for capital crimes, where I don't think one person should decide to try a case, we ought to eliminate the grand jury."

TUCKER MUST have been watching the CBS show "Sixty Minutes" Sunday, for the identical charge was made against a federal grand jury in Pennsylvania which, it was charged, got too cozy with the FBI and the U.S. attorney, thus unseparating the constitutional separation of judicial and executive power and in effect giving a suspect the choice of testifying against himself or going to jail for contempt of court.

The accusation may be true. Federal and state grand juries have been manipulated by strong willed prosecutors, and even judges from time to time have misused juries.

The Florida law that displeases Tucker authorizes grand juries of between 15 and 18 citizens who may be called into session by a circuit judge.

The judge holds the ultimate power, for he may 1) fail to impanel a jury, 2) dismiss it once it has been formed, or 3) extend its term.

That, however, is virtually the only harness. The grand jury is given vast power to look into any topic its members want to pursue, including noncriminal matters of broad public interest.

TUCKER might have good reason to be peeved. His business affairs were investigated by a grand jury that never issued a report and left the matter hanging for anybody's conjecture. The house speaker might find some allies for his cause if he sought to remedy such abuses rather than abolish the concept.

One safeguard would be to change the law to let a witness take his attorney into the jury room with him.

Another would be for the judge to make clear in his charge to jurors that they have the power to plot their own course of inquiry, even if it is counter to the advice of the state attorney.

When it comes down to it, that's the real weakness in the present system — citizen jurors let themselves be overwhelmed by a strong-minded state attorney who may be personally or politically motivated.

THERE HAVE been runaway grand juries, so called, which went their own way, in defiance of the state attorney, and discovered miscreants in high places. This rare exercise of zealotry is a joy or an abomination, depending, of course, on which side of the law one sits.

This independent spirit ought to be encouraged by any judge who impanels a grand jury.

With those reforms, there'd be no need to abolish grand juries, a move that would put justice in fewer hands and remove one layer of protection from the citizens' rights.

THE CHRISTIAN SCIENCE MONITOR
Boston, Mass., February 16, 1977

Attorney General Bell has stepped into the urgent question of grand jury reform by recognizing the general need for it while opposing such a specific key element of reform as permitting a witness to have counsel present. Mr. Bell promises study of the matter, which was also undertaken by his predecessor. The happiest outcome would be for him to lend his support to the new refinement of reform legislation perennially and persistently introduced by Rep. Joshua Eilberg of Pennsylvania.

Subcommittee hearings on this legislation are expected the middle of next month. Representatives of the American Bar Association (ABA) have long backed efforts for reform. Passage of reform at long last would be a good way to begin the third century of a nation dedicated to liberty and justice for all.

Manifest abuses of the grand jury system have worked against justice. In his confirmation hearings Mr. Bell said it had become a tool of the prosecutor. But as the ABA convention considered adopting a slate of strong grand jury standards this week, Mr. Bell expressed reservations.

On the matter of permitting a witness to have counsel, the Attorney General, like his predecessor, makes the valuable point the grand jury should not be turned into a mini-trial. The secret proceedings of the grand jury were never meant to be an adversary procedure but an investigative process to protect the innocent while bringing wrongdoing to the surface.

The new proposed legislation aims to keep it from becoming an adversary procedure by lim-iting the counsel's role to that of advising the witness — and not, for example, challenging evidence. Also, it would allow the court to remove or replace counsel in certain circumstances, while seeing that free counsel, if necessary, is available in general. Evidence could be challenged at a required preliminary, pretrial hearing such as most states already have.

There are also other refinements to provide some flexibility in the application of the reforms as evaluated by the courts. But the thrust remains to combat abuses by assuring the rights of the witnesses and the independence of the grand jury.

Thus not only must the witness be fully informed of his rights and other matters such as whether he is a potential defendant, but the jurors must be informed of their powers and duties — that they, not the prosecutor, are in control. Regulations on contempt and immunity would be tightened.

Beyond the legislation there are such proposals as a constitutional amendment to continue the investigative power but end the indicting power of grand juries. This has been proposed by high-level studies in the past. There are also proposals to eliminate the grand jury, as happened more than four decades ago in Britain, where the grand jury began.

Certainly, unless the United States is to follow Britain's lead in this manner, it must reform the grand jury system that has served it well in many ways but has been subject to too much misuse.

The San Diego Union
San Diego, Calif., October 2, 1977

Grand juries have become a target of so much criticism that if there is no progress in reforming their rules of procedure their critics may succeed in seeing them abolished altogether. That would be a regrettable loss. There is more good than ill to flow from the grand jury system, both as a tool of law enforcement and as a protection for the citizen against harassment or worse at the hands of prosecutors.

The subpoena powers of a grand jury are an investigative sword, but as a panel of citizens who must decide whether to issue an indictment, a grand jury also can shield the citizen from being brought to trial by over-zealous prosecutors on evidence too flimsy to support a case. America's Founding Fathers thought enough of grand juries, which originated in Medieval England, to provide in the Constitution that they be employed in all federal criminal cases. Most states, including California, use grand juries at least as an option in their criminal justice system.

The problem is that the sword has become too sharp, the shield too thin. Widespread complaints that grand juries are abusing their power suggest that their procedures have not kept pace with evolution of the law and public sensitivity to individual rights. An effort to bring the sword and the shield into better balance lies behind the reforms proposed last August by the American Bar Association.

We think the proposals are sound. Principally, the ABA would scrap the rule which prevents lawyers from accompanying their clients into a grand jury room. Two members of the ABA Criminal Justice Committee, in an article appearing elsewhere in this section today, explain how the right to counsel can be extended to persons called before grand juries without turning the proceedings into a "trial." Under the proper ground rules, that reform and others proposed by the ABA to protect the rights of witnesses can go a long way toward meeting current protests about grand jury abuse.

Naturally, prosecutors are worried that these changes could undermine the investigative pur-pose of grand juries. However, the need for the reform arises from excesses within their own ranks. There have been too many cases where grand jurors, who are laymen relying solely on a prosecutor's interpretation of the law, have been led into proceedings which confuse witnesses, expose them to unnecessary publicity and jeopardize their defense in a future trial.

Lawyers can make or break the grand jury system. The sword and the shield make a neat metaphor, but this does not mean grand juries must be an arena for legal fencing by attorneys, nor should the debate on proposed reforms be a contest between the prejudiced interests of district attorneys and defenders. Their mutual concern should be to help grand jurors make a dispassionate judgment on whether they are confronted with an indictable offense. Our legal practitioners will increase public respect for themselves and the law if they support reforms which strengthen that role of the grand jury in our federal and state judicial systems.

Wisconsin State Journal
Madison, Wisc., May 3, 1977

The grand jury system in this country needs reform.

The system, devised under English law to provide a more democratic way of bringing charges against persons suspected of crimes, has been perverted into a prosecutors' tool to get around constitutional guarantees.

Almost nowhere else in the criminal justice system is a person who wants a lawyer denied that right. Someone hailed before a grand jury must submit to questioning under oath with no professional legal help at his side. He can receive advice from counsel outside the jury room but must ask for and be granted permission to leave the room when he wants it.

Richard F. Gerstein, chairman of the American Bar Assn.'s (ABA) criminal justice section's grand jury committee, said this not only unnecessarily prolongs the proceedings but also places the witness in an unfavorable light before the jury.

"It is extremely damaging to the witness to continually get up, go outside, and consult with counsel," Gerstein, a prosecutor for more than 20 years, said.

What would be wrong with permitting someone testifying before a grand jury to have legal counsel at hand? He's allowed it outside the room. Why go through the clumsey motions of leaving the room to talk to a lawyer?

Other reforms are needed. The following changes have been recommended by the ABA:

✔ Witnesses forced by law to give testimony that might violate the guarantee against self-incrimination should be given immunity from prosecution for any crime referred to in the testimony.

✔ Witnesses who refuse on several occasions to testify about the same event.

✔ Increased penalties for unauthorized disclosure of grand jury information.

The Sixth Amendment to the United States Constitution says:

"In all criminal prosecutions, the accused shall enjoy the right to a speedy and public trial, by an impartial jury of the State and district wherein the crimes shall have been committed...to be confronted with the witnesses against him; to have compulsary process for obtaining witnesses in his favor, and to have the Assistance of Counsel for his defence."

The rights spelled out in that amendment should not stop at the door to the grand jury room.

HERALD EXAMINER

Los Angeles, Calif., June 7, 1977

Selection of juries in criminal and civil cases is unduly prolonged through the legal device known as peremptory challenges.

The peremptory challenge enables an attorney to dismiss prospective jurors without stating cause and without further questions. Many court-watchers believe that California law currently provides for an excessive number of these challenges, lengthening the time of trials.

Two bills that would reform this device have been introduced in Sacramento as SB 618 and SB 1063. Both of them have the support of the Los Angeles Superior Court Committee on Court Improve-

ments. They also have our support.

According to Presiding Judge William Hogoboom, the Superior Court selects more than 1,200 civil juries and about 1,500 criminal juries each year. By reducing the number of peremptory challenges for these 2,700 juries, the Superior Court could save an estimated 900 court days each year—equal to the time of four full-time judges.

Beyond the savings in court expenses and time, another benefit of the proposed court reform is the need to disrupt the life of fewer prospective jurors. All these advantages should tend to reinstill greater faith in the American system of justice.

ST. LOUIS POST-DISPATCH

St. Louis, Mo., April 6, 1977

The criminal justice section of the American Bar Association has added its voice to those of other critics in favor of legislative safeguards against abuse of the grand jury. The ABA group has recommended that Congress, among other things, allow witnesses before grand juries to have legal counsel, ban the repeated imprisonment of witnesses for refusing to testify before grand juries, and allow grand jury witnesses to use a violation of the federal wire-tapping law as a defense.

Such protections are needed because of the evolution of the grand jury from what originally was its role as a shield against unjust prosecution to its present role as a tool of the prosecution. The abuse of the grand jury reached a peak under the Nixon Administration, which used the grand jury as an investigative lever to force delivery of evidence in violation of the spirit of the Fifth Amendment's guarantee against self-incrimination.

Legislative reforms, such as the ABA group is proposing, are designed to return the grand jury to its intended constitutional purpose as a shield for the people against the government rather than a sword for the government against the people.

The Boston Globe

Boston, Mass., July 8, 1977

There were undoubtedly those who saw a certain irony in the complaints by General Motors last month that the Federal government was abusing the grand jury process by hauling in GM officials to testify under oath about corporate tax matters. In recent times, at least, complaints about grand jury abuses have come most frequently not from the offices of the nation's corporate executives but from political radicals charging grand juries have been employed to quash their activities.

In theory, the grand jury serves a laudable purpose. It allows possible criminal charges against an individual to be screened in secrecy by an independent panel of the accused's peers before they are publicly lodged.

In fact, however, the grand jury has become a tool of the prosecutor. By both establishing the grand jury's agenda and orchestrating the quality and quantity of the evidence presented, the prosecutor almost invariably determines who is and is not indicted.

But the grand jury can still provide valuable protection to individuals and the most prudent course now is to increase those safeguards. At the Federal level, legislation to do this — which could well serve as a model for similar state actions — has been introduced by Rep. Joshua Eilberg (D-Pa.). It received a cool reception from the Carter Administration at a hearing last week but it points in the right direction.

It would repeal the "use" immunity law enacted at the urging of the Nixon Administration under which witnesses can be compelled to testify before a

Federal grand jury and then, despite the constitutional guarantees against self-incrimination, be tried for activities about which they testified as long as the specific testimony is not used. The Eilberg legislation would return the Federal system to "transactional" immunity under which a witness compelled to testify could not later be tried for crimes detailed in that testimony.

The Eilberg legislation would also allow defense attorneys into the grand jury room to advise their clients (now they wait outside the room and their clients can go out to them) and, not incidentally, to monitor the process. A similar proposal for Massachusetts grand juries was recently approved by the state Senate.

Another meritorious provision of the Eilberg legislation would require that a judge screen Federal grand jury indictments prior to their issuance to make sure that they are based upon sufficient admissible evidence and that the procedures were appropriate. The proposal is designed to avoid needless damage to reputations arising from improper indictments.

None of these proposals has won the general approval of prosecutors. Yet none should generally impair prosecutors' work. Whatever the grand jury's original function, in a complex industrial society, where crime is commonplace and crime fighting sophisticated, the professionals — the prosecutors — will play the dominant role. But it is in exactly such a society that sufficient measures must be taken to protect the rights of individuals.

Roanoke Times & World-News

Roanoke, Va., April 8, 1977

Society has an equal right with a defendant in a criminal trial and it is a pleasure to note a probable rule change in federal court criminal procedure. At present in a capital case, each side is entitled to 20 peremptory challenges—dismissal from jury duty for no stated cause whatsoever.

In a noncapital felony case, the prosecution can challenge six potential jurors peremptorily while the defense can remove 10 without cause. Equality is restored on the misdemeanor level: three each.

An amendment now before Congress would give each side the right to the same number of no-cause challenges: 12 in a capital case; five in a noncapital felony case, two in a misdemeanor case. The reduction in the number of such challenges is more important than equalizing the number for each side; strange things are happening in jury selection.

In some spectacular cases of recent years, the defendants made a sociological survey of attitudes. In the New York City area, for instance, if being Protestant or Catholic, young or old, black or white, educated or illiterate, low to medium or high income,

etc., could be "proved" to increase the odds for the defense, the defendants would then use their large quota of arbitrary strikes to obtain a jury to their liking.

Richard L. Thornburg, acting deputy attorney general, made an interesting point about the technique recently. If the sociological survey helps the rich, one should be made for the poor; in fact, some poor defendants are now demanding that the government put up the money to obtain for them a sociological guide to jury selections. The way to make the survey almost useless, for rich or poor, is to remove the extraordinary number of challenges now permitted.

Mr. Thornburg is correct in saying the procedure makes the criminal justice system look bad. The verdict should be seen as primarily dependent on the quality of the evidence presented and the judge's instructions on the law. It should not be made to seem that the verdict depends upon whether the "proper" racial or cultural makeup was obtained in jury selection. The trial lawyer's hunch and a modest number of absolute strikes are as much as should be allowed in the cultural stacking of a jury.

Crowded Courts:
Any room for justice?

Chief Justice Warren Burger is both the presiding justice of the United States Supreme Court and chief administrator of the entire federal court system. The system is composed of the Supreme Court; 11 circuit court districts with 97 judges; and 94 district courts with 400 judges. The circuit court serves as an appeals court for the trial-level district courts. The Supreme Court is, with a few exceptions, also an appeals court and is the final arbiter of judicial disputes for federal courts and state courts if a federal question is present.

Chief Justice Burger has argued since he was appointed in 1969 that federal judges at all levels, including the Supreme Court are over-worked with too heavy caseloads.[1] Since 1970 alone the number of cases filed in district courts have increased by 40% and by 140% in the circuit courts.[2] One obvious solution advocated by Chief Justice Burger is the creation of more federal judgeships by Congress.

Congress is in the process of creating approximately 115 new federal judges. The new positions are to be filled by President Carter. Traditionally the appointment of federal judges has been influenced by political factors. Presidents since the early days of the country have selected judges almost exclusively from their own parties. President Carter in his campaign expressed a desire to break with the tradition: "political participation should not be a factor" in selecting federal judges. Carter has fulfilled part of his pledge by establishing the United States Circuit Judge Nominating Commission to propose candidates for the United States Court of Appeals. Federal district judges, however, have been excluded from Carter's proposal. Carter did call for "voluntary" merit selection panels to recommend candidates for the district courts. Nevertheless, it is expected that political connections will determine the appointment of nominees for the time being.

Enlarging the panel of federal judges is only one of the solutions Chief Justice Burger proposes. Through court decisions he has attempted to restrict federal court review for numerous classes of claimants. In *Younger v. Harris,* the Supreme Court required defendants in state criminal cases to completely exhaust their state appeals before coming to federal court.[3] More recently, the Court has limited the types of post-conviction relief open to state prisoners. Convicted prisoners in *habeas corpus* writs may no longer ask the high court for relief if their petition is based on a Fourth Amendment claim concerning an illegal search and seizure.[4] Failure to follow a state court precedural rule now precludes a *habeas corpus* appeal to the federal courts except in the most narrow of circumstances.[5] Rules of standing, that is, the right of a claimant to bring a case and raise legal issues before the federal courts, have also been tightened.[6]

Many critics do not dispute Chief Justice Burger's desire to reduce the types of claims that can be adjudicated in the federal courts. But these critics argue that the Burger Court decisions have limited access at the expense of the poor, the minorities and the politically disenfranchised. Rejection of their cases in federal court means litigating the issues in state courts, which are less independent of political pressures than the federal courts. Instead, court reforms should eliminate federal jurisdiction based on the diversity of citizenship. Diversity cases refer to a legal dispute where one or more parties have a different state residence than the opposing party. The historical reason for federal diversity jurisdiction was the early nineteenth century belief that state courts would not treat out-of-staters fairly in suits against their own citizens. Since the historical justification for this jurisdiction has been considerably lessened, critics argue that the federal courts should give greater priority to the claims of unpopular groups who have often faced hostile state judicial forums.[7]

PLEA BARGAINING

Caseloads of federal courts are small compared to those of state courts in urban areas. Waiting periods of two or three years for a personal injury or contract case might be distressing but not as serious as a year spent in jail awaiting trial. The especially heavy dockets of criminal courts are a primary reason for the pervasiveness of plea bargaining.   Plea bargaining is the practice of a defendant's pleading guilty in return for a promise of a reduced sentence or charge. In Manhattan 95% of all convictions result from a plea bargain.[8]

By pleading guilty, a defendant surrenders his right to a trial, his right to cross-examine witnesses and his right against self-incrimination. The Supreme Court has recognized the constitutionality of the practice in *Brady v. United States*.[9] The advantage of plea bargaining to the judges and prosecutors is obvious: it quickly reduces the caseload backlog. If each case went to trial it might take days before a verdict is rendered. A plea of guilty, on the other hand, rarely takes more than five minutes. Refusal to plea bargain would cost the public millions of dollars in higher court administration costs. Plea bargaining is used as a means of making the sentence more realistic. Often politicians are prone to legislate long sentences as a result of a temporary public outcry. Plea bargaining gives the system a built-in flexibility. The prosecutor frequently employs plea bargaining when he believes he has a weak case: better a guilty plea with a light sentence than an acquittal. The police also like plea bargaining because every plea represents an arrest resulting in a conviction—proof of the efficiency of the system.

Defense attorneys often encourage their clients to plead guilty. The principle reason is that the evidence against their clients is often substantial and a plea will result in less punishment than a conviction after trial. But for less noble reasons, some private attorneys like pleas because involvement in a lengthy trial would infringe upon their other cases. Though trial fees are quite steep, they do not cover the cost of business lost during the course of a trial. Public defenders are not influenced by the financial aspects, but their heavy caseloads prevent them from spending the necessary time on each case. Using their professional judgment, they must determine which cases are most likely to result in acquittals and allocate their limited time accordingly. Institutional concerns also play a part. If public defenders insisted on contesting the innocence of each and every client in a trial, they would earn the enmity of the judges before whom they constantly appeared.

From the defendant's point of view, plea bargaining contains certain advantages. Most judges will mete out heavier sentences to defendants who insist on going to trial and are convicted, than to defendants who plead guilty. To many, the judge is informally punishing the defendant for exercising his right to a trial. The Supreme Court in *Brady* has rejected the claim that exposure to a longer sentence by insisting upon a trial is unconstitutional:

"We decline to hold, however, that a guilty plea is compelled and invalid under the Fifth Amendment whenever motivated by the defendant's desire to accept the certainty or probability of a lesser penalty rather than face a wider range of possibilities extending from acquittal to conviction and a higher penalty authorized by law for the crime charged.[11]

More recently, the Supreme court has even sanctioned the common practice of prosecutors threatening to charge defendants with more serious crimes if they should refuse to plead guilty to a lesser offense. In *Bordenkircher v. Hayes,* the defendant charged with forging a check for $88.30, was offered a sentence of five years if he would plead guilty.[12] If he rejected the offer, prosecutor threatened to seek a second indictment against the suspect as a habitual offender, based on two previous felony conviction, a crime that carried a mandatory life sentence. The defendant refused to plead guilty to the first indictment and wound up sentenced to life in prison. The majority of the Court reasoned that punishing the defendant in this way was permissible since the defendant was free to reject or accept the offer made to him.

Defendants who are unable to make bail are also prone to plead guilty. If a defendant is not charged with a serious crime, he might, in return for a plea of guilty, receive only a few days or a sentence of time-served. Insisting upon a trial would take several months, if not longer. All of this period must be spent in a pre-trial detention center, which in most respects is little different than a penitentiary for convicted prisoners. It has even been alleged in a well documented law review article that intolerable conditions in one California pre-trial detention center, condemned by Federal District Judge Alphonzo J. Zirpoli as "barbaric" and "cruel and unusual punishment for man or beast," were maintained so as to encourage prisoners to plead guilty.[13]   Other defendants who are innocent might prefer to pay a small court fine in. return for a guilty plea, rather than a lawyer's fee of a $1,000 or more for a short trial.

It is argued that the public has an interest in preventing plea bargaining because its elimination would result in longer sentences. This is unclear since often a reduction in the charge after a plea of guilty is not a prosecutorial gift to the defendant but a realistic appraisal of the crime actually committed. The prosecutor, aware that plea bargaining always takes place, has a tendency to overcharge the defendant so as to be able to reduce the charge when plea negotiations are initiated. An example of this might be a suspect who is found at night in a vacated building with an open door or window. The prosecutor will charge the accused with burglary. Once plea negotiations commence, the defense counsel will impress upon the prosecutor that the case is no more than a trespass since the vacant building can be entered without an actual breaking, and that there is nothing of value in the building. The end result will probably be a plea of guilty to a trespass, a minor offense.

A more serious charge against the plea-bargaining system is that it reduces respect for the system among defendants. Social scientists have explained that an important element of rehabilitation is that the criminal offender is made to feel that he has been treated fairly and that the operations of the legal system fairly reflect its own values and aspirations.[14] Plea bargaining may serve that principle poorly.

Notes

1. See, e.g., "How to Break Logjam in Courts," (Interview with Chief Justice Burger) *U.S. News & World Reports,* December 19, 1977 p. 21.
2. *Congressional Quarterly,* November 19, 1977 p. 2443.
3. *Younger v. Harris,* 401 U.S. 37 (1971).
4. *Stone v. Powell, Wolff v. Rice,* 428 U.S. 465 (1976).
5. *Francis v. Henderson,* 425 U.S. 536 (1976); *Estelle v. Williams,* 425 U.S. 501 (1976).
6. *Simon v. Eastern Kentucky Welfare Rights Org.* 426 U.S. 26 (1976); *Warth v. Seldin,* 422 U.S. 490 (1975).

7. See Burt Neuborne, "Myth of Parity," 90 *Harvard Law Review* 1105 (1977).

8. See *Santobello v. New York,* 404 U.S. 257, 264 & n.1, n.2 (1971). (Douglas, J., concurring). ring).

9. *Brady v. United States,* 397 U.S. 742 (1970).

10. Jerome Skolnick, "Social Control in the Adversary System," 11 *Journal of Conflict Resolution* 52–70 (1967); and generally on public defenders, see Anthony Platt & Randi Pollock, "Channelling Lawyers," *Issues in Criminology,* Spring, 1974 p. 1.

11. *Brady, supra,* 751.

12. *Bordenkircher v. Hayes,* 46 U.S.L.W. 4084 (January 18, 1977).

13. Gregory J. Hobbs, Jr., "Judicial Supervision over California Plea Bargaining: Regulating the Trade," 59 *California Law Review* 962 (1971).

14. See, e.g., *Donald Newman, Conviction* (Boston: Little Brown, 1966).

BURGER URGES CONGRESS TO APPROVE MORE COURT SEATS, HIGHER SALARIES

Chief Justice Warren E. Burger urged Congress to create more federal court seats Jan. 3. Writing his year-end report, Burger recalled that Congress had been informed in 1972 that the federal district courts needed 52 new judgeships and the court of appeals needed 13. No new seats had been created since the request; although the Senate has passed a bill approving seven new appeals court seats. Another bill establishing 45 district court judgeships has been cleared by the Senate Judiciary Committee but has not reached the Senate floor.

Congress last authorized an increase in appellate judges in 1968, Burger noted, when the caseload was an average 282 per judge. In 1975 the average was 515, and is expected to reach 600 in 1976. The chief justice also urged higher salaries for federal judges, claiming that more judges had left the bench in the last two years for financial reasons than in the previous 35 years. Federal district judges now make $42,000 annually, circuit court of appeals judges $44,600, Supreme Court associate justices $63,000, and the chief justice $65,600.

The Houston Post

Houston, Tex., January 12, 1976

Chief Justice Warren Burger's criticism of congressional failure to increase the number of federal judges is doubly justified. Not only has Congress declined to act on a request made in 1972 for 52 more federal district judges and 13 additional appellate judges, it has imposed an added burden on the federal courts with the passage of the Speedy Trial Act in 1974.

Burger, who has waged a long, vigorous campaign to beef up the federal judicial system, offers convincing evidence to support his contention that the system is severely overburdened. In deploring the unresponsiveness of Congress to requests for new judges, Burger released figures showing that 160,602 cases were filed in U.S. district courts in the fiscal year ending June 30. This is an average of 402 cases per judge, an increase of 95 cases per judge since 1970. The chief justice estimates that the caseload will average 450 cases per judge in another year despite improved procedures for disposing of cases.

Burger says the appeals courts could receive 19,400 filings in the coming fiscal year—an increase of 113 per cent since 1968, the last time judges were added. He also notes that the Supreme Court's caseload has nearly quadrupled in the past half-century. Burger considers inadequate a bill before Congress that would add 45 new district judgeships and seven appellate judgeships. This is a total of 13 fewer than he had requested four years ago. "Action taken in 1976 on 1972 needs and projected needs is hardly a reasonable response," he said.

Congress has a greater obligation than ever to see that the federal judicial system is adequately staffed since it passed the Speedy Trial Act a little over a year ago. The new law requires that criminal cases in federal courts be tried within 60 days of indictment or be dismissed. True, the law is being applied gradually over a seven-year period, giving the courts time to assess their needs and report them to Congress. But Congress has the responsibility to supply the means of implementing the speedy trial program. It is high time the lawmakers heeded Burger's warning of the strains being put on the federal judicial system by the growing caseloads and the shortage of judges. The quality of justice is at stake.

Boston Herald American
Combining the best features of the Herald Traveler and Record American

Boston, Mass., January 5, 1976

"At our 200th anniversary of nationhood we find, in common with most other countries, that confidence in our institutions, public and private, seems to be eroded." Chief Justice Warren E. Burger told us in the first sentence of his annual "year-end report" on the judiciary.

His second sentence said, "The judicial system by and large, however, is working well, and this is reflected in the relatively high popular esteem of the courts. The faults and frailties of our judicial branch are, for the most part, recognized and correctable — and there is much activity toward improvement."

So far, so good. No whereas's, hences, ergos, or wherefores. Not a suspicion of a be it known.

The chief justice's report is only seven pages in length. His report is not a report on the condition of the judiciary so much as it is a plea that justices are overworked and underpaid. Even retired justices are underpaid.

Here's what the chief justice says: "The gross inequity toward salaries of federal judges, in common with 12,000 other high-level federal officials, continues, relieved only by the 5 percent increase late in 1975. At the same time, retired federal judges have received only a 5 percent increase since 1969, in common with active judges. By contrast, all other retired federal employes have received a 69 percent increase in their retirement pensions."

Bad news. Needs correcting. More federal judges have resigned for economic reasons to return to private life during the past two years than in the previous 35 years. The chief justice says this trend will continue "unless Congress acts to remedy this grave unfairness."

More judges are needed. The chief justice notes that federal judges had "longer hours of work" and they disposed of more cases last year than formerly. "The average disposition per judgeship in 1975 was 371 cases, up 27 percent from 292 in 1970. Nevertheless, the rising tide of new filings outdistanced the increased output, so that 355 cases per judgeship awaited disposition in 1975, compared to 285 in 1970."

The late Chief Justice Earl Warren — may he rest in peace — is simply not allowed to rest in peace by this court. Justice Burger notes how the Supreme Court faces a caseload almost four times as much as that which confronted the Court in the 1920s and 1930s. He, too, that "In the first three years of Chief Justice Earl Warren's tenure, 1953-55, there were an average of 91 signed opinions each year. In the past three years the average has been 134."

So much for the end-of-the year report. Now it's up to Congress to respond to Justice Burger's report. His deep respect for our judicial system should win much support for the opinions he hands down on how to strengthen it.

Post-Tribune

Guarding Your Interests Daily

Gary, Ind., January 7, 1976

In some cases it's unfortunate that the year-end remarks which Chief Justice Warren Burger has made an annual event since assuming the nation's top judicial post lack the weight of Supreme Court dictum.

That is especially true of his remarks in his latest such report about the continuing need of more federal judges. It was a repeat, actually, of the chief justice's remarks of the year before and possibly the year before that.

We in this area should be particularly tuned in to the top judge's remarks in that regard.

The United States District Court for the Northern District of Indiana is short at least two judges.

One is to fill a vacancy left since the death of Judge George Beamer. The other is to fill a post which the Senate Judiciary Committee now recognizes that the court should have on the basis of its case load.

But those vacancies seem to be tied up in a dispute between Indiana Sen. Birch Bayh, a member of the Senate Judiciary Committee, who insists the next appointment should go to a Democrat, and President Ford who already has opted for a Republican to fill the Beamer vacancy.

The opportunity for a compromise appears open due to the fact that the committee has recognized the need of an additional judge.

What's holding up the compromise? We aren't certain about all the ins and outs. There is, however, the possibility now that both men are too busy right now campaigning for the presidency and so may have let the issue slide.

But the courts are too busy, too —far too busy— and their delays are costly to many of the public both in civil and criminal cases.

Justice Burger pointed out that in 1972 the federal courts cited a need for 52 additional district judges and 13 more on appeals benches.

Quite inevitably those needs have grown.

But Congress and the executive continue to bicker while the overload of cases in the courts continues to grow.

Doubtless there should be a new reassessment of the needs of the courts.

We are most familiar with the Northern Indiana situation, but there are probably other needs equally urgent and very likely equally snarled in politics.

The chief justice can't fill such vacancies. Under our governmental organization, he should not be entitled to. But he is in a peculiarly apt position to estimate the needs. His advice should be followed.

THE KNICKERBOCKER NEWS

••• UNION-STAR •••

Albany, N.Y., January 5, 1976

Chief Justice Warren E. Burger has issued his annual report on the state of the federal judiciary. Much of the report is devoted to the need for more federal judges to handle the ever increasing work load of the courts. It is, however, the causes for this increasing work load that is of greater interest.

The first of these causes enumerated by Justice Berger is in "the tendency of Americans to try to resolve every sort of problem in the courts." The chief justice continued by saying:

"Overwhelmed by increased demands for regulatory legislation, for broadened governmental programs of all kinds, Congress enacts legislation, much of which reaches the courts for resolution. There the legislation increasingly presents difficult questions of interpretation because of the uniqueness of the issues."

It might be mentioned that this increasingly legalistic world not only makes the work load of the courts heavier but has become a plague to business and the despair of individuals.

Justice Berger also noted the 34 per cent rise in bankruptcies in 1975, leaving 262,000 cases awaiting decisions. Hard times and the discovery by more and more people of the possibility of bankruptcy as a relatively easy way out bespeak the human condition.

The chief judge found two other matters that lead to crowding of federal courts particularly unsupportable. The first was the huge number of petitions from prison inmates on matters which he said "could be handled effectively and fairly within the prison system. The second was in the use of federal courts simply because the opposing litigants happen to be residents of different states. The justice said such cases should be returned to state courts.

Sum it up and the report makes clear that through a few relatively simple procedures much of the court burden could be eased. But it remains doubtful that even the chief justice of the United States or anyone else can do anything much to end "the tendency of Americans to try to resolve every sort of problem in the courts." By nature we're a contentious people and better that we fight matters out in the courts than in the streets.

The Oregonian

Portland, Ore., January 4, 1976

Chief Justice Warren E. Burger's annual report on the federal judiciary gives an alarming portrayal of the flood of litigation engulfing the courts at all levels.

"The tendency of Americans to try to resolve every sort of problem in the courts continues," Chief Justice Burger observes. "Overwhelmed by increased demands for regulatory legislation, for broadening governmental programs of all kinds, Congress enacts legislation, much of which reaches the courts for resolution. There the legislation increasingly presents difficult questions of interpretation because of the uniqueness of the issues."

In fiscal 1970, cases filed in U. S. District Courts averaged 317 per judge. That figure rose to 402 cases per judge in the fiscal year ending last June. Projections for the current fiscal year indicate that the case load will be about 450 per judge.

The situation is even more critical in the appeals courts. The case load there is expected to be about 600 per judge this fiscal year, as compared to fewer than half that number in fiscal 1968, when Congress increased the number of appeals judgeships.

The sharp increase in appeals has also increased the work load of the Supreme Court, sparking recommendations for a federal Court of Appeals on the order of Oregon's Court of Appeals.

The Chief Justice made the standard recommendations of an increase in federal judgeships and an increase in federal judges' salaries to stem what he says has been a record rate of resignations by judges for economic reasons.

But there are other measures that could be taken that would help reduce the work loads of the courts.

Almost one in every five federal cases filed is what is called a "diversity case," one in which the opposing litigants are residents of different states. Burger says that such cases belong in state courts. Logic is on his side.

The multiplication of the number of cases in which a panel of three federal judges sits and renders a decision that may be appealed directly to the Supreme Court is also consuming of the courts' time. Congress could eliminate this practice.

It is also possible that U. S. magistrates, appointed under the terms of a 1970 law, could further relieve federal judges. The 143 U. S magistrates plus part-time magistrates, in fiscal 1975, disposed of more than 250,000 matters that would otherwise have gone to federal judges.

It is axiomatic that justice delayed is justice denied. So is justice drowned in case volume.

LEDGER-STAR
Norfolk, Va., January 5, 1976

In his annual report on "the condition of the judiciary," Chief Justice Burger points to another area of congressional foot-dragging—providing for the needs of the federal court system, which he says is staggering under a caseload so swollen as to constitute a threat to the American standard of justice.

The statistics Mr. Burger offers document his argument impressively. In fiscal year 1975, an average of 402 new cases were filed in the U.S. District Courts for each judge (for a total of 160,602). Five years ago, the figure was only 317 new cases per judgeship. Based on early experience the figure for fiscal '76, which is half over, will be 450.

The judges increased their productivity during this period, disposing of an average of 371 cases per judge in 1975, as compared to 292 in 1970. But

the district courts still fell farther behind.

At the appeals court level, a similar situation prevails, the number of appeals per judgeship rising from 282 to 515, and expected to reach 600 this year. The backlog of cases pending doubled in five years.

★ ★ ★ ★

During this time, Congress did not see fit to increase the number of judgeships, despite a recommendation by the Judicial Conference of the United States that 52 district and 13 appeals judges be added. This recommendation was made pursuant to an act of Congress calling for the federal courts to project the needs through 1976. The law now requires a projection of needs through 1980, causing the Chief Justice to observe:

"What can be expected by way of

congressional action to meet 1976-80 needs when the 1972-76 needs have not been met is problematical."

★ ★ ★ ★

Actually, Mr. Burger does not see the creation of new judgeships as a complete answer to the problem of burdensome dockets. Noting a "tendency of Americans to try to resolve every sort of problem in the courts," he recommends several steps, legislative and otherwise, that would provide some relief. One involves better handling of complaints within prisons to reduce the mass of petitions reaching the courts (an effort that is succeeding in federal prisons, though the number of petitions from state prisons continues to arise).

He also wants so-called "diversity" cases removed from the federal courts, which have jurisdiction for no other reason than that the litigants re-

side in different states. These proposals suggest, hearteningly, that there are some practical things that can be done to remedy the problem at least partially, without relying entirely on the addition of platoons of new judges.

In this vein, Mr. Burger notes that changes in methods and the use of magistrates to handle certain court functions already are making possible more effective use of judges' time. Computerization, applied to such things as monitoring dockets and transcribing reports, holds promise also.

Even so, considering the enormous increase in workload described by the Chief Justice, it no doubt would be unrealistic to hope the courts can manage without adding some new judgeships. Congress, whose legislative products lead to so much of the litigation, could be risking damage to the judicial system if it fails to take the recommendations seriously.

THE COMMERCIAL APPEAL
Memphis, Tenn., January 5, 1976

CHIEF JUSTICE Warren Burger has a good point when he says Congress is falling down on its job in not naming even a few of the additional federal judges which were requested four years ago.

If 1972 needs of the federal courts are to be met in 1976, he argues, that action will not meet the needs of those courts in the four years ahead.

There is a growing awareness that justice is too long delayed. Many members of Congress campaign on platforms that demand swifter justice. They need to follow up on those demands with actions that make it possible.

The increasing work load of the courts is understandable. Crime has been increasing. Legislators keep passing new laws. And there are ever more lawyers to file new cases. The federal courts have instituted rules to expedite matters, but there are limits to what the individual judges can do when the number of cases coming before each of them reaches 450 a year as it will in the year ahead.

Appointment of additional judges would relieve some of that ever-growing load. But the bar associations also have an obligation to discipline their members to require them to expedite justice rather than delaying it by tactics that in some cases border on barratry.

BURGER ALSO has a point in his urgent request for better pay and pension equity for judges. We have never bought his argument that the erosion of judges' salaries due to inflation is a violation of the constitutional provision that prohibits a cut in judge's pay while he is in office. That's a silly argument, simply an appeal for a cost-of-living escalator.

The pay of federal judges should be based on their worth. We believe most federal judges deserve more pay than they are getting. And certainly retired judges should get the same sort of pension benefits all other retired federal employes get. Congress should see that they get those improvements.

The Providence Journal
Providence, R.I., January 7, 1976

Federal law requires the Judicial Conference (the administrative arm of the federal courts) to inform Congress of projected needs every four years. But the law says nothing about a corresponding congressional obligation to meet those needs.

This gap has moved Chief Justice of the United States Warren E. Burger to complain. In 1972 the conference asked for 52 new district judges and 13 more appeals court judges. Beyond the preliminaries, nothing has happened. Now it is time to project the judiciary's needs for the next four years.

"What can be expected by way of congressional action to meet 1976-1980 needs when the 1972-1976 needs have not been met is problematical," said Chief Justice Burger, in an unusually blunt year-end report.

The situation has serious implications for the efficient functioning of the U.S. courts. In 1970, for example, the average annual workload of a U.S. District judge was 317 cases. By this year the figure was up to 402 and by next June 30, according to the Chief Justice, it will be about 450. An even heavier burden weighs on the courts of appeals — estimated at 600 cases per judge this year, or an increase of 113 percent from 1968.

The salaries of federal judges pose another problem. "During the past two years," Mr. Burger said, "more federal judges resigned for economic reasons to return to private life than in the previous 35 years. This will continue unless Congress acts to remedy this grave unfairness."

A co-equal, largely autonomous branch of government, the judiciary remains totally dependent for money and manpower on the legislative arm. New judgeships mean political patronage to be dispensed — reason enough for many members of Congress to dawdle and vacillate until conditions are just right.

But mention a congressional salary increase and suddenly the skies clear, uncertainty vanishes and a collective sense of duty grips this august body. Notwithstanding the lament of the taxpaying public, the motion for an increase passes with scarcely a dissenting vote.

The Hartford Courant
Hartford, Conn., January 14, 1976

Chief Justice Warren E. Burger of the Supreme Court of the United States could be pardoned if an old Latin phrase pesters him constantly these days. It is: "Vox clamantis in deserto"—or, "a voice crying in the wilderness." And such indeed is the lot thus far of the top tribunal in trying to convince Congress of the urgency in increasing the manpower of the bench.

Matter of fact, some of the lawmakers are downright deaf when it comes to discussing the important issue. Fortunately, for the cause of justice, Mr. Burger is not about to be ignored.

In his year-end assessment of the courts, the Chief Justice sharply criticized the House and Senate for failing to act on judgeship proposals submitted to them four years ago. Obviously, as he himself has stressed, the need is far greater now.

Mr. Burger noted that in 1972, as required by statute, the Judicial Conference—the administrative arm of the Federal bench—told Congress the Federal district courts needed 52 new judgeships while the courts of appeals needed

an additional 13. Despite some preliminary consideration, no new seats have since been created.

Small wonder then that the Chief Justice commented caustically: "The same act of Congress that required submission of these figures four years ago now requires that we submit in 1976 the figures to measure the needs for 1976-80. What can be expected by way of Congressional action to meet 1976-80 needs when the 1972-76 needs have not been met is problematical."

That justice once again is in a jam due to overloaded dockets is clearly evident. For instance, the rising number of cases filed increased the number awaiting disposition per judge in the district courts from 285 in 1970 to 355 in 1975.

Clogged courts naturally lead to delayed decisions, with time thus becoming a dubious arbiter. Congress should move rapidly to fill the mounting manpower needs of the Federal bench.

The Courier-Journal

Louisville, Ky., January 8, 1976

ONCE AGAIN, Chief Justice Burger's year-end review of the judiciary takes Congress to task for not doing its part to assure efficient working of the federal justice system. His complaints are fully justified.

Congress is alert to the broader demands of social justice — as witness last year's passage of the Speedy Trial Act, for instance. But it lags inexcusably, mostly for political reasons, in providing the tools needed to do the job.

Thus in 1972 the Chief Justice filed, as required by law, detailed statistics on the federal court workload and projected figures for the next four years. He estimated that at least 52 new district judges and 13 new appellate judges would be required to handle future needs. Since then, despite renewed pleas, Congress has taken no more than the first steps in this direction. Even the bill that has been introduced would add only 45 judges to the district courts and seven to the courts of appeals.

Later this year, Chief Justice Burger will have to furnish his projections for the next four years. How he is expected to do this when Congress still has not acted on his earlier estimates is, as he says, "problematical."

The problem, of course, is that this is the area where political bargaining begins. Additional judgeships mean extra patronage power for members of Congress from the states involved. Although court appointments are made by the President, he relies on nominations from within the states and, traditionally, senators have had veto power over appointments in their own states. Moreover, while nobody denies that the courts need relief, it's sometimes hard for politicians to agree on where the extra judges should be allocated.

In the best of all possible worlds, politics would play no part in the appointment of federal judges. But even in this imperfect world, political considerations should take a back seat, particularly when an obviously outstanding candidate is up for nomination.

That's the case in the Western District of Kentucky where, with the semi-retirement of Judge Gordon this month, a vacancy will occur. The name of Jefferson County Circuit Judge Richard Revell has been sent to President Ford by the state's Republican congressmen. But Kentucky's two Democratic senators, while committed to the "best-qualified candidate" in principle, are known to be unhappy at their effectual exclusion from the nominating process. Senator Ford reportedly let his concern provoke him into an ill-timed spat with Republican Representative Tim Lee Carter at a White House Christmas party.

It would be a shame, however, if such political maneuvering were to kill Judge Revell's chance. He has going for him not only long experience on the bench, but a reputation as the most outstanding jurist in Jefferson County. The Kentucky senators may have a legitimate grievance over what they believe to be their right to a greater share of federal patronage, but they are unlikely to win greater support for their position by blocking this nomination.

A slight delay to make a point can be understood. A certain amount of bargaining within Congress over which state gets how many new judges also can be tolerated. But the time is long past for this playing around to end.

THE SUN

Baltimore, Md., January 6, 1976

Chief Justice Burger's campaign to enlarge the federal judiciary becomes more and more persuasive. Once again, his annual year-end report cites inexorably rising case-loads per judge. Small wonder his tone is getting testy towards Congress.

"Overwhelmed by increased demands for regulatory legislation, for broadened governmental programs of all kinds, Congress enacts legislation, much of which reaches the courts for resolution." But of the additional 52 trial judgeships and 13 appellate judgeships recommended by the Judicial Conference in 1972, none has been created. The Judicial Conference is required again this year to submit figures to measure the need for the next four years. "What can be expected by way of congressional action to meet the 1976-1980 needs when the 1972-1976 needs have not been met is problematical."

Curiously, while the creation of new judgeships stays mired in the congressional pipeline, another of the Chief Justice's favorite projects has moved from abstract debate to the bill stage. Senator Roman L. Hruska, ranking Republican on the Judiciary Committee, has introduced a proposal to create a national court of appeals, above the circuit courts of appeals and below the Supreme Court. This raises fundamental questions about the speed of appeals through the court system and the relation of citizens to the Supreme Court. Compared to this creation of a new level of court, the creation of new judgeships on existing courts is non-controversial and overdue.

One of Chief Justice Burger's more startling figures is that a sixth of the 117,000 civil cases on the federal court dockets are petitions from prisoners, "most of which could be be handled effectively and fairly within the prison systems." The Chief Justice praises the federal prison complaint system and implies that the states should emulate it. Many of the Supreme Court's important decisions in the Warren era, expanding rights of defendants, sprang from such petitions. While decent prison systems should be able to deal fairly with complaints, they can never substitute for the courts in deciding who should be imprisoned.

The Cincinnati Post

Cincinnati, Ohio, January 6, 1976

The federal courts may be headed for serious trouble unless Congress soon appoints more judges to handle the growing volume of cases.

Not a single new judgeship has been created since court officers warned Congress four years ago that 52 new district judges and 13 new appellate judges would be needed by 1976.

Yet the number of new cases filed has increased 42 per cent in district courts since 1970, and the number of appellate filings has more than doubled since 1968, according to Chief Justice Warren E. Burger.

BURGER BLAMES the mounting backlog on "the tendency of Americans to try to resolve every sort of problem in the courts" and on complicated new laws that demand judicial interpretation.

It also should be noted—just for the record—that some judges tend to work short days and take long lunch hours.

But even if all judges were diligent in their duties, it's doubtful the courts could keep up indefinitely with the torrent of new litigation.

The pressure can only get worse as judges move to comply with a 1974 law (fully effective in 1980) requiring that all persons accused of federal crimes be tried or released within 10 days.

Congress is well aware of the crunch. The Senate, in fact, has approved seven new appellate judgships, and a Senate committee has recommended 45 new district judges.

There is a danger both of these proposals will get sidetracked (by election-year politics) until 1977, when a new Congress, and perhaps a new President, will be in office.

The better course, for the country, is for congressional leaders to stop stalling and give the federal courts the help they need in 1976.

The Evening Bulletin

Philadelphia, Pa., January 12, 1976

In the view of Chief Justice Warren E. Burger, the nation's judicial system has, on balance, fared better than a number of other institutions through our first 200 years of nationhood.

Chief Justice Burger offered the following assessment in his annual report on the condition of the judiciary:

"At our 200th anniversary of nationhood we find...that confidence in our institutions...seems to be eroded. The judicial system by and large, however, is working well, and this is reflected by the relatively high popular esteem of the courts. The faults and frailties...are, for the most part, recognized and correctable — and there is much activity toward improvement."

The Chief Justice makes it quite clear that the judiciary itself can take credit for its good standing and that Congressional inaction in several key areas is largely responsible for the faults. There is considerable evidence to support Mr. Burger's position.

Three major problems outlined in Mr. Burger's report are the shortage of judges and the rapidly escalating caseloads, salary and pension scales which have kept a number of qualified individuals off the bench and that have forced others to resign, and jurisdictional regulations that unnecessarily swell federal court dockets.

The remedy for these problems must come from Congress. The remedies are overdue. The number of cases per judge in the district courts has risen from 285 to 355 since 1970. However, no new judgeships have been created during that period.

Similarly, the number of appeals court judges has remained static since 1968, while the average caseload per judge has risen from 282 to more than 500.

In the best of circumstances the judicial system works under an immense burden. As Mr. Burger notes, "the tendency of Americans to try to resolve every sort of problem in the courts continues."

Congress always manages to look after itself. It ought to start looking after its coequal partner in the federal establishment — the courts.

BURGER CALLS FOR MORE JUDGESHIPS, HIGHER PAY, REVIEW OF SENTENCES

Chief Justice Warren E. Burger Jan. 1 issued his annual year-end report on the federal judicial system. The report contained a renewed plea to Congress for the creation of more federal judgeships. Burger said case filings had increased 11.3% in 1976. He reported that the "average federal judge completed work on 36% more cases" in 1976 than in 1968.

Burger warned that a failure to increase the salaries of federal judges would lead to a growing "brain drain" of the judiciary. He said that judges and other high federal officials had been objects of "unparalleled discrimination on salaries." Judges, he claimed, had not received a pay raise since 1968, with the exception of a 5% cost-of-living increase in 1975. Burger endorsed a list of judicial pay increases recommended by the Commission on Executive, Legislative and Judicial Salaries in 1976. Under the proposals, U.S. District Court judges' salaries would rise from $42,000 a year to $62,000; U.S. appellate judges', from $44,000 to $65,000; Supreme Court associate justices', from $63,000 to $77,500; and the Chief Justice's, from $65,600 to $80,000.

In another area, Burger called for the creation of procedures for the review of widely varying sentences imposed by federal judges in criminal cases on similarly situated defendants. He called discretion in sentencing "a double-edged sword." (Federal appeals courts reviewed convictions but not sentences.) Burger also gave apparent approval to campaign statements by President-elect Jimmy Carter recommending the merit selection of judges and U.S. attorneys; noted that an increasing number of law schools and state bar associations required the study of ethics by students; and cited the work of judges over 65, without whom, he said, "the federal court system would have collapsed during the past five or six years."

The Wichita Eagle

Wichita, Kans., January 5, 1977

Chief Justice Warren Burger submitted a blueprint for an improved judiciary the other day when he recommended that President-elect Carter refrain from automatically replacing U. S. attorneys across the country — as new chief executives are wont to do.

Burger's words present the best argument for uninterrupted service of the attorneys:

"No modern society maintains a system, as we do, of changing hundreds of U. S. attorneys and assistants with every change of party control of the executive branch.

"The proper handling of public business in federal courts — whether civil or criminal — requires trained and experienced lawyers. Without substantial continuity, this cannot be attained and the public interest suffers accordingly."

The chief justice's proposal would serve an additional purpose by removing politics from the federal court system, where it certainly has no place.

Minneapolis Tribune

Minneapolis, Minn., January 4, 1977

Federal judges "should be appointed strictly on the basis of merit, without consideration of political influence," President-elect Carter said during the election campaign. In 1977, he will have an unusually large opportunity to prove that he means what he said. With Congress expected to expand the number of federal judgeships, and with at least 20 vacancies expected from retirements or death, Carter could appoint almost a quarter of the federal judiciary by this time next year. Those appointments would be nearly twice the number made by Richard Nixon during his first two years in office.

If Carter initiates a merit system for selecting judges, he will do much to maintain the quality of the federal bench — and to build the public's confidence in it. That would be a major contribution, according to Chief Justice Burger's annual report on the judiciary. "Given the crushing caseloads and the increasingly complicated problems being assigned to the judiciary, and the high importance of perpetuating constitutional freedoms," Burger said last week, "the professional attributes of those selected to be judges continue to be of critical importance." The traditional way of choosing judges has too often produced judges who are, at best, minimally qualified. The system of "senatorial courtesy" gives senators at least veto power, and sometimes virtual power of appointment, over judicial selections in their states. Part of the ritual calls for sending nominees' names, on blue slips of paper, to the senators from their states; unless both senators return their blue slips, the nomination quietly dies. "It may be fine for a parlor game," says an article in the American Bar Association's law-student journal, "but it is far from a rational way to choose men and women who make the most difficult and far-reaching decisions a complex society has to offer." While the system often produces outstanding jurists, it also fails often: Half the judicial nominees in the Nixon administration and 42 percent of those in the Johnson administration were rated as barely acceptable by the ABA screening committee.

As governor of Georgia, Carter overcame a patronage system and established merit selection of state judges, winning an award from the American Judicature Society for his achievement. And during the third televised debate last fall, Carter pledged to initiate a similar reform of the federal judicial-selection process. Since then, however, he nominated an old friend with questionable qualifications for attorney general; thus an official who will play a key role in choosing judges was himself not picked entirely on his merits. That makes it all the more important for Carter to live up to his campaign promise that federal judges will be selected on their merits, not their connections.

The Evening Bulletin

Philadelphia, Pa., January 10, 1977

In his annual report U.S.Chief Justice Burger says "No modern society maintains a system, as we do, of changing hundreds of U.S. Attorneys and Assistants with every change of party control of the Executive Branch ... The proper handling of public business in federal courts . . . requires trained and experienced lawyers. Without substantial continuity this cannot be attained . . ."

We'd add that the break for politics may also be a break for crime and corruption. Time is lost to the prosecution and maybe papers, witnesses and enthusiasm.

Chief Justice Burger says offices of U.S. Attorneys in the larger metropolitan centers have moved toward permanent staffing and this should be encouraged and expanded if the quality of the government's representation is to be kept at a high level. He's right.

President-elect Jimmy Carter has said U.S. Attorneys should be appointed on merit. And they should be retained on merit, too.

THE PLAIN DEALER

Cleveland, Ohio, January 4, 1977

In his year-end report on the federal judiciary, U.S. Supreme Court Chief Justice Warren E. Burger makes a solid case for increasing judges' salaries.

Burger noted that in the past three years more federal judges resigned to return to private law practice than in the previous 50 years. He said that failure to increase pay will lead to an even greater "brain drain" in the courts.

This condition is a handicap to good government. Also, it is unfair and unreasonable to expect judges to accept prestige as a substitute for monetary reward, especially when their own work load grows and lower-level federal employes receive cost-of-living pay boosts.

Federal judges at the district court level currently are paid $42,000 annually, which is not much when compared with what a good lawyer can command in private practice. The same is true of salaries at the federal appellate and Supreme Court levels where pay is $44,600 and $63,000.

Except for a 5% cost-of-living raise in 1975, federal judges' salaries have not increased for nearly eight years. In an interview four years ago in Cleveland, Chesterfield H. Smith, then president of the American Bar Association, commented on the inequity. He said federal judges' salaries had remained frozen at $40,000 while most other federal employes had been raised 34%. Smith suggested annual salaries for federal judges of at least $60,000.

Recent recommendations of the federal Commission on Executive, Legislative and Judicial Salaries, which take effect soon unless disapproved or amended in either house of Congress, provide a more realistic salary scale for members of the judiciary: $62,000 in district courts, $65,000 in appellate courts and $77,500 in the Supreme Court.

The commission's reasons for advocating a high-percentage pay increase for the judges are convincing:

" . . . This group foregoes more outside earning opportunity than any other in federal service. The strains of . . . years are beginning to show, not only in the upper ranks of the federal judiciary but even more in the federal bankruptcy courts where 18 resignations in the past two years appear to be related to money problems. Finally, all of our studies . . . tell us the American public is most supportive of the highest possible quality in the judiciary and is quite prepared, we believe, to pay for it."

It is unfortunate that salary increases for the judiciary are in the same package as pay increases for Congress and other high-level federal officials. The latter could draw public censure if the commission's call to tie pay increases to a new code of ethical conduct is ignored. There is no problem for the federal judiciary in this area. Already it is in substantial compliance with what has been proposed.

While it seems clear that the federal judiciary is going to cost more and be well worth the price, it is likewise evident that consideration also must be given to improving salaries in other courts.

Here in Ohio the General Assembly should address the problem of attracting and retaining good judges. For example, top pay of $34,000 in courts of common pleas, in effect since 1973, has not kept pace with increases in the cost of living; nor is it adequate reward for trained and experienced people upon whom so much of good government depends.

THE DAILY OKLAHOMAN

Oklahoma City, Okla., December 22, 1976

THE annual yearend report on the judiciary by the Chief Justice of the United States usually has a lot of meat in it, and this year's wrapup by Warren E. Burger is no exception.

The chief justice again used the occasion to belabor his long standing plea for higher judicial salaries, arguing that federal judges have not received a raise in seven years. But he also called attention to other developments which are of far broader public interest.

Burger noted that much popular unhappiness with the law "is in many ways dissatisfaction with the legal profession." In other words, lawyers are not exactly at the top of the list in public esteem.

One reason for this is the fact that in too many instances clients are being represented—it might be more accurate to say misrepresented—in state and federal courts by lawyers who are not qualified advocates.

The assumption that an attorney automatically becomes qualified to try a case in court by completing law school and passing a state bar examination always was questionable. And with the complexity of issues involved in modern litigation, the assumption is no longer valid.

Recognition of this fact within the legal profession has prompted a growth in continuing education programs, but to date only three states —Iowa, Minnesota and Wisconsin— make attendance mandatory.

The truth is, as Burger observed, that "we require more to certify plumbers and electricians than we do for lawyers to represent clients in state and federal courts."

Bar associations and law schools are attacking the problem by developing trial advocacy programs, and in the federal courts a committee is now studying how to upgrade standards of admission to practice. Out of these efforts could come an improved level of trial advocacy competence, something which most veteran jurists candidly acknowledge is badly needed.

In his report Burger also questioned the practice of "changing hundreds of U.S. attorneys and assistants with every change of party control of the executive branch." He recommended converting these positions to a career service.

Burger argues strongly that the public interest in matters before the federal courts suffers "without substantial continuity" in prosecution personnel. This is particularly true when it comes to prosecuting organized crime.

But a party denied access to the federal executive patronage trough for eight years will likely ignore the idea of giving up all those appointive plums, regardless of President-elect Jimmy Carter's campaign statement that "all federal judges and prosecutors shall be appointed strictly on the basis of merit."

THE INDIANAPOLIS NEWS

Indianapolis, Ind., January 14, 1977

In a recent address Chief Justice Warren Burger of the U.S. Supreme Court expressed support for increasing the salaries of congressmen, Federal judges and bureaucrats. We think he should not have.

It is the duty of a special commission to make recommendations for adjusting the pay of these officials, and it is the function of Congress either to approve or disapprove the commission's suggestions. The Federal judiciary has no statutory role in making this decision.

Since Burger himself would gain by acceptance of the commission's recommendation of a pay hike, his public support for the increase has the sound of a lobbying effort which is, or should be, beneath the dignity of the court.

Perhaps a more substantive objection is that Burger spoke expressly to the alleged need to increase the salaries of Federal judges — a matter currently in litigation in the Federal courts.

A group of judges has claimed that inflation has weakened the purchasing power of the dollars they receive in salary and the result is an effective pay cut. The Constitution, they note, forbids such a reduction in pay. The implications of the case are enormous. If the executors of contracts are held liable for the long term effect of inflation (or deflation), chaos will prevail in the entire marketplace, both private and public sectors. Real estate values, contracted fees for professional negotiated labor contracts, loan agreements, mortgages — all become subject to endless contest in and out of court.

A case of such magnitude is certain to come before Burger's court before final resolution — particularly if the judges prevail in the lower courts. It is unfortunate and improper that the Chief Justice has already made public his feelings about the merits of the judges' case.

ST. LOUIS POST-DISPATCH
St. Louis, Mo. January 11, 1977

Chief Justice Burger identified a particularly nagging problem of the criminal justice system in his year-end report; and if he will now take the lead for reform, the system will be the better for his efforts. We refer to his call for the creation of procedures to review sentences imposed by federal judges, which is an overdue recognition of the growing concern inside the courts and out over inequities in punishment.

Trial judges under the law have wide discretion in sentencing. As the Chief Justice noted, discretion "permits the judge to accommodate unusual circumstances relative to each defendant. But this sometimes results in the defendants who ought to be similarly treated receiving substantially disparate sentences." Not infrequently, blacks and poor persons suffer harsher sentences for the same crime than whites and defendants with money, studies have shown.

As a practical matter there is no appeal from a trial judge's sentence so long as it falls within the limits permitted by law; and that of course is the trouble. Surely there ought to be some mechanism for review of unreasonable sentences in criminal cases just as there is for reviewing excessive monetary awards in civil cases. Indeed, such reviews have already been proposed for Missouri's state courts.

The problem of providing appellate review of sentences at the federal level, as the Chief Justice said, is that case loads are more than "crushing"; they are "impossible." Whether Congress will create more judgeships remains to be seen. But Chief Justice Burger pointed to a mechanism suggested by the Judicial Conference, which he heads, providing for the screening of sentencing petitions by panels composed mostly of district court judges; petitions that passed this screening then would go to the appeals court.

The judicial branch evidently could adopt this scheme without action by Congress, although Congress if it wished could block it, according to *The New York Times*. That being so, then the Chief Justice has an opportunity to act.

THE ANN ARBOR NEWS
Ann Arbor, Mich., January 5, 1977

CHIEF JUSTICE Warren E. Burger made good use of his latest annual report on the state of the nation's judiciary.

In a few words, the chief justice added his support to efforts to obtain more nearly uniform sentencing for criminals convicted of similar crimes.

This is both a federal and state issue. Bills calling both for elimination and reduction of the amount of discretion available to judges, when issuing sentences, are certain to be debated in Michigan's Legislature this year.

As Burger puts it. "Discretion in sentencing has been a double-edged sword. It permits the judge to accommodate unusual circumstances relative to each defendant, but this sometimes results in defendants who ought to be similarly treated receiving substantially disparate sentences."

IT HARDLY needs to be pointed out that this problem squares neither with the ideal of equality before the law for all citizens, nor with the hope that certainty of punishment will deter some potential criminals.

"Every American," President-elect Carter rightly observed in a campaign statement, "has a right to expect that laws will be administered in an evenhanded manner, but it seems that something is wrong even with our system of justice.

"Defendants who are repeatedly out on bail commit more crimes . . . Citizens without influence often bear the brunt of prosecution. Violators of anti-trust laws and white collar criminals are often ignored and go unpunished."

★ ★ ★

ILLOGICALLY, Carter went on to reiterate the cliche that "the best way to reduce crime in a substantive manner is to reduce unemployment."

Some useful comments on that sort of guesswork about causes for crime were made recently by Wayne County Prosecuting Atty. William L Cahalan:

"Some say it is poverty; yet, the vast majority of the poor do not commit crime. I am of the opinion that it is not poverty that forces wealthy men to rig prices, to violate the Securities and Exchange laws, and to avoid payment of income taxes . . . There are some who say it is lack of education; yet, the vast majority of those who are poorly educated do not commit crime. I don't think it was lack of education that caused Patty Hearst, John Mitchell or Spiro Agnew to commit their crimes."

★ ★ ★

MANDATORY sentences would provide society with assurance that persons convicted of specific crimes would be out of general circulation for specific periods. That is society's most immediate interest following convictions.

Chief Justice Burger hasn't specified which of several possible approaches to uniform sentencing he favors. His brief comments should, nevertheless, improve chances for action on this subject in Congress and state legislatures.

Democrat and Chronicle
Richmond, Va., January 8, 1977

CHIEF Justice Warren E. Burger has once again drawn attention to the problems of defendants who are given sharply different punishments for basically the same offense.

"Discretion in sentencing," Burger told the nation in his year-end report, "has been a double-edged sword. It permits the judge to accommodate unusual circumstances relative to each defendant. But this sometimes results in the defendants who ought to be similarly treated receiving substantially disparate sentences."

Sentencing varies from region to region, from state to state, from county to county, and from city to rural district. The problem came close to home in this area when Rep. Frank J. Horton was sent to jail for drunk driving. A survey made by this newspaper at the time showed that other judges, rightly or wrongly, would have imposed other sentences.

There's no easy, simple way to reduce disparities in sentencing. In New York State, the climate now seems more favorable to a reduction in sentencing discretion. But if the original sentences themselves can't be evened out, it's possible that a solution can be found in a review procedure.

Burger noted one proposal from the Judicial Conference that would provide for a defendant to file a petition with the appropriate court of appeals. If a panel of judges found evidence that the sentence was clearly unreasonable, it would grant a review and the appeals court would then decide if the sentence was indeed unreasonable.

The difficulty, and the challenge, might be to work out a system that didn't hopelessly bog down the various appeals courts. But the case for more even-handed treatment of offenders is undeniable.

The Hartford Courant
Hartford, Conn., January 8, 1977

There is something old, something new in Chief Justice Burger's annual review of the judiciary. The familiar theme is the top jurist's continued dismay at the undermanning of Federal courts. As for his new concern, it rightly centers on widely disparate sentencing practices involving similarly-situated defendants.

Mr. Burger's arguments for a larger bench remain most convincing. He noted, for instance, that the Federal judiciary's administrative arm, the Judicial Conference, recommended in September that Congress create 106 new judgeships for district courts and 16 for the courts of appeals. He also remarked pointedly that about half that total "had been identified as needed four years earlier."

The consequences of crowded dockets are readily apparent. The Chief Justice concluded that caseloads were "crushing" and, particularly in the case of the courts of appeals "impossible." Furthermore, he contended that some Federal district courts, in their efforts to comply with Federal legislation setting time limits for trials of criminal cases, had been unable to try civil cases for months, except in emergency matters.

Regarding sentencing, Mr. Burger declared that discretion in that area has been a "double-edged sword. It permits the judge to accommodate unusual circumstances relative to each defendant. But this sometimes results in the defendants who ought to be similarly treated receiving substantially disparate sentences."

Mr. Burger did not offer any specific solutions to the problem. One remedy often heard, however, is the passage of legislation pinpointing how a judge is to handle the sentencing process. Some courts are experimenting with sentencing "panels," in which the trial judge discusses a case with other judges and hears their recommendations on what sentence he should impose.

Justice is ill-served when court cases are delayed interminably for a lack of manpower. Nor is the law enhanced by glaring inequities in the sentencing procedure. We hope that a year hence the Chief Justice will be able to report significant progress in both problem areas.

THE  SUN

Baltimore, Md., January 7, 1977

In his annual Year-End Review, Chief Justice Warren E. Burger noted that there were significant steps taken in 1976 in the direction of increasing the public's respect for the law and lawyers. The professional organizations of the bar and of the federal and state judiciaries met—for the first time—to begin a series of studies of why the public is dissatisfied with the administration of justice and how such causes can be eliminated.

Exactly what all these studies will turn up can only be guessed. But, as the Chief Justice noted, several shortcomings in the legal profession are obvious now and efforts to deal with them are already under way or could be quickly initiated. These include improving legal education (including the study of ethics), upgrading of standards for admission to practice before some courts, disciplining of lawyer misconduct, and easing the burden on judges by shifting some responsibilities from courts to other institutions and by increasing their numbers and their pay.

One thing that creates cynicism among offenders and observers of the administration of justice system is the range of sentencing for the same crime from court to court and often in the same court from case to case. Mr. Burger rightly called for some form of review procedure to avoid differences of punishment that are so great as to breed disrespect not only for individual judges (and lawyers and prosecutors) but for the law, itself. And for society. Prison officials say few things make inmates more anti-social and less likely for rehabilitation than learning that others who did what they did received lighter sentences. An expanded federal judiciary, likely this year, ought to be able to review sentences without having to shirk other duties.

Rocky Mountain News

Denver, Colo., January 5, 1977

CHIEF JUSTICE Warren E. Burger made good use of his year-end report the other day by pointing out that inconsistent sentencing of criminals in this country is undermining public respect for law.

Burger made no specific recommendation, but he did suggest that one way to make sentencing fairer and more logical would be to set up a review panel of three judges in cases in which the punishment appeared to be harsh or unreasonable.

Disparities between sentences for similar crimes have been a cause of judicial concern for years — primarily because of the wide latitude judges are given in punishing convicted criminals

In a study conducted several years ago, for example, it was discovered that one federal judge might sentence a crooked union official, with a long criminal record, to 20 years in prison and a $65,000 fine for loansharking and income tax evasion while another federal judge might sentence the same man to three years in prison and no fine.

Disparities in sentencing tend to be particularly hard on poor blacks, who often seem to receive more severe sentences than affluent whites convicted of similar crimes.

There are a number of ways to make sentencing more evenhanded. One is to cut back on the use of indeterminate sentences, which may result in only a few months in jail for one convict while another is locked up and forgotten for 10 or 20 years.

Some courts have experimented with sentencing panels so that a judge might discuss punishment with several of his colleagues before pronouncing sentence on a convicted criminal.

This would seem to be a less cumbersome process than waiting until a sentence is imposed and then getting into a long legal hassle over whether it was reasonable.

No two cases are exactly the same, of course. Nor is it wise to strip judges of all discretion in sentencing when so many complicating factors are involve.

But if "equal justice under law" is to be more than just a motto on the Supreme Court Building in Washington, our haphazard system of sentencing criminals will have to be substantially judicially improved.

BUFFALO EVENING NEWS

Buffalo, N.Y., January 7, 1977

The growing national movement for reform of criminal sentencing procedures has gained welcome impetus from Chief Justice Warren E. Burger in his annual report on the State of the Judiciary.

The broad discretion permitted federal and state judges in fitting punishment to the individual criminal as well as to the crime has become common practice since early in this century, when it was regarded as an enlightened advance fostering rehabilitation of prisoners before their return to society.

Justice Burger, however, has joined the ranks of penologists and correction officials who deplore the "substantially disparate sentences" meted out to defendants charged with similar crimes and having similar records. While proposing no specific remedy, he called for "some form of review procedure" in the federal courts for sentences offending standards of reasonableness.

Three states last year switched from indeterminate to either fixed or a narrower range of sentencing, and similar action is being considered in at least nine other states. This trend stems mainly from two factors: (1) a growing loss of faith in the ability of prisons to rehabilitate and of parole boards to predict a released felon's future conduct; and (2) the tension-heightening resentment among prisoners over widely disparate sentences and perceived vagaries in parole operations.

New York Corrections Commissioner Benjamin Ward, in declaring last month that this state's sentencing structure has caused many of the problems besetting the prison system, has urged adoption here of a system that "allows for less indeterminate sentencing and in which a person knows that if you commit this crime, this is what you will get."

In effect, Mr. Ward endorsed last year's proposal of a Twentieth Century Fund task force for so-called "presumptive sentencing." Under this procedure, a guilty verdict would bring a particular sentence established by the Legislature for each specific crime category, with discretion reserved for the courts to vary sentences within limits in accordance with mitigating or aggravating factors.

The search for perfection in any sentencing revision is likely to be futile, and there are dangers in swinging the pendulum too far from the discretion now allowed judges and parole officials to fixed sentences inflexibly oblivious to defendants' individual circumstances and to prospects for a convict's safe release into society.

Rejecting extremist calls for a total discarding of parole as "equivalent to throwing the baby out with the bathwater," the Assembly Codes Committee rightly proposed measures to overcome "unquestioned weaknesses and failures of our present parole system." The committee contended that "it is totally unrealistic to expect the people" to support any plan that makes "total and abrupt changes in the present sentencing and parole structures."

Any moderate restructuring of both, however, must start with a thorough-going legislative-commission review of present sentence guidelines, including the aggravating effect of widespread plea bargaining on sentence disparities. In any case, the trend endorsed by Justice Burger, and earlier by President Ford in directing a Justice Department study of fixed sentencing procedures, reflects a valid concern for establishing firmer and more uniform guidelines which leave some room for discretion but generally relate minimum imprisonment to the severity and circumstances of individual offenses.

The Providence Journal
Providence, R.I.,
February 24, 1977

Carter plan for choosing judges

President Carter, apparently with the aim of reducing the role of political pressure in the selection of federal judges, is trying an interesting experiment for sifting the names of nominees to the appeals courts.

He plans to establish 11 commissions across the country that will prepare for the White House a list of recommended names whenever an appellate court vacancy should arise. Names may be submitted by members of Congress, by figures in the administration, or by the commission itself. What is significant is that the Carter plan would force the President (or an attorney general) to make his choice only from the names the commission recommended. Thus, for example, if a senator put forth the name of a would-be judge, but the commission decided to scratch the name from its list, the President could not nominate that person.

Since each commission would be made up of both lawyers and non-lawyers, there would be a chance for a cross-section of opinion from experienced people in the area where potential nominees would be best known. With a high-quality membership (the President himself would appoint each commission's members and chairmen), these panels would have the chance to expose any possible serious shortcomings in a potential nominee's background — as well as spot candidates of real stature. And by committing himself to selecting judges only from the names on a commission's list, the President would strengthen the effectiveness of the screening process.

The only possible risk in such an approach is that the panels, being made up entirely of a President's own appointees, might tend to be a distillation of presidential views. This could narrow the selection process, instead of broadening it. If the new commissions are to function effectively as a high-level talent hunt, Mr. Carter will want to be as careful in appointing their members as he should be in making his choices of the judicial nominees themselves.

On its face, the Carter plan seems to be worth a try. It marks an attempt to shake the judge-picking exercise loose from the pressures of political cronyism that have been known to exert some influence in the past. If the procedure seems to aid the selection of appeals judges, then the President may want to extend it to choices of district, or trial, judges. There the patronage system is still in full sway.

BUFFALO EVENING NEWS
Buffalo, N.Y., December 11, 1977
Pick U.S. Judges by Merit

Congress is finally acting on a long-standing plea from Chief Justice Warren Burger that several dozen new federal judgeships should be created to handle the growing caseload in the federal courts. Since new judges were last added in 1970, the number of cases filed at the district court level has soared by 36 percent and, at the appellate level, by 140 percent.

So the arguments repeatedly cited over the years by Justice Burger are convincing, both in terms of the rising caseload and the legitimate criticism focused on inordinate delays in disposing of those cases.

One interesting point in all this is why the long-standing Burger arguments have suddenly become so persuasive. The well-grounded suspicion is that political considerations are playing even a larger role than caseload data and judicial reasoning.

Chief Justice Burger asked for 65 new judgeships in 1972, for example, and it took the Senate Judiciary Committee three years to recommend 59. Then, resounding silence. Nothing much else happened. This year the Judicial Conference, administrative arm of the federal judiciary, asked for more, and the full Senate, in May, approved legislation creating 113 new district and 35 new appellate posts. The House has not yet acted, but a Judiciary subcommittee, thinking this too many, urged only 81 new district and 34 new appellate seats on the bench. The full Judiciary Committee was having none of that, however. In readying its final proposal for the full House, Peter Rodino, committee chairman.

The chief reason why the Democratic Congress, so reluctant to add new federal judges in recent years, is so eager to do so now seems obvious: With President Carter instead of a Republican in the White House, the Democrats will get the lush patronage involved in the presidential appointments.

Let it never be said that Congress doesn't play politics with the federal bench, either in creating the jobs or in suggesting candidates for a president to consider in filling them. Nor is this anything new.

But this kind of partisanship is not calculated to elevate public esteem for the courts. In his 1976 campaign, Mr. Carter said "all federal judges ... should be appointed strictly on the basis of merit without any consideration of political aspect or influence." He was on the right track there. We would like to see the full House adopt the more modest recommendations of its Judiciary subcommittee, which minimized political clout and applied reasonable caseload standards in determining the number of new judges required, along with legislative language paralleling President Carter's own merit-not-politics pledge.

There is a need for more federal judges. There is no need, however, to end a judicial famine with a partisan feast.

The Cincinnati Post
Cincinnati, Ohio, January 27, 1977
Pick judges on merit

Jimmy Carter insisted during his presidential campaign that "all federal judges and prosecutors should be appointed strictly on the basis of merit without any consideration of political aspects or influence."

It now appears that Carter and his attorney general, Griffin B. Bell, are willing to settle for something far short of the original goal.

At his confirmation hearing the other day, Bell told the senators that special commissions of lawyers and laymen will be set up to help select new judges for federal appeals courts around the country.

But, said Bell, the screening of judges for the district courts will be left up to the senators themselves. He urged them to set up nonpartisan selection committees like ones which now function in Florida and Kentucky.

This is an obvious retreat from true reform. The two Democratic senators from Colorado—Floyd K. Haskell and Gary Hart—have asked Carter to extend the merit system to the selection of all federal judges, not just to those at the appellate level.

Ohio's Democratic senators—John Glenn and Howard Metzenbaum—ought to do likewise. Not only would this serve the quality of justice in the Buckeye State; it ought to make life easier for senators beset with requests to help reward the party faithful.

There are, after all, four times as many district judges as appeals court judges. It is going only part-way to choose appeals judges on merit and district judges on a political patronage basis.

Setting up a full-scale merit system (as Carter did for the state courts while governor of Georgia) would be of special benefit this year because Congress is expected to create 50 to 100 new judgeships to help clear up the backlog in overburdened federal courts.

The major hitch in trying to change the judicial selection system is that senators of the party in power traditionally have the right to recommend—or at least to veto—the selection of new district judges when vacancies occur in their home states. This is a practice that sometimes leads to rejection of qualified candidates for petty or political reasons.

Some political appointees distinguish themselves on the bench, but too often those nominated have been unimpressive: the American Bar Assn. gave exactly half of former President Nixon's nominees its lowest acceptable rating, "Qualified." Committee members were similarly unenthusiastic about 42 per cent of former President Johnson's choices for the courts.

The current selection system is so partisan that Philip B. Kurland, law professor at the University of Chicago, has described the federal judiciary as "a place to put political warhorses out to pasture."

The courts would be better served if the warhorses were pastured elsewhere and federal judges were chosen for their legal competence and their demonstrated dedication to equity and fair play.

The Kansas City Times
Kansas City, Mo., December 8, 1977

Merit, Not Politics, Should Rule Judge Selection

The mixing of political patronage with selection of judges is most bothersome. How can individuals standing at the bar of justice know for sure that rulings are based on merit when they suspect political influence in the appointment of the jurist?

The answer is, of course, they cannot. They must hope and trust that the judge, irrespective of party or other loyalties, will make a fair and impartial decision.

This issue was raised recently by the House Judiciary Committee. It adopted an amendment that calls for, but does not require, the selection of all federal judges and prosecutors on merit. We heartily endorse the committee action and it reflects the sentiments of many Americans.

Traditionally these appointments have been the prerogative of U. S. senators whose political party controls the Senate. Following up on a campaign pledge on judicial selection, President Carter has issued an executive order that requires special commissions to recommend judges for appellate courts. Authority to recommend district court judges and U. S.

attorneys still rests with the Senate. Thus the president has carried out part of a campaign promise to remove political influence from judicial selection.

Merit selection, more commonly known as the Missouri plan because it was first used in this state, removes partisanship from this important process. In this area voters have overwhelmingly approved nonpartisan selection when they have been given the opportunity. In recent years the plan, which was first adopted in Jackson County and St. Louis in 1940, has been approved in St. Louis, Clay and Platte counties. In Kansas a majority of court districts adopted the plan in a statewide vote in 1974.

It would be unrealistic to contend that nonpartisan selection is free of personalities or some politicking. But it prevents judicial candidates from seeking financial and political support in partisan elections. In the case of federal judges it removes political considerations that would figure in appointments by U. S. senators. The further away from the political turmoil judges are, the better.

Democrat and Chronicle
Rochester, N.Y., January 18, 1977

The case for merit selection

THE CASE for merit selection of both judges and prosecutors was given a boost by Chief Justice Burger in his year-end report.

No other modern society, he pointed out, persists with our system of changing hundreds of U.S. attorneys and assistants every time party control of the executive branch changes hands.

"The proper handling of public business in federal courts — whether civil or criminal — requires trained and experienced lawyers. Without substantial continuity this cannot be attained, and the public interest suffers accordingly."

Burger also noted that while more states are adapting or expanding merit selection systems for judges, "some state courts continue to carry the irrational burden of partisan election of judges and absence of merit selection and tenure for support personnel. The effect of this neglect and inattention .. is a problem for national concern."

Given the right circumstances, merit selection can work, and it's encouraging to know that Mr. Carter has urged that "all federal judges and prosecutors shall be appointed strictly on the basis of merit."

THE COMMERCIAL APPEAL
Memphis, Tenn., December 4, 1977

The Big Plum

CONGRESS APPEARS headed toward handing President Carter one of the ripest patronage plums in U. S. history by allowing him to appoint more federal judges than any previous president. But neither house has yet to answer whether all these judgeships are needed, nor have they tackled a selection system rooted in politics and not in ability.

Despite a House Judiciary subcommittee recommendation that only 81 district courts and 34 circuit courts be created, the full committee Wednesday approved a measure calling for an additional 110 district and 35 circuit courts, just 3 short of the total approved by the Senate last spring. Not only did the committee lower the threshold of 400 cases a year the subcommittee found to be manageable, but its members also had the crust to tack on judgeship after judgeship — not to show Carter what good boys they are but to deliver to the folks back home. As Rep. Jack Brooks (D-Texas) said, "This is one of the best classic examples of logrolling."

THE COMMITTEE also included a toothless provision for selection on merit, not party, which Carter can ignore by notifying the Senate of his reasons. This provision — toothless though it may be — faces a doubtful future in conference, where the Senate is expected to be unwilling to sacrifice its patronage in advising the President on whom to name to the federal bench.

Carter's widely-hailed campaign promise to appoint judges "strictly on the basis of merit, without any consideration of political aspect or influence," has become a voluntary system. Only 13 states have advisory merit boards, and even

then, those states' senators have a say as to who recommends selection. Under such circumstances, how can merit be given a fair trial?

SURELY MORE federal judgeships are needed to ease the heavy caseload and relieve the backlog that, in the case of Florida's Middle District, has forced abandonment of civil cases because the criminal docket couldn't be handled. According to statistics from the Judicial Conference, on which the Supreme Court's Chief Justice and 24 other federal judges sit, case filings have increased 36 per cent for the nation's 400 district judges and 140 per cent for the 97 judges in the 11 appeals-court regions since the number of federal judges last was increased in 1970.

The figures don't say whether all the new judges Congress wants really are needed, but they raise the question of why more openings weren't created earlier. The answer again is politics. The Democratic Congress sat in the corner, ignoring the public's need for swift and thorough justice, until a member of its own party sat in the White House. Now that Congress has decided to move, it is asking the public to pay without justifying new judges' salaries and the attendant costs of more court clerks, bailiffs and secretaries, not to mention new courtrooms.

The folks back home expect their representatives to give sound reasons for expenses and appointments, just as they don't expect to be held hostage to political favoritism. If those in Congress can't defend their actions, they may find themselves deprived of the biggest plum of all: Their re-election.

Chicago Defender
Chicago, Ill., February 7, 1977

Carter and the judiciary

President Carter has a rare opportunity to recast the judiciary into the image of a nation bent on preserving the broad outlook of its constitutional traditions.

There are 24 district court judgeships and 3 circuit court judgeships open. In addition, there are 31 active Judges who will leave the bench this year as a result of retirement. Legislation is pending in Congress for the creation of at least 49 new federal district court judgeships.

It is estimated that by the end of his first year in office, President Carter will have appointed 20 per cent of the total federal judiciary. And, by the end of his first term, Carter might have appointed a substantial majority of the bench.

The President has, therefore, a substantial numerical opportunity to appoint judges who will show regard for their obligation to enforce the law, not in accordance to their personal whims or biases, but in the light of the imperatives of established constitutional principles.

Incidentally, this is as well an opportunity for President Carter to put on the federal bench a number of black lawyers whose legal training and talents have been deliberately ignored by previous Administrations. Moreover, it is not too much to suggest that the next vacancy on the Supreme Court should be filled by a black lawyer or judge. In fact there should be three blacks on the high court to counterbalance the baleful influence of the Nixonites whose decisions are playing havoc with the Constitution.

Judges can do much to influence the ebb and flow of historical events in an open and free society. They should be selected on the basis of merit, intellectual integrity, not political pull.

The Boston Globe

Boston, Mass., October 7, 1977

Choosing judges on merit

Sen. Kennedy's decision to form a screening committee to recommend a list of candidates from which he will recommend a nominee for the Federal bench here has paid off handsomely. The five candidates put forward by Kennedy's special judicial nominating committee are, by all accounts, exceptionally able. Now that the merits of removing pure politics from judicial selections has been demonstrated, the sitting Federal judges here should see the wisdom of insulating their own selection of a new bankruptcy judge from politics.

Certainly consideration of merit, rather than clout, does not make judicial selections easier. Kennedy will have a tough time deciding between the five men recommended by his nominating committee: Superior Court Justices Joseph P. Lynch, David A. Mazzone, David S. Nelson and John J. McNaught and Harvard law professor Robert E. Keeton. But the public can be confident that whichever man Kennedy chooses will be qualified to assume the duties of a Federal judge.

Regrettably, the public cannot be quite so sanguine about the prospects for the selection of a judge for the Federal bankruptcy court, a selection that will be made by the judges of the US District Court. The appointment has been delayed for months by in-chambers maneuverings that seem to have nothing to do with merit selection.

Sen. Kennedy is not entirely blameless in this affair, since the aim of the maneuverings within the court is apparently to assure that Kennedy's choice for the job is selected over an entry being boosted by Sen. Brooke. Neither of the two candidates has gone through any kind of screening process.

Yet, the final decision lies with the Federal judges themselves, and they are under no constraint to accept the recommendations of either senator. Given the added status and increasing importance of bankruptcy judges and given the unquestioned success of Kennedy's judicial nominating committe, the judges themselves should establish a system of merit selection for the bankruptcy court.

The Philadelphia Inquirer

Philadelphia, Pa., March 5, 1977

Pick U.S. judges on merit

If a proposal to create additional federal judgeships wins congressional approval, as seems likely, President Carter will have a unique opportunity to mark the federal judiciary with his own indelible stamp that will far outlive his tenure in office.

Because of existing vacancies, Mr. Carter inherited five circuit court and 19 district court positions to fill as soon as he entered the White House. Approval of the proposal would create another 16 circuit court and 106 district court judgeships for Mr. Carter to fill. President Carter, in other words, would be able to name a quarter of the federal judiciary before his first year of office is up.

The important question will be whether Mr. Carter uses the opportunity to improve the quality of the judiciary and, consequently, the administration of justice or, uses it to win political points.

Until Attorney General Griffin Bell's testimony before the Senate Judiciary Committee at his confirmation hearing, the indications were that Mr. Carter would make the most of this opportunity. As a presidential candidate, he continually stressed his commitment toward merit selection of judges. "If I am elected, I intend to work . . . to create an equally effective plan of merit selection of federal judges."

His record as governor of Georgia gave credence to that pledge. As governor he established a merit selection panel comprised of lawyers and lay citizens. Even his detractors concede that he did a good job.

Judge Bell, who as attorney general would be Mr. Carter's chief advisor in this area, seemed less committed, however, to pursuing a merit selection system. He told members of the Senate Judiciary Committee that a merit selection system would be used for nominees to the Supreme Court and the circuit court—the nation's second highest court. But for district court judges, he indicated it would be, as one senator remarked, "politics as usual."

Between the compaign trail and the confirmation hearing, Mr. Bell and President Carter obviously learned that senatorial resistance to merit selection was much greater than anticipated. They have deemed it wiser to strike a compromise so some form of merit selection can be implemented now rather than run the risk of no merit system at all.

We would have preferred a plan covering the entire federal judiciary but recognize the political realities and accept Mr. Bell's plan as a step in the right direction.

We trust that one of Mr. Bell's aides was correctly reflecting the sentiment of the attorney general when he insisted that Mr. Bell's position was not a "lessening of the goal" but "a matter of timing."

The Houston Post

Houston, Tex., January 23, 1977

Above politics

The Carter administration, in keeping with a campaign promise by the President, is preparing changes in the system of picking federal judges. The objective is to devise an impartial selection process based on merit rather than political influence.

Mr. Carter pledged to appoint judges "strictly on the basis of merit," but the details of the nomination and screening system to accomplish this have not been worked out. Members of the President's staff, headed by Joseph J. Levin Jr., Mr. Carter's transition chief for justice matters, is considering several options. Under one proposal presently receiving close study, the President would appoint panels in each of the 10 federal judicial circuits to recommend nominees for appellate court vacancies. Similar nominating panels would be established in each state to recruit, screen and recommend candidates for federal district judgeships. The two U.S. senators from each state would possibly choose the nominating panel for their state.

Giving the senators a voice in the judicial selection process is considered politic to defuse potential Senate opposition to reform of the present system. Senators, particularly if they are members of the President's party, now have great influence over the naming of judges. Levin says the Senate seems receptive to the merit selection idea, but members are "understandably concerned about keeping their prerogatives."

Twenty-one states already have judicial selection commissions of one form or another. In addition, Florida and Kentucky have panels chosen jointly by the states' U.S. senators and bar associations to screen candidates for federal district and appellate judgeships.

Levin says the screening panels envisioned by the administration would recommend prospective appointees for consideration by the President. The Senate would still have the power to confirm or reject them. He says the system would probably not be used to recommend nominees for the Supreme Court or for U.S. attorney jobs.

The new administration is expected to move quickly on its judicial selection reform proposals since it will have a large number of vacancies to fill on the federal bench. An estimated 18 to 22 existing judgeships are vacant or will be shortly, and Congress may create several of the 106 new positions recommended by the Judicial Conference of the United States. The new system can be put into effect either by executive order or by law, but for obvious reasons, Mr. Carter wants Senate support for whatever reforms he initiates. If the administration's proposals meet the criteria for a truly nonpartisan, impartial merit selection process for federal judges, the senators should be willing to surrender some of their prerogatives to elevate the top tier of our justice system above politics.

The Washington Post
Times Herald
Washington, D.C., June 7, 1977

More Federal Judges

IT IS NO SURPRISE that Congress is moving this summer to provide the federal courts with the amount of judicial help they need. A Democrat is now in the White House and federal judgeships are among the most prized of political appointments. So, within a few weeks, it is likely that President Carter will have an opportunity to appoint more judges to the bench at one time than any other President in history.

The need for these new judgeships is clear. Some of the 148 that the Senate has already approved and the House has under consideration were needed as long ago as 1972. Late that year, the Judicial Conference asked Congress for 51 new judgeships. Since then, the request has been renewed every few months, growing in size as the business and backlog of the courts became greater. But Congress set the requests aside each year, forcing a reduction in the quality and speed of justice as it waited for a presidential election to go by. The need for so large an increase this year—36 per cent more judges for the circuit courts and 29 per cent more for the district courts—underlines the neglect of the recent past. If the House fails to go along with the Senate in providing this major increase in judicial personnel, the administration of

justice will be critically overburdened.

So we hope the Congress will approve the new judgeships. And we also hope that President Carter and Attorney General Bell will be sensitive to the challenge that this opportunity will present to them. They have promised to make judicial nominations on the basis of merit, not politics, although the Attorney General tempered that promise a bit after encountering resistance on Capitol Hill. Nevertheless, if the numbers approved by the Senate hold up, the administration will have 36 new circuit judges to pick (12 of them in the West and 11 in the South). These are judgeships on which the rule of senatorial courtesy is not so strong and on which Mr. Bell has said the President will use judicial nominating commissions. Given the number of judges to be picked, this will provide an opportunity to demonstrate that such commissions can help to improve their quality. That is important, not only because it would create an impetus for using them to help select district judges as well, but also because the questions of competence and quality are all the more important any time a President is selecting at one time so large a percentage of all the federal judges.

The Oregonian
Portland, Ore., January 24, 1977

Promise to remember

President Carter's appointments to the bench will determine the quality of justice for a long time to come, because federal judgeships are lifetime posts and because the new chief executive probably will have an unprecedented number of judicial selections to make in his first year. Thus, it becomes particularly important that Carter quickly recalls and acts on the implied promise in his campaign statement that federal judges and prosecutors "should be appointed strictly on the basis of merit, without consideration of political influence."

Last year Congress came close to final passage of a bill creating some four dozen new federal judgeships, based on a 1972 survey of federal judges' caseloads. The survey is conducted every four years, and the 1976 report is expected to recommend that the number be more than doubled, to 106 District Court judgeships. Additional positions at the appeals court level would give Carter 128 new judgeships to fill before the year is out, and routine vacancies resulting from death or retirement would bring the total to about 150 — almost one-quarter of the federal judiciary.

As Chief Justice Burger has stressed in his recent messages on the state of the judiciary, federal court caseloads are becoming extremely

heavy and the disputes before the courts more complex. In the Pacific Northwest, disputes in federal courts over rights to salmon resources and over a variety of environmental impact issues bring home Burger's message about the complexity of issues.

On matters such as these, the professional attributes of those selected to be judges become critical. This is not an area of American life that should be governed by those archaic anachronisms of senatorial courtesy, the "blackball" and the "standoff," devices less designed to seat men of merit than to provide a means of political back-scratching.

Various proposals have been put forward to reform the selection process. The best of them seek to make the system one that affirmatively searches for the finest talent available. They remove the dominance of senatorial courtesy — a system primed to repay old political debts — and also avoid the trap of giving the Justice Department excessive influence in the screening process.

If President Carter means what he said about merit selection, he must quickly — before the mass appointments begin — let the Congress know which reform plan he prefers, and then push for its prompt enactment.

Minneapolis Tribune
Minneapolis, Minn., February 21, 1977

Merit selection of judges

Chief Justice Burger gave some welcome support last week to the selection of federal judges by nominating commissions that would consider candidates' merits, not their political ties. If competant screening commissions are established, Burger said, "I believe we will find a higher proportion of nominees who will be ranked 'exceptionally well-qualified' by the American Bar Association." That would be an improvement: Half the nominees in the Nixon administration and 42 percent in the Johnson administration were rated as "barely acceptable" by the ABA.

Burger, in his annual report to the ABA, also hoped that the concept of merit selection of judges by nominating commissions would spread to states. And he suggested that nominating or screening commissions include not only lawyers and judges, but also non-lawyers. Incusion of non-lawyers would be appropriate; non-lawyers, after all, constitute the bulk of the public that the courts serve.

The main hurdle for merit selection of federal judges is likely to be the Senate. Senators, under the present selection system, have veto power over appointment of judges for their states. But the idea has already been endorsed by President Carter, who ended a judicial patronage system and instituted a merit plan when he was governor of Georgia. Burger's support is additional impetus for an idea whose time has come.

Des Moines Tribune

Des Moines, Iowa, November 23, 1977

More federal judges

How many federal judges does the United States need? The U.S. made an effort years ago to see that the matter is decided in the public interest instead of by political grabs by creating conferences of judges (1922) and the administrative office of the U.S. courts (1939) to make recommendations on the basis of the workload of judges.

This year the system is working to create a sudden flood of new judges, with partisan politics a strong element in the background.

Democratic Congresses since 1970 have refused to expand the federal judiciary. To do so during the Ford and Nixon years would have given Republican presidents cushy appointments to make. Now federal court business has expanded to the point where the Judicial Conference of the United States is recommending a large increase, including an extra federal judge for Iowa.

The Senate voted in May, following the judges' recommendations in most respects, to add 113 federal district judges to the 398 now in office, and to add 35 circuit court judges to the 97 now in office: thumping and costly increases.

Chairman Peter Rodino, jr., (Dem., N.J.) of the House Judiciary Committee thought the Judicial Conference was asking for too many and that the conference's method was wrong. It anticipated rising workloads through 1980.

Representative Rodino's subcommittee set its staff to work out a new formula disregarding the uncertain future. The formula called for only 81 new district judges instead of 113; and 34 new circuit court judges instead of 35.

But the full committee had other ideas. Pork-barrel ideas. A series of amendments during the mark-up sessions kept adding judgeships — in the districts of congressmen on the committee — until the House bill was nearing the Senate bill's total, but without reasoned justification.

"The dam broke," Rodino put it.

Yet a straight increase in number of judges in proportion to the increase since 1970 in number of cases filed would call for more new judges than the Judicial Conference did, more than the Senate voted, more than the Rodino subcommittee recommended.

Americans were always a litigious people and seem to be becoming more so, especially since the efforts in recent years to make the courts and the law more nearly accessible to the poor.

THE DAILY HERALD

Biloxi, Miss., May 29, 1977

In fairness to the justices

We hope the U.S. House of Representatives agrees with the Senate and enacts the legislation that will expand the federal judiciary.

Political considerations aside, and there are many in such a step as this, we accept as fact the Senate Judiciary Committee's finding that the increased caseload of the federal courts is "...now one of near-crisis proportions."

The Senate passed the bill by voice vote, an indication, we hope, of an approving mood in Congress.

What the Senate-passed bill would do is authorize 113 new federal judges in 39 states and Puerto Rico and add 35 new federal appeals court judges. Of more importance to Mississippians, it will contract the U.S. Fifth Circuit Court of Appeals by removing Louisiana and Texas and putting those two states in a new 11th Circuit. Federal cases appealed from Mississippi's courts go to the Fifth Circuit.

For many years, the late Sidney C. Mize was the only federal judge serving the needs of the southern half of Mississippi; the northern half was likewise served by only one federal judge.

Increasing caseloads eventually mandated two judges for South Mississippi. Cases continued to proliferate until a third judge became necessary for this half of the state. Two judges serve the northern portion.

Even the increase to five judges, some court observers contend, is not enough to stay ahead of the number of cases being filed.

The new expansion would not alleviate the crunch in Mississippi's federal courts, but the reduction in size of the Fifth Circuit will expedite appellate review from Mississippi.

Mississippi's experience of increasing caseloads has been repeated in other areas of the country, many to a more acute degree than here. There has been no corresponding increase in district court judgeships since 1970 and none for the circuit court since 1968.

In those time periods, our society has been experiencing a host of changes, among them a citizenry more prone to instituting federal litigation. And the basis for litigation has been expanding into considerations, such as environmentalism, civil rights and consumerism, that were previously seen only relatively rarely in the courts.

These developments have not been accompanied by any decline in the bulk of civil and criminal matters that are the grist of the judicial mills.

Overtaxing the capacity of the federal judicial system by failing to recognize and remedy these developments would not be fair and just on the part of Congress.

Roanoke Times & World-News

Roanoke, Va., November 26, 1977

Merit Selection for New Judges

Congress is on its way to authorizing the largest single increase in the federal judiciary in the nation's history. There would be 113 new district judgeships (two in Western Virginia) and 35 new circuit or appeals court seats.

Peter Rodino, chairman of the House Judiciary Committee, led an effort to limit the total to 115 and establish standards to determine where new judgeships were needed. In conference, amendment after amendment overwhelmed Rodino. "The dam broke," he said afterward.

Another kind of dam also was breached. For several years, while Republicans were in the White House, the Democratic-controlled Congress held up creation of new judgeships. Now they come in a flood. The independent reporting service *Congressional Quarterly* called it "a huge political patronage plum for President Carter," who will appoint 148 new judges.

Influential members of Congress—usually, senators—expect to have a large say in whom a president of their own party names to the bench. They may be disappointed this time. A year ago, Jimmy Carter declared that merit, not politics, would determine selection of judges during his administration.

Attorney General Griffin Bell has repeated this pledge, and early indications are that it will be fulfilled. In February a presidential executive order established the U.S. Circuit Court Judge Nominating Commission, consisting of 13 panels, to propose candidates for the U.S. Court of Appeals. Senators from several states—including Independent Harry F. Byrd Jr. of Virginia—have formed commissions to nominate judges for district court vacancies.

These commissions are to be broad-based, including lay people as well as lawyers, and their work is intended to be non-partisan. Senator Byrd has said he will ask each of his two advisory groups to recommend four or five individuals for its two area judgeships; he will then forward some or all of these names to the president, but will not add any of his own.

That is a good method, but although there is some similarity among the handful of state plans, they are not uniform. In most instances, this is an entirely new approach to selection of judgeship candidates, and more experience is needed to determine the best process.

Former U.S. Sen. Joseph D. Tydings of Maryland sees advantages to politicians as well as the public in the new procedure. In a recent issue of *Judicature*, he writes:

Although it has always been important for Americans to know how their judges are chosen, it has become even more important in the last two decades as federal judges have undertaken traditional "legislative functions." Ordering the funding for road and prison construction and mandating the integration of schools and the reapportionment of legislatures are decisions which go to the heart of our national governance; such decisions are made regularly by federal district judges. Citizens are entitled to know how these judges were chosen. . . .

If the public perceives a judgeship appointment as a political payoff, Tydings says, that shakes confidence in the system and in the senator thought to be behind the appointment. The example set by senators such as Harry Byrd will put pressure, he adds, on those who cling to the traditional method. While solons are studying the new methods tried by Byrd and others, they might also direct attention to the Virginian's long-standing effort to subject members of the newly powerful federal judiciary to periodic re-examination of credentials.

The Charlotte Observer

Charlotte, N.C., November 30, 1977

The Politics Of Judge-Making

The Democratically controlled Congress would have held its breath until it turned red, white and blue rather than create federal judgeships to be filled by Republican presidents. So for years no new judgeships were created, even though the federal courts were overloaded.

Now there is a Democratic president to pick the judges. The sudden release of pressure seems to have made the House, at least, giddy.

The Senate accepted most of the recommendations of the Judicial Conference and approved creation of 113 U.S District Court judgeships and 35 for the U.S. Circuit Court of Appeals. (The Judicial Conference, a kind of board of directors of the federal judiciary, is made up of the Chief Justice and 24 federal judges.)

The Senate bill includes three new District Court judges for North Carolina (one for each judicial district), three for South Carolina, and three judges for the 4th Circuit Court of Appeals.

The House devised its own formula, however. A House Judiciary subcommittee recommended creation of only 81 federal District Court judgeships and 34 Circuit Court judgeships.

The subcommittee, chaired by Peter Rodino, D-N.J., left out more than a dozen judgeships sought by members of the House Judiciary Committee, mostly for their home states. That was fine — until the committee got hold of the recommendations. When it recessed for Thanksgiving, it had added 16 judgeships not approved by the subcommittee.

The House bill now would provide the same number of new judges for the Carolinas and the 4th Circuit as the Senate bill. The House committee may add even more.

The House is also expected to offer an amendment to provide for selection of judges by merit instead of politics. But that's like a Honda driver favoring smaller parking places. The Senate, not the House, has judicial patronage; the senators aren't likely to give it up.

Chances are, the House and Senate bills won't wind up far apart. The House would do well to accept the Judicial Conference's recommendations. If it doesn't adopt some rationale for its bill, the Judiciary committee's haphazard addition of judgeships could be repeated on the House floor.

The Detroit News

Detroit, Mich., December 4, 1977

86 Democrats appointed — but only one Republican

When President Carter remarked at his televised press conference last week, "I'm trying to fulfill all my promises," you could almost hear a collective raising of eyebrows.

The disenchanted include dozens of qualified judicial candidates bumped aside to make way for political appointees despite Mr. Carter's 1976 campaign promise that "All federal judges and prosecutors should be appointed strictly on the basis of merit, without any consideration of political aspects or influence."

The President has violated that promise so frequently and shamelessly that the House Judiciary Committee, dominated by his own party, last week felt compelled to express its dismay.

Before approving a bill creating 110 new district judgeships and 35 new appellate judgeships, the committee deplored the continuing practice of treating the administration of justice as political patronage. It wrote an amendment urging the selection of the additional judges on merit.

As if to illustrate the committee's point, one political nomination, that of George Schumacher for U.S. attorney in the Pittsburgh area, threatened to explode in Mr. Carter's face. Atty. Gen. Griffin Bell, who had named Schumacher upon the urging of six Democratic congressmen, wisely delayed the appointment. There is a little matter of looking into payments made to a congressman by Schumacher's law firm.

Meanwhile, the sour taste of numerous other acts of patronage lingers. Michigan, for example, cannot easily forget the ruthless firing of an excellent U.S. attorney, Philip Van Dam, to make way for a candidate suggested by Democratic Sen. Donald W. Riegle. Utah has no illusions about how the brother of a Democratic congressman, who happens to be a close friend of House Speaker Tip O'Neill, who works closely with Jimmy Carter, got nominated for a judgeship.

We are indebted to "Time" for keeping score on the President's appointments of judges and U.S. attorneys. Here are the results thus far:

U.S. circuit courts — Democrats: 10. Republicans: 0.

U.S. district courts — Democrats: 21. Republicans: 0.

U.S. attorneys — Democrats: 55. Republicans: 1.

Total — Democrats: 86. Republicans 1.

Now go back and read candidate Jimmy Carter's promise again.

THE ARIZONA REPUBLIC

Phoenix, Ariz., November 27, 1977

Judicial Patronage

PETER RODINO, a Democratic congressman from New Jersey, made a valiant fight to hold down the number of new federal judgeships that will be created before members of the 95th Congress face voters in November of next year.

But Rodino lost to Democrats who see a bonanza in allowing President Carter to appoint 150 or more district and circuit judges when the 1978 congressional elections are beginning to heat up.

The Senate has passed a bill creating 113 new district and 35 new circuit or appeals court judgeships. Rep. Rodino, as chairman of the House Judiciary Committee, wanted to create only 81 district and 34 circuit judgeships.

When his committee started to mark up its bill, he found members demanding the creation of additional judgeships from Massachusetts to Maine.

"The dam broke," Rodino said sadly. By the time his committee adjourned for the Thanksgiving recess it had added 16 judgeships not approved by the subcommittee. When the Judiciary Committee meets Tuesday it may well go above the number of new judgeships in the Senate bill.

When the bill hits the floor of the House of Representatives, there may be an effort to add even more judgeships by amending the bill.

The pay is good ($44,600 for circuit judges; $42,000 for district judges) and the tenure is unbeatable (appointments are for life). If the Democrats are allowed to pass out 150 of these plums, it won't hurt the party's chances in November.

The appellate federal judges are subject to nomination by judicial review committees, but the district judges are still all-out patronage. That's not new, of course.

Congressional Quarterly, in its current issue, carries the following list of federal circuit and district judgeships filled by American presidents beginning with Roosevelt:

(Two of the totals are incorrect because appointees were made who did not belong to either major party.)

	Total	Dem	Rep
Roosevelt	194	188	6
Truman	125	116	9
Eisenhower	174	9	165
Kennedy	123	111	11
Johnson	168	159	9
Nixon	214	15	192
Ford	64	12	52
Carter	27	27	0

Politics is still the name of the game, when it comes to getting on the federal bench.

The Evening Bulletin
Philadelphia, Pa., November 27, 1977

Who will judge the judges?

Remember how all the politicians hooted last spring when Pennsylvania's two Republican U.S. Senators formed a commission to recommend federal court nominees to the President? After all, Republicans usually don't get to tell Democratic presidents *anything* about federal judgeships.

There was a double irony, too, because it was President Carter's Attorney General, Griffin Bell, who suggested U.S. Senators form these commissions to pick federal judges on the basis of merit, not politics.

So here were these two minority-party senators taking him up on the idea. And Senators Schweiker and Heinz were accused of rallying behind merit selection simply because their political party didn't control the White House anymore.

Well, with five vacancies now on the federal courts in Philadelphia and Pittsburgh, we're going to see how serious members of both political parties are about picking qualified federal judges. This applies to President Carter, too, because he has backed off somewhat on his campaign pledge of full merit selection of all U.S. Court judges.

It's clear Pennsylvania's Democratic congressmen have no intention of letting the Schweiker-Heinz commission make all the recommendations to President Carter. They'll be offering their own suggestions to the Justice Department, which then forwards the candidates' names to the President, who makes the appointments.

On the other hand, the Schweiker-Heinz Federal Judicial Nominating Commission of Pennsylvania appears to be truly bipartisan. Eight votes are needed to recommend a candidate and no political party can have more than seven representatives on the 14-person commission. But most important, the commission has a promise from the two senators that its list of recommendations will go to the Justice Department without any alterations.

We know Pennsylvania's Democratic congressmen claim to be just as devoted to merit selection of judges. And there is really no reason why they can't search for qualified judge candidates, too. But why not run their choices through the Senators' nomination committee? If their people are qualified, won't they get the commission's vote?

For their part, Senators Heinz and Schweiker should maintain their distance from the commission's work. And they might also offer more tangible proof of their enthusiasm for merit selection by coming up with a few thousand dollars each year to reimburse the commission members — not all of whom can write it off as a business expense — for travel and the expense of sending out questionnaires. We suggest the senators scrutinize their own $705,000 yearly office allowance for a few extra dollars.

The White House has a challenge to meet as well. Mr. Carter has already chosen one Pennsylvania judge who was recommended by the new nominating commission. However, that was a relatively uncontroversial choice and the five remaining selections will be a better test.

We've seen a gradual move away from patronage in many areas of government, and nowhere is this more important than in the judiciary. But the prevailing method for choosing a federal judge still involves political considerations. That's why we'll have to see whether Pennsylvania's new judicial nominating commission actually helps implement merit selection.

Then maybe we'll know whether the rules of the game have really been changed in the picking of federal judges.

The State
Columbia, S.C., May 29, 1977

Democrats Not So Noble In Judiciary's Rescue

ONE THING just as certain as death and taxes is that the Democratic-controlled Congress will add a host of new judgeships this year to the federal judiciary.

The U.S. Senate passed a bill on Thursday which would add 108 U.S. district judges and 35 U.S. circuit court judges in the federal court system. Similar legislation is moving through the U.S. House of Representatives and no substantial opposition is expected.

There is little question that the federal courts are overburdened. They have been for a number of years and are overdue some expansion. South Carolina, as things stand now, would get an additional three district judges to help the present five. The Fourth Circuit, which includes South Carolina, would have three judges added to the present appellate bench of seven.

But what makes the expansion of the federal judiciary a virtual certainty this year is not altogether the needed relief for the judicial burden. There's the matter of politics.

It works this way. The judges are appointed by the President subject to confirmation by the U.S. Senate — in practicality, the senators from the state involved. Since Republican Presidents usually appoint Republicans as judges, and Democratic Presidents appoint Democrats, the Democrats in Congress weren't about to let Presidents Nixon and Ford have such sweet patronage.

Now that there is a Democratic President, the Democratic Congress is ready to move ahead with relief for the federal judiciary for the first time since 1970. The Democratic senators, of course, will have a word or two to say on the appointments in their states. Presidents just don't send up appointees who will be rejected.

And that's the way it works, although the courts' need for help has been long and well documented. For example, since 1964 the Judicial Conference of the United States, composed of federal judges and concerned with court administration, has been making quadrennial surveys of the courts' needs. In 1972, the conference recommended 51 new judgeships, but Congress did nothing.

For their part, congressional leaders pleaded that the "Watergate events" took up too much time of the judiciary committees of the House and Senate. Those are the committees where the judgeship bills start.

But that's not the whole story, as the authoritative *Congressional Quarterly*, which monitors Congress, points out: " . . . The reluctance to deal with the creation of new judgeships during the Watergate crisis was succeeded by the reluctance of the Democratic majority to create a large new body of federal patronage while a Republican President was in office."

The Democratic Congress which now is rushing to the rescue of the federal judiciary isn't so noble. Call it what it is — politics and patronage.

The Washington Post
Times Herald

Washington, D.C., November 25, 1977

Judges and Speedy Trials

W E CAN UNDERSTAND the frustrations that led federal Judge Joseph M. Young to his peculiar ruling that the speedy trial act of 1974 is unconstitutional. The act has placed a heavy burden on federal judges all over the country. It has disrupted court calendars in many districts, so that civil cases have been pushed aside almost indefinitely. And it has meant that some persons charged with crimes escaped trial altogether because courts could not meet the act's requirements. But the response to all this should not be to reach out, as it seems to us Judge Young did, for a theory on which to strike down the act. Nor should it be to repeal the act, as some have suggested. What is needed is for Congress to provide the federal courts with enough judges to do the work it has said must be done.

The 1974 act, a legacy from former Sen. Sam J. Ervin, was designed to give reality to the Sixth Amendment's guarantee of a "speedy" trial. It sets up the maximum periods that can elapse between the time a suspect is arrested, indicted, arraigned and tried. If the time limits are not met—except for some extraordinary reason—the case must be dismissed.

Judge Young ruled that these conditions are a "legislative encroachment" on the judiciary and thus violate the separation-of-powers doctrine. Because Congress has adopted so many other procedural and substantive judicial rules during the last two centuries—which are presumably also unconstitutional—we do not take Judge Young's challenge seriously.

But we do think the inaction of Congress in providing new judges is a serious default. No new federal district judgeships have been created since 1970. As long as the Republicans held the White House, the Democratic Congress ignored this situation, hoping that the election in 1976 would bring in a Democratic President who would appoint the new judges. The election provided a Democratic President, all right, but the courts are still waiting—more and more impatiently. The Senate approved a bill to create 148 new judgeships last May. A House Judiciary subcommittee recommended cutting that number to 115 last June. But the full House committee has yet to complete action. There is no justification for that kind of delay. It serves to frustrate justice, not just individual judges.

THE KANSAS CITY STAR
Kansas City, Mo., July 17, 1977

Overloaded U.S. Courts Are A Drag on Justice

An observation by Alexis de Tocqueville nearly a century and a half ago seems even more appropriate now. "Scarcely any political question arises in the United States that is not resolved, sooner or later, into a judicial question," wrote the French visitor.

Indeed, in this, the last quarter of the 20th century, no difference of opinion is far from the courtroom door. We are a litigation-minded society. Disgruntled fans sue over assignment of football tickets. Highly complicated interlockings of sprawling business conglomerates virtually assure lawsuits.

In recent years Americans have turned increasingly to the courts for resolution of some of their more pressing social problems—racial segregation, capital punishment and abortion, among them.

Nowhere has this crush of frustration been felt with greater intensity than in the federal judicial system. On June 30 of last year there were 128.9 per cent more cases (140,189) pending in U.S. District courts than on that date in 1960. This explosion reverberates upward through the appellate jurisdictions, including the United States Supreme Court. The system is overburdened, a condition that puts our quality of justice at stake.

Yet despite some rather obvious signals, relatively few significant adjustments have been made in the mechanism to accommodate the escalating work load. Congress has shown little imagination or inclination to deal with this most important public matter.

Many Americans may feel they are not touched by this issue. Of course they are. The federal judiciary regularly turns out decisions of momentous impact on their lives. Racial integra-

tion is but one example, but it underscores the point.

The controversy over the crowded federal dockets is breaking along lines that have been fermenting for several years. Should federal courts be called on to resolve more or fewer confrontations? Should there be restrictions on the types of cases that are filed? The way this conflict is settled will have a profound effect on who will or will not have access to federal courts.

The issue is under study in Congress. A newly created office in the Justice Department is looking for ways to improve the administration of justice.

As Supreme Court decisions during most of this decade have indicated, Chief Justice Warren E. Burger is at the forefront of those who contend that more discretion is needed in the use of federal courts. The chief justice has suggested that many federal cases could be headed off through action by Congress, state and local governments.

The opponents of restrictions, including representatives of antipoverty, environmental and consumer organizations, are apprehensive that limitations on the number and types of cases could shut many Americans out of the judicial process. Some members of Congress share this concern. Pending in Congress are several pieces of legislation that would counter what are considered restrictions set up by the Supreme Court.

One of the most direct, immediate solutions also is before Congress. That is a bill to add judges. In May the Senate approved a measure that would create about 115 new district and 35 additional circuit court judgeships, in-

cluding two in the Western District of Missouri. A subcommittee in the House eliminated one of them, a move that if allowed to stand would hamper the administration of justice in this area. The House Judiciary Committee must approve this legislation before it is sent to the House floor for debate. The subcommittee's decision to eliminate one of the judgeships here should be overturned. The work load in Kansas City clearly merits the two extra judges.

The jurisdiction of federal magistrates would be expanded by another measure that has been introduced in Congress. Other ideas are being explored. Among them are the substitution of more compulsory arbitration for court suits, expansion of no-fault liability, addition of nonjudicial workers to assist judges, new tribunals, alternatives to class actions and ways of discouraging appeals that are considered to be extraordinarily frivolous.

Still another piece of legislation moving through Congress at the moment is aimed at keeping small claims of consumers out of court proceedings. The objective is to assist in the settlement of such disputes by conciliation and mediation. The Justice Department is also planning to experiment with neighborhood justice centers where informal hearings would be used to dispose of cases without the full trappings of the judiciary.

On Feb. 14 President Carter issued an executive order that established the merit selection of judges for circuit appeals courts. Under terms of the order the panels will suggest the "best qualified" individuals for those judgeships. It does not apply to appointments to the district courts. U. S. senators will continue to have a major role

in the selection of federal district judges.

It is most difficult to predict what will come of all these ideas and experiments, if anything. Solutions, however, are clearly needed.

One scholar on the judiciary has made some rather unnerving projections. If the current growth rate continues, by the year 2010 some 5,000 judges would be needed to rule on the 1 million appeals each year alone! For some perspective on that, 18,408 cases were taken to the appeals courts in 1976. The system, as it exists, could not survive the crowded dockets into the next century.

Cumbersome though the task may be, the major responsibility for improvements rests with the Congress. Judges overstep their authority when they hand down decisions that discourage litigants from using the courts. The courts are the preserve of the people, not the judges who serve them.

Within the federal structure, the judicial system is, and must be considered, an important, integral part of the decision-making process.

Of course the ultimate direction must come from the public. If citizens want courts that provide equitable justice in a reasonable time, they must make those wants known. Congress must be informed and the pressure cooker turned on. One of the drawbacks from the public's viewpoint is the lack of a special lobbying effort for judicial needs.

For the most part the record of Congress in this field is unimpressive. The judiciary—and thus public justice—is attended to belatedly and often as a political exercise. That disregard for the public interest no longer should be tolerated.

The State

Columbia, S.C., June 28, 1977

Our Overloaded Courts

THE TERM, ''impact statement,'' generally is construed to mean a report describing the effect upon the environment of some major construction project.

It also has a legislative connotation in the sense of evaluating the cost consequences — present and future — of a proposed statute.

But it has still a third meaning, this one with judicial overtones. Chief Justice Warren E. Burger has asked Congress to develop an ''impact statement'' for every piece of legislation affecting the federal judiciary. In short, the chief justice feels that the judiciary should be alerted (along with the public at large) to the probable results of a given act in terms of jurisdictional, procedural, financial and personnel needs.

It seems quite evident these days that the federal courts are becoming overloaded with litigation. Since Congress itself is partially responsible for this state of affairs (through passage of new federal laws without corresponding increase of federal courts) it seems only fair that notice of consequence be given at the time a new law is under consideration.

Democrat and Chronicle

Rochester, N.Y., June 10, 1977

No justice without the victim

WITHOUT the assistance of the victim, the violent criminal often cannot be brought to justice.

But that cooperation will only be forthcoming if the victim has confidence in the effectiveness and fairness of the judicial system.

One of the disquieting aspects of the recent study commissioned by the Victims Assistance Program (VAP) of the Rochester Police Department was the dissatisfaction expressed by many victims with the criminal justice system, particularly the courts.

Some of the reasons why can best be demonstrated by several cases that were put into evidence earlier this year before the State Republican Task Force on Crime Victims by Susan L. Costa, coordinator of the local VAP, and Sergeant Joseph J. Davis, project director. Thus:

> "A 42-year-old physically and emotionally handicapped woman is raped while being shown an apartment for rent. Accompanied to the grand jury by the Victim Service worker, she goes to testify and finds she must wait in a crowded hallway where the defendant and his family have decided to appear. The victim is upset and wants to leave but is convinced to stay and testify by the Victim Service worker. They go to the public ladies' room and are followed and harassed by the defendant's wife and daughter."

A lesson from that bad experience is that victims and witnesses must be provided with separate waiting rooms and spared face-to-face confrontations.

The importance of prompt property return is emphasized by this case:

> "A 22-year-old woman has her purse snatched and a police officer almost immediately apprehends the suspect. The purse and its contents are recovered and confiscated as evidence. The woman was carrying $400 to make an already overdue mortgage payment. She is a factory worker and does not have access to additional funds. The bank is threatening to foreclose and she appears at the Victim Service in tears and very angry after half-a-day of futile efforts to get the money released. She threatens to drop the charges. Luckily, we were able to secure the release of her money, after arranging for it to be photographed as evidence, within 24 hours."

The need for a standby telephone system that would eliminate unnecessary trips and frustrating waits is shown by this case:

> "A 94-year-old man is mugged, his wallet stolen, in the bus terminal. He is subpoenaed to testify before the grand jury and a Victim Service worker goes to the city of Canandaigua to get him. Upon arrival at the grand jury it is found that the package for his case has been misplaced and he cannot testify that day. He returns to his home and must come back another day. He is angry, inconvenienced and bewildered."

These needs, and others, were also pointed up at the recent Victims' Assistance workshop co-sponsored by the VAP and the U of R, University College of Liberal and Applied Studies. It was noted for example . . .

• that the general community is not as well informed as it should be about the VAP.

• that social and criminal justice agencies should work more cooperatively.

• that victims be advised regularly of the status of their cases.

• that time be taken to explain to victims the court procedures and the kinds of questions they might expect.

• that suspects be dealt with as soon as possible.

• that threats of retaliation be dealt with by, for example, review of bail, filing of a criminal complaint, or a call to the defense attorney.

• that some central point be established where witnesses could lodge complaints.

• that the court case backlog be seen as the most important barrier to quick justice.

As Ms. Costa has said, "victims and witnesses are frustrated, alienated, ignored and victimized by the system. Sometimes they are even blamed for their criminal victimization . . ."

The VAP is doing valuable work in reducing the alienation and in increasing the number of victims and witnesses helping in prosecution.

But only with wide community support and only with changes in the system can it say to the victim, "without you there can be no justice," and be sure of a quick, cooperative response.

THE TENNESSEAN

Nashville, Tenn., February 27, 1977

Justice Burger's Suit
May Also Be Ruled Out

CHIEF Justice Warren Burger has been complaining for the last several years about the heavy workload of the Supreme Court and the need for reform of the court system to make it work better.

In Seattle recently, the Chief Justice was quoted as deploring the "unfortunate propensity" of Congress to pass laws increasing the court's work load without providing the people to do the work.

There is no doubt the court system could be made to work better, and more judges may be needed in the lower courts to handle expanding dockets.

The Supreme Court itself may have to work a little harder at times than at others. But the Burger court seems to have been taking action on its own which cuts down on the work load of itself and the lower courts.

The court, in its rulings, has been excluding more and more Americans from seeking relief in the federal courts. The critics of the court claim it has been destroying the effect of previous decisions, primarily through procedural rulings. They say these rulings have closed the doors of the courts to

many claimants among racial minorities, the poor, consumers and others.

The court's procedural rulings have made it more difficult for persons convicted of crimes to challenge the constitutionality of searches, restricted class actions and denied the awarding of fees to lawyers in public interest cases.

Restricting class actions makes it more difficult for persons with small claims to get a hearing in court. In one antitrust case, the court ruled that the plaintiffs had to notify at their own expense more than two million people they sought to represent as a single case.

The ruling denying fees to lawyers in public interest cases is sure to cut down on the number of such cases brought.

The effect of these rulings and others has been to deny the facilities of the judicial system to the poor and the powerless and to make the court more of an institution for serving the wealthy and the influential.

Very serious questions are raised as to how many more people and how much more money the judicial system

needs to carry out this kind of justice.

It would be one thing if the court were issuing these procedural rulings excluding more and more people from access to the courts because the justices were overworked and just didn't have time to fool with a lot of bothersome cases brought by ordinary people. This would be bad justice, but one could understand its causes.

Something quite different from this seems to be the true case, however. It seems certain the Burger court has been tightening up with procedural rulings not to cut down on the number of cases but for ideological reasons.

It is likely that the majority of this court really believes that justice would best be served if traffic in the courts were reduced — even though that makes it more difficult for many people to seek to assert their constitutional rights.

The only way the public ought to be asked to pay more in tax dollars to the administration of justice is if the system responds by providing more judicial services to the broadest number of citizens.

The Dallas Morning News

Dallas, Tex., February 20, 1977

Krytocracy

MR. CHIEF Justice Burger's "state of the federal judiciary" address abounds with admirable suggestions for improving the technical performance of the courts. More judgeships, reform of appellate court boundaries, creation of a National Institute of Justice—such are Burger's prescriptions for change.

It is in no way to criticize the chief justice, however, to suggest that his 1977 address is as disappointing as all its predecessors have been. Not for their lack of creative suggestions; rather, for their failure to address the main problem regarding the courts, the problem of bloated judicial power.

Can the federal courts be trimmed down to size? If so, how? These are the paramount questions. For whatever reason the chief justice fails annually to address them, his state of the judiciary message has an emptiness at its core. It is "Hamlet" without the Prince of Denmark.

The problem to which Burger ought to be speaking—the problem of judicial meddling—was amply

illustrated in Tennessee a few weeks ago. In the City of Nashville there are two colleges—a University of Tennessee campus and Tennessee State University. The former is mostly white, the latter mostly black. Both schools have open admissions policies. Yet to U.S. Dist. Judge Frank Gray this does not matter. Gray finds that there is insufficient integration on the two campuses.

Accordingly, Gray has ordered, not a busing program, no, no; he has ordered the merger of the two universities—their compaction into a single educational entity.

This is a breathtaking order, even by federal standards. And yet this sort of thing the federal judiciary does regularly nowadays. Seemingly, numerous federal judges have no shame whatever in writing laws for the various inferior governmental subdivisions, which means all subdivisions besides the courts themselves. A judge in Mobile has ordered the city to alter its form of municipal government. In

Texas, Judge William Wayne Justice has commanded the state to reform its juvenile detention system along lines stipulated by himself.

What should be understood at the outset is that decisions like these are in sharp contrast with decisions of the more remote (i.e., pre-Earl Warren) past. The court's old role was a negative one. What it disliked it ordered stopped. The court's new role is a positive one. What it wants done it orders done—even if to do this is, in effect, to usurp the legislative prerogative of drafting and enacting legislation.

The courts before Warren's day would no more have ordered two state universities merged than they would have pronounced judicial salaries unconstitutional. After all, as the learned Francis Bacon had written several centuries before, "Judges ought to remember that their office is 'jus dicere,' and not 'jus dare' to interpret law, and not to make or give law." In short, the judges would tell you what not to do; they would not go further still and tell you, in excruciating detail,

what to do.

This they do nowadays because they have drunk the heady wine of Warrenism. Judicial modesty is a phenomenon of the past. Even Archibald Cox, a certified liberal, has declared the trend to be fraught with danger "because these quasi-legislative decrees cannot be said, like true legislation, to have the legitimacy which flows from the processes of democratic self-government."

Indeed not; autocracy and oligarchy are not, after all, the only forms of government hostile to democracy. So is krytocracy—government by judges.

We are not there yet—we have, for one thing, a chief justice who is an antikrytocrat—but we are closer than we ought to be. And surely it is for the chief justice to speak, besides a word about judicial boundaries, a message of comfort and hope to those who see the federal courts arrogating more and more power unto themselves.

Maybe next year?

THE SACRAMENTO BEE
Sacramento, Calif., April 6, 1977
Crime And The Courts

While there may be occasional abuses of plea bargaining, as practiced in California courts, its use permits needed latitude in the criminal justice system and it should not be completely abandoned in the name of cracking down on crime.

Sen. Dennis Carpenter, R-Newport Beach, is making another legislative attempt to kill plea bargaining. He says the practice makes a "bargain basement" of the courts. His argument reflects the view that crime would be significantly reduced if only the courts would stop coddling criminals.

This is simplistic. It just isn't true that judges are letting serious offenders off the hook in any wide-scale fashion.

California's judges on the whole are just as reasonably concerned about crime as anybody else. Serious offenders who get off too lightly are few and far between.

There are times, certainly, when plea bargaining is abused. It would be foolish to argue otherwise. But this happens mainly in the case of lesser crimes, and for an understandable reason.

It goes to the practical and necessary purpose behind plea bargaining, which is in part a result of seriously overburdened courts.

Its practical purpose, reaffirmed and legalized in California as recently as 1971, is to permit judges and prosecutors to determine when the best interests of justice would be served by a lesser plea or a reduced charge. Given the logjam of the courts, this is one way to permit court calendars to be cleared of less serious offenses in order to make way for the serious crimes that need to be dealt with.

It is entirely possible to put less harsh restriction on the practice of plea bargaining than Carpenter's SB 295, which is essentially the same proposal that died in the Assembly last year.

But to halt plea bargaining entirely goes too far, and the bill deserves the same fate this year.

The Des Moines Register
Des Moines, Iowa, July 8, 1977
Plea bargaining in public

Plea bargaining often gets a bum rap. Many perceive it as letting criminals off easy; some say it's an invidious tool the prosecutor can use to coerce defendants to plead guilty, regardless of the evidence.

In plea bargaining, the defendant pleads guilty in exchange for a sentencing recommendation or an expectation of leniency.

A new study by Georgetown University Law Center's Institute of Criminal Law and Procedure indicates that plea bargaining often does not benefit the defendant.

"In some cases defendants may believe they are getting a 'bargain' and they may be encouraged in that belief by their attorneys (who may or may not know otherwise)," the study said. "In fact, they may get nothing in return for their plea of guilty.... The sentence imposed may be no different than if the defendant had been convicted at trial."

The director of the study, Prof. Herbert S. Miller, recommended that public records of plea bargaining be kept, to reduce the likelihood that the defendant will be coerced, and to make the public aware of the factors that go into the plea — weak evidence, for instance, or a reluctant witness.

Iowa's current criminal code, like that of many states, makes no mention of plea bargaining, although it is widely used. The revised criminal code, which takes effect Jan. 1, formalizes the practice.

The new code says that the prosecutor and defense attorney may negotiate a plea bargain. The agreement is to be disclosed in open court, and the judge may accept or reject it. He may withhold that decision until he sees the presentence report.

If the judge accepts the bargain, he must sentence according to it or impose a lesser penalty. If he rejects the bargain, he must so inform the defendant, tell him the sentence may be harsher than that negotiated and tell him he can withdraw the plea.

If the defendant withdraws the plea and goes to trial, or if the prosecution and defense negotiate but are unable to agree, neither the negotiations nor the previous plea are admissible in any criminal, civil or administrative proceeding.

Iowa's new statute is needed. Plea bargaining occurs in most criminal cases; the law should acknowledge and regulate it.

But Iowa's statute doesn't go as far as Miller's recommendation: Only the result would be public. Making records of negotiations, and making them public, would also be wise.

The Times-Picayune
New Orleans, La., July 10, 1977
Is Plea Bargaining a Gyp?

Mention "plea bargaining" to almost anyone in casual conversation, and he will likely declare knowingly that it is the arrangement whereby a vicious murderer gets off with a light sentence by pleading guilty to a lesser charge such as manslaughter. Now comes a scholarly report that says defendants may be drawing harsher sentences by plea bargaining than by going to trial.

The 21-month study on plea bargaining in the United States was financed with $303,000 from the Law Enforcement Assistance Administration and conducted by the Institute of Criminal Law and Procedure at the Georgetown University Law Center in Washington. Researchers covered 26 localities, including New Orleans and several other large cities.

The report said some defendants may gain nothing for their plea of guilty because some prosecutors overcharge hoping to induce a guilty plea on one count of an indictment. For example, a prosecutor might persuade a grand jury to indict on assault and armed robbery, even though he knows he could not get a conviction on the robbery charge. He then offers the defendant a deal: plead guilty to the assault charge in exchange for dropping the armed robbery indictment.

The public's view of plea bargaining as a slipshod method of speeding up court dockets at the expense of justice should not be altered by this report. If it is wrong to permit a murderer to plead guilty to manslaughter simply because the courts cannot be bothered with a trial, then it is hardly any more just to trick a defendant into pleading guilty so that a more serious charge which could not be proved may be magnanimously dropped.

The report recommends opening up the plea-bargaining process so that the public can understand it. This, it is theorized, would disabuse citizens of the notion that criminals get a break by the practice. That might be an improvement, but it seems a better idea would be the old-fashioned judicial process in which a defendant is tried in open court on the evidence and not on the expedient of swapping.

San Francisco Chronicle

San Francisco, Calif., May 9, 1977

The Role of Judges in Plea Bargaining

TWO STATE SENATORS have made it their purpose this year to curb the powers of judges in dealing with the flood of felonies that come before them for judgment.

One, a bill by Senator Dennis Carpenter (Rep-Newport Beach), SB295, would outlaw "sentence bargaining," i. e., preclude a judge from discussing or agreeing to a sentence to be imposed on a defendant charged with felony until after he has been found guilty. This measure recently passed the senate Senate 25 to 13 and may have a chance this year of surviving in an Assembly committee where it died last year.

A related bill, SB 195, is Senator Newton R. Russell's so-called Judges' Open Record Act, which would require that any time a judge in a felony case accepts a plea or decides on a sentence, he shall state on the record the reasons for his decision. Russell's object is to create a file of each judge's explanations for the felonies he disposes of, separately indexed from other files in the courthouse and made easily available for the public's inspection when the judge comes up for election.

SINCE THESE MEASURES would invade and alter the present practices and powers of judges, we believe they deserve the most serious consideration.

There is no doubt that the Carpenter bill deals with a growing concern of the public in cutting judges out of the process of what is loosely called plea bargaining. This is a disturbing concept to many people. They suspect that oftentimes a defendant charged with a serious crime is allowed by the judge to plead guilty to a lesser one merely in order to get the case disposed of and move the line of criminals along.

To the extent that this is true, it is certainly objectionable. The American judicial system should be provided with whatever means are required to give due, careful and unhurried consideration to the facts of each criminal case, and not only to the rights of the defendant but also to the rights of the public. The public demands protection from hasty or easygoing judgments reflecting pressure on the courts, and if more courtrooms, judges, clerks and bailiffs are needed to manage the criminal courts' business in this deliberate manner, we believe society must pay the price.

PLEA BARGAINING, it needs to be said, is unfortunately a loaded phrase describing a process which is very useful when properly conducted, as we are convinced it mostly is. The typical plea bargaining situation puts a felony defendant and his lawyer, the prosecution and the judge together in a pretrial conference, wherein the judge learns what the facts are, what sentence the prosecution would ask for upon a plea of guilty, and what the defense counsel hopes to hold out for.

This is a delicate process of finding the path of justice and assessing the appropriate penalty. It calls for judges with a firm knowledge of the law and the facts. It seems to us that to remove the judge from this process, by precluding him from any discussion of the sentence to be expected on a plea of guilty, would unnecessarily hobble the courts in doing justice.

CERTAINLY, to take away from a criminal defendant the incentive to plead guilty, knowing what his sentence is likely to be, would incline him in many cases to elect to go to trial and take his chances. This could require a tremendous expansion of the courts to accommodate the increased number of trials. Currently in San Francisco 90 per cent of the felony cases result in pleas of guilty and are handled in one court; the other ten per cent going to trial use up seven courts.

The California Judges Association has expressed its opposition to both Carpenter's and Russell's bills. We believe it is warranted and the bills should be defeated. The objection we make to Russell's bill is that it would add to the judge's burden by requiring a full explanation for every disposing act; we fear he would worry more about how he was going to look in print and about fitting his judgment into the pattern of what is expected than he would about doing justice in the individual case.

Lawyers:
Justice only for the rich?

Lawyers have frequently been accused of only serving the needs and interests of the rich. In 1965 a major effort was undertaken to supply free legal aid to the poor with the Office of Economic Opportunity's legal services program. By the early 1970's legal services were the only remaining branch of the O.E.O. In order to guarantee its continued funding and political independence, the Congress established the Federal Legal Services Corporation in 1976 as a separate public corporation with the Board of Directors nominated by the president and approved by Congress. The Congress did include certain restrictions as to what type of cases legal service lawyers could advocate: homosexual rights and abortion were two of the most controversial issues to be denied legal services support. It is very likely that the restrictions are unconstitutional, if not in violation of the Canon of Ethics for attorneys, requiring them to provide representation even for unpopular issues and clients.

Currently 2500 lawyers throughout the country provide free legal help to indigents in the civil area of law: landlord-tenant, welfare, employment and family law. While the program has established a precedent in making legal services available to the poor, many offices are so overworked that only emergency cases can be handled. The Corporation allocates on the average of seven dollars per capita for each person below the poverty line living in the area of a legal service office.

A wave of change is also beginning to improve access to lawyers by middle-income groups. The Supreme Court in *Goldfarb v. Virginia State Bar* held that bar associations could not establish and enforce minimum fee schedules among lawyers.[1] Established fee schedules have played a significant role in restraining competition among lawyers and maintaining the high cost of legal assistance.

In *Bates v. State Bar of Arizona* the Supreme Court ruled that forbidding lawyers to advertise their services and prices was a violation of the First Amendment free speech principle.[2] The restrictions on legal advertising have not been completely removed. The Court did not set any explicit guidelines, but it did suggest that lawyers should still be prevented from making claims about the quality of their services or advertising prices for services that are not routine.

The prohibition on legal advertising had dissuaded many from seeking assistance because they were fearful of the actual cost.[3] It is still too early to predict if advertising will reduce the cost of legal services. Perusal of legal advertisements seems to indicate that fairly standardized functions like non-contested divorces, name changes and small will and deeds are dropping in price.

Even prior to the *Goldfarb* and *Bates* decisions, there was a flurry of activity to expand legal services for middle-income groups. Numerous trade unions had established legal services clinics for their members. This practice had also been opposed by the state bar associations. Once again the Supreme Court provided constitutional sanctuary for legal clinics in the decisions of *United Mine Workers v. Illinois State Bar Assn.*[4] and *United Transportation Union v. State Bar of Michigan.*[5]

The current trend of greater access to lawyers for all classes of people does not answer the question of whether lawyers have too dominant a position in resolving disputes among the American people. Chief Justice Burger has charged that the extension of due process rights to many new areas has caused the society to be overrun by lawyers, comparing them to locusts. Apart from Israel, the United States has more lawyers per capita than any other country in the world: 450,000 in total.[6] Chief Justice Burger's solution is to substitute more non-judicial arbitrations which would be less formal and time-consuming. Non-judicial decision making could also eliminate costly lawyers' fees. However, there is a tendency among lawyers to penetrate into areas that they are discouraged from entering. This has frequently been the situation in small claims courts, originally established to enable the lay person to proceed without an attorney. The growing assumption that lawyers have a unique ability to advocate ideas has persuaded many people to seek professional legal advice even when they do not need it.

The resistance of the organized bar to expanding legal services to wider strata of society is probably near an end. The size of the bar has been burgeoning in the last few years as law school enrollments have tripled. The traditional corporate law firms rendering assistance to the wealthy and the various government bureaucracies are unable to hire most of the law school graduates. Except for graduates of the prestige law schools, employment opportunities are few. Justice Robert Clifford of the New Jersey State Supreme Court noted in a swearing-in ceremony of new lawyers that "Law schools are producing twice the number of graduates as the system can absorb." However, it appears to be due to prohibitively high legal fees that more lawyers are not being "absorbed." Perhaps if the price were right, a new market—the middle class—could afford the services of a new generation of young lawyers who might otherwise find themselves out of work.

Notes

1. *Goldfarb v. Virginia State Bar,* 421 U.S. 773 (1975).
2. *Bates v. State Bar of Arizona,* 46 U.S.LW. 4895 (June 27, 1977).
3. Earl Koos, *The Family and the Law* (New York: 1948) p. 7.
4. *United Mine Workers v. Illinois State Bar Assn.,* 389 U.S. 217 (1967).
5. *United Transportation Union v. State Bar of Michigan,* 401 U.S. 576 (1970).
6. *The New York Times,* May 17, 1977 p. 1.

SUPREME COURT RULES AGAINST MINIMUM LEGAL FEE SCHEDULES

The Supreme Court June 16 unanimously ruled that the setting of uniform minimum fee schedules by lawyers was price fixing and a violation of U.S. antitrust laws. Chief Justice Warren E. Burger, author of the court's opinion, called the fee schedules "a classic illustration of price fixing" and "a pricing system that consumers could not realistically escape."

The classic argument, Burger said, that professions could not be considered "trade or commerce" lost "some of its force when used to support the fee control activities involved here." Although the court rejected the contention that Congress had intended to exempt all "learned professions" from antitrust regulation, it cautioned against interpreting the ruling too broadly. "It would be unrealistic to view the practices of professions as interchangeable with other business activities, and automatically to apply to the professions antitrust concepts which originated in other areas," Burger wrote in a footnote to his opinion.

The ruling stemmed from a suit originally brought by a Reston, Va. couple, who discovered they could not find a Fairfax County, Va. attorney to conduct a title examination search for their home for anything less than $522.50, the minimum 1% of the value of their $50,000 home, which was the fee "suggested" by the county bar association. Ruth and Lewis Goldfarb, the homebuyers, subsequently brought a class action suit against the Fairfax and Virginia state bars on behalf of home purchasers in their area who had been charged title-examination fees in accordance with a fee schedule.

Justice Lewis F. Powell Jr. did not participate in the case. His former law firm represented the Fairfax County Bar Association.

Arkansas Gazette.

Little Rock, Ark., June 21, 1975

Great annoyance and expense accompany the ordeal that millions of Americans have gone through in the buying or selling of a home. The process is so complicated that most of us are literally at the mercy of lawyers, real estate agents, engineers, and other specialists.

In many states and cities the results are really outrageous total charges for the transaction — the closing costs. One important part of those costs — fees charged by lawyers to examine titles — came under challenge by a couple in Reston, Virginia, however, and on Monday the United States Supreme Court made a far-reaching ruling.

It was the Supreme Court's 8 to 0 ruling that minimum fee schedules established by state or local bar associations violate federal antitrust law in cases where the fees have a substantial effect on interstate commerce. Such fee schedules, said Chief Justice Warren E. Burger for the court, afford "a classic illustration of price fixing."

The Reston couple asked more than two dozen lawyers in an effort to find one who would charge less than the $522 listed in the minimum fee schedules for searching a home title. None would and the suit followed, to the obvious chagrin of those in the legal profession who have valued the fee schedules and to the delight of others, mostly younger lawyers, who felt the need for competition to attract clients.

The Supreme Court's ruling does not guarantee that the home seller or purchaser, whichever the case may be, will be getting the advantage of lower fees for title examination, but at least the formal pressures against those lawyers who would lower the fee have been neatly removed.

In the ruling, the court took pains to point out that the same antitrust concepts it applied to legal charges would not necessarily apply to charges made in other professions. There is something that rubs against the grain of the free enterprise spirit, however, in the setting of minimum fees for services of any profession, and additional challenges to such practices may be encouraged by the ruling on legal fees.

The Washington Star

Washington, D.C., June 19, 1975

Almost anyone who spends much time around a courthouse can tell you that $522.50 is high pay for searching a house title. In the ordinary run of title searching, it's not all that time-consuming and it hardly requires a lawyer to dig very deeply into the store of expertise he presumably acquired in law school.

So it was a blow for common sense and free competition — and lower legal fees, we hope — that the Supreme Court struck when it ruled Monday that the Fairfax County Bar Association may no longer require lawyers to charge a fixed minimum fee for a title search. The minimum fee of one per cent of the purchase price — which in the case at hand amounted to $522.50 — is a "classic illustration of price fixing" that violates federal anti-trust laws, the Supreme Court held.

It is not clear what effect the ruling will have on legal fees in general or on the practices of other so-called "learned professions" that try to force their members to charge minimum (which is to say, high) fees for their services. But the consequences could be considerable. In any event, the tens of thousands of persons who will be buying homes across the country this year ought to realize a large collective saving.

Bar associations that establish fee schedules have never satisfactorily explained why every lawyer in a given area should charge the same for routine services such as property settlements, simple wills or uncomplicated divorces. The schedules obviously are designed to insure artificially high incomes for a relatively small group of professional people whose services have become a necesssary part of life.

In the case before the court, Chief Justice Burger observed that the "fixed, rigid" title search fee was a "pricing system that consumers could not realistically escape." That is completely contrary to the spirit of free competition which is supposed to underlie the American economic system. A citizen ought to be able to shop around for the best price he can get on legal services, just as he can for most other needs.

Shopping for a lawyer is unlikely ever to become comparable to shopping for tires or tooth brushes. Lawyers are prohibited by their canons of ethics from advertising their services, so don't expect suddenly to find "cut-rate divorce" ads in the yellow pages or the newspapers. But the Supreme Court ruling should result in some healthy competition that should tend to force prices down, which would mean that legal services would be available to more people at reasonable costs. At least the consumers will be in a better position to bargain for what they get.

Pittsburgh Post-Gazette
Pittsburgh, Pa., June 18, 1975

THE U.S. Supreme Court, seldom accused of not taking seriously the dignity of the legal profession, has rightly found one assertion of that dignity unwarranted. That is the claim made by lawyers that theirs is a "learned profession," not a mere business, and should therefore be exempt from federal antitrust laws.

The court rejected that claim this week in ruling illegal minimum fee schedules set by state and local bar associations for legal services associated with home buying. Chief Justice Burger's opinion in the 8-0 decision merely confirmed what has long been clear to consumers of legal services, that "the activities of lawyers play an important part in commercial intercourse and that anticompetitive activities by lawyers may exert a restraint on commerce."

Consequences of the court's prohibition of legal price-fixing might well extend beyond relief for home buyers in areas where bar association fee schedules have prevailed. (Pennsylvania residents largely do not fall into this category, fee schedules having been abolished in most counties years ago on the recommendation of the state bar.) Lawyers are not the only profession to claim exemption from antitrust laws; architects, engineers and accountants could also be forced to offer more competitive fees.

There is no legal or common-sense reason why such professions, however "learned," should be able to maintain, by agreement among supposed competitors, artificially high prices.

The Knickerbocker News
••• UNION-STAR •••
Albany, N.Y., June 18, 1975

Some months ago, Chief Justice Warren E. Burger was highly critical of the costs associated with buying a home and advised lawyers particularly to see to it they were brought down.

Now the court itself has found, in effect, that a high contributory factor to the "closing costs" in a home purchase has been the illegal price fixing by lawyers and their bar associations. The price fixing was done through minimum fee schedules established by bar associations in 19 states (but not New York State) and hundreds of local bar associations.

The high court ruled in a 8-0 verdict that such price fixing violates the anti-trust laws and eliminates competition. Chief Justice Burger described the practice "a classic example of price fixing" and said:

"It cannot be denied that the activities of lawyers play an important part in commercial intercourse and that anti-competitive activities by lawyers may exert a restraint on commerce."

Although the impact of the decision is not fully clear, the ruling could extend to real estate agents, architects, engineers, accountants and the like.

And so the court recognizes that consumers too frequently are victims of the "learned professions," which often appear most learned in ways of feathering their own nests by charging unconscionable fees for work that frequently is done, not by a member of the profession, but by a hired hand .

The man in the street has reason to hail this decision. To keep his views in balance,however, he might also give recognition to the fact that this case, which clips the wings of some lawyers, was argued successfully in that high court by other lawyers. In that, too, the man in the street can find a substantial measure of satisfaction.

The Cleveland Press
Cleveland, Ohio, June 19, 1975

Consumers won an important victory this week when the Supreme Court ruled unanimously that fee-fixing by lawyers and other professionals is a clear violation of federal antitrust laws.

Specifically, the court ruled in a Virginia case that bar associations have no right to tell lawyers how much they must charge for examining the title of a newly purchased home.

But the significance of the ruling could go far beyond that.

It could mean that fee-fixing by lawyers, doctors, realtors, architects, engineers, accountants and other professional groups will be more vulnerable to legal challenge in the federal courts.

The ruling could drastically reduce real estate settlement fees in some states and give home-buyers a better chance to purchase such services at a price they can afford to pay.

Why, for example, should a home-buyer be forced to pay $500 for a routine title examination that may cost half that much (or less) to carry out?

In the Virginia case, no lawyer was willing to conduct a title search for less than 1% of the selling price, as stipulated by the Virginia Bar Assn.

This refusal to deviate from a published fee schedule — for fear of discipline by the bar — was a "classic illustration" of price-fixing, according to Chief Justice Warren E. Burger.

Fee-fixing, as President Ford pointed out last October, is a root cause of inflation in the United States.

That's why the Supreme Court ruling is good for the consumer, good for the country and good for the free enterprise system as well.

The Saginaw News
Saginaw, Mich., June 19, 1975

The Supreme Court's unanimous decision striking down the practice of minimum fees for attorneys providing routine services will have little more than a ripple effect in Michigan — if that.

Michigan has not been foremost among the states whose bar associations have routinely approved establishment of minimum fee schedules.

That practice, in fact, has been falling out of favor in recent years — and it no longer has the official blessing of the American Bar Association.

The court's decision is no less timely, however. It strikes a solid blow on behalf of the consumer. At least 20 states embracing the minimum fee practice have been put on notice that it must end.

The arguments are all in favor of the decision. Minimum fees for such things as title searches, writing a will, getting a divorce or drawing up papers to establish small businesses are antithetical to competition. Worse, where such practices are in force, the attorney is under compulsion to charge the going rate or face subtle if not severe reprisal.

We believe the Supreme Court has seen clearly that minimum fees are inimical to free enterprise, contrary to the public interest and not different, really, from price-fixing.

Without infringing upon the right of any attorney to charge what the client is willing to pay for extended, complex legal service, it has simply said that the professions are not exempt from the same price-fixing, restraint-of-trade regulations that apply to other businesses.

The Seattle Times
Seattle, Wash., June 17, 1975

ALTHOUGH the long-term implications of yesterday's United States Supreme Court decision on fees charged for legal services are not entirely clear, there is at least a hope that the ruling could portend some good news for consumers who avail themselves of services from lawyers and other professional practitioners.

The gist of the court's unanimous finding was that professional fee schedules are no more exempt from price-fixing laws and regulations than the rates charged for goods and services in commerce and industry.

Lawyers' minimum-fee schedules were adopted by local bar associations years ago in hopes of deterring attorneys from "soliciting" clients by charging fees consistently below what their colleagues considered to be acceptable levels.

In this state, both the Seattle-King County Bar Association and its state-level counterpart abandoned the publication of fee schedules some time ago, partly because of the Justice Department view that they violate the restraint-of-trade provisions of the Sherman Anti-trust Act.

The Justice Department had taken the plaintiffs' side in the case that was decided yesterday. Bar Associations in more than 30 other states will be affected.

Some experts believe that the court's action now will cast a cloud over the rates charged for certain medical services, particularly those delivered in co-operation with health-insurance plans.

No one expects that professional services suddenly will become available at bargain prices. But the prospect of some relief for consumers has at least been improved by a striking down of price-fixing practices in the so-called "learned professions."

The Salt Lake Tribune
Salt Lake City, Utah, June 19, 1975

Utah State Bar abolished its "advisory" legal fees schedule in 1971 because, an official recalled, of its "antitrust overtones."

A number of other professions face the prospect of taking similar action in view of the U.S. Supreme Court's ruling banning minimum legal fees which lawyers in some other states charge for real estate transfers.

Although the high court's ban was confined to certain real estate services performed by lawyers, its implications are broad.

The court didn't accept the lawyers' argument, upheld by the Fourth Circuit Court of Appeals, that they were exempt from antitrust laws because of membership in a "learned profession." Thus the ruling has potential impact on the fee schedules followed in many areas by architects, physicians, engineers and certified public accountants.

Perhaps a more immediate extension of the ruling will be against compacts among real estate sales companies in a given community under which a uniform percentage of the purchase price of a home is charged as sales commission.

The decision, coupled with a proposed rule by the Federal Trade Commission abolishing agreements among pharmacists not to advertise price of prescription drugs, could open new segments of the economy to rugged price competition.

Consumers could benefit from such a development but there are dangers too.

Minimum fee schedules, as in the case before the court, prevented a buyer from getting a job performed at a lower price. But the minimum also offered the same buyer a measure of protection against overcharge.

In the absence of competitive advertising, and without so much as a suggested minimum fee schedule, the buyer is left without an index to what a given professional service should cost.

The basic sin of fee schedules is not the schedule itself but the manner in which it is applied and enforced. A schedule which is truly only a suggested fair price, with practitioners free to charge lower or higher prices, can be a service to the consumer. But where the minimums are rigidly adhered to under pain of professional pressure or punishment, they deprive a consumer of opportunity to take advantage of price competition. That is the evil the Supreme Court was getting at in its ruling on lawyer fees.

ARKANSAS DEMOCRAT
Little Rock, Ark., June 18, 1975

The Supreme Court has opened up a big area of law-practice to competitive pricing with an 8-0 decision knocking out fee-scheduling in services touching interstate commerce. A classic case of price-fixing, the court said of the Virginia bar's minimum-price arrangement — hence a violation of the federal anti-trust laws.

Though the court said the ruling doesn't apply to other professions, the reverberations will echo through them anyway. Doctors, optometrists, accountants and other real or would-be professionals cannot escape the reasoning behind the ruling. The future of any kind of professional price-fixing is in doubt. So are bans on the advertising of professional services. All this can be read, inferentially at least, into the Justices' rejection of all lawyerly (and thus other professional) defenses of fee-scheduling.

The court brushed aside the Virginia Bar's claim that the fee schedules are only advisory. It rejected the bar's truly indefensible argument that "learned professions" aren't in the same anti-trust class with money-grubbing trades. The Justices simply identified professional fee-scheduling for what it is: Price fixing; the setting of an arbitrary value on a service whose real value should be decided competitively in the market-place.

Ironically enough, it was a house-hunting federal bureaucrat who carried the issue to the high court. The Justice Department, which has long threatened to take action against fixed fees, joined him in his complaint that every Virginia lawyer he shopped named the same price for the title-search required by state law.

Some 20 state bars (excluding Arkansas) and many local bars had fee-schedules at last report. The ruling does not kill the practice "as such." Legal services not in interstate commerce can be sold at a fixed fee and will probably continue to be so sold, though the American Bar Association has recommended that the practice cease. But the assumption that legal services lie generally outside interstate commerce will probably prove illusory.

"Interstate commerce" is involved so pervasively in the manufacture and sale of goods and services that few pursuits-for-profit can be safely regarded as untouched by it. There will be suits against fee-scheduling for what appear to be purely local legal services. The plain outlook is that legal fee-scheduling is doomed. And the outlook for all professional price-fixing is hardly brighter

The principle the justices laid down prospectively takes in all the professions. Sooner or later, suits will be brought against price fixing in medicine, optometry and other services where prices are standard.

Legal action will also be taken against laws and customs that limit competition and encourage price-fixing in yet another way: By forbidding advertising.

Such advertising bans are not yet an issue as they concern the prices professionals charge. But since the bans stifle competitive pricing and keep public prices artificially high, they logically face the same attack as fee-scheduling.

Younger members of the legal profession are, in fact, already arguing that lawyers should advertise. So are some doctors.

In Arkansas, the crying example of artificial pricing is the non-advertised sale of eyeglasses. They cost double and more the $20 the public pays in Texas, where advertising is legal. No high professional mysteries are involved in fitting eyeglasses; competition would do wonders for pricing.

Competition is coming in all professional fields. The lawyers are only the first to be hit by the big wave generated by the high court ruling. That wave and its ripples will ultimately reach into all the nooks and crannies of professional price-fixing. The court shattered its defense once and for all when it simply called it price fixing.

LAWYERS ALLOWED TO ADVERTISE CHARGES FOR SPECIFIC SERVICES

The Supreme Court June 27 held, 5–4, that lawyers could not be constitutionally prevented from advertising their fees for routine legal services. The case was *Bates v. Arizona State Bar*.

The challenge to a regulation of the Arizona bar prohibiting such advertising occurred when two lawyers, John R. Bates and Van O'Steen, inserted an advertisement in a Phoenix newspaper which began, "Do You Need a Lawyer? Legal Services at Very Reasonable Fees." Stated fees for Bates and O'Steen's services followed: $175 for an uncontested divorce, $225 for an adoption, $250 for an uncontested, nonbusiness bankruptcy, and $95 for a change of name.

The court was unanimous in finding that the Arizona ban did not violate federal antitrust law, since it was a product of state law. However, the court ruled, 5–4, that such a ban did violate the free speech guarantee of the First Amendment. Chief Justice Warren E. Burger and Justices William H. Rehnquist, Potter Stewart and Lewis F. Powell Jr. dissented. Chief Justice Burger predicted that the court decision would "breed more problems than it can conceivably solve."

The majority, led by Justice Harry A. Blackmun, rejected arguments that such advertising would increase legal fees or encourage lawyers to use false or deceptive advertising. The ruling was limited to the advertising of fees for specific, routine services. Lawyers could not promote their services generally, or solicit clients in person, a practice usually called "ambulance chasing."

THE EMPORIA GAZETTE
Emporia, Kans., June 30, 1977

NEEDLESS to say, newspapers applaud the Supreme Court's decision to let lawyers advertise their services. Heaven knows the poor newspaper people can use the money and most lawyers seem to have some to spare.

There are reasons for others to cheer the decision too.

Young lawyers just hanging out their shingles now may run discreet advertisements in their local paper announcing that they are open for business. Before the recent decision, about the only way a new lawyer could get his name before the public was to run for county attorney, and many did.

Lawyers who choose to switch from general practice to a specialty of some sort also can use advertisements to good advantage.

—

The public will benefit too, because some lawyers will choose to advertise their prices. People looking for a cheap divorce attorney will be able to find one. The increased competition may help hold down some fees. Furthermore, the ads will give the uninitiated some idea of the legal costs involved in lawsuits, wills and title searches.

Most attorneys will not advertise their fees — or anything else for that matter. The successful ones will look upon advertising as undignified and degrading. Thus the court's ruling probably will not cause an outbreak of full-page ads hawking suits for whiplash injuries or breach of promise actions.

—

Advertising is a tool that should be available to lawyers to use as they see fit. Used properly, it will not degrade the profession. — R.C.

San Francisco Chronicle
San Francisco, Calif., June 28, 1977

THE DECISION written by U.S. Supreme Court Justice Harry Blackmun, allowing attorneys to advertise their services, with certain spelled-out restrictions, appears to us to be a fair and reasoned one. We agree with the court's majority in its holding that advertising will tend to reduce, rather than increase, the cost of legal services.

And it may well be true that public disillusionment with the legal profession exists in part because potential consumers are unaware about what a lawyer does and what he charges for the service. Justice Blackmun noted that the organized bar still has the right to monitor ads and to discipline lawyers who make false or misleading claims.

Thus we do not foresee televised ads on Saturday mornings huckstering the virtues of one law firm over another in the manner that some used car operations' spokesmen are given to employ.

IT IS AN interesting fact that Justice Blackmun is also the author of a May, 1976, majority opinion which held unconstitutional state laws banning the advertisement of prescription drug prices by pharmacists. In that opinion, he said the dissemination of information "as to who is producing and selling what product, for wht reason and at what price," is in the public interest. The exchange of such data tends to promote the intelligent, private economic decisions that bolster free enterprise.

That principle is no less applicable in the case of attorneys advertising their services and fees. For many years, legal associations in various sections of the country posted what were known as "recommended fee schedules" for various types of legal action. This sounded suspiciously like price-fixing, and in fact the courts held that was what it was.

We do not expect a wave of advocates inundating advertising firms in light of the high court's ruling. But we would hope that informative, yet discreet and tasteful, listings by attorneys so inclined will prove to be what one member of the legal profession described as "a tremendous boon for the consumers."

Sentinel Star

Orlando, Fla., June 29, 1977

THE FREEDOM given lawyers to advertise their services and fees won't bring about the profound professional changes feared by Justice Lewis F. Powell; it will merely give the public a better idea what attorneys do and how much their expertise costs.

The Supreme Court majority is right in its position that the public is entitled to the information they might gain from lawyers' ads, and that it is interfering with a lawyer's free speech when he is prevented by his peers from advertising.

As a practical matter, most lawyers will go on much as before, with a shingle in front of the office and a listing in the yellow pages. Those with something special to offer — patents, divorce, accident recovery, maritime law, real estate and the like — surely have a right to communicate with those who might require such services.

As for price advertising, most lawyers are too shrewd to fall into that trap. The firm that features a $295 divorce would pay far more for a cheapened image than the extra business would justify.

For the last year Floridians have been able to shop the ads for eyeglasses, something that had been forbidden for years. Now that the customer knows he can buy a pair of glasses in a simple frame for under $20, there has been no great upheaval among optometrists. Nor will the lawyer's ad revolutionize that profession. It just isn't that big a deal.

The Burlington Free Press

Burlington, Vt., June 30, 1977

THE U.S. SUPREME COURT'S ruling that lawyers may advertise fees for routine services, such as uncontested divorces and drawing up wills, not only will assist consumers in finding legal advice when they need it but also may signal a change in advertising policies in other professions.

For years, lawyers have lived with regulations against advertising because somehow it was felt it would degrade their profession. That policy, said Justice Harry A. Blackmun in writing the majority opinion for the court, has sometimes blocked access to legal services for the non-poor and unknowledgeable. The new policy, he said, may benefit the administration of justice and reduce the cost of legal advice for the consumer without lowering the standards of the legal profession.

Officials of the Vermont Bar Association also seem to agree that lawyer advertising will benefit the public and aid young lawyers who have not had adequate time to establish a reputation in their field.

Advertising will mean that the consumer will be able to choose a lawyer who specializes in the services he needs instead of going from door to door to find a lawyer who can help him.

Some persons feel that the court's ruling also may open the way for advertising by the medical profession which has maintained the same tradition against it as the legal profession.

The use of advertising by doctors could achieve the same results as those predicted for lawyers by giving the consumer an opportunity to make a choice and by allowing him to choose the doctor who offers acceptable service at lower cost.

For now, there can be little doubt that the court's decision on advertising by lawyers represents a genuine service to the consumers of this country.

Arkansas Gazette.

Little Rock, Ark., June 30, 1977

The Supreme Court's decision to let lawyers advertise services and prices is one of the surprises emerging from this year's docket. This particular Court was hardly the one that we would have expected to upset a conservative practice of such long, long standing in the legal profession itself. Indeed, as the wire services suggested, the voice of the consumer is being heard across the land.

Let us stipulate that the decision is not one of earth-shattering importance, outside the profession, but it *is* important and, we think, constructive, even if it is deeply disturbing to many old school lawyers. We respect the dissenting sentiment on this issue but, as Mr. Justice Blackmun noted for the majority, this advertising will lend itself only to relatively simple services, the uncontested divorce, simple adoptions, the uncontested bankruptcy—that sort of thing.

The majority in the 5-4 decision was on sound ground, we believe, in citing the First Amendment's guarantee of free speech as authority for striking down restrictions on lawyers' advertising. And there is every reason to expect the public will learn much more about the availability of routine legal services and how much to pay for them.

★   ★   ★

There is lagniappe in the decision for young lawyers, who are thicker than torts in this litigious society. The law schools are turning out lawyers in swarms, even though it is harder all the time to make the grades, and it takes longer to get through the courses. The good old days of one-year degrees at Cumberland are long gone but still there are even more young lawyers than cub reporters, in the general popular assumption that practicing law is more fun than selling lingerie, or even insurance.

A young lawyer turned out into the cruel world to earn his bread needs some way of getting public attention in a crowded field. He may choose to advertise.

★   ★   ★

There is even more lagniappe in the implications of the decision in other areas of restraint against competition. If the First Amendment allows competitive advertising in the profession of law, how much more compelling is its force against the arbitrary restraints against advertising prices for such products as eyeglasses and liquor. The state statutes purporting to forbid price listing in the dispensing of eyeglasses and the sale of spirits and wine would appear to be wholly vulnerable to the first dissatisfied party expecting to advertise and let the state try to punish him, if it dared.

The Salt Lake Tribune

Salt Lake City, Utah, June 30, 1977

There is not much doubt that allowing lawyers to advertise prices will bring about profound change for both the legal profession and the public. But don't expect to see a full page advertisement complete with bargain specials in tomorrow's newspaper.

The Supreme Court of the United States declared Monday that state laws and bar association rules against advertising lawyers' fees violate the First Amendment's free speech guarantee. But the majority opinion also noted that states may regulate the type of advertising lawyers do.

Further, the five-man majority made it clear that its ruling extended only to the kind of advertisement in the case before the court. The ad in question was a modest, brief, factual statement of fees charged for specific and mostly routine types of legal work.

Even so, the appearance of exact dollar amounts charged for a certain legal chore will provide tremendous insight into what has been a murky area of misinformation and total ignorance on the part of many, perhaps most, potential legal services consumers.

Ability to advertise not only their names but their possibly lower fees can be an immense boon to young lawyers just beginning practice. And the pressure from the hungry hordes cannot help but have price-shaving effect on established attorneys providing the same type service.

The four-man minority based its opposition on fear of what might happen if lawyers are allowed to discreetly promote their wares. But anxiety over a situation which may never arise is insufficient justification for continuing a ban that can be shown to be detrimental to many would-be clients.

There was a time, as Justice Harry A. Blackmun noted, when the legal profession was considered a type of "public service" instead of a means of earning a living. But that day has passed and with its passing should go the trappings which are no longer relevant.

The learned professions still provide dedicated, quality service. But they do it for a fee. And the Supreme Court is saying, in a round-about way, that the person paying the fee has a right to know well in advance how much it is going to be.

The Wichita Eagle
Wichita, Kans., July 2, 1977

The U.S. Supreme Court's recent ruling that lawyers have the right to advertise prices probably won't inspire any legal services sale ads ("Celebrate Independence Day By Getting Your Independence — Divorce Cases Marked Down 50 Per Cent During July"), but there might be merit, in some cases, in the publicizing of fees for routine services.

Usually, of course, clients' problems are so different it would be difficult to catalog fees in the same way prices of car repair parts can be.

EVENING EXPRESS
Portland, Me., June 29, 1977

The U. S. Supreme Court decision striking down the traditional ban on advertising by lawyers was a fair and wise ruling so far as it goes, but it still leaves some confusion about what kind of advertising is permitted.

The decision will have a greater impact on other states than it will here. The Maine Bar Association became the national leader in permitting lawyers to advertise when it amended its code of ethics last winter.

Nevertheless, the court ruling settles once and for all the question of whether attorneys may list fees in their ads, something the Maine Bar Association had sought to prohibit.

That restriction was being challenged by three young Portland attorneys, and their position has been upheld now that the Supreme Court has ruled lawyers may advertise fees for routine services such as wills and uncontested divorces.

But the high court decision apparently leaves unanswered other questions raised by Attorney General Joseph Brennan in a separate suit against the Maine Bar Association relating to advertising.

The MBA's rules specifically restrict such ads to the print media. Brennan feels that the prohibition against television and radio advertising is a violation of the First Amendment guarantee of free speech.

His complaint maintains that the MBA rules not only restrict a lawyer's freedom of expression, but also limit the amount of information which potential clients are able to secure.

By remaining silent on the subject of broadcast advertising, the Supreme Court has left that aspect of the question open. It may take another court challenge to resolve the matter.

Meanwhile, however, Maine lawyers — and their colleagues throughout the nation — are now free to advertise their services competitively.

And that's good.

The Evening Bulletin
Philadelphia, Pa., June 29, 1977

Since 1908, lawyers in this country have felt — at least officially — that it was beneath their dignity to advertise fees. And like a restaurateur whose menus have no prices, attorneys no doubt enjoyed the aura that went with the nationwide caveats against hawking their wares.

These days, though, how many people can afford to sit down to such a "meal?" That's why the U.S. Supreme Court's decision yesterday, which frees up lawyers to advertise for certain services, is so welcome.

One Philadelphia attorney says he'll have ads in this Sunday's newspaper editions but few colleagues will rush into the fray that quickly. What the high court ruling should do, however, is give new life to the liberalization of ad prohibitions from within the profession.

Pennylvania is well on the way. Last May, Pennsylvania's state supreme court — at the urging of the Pennsylvania Bar Association — approved expanded advertising in the Yellow Pages, to include specialties, things like office hours, credit card acceptance and notice that fees are available on request. And in New Jersey, the bar association has been drafting recommendations for judicial review.

Right now, the United State's Supreme Court ruling is too fresh for any observer to predict accurately its impact. To be sure, price-shopping is more likely to become a reality for the many cost-conscious people in need of legal service. Young attorneys will be able to bring their names to public attention easier.

Of all the arguments against advertising for attorneys, the most curious comes from Associate Justice Lewis Powell Jr., who wrote the minority opinion after the Supreme Court's 5-4 vote. Justice Powell fears advertising will increase the chance for deception in the profession.

Deception among attorneys, the men and women charged to uphold and defend the law? Surely the justice has more faith in his colleagues. And if not, that's the best argument for making an open book of the legal profession's ledgers.

SAN JOSE NEWS
San Jose, Calif., June 29, 1977

The U.S. Supreme Court's decision in behalf of the advertising of legal services is another significant victory for consumers.

The ban on advertising by attorneys has worked primarily to the benefit of the profession. Rather than safeguarding standards, it has chiefly discouraged fee competition. It also has worked to the disadvantage of new lawyers.

As in previous rulings upholding advertising of eye glasses and prescription drugs, the Court stresses that only truthful advertising of fees is protected. Claims about quality of services, and efforts to solicit clients in person (ambulance chasing) are not sanctioned.

The California Supreme Court should move quickly to establish rules for lawyer advertising within the state. Such advertising should be permitted in the daily media — newspapers, radio and television — where it is readily accessible to the public rather than confined to obscure "legal directories" as the State Bar has proposed.

Oregon Journal
Portland, Ore., June 30, 1977

The U.S. Supreme Court made a logical decision this week when it ruled 5 to 4 that states prohibiting attorneys from advertising are limiting free speech.

But the decision is one which is filled with complications, for both the legal fraternity, which is obviously divided as was the court, and for the general public.

Prohibiting advertising by attorneys has meant in Oregon that a lawyer could only have his practice known to the public in the alphabetical advertising in the back of the telephone book. It has been a part of attorneys' code of ethics reinforced by Oregon law and the State Supreme Court, which runs the state bar.

But the U.S. high court said properly that this infringes on a lawyer's constitutional guarantee of free speech. The court decision, however, was a relatively narrow one, even though it will likely make a broad impact on the legal profession, and probably in the future the medical profession, which restricts its members similarly.

The high court said advertising must be limited to basic fees for basic services such as wills, divorces and the like. Any lawyer will tell you he is afraid to quote a basic fee, because most such services are as complicated as the human problems they are dealing with, and costs balloon accordingly.

More than one Oregon attorney is afraid of malpractice suits if his advertising quotes one price but his client's final bill says another.

The Oregon State Bar this week came out with a service it probably should have provided long ago: A directory, although an incomplete one, which lists attorneys wishing to be included, their specialties, backgrounds, fees and office hours.

In a year's time, the Bar will also make it possible for attorneys who wish it to be listed by specialty in the telephone directory.

Both of these changes came about, the Bar says, without the prodding of the Supreme Court.

Attorneys are generally conservative when it comes to changes in their profession, and the court's ruling Monday is one they will answer with caution. But the decision does make it possible for potential clients, and those lawyers who want to advertise, to meet each other. Therefore the ruling is a positive gain.

The Honolulu Advertiser
Honolulu, Hawaii, July 2, 1977

The U.S. Supreme Court's decision that lawyers may advertise their fees for routine services will bring welcome changes to the relationships between the bar and the public.

The immediate change may be price advertising by lawyers for simple services such as real estate work, will drawing, collections and uncontested divorces.

The advertising is almost bound to bring down prices for these services. And it will not stop there. Aggressive attorneys will quite likely set up "clinics" which will offer more complex services at lower prices. They would rely, as do the big corporate law firms on another level, on volume to support a large staff.

SOME LAWYERS are not going to welcome the court decision. They will feel that it deprofessionalizes and cheapens the lawyer's work. That claim has a certain validity, but from the public's view it has often seemed difficult to obtain services at reasonable rates.

Nationally, the way could be opened for regulation of certain kinds of law practices by the Federal Trade Commission and other agencies.

Among other changes will be a re-examination by the American Bar Association and state bar associations of their ethical standards. With the advertising door opened, the ramifications are many.

Washington observers have suggested that the decision involving lawyer advertising, following one that permits prescription drug advertising, is creating basic alterations in our society. They predict it will not be long before physicians, optometrists, dentists, accountants, and other professionals will be advertising and competing on a fee level.

In a way, this is a leveling off of social change. All these professionals have increased their business approach to their work. Years ago, doctors and lawyers were the last creditors to be paid. Now, they are as quick as any others to bill, to use collection agencies and, if need be, to sue for fees.

HERE IN HAWAII, the U.S. Supreme Court ruling will liberalize the State rules for advertising. At present the only form acceptable is listing in the Yellow Pages of the telephone directory, or newspaper ads announcing the opening of a law office or the joining of a firm.

One case is pending, which involves alleged violation of the State advertising ban by a local lawyer, and presumably it now will be settled to the advantage of the lawyer involved.

The bottom line is that the door has been opened to price competition in the legal profession, and some lawyers presumably will be eager to make the aperture a wide one.

Pittsburgh Post-Gazette
Pittsburgh, Pa., June 29, 1977

BY THROWING over the prohibition against the peddling of legal services in the public prints, the U.S. Supreme Court has given consumers a break and the legal profession a new standing.

Generally, the decision to permit advertising of fees for routine legal service, such as uncontested divorces, wills and deeds, will encourage justice which too often could not be had without payment of steep prices to the bar.

Public rates will encourage price comparisons, competition and minimum rates. Moreover, legal advertisements could accelerate the trend toward legal clinics and the use of paralegals, trained assistants for preparation of those aspects in proceedings which require mostly knowledge of courthouse procedure rather than trial work.

The most persuasive argument against advertisement by lawyers had been the fear of hucksterism and unseemly appeals. But the Court has guarded against this by applying the decision to the most general services. The profession itself will also be able to monitor truth in advertising.

Court appearances have become a more likely, less awesome prospect for increasingly litigious Americans. As a consequence, clients often leave the courtroom wondering why they have paid so much for such routine work. The Supreme Court's decision gives hope that common recourse to justice will no longer be so routinely expensive.

The Cincinnati Post
Cincinnati, Ohio, July 1, 1977

The lawyers have a favorite saying that "justice delayed is justice denied."

But we would guess that far more justice is being denied because many people are not obtaining legal help in the first place — they have no idea what it might cost and are afraid to ask—than by lengthy waits on crowded court dockets.

For this reason, we hail the U.S. Supreme Court's ruling that lawyers may advertise their services. We believe it will open up the legal profession in a way that in the long run will benefit both it and the public immensely.

It is significant that the case on which the court based its narrow 5-4 decision involved a legal clinic in Phoenix, Ariz., run by two maverick lawyers who placed a newspaper advertisement listing "reasonable fees" for such services as an uncontested divorce, adoption, change of name, etc.

Some lawyers may hate to admit it, but it is unexciting work like this that is the bread and butter of most legal practitioners. And most of the routine paperwork involved can be handled just as well by secretaries or "paralegal" personnel.

Thus the lifting of the ban on advertising is expected to give a tremendous boost to the growth of legal clinics, where certain standard services are available at low cost. The clinics can now go after the high volume of clientele they must have to be able to offer cut-rate legal services.

The American Bar Association and its state, county and city counterparts will still exercise considerable say-so over professional ethics, however, and this is good.

The high court's ruling is specifically limited to simple newspaper advertisements. False, deceptive or misleading advertising remains subject to restraint and "there may be reasonable restrictions on the time, place and manner of advertising."

There will always be plenty of scope for the reward of legal brilliance. The prestige law firm and the specialist attorney will still command high fees and never stoop to advertise.

But for the kind of legal services most people need at some time or other in their lives, anything that places the system within closer reach and which fosters competition is a worthwhile development.

Minneapolis Tribune
Minneapolis, Minn., July 2, 1977

This week's decision by the U.S. Supreme Court, striking down the traditional ban on lawyer advertising, was long overdue. Some of the arguments against advertising legal services are sound — for example, that lawyers are part of the judicial system and should not demean that role by making it seem too commercial. But a more compelling argument — hinted at if not stated outright in Justice Blackmun's majority opinion — is that those who need legal services should know something about a lawyer's specialty, qualifications, experience and fees.

While the high court did not rule specifically on whether a lawyer's advertisement might be protected under the First Amendment if it contained relevant information other than fees, several lawyers' groups had already conceded that such information might be necessary to help consumers make a choice. Some of these same groups had balked, however, at publicizing fees. Consumer groups are praising the decision on the grounds that, without advertising, the prospective client often must rely on second-hand advice from friends and relatives or on an inadequate referral service that gives no indication of the kind of lawyer being recommended or how much he will charge.

Among members of the Hennepin County Bar Association, opinions on lawyer advertising are mixed. In a recent survey of 237 association members by the University of Minnesota School of Journalism and Mass Communications, a majority favored advertising. Of those surveyed, younger lawyers, specialists, government-employed lawyers and lawyers who earn under $25,000 a year were predominantly in favor. Older, established members of the profession were predominantly against it.

Undoubtedly the decision will benefit some lawyers, and it will involve some risks. But, more importantly, it should give would-be clients a better choice of lawyers.

LEGAL SERVICES CORPORATION ACT TO PROVIDE LAWYERS FOR THE POOR

Legal services for the poor will continue to be provided by the Legal Services Act, signed into law by President Nixon July 25. The Office of Economic Opportunity had administered the program; the new legislation created a corporation independent of the now dismantled Office of Economic Opportunity. The Legal Services Corporation was granted $90 million for fiscal 1975, $100 million for 1976, and open-ended funding for 1977.

The bill was passed by a vote of 265–136 July 16 in the House and 77–19 July 18 in the Senate. Several major compromises were needed to win support for the bill. Particularly controversial was the deletion of research back-up centers for poverty lawyers. Opponents of the research program termed the centers "hotbeds of agitation." Conservative members of Congress also insisted that the 11-member board of directors be appointed by the President and confirmed by the Senate.

Other provisions of the act:

■ Employes would be exempt from laws and executive orders affecting federal agencies.

■ The corporation could not lobby for or against legislation at any governmental level, except in response to formal requests from legislative bodies for testimony.

■ Lawyers involved full-time in corporation-funded activities could not engage in outside practice for compensation.

■ Corporation funds could not be used for suits involving criminal charges, political activities, school integration, Selective Service laws or abortions.

CHICAGO Sun-Times
Chicago, Ill., July 24, 1974

Legislation that would create a permanent corporation for providing legal aid services to the poor has finally been passed by Congress and now awaits only President Nixon's expected signature to become law. Even in its compromised form, the legislation means that not only will large cities such as Chicago continue to have one of the most important tools for combating injustice, but that increased funds would be available. Chicago could go from its present $3 million to $29 million for legal aid.

Up until now, legal services has been one of the programs existing under the precarious umbrella of the Office of Economic Opportunity, now being dismantled by the federal government. Its future has been in doubt as supporters and conservative opponents in Congress battled over how it should continue — but even though the present measure does not satisfy everyone, it is an important start. An unfortunate deletion has been the back-up centers which provided legal research assistance to lawyers in such areas as health, consumer and juvenile law. But the compromise measure does allow the corporation to hire consultants in these fields.

The lack of adequate legal services for the poor in this country has been a grave problem. The legal services program under OEO proved its worth, but even then never received the support it merited. The new legislation should get that support — so a job that needs doing can be done.

The Washington Post
Washington, D.C., August 2, 1974

AFTER MORE SNARLS and setbacks than most legislation could survive, a bill to establish an independent legal services corporation has finally been approved by Congress and signed by the President. The new law is not what its champions envisioned when their efforts began several years ago. In the course of its slow, stormy passage, the program was greatly diminished and burdened with arbitrary restrictions on what legal services attorneys may do. To overcome the last burst of conservative resistance, House-Senate conferees even agreed last month to prohibit any corporation support for the outside back-up centers which have given such depth and support to the young field of poverty law. This final concession was a serious loss, although local programs should be able to find other ways to obtain this valuable research aid.

For all of its defects, the new law is better than no law at all. From Mr. Nixon's standpoint it can be regarded as a triumph, a case in which his veto power and veto threats were used successfully to forge a law in line with his own narrow designs. During the fight, however, the White House did very little to dispel widespread suspicions that the President's adamant stand was really meant to frustrate negotiations and kill the program entirely. Thus Mr. Nixon, having signed the bill, is now receiving weary thanks from the liberals whom he battered down —and bitter cries of betrayal from some of the conservatives who recently claimed to be pressing his case.

Now that a legal services corporation has been approved, the next arena of controversy will be the crucial matter of appointments to that corporation's board. In line with Mr. Nixon's long insistence, the law gives the President the power to nominate all 11 board members, subject to Senate confirmation. But there is much uncertainty about how this power will be used—and Mr. Nixon's personnel policies in the anti-poverty field are hardly encouraging. Last year he turned over the Office of Economic Opportunity to Howard Phillips and his wrecking crew. And last month he summarily fired Mr. Phillips' successor, Alvin J. Arnett, whose major offense as OEO director was apparently to lobby too effectively on behalf of community action and OEO. Given this record, there is little assurance that Mr. Nixon will name a legal services board of the quality and independence required to make even a modest program really work.

From one standpoint, it is strange that the anti-poverty programs should arouse such persistent hostility among White House and congressional conservatives. The programs' purpose, after all, is to help people to work within the system and solve problems in their own communities. This is the aim of community action, which in its present form has won the strong support of governors, mayors and congressmen who once resisted and resented peaceful organizing by the poor. It is also the aim of legal services; indeed, nothing is more conservative or traditionally American than the idea that disputes should be resolved through processes of the law. The conviction that everyone is entitled to have access to the law is what impelled so many legislators to fight so long to win approval of a legal services corporation act. It is now up to Mr. Nixon to implement the important law which he has signed.

Detroit Free Press
Detroit, Mich., July 28, 1974

THE PLAN for legal services for the poor that just passed in both houses of Congress and was signed by the president is slightly better than no plan at all because it gives a degree of permanency to one of the most effective programs developed under the general war on poverty.

But those in and out of Congress who truly want equal justice for all—despite economic differences among individuals—will have to fight on for legislative improvements in future sessions. But a more immediate objective will be a careful Senate screening of the 11 individuals Mr. Nixon will appoint to set broad policies for the Legal Services Corp.

Mr. Nixon vetoed an earlier plan that would have forced him to make some selections from lists provided by the bar association and by groups representing the poor. In his veto message, he said: "The sole interest to which each board member must be beholden is the public interest."

Such a statement might have more appeal if it were not for the sorry record Mr. Nixon has compiled with his appointments to other boards and agencies that have tended to strengthen the hold of special interest groups on those public bodies. In exercising the discretion given him under the new legislation, Mr. Nixon should name at least some individuals who understand the continuing need not only to help particular poor people with particular legal problems but also the need to review existing laws and procedures that discriminate against poor people as a group.

If Mr. Nixon ignores that obligation to those who are supposed to benefit from the legal services program, then the Senate will have to meet it through the power to refuse to confirm any who do not show a clear concern for equal justice.

PORTLAND EVENING EXPRESS
Portland, Me., July 29, 1974

Ever since President Richard Nixon entered the White House he has displayed a cold indifference to the problems of the poor and the underprivileged, with one possible exception — the income maintenance bill he introduced four years ago that would have put a floor of about $80 a week under every household's income.

But when that concept ran into trouble in Congress the White House ditched it, and the President went on from there to scrap the Office of Equal Opportunity — a project he has just completed—housing subsidies for low- and middle-income people, and a number of other holdovers from the Kennedy and Johnson Administrations.

But now he seems to have got religion, and has rescued from the destruction of the OEO a program of legal aid to the poor that was once a vital part of that useful law.

Admittedly the bill that has just passed the House and Senate, to be signed by Mr. Nixon, is not a very good measure, but it is much better than nothing, and it can be improved next year, assuming Mr. Nixon is still in office, and in a conciliatory mood. The bill had to be severely trimmed to meet the specifications laid down by the White House, and one of the restrictions amply reflected the President's attitude toward the poor. Even so, conservatives have attacked the new law, and it may affect the impeachment vote.

Legal services will be furnished by an independent corporation, though Mr. Nixon will name its members. And get this — while the objective is to give the poor legal aid they can't obtain elsewhere, the corporation lawyers are prevented from aiding the poor in court cases involving crime, abortion, draft evasion, and school segregation.

That restraint alone almost makes the bill a travesty, but as we said, it is a foot in the door, and for that the poor can be grateful.

San Jose Mercury
San Jose, Calif., July 22, 1974

President Nixon should sign the independent legal services corporation bill now on his desk.

It represents a major step toward making the principle of equal justice under law applicable to the poor as well as to the rich.

The compromise measure passed by Congress and sent to the President last week takes care to remove the corporation from the so-called "social activist" atmosphere that surrounded legal services to the poor when they were part of President Johnson's war on poverty. President Nixon will name all 11 members of the corporation's board, and the Senate must confirm them. This should provide adequate safeguards against improper political activity.

San Francisco Chronicle
San Francisco, Calif., July 29, 1974

THE LEGAL AID BILL signed by President Nixon last week required three years to pass Congress but at last it firmly establishes an independent Legal Services Corporation with a budget of around $100 million.

The publicly financed lawyers are authorized to represent the poor in civil cases involving rent, child custody, property, housing and welfare rights but are barred from filing actions involving labor, the draft, desegregation and abortion. These strictures reflect a conservative obsession that it is somehow outrageous for the government to pay the way of the poor into the courts. We believe President Nixon's judgment is the more likely one to prevail, however: that legal aid is "one of the most constructive ways to help (the poor) help themselves."

The Pittsburgh Press
Pittsburgh, Pa., July 21, 1974

President Nixon can affirm his commitment to equal justice by promptly signing into law the new legal-aid legislation approved by Congress last week.

The bill would set up a non-profit corporation, with 11 directors appointed by the President, to provide poor people with the basic legal services most of us take for granted.

In effect, it would extend on a permanent basis one of the most successful anti-poverty programs of the past decade—a program that involves 2,500 neighborhood lawyers and reaches into 300 American cities.

★ ★ ★

Despite opposition from arch-conservatives, who consider all poverty lawyers troublemakers, the President is expected to sign the bill. He should do so, for two reasons:

The first is that legal-aid-for-the-poor is a useful program. The lawyers spend most of their time on contracts, divorces, bankruptcies and routine matters.

Stricken from the bill, at Mr. Nixon's request, were the so-called "back-up centers" (usually law schools) considered by critics to be hotbeds of "radical" thought. These centers gave rise to much of the controversy over the legal-aid program.

The second reason for signing the bill is that legal aid should not be a partisan issue. Access to a lawyer is a fundamental American precept, not a subject for political horse-trading.

★ ★ ★

In his current battle against impeachment, Mr. Nixon may be tempted to veto the legal aid corporation (as he did in 1971) in a bid for right-wing support.

That would be a mistake for the President, and a mistake for the nation as well.

TWIN CITY SENTINEL

Winston-Salem, N.C., August 3, 1974

President Nixon's signing of the Legal Services bill last week brought to an end a three-year controversy over this remnant of the anti-poverty program. The White House was pressured to veto this bill, despite the many concessions that had already been made to conservative foes of legal help for the poor. The President deserves credit for not bowing to that last-minute pressure.

Sen. Jesse Helms of North Carolina continued his tiresome, long-winded opposition to legal aid to the final hour. It still mystifies us what conservative principle Helms sees at stake in a program that will provide free legal aid to people with incomes below the poverty line. Surely there is nothing revolutionary about equal access to competent legal counsel, a principle that the legal profession itself espouses.

But Helms discovered at the last moment that the Legal Services Corporation would be able to continue doing research on general legal issues pertinent to people living in poverty. Helms wanted to prohibit any such work, which provides a most useful service to the local legal aid offices, and without which their effectiveness would be greatly diminished. Fortunately his amendment failed.

Reading Helms' lengthy arguments against the bill, we got the impression that Helms is afraid of what can be accomplished on behalf of poor clients in a court of law. His mighty rhetoric against the program would lead one to believe that legal aid is some insurrectionary activity, when in fact it merely ensures that the judicial machinery works even for people who cannot afford a private lawyer. It seems to us that no one need fear any victory of a poor client over the welfare bureaucracy or any other agency, however controversial.

The bill signed by Mr. Nixon established legal services as a permanent federal office. The young lawyers working in the program may be handicapped by the many restrictions placed on them in the new law, but at least the future of the program is assured. This was one wing of the anti-poverty program eminently worth making permanent.

ST. LOUIS POST-DISPATCH

St. Louis, Mo., August 2, 1974

Three years ago, when President Nixon asked Congress to create an independent legal services corporation, he declared that the proposed system would secure "justice within the system and not on the streets" and that it should be "immune to political pressures" and should stand as a "dramatic symbol of this nation's commitment to the concept of equal justice."

Last week, after a long and difficult struggle which included a veto by Mr. Nixon, supporters of the legal services corporation finally saw the proposal signed into law, but the end product bore only a faint resemblance to the lofty institution the President originally described.

Under the law, legal services lawyers will not be permitted to represent clients in cases involving school desegregation, abortion, the Selective Service, labor disputes, criminal law and, with a few exceptions, juveniles. The corporation may not fund outside research centers, which frequently are operated at universities and provide high quality research services. Groups receiving corporation funds would be obliged to give preference to hiring local attorneys, a system which will provide a boom to home town lawyers but is scarcely designed to attract the best legal talent. Legal services lawyers may not participate in nonpartisan political work such as voter registration in nonworking hours; indeed, corporation funds may not be used for voter registration activities.

As insisted on by Mr. Nixon, the 11 members of the corporation board will all be appointed by the President subject to confirmation by the Senate. Theoretically the Senate could prevent the corporation from being abused politically by a president, but in reality the program will be greatly susceptible to Administration influence or even control. Six members of the board may be from the same party, thereby permitting a president to set both the partisan as well as the philosophic tone of the corporation, which has hardly been rendered "immune to political pressures."

These are serious shortcomings and the law embodying them, in our opinion, is deficient. Nonetheless, the creation of legal services corporation, inadequate as it is likely to be, is an important event and a step, albeit a small one, in the right direction.

Most importantly, the corporation will exist, and may well be improved in the future by enlightened amendments. It will stand as a guarantee that legal services will be available to those who otherwise would not be able to afford it; and while in its present form the corporation cannot assure equal justice to all in every situation, it should at the very least improve the opportunities of the poor to compete more equally with those who can pay for their legal assistance.

THE CINCINNATI ENQUIRER

Cincinnati, Ohio, August 3, 1974

LIKE NEARLY ALL compromises, the Legal Services Corp. Act finally agreed to by both the Senate and the House and signed by President Nixon satisfies neither the zealous advocates of institutionalizing the legal-aid services originally established as a feature of the Johnson administration's war on poverty nor the equally zealous congressional conservatives who see legal services as a device for fomenting social activism at public expense.

But also like most compromises, the measure preserves the basic purpose of the original proposal while eliminating some of its more objectionable aspects.

The idea of making legal services available to the poor is very nearly as old as organized charity itself. Almost every major community in the nation has had a legal-aid society. Cincinnati's, as an illustration, is a half-century old, funded for most if not all of its life by the Community Chest, with the counseling and co-operation of the Cincinnati Bar Association.

Such agencies are rooted in the long-standing American tradition of equal justice under law. Just as destitute defendants at the bar of justice have been assisted by public defenders in criminal cases, so, the theory has run, should they have access to legal assistance in civil actions.

The Supreme Court has elevated what was once widely regarded as the privilege of a publicly provided defense in criminal actions to the status of a constitutional right. It would seem, as a corollary, that legal representation in civil cases should be just as readily available to those who need it. That, in essence, is what the Legal Services Corp. will seek to provide.

When originally presented, the Senate version contained many questionable features. Among them was the federal funding of university-based research centers, which many lawmakers feared might easily become mischievous beehives of near-revolutionary agitation.

Thanks in large measure to a filibuster undertaken by Sens. Jesse Helms (R-N.C.) and William Brock III (R-Tenn.), the Senate significantly refined its version. House-Senate conferees went even farther in restricting the scope of what the legal-services concept should entail. The result, overall, has been salutary, and the version that finally passed both houses is devoid of the looseness that was the original measure's most notable characteristic.

Like all new governmental enterprises, the Legal Services Corp. should be subject to periodic review by Congress to make certain that it is performing the mission for which it was created. Such a review, it seems to us, is particularly appropriate in the case of an agency like this one.

If such congressional overview is a fact, the Legal Services Corp., despite the fervid controversy in which it was born, is capable of being a useful if not indispensable part of the American scene.

THE SACRAMENTO BEE

Sacramento, Calif., August 2, 1974

Government is supposed to be the art of the possible, which means compromise. And that is what the legal services bill, signed by President Richard Nixon, creating a new, independent corporation to provide legal aid to the poor, is all about.

As it finally emerged from Congress after three years of debate, the measure was a conservative, Republican, Nixon-leaning compromise.

As the Los Angeles Times described the bill when it came out of the House of Representatives, the measure signed by the President is " a grudging extension of legal services to the poor, filled with suspicion, reservation, and restriction. It is largely a recitation of thou shalt nots."

___

Under the new act, Legal Services lawyers no longer will be able to file actions in connection with military draft, desegregation, labor and abortion cases.

The President sent word he would not sign the bill unless 15 legal research backup centers, concentrating on certain areas of poverty law, were stricken from the bill. So they were.

Still, the bill removes the legal services for the poor from the beleaguered Office of Economic Opportunity to a new public corporation.

Lawyers in the new corporation will be able to represent the poor in civil cases involving rent, child custody, property, housing and welfare rights.

___

The idea of providing legal assistance to the poor through an organization which is isolated from political pressure is a tough one to work out to every politician's satisfaction.

Congress tried, and the new Legal Services Corp. has been established with objectives consonant with the goals of this nation from the time of its creation.

CHICAGO Daily Defender

Chicago, Ill., August 29, 1974

The evils of the Nixon-Agnew Administration linger on, even after the perpetrators have departed. As the 10th anniversary of Legal Services to the Poor is being observed, the depth of the opposition to it is just coming to light.

It was Spiro Agnew as Vice President who ordered the appropriation for the new Antioch Law College in Washington to be killed. Irked that certain community groups whom he disliked were being serviced by lawyers for legal aid, Mayor Daley moved to frustrate the efforts. Slowly and surely, the Nixon hangmen tightened the noose around all OEO programs. The expiration date is due in December of this year.

Fortunately, the concept of legal services for the poor has not died. A patchwork arrangement between the public and private sector will assure that in a modified form, the needy can still get redress for their grievances.

The new national legal Assistance Corporation is scheduled to go into operation Jan. 1 with a budget of $90 million in federal grants.

Under the enabling Act, middle class citizens can be represented under certain conditions. To appease the conservatives in Congress, the law restricts the corporation from servicing draft resisters, abortion cases and school desegregation suits. Corporation employees may not participate in community organizing nor assist tenants in forming unions to fight landlords. They may not lobby for changes in federal, state or local laws. It is forbidden to represent juveniles without the parents' consent, a limitation that is particularly frustrating in the case of child abuse.

On the whole, however, it is good that there is a service. The shortcomings can be rectified by putting pressure on Congress to make the changes.

THE RICHMOND NEWS LEADER

Richmond, Va., August 2, 1974

Conservative supporters of President Nixon still are reeling in disbelief at his decision to sign into law a measure that will establish a Legal Services Corporation. This is a measure that conservatives fought bitterly, and, up until a few hours before the measure was signed, they were assured of a presidential veto. They may be forgiven if they feel a sense of betrayal.

The legal services program had been operating under the umbrella of the Office of Economic Opportunity. The measure signed by the President will establish the independent Legal Services Corporation, to be funded with $90 million in fiscal 1975 and $100 million in fiscal 1976. Most of the excesses permitted in the former legal services program will be institutionalized in the new corporation.

The long history of activism and militancy in federally-financed legal services has not ended; the few feeble safeguards placed on the new corporation insure that the new corporation merely will take up where the old program stopped. Legal services projects funded under the former program are covered under a grandfather clause that insures them continued funding, no matter how poorly they may have performed.

The measure, as reported by a House-Senate conference, was so bad that a recommittal motion in the House failed by only seven votes. Many Congressmen were outraged that the conferees had watered down most of the safeguards contained in the original House measure. The House bill would have put the corporation out of business in 1978. The conference measure establishes the corporation on a permanent basis, with funding provided on an open-ended basis after fiscal 1976. Political and social activist groups such as the American Indian Movement, the National Tenants Organization, and the Berkeley Anti-Police Hippy Youth Coalition will continue to receive legal aid.

The House version had stipulated that plaintiffs found innocent in suits brought by legal services employees would be reimbursed; this provision was intended to reduce the corporation's potential for mischievous litigation. The measure signed by the President would permit reimbursement only if the innocent plaintiffs could prove malice — which is as hard to prove as "intent." To be sure, the measure prohibits corporation employees from engaging in riots, picket lines, boycotts, disturbances, and demonstrations — during working hours. What these employees do on their own time — including "uncompensated" legal work — is not covered by the new law.

The measure, as finally agreed to by the House and Senate, was appalling. Conservatives mounted a strong drive to insure a presidential veto. Two weeks prior to signing the bill, the President assured opponents of the measure that he *would* veto it. Congressional Liberals then reportedly told Alexander Haig, the White House chief of staff, that they would sabotage some key administration proposals, including a bill authorizing payment of the President's Watergate legal defense, if the President vetoed the bill. When the President reneged on his promise to conservatives and signed the bill, he was playing impeachment politics.

For one outraged Congressman, the President's action was inexcusable. Before the bill was signed, the Congress said, "If he lets this bill become law, I would not only vote for impeachment, I will help to organize it." The President's decision clearly will cost him support among conservative ranks, whose support he long has taken for granted. He may have mollified some Liberals for the moment, but he could not count on Liberal support in a showdown, anyway. Conservatives are slow to abandon the President in his distress, but they have begun to lose conviction in their support for him. In actions such as signing the legal services bill, the President did not give conservatives any encouragement to stand fast in his behalf.

DAILY NEWS
New York, N.Y., July 27, 1974

President Nixon has signed a law making the legal aid program for the poor an independent corporation. We hope our misgivings about possible abuse of the service will prove unfounded.

Congress has barred poverty lawyers from filing suits connected with the draft, desegregation, labor or abortion. A dangerous provision setting up research centers at law schools that could become hotbeds of radical indoctrination was eliminated.

If the new program only provides legal aid to those who can't afford it, well and good. But Congress should monitor the program closely with a watchful eye to see that political activists don't worm their way in and pervert the purpose of the agency.

THE MILWAUKEE JOURNAL
Milwaukee, Wis., July 18, 1974

Again and again, congressional proponents of a strong program of legal services for the poor have tried to satisfy President Nixon's shifting objections. However, each swing of the compromise axe seemed to produce a demand for more chopping. Now, astonishingly, the legislation before Congress is far more restrictive than Nixon himself proposed a year ago.

Impeachment politics is the chief explanation. Many conservatives in Congress view poverty lawyers as troublemakers and dislike the idea of establishing an independent legal services corporation that would continue the program on a more solid footing. Since Nixon desperately needs the right wing on his side in any impeachment battle, he has been hanging tough on legal services, implying readiness to use his veto.

All of that has exacted yet another concession — elimination of a dozen backup centers for poverty lawyers. Located at universities around the nation, these centers lay the groundwork for important cases and provide other technical assistance to overworked, possibly inexperienced lawyers on the firing line.

It's tragic that such a legislative deal must be struck. But if the bill is mangled no further and a cringing Nixon finally agrees to sign it, the result will be tolerable. Legal services will go forward. Compromise will not have meant utter capitulation.

THE DALLAS TIMES HERALD
Dallas, Tex., July 21, 1974

CONGRESS has now passed a bill drastically changing the structure of legal services, one of the most controversial of the old War on Poverty programs.

The bill, which has gone to the President, sets up an independent government corporation to administer legal services for the poor. The corporation will be run by an 11-member board, appointed by the President with the approval of the Senate.

The new operation will be funded by $90 million the first year, $100 million the second year and whatever Congress thinks it needs the third year of the three-year authorization.

The original idea and purpose of federal legal services was good.

Those who need the service of an attorney but cannot afford to pay for it should be provided that help at government expense. Unfortunately, as a part of the War on Poverty, legal services became deeply involved in activist efforts.

Attorneys for the agencies were chiefly interested in, and dedicated to, prosecuting legal battles for social causes rather than providing legal counsel for the poor. Bitter controversy, as we well know in Dallas, resulted from this activist concept.

If the President signs the bill, hopefully the new corporation will be able better to carry out the original purpose of legal services—helping the poor with their legal problems.

DAYTON DAILY NEWS
Dayton, Ohio, July 19, 1974

Already shamefully undersupported, Dayton's Legal Aid society has had a leg cut off by reactionary congressmen and a president desperate to curry their favor in order to avoid impeachment.

Congress has voted to abolish legal "backup centers" set up under the dying Office of Economic Opportunity. The centers help struggling legal aid attorneys keep up with the latest legal doings in areas such as welfare, mental health, consumer protection, and landlord-tenant relations.

Dayton Legal Aid has leaned heavily on Ohio State Legal Services, a backup center in Columbus that provides help to attorneys and lobbies for bills that help the poor—legal aid attorneys' clients. Like most other similar offices, its crushing caseload leaves no time for fancy research or the preparation of complex cases that might overturn laws that deal unfairly with whole groups of people.

The backup center helps with that sort of thing. But that sort of thing apparently made reactionary congressmen angry. So they sent a message to Mr. Nixon: Please threaten to veto the legal services corporation bill (which would continue federal funds to poverty law offices) unless continued funding for backup centers is dropped from it.

Mr. Nixon did. He needs only 34 senators to avoid conviction. After fuming several weeks, Congress complied, hoping to salvage at least a minimal federal legal services program.

So Dayton's Legal Aid office will continue to get its meager federal funds, but Ohio State Legal Services will almost certainly not. Unless somebody comes up with another source of money, it will fold.

No more help to legal aid attorneys. No more representation of poor people and ordinary consumers before the legislature.

Of course, special interest groups—whose legal fees are tax deductible as business expenses—will continue to deploy batteries of lawyers to present their side of things. Just like the good old days.

The Philadelphia Inquirer
Philadelphia, Pa., July 22, 1974

After more than three years of struggle, Congress has finally sent a bill establishing an independent corporation to provide legal services for the poor to the President's desk, with the understanding that the President will not veto it.

That, we must say, is an accomplishment, although made at considerable sacrifice. Even though Mr. Nixon himself, in a special message in 1971, had urged Congress to adopt the proposal as "a dramatic symbol of this nation's commitment to the concept of equal justice," he had vetoed the legislation once and held the threat of veto over it down to the wire.

As Republican Sen. Jacob Javits of New York noted, the issue had, like so many others these days, become enmeshed in "impeachment politics." A Senate-House conference committee had tailored a bill very much to the President's specifications, and the bill passed the House and would have passed the Senate. Yet even then, to mollify Mr. Nixon's conservative supporters the White House insisted that authorization for "backup centers" be dropped. Reluctantly, Senate sponsors conceded the point in exchange for assurances that Mr. Nixon would sign the bill.

The "backup centers," located in 15 law schools and universities, provide research, model briefs and on occasion experienced attorneys to help the poor obtain their legal rights. The sacrifice is like removing the law library from a law firm.

Nevertheless — and despite unnecessary restrictions on the ability of poverty lawyers to provide the full gamut of legal services to the poor — the bill does keep this nine-year-old program alive, and it should keep it reasonably secure from political interference. We can expect it to engender more controversy, but surely there should be no controversy over the principle of "equal justice under the law."

THE ARIZONA REPUBLIC

Phoenix, Ariz., August 5, 1974

On the very day he promised, in a nationwide televised address on the economy, to veto any bill that would further inflate the federal budget, President Nixon succumbed to pressure from Senate liberals and signed a bill to create a legal services corporation to provide lawyers for the poor in noncriminal cases.

The initial cost will be small—$90 million—a flyspeck on a $305 billion budget, but the eventual cost will be much greater.

For the corporation inevitably will attract activist lawyers, who will be bringing actions against city and state governments, as well as federal agencies, in behalf of gay liberationists, women's liberationists, black nationalists, Indian militants and whatever other cause strikes their fancies.

The taxpayer will have to foot the bill for the defense, too.

In signing the bill, the President gave another demonstration of his habit of talking one way about inflation and acting another.

He gave still another demonstration within 24 hours by signing a bill to guarantee $2 billion in loans to livestock producers and other agricultural interests.

He did this, he said, with misgivings, because he feared the bill could be used "to bail out short-term speculators who are not normally engaged in livestock production" and even banks, which "are in a position to absorb some loss as a normal business risk."

How much this bill costs the federal treasury will depend on how many of those who receive the loans default on them.

If the signing of the bills didn't confuse people enough about the administration's policies on inflation, deputy White House economic counselor Sidney L. Jones had to open his mouth.

In his televised address, Nixon had urged those who could to save 1.5 per cent of their incomes. This, he said, would have the same effect in helping to curb inflation as a $12 billion cut in the budget.

Now listen to Jones.

"I don't want to see it," he told a news conference. "We don't want a consumer boycott."

The President cannot hope to keep inflation from running away unless he and his administration follow a consistent policy on inflation. The present chaotic policy is only making things worse.

THE TENNESSEAN

Nashville, Tenn., July 16, 1974

THE RIGHT of this country's poor people to legal services is not a matter for petty politics or for ideological trench fighting. Or, more accurately stated, that right shouldn't be subject to such considerations in this country, but it is.

After three years of legislative efforts and consultations with the White House, Senate sponsors believed in May they had succeeded in establishing a government-financed, but independent, legal services corporation for the poor. The White House then began giving signals that President Nixon would veto the bill to appease conservatives — upon whom the President must depend to fight impeachment.

The final version of the bill, reached in a House-Senate conference, contained compromises for both liberals and conservatives. The liberals allowed restrictions to be placed on lawyers for legal services in return for the funding of research centers, usually run by university law schools.

Now, the White House has let it be known that it will veto even this compromise bill unless the funding of the research centers is dropped. The Senate sponsors realize that they don't have the votes in the House to override a veto and have decided to drop the funding of the centers to try to insure passage.

Quite simply, these centers provide research services that local legal services operations could never dream of duplicating. The local operations have neither the personnel nor the finances. But opponents of legal services have pictured the research centers as bastions of left-wing activism and the local legal services as their vanguard.

Such a picture distorts the fact that legal services provide mainly day-to-day legal aid that most Americans can afford, but which the poor cannot. If, in other instances, lawyers for legal services have challenged the system and the government to win sweeping changes, so be it. In courts of law and justice, the poor are supposed to be on an equal footing with the rich and established.

Given the present administration, given the social and political realities in this country, perhaps this is the best bill possible. Given the pious sentiments of equality and justice preached by so many and so recently as the Fourth of July, the bill is a shame.

St. Louis Globe-Democrat

St. Louis, Mo., July 24, 1974

Congress has sent to the President a bill that converts the federal program of legal aid to the poor from one that is under the Office of Economic Opportunity to one run by an independent government corporation.

The legal services bill lacks the onerous provision for "back-up centers," or research centers, for the propagation of left-wing legal briefs. These centers, at various universities primarily, have been funded through grants or contracts with the Legal Aid Society. But the bill, while prohibiting these grants and contracts, still permits the new Legal Services Corporation to hire consultants to do the work of the back-up centers, which is just as bad. President Nixon vetoed a similar bill in 1972 because the government would have no control over such abuses, and he should exercise his veto again on this bill for the same reason.

The back-up center staff members would merely become direct employes of a corporation which could do just about what it pleased. In the past, the back-up centers have had the following functions:

Amicus briefs (as in the DeFunis racial quota case), co-counsel work with allied organizations (such as Planned Parenthood on abortion suits), legal research for private advocacy groups (like the NAACP in the Detroit school busing suit), preparing "model" legislation (such as the Massachusetts "student rights" law), serving as "house counsel" to direct action organizations (like the National Welfare Rights Organization), and working on changes in the regulations issued by state and federal bureaucracies (OSHA, HEW, etc.).

The staff members lobby (as on no-fault), conduct national issue strategy conferences (like those run by the Kennedy-oriented National Legal Aid and Defenders Association), publish books (such as one advocating national socialized medicine), publish newsletters and studies (some of which attack President Nixon's policies), and represent individuals in important test cases (such as gaining for felons the right to vote).

Obviously, much of these activities have little relevancy to the rights and protection of the poor. They are merely battle plans of liberals to mold society into their own image. And for their efforts these liberals and radicals would be paid by the federal government—with no responsibility to the government (and thus, in a sense, the people).

President Nixon has vowed to veto any bill that is "one word to the left" of the one he had introduced in May 1973 or the one passed by the House in June 1973. The bill passed by Congress should be vetoed. If the bill is signed, the corporation will forever be able to get heavily involved in matters which are of no concern to federally bank-rolled employes.

BURGER RAPS PLETHORA OF LAWYERS, URGES LESS LITIGATION OF DISPUTES

Chief Justice Warren E. Burger May 27 told a conference of the American Bar Association that unless more legal disputes were settled outside the courtroom, the nation could be "overrun by hordes of lawyers hungry as locusts." The conference, which was held in New York City, heard Burger plead for a change in the "smug assumption that conflicts can be solved only by law-trained people."

The Chief Justice noted that the U.S. had 14 times as many lawyers as Japan. That number, he suggested, was far in excess of the needs of the public. (The ABA estimated there were almost 450,000 lawyers in the U.S.) Burger said he believed "most people will prefer an effective, efficient tribunal of nonlawyers, or a mix of two nonlawyers and one lawyer, to the traditional court system to resolve ... modest" claims. He also cited arbitration, mediation or conciliation panels as possible alternatives to the overburdened small claims courts.

THE BLADE

Toledo, Ohio, June 20, 1977

The harsh truth is that if we do not devise substitutes for the courtroom process, and do not do it rather quickly, we may well be on our way to a society overrun by hordes of lawyers as locusts competing with each other and brigades of judges in numbers never before contemplated.

—Chief Justice Warren Burger

THE chief justice sounded that alarum at a seminar on ways of resolving minor disputes such as small claims, consumer complaints, and tenant-landlord conflicts. The seriousness of the problem to which he referred is indicated by the fact that there is increasing recognition within the legal profession itself of the public's need for informal, inexpensive alternatives to full-scale litigation.

The meeting at Columbia University which Chief Justice Burger addressed was, for instance, sponsored by the American Bar Association. The president of that organization, speaking in Toledo during recent Law Day observances, included a search for simpler means of handling minor disputes among the profession's priorities as he sees them. And the Justice Department reportedly is about to launch an experiment with "neighborhood tribunals" composed of nonlawyers to mediate relatively uncomplicated conflicts.

A significant point emphasized by Chief Justice Burger is that such approaches should be sought not merely to relieve the burden on court dockets. Rather, he said, there are situations in which it would be better if judges and lawyers kept hands off: "The role of law, in terms of formal litigation with the full panoply of time-consuming and expensive procedural niceties, can be overdone." People should be able to get relief for many of their everyday legal difficulties without having to turn to "black-robed judges, well-dressed lawyers, and fine-paneled courtrooms," the chief justice added.

Such views are by no means shared throughout the profession, however. The proliferation of lawyers in this country already threatens to approach the locust-horde level the chief justice warned of. Many laws are designed to make the use of lawyers virtually mandatory — probate statutes being a prime example. Legislators are far more willing to expand the number and size of the various benches and to vote ever higher pay scales for the judiciary than they are to deal with real reforms in the interests of justice for the public. Judges themselves are stubbornly resistant to changes in court structure that might affect their own little bailiwicks.

There is, in short, a long way to go before the lofty ideas espoused by high-ranking justices, bar officials, and law professors are brought to bear in a practical way on the problems of ordinary citizens.

The Chattanooga Times
Chattanooga, Tenn., June 5, 1977

Chief Justice Warren E. Burger is not known as a man who shrinks from speaking his mind; in such fashion he could be called — shades of Earl Warren! — an "activist chief justice."

In a recent conference sponsored by the American Bar Association at Columbia University, Mr. Chief Justice Burger warned that unless new ways are found to settle disputes, the country might be "overrun by hordes of lawyers hungry as locusts." Aside from his use of vivid imagery, the chief justice has hit on a troubling problem: How the courts can cope with a rising tide of litigation which necessarily dictates an increasing number of lawyers.

In last week's cover story, Business Week noted that since 1967, the number of federal civil cases filed has jumped from some 70,000 cases to more than 130,000. Part of the cause, the magazine said, can be laid to suits filed in response to numerous acts passed by Congress in the 1970s.

But the problem extends beyond the federal system, reflecting the apparent belief on the part of many people that solutions to legal grievances can only be solved by the courts and requiring the services of a lawyer. It is a belief fostered in part by lawyers themselves.

Mr. Chief Justice Burger argues otherwise: "The notion that most people want black-robed judges, well-dressed lawyers and fine-paneled courtrooms as the setting to resolve their disputes is not correct," he said. "People with problems, like people with pain, want relief, and they want it as quickly and inexpensively as possible."

There are people, he continued, "who seem to regard litigation as one of the essences of life, and who scorn any solution short of the traditional; but the harsh truth is that if we do not devise substitutes for the courtroom processes, and do not do it rather quickly, we may well be on our way to a society overrun by hordes of lawyers hungry as locusts, competing with each other and brigades of judges in numbers never before contemplated."

That scenario is not as outlandish as it may appear. East Tennessee, for example, is well known as one of the "litigatin'est" parts of the country. That part of the state, and Hamilton County in particular, has seen a dramatic rise in cases filed over the years.

Obviously the best solution is to simplify court procedures, even to the extent that lawyers — and even juries — might not be needed if the litigants agree on such a course; in fact, the chief justice noted that lawyers "may be a handicap" in trying to resolve minor disputes.

Some avenues for removing disputes from the traditional legal framework include expanding small claims courts, relying more on arbitration and mediation, and forming neighborhood tribunals that settle conflicts too trivial for a regular court's attention.

In a nation of more than 400,000 lawyers, and with more students than ever clamoring to join their ranks, it stands to reason there has to be enough litigation spread around to support the profession. The cost to society, however, is enormous: Business Week quoted a Stanford Law School professor as saying that if the growth rate of federal appeals remains constant, by the year 2010 there will be 1 million appeals decided each year, requiring 5,000 judges (against today's 97 federal appeals judges). With appeals running at 10 per cent of total cases initiated, he noted, that would mean the courts would be hit with 10 million cases annually but "long before then, of course, the system would have collapsed."

To keep that from happening, Congress, state legislatures, the public — and especially the legal profession — must take steps soon.

THE ATLANTA CONSTITUTION

Atlanta, Ga., May 31, 1977

First, there were great waves of litigation involving automobile accidents. Then along came no-fault auto insurance, and there was a startling upsurge in malpractice law suits against physicians. Now the physicians in turn are filing suits against patients who sue them. Meanwhile, a no-fault divorce law was enacted in Georgia with the apparent intent of cutting short the work of divorce courts. Instead, it seems to have triggered more, not less, legal entanglements.

So it goes. The mountains of litigation grow higher. The courts call for more judges and more help. Could it be that we need not more judges but fewer litigation-minded lawyers?

That is what Chief Justice Warren E. Burger suggested last week in an address at a conference sponsored by the American Bar Association at Columbia University. Said Justice Burger: "The notion that most people want black-robed judges, well-dressed lawyers and fine-paneled courtrooms as the setting to resolve their disputes is not correct. People with problems, like people with pain, want relief and they want it as quickly and inexpensively as possible."

There are people, Justice Burger said, "who seem to regard litigation as the essence of life, and who scorn any solutions short of the traditional; but the harsh truth is that if we do not devise substitutes for the courtroom processes, and do not do it rather quickly, we may well be on our way to a society overrun by hordes of lawyers hungry as locusts competing with each other, and brigades of judges never before contemplated."

Hear! Hear! Mr. Chief Justice.

ALBUQUERQUE JOURNAL

Albuquerque, N.M., May 31, 1977

Some attorneys won't like what Chief Justice Warren E. Burger has to say.

Burger told a group of lawyers that people with problems often do not want "black-robed judges, well-dressed lawyers and fine-paneled courtrooms as the setting to resolve their disputes. . ."

People with problems, the chief justice observes, "like people with pains, want relief and they want it as quickly and inexpensively as possible."

He suggests that most people prefer an effective, efficient tribunal of nonlawyers or a mix of two non-lawyers and one lawyer to the traditional court system to resolve modest but irritating claims. In some instances, lawyers may even be a handicap, he believes.

Minor disputes that are clogging many small claims courts and other tribunals must find a new outlet for settlement "to avoid the frustrations, tensions and hostilities that often flow from unresolved conflicts. The harsh truth is that unless we devise substitutes for the courtroom processes, we may be on our way to a society overrun by hordes of lawyers hungry as locusts and brigades of judges in numbers never before contemplated," Burger said.

To which many would add, "Amen."

TULSA WORLD

Tulsa, Okla., June 12, 1977

AMERICANS have turned to the nation's courts in such numbers in the past decade that the judicial system eventually will collapse unless something is done.

Most readers are aware of the boom in legal cases of all kinds. It has become fashionable to take all manner of complaints—large and small—to court for relief.

But how many of us realize that the number of court cases has nearly doubled since 1967? And if the trend continues there will be 10 million lawsuits filed annually by the year 2010 and that it would take 5,000 Judges to hear the appeals to Federal courts alone? (There are now 97 Federal Appellate Judges).

What has caused the surge? While it can't be blamed for all of the actions, the Federal Government can be faulted for causing much of the increase because of legislation it passed beginning in the late 60s which encouraged—in fact almost required—court interpretation.

Such programs as clean air, consumer credit protection, health and safety on the job, equal employment, consumer product safety, water pollution control, employes retirement, law and order, energy conservation, equal credit and a raft of others have forced thousands of court rulings.

Congress and Local Governments have taken advantage of the courts refusing to decide matters that elected officials knew would be taken up by the courts. In short, litigation has become the favored way of dealing with social problems in an increasingly complex society.

There are few winners in the litigation game except lawyers, the number of which also is growing alarmingly.

A $2 million settlement of a Gulf Oil Corp. suit brought in the name of shareholders against former officers for operating a political slush fund netted the shareholders $300,-000. The rest went to lawyers on both sides. Most stock brokers will tell you Gulf stock suffered from the publicity enough that stockholders, instead of being helped, were hurt badly.

What is to be done? Legal students all over the country are worrying with the problem, suggesting various schemes to speed up the process and put some of the litigation outside the court system.

But few suggest that any concrete solutions are in the offing. One thing is certain: the legal profession owes it to itself and society to come up with some ways of coping before the country literally litigates itself to death.

Democrat and Chronicle

Rochester, N.Y., June 3, 1977

WHATEVER happened to the old-fashioned handshake?

Are families and neighbors no longer capable of settling some of their own problems without running to the courts?

Such questions are important in the light of today's hopelessly overburdened judicial system.

U.S. Chief Justice Warren E. Burger made this comment the other day:

"There are people who seem to regard litigation as one of the essences of life, and who scorn any solutions short of the traditional, but the harsh truth is that if we do not devise substitutes for the courtroom processes, and do not do it rather quickly, we may well be on our way to a society overrun by hordes of lawyers hungry as locusts competing with each other, and brigades of judges in numbers never before contemplated."

Burger seemed to put a fair share of the blame on the lawyers. But the point can also be made that too many people turn too quickly to the courts for the settlement of problems that once would have been resolved within the family, the neighborhood, the community.

Monroe County Bar Association president Justin L. Vigdor has said that people do tend to depend too much on the courts, that the judicial system should be used only when everything else has failed, that courts were never designed for the kind of use they're now being put to in the big urban centers.

While it contributes nothing to a solution to make the point, it's also a melancholy fact that the anonymous bigness of today's society aggravates the problem.

Columnist Sydney Harris once said as much about the award of $1 million in damages to a woman falsely accused of shoplifting. The jury's award, he suggested, flowed from the increasingly impersonal nature of society.

"People," he said, "don't sue other people for huge sums; they sue establishments and institutions that wear no human face. Nobody ever sues a small-town doctor who has been trying to take care of the family within his own limitations; it is the specialist attached to the large urban hospital, hardly known and scarcely seen by the patient, who bears the brunt of malpractice. Or if a small mama-papa shop had caused the woman's arrest (for shoplifting), we may be sure the case would have been settled for a few hundred dollars."

We've become sue-happy, with one result that the courts are clogged with cases that probably should have been settled before they got there.

The search for alternatives to the courts ought to be pushed just as hard as it can be.

The Seattle Times

Seattle, Wash., June 1, 1977

NOTING the increasing tendency among Americans in recent years to file lawsuits over real or imagined grievances regardless of size, a growing number of experts are becoming worried over what might happen to the nation's legal system.

The latest to voice those concerns is Chief Justice Warren Burger of the United States Supreme Court.

Addressing a Columbia University Law School forum, Justice Burger suggested that people looking for swift settlement of disputes should not turn to the courts in every instance.

"The notion that most people want black-robed judges, well-dressed lawyers, and fine-paneled courtrooms as the setting to resolve their differences is not correct," he said.

Groaning court backlogs and the long delays involved in getting matters before a judge (as well as needlessly complicated procedures surrounding lawsuits) are sure symptoms of the need cited by the chief justice to devise substitutes for the courtroom process.

What might those alternatives be? Justice Burger did not suggest specifics, but some tentative ideas have been mentioned by others. A good local example: The use of mediation techniques by non-lawyer negotiators to settle some of the arguments over Interstate 90 and Snoqualmie River flood-control issues.

If the trends toward ever-greater amounts of litigation continue without the addition of alternatives to dispute settlement, the future foreseen by Justice Burger is scarcely appealing.

"We may well be on our way," he said, "to a society overrun by hordes of lawyers, hungry as locusts, competing with each other and brigades of judges in numbers never before contemplated."

The Cleveland Press

Cleveland, Ohio, June 4, 1977

Chief Justice Warren Burger warned the other day that unless new ways are found to settle disputes, the country might be "overrun by hordes of lawyers hungry as locusts and brigades of judges."

We share Burger's worry and go him one further: The grim situation he fears may already be at hand and impossible to reverse.

In any event, the chief justice deserves praise for spotlighting a national sickness, that of taking minor disputes to court and turning them into costly, time-consuming legal struggles.

"The notion that most people want black-robed judges, well-dressed lawyers and fine-paneled courtrooms as the setting to resolve their disputes is not correct," Burger told a legal conference.

"People with problems, like people with pains, want relief, and they want it as quickly and inexpensively as possible."

Unfortunately, while Burger's diagnosis of the illness was right on target, he did not have a sure cure. He is dubious about stepping up the use of small-claims courts, which some recommend, because they are already overloaded and often lack ways of enforcing their rulings.

Burger urged that the legal profession explore the use of arbitration in place of litigation, noting that arbitration has made great contributions to trade and to labor peace. He also called for more use of newspaper and radio action-lines to settle disputes out of court.

Both ideas have merit and should be tried. But the chief justice can be viewed as swimming against the tide if one looks at two simple statistics: Enrollment in U.S. law schools is up by some 50 per cent over the last six years, and some law schools have doubled their enrollment in that time.

What does that mean? Well, a slight variation on Parkinson's Law would put it that the amount of litigation will increase to equal the number of lawyers.

And that suggests that Burger and the country have their work cut out for them if they are not to be swamped by "lawyers hungry as locusts."

San Francisco Chronicle

San Francisco, Calif., March 18, 1977

CROWDED COURTS, overworked judges, clogged calendars and what often amount to interminable delays before access to the bar of justice—particularly in civil cases—are accepted these days as sad facts of life in our system of jurisprudence. So it was with a receptive spirit of approval that we heard a suggestion the other day aimed at making certain this lamentable legal traffic jam gets no worse. It carried particular weight since it came from a man who both has these matters very much on his mind and deeply senses that we are "a terribly litigious nation"—the president of the American Bar Association.

Why not enact a law requiring Congress to consider a "judicial impact statement" before blithely passing bills that may gum up the works even more, asks Justin A. Stanley, a distinguished Chicago lawyer who is this year's head of the national bar group? Why not, indeed? This is the day of the impact report—environmental and otherwise—and it would seem only fair to allow lawyers such a kind of defense against lawmakers who impose rules on the court system.

AS STANLEY NOTES, there are presently "26 or 27 Congressional acts" on the books that decree what priority should be given to cases on appeal. That's a lot of rules, and it boggles the mind to contemplate the legal thicket.

As another case in point, the bar leader pointed to the "speedy trials" act sponsored by Senator Sam J. Ervin (Dem.—N.C.) and passed by Congress in 1974. That did a lot of good things about seeing to it that criminals get prompt justice in Federal court, said Stanley, but it also effectively removed any chance of a great glut of civil cases ever getting into the courts at all. The Fifth circuit, and other jurisdictions plain had to suspend civil trials for a while. The point is that Congress didn't consider the long-term effect of giving high priority to some cases and relegating others to a back burner.

All Stanley is asking is that lawyers—and his group is a notably experienced vehicle of expression for the profession—be allowed to tell Congress just how it might be making things more difficult in their field. To put it briefly, as lawyers aren't so often wont to do, that's a good idea.

The Detroit News

Detroit, Mich., June 6, 1977

"The first thing we do, let's kill all the lawyers."
— King Henry the Sixth, Part II

Chief Justice Burger, speaking at an American Bar Association conference in New York, rightly rejected as "Shakespearean slander" suggestions that the first step in improving society is to "kill all the lawyers."

He went further, lauding the contributions that lawyers and judges are making toward achieving "a fair and humane society."

But Burger also challenged the lawyers, who dominate Congress and state legislatures. Unless new ways are found to settle disputes, he said, the nation might be "overrun by hordes of lawyers hungry as locusts."

The country has become so litigation-prone that the courts are being overwhelmed by law suits — many of them frivolous — and lawyers are getting even fatter fees.

Taking note of lawyer greed, the chief judge of the New York State Court of Appeals warned recently that "if lawyers just grab, grab, grab, they may be killing the goose that lays the golden egg."

What's to be done about it?

ABA conference participants suggested that small-claims courts be expanded, taking advantage of less formal procedures and the fact that small-claims parties often appear without lawyers.

They also suggested that small-claims courts might be placed in firehouses and even put on wheels, the mobile courts "riding circuit."

The participants also proposed something akin to one of China's legal underpinnings: neighborhood tribunals staffed by non-lawyers.

Human nature being what it is, the public will not relinquish its right to file suit and the lawyers their right to get rich.

But Chief Justice Burger at least capsulized the problem when he told the ABA conference:

"People with problems, like people with pains, want relief and they want it as quickly and inexpensively as possible."

The Federal Criminal Code: Advance or retreat?

The Senate approved in January 1978 a measure providing for the codification of federal criminal law. Codification is the collecting and arranging of a set of laws in an orderly way so that the relationship among the laws can be made more consistent and readily understandable. Presently the federal criminal laws are spread throughout 50 different chapters of the United States Code. This lack of centralization makes it fairly difficult for defense attorneys unfamiliar with federal law to research all of the applicable case law and defenses. If passed, the legislation would be the first full codification of the nation's criminal laws which have been enacted piecemeal over two centuries.

While there is little controversy over the need to codify the criminal code, the revisions and reform contained within the proposed legislation, Senate Bill 1437, have generated heated debate and argument. S-1437 is a revised version of an earlier proposal, Senate Bill-1, that was defeated in 1975. S-1 faced massive criticism because of certain features that opponents argued would sharply circumscribe the civil liberties of Americans and also unduly strengthen the secretive aspects of the federal government. The critics argued that S-1 would have legitimized the illegal acts of ex-President Richard M. Nixon and his advisors through the so-called "Nuremburg defense"; government officials accused of crimes would have been permitted to argue in court that their acts were justified because they were obeying orders and acting in the national interest.

S-1, if it had passed, would have subjected future opponents of the government to harsh penalties for revealing internal government documents. This section, the "Official Secrets Act" could have been applied to Daniel Ellsberg who uncovered *The Pentagon Papers,* and to the editors of the *New York Times* who had published them. Exposure to prosecution could have also faced many of the nation's best newspapers and reporters who revealed government illegalities, especially in the area of foreign policy and Central Intelligence Agency activity.

In the revised bill these two objectionable sections have been deleted. The proponents of S-1437 attempted to meet the demands of civil libertarians through the repeal of the Smith Act, which prohibits seditious speech, and decriminalizing possession of small amounts of marijuana. These changes have increased support for the new codification bill. Senator Kennedy, a strong opponent of S-1, is a sponsor of S-1437. Many national newspapers have switched from opposition to support, arguing that the new bill is the best that can be expected from a balky Congress. Others remain adamant that S-1437 is almost identical to the disgraced S-1 bill. They argue that flaws in the bill, unless corrected now, will be compounded because federal statutes have always served as model codes for state legislation.

Constitutional law experts, like Professor Thomas Emerson of Yale University, remain deeply troubled by the vague language of S-1437. These ambiguous statutes could be exploited by a future administration confronted with popular dissent. The new proposal would make "obstructing a government function by physical interference" a crime. This phrase could be interpreted to punish political demonstrators. The acts of "hindering law enforcement" and "concealing the identity of a criminal" would become illegal. News reporters and news gathering activities could be threatened by this section if forced to reveal their sources of information. Even legitimate labor union activity like picketing might come under the purview of the code because it prohibits extortion where property damage occurs. Until now, court decisions have refused to define such activity as criminal. The bill would also give increased power to the federal government over the states by expanding the definitions of existing federal crimes. Accordingly, the size of the Federal Bureau of Investigation could be expected to increase in order to enforce the new statutes.

In deference to those who favor a shifting of the equilibrium between the state and the accused, the new bill changes the Anglo-Saxon common-law rule that ambiguous criminal statutes be construed in favor of the defendant. Instead, a reading of the law according to the "fair import" of the terms would be substituted. The role of jurors would also be partially circumscribed by having judges determine some of the factual elements of the crime. Federal law now leaves it to the jury to determine if the defendant used interstate commerce to commit the alleged crime. S-1437 would place this decision with the trial judge.

Reform of sentencing laws has earned the support of many who normally would be offended by key sections of S-1437. Under the bill judges would no longer have the vast discretion in sentencing convicted defendants. The law would contain nine specific classes of crimes from an A-felony, punishable by life imprisonment, to an infraction, punishable by no more than five days in prison. Indeterminate sentences—while not entirely eliminated—have been reduced by employing fixed maximum and minimum sentences that have narrower limits. Parole and good time provisions have been restricted. Judges would be permitted to make a prisoner ineligible for parole for the entire length of the sentence. Prisoners are currently eligible for parole upon the expiration of one-third of their term. The length of sentences, for the first time, would be appealable by both prosecutors and defendants. This provision is to help reduce the disparity of sentences within federal courts. The legislation would permit, but not encourage or require, use of alternatives to prison: fines, restitution, forfeiture, and intermittent incarceration.

Democrat and Chronicle
Rochester, N.Y., May 15, 1977

Courts, too, can foster violence

NOT ALL the violence in America springs out of casual, unexplainable brutality.

Some of it is the product of bitterness and frustration created by the judicial system itself.

From one part of the country to another, and often within the confines of one or two countries, punishment fluctuates widly. A marijuana offense in Orleans County, under the tough sentencing of Judge Hamilton Doherty, is likely under existing law to draw a prison term. Elsewhere, as in the Rochester area, a fine might be imposed.

Disparity in sentencing puts marijuana offenders and child-beaters behind the same prison bars and builds up enormous resentment.

The nation can take a significant step towards reducing these inequitities by persuading Congress to approve a 297-page revision of the U.S. criminal code titled officially the Criminal Code Reform Act of 1977 (S1437 in the Senate and HR6869 in the House).

A basic provision of the legislation is the appointment of a commission that would set sentencing guidelines. Unless they could justify an alternative sentence, judges would be bound to sentence offenders within the limits of the guidelines. Sentences would also be subject to appellate review.

At a press conference by Sen. Edward M. Kennedy, one of the main sponsors, Attorney General Griffin B. Bell and House Judiciary chairman Peter W. Rodino Jr., the point was made that such provisions would be a significant step towards a criminal justice system perceived as fair rather than one favoring the rich and influential. Bell indeed said that the legislation "is important for the life of the Republic."

S1437 is the successor to last year's S1, that ill-designed and controversial bill now deservedly dead. Some of its features would have made abuses of government power even harder to lay bare than they are now. The proposed new criminal code avoids the repressive provisions of the old bill.

The whole range of federal criminal laws is covered by S1437, but the narrowing of sentencing discretion is one of its most important aspects.

It's true, as Bell has explained, that since criminal enforcement is mostly a function of the states, the sentencing proposals would not apply to a large part of the justice system. But federal statistics have traditionally served as a model for state legislation, and it's hoped this will hold true in this instance.

Even though the case for codifying the federal criminal laws and making them more uniform is a strong one, the bill is expected to face some rough sledding. Citizen support may be important when the testing time comes.

AKRON BEACON JOURNAL
Akron, Ohio, July 6, 1977

Proposed criminal code gives justice solid base

NOT SINCE the first criminal law was passed by Congress in 1789 has the whole federal criminal code been overhauled.

Now, after Congress has piled 3,-000 laws atop that first one, dealing with bribery of a customs inspector, the code appears on its way to a revised form both liberals and conservatives can endorse — or at least build upon.

If the reforms are accepted by Congress they may provide a model for all states, thus bringing greater consistency to state laws and some uniformit into federal court sentencing throughout the country.

Attempts to revise the code began a decade ago and reached an 800-page proposal — Senate Bill No. 1 in the 94th Congress.

Now hearings have begun on a bill sponsored by Sens. John L. McClellan (D-Ark.) and Edward M. Kennedy (D-Mass.) that removes many of the excesses of S1, is reduced from 800 to less than 300 pages and makes major reforms in the proposed establishment of a Federal Sentencing Commission that would set guidelines for imposition of sentences for all federal offenses.

The compromise version is certain to stir controversy in some, maybe even many, areas but it appears to take a big step forward in fair treatment for comparable crimes.

For instance, the commission, which would probably be made up of members of the Judicial Conference (judges), would recommend sentences within specific ranges. Instead of a six-to-25-year sentence for a felony, the code might specify six to eight years with parole after six.

More important, the code would require a judge to set forth purposes of sentencing — deterrence, protection of the public, assurance of just punishment and rehabilitation.

If the offender is sentenced above the recommended range, the judge must give his reasons and the offender has the right to appeal. If the sentence is below the specified range, the judge must again state his reasons and the government has the right of appeal.

Actually, guidelines set by the commission would tend eventually to eliminate parole and establish a great deal more uniformity in the treatment of criminals everywhere.

One section almost certain to win approval would provide for more realistic fines for offenses in which a defendant derived personal gain or caused bodily injury or property loss. The amount of the fine could be up to twice the gain derived or twice the gross loss caused. Such a statute would eliminate the "profit incentive" for an embezzler who cheated someone out of $200,000, then got off with a $50,000 fine.

There are many, many other changes, some dealing with rape that would make special corroboration of the victim's testimony unnecessary for prosecution. While there are few federal rape cases, this is a case where the federal code could serve as a state model.

Other changes deal with release of classified information, as in the Ellsberg case. Proposals in S1 that would have made it a criminal act to possess information that had been classified as secret have been changed.

While congressmen and lawyers may argue over the revised version, at least they have something substantive to talk about, something that appears more acceptable than S1. None can deny that after nearly 200 years the code should be modernized, that gross disparities in sentencing should be eliminated and that more uniformity should be brought into the application of all law.

THE BISMARCK TRIBUNE
Bismarck, N.D., November 3, 1977

U.S. Criminal Code Revision

Despite the continuing opposition of civil liberties groups, a long-discussed proposal to reorganize federal criminal laws is expected to be approved by the Senate Judiciary Committee before Congress adjourns this year.

The revision is the culmination of a decade of debate about how to organize the myriad federal criminal laws now scattered throughout the U.S. statute books. Because the nation's criminal laws have been enacted piecemeal over two centuries of legislative activity, they are often difficult to find, confusing and even inconsistent.

The reorganization would eliminate much confusion by more clearly defining what constitutes a crime and by setting more exact standards for determing a person's guilt and imposing punishment. Even critics of the Senate bill agree this is needed.

Because criminal law in the United States is largely a state and local rather than a federal responsibility, the vast majority of American law enforcement would not be directly altered by passage of a new federal criminal code. Historically, however, federal statues have served as a model for state and local laws.

American Civil Liberties Union (ACLU) lawyers and other civil rights advocates contend the bill would create "new law" rather than simply reorganize existing law, and that some of the new sections would endanger political and personal rights.

These are the "new law" items that most worry them:

Obstructing Government. A section on "obstructing a government function by fraud" is drafted to include actions of individuals as well as those of conspirators, so that any stealthful action to thwart a government purpose might be encompassed. The ACLU argues that this provision could be used to punish a Pentagon Papers-style unauthorized publication of governmental documents and could be a type of "official secrecy" law.

Physical Interference. A section on "obstructing a government function by physical interference" would apply to any action that would impede the performance of a public official's functions, as in the case of a mass demonstration that hindered government officials.

Hindering Enforcement. A section on "hindering law enforcement" is written to include "concealing (the) identity" of a criminal, which, critics say, could cover news gathering activities where criminal identities, even though privileged information, would be known to reporters.

False Statements. A section on "making a false statement" would make oral as well as written false statements to law enforcement officials a crime, inviting "abuse by law enforcement officials" and the "fabrication of charges," according to the ACLU.

Not Obeying Orders. A section on "failing to obey a public safety order" could impede mass demonstrations for political purposes by empowering any federal official to issue a binding order to "disperse or refrain from a specified activity" if the official perceives a danger of injury to a person or to property.

Extortion. "Extortion," as currently included in the bill, also arouses opposition of labor unions as well as civil liberties groups because it appears to overrule past court decisions and include lawful labor picketing where property damage occurred.

If the bill does become law, it will be the first time in history that the nation's criminal laws have been pulled together and organized in a consistent, unitary code.

Register-Republic
Rockford, Ill., May 8, 1977

Crime code reform

On energy, the Carter administration's program stands to touch almost every facet of American economic life and, therefore, almost every American citizen.

But the administration also is launching a long overdue effort to change the way the federal government approaches crime. The reform package is now before both houses of Congress.

It's a mixed bag. And, though it has been stripped of some controversial aspects, there's still enough to debate—and divide—to keep the congressional pot boiling.

Hardly anyone will argue that the United States criminal code needs a reworking. As with any time-worn instrument, the code has become cluttered and archaic.

The clutter includes a prohibition, for instance, against detaining a government carrier pigeon. Such anachronisms would go, under the revised code.

But one of the key provisions would provide a predictable sentence for anyone convicted of a specific crime.

This approach already has seen its ascendancy in policies being formulated by Illinois Gov. James R. Thompson in Springfield.

What it tells the prospective criminal is that crime does not pay, and that the commission of crime will produce a set sentence upon conviction.

We think the nugget of real deterrence is contained in this approach—and so do those who are backing the federal criminal code revision. They include Atty. Gen. Griffin B. Bell and Senators John J. McClellan and Edward M. Kennedy, both Democrats, McClellan for the conservative side, Kennedy for the liberal.

Under the compromise they have worked out, a sentencing commission, to be established under the Judiciary Conference—policy-making arm of the Federal Judiciary—would work out specific sentences for specific crimes.

These sentences would take into consideration these variables: Was the crime a first offense? Was violence used? Was a weapon brandished? What is the age of the offender?

These combinations would determine a set number of years to be served in prison, six to seven-and-a-half years for each offense, for instance. Congress could veto these set sentences.

If they are applied, however, this much latitude would be allowed. The judge could sentence the defendant to more time in prison than is automatically provided. He would have to state his reasons, however. And the defendant could appeal.

Conversely, the judge could sentence the defendant to less of a sentence than prescribed. In that instance, the federal prosecutor could appeal.

These compromises were worked out to satisfy both liberals and conservatives. But the forecasts indicate neither side will be completely happy—which may be a good credential for passage.

The proposed code also would decriminalize the possession of small amounts of marijuana, say 10 grams or less, enough for 10 or 15 cigarettes.

To liberals, this may seem like a mandated principle. But to conservatives like McClellan, a different reality came into play. McClellan discovered that federal prosecutors simply do no prosecute what is now on the books, a law that technically subjects a marijuana offender to a year in prison and a $5,000 fine for having up to eight ounces of marijuana on his person.

Ever since 1971, when hearings first were held on revising the federal criminal code, progress has been thwarted by controversies with a full head of steam.

One of the earlier proposals was to make it illegal to "leak" classified government information to the press. Because of the storms of protest that ensued, this idea has simply been dropped.

So has the proposal that would have given a government official the defense that he committed a crime because of national security considerations.

Destined for removal from the criminal code are the Smith Act of 1940, forbidding anyone to advocate the violent overthrow of government—an act that has been circumscribed by court opinions, and the Logan Act of 1799, forbidding American citizens to correspond or have other contact with foreign governments.

On the reform agenda, also, are provisions that would make corporate bribery abroad a violation of United States law and a plan to retain death as a federal penalty for only one crime—hijacking an airplane.

State law could cover other crimes.

In all of this, the aim has been to avoid writing new law if that exercise is too fraught with hazards of passage and to recodify much of what is already on the books.

It could be a long road—but one eminently worth traveling. Confusion, imprecision and archaic provisions do as much to kindle disrespect for the law as an open door on a bank-vault. Let us hope Kennedy and McClellan will be able to meld the diverse opinions that have hobbled criminal code reform for seven years.

The Virginian-Pilot

Norfolk, Va., November 6, 1977

In Search of Order

Unification of the Federal criminal code's scattered parts, already a year behind schedule, makes progress painfully.

Beset by many criticisms from hardliners and civil libertarians alike, the massive legislative proposal faltered in 1976. Patched and scrubbed up, it has now emerged from the Senate Judiciary Committee on a 10-2 vote.

The committee division could foreshadow the shapes of opposition on the Senate floor. Of the dissidents, liberal James Abourezk (D-S.D.) considered the bill too restrictive while conservative James B. Allen (D-Ala.) reckoned it is too permissive. Gradations of opinion between those poles is reflected in the majority.

Whatever the excesses and shortcomings they perceive in the bill, even its critics agree that it would provide an overdue reorganization of Federal criminal laws, eliminate much confusion, and set firm standards for determining guilt and penance. There have been partial revisions from time to time, but in 200-plus years of making laws Congress has not codified them in a single text. The result is a hodge-podge of acts, some of them elusive, some obscure, and some inconsistent and conflicting, scattered in a variety of code books.

Debate can be expected over parts of the bill being attacked, primarily by the American Civil Liberties Union, as "new law." That category includes inhibitions on thwarting or interfering with governmental functions and functionaries, interpreted in some quarters as threatening peaceful protest demonstrations and publication of dissenting material. Labor unions are skeptical of a broadening of the definition of extortion, which they see as a potential check on lawful picketing.

Conservative fire is probable against recommendations for weakening penalties for marijuana possession, for allowing the mailing of pornography to adults in states that don't object, and for repealing the Smith and Logan acts, Cold War antisubversive hangovers directed chiefly against domestic Communists.

However, something approaching unanimity is likelier on a fundamental change incorporated in the bill. That is a proposal for uniformity of sentencing, with a commission established to guide trial judges. The anomaly of a criminal's being liable to five years in one judicial district and two in the next—or even probation—for the same violation of Federal statute tends first to confusion about the law, then to disrespect for it. Consistency of punishment would be as welcome as the certainty of it.

Burdened as it is with objections to raise liberal and conservative hackles, and perhaps occasional moderate ones, the bill is poised on an uncertain path. Senate passage early next year is no cinch, and there remain the hurdles of the House, whose Judiciary Committee has only begun contemplating the proposal.

Since the job took two centuries to pile up, the Honorables may be in no especial hurry to get it done. If there is a sense of urgency they could, as they did with President Carter's energy package, extract what pleases them and finesse the rest. Some positive response from this Congress is in order, however. Reform is more desirable than urgent, but it shouldn't wait for another centennial to roll around.

The Boston Globe

Boston, Mass., November 6, 1977

Remaking the criminal code

The Senate Judiciary Committee's 12-to-2 vote the other day approving a total rewriting and modification of the nation's criminal code represents a major political victory for Sen. Edward M. Kennedy. More important than the politics of it, however, is the substance of it, and substantively it represents solid progress toward providing the nation with a better, more workable set of criminal laws.

By winning Judiciary Committee support for the legislation, Kennedy successfully pushed the 300-page bill over a very formidable hurdle indeed, a committee whose membership includes some very liberal liberals and some very conservative conservatives, a group in which the center might have very well collapsed and in which, for the sake of a few slices at either end, the loaf might have been lost. Despite all the work involved, the bill still has a long way to go. First, it must get through the Senate early next year without the kinds of amendments, from either the left or the right, that will sink it; and then, of course, it must start the march through the House, where interest in the bill has thus far been tepid at best.

No one should underestimate the value of the legislation. The Federal criminal laws are a mess, including scores of overlapping crimes, some 80 different standards of culpability and such outmoded provisions as the one making it a crime to detain a government carrier pigeon.

The new codification eliminates the ambiguities and anachronisms in current law. But it does more than that; It repeals the most repugnant laws that attempted to throttle dissent; it makes sex discrimination a crime; it gives the government new tools for combating white-collar and organized crime; it outlaws political "dirty tricks."

It is by no means a perfect bill. It does not restrict use of wiretapping beyond what is currently permitted; it does not, as it should, broaden protections to persons who testify after being granted immunity; it regrettably retains a criminal penalty for the possession of small amounts of marijuana, though the penalty is substantially reduced from the current level.

Liberal groups, particularly the American Civil Liberties Union, are not fully pleased with the final result. But during the Judiciary Committee review of the bill concessions were made toward those groups. Press protections in the legislation were markedly strengthened. Federal prosecution of obscenity cases was restricted somewhat.

And the key provision of the bill — a Kennedy proposal to create a commission to establish sentencing standards and phase out parole — was improved by broadening membership on the commission itself. The ACLU contends the sentencing commission idea may end up with tougher, even unrealistic sentences. There are, however, some safeguards against that in the legislation and, in any event, Congress will have to approve the final commission recommendations before they are implemented.

No fair-minded person could now dismiss the bill as the "son" of S-1, the abominable redrafting of the criminal code that died a well-deserved death at the hands of liberals in the Senate last year.

It is instead an artful compromise that squarely hits its primary target — the codification of the Federal criminal law — and along the way makes sensible reforms of the law as well without, if the Judiciary Committee vote is a fair measure, sacrificing broad support for the legislation. It isn't perfection, but it's a good and wholly supportable piece of work.

The Washington Post

Washington, D.C., May 4, 1977

Son of S. 1

S. 1, AS THE BILL to revise the federal criminal laws has become known, has a longer history than is decent. It has been before Congress, in one form or another, since 1971. Work on it began five years before that, and it embodies an idea that developed in the 1950s. It is back again with us this year, stripped of most of its controversial parts and assigned a different number. Perhaps the combination of the two will create a legislative climate in which something definitive can happen to this bill at long last.

What is most impressive about this year's version of S. 1 is its sponsorship. Instead of fighting over various parts of the bill, as they have in years past, Sens. John L. McClellan and Edward M. Kennedy have produced a massive compromise. Each has dropped many of the proposals he liked best but which the other thought unacceptable, and they have found a way to get together on other provisions on which they disagreed just last fall. That must not have been easy for either senator to do, given the strong feelings held by the constituencies that have lined up behind them—the civil libertarians urging Sen. Kennedy on and the law and order people supporting Sen. McClellan. But it strikes us an example of the way in which legislation of this magnitude has to be handled, particularly since its new form also has won the support of Attorney General Griffin Bell.

While their efforts have cut the text of the bill by more than 50 per cent, it is still an unusually long and complicated measure. That is because it codifies, for the first time in the nation's history, all of the existing federal criminal law while changing some of it. Almost everyone accepts the idea that the law needs codifying, but various groups have seen this as an ideal opportunity to make fundamental changes. Most, but not all, of those changes have now been deleted so that what remains is more the rewriting of legislation that is already on the books than the creation of new legislation.

No doubt there are still parts of the bill that some will consider objectionable. For example, it alters drastically the discretion federal judges now have in imposing sentences on criminals, and it decriminalizes—as far as federal law is concerned—the possession of small amounts of marijuana. But the two senators have reduced the areas of potential conflict to a handful, and Congress ought to be able to deal with these in a rational manner. It may be that some provisions will have to be changed once there has been time to analyze all of the 300 or so pages that remain in the bill. But our impression now is that this package is one that deserves to be passed and will be worth all the years of work that went into it.

Herald News

Fall River, Mass., November 5, 1977

Criminal Code

The Senate Judiciary Committee has approved a comprehensive revision of the nation's criminal code. The measure, which runs to 400 pages, will not reach the Senate floor until early next year, but its chance of passage is regarded as excellent.

Meanwhile, the House committee working on a parallel measure has not proceeded as rapidly. All the same, it is believed that action on its version of the revised code will also be acted on next year.

If Congress seems to be even slower than usual in making up its mind about the code, it should be remembered that this is the first time in the country's history that any such revision has been undertaken. Presumably, the new code, when it is finally enacted, will last another century or two.

In a country like this, where so much changes so fast and so constantly, the continuity and stability needed for survival are provided by the system of law. Of the nation's legal system, the criminal code is obviously a vital part. No one seriously disputes that the code needs changes. In some aspects it is obsolete, in others inefficient. But those changes must be made with sufficient care so that they will last for a long time.

The Senate committee's action is welcome. So will the House's, when it comes. But both the Senate and the House should not be urged into precipitate action over revision of the criminal code. They should work with due regard to the fact that whatever changes they make will be expected to last for generations to come.

THE INDIANAPOLIS NEWS

Indianapolis, Ind., November 9, 1977

'Close' doesn't count

Congressional efforts to revise the Federal criminal code have come a long way.

Compromise reform legislation has, for example, just been approved by the Senate Judiciary Committee, which represents more progress than has been made since the codification process started over a decade ago.

In terms of content as well, criminal code reform has also come far. The laws pertaining to the press illustrate how the compromise legislation has been shaped even in the course of just one year.

The proposed section on national security in last year's bill would have made the leaking of classified information and the non-return of such information a felony. Likewise, the press would have been subject to prosecution for publishing material later deemed by the courts to cause direct, immediate, and irreparable injury to the United States.

The repressive nature of those provisions can be realized simply by considering that such laws might have prevented publication of the Pentagon Papers concerning the Vietnam war or the many leaks which revealed the true extent of Watergate. Such legislation would have placed the courts above the First Amendment and given the judiciary the power to decide when the American people should be informed.

Provisions in this year's version, S. 1437, reflect a liberal-conservative compromise shepherded through committee by Sens. Edward Kennedy, D-Mass., and John McClellan, D-Ark. The new bill dropped the official secrets provision, for example, but it still retains the basic philosophy that the government must be protected from the press — not that the press and the public's right to know should be protected from abuse and prosecution.

The section on criminal contempt illustrates how the bill appears to have been improved but is actually still flawed.

Originally, this section would have made possible jailing of reporters for contempt for violating a Federal court gag order — even though the court order was later declared "invalid" — unless the court found the order "clearly invalid."

An amendmment offered by Sen. Birch Bayh would bar jailings for violation of invalid gag orders. Considering the alarming proliferation of such orders in recent years, this provision becomes extremely important. Under the new language, a newspaper could disobey a gag order without fear of contempt prosecution if the order was invalid and "reasonable" steps were taken to obtain judicial review.

But this modest improvement tends to obscure the fact that the bill would further imbed in the Federal statutes the very power of courts to issue gag orders. Likewise, this provision could encourage the jailing of reporters who refuse to reveal sources of confidential information. The bill not only imposes no effective restraints on judges, but rather makes reporters subject to jail terms and fines for protecting sources.

The Senate Judiciary Committee favorably modified several provisions of the bill after testimony from various media groups. The changes that have been made, however, should not blind us to the changes that have not been made. Revision of the criminal code is long overdue, but measures which shackle the press assault every citizen of this nation.

The new code has come a long way, but not far enough.

Chicago Daily News

Chicago, Ill., May 3, 1977

Reforming the criminal code

Under the existing federal criminal code, it is a punishable offense to detain a government carrier pigeon, to pick only one notorious example. What the nation has is less a code than a tangle of patch-on statutes enacted since the birth of the republic, many dealing with crimes that have gone out of style, others unenforced or unenforceable.

Efforts to unsnarl the mess have been under way since 1966, when the National Commission on Reform of Federal Criminal Laws was appointed. The fruits of its labors emerged in Congress as the 1973 Criminal Code Reform Act, or Senate Bill 1.

Over all S.1 was a laudable effort at re-codification, but it was odious in details — in the making of new law during the the Nixon administration under the conservative management of Sen. John J. McClellan (D-Ark.), chairman of the Judiciary Committee. One provision would in effect have created an official secrets act, which—had it existed in the past—would have prevented the revelation of such public scandals as Teapot Dome, the Pentagon Papers and Watergate. Liberal senators never let the bill get out of committee.

But the need for reform remained, and last year Sen. Edward M. Kennedy (D-Mass.) sat down with McClellan to begin redrafting the bill into a form more acceptable to liberals—and, indeed, more amenable to American democratic traditions. The compromise bill was introduced on Monday.

The new legislation is stripped of the most objectionable features of the old one, but it is still so encompassing and many of its provisions are so controversial that months—if not years—of spirited debate lie ahead. For example, the bill decriminalizes, federally, possession of small amounts of marijuana, a hot item for debate everywhere. It also provides for more uniform sentencing of criminals along lines that will be opposed by the more zealous protectors of civil rights.

Other provisions will gain wider immediate appeal: revision of rape laws to make it less traumatic for women to testify against their attackers; outlawing of "dirty tricks" perpetrated to influence the outcome of elections; widening the scope of and increasing the penalties for white collar crime.

The new bill also would strip the lawbooks of carrier-pigeon statutes and such unenforceable laws as the Logan Act of 1799, which bars private citizens from "correspondence or intercourse with any foreign government."

The need for over-all reform is so great that Congress should not allow itself to get bogged down in its most controversial provisions. Rep. James R. Mann (D-S.C.), chairman of the Criminal Justice Subcommittee, said that in order to get any bill through a single session of Congress it may be necessary to concentrate on "a maximum of recodification and a minimum of revision." We urge that course when it becomes essential to getting the bigger job done.

THE ATLANTA CONSTITUTION

Atlanta, Ga., May 4, 1977

Criminal Code

A long overdue revision of the federal criminal code has been thrown into the congressional grinder. Let's hope it emerges with at least a few teeth.

The bill, introduced in the Senate Monday, would modernize and simplify the criminal code in a number of ways. For instance, possession of 10 grams or less of marijuana (equal to about a pack of cigarettes) would no longer be a federal offense. The maximum penalty for possession would be cut from the present 7 years imprisonment and $15,000 fine to 30 days and a $500 fine.

However, traffickers in hard drugs would receive mandatory sentences, as would anyone convicted of using a weapon while committing a crime.

Several improvements would be made in the handling of rape cases. Corroboration of a victim's testimony would no longer be required. Inquiry into a victim's past sexual conduct would be restricted. The crime would be redefined to cover homosexual attacks.

The bill, co-sponsored by "conservative" Sen. John McClellan of Arkansas and "liberal" Edward Kennedy of Massachussetts, calls for some needed improvements in sentencing. Two people in this country can commit the same type crime and receive appallingly disparate sentences. That's no secret and it is no secret that a person's wealth can often be influential in the length of his sentence (or too often whether he is sentenced at all).

The bill introduced Monday would change that. Or to put it more accurately, the bill would create a commission to set guidelines to sentence criminals for different kinds of offenses.

In addition to these and other broad changes, the bill would eliminate some of the country's unused laws that, like certain bureaucratic practices, have just hung around the government without any benefit or any hope of benefit.

In keeping with bureaucratic practices, this bill must now fight its way into law. The chance for passage is said to be good. Perhaps Congress really recognizes the need to reform federal criminal laws. Now if, after the bill becomes law, that need can be communicated to those responsible for enforcing that law, the country will be on to something good.

THE STATES-ITEM

New Orleans, La., May 3, 1977

New criminal code

Efforts to simplify the federal criminal code made significant progress this week. A bill introduced in Congress apparently carries out the needed modernization without stifling investigative journalism.

The proposed legislation retains the present law as it relates to espionage and the disclosure of classified information.

Changes considered last year would have set up a form of Official Secrets Act that could be used to discourage the reporting of government misdeeds. The proposal went far beyond legislation needed to protect secrets bearing on the nation's security. Its purpose was to "chill" news sources, thereby protecting incompetence and wrong-doing in government.

A positive proposal in the bill advanced Monday would protect the press against contempt-of-court convictions for the publishing of information in violation of a judicial "gag" order, where the order was clearly invalid and there was no opportunity for timely review by a higher court. Such orders have become weapons for blocking the press from doing its job — the informing of the public.

Other proposals in the bill are clearly needed.

Possession of a very small amount of marijuana (10 grams or less) would no longer be a federal offense. Trafficking in heroin or other hard drugs, on the other hand, would result in a mandatory jail sentence.

The proposed legislation still must be debated, but the list of proposed changes indicates that the authors are on the right track.

St. Petersburg Times

St. Petersburg, Fla., May 4, 1977

Another try on S-1

Eventually they labeled it Richard Nixon's revenge. More formally it was known as Senate Bill 1. It was described as a bill to revise the criminal code. As it turned out, S-1 also would have legalized a lot of what the Nixon crew went to prison for, and might have jailed instead some of the newspapermen who dug up their crimes.

Three years later, after endless revision and national controversy, S-1 finally was laid to rest by the Congress.

Well, believe it or not, S-1 is back. But it not only has a new number (this time it's S-1437); it also has been rewritten from scratch. And it has the backing of such diverse members as Sens. Edward Kennedy, D-Mass., and John McClellan, D-Ark. Attorney General Griffin Bell has also embraced it.

Its sponsors say all the bad stuff has now been edited out.

ORIGINALLY, of course, nobody thought it contained anything bad. When President Nixon sent the proposed code revision to Congress on March 14, 1973, the bill was widely hailed as an overdue compilation and rejiggering of the several thousand criminal laws enacted by Congress over almost 200 years.

We were told, for instance, that it still was a crime to interfere with a government carrier pigeon. And that a lawyer or judge might have to search through all 50 volumes of the U.S. Code to make sure he had covered the criminal laws, which in theory are all bunched into one volume, known as Title 18.

So why not throw out all the obsolete stuff, and package the rest into comprehensible form? That sounded fine to the Congress, which seven years before, in fact, had started work on just such a revision.

BUT THE BILL ran into hundreds of pages, and it was a while before one interested lawyer, Sen. Edmund S. Muskie, D-Maine, managed to make his way through it. What he found, mixed in with all the technical stuff, were new provisions to let off a law-breaking official who could claim bosses' orders, and to make it a crime for unauthorized persons to possess government secrets.

And gradually a lot of other offensive stuff was discovered.

Months of staff work now have gone into rewriting the bill. Kennedy, McClellan and Bell give their assurance the provisions that derailed the original measure have all been deleted.

NEW PROVISIONS have also been added. One would encourage uniform sentencing in federal courts. Another would repeal a law (not generally enforced anyway) making minimal marijuana possession a federal crime.

Hearings are planned shortly in the Senate Judiciary Committee. Meantime, most senators and House members too, who haven't forgotten S-1, can be excused for reserving their judgments.

We concur in the prevalent view among lawmakers that this codification of the criminal laws is urgently needed. But we commend their apparent intention to read all the fine print before voting on it.

The Philadelphia Inquirer

Philadelphia, Pa., May 3, 1977

Congress should welcome 'Son of S-1'—skeptically

For the sake of most arguments, Sen. John L. McClellan, the bristly Arkansas Democrat, and Sen. Edward M. Kennedy stand at opposite ideological poles on the general subject of criminal law. Sen. McClellan is a law-and-order man in the fundamental sense of strong prohibitions, severe sentences and a predisposition to legislate on a grim presumption of the evil that is human. Sen. Kennedy is liberal, predisposed to optimism about the redemption of miscreants and to distrust of police powers.

Yesterday, in an act of both substantial and symbolic significance, Senators McClellan and Kennedy spoke in unison in sponsoring a measure titled the Criminal Code Reform Act of 1977. The fact that they have found common ground, and won Attorney General Griffin B. Bell's support, is cause for encouragement among Americans from all over the ideological spectrum who would like to see reason prevail over the statutory chaos which now exists in federal criminal matters.

The bill cannot be judged in ultimate detail by cursory examination. If it becomes law—and reserving the opportunity to find objectionable elements, we strongly believe it should—it will be one of the most complicated single pieces of legislation ever to come out of the Congress.

That, indeed, is the nature of the need. For as complicated as a broad and inclusive codification of all federal criminal law is, its purpose is to integrate and make coherent the 200-year-long, piecemeal development of federal criminal law.

At present, almost every one of the 50 titles of the U. S. Code contains some criminal provision — by one estimate, there are 70 separate provisions which deal with theft alone. There is a clutter of prohibitions against such archaic and arcane acts as the criminal deflection of a government carrier pigeon.

The contemporary effort to codify the federal criminal law began in earnest 11 years ago with the formation of a commission chaired by Edmund G. Brown, Sr., then governor of California. The product of that group's efforts became the working basis for development of a legislative draft in the Senate, in 1971 and after. It was designated Senate Bill 1, and known as "S.1."

In the darkest days of the late Nixon Administration, there came into S.1 a series of proposals which were profoundly threatening to fundamental liberties. They would have struck at the heart of freedom of speech, of the press and of the right of assembly. Rightly, emphatic libertarian objections were put forward, and the codification effort was sent reeling.

It is now the sponsors' contention, and the Justice Department's as well, that those elements have been exorcized—and that the "son of S.1," as it is being called in the cloakrooms, addresses its original purpose: To make sense of chaos, and to leave substantial new law to the orthodox reform process.

That purpose is an honorable and important one. We urge the members of the Senate, while keeping sharp eyes skeptically open, to join behind what appears to be a constructively hard-nosed act of horsetrading by Senators Kennedy and McClellan. The House, which properly may be led in the effort by Judiciary Committee Chairman Peter Rodino, should move with all deliberate enthusiasm to examine and press forward a sound—and far too long overdue—act of making sense of the nation's criminal law.

THE COMMERCIAL APPEAL
Memphis, Tenn., May 3, 1977

Updating The Laws

AT LONG LAST Congress is moving on a new federal criminal code that would wipe out antiquated laws and recognize that we live in the 20th Century with problems that are different from those that existed earlier in this nation's history.

The need for that new code was recognized as early as 1966 when the National Commission on Reform of Federal Criminal Laws was established. But the task got out of hand. Instead of simply bringing the laws up to date, the commission was prevailed upon to add some provisions to the federal laws which clearly were in conflict with the constitutional safeguards.

Undoubtedly the worst of those new provisions were some that would have dealt with the leaking of classified information in such a way as to make the federal law what is known in some other nations as an official secrets act. The effect of such a law, had it been on the books five years ago, would have been to make impossible the press revelations about Watergate that led to the Senate investigations and the subsequent presidential resignation under threat of impeachment. Such a law also would have made impossible the revelations about CIA and FBI wrongdoings. It would have prevented disclosures about Defense Department fumbles that cost the taxpayers millions of dollars. It would, in fact, have

provided a curtain of secrecy to hide all sorts of errors and corruption that government officials wanted kept from the people, and in the end it could have led to creation of a new form of federal government that would have had the power to limit the personal freedoms of all citizens.

AN OUTCRY by the press and by citizens and members of Congress who were aware of the inherent dangers of the proposal prevented it from coming out of the Senate Judiciary Committee since hearings on the report of the code commission began in 1971.

The nation is heavily indebted to those critics of what for a long time was referred to as Senate Bill 1.

As a result, the present proposal is stripped of most of its controversial proposals. And by agreement among Sen. Edward M. Kennedy (D-Mass.) and Sen. John J. McClellan (D-Ark.) and Atty. Gen. Griffin Bell, Congress now has before it a bill which seems assured of support from both conservatives and liberals.

McClellan has been won over to support revision of the federal laws regarding possession of small amounts of marijuana, for example, because he now recognizes that federal law enforcement officials no longer feel the need for prosecuting such minor offenses and believe they should be spending their time on hard drug traffic. Kennedy, meanwhile, has been getting the support of liberals on the proposed new code's provisions deal-

ing with organized crime, recognizing that it is indeed a national problem and a real political issue.

The new code, for example, finally would make it a federal crime to traffic in stolen property, or to operate a racketeering syndicate. It also recognizes the lessons of recent political campaigns and the "dirty tricks" tactics they produced.

THE NEW BILL would seek to make sentences for the same crime uniform throughout the nation, with provision for eliminating uneven justice being dispensed on the whim of federal judges. It would prevent federal judges from issuing invalid gag orders that result in contempt actions without judicial resort. It seeks to avoid some of the pitfalls of present laws regarding obscenity. It would prevent "laundering" of criminal profits through legitimate businesses. It would make overseas corporate bribery a federal offense.

All in all, it appears to be a progressive, realistic piece of legislation now. Congress, of course, will have full opportunity to review it, bit by bit, and to revise as it deems necessary. It is likely to take the remainder of this session of Congress to achieve that sort of careful examination. But Congress should get on with the task as swiftly as possible so that our federal laws will keep pace with the problems of our times.

THE CHRISTIAN SCIENCE MONITOR
Boston, Mass., December 5, 1977

A new crime code

After 10 years of trying, Congress appears somewhat closer to rewriting the cluttered, often overlapping, and outdated federal criminal laws of the United States. The compromise bill finally pushed through the Senate Judiciary Committee by Senator Kennedy of Massachusetts and the late Senator McClellan of Arkansas represents major progress toward finding a fair and equitable approach to the criminal code — one that both conservatives and liberals may be able to live with.

Winning Judiciary Committee approval was no little achievement in itself, but clearly the Criminal Code Reform Act of 1977 is still a long way from final passage. Senators Kennedy and McClellan deserve credit for their efforts in shaping the compromise bill. As it stands now, the legislation is a good start toward organizing and updating the some 3,000 U.S. criminal statutes. And it is a big improvement over the Nixon administration's attempt to revise the code — a bill that drew such opposition that it never got out of committee.

The public can be especially encouraged that the Kennedy-McClellan bill incorporates some of the reforms called for in the aftermath of the Watergate and other scandals, and hits at the funding of organized crime. In addition to providing badly needed new law-enforcement tools for combating white-collar crime, the bill attempts to curb official corruption and graft by outlawing political "dirty tricks" and prohibiting the laundering of money from criminal pursuits into legitimate uses.

⚹   ⚹   ⚹

The bill also significantly strengthens safeguards for the press against so-called "gag orders," but adds new possibilities for a reporter to be sent to jail for refusing to identify a confidential source to a judge or federal agent. It expands civil-rights laws to make sex

discrimination a criminal offense. It also removes several restrictions on free speech —laws that have too often provided an excuse for police harassment of antiwar and other protest groups.

However, some provisions in the bill are still too broad to completely rule out such excesses.

For instance, the revised code would severely limit the right of assembly and protest around government installations in time of war. But the bill fails to define what constitutes "war" and leaves open the question of whether such restrictions would apply during hostilities short of declared wars.

⚹   ⚹   ⚹

We are glad to see the Senate conferees held the line on decriminalizing possession of marijuana inasmuch as federal statutes frequently serve as models for state laws. Instead of going the route of decriminalization, the Judiciary Committee decided to soften criminal penalties for possession of small amounts of marijuana. It is to be hoped that further legislative action will ensure that the federal government is not seen to be condoning the use of harmful drugs even while it writes laws that are realistic and enforceable.

One key aim of the revised code is to eliminate the wide disparity in sentencing, which results in some defendants receiving far stiffer prison terms than do others convicted of the same crime. Judges now have wide discretion in sentencing, leaving both the public and criminals with the impression that sentences are often inconsistent and unfair.

The revised code would correct this by creating a commission of seven prominent jurists to set guidelines for federal sentencing — guidelines that would also serve as an example for state courts as well, where disparity in sentencing is often even greater. Judges would be required to explain in writing any sentence

handed down that did not fall within the commission's guidelines, and both defendants and prosecutors could appeal any sentence that did so. This is a radical departure from the traditional practice of flexible sentencing and the general assumption that the length of a prison term should depend not only on the crime but on a prisoner's conduct and rehabilitation during incarceration.

Growing acceptance of the determinate sentence in legal circles in effect reflects recognition of the shortcomings of prison rehabilitation as now practiced. It is also in keeping with the growing view that firmer sentencing helps deter would-be criminals.

⚹   ⚹   ⚹

However, further legislative study should be given to the complex question of parole, which the House committee proposes be abolished (even while retaining reduction of sentence for good behavior). The system of parole is one way to help hold down the population in the nation's overcrowded penal institutions. More than that, however, it represents the desirable goal of rehabilitation which society should never abandon simply because past efforts have not generally proved successful. The proposed legislation gives far too little attention to alternatives to prison, such as work-release and community-service programs for nondangerous individuals. More such innovative rehabilitative efforts are needed.

On balance, the Kennedy-McClellan bill is a big improvement over the current disorganized mishmash of criminal laws. But it obviously will require further scrutiny when it reaches the Senate floor probably early next year, and the House, too, which thus far has shown little enthusiasm for tackling the criminal code, must take it up. Reform is long overdue. The bill is a good beginning. Congress should not stop now.

THE RICHMOND NEWS LEADER

Richmond, Va., June 8, 1977

A Mixed Bag

For four years, a monstrosity of a bill called S.1 has been languishing in a Senate committee, the target of bitter criticism from Liberals and conservatives alike. It now appears, however, that a compromise effort may succeed in bringing S.1 to the floor.

Although much disagreement may ensue about the provisions of S.1, there is no doubt that such a measure is needed. It is an attempt to update the federal criminal code, currently a crazy-quilt of archaic, conflicting, and overlapping laws. The code now provides penalties for trapping a federal carrier pigeon, for instance. But the recodification attempt made by the Nixon administration contained many objectionable features, such as offensive official secrets provisions that would have restrained the free flow of information. The Nixon bill also would have permitted high government officials to engage in illegal activities with immunity.

The new compromise version is better, but nonetheless it contains provisions that will please Liberals and dismay conservatives. The official secrets provisions — highly objectionable because of their threat to First Amendment rights — have been eliminated, as have the provisions granting immunity to government officials. But the new measure would repeal the Smith Act, which forbids actions intended to overthrow the government by force, and the Logan Act, which governs a private citizen's contacts with foreign governments.

Neither of these acts has been invoked frequently, but each is an important symbol of American sovereignty. Other controversial provisions would decriminalize the possession of marijuana and add sex discrimination to crimes now defined by civil rights laws banning racial bias — in effect making the Equal Rights Amendment law without ratification. These aspects are highly questionable at best.

But the compromise bill contains some provisions worthy of praise. A section on obscenity strongly reinforces the right of localities to judge pornography on the basis of community standards, as Supreme Court rulings tend to allow. Another provision would set up a commission to study ways of equalizing criminal sentences, thus eliminating widespread disparities of sentences imposed for similar offenses. Current laws against conspiracy and espionage would not be softened.

The new version of S.1 is, in short, a mixed bag. It represents an effort to eliminate earlier provisions that attracted the greatest criticism, and — like all compromises — it incorporates pet causes of both left and right. In the coming months, the faults and virtues of the compromise effort will provoke much discussion across the political spectrum, and a number of further compromises may make some of the most questionable aspects more palatable. It may take longer that way, but such an important bill deserves much refinement before it goes to a vote in the Senate or House.

Detroit Free Press

Detroit, Mich., June 3, 1977

Time Has Been a Help In Criminal Code Revision

A DECADE has passed since a national commission went to work on overhauling the U.S. Criminal Code, a massive embodiment of the country's criminal statutes. Six years have passed since congressional hearings began on the commission's recommendations. Two Congresses have been unable to resolve disagreements and approve a new code.

One might surmise that these delays represent a serious failure. We think not. The passage of time and the sharpening of choices to be made in revising the code have been valuable. In fact, Congress may have averted serious damage not only to criminal law enforcement but also to the protection of basic freedoms.

Now the revision is moving again. Attorney General Griffin Bell and Sens. Edward M. Kennedy, D-Mass., and John J. McClellan, D-Ark., recently announced agreement upon a compromise version that stands a good chance of winning congressional approval after some dissection and change.

As much as the code revision is needed because of the hodgepodge of criminal statutes created through the years, this is clearly an instance in which haste—even after a decade—can make waste. We would like to see a new code approved by the present Congress, but not at the expense of careless drafting or lack of deliberation on key points.

The code, after all, deals with everything from the number of witnesses required for a perjury conviction to the definition of conspiracy. There was a clear danger at one point that a new code would be enacted before we had learned the lessons of Watergate: lessons involving the limitation of power and the public's right of access to information that a Washington administration might find embarrassing, among other things.

The fact that Sens. Kennedy and McClellan have agreed upon the latest version is very significant. Liberal and conservative viewpoints have been reconciled on many points. (It should be noted that Sen. Philip Hart, D-Mich., contributed mightily to the compromise efforts before his death.)

Some of the most abhorrent aspects of Senate Bill 1, an earlier version of the code, have been eliminated in the McClellan-Kennedy version. For instance, a section that would have made it a criminal act even to possess information that someone in government had classified as secret apparently has been removed.

The full text of the legislation that was introduced by Sens. McClellan and Kennedy must be examined carefully before even an overall judgment can be made. But we are encouraged by indications that this massive undertaking may be nearing fruition.

There will be hot debate over some of the proposals: for instance, removing a federal criminal penalty for possession of small amounts of marijuana (enough to make 10 to 15 cigarets); the narrowing, rather than the broadening, of federal application of the death penalty; making corporate bribery overseas a violation of U.S. law; and narrowing conspiracy laws that lend themselves to government abuse.

There also will be serious debate of sentencing provisions that are being considered separately. They follow current thinking, alive in Lansing as well as in Washington, about limiting the discretion of judges in determining the length of sentences. Described in simplest form, the proposal is an effort to increase the certainty and consistency of punishment without necessarily increasing the length of sentences.

If we have learned nothing altogether new about federal powers and criminal law during the decade since code revision was begun, at least we have been strongly reminded of some fundamentals. The fact that a new criminal code is reaching the home stretch now rather than during the emotion-charged Vietnam and Nixon-Agnew days is probably a blessing.

Federal Criminal Code—171

The Kansas City Times

Kansas City, Mo., November 5, 1977

More Work on Criminal Code

A thoroughly bad piece of legislation on federal criminal law has been improved somewhat by the Senate Judiciary Committee. But other changes are clearly necessary before this measure can be acceptable in a democratic system that values highly political freedom.

The legislation is a proposed revision of the criminal code. It is a complex but very important issue that has a direct bearing on the rights of Americans. A measure, designated Senate Bill No. 1, was introduced in 1973 during the Nixon administration. It was a repressive act. That effort and others failed, and deservedly so.

Senate Bill 1437 carries the provisions in the current Congress. It represents a compromise worked out between Sen. John McClellan, D-Ark., and Sen. Ted Kennedy, D-Mass. As it was introduced it too placed severe limitations on public freedoms, including those of the media.

Now some of the undesirable provisions have been eliminated. No longer would print and electronic media be liable for criminal contempt prosecution if they defied a judicial gag order that later was found to be invalid. Another favorable change provides a defense for newspapers against charges of receiving stolen property or defrauding the federal government if it

can be proved there was intent to make information available to the public.

There are other unsettling parts to the bill, however. Many involve the flow of information to the public. Government employees could be prosecuted for leaking information to the press. Criminal contempt charges could be drawn against reporters who attempt to protect confidential news sources.

The overall objective of this effort is to revamp all federal criminal statutes, some dating to 1789. It is a big undertaking. The comprehensive document includes new protections for marijuana smokers, rape victims and stiffer terms for some violators of the law. The bill calls for mandatory minimum sentences, without parole, in hard drug trafficking cases and use of a firearm in commission of a crime. A commission would be established to draft guidelines for sentencing criminals. That provision is to curb disparities in assessment of prison time. Senate floor action is not expected until next year. A subcommittee of the House Judiciary Committee has held a day's hearing on a similar proposal. This means that there still is time, if it is taken advantage of, for further improvements. They must be made if the basic tenets are to be assured in this free society.

The Topeka Daily Capital

Topeka, Kans., May 5, 1977

Caution needed on new crime code

The nation would benefit if the federal criminal code were modernized and simplified, as a new Senate bill attempts to do. Though many of its provisions are good, others represent backward steps.

The bill is a revision of S1, which many Americans opposed as dangerous to freedom because of provisions on disclosure of government secrets. The new bill omits these portions.

The measure's requirement of mandatory jail sentences for trafficking in hard drugs is good, for this is a despicable offense.

The bill rightfully protects the press against contempt-of-court convictions for publishing information in violation of illegal court orders, thus defending the people's right to know.

Civil rights laws would include non-citizens and cover discrimination because of sex as well as race or religion.

The offense of rape is redefined to include homosexual attacks, and the law makes it easi-

er and less degrading for rape victims to prosecute attackers.

In general all these changes are good ones, though definitions and distinctions must be made clear, to reduce litigation.

A program to compensate victims of federal crime by money grants would help these people, though largely at taxpayers' expense.

Two glaring faults in the code are provisions on marijuana and capital punishment. It would drop provisions for a limited restoration of the death penalty, though courts need this tool in cases involving the most heinous crimes.

Despite a large body of thought which holds marijuana is a dangerous, degenerative drug, the proposed code would remove possession of small amounts of it from the list of federal offenses and drastically reduce penalties for possessing larger amounts.

The bill should be considered carefully, and objectionable portions removed.

THE DAILY HERALD

Biloxi, Miss., July 10, 1977

Code reform bill is an atrocity

Congress has a way of adopting a sensible idea then turning it into folly when it drafts the legislation to accomplish its purpose. That has been the case in the effort to reform the federal criminal code.

It happened with S-1, the legislation that was originally designed to accomplish the criminal code reform. S-1 was an atrocity, the drafters had to return to the drawing board, emerging with a newer version, S-1437, which has been referred to as "Son of S-1." It too is atrocious.

It is, in the words of Jack C. Landau, a representative of the Reporter's Committee for Freedom of the Press, "...a frontal assault on the First Amendment..." It would give the government wide-ranging powers to restrict severely the First Amendment rights of the press to report the news and of

the public to receive the news. The philosophy of the new bill, as it pertains to restricting press coverage of government, runs counter to every lesson this nation should have learned from the transgressions of Watergate.

Government officials, even in the highest posts, are not above placing personal and political interests above the common good and their sworn duty. Watergate screams that message so forcefully that it would seem to be unforgetable.

Government officials already have at their disposal an arsenal of weapons to evade press coverage of unpleasantries, of mistakes, of unethical political machinations, of conflicts of interest and of outright criminal activities. They do not need the protective cloak of legality to assist them in cover-

ing up deeds of misfeasance and malfeasance. But S-1437 would do exactly that.

One section would make it a crime for a news organization to publish a report or editorial which "improperly" attacks a government employe. Another would make it criminal to publish a news article or editorial in violation of a court order that later was declared void.

Yet another section would make of news organizations an involuntary arm of law enforcement, forcing the release of unpublished information, notes or news film out-takes (portions of news film shot but not broadcast). Several other sections would make it criminal to publish government information without the permission of the government.

In effect, the bill would make the government the official censor of the press. Can any

American citizen believe that former attorney general John Mitchell, now federal prisoner Mitchell, would have ever called a press conference to announce that agents of the Committee to Re-Elect the President had burglarized Democratic headquarters in Watergate? Nor in a million years.

Democracy has endured many serious trials during our 201-year experiment in what is undoubtedly the freest nation in earth's history. But democracy cannot survive in a nation where the citizens no longer have the right to know what their government is doing, legally, illegally or otherwise.

When the right of citizens to that essential information is terminated, democracy's demise cannot be avoided.

The Miami Herald
Miami, Fla., November 8, 1977

Criminal Law Requires Flexibility

All down the line a tightening up is in evidence. For example, under the Judiciary Committee version, further restrictions would be placed on the insanity defense and there is provision for fines and possible jail terms for possession of very small amounts of marijuana.

The code revision is expected to pass in time to help congressmen in next year's election. They will be able to say they voted for tough action on crime.

Perhaps these stronger measures are as necessary as they are inevitable. But we do not delight in their potential. The flexibility found in many of the present criminal laws indicates a basic confidence in the ability of judges and others to exercise sound judgment and arrive at equitable decisions on a case-by-case basis. It is well to bear in mind that flexible laws are the product of a free society.

With them come opportunities for exploitation by unscrupulous lawyers, weak judges and others who put special interest ahead of the general public welfare. If the situation in the criminal justice system is out of hand, then stronger measures may be justified to save it. But such remedies should be viewed as a step backward, not forward, in the continuing effort to keep this democracy both safe and free.

SOME TIME next year Congress is expected to approve a revised federal criminal code that will be responsive to the angry mood of law-abiding citizens.

The revisions will reflect the national suspicion that criminals who are smart enough or rich enough never stay long in prison, if they are sent there at all. The public has become so cynical about sentencing and parole that news of a particularly horrifying crime often is followed by predictions that the perpetrator, if caught and convicted, would be back on the streets in no time.

This picture of the present criminal justice system is part myth, of course. The federal prisons, like most others, are overflowing and many of the inmates have been left there to rot. But there is enough truth in the conventional concept to warrant concern by everybody from the cop on the beat to senators on the Judiciary Committee.

The committee Wednesday reported out a bill that would send more convicted federal criminals to jail and keep them there. Sentencing would have to be based on very narrow guidelines devised by a special commission. A judge would have a choice, say, of sentencing a person to four years or five years, but that is all. Once in, the prisoners would have very little hope of parole unless the sentencing judges specified they were eligible for early release. Parole could be granted only under "exceptional circumstances."

These provisions are similar to laws already passed in California and Maine in attempts to jam what is seen as the justice system's "revolving door." They are part of a very large package developed after a very long study of the federal justice system and its more than 3,000 criminal laws.

The Providence Journal
Providence, R.I., June 24, 1977

Weaknesses in federal criminal code bill

In trying to reorganize the tangled web of federal criminal laws, some U.S. senators have left loopholes that could cause problems for news reporters and editors. Some adjustments are in order before the bill comes up for action.

The problem is that the bill, in redefining several criminal offenses, contains language that could be used to restrict reporters in their writing about government. One section dealing with theft of government property, for example, could be applied to documents that are leaked to a writer who is paid for the resulting article. Conceivably, under the proposed law, such a writer could be prosecuted.

Another risky section, one that might open the way for judges to impose "gag orders" on the press, seems to restrict the press's ability to appeal citations for criminal contempt. Still another section, dealing with conduct that "improperly subjects another person to economic loss or injury in his business or profession," could be applied to writers of articles critical of government employes.

These and other significant weak spots in what otherwise is a sound attempt to Make order out of the federal criminal code pose a real danger to the operation of a free press. It would be reassuring if the debate, mindful of the press's important role in covering governmental activities, would include exemptions for the press in the sections that could cause trouble.

ST. LOUIS POST-DISPATCH
St. Louis, Mo., November 6, 1977

Threat To Liberties

Prodded by Attorney General Griffin Bell to act on the long stagnated effort to modernize and codify the jumble of outdated, inconsistent and ambiguous federal criminal laws, the Senate Judiciary Committee has approved a bill that represents some progress toward the desirable objective. The measure does eliminate statutory deadwood. It repeals, for example, the 1940 Smith Act, which had already been largely invalidated by Supreme Court decisions because of its infringements on First Amendment rights.

The bill would set up a federal commission to establish guidelines for sentencing in an attempt to eliminate wide disparities in sentencing for similar crimes. It would shield rape victims against courtroom questioning about their past sexual conduct. It would limit the power of the government to prosecute newspapers for receiving government documents alleged to have been stolen and curb the power of federal judges to jail reporters for violating gag orders by saying punishment could not be imposed if the order was found invalid on appeal.

Despite improvements over some existing statutes and despite concessions as a result of objections to some of its original repressive features, the bill does not deserve to pass the Senate in its present form. The legislation is still riddled with potentially repressive provisions reflecting an overall attitude that the government should be given greater authority to control the political activities of citizens and to act against the press when it is deemed to be too prying or to be telling too much.

For example, while judicial gag orders would be more difficult to impose, the power of judges to issue them would be legislatively recognized—which means implicit approval of a kind of prior restraint on publication that is inconsistent with the First Amendment. On the matter of press possession of government documents alleged to have been illicitly acquired, newspapers would be allowed to plead intent to publish as a defense. But the questionable doctrine that official information is the property of the government and that it has the exclusive right to disseminate such data would be by inference recognized.

Senate Bill 1437—the latest version of what used to be S-1—still confers far too much loosely defined authority on federal officials to move against unpopular protest groups. The conspiracy provision, for example, would allow the prosecution of one alleged to have agreed to commit an act that was later found to be an illegal protest demonstration, although he or she never took part. The bill would allow the prosecution of demonstrators for failing to obey a minor official's public safety order.

These are only a few of the objectionable features still remaining in the legislation. Senators Edward Kennedy, Birch Bayh and other liberals have sought to eliminate some of the restrictive provisions of the original bill in order to gain broader support and bring to fruition the criminal law codification effort that has now been under way for 10 years. Although their work has softened the impact of the measure as initially sponsored by hard line Sen. John McClellan and the Nixon Justice Department, the Judiciary Committee bill still threatens the liberties of Americans to such an extent that it does not merit the support of senators who respect the Bill of Rights.

S.1, BILL CODIFYING CRIMINAL LAW, DENOUNCED BY ACLU, ABA, SEN. BAYH

S.1, the bill which would codify the federal criminal law for the first time, has been denounced by the American Civil Liberties Union, the American Bar Association, and Sen. Birch Bayh (D, Ind.) Bayh had originally sponsored the bill, together with Sens. John L. McClellan (D, Ark.), Roman Hruska (R, Neb.), Mike Mansfield (D, Mont.), and Hugh Scott (R, Pa.) A Senate Judiciary subcommittee is now considering S.1.

The ACLU's published pamphlet, *Stop S-1*, says, "The bill's alleged purpose is to revise and reform the United States Criminal Code, but the real purpose of important parts of the bill is to perpetuate secrecy and stifle protest." The ACLU notes, "Although parts of the 753-page S.1 would improve the law in several areas, some 30 provisions—including the secrecy sections—are so detrimental to civil liberties that, so long as they remain, we are better off with no bill." The pamphlet lists four sections, 1121–1124, composing "what would become an Official Secrets Act." Section 1122 would prohibit disclosure of "national defense information" to anyone not authorized to receive it. The ACLU charges that the definition of national defense information is the "most objectionable feature" of those sections because the definition "encompasses a vast array of information limited only by the imagination of the prosecutor."

The American Bar Association's 340-member House of Delegates recommended by a nearly unanimous voice vote Aug. 13 that any codification of federal law "not go beyond present law." While the group endorsed "in principle" the provisions of the bill, it listed 39 specific recommendations for changes. Harold Tyler, deputy attorney general, had told the ABA that the proposed bill "represents a start."

Sen. Bayh said Aug. 19 that S.1's definition of defense information is much broader than the Supreme Court used in permitting publication of the Pentagon Papers. The court specified that the data would have to pose "direct, immediate and irreparable harm to the security of the United States" to be considered dangerous to national security. Bayh said he would introduce an amendment using the Supreme Court's formula to prevent what he termed the dilution of First Amendment rights under the present S.1.

THE SACRAMENTO BEE
Sacramento, Calif., June 17, 1975

Provisions tucked away deep in a legalistic 750-page proposal before Congress carry an ominous threat to the American traditions of a free press and basic rights of all citizens.

You would never know from the title of the massive Senate bill — the Criminal Justice Codification Revision and Reform Act — that certain language introduced in it has been denounced by critics as the gravest threat yet to our civil liberties.

The measure is the outgrowth of a five-year study by a bipartisan commission named to review and revise federal criminal laws. But the Nixon Justice Department turned the ostensible new code into what the St. Louis Post-Dispatch called a "legislative monster with a potential for vast intrusions on the liberties of the American people."

If approved, newsmen could be prosecuted for reporting something the government didn't want made public. (Like Watergate? Like My Lai? Like CIA violations?) It would legalize for the first time the concept that the government and not the people own government information. That way lies the land of Big Brother.

A reporter who wrote on unclassified — mind you, unclassified — national defense matters in peacetime could face felony charges, a fine of up to $100,000 and a seven-year prison sentence. The proposed code broadens espionage laws by making it illegal to disclose information stamped "secret." Thousands of officials have the power to cover up their actions by classifying documents whose disclosure may not in the least be dangerous, except possibly to the classifier's own political safety.

Disturbing, too, is a section giving the government broad latitude to prosecute dissenters. A spokesman for the American Civil Liberties Union recently testified this invited wholesale abuse of the First Amendment. It would, he said, allow prosecution and conviction of individuals whose purpose in speaking of so-called "national defense information" is to inform the American people of governmental activities which the public has the right to know.

There would seem to be ample protection for national security in the Espionage Act and laws governing atomic secrets. The new code would create a state of siege against freedom of information and envelop the country in an unhealthy climate of concealment. It should be drastically revised — or scrapped.

Des Moines Tribune
Des Moines, Iowa, August 9, 1975

Most of the criticism of S. 1, the 753-page bill to rewrite the federal criminal code, has centered on provisions to make it easier for the government to suppress information. Other equally questionable provision would arm the government with power to suppress alarmed in . . . political dissent. .

A popular — and effective — method of expressing dissent is through protest demonstrations. Such demonstrations could be a thing of the past under the 'disorderly conduct' section of the proposed federal law. The section makes it a federal offense if a person "with intent to alarm, harass, or annoy another person or in reckless disregard of the fact that another person is thereby alarmed, harassed, or annoyed, . . . engages in . . . tumultuous . . . conduct; uses abusive . . . language [or] obstructs . . . pedestrian traffic."

It is hard to hold an outdoor meeting in a public place without obstructing pedestrian traffic to a degree. It is equally hard to discuss an issue of public controversy without annoying someone.

A major purpose of the First Amendment is to encourage wide-open and robust debate. The speaker who has to be fearful about alarming or annoying his listeners would be inhibited from engaging in just the sort of discourse the free-speech guarantee is intended to protect.

The country has little to fear from "abusive" language. It has much more need to worry about conformity and blandness. The disorderly conduct section of the proposed federal criminal code is a recipe for speech that annoys nobody, stirs nothing up and imparts no message.

The disorderly conduct section of the proposed law would permit the arrest of the speaker. A companion section would make it possible to arrest his listeners. The section provides:

"A person is guilty of an offense if he disobeys an order of a public servant to move, disperse or refrain from specified activity in a particular place, and the order is, in fact, lawful and reasonably designed to protect persons or property."

This seems to give any federal official a blank check to break up a meeting if he perceives a threat.

These provisions concerned with dissent and protest are a throwback to the days when the Nixon administration was alarmed about anti-war demonstrations. The administration reacted hysterically by ordering mass arrests and jailings. The courts overturned the actions, but those who wrote the revised federal criminal code seem determined to find legal ways to make it easy to toss people in jail for registering political dissent.

THE BLADE

Toledo, Ohio, July 3, 1975

A 750-page bill known as S1, now being considered by the Senate Judiciary Committee, would accomplish nothing less than a complete revision of the U.S. criminal code. Designed to remedy contradictions, ambiguities, anachronisms, and omissions in present laws, S1 is a largely laudable piece of legislation. Some of its provisions, however, are disturbing and should be eliminated.

The first of these would establish a 30-day maximum penalty for simple possession of marijuana, with a six-month penalty for a second offense. This provision ill suits an attempt to bring federal law into conformity with modern realities. Among the realities it ignores are the consensus against harsh penalties for marijuana use, reflected in positions taken by President Ford's drug-abuse advisers and the acting U.S. attorney in Washington, and the debunking of the belief that marijuana use leads to insanity and violence.

The precise physiological effects of marijuana use are still a subject of medical controversy. But those responsible for the relationship between the state and individual behavior — judges, legislators, and prosecutors — are increasingly agreeing that an individual's choice to use marijuana should not lead to his being treated as a criminal. As in the case of Prohibition, laws against marijuana have succeeded only in creating cynicism about the law. The anti-marijuana provisions of S1 — those

banning use and sale of the substance — would perpetuate that cynicism and the gratuitous harassment that produces it. They should be removed from S1 before it reaches the Senate floor.

An equally objectionable provision of S1 would hamper the nation's free press from reporting on government actions by making it a felony to disclose without authorization "classified" official information. As with the Nixon administration's attempt to prevent publication of the so-called Pentagon Papers, the appeal in this provision is to natural fears about the disclosure of information the secrecy of which is vital to the national security.

Disclosure of such information, however, can be punished under treason and espionage laws already on the books. What S1 would create is a British-style official secrets act, shutting off from public scrutiny any piece of information, however irrelevant to genuine national security, that would fall under the indiscriminate "classified" stamps wielded by a virtual army of bureaucrats.

The American system — deliberately — has subjugated official secrecy to the requirements of a free and aggressive press. The results have been beneficial to the nation. The official secrets act proposed in S1 is a dangerous response to an inconsequential problem, and — like the anti-marijuana provisions — richly deserves to end on the legislative cutting-room floor.

DESERET NEWS

Salt Lake City, Utah, July 28, 1975

Americans have always believed that government should be accountable to the people. But the first bill introduced into the United States Senate this year could change all that.

The bill, S.1, is a revision and codification of the federal criminal laws. In its 753 pages, it contains many desirable changes, and some controversial ones.

But one section would severely diminish the fundamental rights of American citizenship, the rights of speech, press and assembly.

The bill would provide that government "owns" information about itself; that a citizen who used this information without consent of the government would commit a crime.

Suppose, for example, that the Environmental Protection Agency made a study with taxpayers' money before making a controversial decision. Then suppose the agency published only the facts that were favorable to its decision and kept the other facts hidden.

If S.1 were passed, any citizen who published the hidden facts from the

report would be guilty of defrauding the government of its property. A government employe who released the hidden facts could also be liable to prosecution.

Under S.1, a government worker could be prosecuted for revealing crimes the government committed. He could be put in jail for releasing information which contradicted administration policy, even if the information was true.

Under this bill, what citizens would know about government would be only what government wanted them to know.

Some of the desirable provisions in S.1 have led Sen. Frank E. Moss, D-Utah, to cosponsor the bill. He has promised to work to amend out the objectionable features that diminish citizens' rights.

He must succeed. Defeat of the objectionable parts of S.1 will be the most important decision Congress makes this session in deciding whether Americans are to control their government or be controlled by it.

The Charleston Gazette

Charleston, W.Va., September 6, 1975

Since national security and civil liberty are concepts which inevitably clash, at what point do national security concerns loom more importantly than civil liberty concerns?

The question was asked in this space as part of an editorial welcome to a new Kanawha Valley newspaper whose publisher has identified himself as being concerned with national security and civil liberty.

The publisher was one of three persons who replied, in the Readers' Forum, to the question. None of the three addressed himself precisely to the point, however. All offered polemic support to ideological convictions already tenaciously held.

Two respondents reacted defensively to what they apparently perceived as crazed Gazette attachment to civil liberty at the expense of the Republic. They argued forcefully for the proposition that without national security, all civil liberty might well be abolished by the repressive forces which have only contempt for constitutional safeguards.

The third respondent argued for the necessity of maintaining constitutional safeguards against the pressures of national security advocates, suggesting that it is pointless to protect civil liberty by destroying civil liberty. (It is a small irony that the third argument, now seen as the liberal position, once was the classic conservative view.)

If time and space prevented the three respondents from pointing exactly to where the line should be drawn, it may please some Americans to learn that a curious coalition of U.S. senators, who have plenty of time and space, has unhesitatingly drawn the line. It is a line which cuts deeply into civil liberty in the name of national security.

The coalition of staunch conservatives and equally staunch liberal senators has come up with a bill aimed at protecting the state against the Daniel Ellsbergs of the future. What they have produced is an appalling affront to the Constitution. It shreds completely the ideals of the Founding Fathers, who took pains to write individual rights into law.

The bill, S.1, is a 753-page measure which reveals an incredible desire to subjugate the individual to the state.

It denies access by the media to much of what the government does or says.

It prescribes severe punishment, even in peacetime, for anyone who reveals "national defense information" as defined by the government.

It widens the definition of sabotage to include the transmission of information, by government definition, as related to security.

It prohibits the "incitement" of persons to engage in conduct "that then or at some future time would facilitate" the destruction of the government. Membership in an investigative group would be grounds for arrest.

It permits wiretapping without court orders. Landlords and telephone companies would be required to cooperate "forthwith" and "unobtrusively."

It makes peaceful demonstrations legally hazardous.

It effectively eliminates the Fifth Amendment.

It legally condones entrapment by government agents.

The above listing is but a sampling of the repression of individual rights in S.1, a bill which could bring Thomas Jefferson roaring angrily from his grave.

We believe S.1 goes far beyond the security measures envisioned by thoughtful persons who desire simplification of federal law. We believe it seriously threatens the right of both conservatives and liberals to advocate causes. We hope West Virginians in Congress will oppose this monster bill with all the force at their command.

The Salt Lake Tribune

Salt Lake City, Utah, July 23, 1975

What began as a basically sound objective has been corrupted into some of the most repressive legislation ever presented to the United States Congress.

The concept behind Senate Bill 1 has been around for a long time. It was initiated during the administration of Lyndon B. Johnson, when Congress in 1966, at his request, created a national commission on reform of federal criminal laws.

At the moment, federal criminal laws are a mish-mash of continuing congressional efforts since the nation's founding. Many of the statutes have been made obsolete by the changing times. Still on the books, for instance, are laws specifying penalties for river piracy.

Also, simply locating applicable statutes in criminal prosecutions can entail many non-productive hours of searching. And then, federal attorneys are likely to find mind-boggling contradiction and confusion, simply because over the nearly 200 years of this country's existence Congress has amended and reamended federal criminal laws, often unmindful that it was only inserting confusing provisions into the law.

Senate Bill 1 has been before Congress in some form since 1973, when it was originally presented in two bills, the Criminal Code Reform Act of 1973 and the Criminal Justice Codification, Revision and Reform Act of 1973.

Since their introduction the bills have been in the hearing process.

But, to date, that hearing process has not eliminated provisions that are as repugnant as anything Congress has attempted since the Alien and Sedition Acts of the late 18th Century. Under the Sedition Act anyone opposing governmental enactments — or who wrote anything against the president or Congress that could be called "malicious" — could be severely fined or imprisoned. The Alien Act authorized the arrest and deportation, at the discretion of the president, of troublesome and dangerous aliens.

These laws triggered a reign of terror, resulting in lynchings, mob rule and wholesale repression of free expression, that did not end until the laws expired in 1802.

The Defense Secrets Act contained in S1 is very reminiscent of these former repressions. It would make it a crime for a reporter to write and an editor to publish any "national defense material (that) may be used to the prejudice of the safety or interest of the United States, or to the advantage of a foreign power . . . ." The only defense against almost certain conviction is that the reporter or editor must know that the information "may he used" to the "prejudice" of the United States or the "advantage of a foreign power." But who is to say whether such disclosure is prejudical or disadvantageous to the United States? Why the bureaucrats of the State and Defense Departments, of course.

And government employes, present or former, who convey such information, no matter how old it is or how insignificant it might be, would be liable for criminal prosecution.

The repressive provisions of S1 are not limited to press freedoms and restricting the free flow of information. The act would strip away many of the protections enjoyed by any and all Americans involved in possible criminal prosecutions, particularly those limiting the admissability of criminal confessions.

Senate Bill 1, as now before the Congress, has strayed too far from its initial objectives of codifying, consolidating and clarifying federal criminal laws. In its present form it is a tool for totalitarian government. And while its liberty taking provisions would probably never survive a constitutional test, before they could be struck down freedom of expression in this country would have suffered a multitude of unwarranted devastating attacks, which would make all Americans, not just reporters and editors, the losers.

Long Island Press

Jamaica, N.Y., July 27, 1975

It is almost a year since the Watergate scandal reached its climax, the resignation of Richard M. Nixon.

There was hope then that it was the end of an era of secrecy and deceit, of misuse of public office and abuse of public trust.

The press was in its glory, for the persistence of diligent reporters had helped uncover the "White House horrors." There was respect for public officials who put their country above loyalty to an individual and helped bring to light the subversions of government agencies by those in power.

There were pledges of renewed diligence so such a situation could never happen again.

A year later, the public has almost forgotten the horrors themselves, much less how they were uncovered. And there are disturbing signs that Orwell's "1984" may be more truth than fiction . . . and before 1980.

The Senate Watergate Committee made some recommendations to assure that Watergate could not happen again. Most of them have not been enacted into law; some have. For example, the election laws were strengthened to prevent some of the Nixon fund-raising abuses.

* * *

One proposed law would not prevent another Watergate, but it might prevent the public from finding out, should there be one.

It is called S. 1, because it was the first bill introduced in the current Senate session, and its purpose is to reform the federal criminal law.

There are some worthwhile provisions and some necessary changes because there has never been a complete revision of the criminal code in over 200 years. But there are other provisions which are frightening, particularly in the wake of Watergate.

Indeed, had S. 1 become law after it was first introduced — by the Nixon administration in 1973 — Mr. Nixon could never have been brought to justice, or as close to it as resignation and public disgrace are.

For example, as the recent Press Spotlight Series by Jack C. Landau of Newhouse News Service, pointed out — S. 1 would allow conviction of editors and reporters who published the Pentagon papers, details of the Watergate cover-up and other secret information on government policies.

It would mean jail terms for present or former government employes who leaked secret information to the press.

Thus, we would never have known about the Pentagon Papers, the White House plumbers, the CIA's domestic spying, the administration's lying about its role in Chile or the India-Pakistan War . . . indeed, anything the White House didn't release officially.

* * *

The restrictions on the press, government employes and political dissenters are not S. 1's only drawbacks.

It also reverses the Supreme Court's landmark Miranda decision, which spelled out the rights of those accused of crimes. It provides for death penalties, no-parole minimum sentences and appellate review of sentences, including the government's right to appeal for a stiffer term. It changes trial procedures to make it tougher on criminal defendants, thus eroding civil liberties gains over past decades.

Reporter Landau — himself a lawyer — calls the bill "Nixon's legacy," because it embodies the law-and-order philosophy of the ex-President and two of his attorneys general, John N. Mitchell and Richard G. Kleindienst, both of whom brought dishonor to the office.

It is a legacy which America can do without. The domestic policies and politics of the Nixon administration have been discredited. His attitude toward the press, his opponents and anyone who cares about civil liberties demonstrated the need for better protection for them, not more restrictions.

* * *

We are shocked that men like Senate Majority Leader Mike Mansfield and Sen. Birch Bayh, who may be a contender for the Democratic presidential nomination, would put their names on the bill. And we cannot accept Sen. Bayh's explanation that he thought he'd be in a better position to negotiate modifications as a co-sponsor.

S. 1 doesn't need modifications. It should be discarded, and a new start made toward revision of the criminal code.

Los Angeles Times

Los Angeles, Calif., September 15, 1975

Legislation now pending in Congress to revise the federal criminal code should be junked.

Senate Bill 1, a massive and complicated measure 753 pages long, is so pervasively and fatally flawed that it lies beyond the scope of any rational amending process.

Known as the Criminal Justice Reform Act of 1975, the bill, and companion legislation in the House, purports to standarize federal criminal law. It does that to an extent—but far more. It proposes revolutionary change that would vastly enhance the power of government and sharply decrease the freedom of the American people.

Federal law is a hodgepodge of discrepancies that need revision and codification. That was the purpose of the National Commission on Reform of Criminal Laws appointed in 1966, with former Gov. Edmund G. Brown as chairman. After five years of study, the commission presented its report to President Nixon and Congress in 1971.

In the next two years, the bipartisan commission's effort was undercut. The three Senate members of the commission, often dissenting from its recommendations, embodied their views in a bill (S 1) introduced in 1973. They were John L. McClellan (D-Ark), Roman L. Hruska (R-Neb.) and Sam J. Ervin Jr. (D-N.C.). Even this did not satisfy Nixon, who had the Brown commission report thoroughly revised and presented as the administration-backed Criminal Code Reform Act of 1973 (S 1400). McClellan and Hruska held hearings to consolidate both bills, and what emerged was the present legislation, which far exceeds the goal of the Brown commission.

The American Bar Assn. house of delegates recognized this last month by voting nearly unanimously that codification should not go beyond present law. And the board of governors of the Society of American Law Teachers concluded recently that "the bill is so riddled with defects" that it is doubtful whether it is "amenable to piecemeal improvements."

Its most drastic provisions would virtually give ownership to the government of all public information. The legislation would accomplish this by creating a new felony: unauthorized disclosure of "classified" official data. With some 15,000 government employes authorized to classify documents, this provision, with its severe penalties, would permit the government to engage in unprecedented suppression of information.

The sections dealing with "national defense information" would make government employes and news reporters vulnerable to prosecution that would be limited only by the imagination of the prosecutor.

One section would make it a crime to collect or communicate "national defense information" with the "knowledge that it may be used to the advantage of a foreign power . . ." Is there any information, defined as a prosecutor may want to define it, that could not be "used" by a foreign power or would not be related in some way to national defense?

Government employes who revealed information and reporters who received and published it would be liable under the law. Only the official version of events would be available to the public. The government would be able to operate behind a screen of secrecy.

This attempt to scuttle the First Amendment is the most dangerous aspect of S 1, and naturally has drawn the most fire from the press. As a result, some modifications of sections relating to control of government information may be accepted by the bill's sponsors. Even so, the legislation should be rejected, because freedom is not a commodity to be parceled out in varying degrees to the American people, and S 1 contains a long array of hazards to a free society. The bill would:

—Protect federal officials from criminal prosecution for illegal acts as long as they believed "the conduct charged was required or authorized by law"; this clause, dubbed the "Watergate defense," would provide a rationale for almost any kind of abuse of authority.

—Reaffirm authorization of domestic wiretapping for 48 hours without court order and require landlords and companies to cooperate "forthwith" and "unobtrusively" with government agents.

—Impose restrictions on demonstrations by making the picketing of government buildings illegal; also illegal would be interstate travel to assemble 10 or more persons who "create a grave danger of imminently causing" damage to property.

—Outlaw demonstrations that would take place adjacent to wherever authorities say is the "temporary residence" of a President.

—Revive in part the Smith Act by making it a crime to incite others to engage in conduct that then or at some future time would facilitate the destruction of the government.

—Define sabotage broadly as activity that "damages" or "tampers with" almost any property, facility or service "that is or might be used" in the national defense of this country or "an associate nation."

—Permit entrapment by government agents, and place the burden on a defendant to prove he was "not predisposed" to commit the crime.

—Broaden the conspiracy law by eliminating the requirement of proof of an "overt act"; substituted is "any conduct" that shows intent to effect a criminal agreement.

—Reaffirm limited "use" immunity in criminal proceedings and congressional hearings—a procedure that weakens the Fifth Amendment protections against self-incrimination.

These provisions do not by any means exhaust the list; worse, the legislation is marked throughout by a chronic vagueness of definition that would insure decades of battles in the courts.

Whatever this bill is, it is not simply an effort to pull together and rationalize existing federal law. It is, rather, a reflection of an authoritarian view of the way government should function, and a radical departure from the letter and spirit of the Constitution.

In this bicentennial year, Congress could honor the founding fathers in no more effective way than by throwing out this legislation in its entirety.

Arkansas Gazette.

Little Rock, Ark., August 13, 1975

Senator John McClellan, in an interview with the Gazette, has said that he is willing to change certain fiercely contested sections of a bill, "S. 1," that he has introduced in the Senate to recodify the U. S. criminal code. The senator's stated readiness to accept amendments is welcome, for the disputed sections pose an unmistakable threat to freedom of the press.

Nevertheless, the mere inclusion of these sections in the bill has given ample warning that S. 1 must be kept under closest surveillance, in committee and afterward if it is sent to the Senate floor. Much of the bill appears to be constructive but no one knows how many other sleepers there may be hidden away, along with press restrictions, in other parts of a purportedly innocent recodification of law. Americans, especially lawyers, have a passion for collecting and grouping statutes in neat and orderly array but what counts is the substance of the law rather than the convenience of its arrangement.

McClellan argues that his bill makes only minor changes in the language of the existing law but a close scrutiny of the changes suggests they are major, because they broaden the scope of prohibitions against "communicating" information relating to defense. The existing statute makes it a felony to "communicate" to unauthorized persons certain recorded national defense information but the McClellan bill makes reference simply to "national defense information." Clearly a news reporter for press or the broadcast media could be prosecuted under the statute for disclosing to the public whatever information that Defense Department bureaucrats designated as classified.

S. 1 has been described, fairly, we think, as the United States' first proposed Official Secrets Act. It is revealing what Senator McClellan admits about the bill in the context of one specific application, the Pentagon Papers case. In the interview McClellan said that, no, S. 1 would not have prohibited the disclosure of the celebrated Pentagon Papers but that it might have required that "certain facts in the stories"—be kept in confidence. Exactly The "certain facts" being, in all likelihood, the revealing ones in the Pentagon Papers that the Pentagon had been disregarding all those agonizing years of the Vietnam war.

And what would S. 1 have done to the disclosures about the horrors of the CIA intrigues, which, most certainly involved "defense information"? It would have made many of these disclosures un-publishable except under threat of durance vile.

* * *

The bill is in the Judiciary Committee and various figures in the press and television and radio businesses have been making proper protest about the dangers of the bill. Consultations are under way to reach some kind of agreement on the language of the bill, McClellan saying that he hopes for something better than the existing provisions of law. Here we would raise a precaution, for McClellan and everyone else having responsibility for the bill, against regarding any of the media people as "representatives" of the press. There *are* no representatives of the press, for no newspaper or TV station, or association of news and broadcast people can speak for the press. Indeed, no one can speak for any newspaper or broadcast station except his own. The American Society of Newspaper Editors, the American Newspaper Publishers Association, the Reporters Committee for Freedom of the Press, are estimable agencies, all, and are making due protest on S. 1 But if they should reach some sort of compromise with the Judiciary Committee it would not be binding on any publication or station or reporter except the few who took part in the negotiations.

In any case, as the argument continues, it is well to recognize that Senator McClellan has an established bias against the press that is known to all who have followed McClellan's service closely. This means that his compromises will have to be examined with vast skepticism. The dead giveaway for the senator was in the case of Florida's notorious "right of reply" law, which was upheld by the state Supreme Court and later unanimously rejected by the U. S. Supreme Court, with conservatives and liberals standing in one accord on the statute's unconstitutionality. While the case was pending before the Supreme Court, McClellan revealed he would have his own federal "right-of-reply" statute ready if the Florida law cleared the federal test.

Officials of the ASNE, ANPA and RCFP have made suggestions to the Senate Committee for proposed changes in the language, and these changes will be under study by us all as the bill continues under consideration. It is possible that the existing statutes can be improved, with stronger safeguards for press freedom. At this point, however, it is our own disposition to believe that the best course may be simply to leave the law like it is, in accordance with what McClellan described as one entertainable course of action. The recent record of performance by the press, in the Pentagon Papers case and the Watergate affair particularly, suggests that the press is performing its duty and functioning quite well under the existing law. There may be no persuasive case for changing the law at all.

HERALD-JOURNAL

Syracuse, N.Y., August 13, 1975

The American press has found new friends among the country's lawyers.

The American Bar Association, winding up its annual meeting in Montreal, decided restrictions, now imposed, are sufficient.

The Department of Justice, however, had pressed hard for the bar's endorsement of Senate Bill 1, a 753-page revision of the country's criminal statutes.

As written, the section on the press would:

— Make it a crime for anyone, including a reporter, to use government-owned documents to write a story without the permission of the government.

— Make it a crime for a reporter to read or use the contents of a private letter without the knowledge of the letter's sender or recipient.

— Make it a crime punishable by up to seven years in prison and a fine of up to $100,000 for writing about unclassified national defense information if that information is determined to have harmed the U.S.

— Make it a crime for a reporter to communicate unauthorized national defense information to his readers.

Various versions of these prohibitions, especially the latter ban, are already on the books.

The American Bar Association's House of Delegates criminal justice section opposed some sections of S. 1, but approved the proposed statute in principle, ignoring the restrictive sections on the press.

The Law Student Division of the ABA viewed adoption of these prohibitions as a sellout of the First Amendment and pledged to oppose ABA approval.

A donnybrook was forecast. But the criminal justice section decided, with the students, that no further federal restrictions on the press are necessary. It embraced the law students' compromise, opposing the new restrictions on the press projected by S. 1 for by then, practically everyone at Montreal had decided the press is too necessary to the workings of even a faulty democracy.

The Department of Justice should take note.

Thanks, students.

Rocky Mountain News

Denver, Colo., August 20, 1975

AMERICANS WHO ARE sincerely concerned about preserving their liberties against government encroachment should be grateful for a recent action by the 340-member House of Delegates of the American Bar Association (ABA).

It voted nearly unanimously against restrictions on news organizations as proposed by sections of the new Federal Criminal Code, now before Congress.

These would criminalize as felony theft the unauthorized reporting of national defense information.

The policy-making body of the ABA has now joined nearly every section of the public press in opposing those parts of the code that could make it a felony for reporters to write about such matters as Watergate and the My Lai massacre in South Vietnam, and for newspapers to publish such documents as the Pentagon Papers.

To put it another way, the code would establish the principle that the government, and not the people whom it serves, owns government information.

One needn't read George Orwell's "1984" to picture where this chilling philosophy leads. The effect of news repression in Nazi Germany, Soviet Russia, and, right now, in Indira Gandhi's India, is all too clear.

One can't help wondering what forces are so intent on establishing the same sort of repression in this country, and what their aim can be — other than a monolithic government above the law and the people.

RAPID CITY JOURNAL—

Rapid City, S.D., August 24, 1975

One of the most controversial pieces of legislation pending in Congress is the Federal Criminal Code Act of 1975.

The 753-page bill, sponsored by both liberals and conservatives, has the backing of President Ford. Hearings on the Senate bill (S.1) ended this spring after four years, and a companion bill has been introduced in the House.

The bill attempts to combine interpretations of court decisions and past federal legislation into a package of laws. Currently, federal law is so scattered and so unorganized that it is incomprehensible to laymen and very difficult for lawyers.

The bill also attempts to provide equal sentences for equal offenses, something now lacking in many instances. But because it involves interpretations and a number of new laws, it is controversial.

For example, the death penalty would be mandatory in certain cases, the penalty for simple possession of marijuana would be cut from one year to 30 days, definition of obscenity would be left to local communities and prosecution of civil rights violations would be simplified.

One of the most bitter confrontations is shaping up over provisions in the proposed code that have been considered alien to the nation's freedom-of-the-press tradition.

If the code is approved as written, a newsman could face federal criminal prosecution if he reported something the government did not want made public. And for the first time in the history of this country since the Constitution was adopted, the principle that the government, and not the people, owns government information would be legalized.

Had such provisions been in effect in recent years, many government scandals and abuses would not have been exposed. The public could not have been informed about the Watergate crimes, the Pentagon Papers, the My Lai massacre and the domestic spying of the Central Intelligence Agency.

Founding fathers of this democratic nation wanted to protect the right of citizens to know what the government was doing when they granted the freedom of press responsibilities of the First Amendment.

The press of this country obviously opposes the press-restrictive sections of the proposed code. Such opposition might be labeled as selfishness. However, the American Bar Association, at its recent Montreal convention, rejected those sections that would make Watergate-type prosecutions and press investigations more difficult.

In opposing muzzling of the press, the bar association joins the media in championing the right of American citizens to know what their government is doing.

When that right vanishes, democracy will cease living in this nation.

The Chattanooga Times

Chattanooga, Tenn., August 27, 1975

Few people would question the need for governments to control information absolutely essential to national defense or the right to punish those who violate such secrecy guidelines. Such information can be absolutely vital to a nation's survival.

But the danger inherent in the control of information is that a government can begin to use secrecy powers to hide its mistakes, conceal information vital to the exercise of freedom, engage in practices which encroach on personal liberties or cover up bureaucratic inefficiency or crime.

That is why we are happy to see that Sen. Birch Bayh, D-Ind., has announced his opposition to the revised federal criminal code unless it is rewritten to eliminate what he calls "repressive" sections that restrict the availability of government information. The fact that Senator Bayh was a co-sponsor of the controversial criminal code legislation (known as S. 1) makes his opposition all the more significant.

Actually, we feel that all senators should consider the ramifications of this bill, should it pass as presently written. In effect, it would impose on government employes and the press (i.e., the American people) a sort of "Official Secrets Act" similar to the measure that prevails in Great Britain.

For example, the bill provides that a reporter could be fined $100,000 or sentenced to jail for seven years (or both) for publishing unclassified "national defense" information if it could be used "to the prejudice of the safety or interest of the United States . . ." The problems of such a vague definition are obvious, for what constitutes "national defense"?

Sen. Alan Cranston, D-Calif., is quoted in the bulletin of the American Society of Newspaper Editors as saying such provisions would enable the government to prosecute those who leak information on cost overruns on weapons and foreign aid negotiations. Those who doubt that should recall the disgraceful treatment of A. Ernest Fitzgerald, the Air Force cost analyst who was practically run out of the Pentagon when he disclosed cost overruns on the C-5A.

The trouble with the espionage and defense sections of S. 1 is that it reflects the philosophy of many in government that they could do a more efficient job if statutory controls were imposed on the press to keep it in line. In light of the events in India, one might call this an American version of "Gandhi-ism."

By whatever name, however, the effort to broaden the definitions of alleged criminal offenses involving government information is a serious attack on the freedom of the press and, by extension, the freedom of all American citizens.

We congratulate Senator Bayh on his decision to oppose the repressive vagueness of the bill's sections that are repressively vague. We hope Sens. Baker and Brock will join him.

New York Post

New York, N.Y., August 27, 1975

Nothing is really cryptic or indecipherable about the proposed U. S. Criminal Code now awaiting action by a somewhat divided Congress; it is printed in perfectly visible ink. But it is not particularly easy to comprehend, either.

For one thing, it consists of hundreds of pages. For another, many of its legal implications are a matter of intense controversy, philosophical and political. There is no question, apparently, that a coherent, uniform and up-to-date codification of federal penal law would be an important national asset. But is the proposed document, in its current form, acceptable upon stringent examination?

The latest legislator to say "No," although many of his prominent colleagues are assenting, is Sen. Bayh (D-Ind.), who has now withdrawn as a sponsor of the legislation because of well-justified reservations—also shared by the American Bar Association—about the code's restrictions on reporting. Strictly speaking, the Code would have forbidden disclosure of the Watergate scandals or the Pentagon Papers. It would subject newspaper writers to prosecution for felonies if they published information withheld by the government.

No brief comment on the bill can fairly list all its deficiencies—or its creditable features. But it is fair to say that it does not merit enactment without extensive amendment.

Mandatory Sentences:
Punishing the crime or the criminal?

A piece of doggerel favored by prison inmates is that if "you done the crime, you do the time." This wisdom must be tempered by the reality that the vast majority of criminals are never even apprehended by the police, so the question of punishment is often experienced by only a small fraction of offenders. The President's Commission on Causes and Prevention of Violence stated that for an estimated nine million crimes committed in one year, only 1½% of the perpetrators were imprisoned.[1] But for those convicted of criminal acts the form of punishment has not always resulted in prison sentences. Until recently only 10% of convicted felons were incarcerated.[2] The connection between the severity of the crime and the probability of imprisonment has been rather tenuous.

The justification for having a flexible approach toward sentencing is that the punishment should fit the offender and not merely the crime. This philosophy has been recognized by the Supreme Court:

"The belief no longer prevails that every offense in a like category calls for an identical punishment without regard to the past life and habits of a particular offender . . . Today's philosophy of individualizing sentences makes sharp distinctions for example between first and repeated offenders . . . Retribution is no longer the dominant objective of the criminal law. Reformation and rehabilitation of offenders have become important goals of criminal jurisprudence."[3]

Contained within the view enunciated by the Supreme Court is the assumption that the criminal is in need of a cure for his disease. In the same way a standard prescription for all ill patients is unscientific, so is a rigid sentencing structure that fails to allow penologists to decide when the offender has been rehabilitated.

The practice of fitting the punishment for the criminal and not the crime has often served as a rationale for keeping wealthy and middle-class offenders out of prison. Court imposed probation upon Patty Hearst and Bernard Bergman, the former convicted of armed robbery and assault and the latter of embezzling millions of dollars, have only been two prominent cases among many where judges, despite the enormity of the crime, have determined that prison sentences would not serve society's interest. According to Lesley Oelsner, a lawyer and reporter for the *New York Times,* "Most judges justify the minimal sentences they give to businessmen-criminals— fines, probation, or exceedingly short jail terms—on the grounds that when such a man is convicted, he generally loses his job, his standing in the community and his family's respect."[4] A recent Law Enforcement Assistance Administration study reveals the discriminatory class aspects of sentencing: 91% of those convicted of bank robbery went to jail, compared with only 17% of those convicted of embezzlement of bank funds.[5]

Indeterminate sentences and use of parole are the two penal tools integral to the philosophy of rehabilitation. An indeterminate sentence is actually a prison sentence with a fixed minimum and maximum sentence contained within wide limits. An indeterminate sentence may be from one to six years or one to life. The public often construes the maximum part of the indeterminate sentence as the "real" sentence. Thus, when an offender is released after five years of a one-to-15-year indeterminate sentence, an impression is created that society is coddling criminals. This is a basic misconception in that none of the participants in the criminal justice system ever envisioned most prisoners serving their full sentences.

When the prosecutor accepts a plea of guilty, as he does in 90% of all convictions, he understands that with parole and good time an offender will be released before the maximum term. If the prosecutor feels that the period of time actually to be served is insufficient, he will attempt to charge the defendant with a more serious crime. This is not a difficult task because the statutory language of penal codes is purposely vague so as to allow for great discretion. In New York, up until enactment of the marijuana decriminalization law, it was common to charge first offenders with public intoxication, a violation, rather than with one of the criminal drug statutes that carried a heavier penalty.

The sentencing judge, when setting the punishment, takes into consideration the operation of parole and indeterminate sentences. To assure that the defendant will not be released prematurely on an indeterminate sentence, the judge will double or triple the time actually intended to be served. Similarly, the defendant, should he plead guilty, understands that the charge he is pleading guilty to will not require that he complete the maximum sentence.

The next actors in the sentencing process are the parole boards and prison authorities. These non-judicial agencies have really replaced the judge in determining the extent of the sentence that the convicted offender will serve. Understandably these bodies wield great influence over the inmates. Failure of psychologists and social workers to be impressed by a prisoner's rehabilitation could postpone the day of release or parole. The use of parole and good-time release provide important levers for assuring prison discipline. The displeasure of the prison authorities with an inmate could require the prisoner to complete a one-to-25 year term on a relatively minor sentence. Indeterminate sentences and parole are basic implements in controlling the flow of prisoners into an already overcrowded prison system; the authorities require some rational means of releasing prisoners to make room for newly sentenced convicts. Connected to the problem of prison overcrowding are prison costs. To imprison an inmate for a year may cost anywhere from $7,000 to $10,000.[6] Parole and indeterminate sentences help reduce the costs of institutionalization to the taxpayer.

However, for a number of reasons the philosophy of indeterminate sentences and flexible punishment have come under sharp attack. In the penal institutions prisoners are critical of the possibilities for abuse which the indeterminate sentence structure contains. Two offenders receiving the same sentence for the same crime may serve widely disproportionate prison terms. The system also encourages great uncertainty in the lives of prisoners and places them at the mercy of rehabilitative processes that are at best far from exact in assessing the time for release. Jessica Mitford, author of *Kind and Usual Punishment,* reported that the demand heard most among the many ex-convicts she interviewed was for abolition of the indeterminate sentence and parole boards.[7]

Others have criticized the existing system because of its premise that offenders are in need of rehabilitation and that society is capable of providing it. They argue that people who commit crimes are not essentially different from those who do not.[8] Only the sure expectation of swift and certain punishment will deter these people from committing crimes. Even if criminal offenders did reveal some defect in their social and psychological complexion, social science has not advanced to the point where it is capable of offering a proven cure.

Students of various sentencing models seem to provide limited support for the argument that certainty of punishment reduces crime. Sure punishment also helps eliminate the feeling among those incarcerated that they have been unfairly singled out.[9] However, certainty of punishment must include certainty of detection. The basic problem that most crooks do not get caught remains unresolved in any fixed punishment scheme.

Studies of deterrent techniques indicate that certainty of punishment will reduce crime, but only if the potential offender is aware of the following provisos: he must know that the particular act is prohibited and that those who engage in it might be punished; the degree of severity of potential punishment must be known; and in order that increased detection serve as a deterrent, the probability of being caught must be known.[10] Further analysis shows that "certainty, considered by itself has a moderate deterrent effect for all crimes, while severity acting alone is not associated with lower rates of crime."[11] In fact, extremely severe punishment has been shown to have adverse consequences on the probability of post-prison crime.[12]

The United States imposes sentences two to three times as long as any Western industrialized nation.[13] The reasons for this anomalous position are difficult to assay. The shift from statutes imposing capital punishment to those imposing prison terms was viewed as an enormous reform in the 1800's. Though a 20-year sentence for robbery or arson appears harsh in absolute terms, compared to the previous capital sentence it was a mark of extreme leniency. The death penalty soon became the measuring stick by which to grade all non-capital punishments. Perhaps unavoidably, the strains of violence in American society which help fuel the crime rate also appear in our sentencing determinations.

The proposed channel for implementing the swift and certain punishment philosophy is the creation of mandatory and definite sentencing structures and the concomitant abolition of parole. The pending federal criminal codification revision contains an elaborate section on instituting mandatory sentences and curbing judicial discretion in the area of punishment. California revised its criminal code in 1977 to create mandatory sentences. The California revision is noteworthy since the state employed the most sweeping use of the indeterminate sentence in the country.[14]

One of the arguments on behalf of mandatory sentences is that the disparity in punishment suffered by people who commit the same crimes will be reduced. Figures released by the United States Bureau of Prisons reveal that someone convicted in Federal Court in Manhattan for interstate car theft received an average of 30.7 months. A similar criminal on the other side of the river, prosecuted in Federal Court in Brooklyn, received an average of 51 months.[15] However, while mandatory sentences and abolition of parole will reduce the discretion of judges and prison officials, it will correspondingly increase the discretion of prosecutors and police. The position of prosecutors in the criminal justice system will be enhanced as their prerogative of setting the criminal charge and corresponding sentence can no longer be regulated by a judge. Likewise the cop on the beat, long known for his discretionary use of power, will gain immeasurably by the new reforms.[16]

While no results are available on the new California law, it is clear that the mandatory sentence change has disappointed some of its supporters because it has resulted in even longer prison terms. Under the former indeterminate sentencing law, prisoners in California served more time than in any other state.[17] Liberal supporters of mandatory sentencing like Harvard Law Professor Alan Dershowitz have argued that what is necessary is more people serving prison sentences but for shorter periods of time.[18] Perhaps because of the popular belief that severe sentences are good antidotes to crime, legislators are using mandatory sentencing revisions as an opportunity to increase penalties but without allowing for judicial flexibility. The American Civil Liberties Union estimates that the federal prison population will increase by a third if the stiff penalties of the federal criminal law codification bill are enacted.[19]

According to the highly respected David Bazelon, Chief Judge of the United States Circuit Court of Appeals in Washington, D.C., the very essence of the ideal of justice is to permit judges to apply individualized justice to offenders.[20] Yet the unwillingness of legislators to allow judges this discretion may backfire. A study of mandatory sentences reveals that judges will acquit if the sentence is unjust. "Acquittal of defendants in spite of evidence to convict is a common practice if the defendant is excessively harmed by a mandatory sentence following conviction."[21] New York's experience with the mandatory drug sentence law was not dissimilar; judges and juries became more sympathetic to defendants.[22] However if historical antecedents are a guide to the present, it is likely that state legislators, though desirous of pleasing their constituents with tougher sentencing laws, are hoping that judicial creativity will provide the system with loopholes. When the English Parliament in the early 1700's extended the death penalty to nearly every crime, it was with the understanding that it would rarely be enforced.[23] Judge-recommended royal pardons obviated the casual imposition of the death penalty. The debate about fixed punishment is, in fact, an old one. Eighteenth century England was also torn by serious debate over the ideas of Cesare Beccaria contained in his seminal book *An Essay On Crimes and Punishments,* written in 1764.[24] Beccaria argued that there must be a "fixed code of laws, which must be observed to the letter." Sir Samuel Romilly and Sir F. M. Eden conducted a long and ultimately unsuccessful campaign to implement Beccaria's proposals.[25] They believed that a fixed and graduated scale of more lenient punishment would deter crime and increase convictions. Despite the logic of the argument, eighteenth century England adhered to the arbitrary use of the rope and gallows. One commentator's explanation for English policy is strikingly contemporaneous to the current debate: "A complete rationalization of the criminal law would remove those very elements of discretion, such as the pardon, which contributed to much of the maintenance of order and deference."[26]

Professor Caleb Foote, a noted professor of criminal law at the University of California at Berkeley feels that in the future, criminologists will regard the trend toward determinate sentences as "a fad."[27] Application of the determinate sentence without a reduction in punishment, he argues, will require a five-to-ten-fold increase in the present correctional budget, and the prisons will still be jammed. He believes that the better alternative is the massive decriminalization of many acts and implementation of non-incarcerative punishments. Considering the political improbability of such measures, Professor Foote expects the criminal justice system to keep its balance by continuing to pronounce excessively harsh sentences for some and excessively lenient ones for others.

Notes

1. *Crimes of Violence,* A Staff Report Submitted to the President's Commission on the Causes and Prevention of Violence (Washington, D.C.: Gov't Printing Office, 1969) pp. XLI–XLII.
2. "Berkeley Conference: Prison Sentences," *Corrections Magazine,* September, 1977 p. 64.
3. *Williams v. New York,* 337 U.S. 241 (1949).
4. Lesley Oeslner, *The New York Times,* September 27, 1972 p. 1.

5. Elizabeth Fowler, "Fighting Crimes Against Business," *The New York Times,* January 27, 1978 p. D.5.
6. Rob Wilson, "U.S. Prison Population Again Hits New High," *Corrections Magazine,* March, 1977 p. 22.
7. Jessica Mitford, *Kind and Usual Punishment* (New York: Alfred A. Knopf, 1973) pp. 86– 87.
8. Thomas S. Szasz, *Law, Liberty, and Psychiatry* (New York: Macmillan, 1963) p. 108; Harry Barnes & Negley K. Teeters, *New Horizons in Criminology,* 3rd ed., (Englewood Cliffs, N.J.: Prentice Hall 1959) p. 7.
9. George Antunes & A. Lee Hunt, "The Deterrent Impact of Criminal Sanctions," 51 *Journal of Urban Law* 145, 158–159 (1973).
10. Franklin Zimring & Gordon Hawkins, *Deterrence* (Chicago: University of Chicago Press, 1973) p. 142.
11. George Antunes & A. Lee Hunt, *supra.*
12. Ibid.
13. David J. Rothman, "Doing Time," *The New York Times,* September 14, 1977 p. 21.
14. See Mitford, *supra,* pp. 85–94.
15. Quoted in Oelsner, *supra.*
16. See especially Jerome H. Skolnick, *Justice Without Trial* (New York: John Wiley, 1966).
17. Mitford, *supra,* p. 86.
18. Alan Dershowitz, *Fair and Certain Punishment: Report of the Twentieth Century Fund Task Force on Criminal Sentencing* (New York: McGraw-Hill, 1976).
19. Barry M. Hager, "No Agreement on Revising Criminal Code," *In These Times,* November 2, 1977 p. 7.
20. *Corrections Magazine, supra,* p. 67.
21. Donald Newman, *Conviction* (Boston: Little Brown, 1966) pp. 131–172.
22. *Nation's Toughest Drug Law: Evaluating N.Y.'s Drug Law* (New York: Association of the Bar of the City of New York, 1977).
23. Douglas Hay, "Property, Authority and the Criminal Law," in *Albion's Fatal Tree* (New York: Pantheon, 1975) p. 56.
24. Cesare Beccaria, *On Crimes and Punishments,* trans. Henry Paolucci (New York: Bobbs-Merrill, 1963).
25. Douglas Hay, *supra,* p. 57.
26. *Ibid.,* pp. 57–58.
27. *Corrections, supra,* p. 68.

FORD PROPOSES MANDATORY PRISON UPON CONVICTION FOR VIOLENT CRIME

In a speech at Yale Law School in New Haven, Conn. April 25, President Ford recommended that virtually all persons convicted of a violent crime, particularly where a gun was used, be sent to prison. "There certainly should be imprisonment if the convicted person has a prior record of convictions," he said. The President graduated from the school, which was celebrating its 150th anniversary.

Violent crime "obsesses America," Ford said. "I sense, and I think the American people sense, that we are facing a basic and serious problem of disregard of the law." Referring to Watergate, he stated, "We have recently suffered the national disgrace of law-breaking in high places," and "There is no way to inculcate in society the spirit of law if society's leaders are not scrupulously law-abiding." He said that he had made "it a matter of the highest priority to restore to the executive branch decency, honesty and adherence to the law at all levels." Ford also spoke of the need for prison reform and humane treatment of prisoners. He advocated less use of plea bargaining and a drive against repeated offenders.

The Washington Post
Times Herald
Washington. D.C., May 5, 1975

IN SEVERAL SUBTLE and important ways, President Ford has been guiding the country away from the policies and practices of the Nixon administration. He has not always been successful in making the distinction clear in the public mind. But it is obvious that he is deeply engaged in a process of becoming his own President, of coming out from the shadow of the tragedy that preceded him. The other evening at Yale Law School, Mr. Ford took a giant step. The subject was crime, and his words were badly needed. There will be those who will maintain that the President didn't go far enough to rid the subject of its Nixonian overtones, but it is fair to say that Mr. Ford has set an encouraging course.

Richard Nixon came to power with the words law and order ringing from his lips. He made that cry such a slogan among his white suburbanite Republican supporters that hardly anyone would have guessed that the principal victims of crime in America are urban blacks, especially poor black women. From the empty rhetoric, the Nixon administration moved on to programs. The main program was the Law Enforcement Assistance Administration's hardware distribution gimmick and such constitutional novelties as preventive detention and no-knock warrants. The result of the LEAA program is that hundreds of communities now have helicopters and submachine guns, sophisticated radios and fancy uniforms, but the crime rates are way up. When the preventive detention issue got down to real cases, it turned out that many of the people this approach intended to keep in jail weren't getting out anyway; it was largely unworkable and inherently questionable. As for no-knock warrants, they turned out to be a menace to police officers and citizens alike, and very few law enforcement professionals want anything to do with such practices anymore. So much of what Mr. Nixon said he wanted to do turned out to be wasted effort in real terms. Its basic result was to polarize and mislead the public.

It is for all those reasons that Mr. Ford is to be applauded for his Yale speech. "In thinking about this problem (of crime), I do not seek vindictive punishment of the criminal, but protection of the innocent victim," the President said. Then he added:

The victims are my primary concern. That is

why I do not talk about law and order, and why I return to the constitutional phrase, insuring domestic tranquility.

When you think of a President's speaking of "domestic tranquility" as a goal, you are likely to be reassured that his purpose is to solve a problem and not to make political capital from the fear that exists among citizens.

And Mr. Ford put his finger on the right place in the system where the breakdown occurs, in the criminal justice system. It is here that overcrowding and poor organization make it possible for the guilty to plead lesser offenses and "walk," while the poor, irrespective of guilt or innocence, rot in the detention facilities and explode with each change of season. The result is that there is little justice in that system, as the President pointed out. Serious offenders are on the street because the system makes it difficult to keep track of the most dangerous felons: those who are the violent repeaters. Mr. Ford called for a system in which punishment is swift and sure for the dangerous felon. He offered federal leadership in the effort to make more judges, prosecutors and legal defenders available.

This is a markedly different tone, and probably different in substance, too, from the Nixon effort. We will rely on Attorney General Edward H. Levi to elaborate for us on how the administration intends to implement Mr. Ford's reasoned approach. We have permitted our criminal justice system to deteriorate to the point where in some cities referring to it as "justice" at all is a joke. There is little justice for the accused usually and—much more important—none for society. If the Ford administration sets as its goal assisting the states and cities with realistic remedies for the bottlenecks and for the overcrowded facilities, that will be a major factor in the fight against crime.

But Mr. Ford did not restrict himself to the problem of street crime. He said he hoped to set a new example with respect to crime in high places. He said he realized it was impossible for our society to make any serious inroads in our crime problems if people see a lack of respect for the law among their leaders. When you put that statement beside his enlightened sense of priorities in the criminal justice system, you begin to see that on this issue, Mr. Ford is shaking his shadow, and none too soon.

The Virginian-Pilot
Norfolk, Va., April 29, 1975

In Nixonian code, "law 'n' order" meant get those dirty hippies and uppity blacks off the streets. President Ford, evoking if not invoking the phrase at a Yale Law School convocation last week, restored some of the dictionary meaning to the operative nouns.

Partly sketching proposals he will lay before Congress in a few weeks, Mr. Ford said more judges and prosecutors are needed and brakes should be applied to the abused plea-bargaining practice that frees chronic criminals to ply their trade. His legislative suggestions are expected to include mandatory prison for criminals who use guns or other force.

Mr. Ford's chief concern was with "persistent criminals," the repeat offenders who are the rank and file of the street-crime army. His solution was the one espoused by James Q. Wilson, the Harvard government professor and penology theorist: put them most emphatically in prison, if only for one or three or five years. They may or may not repent their misdeeds while behind bars, Mr. Wilson's reasoning runs, but crime has to drop as more of its practitioners are incarcerated. The logic is simplistic but the argument is appealing.

As he did in his recent press conference, Mr. Ford in his speech put the responsibility for containing crime where it belongs, with the states. Which is not to say that the Federal Government can't contribute materially to the effort, specifically by a meaningful attempt to halt the abominable traffic in handguns.

The gun lobby notwithstanding, the country should close down the shooting gallery. It should be made harder, if not impossible, to translate a murderous impulse to reality by possession of a pistol. Legislation now before Congress would speed that end. Mr. Ford's influence could be a weighty factor in favor of passage. It is regrettable that he did not exercise it while he was on the subject of law 'n' order.

The Seattle Times
Seattle, Wash., April 29, 1975

AS the United States prepares to celebrate its 200th year, the sorry fact is that the nation has fallen far short of meeting the constitutional objective of domestic tranquilety.

"Violent crime on our streets and in our homes makes fear pervasive," President Ford said last week in a Yale Law School address that articulated the most pressing concerns of millions of his fellow citizens.

Although Mr. Ford on this occasion was a lawyer talking to legal scholars, he did not wander in the thickets of legal theory.

He pointed out that perpetrators of violent crimes are very few in number. Most Americans have no reason to fear other Americans.

"The relatively few persistent criminals, who cause so much misery and fear," the President said, "are the core of the problem. The rest of the American people have a right to protection from their violence."

THIS right—the right to protection—is the very right that has so often been obscured by obsessive concerns in some legal quarters with the rights of criminals.

Now of course President Ford did not go to the Yale Law School to advocate that criminals, more than anyone else, should be denied their rights.

What he did urge was that

"virtually all of those convicted of a violent crime should be sent to prison," and that "there certainly should be imprisonment if the convicted person has a prior record of convictions."

Mr. Ford noted that much of the responsibility for crime control rests with state and local authorities.

But among steps that could be taken at the federal level, he observed, the federal code could be modified to make more sentences mandatory "and therefore punishment more certain for those convicted of all violent crimes."

We suggest, too, that the example set at the federal level is important in setting a standard for state lawmakers.

THE President rightly observed that protection of the public, not vindictive punishment, is the objective. In fact, he urged humane treatment of convicts in prison, with loss of liberty the chief punishment.

The crux of the matter is that most serious offenders are repeaters. And, in Mr. Ford's words, "We owe it to their victims, past, present and future, to get them off the streets."

"This," he added, "is just everyday common sense."

Not vindictiveness. Not mob justice. Just everyday common sense. Is that too much to ask of our lawmakers and judges?

DAILY NEWS
New York, N.Y., May 5, 1975

"I am urging that virtually all of those convicted of a violent crime should be sent to prison . . ."

At Yale Law School recently, President Gerald Ford did much to clear away the woolly thinking about the soaring problem of "street crime . . . crime that invades our neighborhoods and homes . . . murders, brutal violence that makes us fearful of strangers and afraid to go out in the night."

The President asked not "vindictive punishment" but protection of the "innocent victim." We agree. Victims have become the battered children of society, all too often overlooked by judges with hemorrhaging hearts and mushy heads. It's time we cried over them and not the criminal.

THE ATLANTA CONSTITUTION
Atlanta, Ga., April 30, 1975

President Ford's call for mandatory sentences for those twice convicted of violent crimes reflects the nation's concern and his concern for the shocking crime rate that afflicts us.

The President spoke at Yale, where he had earned a law degree, and three members of the law school faculty there expressed opposition to mandatory sentences after he spoke. No doubt when he presents his anticrime program to Congress in a month or so this as well as other points will be open to heated debate.

Criminal violence is actually a worldwide problem. The current debate in the U.S. over restoring the death penalty has been echoed in Great Britain and other countries which had done away with it. In our country 29 states have sought to restore the death penalty by revising laws to meet the Supreme Court's ruling that its application in the past has been discriminatory.

Are there any great nations in the free world in which the crime problem is firmly under control? Yes. Japan has a very low rate of violent crime, and the government attributes the low rate to three factors: efficient police and strict controls on weapons and drugs. President Ford didn't say in his Yale speech what his program would advocate in these areas, although his attorney general has proposed limited gun control in high crime areas.

"Most serious offenders are repeaters," the President said. "We owe it to their victims, past present and future, to get them off the streets. This is just everyday common sense."

Mandatory sentences may be part of the answer. But all law-abiding Americans will agree with the President that something must be done quickly to get violent criminals off the streets. It is a disgrace to a great nation that so many of its citizens are afraid to venture out on the streets of our large cities, Atlanta included.

The Cleveland Press
Cleveland, Ohio, April 29, 1975

There was an impressive role of deep determination in President Ford's address at Yale Law School last weekend, and it should bring hope to Americans who live in increasing fear of violent crime.

He urged that virtually all persons convicted of violent crime, particularly where a gun is used, be sent to prison, and most especially when the criminal has a prior record of conviction.

He argued that today there are too many short sentences for violent crime, or no sentence at all, and too much reliance on plea bargaining. He noted that half the persons convicted of felonies in recent years in New York didn't go to jail at all.

And he said that if fewer persons convicted of minor crimes were jailed there would be more room for felons.

But it was when he referred to the scandal of Watergate — without mentioning it by name — that Ford received his big applause.

"We have recently suffered the national disgrace of lawbreaking in high places" and "I have made it a matter of the highest priority to restore to the Executive Branch decency, honesty and adherence to the law at all levels," he said.

"There is no way to inculcate in society the spirit of law if society's leaders are not scrupulously law-abiding."

It was interesting that the President said he would not use the term "law and order" which former President Nixon often used to describe the war on crime. Rather, Ford said, "I return to the constitutional phrase (in the preamble)—insuring 'domestic tranquility'."

Certainly the President's address was high-minded and sincere. It remains now for the nation's law enforcement agencies — especially judges — to do their duty in helping reverse the increasingly alarming trend toward more violent crimes, and thus help assure that domestic tranquility for which we all yearn.

(FOOTNOTE: A recent poll taken by American University found that half of the residents of President Ford's present home town — Washington, D.C. — said they are afraid to walk alone in their own neighborhoods at night.)

The Dispatch

Columbus, Ohio, April 29, 1975

PRESIDENT FORD will find the vast majority of Americans in full agreement with his contention there has been failure to provide the domestic tranquility guaranteed by the U.S. Constitution.

Nor will there be appreciable dissent against his argument that the skyrocketing crime rate cannot be expected to come down until persons who habitually commit most of the predatory crimes are kept in prison.

THE NATION'S Chief Executive will send to Congress in June a proposal for major reforms regarding the sentencing of persons convicted of crimes of violence such as murder, robbery and rape.

Mr. Ford's main recommendation will be imposition of mandatory prison sentences for repeat criminals and he will urge legislated imposition of prison sentences for "virtually all of those convicted of a violent crime especially if a gun was involved or danger or injury" to a victim.

THE PRESIDENT correctly looked at the broad picture, observing punishment should not be vindictive

He said he would recommend additional federal funds for more judges, prosecutors and public defenders along with better prison facilities.

A significant statement by the President was that the "popular notion that trial follows arrest is a misconception in a vast majority of cases."

VERY FEW cases come to trial, he said, adding that the reason is plea bargaining.

Imprisonment, said Mr. Ford, "too seldom follows conviction for a felony. . . .Virtually all of those convicted of a violent crime should be sent to prison."

THE PRESIDENT'S forthcoming recommendations, of course, will apply only to federal law enforcement. However, he was correct in urging state and local law agencies and courts to seriously consider alteration of their sentencing procedures.

After all, guarantees of domestic tranquility are the burden of state, county and city agencies no less than they are of the federal establishment.

The Boston Globe

Boston, Mass., April 28, 1975

President Ford has thrown his weight on the side of mandatory minimum sentences for certain violent crimes. And his suggestion will probably be more warmly received by the general public than it was at Yale where he made it last week in a speech before a notably skeptical audience of lawyers, judges, politicians and students.

After all, crime is on the rise, the statistics say. People are apprehensive and they want answers. Mr. Ford's remarks provided one answer at least. But the wisdom of his approach is as dubious as the rising tide of crime is intimidating.

Convicted felons, especially those involved in violent crimes, rarely inspire the public's sympathy. But the element of compassion is inseparable from our notion of justice and it is applied by judges in ordering appropriate penalties for crimes committed. To the extent that mandatory sentences ignore differing circumstances under which crimes are committed, they diminish the ability of compassion to play its part in the disposition of justice.

Furthermore, there is no evidence that mandatory statutes are effective countermeasures to rising crime and many indications are that they are counterproductive.

The National Advisory Commission of Criminal Justice says mandatory sentences "hinder correction programming without any corresponding benefit," that they are "wasteful of resources" where they require incarceration longer than necessary and that they retard an offender's chances of being successfully reintegrated into the community.

The President is correct in his concern for the protection of society from those whose antisocial behavior is violent and repeated Judges and juries are concerned with this, too, despite the often-heard complaint that offenders are being "coddled." But the President would do better to lend his weight and prestige to judicial reform, concentrating on court backlogs and workloads, the inadequate number of judges, the handling of records and documents and the overall administration and management of courts, a badly neglected imperative.

This is particularly relevant in Massachusetts where the median time to dispose of criminal cases is the longest in the First US Court District and one of the longest nationwide. It would be more useful for the President and his Administration to address this weakness in the criminal justice system than to lead us into the underbrush of easy answers and emotionally appealing solutions.

OKLAHOMA CITY TIMES

Oklahoma City, Okla., April 28, 1975

LOSS OF LIBERTY should be the chief punishment assessed against criminals, President Ford said at a Yale University Law School dinner Friday. He added: "Most serious offenders are repeaters. We owe it to their victims, past, present and future, to get them off the streets."

Oklahoma City Police Chief I.G. Purser and other law enforcement officials have often said they are arresting the same persons over and over. The continued rise in crime is evidence that our present easy parole and weak rehabilitation system are not holding the line on criminal activity.

The legislature has noted this and a bill has been introduced to require criminals to serve at least a year or one fifth of their terms. However, this bill is in committee and this late in the session, it may not reach the floor. If it does, it will have a hard time, because of the number of defense attorneys who are members of the legislature.

IN A SPEECH before the Anti-Crime Council of Oklahoma, Inc., Purser last week cited case after case where persons convicted of felony crimes were back on the streets in a few weeks or months.

President Ford said: "The crime rate will go down if persons who habitually commit most of the predatory crimes are kept in prison."

Purser pointed out that besides thousands of prisoners who were released on parole last year, Oklahoma had 144 "walkaways," prisoners who simply depart from minimum security facilities with no one to stop them, or prisoners who don't return from authorized shopping trips, speaking tours or work assignments.

PURSER SAID more officers are needed to provide adequate police protection and the President emphasized that penal facilities need to be overhauled. Both are right, especially in Oklahoma, but neither will bring down the crime rate as long as the system frees law violators before their victims recover.

Courts need strengthening, too, but most of all, we need to stop turning the criminals loose to commit more crimes. Many citizens no doubt would favor a minimum sentence law, but the legislature is not likely to pass it unless members hear a strong demand for it from their constituents.

The Des Moines Register

Des Moines, Iowa, May 2, 1975

President Ford has come out in support of sending to prison "virtually all of those convicted of a violent crime." He said imprisonment should be mandatory for one to five years "especially if a gun was involved or there was other substantial danger of injury to a person or persons."

The President believes that such an imprisonment policy would serve as a deterrent to lawbreakers and protect society from violence-prone offenders. The relatively short terms he advocates would provide minimal protection. Many prisoners would be released under his program sooner than they are released now under parole.

A mandatory imprisonment policy would prohibit judges from granting probation and would require a huge expenditure for maximum-security prisons to house the swelling numbers of inmates. The existing prison system has failed dismally to prevent recidivism. The President has no basis for believing that his program would accomplish anything except the waste of hundreds of millions of dollars on custodial facilities and guards.

In calling for mandatory imprisonment, President Ford is ignoring the advice of such tough law-and-order types as Chief Justice Warren Burger, who has stated:

"If anywhere in the whole spectrum of criminal justice fresh ideas deserve sober analysis, the sentencing and correctional area ranks high on the list. But it has been widely accepted that mandatory sentences for crimes do not best serve the ends of the criminal justice system."

The President's Crime Commission in 1967 called for criminal code revision with a view "to removing mandatory minimum prison terms, long maximum prison terms, and ineligibility for probation and parole."

The President's Commission was sharply critical of the imbalance in the nation's spending on corrections, citing the two-thirds of expenditures being used to house the one-third of inmates in institutions. The commission called for a redirected effort to develop community-based correctional services.

President Ford's suggestion is a prescription for creating still greater imbalance. It reflects a turn-the-clock-back incarceration philosophy that would cause the government to pump still more money into warehousing people at the expense of programs for assisting them.

The President said he wants to put gun-users in prison, but nowhere in his address about crime did he suggest the need for government action to curb access to guns. This omission, together with his appeal to the emotions for mandatory imprisonment, suggests that the President may be more interested in playing politics with the crime issue than in dealing realistically with the needs of the criminal justice system.

ST. LOUIS POST-DISPATCH
St. Louis, Mo., May 4, 1975

If the crime legislation message which President Ford sends to Congress in the next few weeks reflects the sentiments he expressed in a speech at Yale Law School the other day, the Administration is not likely to provide much helpful guidance on what the lawmakers can do to control crime. Mr. Ford accurately characterized rising crime rates and disregard for law as a complex problem and then proceeded to offer a simplistic answer: see that "all, or practically all, of those actually convicted be sent to prison."

Although studies have indicated that the certainty of imprisonment can have a deterrent effect, an examination of the statistics of crime clearly indicates that the fact of imprisonment is anything but a cure for crime. Since most crimes are committed by people who have been in prison, the record shows that prisons themselves are part of the problem. Instead of enabling their inmates to carry on a more productive life after release, they actually educate them in ways of crime and turn them out less able to cope than they were before — in part, because they have learned nothing useful while incarcerated and in part, because society generally is unwilling to accept former prisoners in jobs or in other respected pursuits. Lacking in skills and rejected in his quest for legitimate employment, the ex-prisoner turns in desperation to the employment he knows — crime.

In the face of these widely recognized conditions, the President was being discouragingly unimaginative in advancing as his key proposal more mandatory prison sentences for those who commit violent crimes. It is distressing also to have Norman A. Carlson, director of the Federal Bureau of Prisons, saying that the federal system should return to the more traditional methods of punishment — methods that haven't worked.

Although it is true enough that imprisonment away from society seems to be the only treatment suitable for some types of violent offenders, such treatment hardly offers a promising solution for the nation's serious crime problem. The solution is obviously complex. But it includes a major effort to keep young offenders out of the prison system so that they will not be educated in crime, a substantial program of training for available jobs and, most important of all, a reduction in general levels of poverty and unemployment, which recent statistics have shown have a direct relationship to crime.

Newsday
Garden City, N.Y., May 6, 1975

President Ford recently suggested that violent crime would be less of a problem if more violent criminals were sent to jail. In fact, he argued that "virtually all of those convicted of a violent crime should be sent to prison." And he cited statistics to show that only three per cent of those indicted in Manhattan during a recent three-year period were convicted after trial, and that half of the felony convictions in a New York State study resulted in jail sentences.

Few cases go to trial in New York because so many are resolved by plea-bargaining. That's not because laws or judges are lenient, but because court calendars are full. We're inclined to agree that violent criminals belong behind bars, if only to protect their potential victims. But mandatory sentences aren't going to put them there if the courts are so jammed that their cases never come to trial.

BUFFALO EVENING NEWS
Buffalo, N.Y., April 28, 1975

We doubt that many Americans would disagree with President Ford's theme, voiced at Yale University, that the country is "facing a basic and serious problem of disregard of the law."

Nor would they disagree with his assertion that the problem, too often simplistically politicized in campaign rhetoric, is in reality very complex, that it demands a "precise and effective solution."

Where people begin to divide, in part because the answers are not measurably clear, is over the main causes for the increased crime and the most effective solutions.

One contributing factor, however, can be the example of others, as the President seemed to emphasize when, in an obvious allusion to Watergate, he forthrightly remarked that "crime in high places . . . sets an example that makes it all the more difficult to foster a law-abiding spirit among ordinary citizens." His pledge to restore "decency, honesty and adherence for law at all levels" of the federal executive branch can surely contribute immeasurably in this regard.

Beyond that, President Ford advanced several specific ideas which reflect an enlightened balance in protecting society from the outrages of crime, although their precise definition must await his subsequent proposals to Congress.

Something must be done, as we have said many times, about the overloaded courts and the prolonged delays in determining the guilt or innocence of the accused. The legal community needs to examine the use of plea-bargaining, and, as the President said, reform of the prison system "is long overdue." We have reservations about mandatory sentences that tie the hands of a judge in particular cases, but we agree with Mr. Ford that those convicted of violent crimes — especially those involving repeat offenders, or those in which guns were used or "substantial danger of injury" to others resulted — should be sent to prison.

These are the crimes that most frighten people. These are the crimes that most gravely threaten the rights and lives of the victims. These are the crimes for which society most looks to law-enforcement for vital protection. These are the criminals displaying the most persistent anti-social behavior. For them, justice means leniency least of all.

Not that such measures by themselves will solve all the complex problems of crime. There are deeper issues, such as what kinds of marginal conduct should be included or exempted from criminal definitions. That returns to the importance of public attitudes. If the vast majority of people share common values in a society, and if they know the laws and enforcement processes mirror those common values, then that attitude itself both deters crime and promotes support for the just enforcement of those laws.

THE CHRISTIAN SCIENCE MONITOR
Boston, Mass., April 30, 1975

Alumnus Ford's Yale Law School speech on crime last week was billed as a forerunner of a presidential message to Congress on the subject. Such a message will be enhanced if its proposals confirm the sensitive and broad-gauged approach to the problem indicated by the President's words at Yale — rather than the headlined impression of simplistic punitive crackdown from which he sought to separate himself.

Politicians may say Mr. Ford tried to have it both ways — to woo his conservative critics with statements permitting hard-line headlines about mandatory prison sentences, and at the same time to be able to claim a middle ground with a context favoring prison reform as part of the "precise and effective solution" demanded by a complex problem.

Cynics may note that, on the very day that Mr. Ford spoke of the "national disgrace of lawbreaking in high places," a federal judge was setting aside the two-month sentence of a congressman convicted of campaign law violations.

Yet there is no doubt that this President meant it when he pledged the restoration of decency, honesty, and adherence to law at all levels of the executive branch. And he set himself another worthy goal when he implied a turning away from the previous administration's attitude of attacking criminals "without pity": "I do not seek vindictive punishment of the criminal but rather protection for the innocent victim. The victims are my primary concern."

The measure of protection provided by imprisoning people after they have committed crimes must be weighed along with the protection provided by social, economic, and educational measures to reduce the causes of crime. Even the criminal who must be put behind bars needs to have the improved prison facilities recommended by Mr. Ford and the opportunity for enlightened rehabilitation.

FORD CALLS FOR MANDATORY PRISON, STRICTER GUN CONTROL PROVISIONS

President Ford submitted to Congress June 19 an anti-crime program changing priority from the rights of criminals to concern for "the victims and potential victims." It called for mandatory jail sentences for certain crimes and for tighter gun-control provisions. Ford's April 25 speech at Yale University also called for mandatory prison for persons convicted of violent crimes.

The mandatory jail terms were to be imposed on persons committing crimes using a dangerous weapon, on persons committing such serious crimes as aircraft hijacking, kidnaping and trafficking in hard drugs and on persons who were repeat offenders who committed federal crimes whether with or without a weapon that caused personal injury or had that potential. Exceptions would be extended to those who were under 18 years of age at the time of the crime, were mentally impaired, acting under "substantial duress" or implicated by others and whose participation was "very minor."

The President said in his message that "there should be no doubt in the minds of those who commit violent crimes—especially crimes involving harm to others—that they will be sent to prison if convicted under legal processes that are fair, prompt and certain."

On gun control, the President asked for a ban on the manufacture or sale of cheap handguns known as "Saturday night specials," and he urged tighter enforcement of current gun control laws. He said he had ordered intensified investigative efforts in the country's 10 largest metropolitan areas and increased manpower to deal exclusively with gun control. Ford reaffirmed, however, that he was "unalterably opposed to federal registration of guns or the licensing of gun owners."

The Detroit News
Detroit, Mich., June 22, 1975

Of all the measures urged by President Ford in his request for sweeping changes in federal crime laws, none is more important than his proposal to impose mandatory prison sentences on violent criminals.

Society can spend billions on police systems and apprehension but the benefits will be slight if the courts fail to follow through. Mandatory sentences, wisely applied, can pay the taxpayer a return on his investment in law enforcement.

Put the emphasis on "wisely applied."

Studies of factors affecting crime rates show that the certainty of punishment deters crime—provided the severity of punishment fits the crime committed. If a mandatory sentence seems too harsh, the jury may not convict, even if it knows in its heart that the accused is guilty.

James Q. Wilson, who has served on presidential task forces on crime and enforcement, observes in his book, "Thinking About Crime":

"The more severe the sentence, the greater the bargaining power of the accused, and the greater the likelihood he will be charged with a lesser offense. Extremely long mandatory minimum sentences do not always strengthen the hand of society; they often strengthen the hand of the criminal instead."

Of course, the complete absence of mandatory sentences too often allows the courts to turn back onto the streets dangerous criminals who should be taken out of circulation. Mr. Ford's proposal would help correct that.

Every time a leader suggests firm measures to cut the ever-growing crime rate, he opens himself to the charge of appealing to vindictiveness and racism. Thus, President Ford is criticized for having used the term "domestic tranquility" several times in his message on crime.

The implication of the criticism is that he used the term as a code word similar to the term "law and order" so often repeated by his predecessors. Well, perhaps.

However, we see no reason why the President needs to make the term into a code word. Lord knows that "domestic tranquility" is at least as urgent and as valid a goal today as when the term was written into the preamble of the United States Constitution.

In our opinion, the critics are being hypercritical and supersubtle toward an earnest effort by Mr. Ford to do something about a major national problem.

The Chattanooga Times
Chattanooga, Tenn., June 24, 1975

The sensible response to President Ford's anti-crime proposals is to express every hope the plan will work as it is intended with the reminder that no single approach to the problem is likely to prove effective.

Mr. Ford made a good many recommendations, but the emphasis was on the need for mandatory imprisonment for conviction on certain crimes of violence, and the imposition of minimum sentences for others.

The reasoning behind it is that lenient treatment of defendants is the main reason for a rising crime rate and that harsher punishment by the courts will be the most effective deterrent.

In commenting on the program, Atty. Gen. Edward Levi confirmed the viewpoint. Mandatory sentences are necessary, in part, he said, because "judges have failed to live up to their part of the job." But the administration blames some of this on judicial hesitation to impose jail sentences "because they (the judges) consider prison conditions inhumane."

The President lends some weight to this fear by citing overcrowded prisons as one reason for administration willingness to undertake a crash program to improve penal institutions and to build newer and smaller detention facilities to replace the antiquated prisons to which inmates are now sentenced.

Atty. Gen. Levi guessed it might cost $12 billion altogether; he didn't say where the money was coming from.

The point, all too often overlooked, is that the commission of a crime is but one in a series of inexorably related events.

Something triggered the misdeed; could it have been prevented? As little as we think of it, this is where the "rights of the victim" lie — the right to go about unmolested and secure.

The victim is hurt or suffers financial loss; compensation, as Mr. Ford suggests, would be a wise and humane action.

The suspect is tried. Does he get a prompt trial or are dockets so overcrowded that justice delayed becomes justice denied?

He is found guilty. Are there mitigating circumstances which warrant probation or parole? Are probationary programs well planned and adequately staffed? If he goes to prison, what kind of person will he be when he gets out, as he must sooner or later? Will he be viciously inclined to take up a life of crime again, or will rehabilitative programs have reached him?

He is freed, having served his sentence. Does the community turn its back on him or give him a decent chance?

Strict law enforcement, rigorous prosecution, just punishment for the guilty, and humane treatment of the deserving are all part of the picture. None can be emphasized to the neglect of the others, if we are to resist with success a rising crime rate.

Portland Press Herald

Portland, Me., June 24, 1975

There is much that is commendable in President Ford's proposals aimed at reducing the amount of violent crime in the United States.

Serious crimes in this country went up by 17 per cent last year, just about the largest increase in a half century.

While restating his opposition to "federal registration of guns or gun owners," the President has put forth several sensible suggestions for bringing under some control the type of weapons most often used in crimes of violence.

He calls for mandatory prison sentences for persons committing crimes while armed. He wants to tighten restrictions for licensing gun dealers, ban the manufacture and sale of cheap "Saturday night Specials" and institute a waiting period before delivering a handgun to a buyer.

We have supported this last proposal whenever it has been considered by the Maine Legislature, and we support it now that it has been presented at the federal level.

We also endorse Mr. Ford's suggestion for compensating victims of violent crimes. The President strikes a responsive chord in many Americans when he maintains that the law has concentrated on the rights of accused persons at the expense of the victims of crime, The concept of equal justice is left in tatters so long as that imbalance is allowed to persist. Compensation of victims would be one step toward achieving such a balance.

In truth, as Mr. Ford acknowledges, the federal government is limited in its ability to attack crimes of violence directly. For the most part such crimes fall under state and local law enforcement jurisdictions.

But Washington can provide the inspiration and leadership in the struggle to curb crime in America, and we feel that the President is making an honest effort to do just that.

The Dallas Morning News

Dallas, Tex., June 23, 1975

THOSE FORGOTTEN Americans—the victims of crimes—were remembered in President Ford's crime message.

While the development of law in recent years has concentrated on protecting the rights of the criminals, the President pointed out, the Constitution also pledges to provide "domestic tranquillity." And that feat can hardly be accomplished with the crime rate spiraling upward at a 17 per cent a year clip.

Ford outlined a broad federal program to crack down on the lawless. But Washington's ability to cut crime is limited. It can only lead. Most street crime—mugging, armed robbery, rape, car theft—is not within the federal government's jurisdiction. It is a local responsibility.

But the federal government can write model laws that can be followed by state lawmakers. Among Ford's proposals were: mandatory sentences for perpetrators of violent crimes; court reform to speed prosecution; revision of the criminal code and standardizing of sentences; prison reform, and strict enforcement of existing gun laws.

It is interesting that while the President was tossing the ball back into the lap of the states and local communities, most already had dropped it.

The Texas Legislature, for example, considered in some form most of the President's proposed reforms in the criminal justice system. None passed.

On the local level, the Dallas County commissioners court is in the process of cutting—not increasing—the sheriff's budget, as it did the district attorney's earlier in the year. And the City of Dallas faces a tax hike to increase the police budget.

While the President's words were pleasing, the real action must come on the state and local levels of government. Elected officials must strengthen the criminal justice system. Money and new laws are needed, plus changes in attitudes toward victims and criminals.

If recent events are any indication, however, those officials closest to the public are the least likely to act. President Ford has urged the federal government to provide leadership. If it does, Texas will need some followship.

The Evening Bulletin

Philadelphia, Pa., June 23, 1975

The basic thrust of the anticrime proposals sent to Congress Thursday by President Ford is certain to have widespread public appeal. With the nation's crime rate — which jumped 17 percent last year — still on the rise and with the issue of crime second only to the economy on the list of national concerns, Mr. Ford's determination to take a "tough" stand on the issue is most surely welcome.

Few people would argue with the President's call for swift and strong action against individuals who commit violent crimes and, especially, against repeat offenders. One of the measures sought by Mr. Ford would require that persons in both categories receive mandatory minimum jail sentences.

Another proposal, which has already been adopted by 11 states, would compensate crime victims for losses sustained through bodily injury up to $50,000. Other measures outlined by the President would place added restrictions on handguns referred to as "Saturday night specials," extend the life of the Law Enforcement Assistance Administration and authorize $1.3 billion for its operation, and permit review and revision by appellate judges of prison sentences handed down by lower court judges.

While Mr. Ford's plan is similar in some respects to the "crackdown" promised by the Nixon Administration, Mr. Ford has wisely avoided the strident rhetoric of his predecessor — stressing the need for "domestic tranquility" rather than "law and order."

It also is encouraging that Mr. Ford recognizes, in principle at least, the need for reform of the judicial system as part of the attack on crime. Under the measures proposed by the President, some first offenders would be placed in rehabilitation programs rather than jail through a system of pretrial diversion.

In some areas, the Ford Administration proposals reflect the thinking of members of Congress. Some of the proposals already are contained in an omnibus crime bill under consideration in the Senate.

While it is important for the President and Congress to provide the impetus for more stringent laws to deal with crime, to insure greater protection for crime victims and to upgrade the quality of the failing criminal justice system, the impact of such initiatives will be limited.

Mr. Ford noted in his message to Congress that the primary task of combatting crime rests with state and local officials, and statistics emphasize the point. Federal prosecutions account for only a miniscule part of the nation's prosecutions each year, less than 3 percent in 1973.

In order for the proposed federal action to have a significant impact, state and local governments will have to enact similar measures, as the President urged. However, even then the effect of the laws will be limited as long as elected leaders at all levels refuse to enact adequate gun control laws, as long as the flaws in the criminal justice and penal systems go uncorrected and the host of social ills that contribute to crime remain unchecked.

The News and Courier

Charleston, S.C., June 22, 1975

An anti-crime bill submitted by President Ford is described as tough. It is certainly innovative. Besides prescribing mandatory sentences for armed criminals who commit violence, Mr. Ford's measure also incorporates compensatory payments from the government to victims of such crimes.

Those features and others will no doubt receive applause over a wide spectrum of people who believe both that criminals are being treated too gently and victims too casually. Looked at in the light of limitations of federal authority, however, Mr. Ford's proposal loses a lot of its promise. As the President himself says, the federal government can't touch many of the crimes that are causing much of the grief and sorrow these days. Murder, rape and assault, for example, continue to be primarily local and state affairs. There is no way of handling most such cases in federal courts.

The President nevertheless hopes that passage of his bill will serve as a model for state legislation. He is offering leadership, he says, toward lowering the crime rate.

It is a commendable approach, but uncertain in its promise. States certainly need to be encouraged to take stricter measures against criminals. On the whole, however, it is not presidential leadership that state legislatures respond to, but demands from the folks back home. If law-abiding citizens want real action against the common run of murderers, rapists and thugs, they can't count on a good example from Washington to produce it. They must get it from their own state legislators — and the sooner, the better, judging from the way the crime curve is rising.

The Charlotte Observer

Charlotte, N.C., June 24, 1975

The anti-crime proposals made by President Ford last week seem reasonable, for the most part; and that reasonable approach — accompanied by a minimum of political bombast — is in itself encouraging.

Crime is an emotional topic, as anyone who has followed the North Carolina Legislature's muddled debates on bills involving prisons and sentences can attest. Almost everyone holds strong opinions on how to deal with crime and criminals; yet those who have looked most closely at crime generally agree that we know little about what causes it and less about how to prevent it.

Given that ignorance, the wisest way to proceed, we think, is by a series of temperate steps designed to reach specific, attainable goals.

The legislation outlined by President Ford seems to fit that description. He would reduce the disparity in sentencing by making prison sentences mandatory for career criminals and those who commit violent crimes. The idea, as Attorney General Edward Levi explained, is that for many crimes a prison sentence need not be long, but it should be certain. Further, Mr. Ford would empower appellate courts to review sentences and change them, if necessary. He would attack organized crime by making racketeering a federal offense. He would crack down on armed crimes by providing tougher sentences for criminals who use weapons and by making it more difficult to obtain cheap handguns.

For those who remember the Nixon Administration's disregard for constitutional processes, Mr. Ford sounded an ominous note when he said that it is time to put less emphasis on the rights of criminals and more on the rights of victims.

But there is nothing in the proposals we have seen to indicate that Mr. Ford wants to trample on anyone's rights. Instead, his concern for crime victims takes a concrete form. He recommends a federal program to compensate persons who are physically injured by criminals. Depending on the extent of their injuries, victims of federal crimes could receive benefits of up to $50,000.

Our chief regret is that Mr. Ford's view of the crime problem was so limited. For instance, the appalling crime rate in urban ghettoes might be influenced by the fact that in some of them, nearly half the young men are unemployed. Providing jobs for those men might do more to reduce the crime rate than any change in the courts or law enforcement. In any case, modifying federal criminal laws is unlikely to influence the crime rate very much, since only about two per cent of the criminal prosecutions each year are for federal crimes. But changes in federal social policy might have a broad impact on the conditions that contribute to some crimes. We hope Mr. Ford now will turn his attention to that need.

DESERET NEWS

Salt Lake City, Utah, June 21, 1975

Although most of the measures President Ford proposed Thursday against crime are sensible, Americans should not expect too much in the way of dramatic results, even if the package is approved by Congress.

President Ford is deeply concerned about the problem. He noted the nation has been "far from successful in dealing with the sort of crime that obsesses America day and night." But under the Constitution, major power and responsibility for most crimes are vested in state and local governments.

The President proposed mandatory jail sentences for perpetrators of serious federal crimes such as kidnapping and airplane hijacking. Fines for other federal crimes would be increased.

But most murders, rapes, muggings, holdups and breakins are not federal crimes. They violate state laws, and are the responsibility of state and local agencies.

The President would increase the scope of federal law against organized crime. But the bulk of the crime that, in the President's words, "invades our neighborhoods and our homes," is not the work of organized racketeers but of disorganized local crooks.

Congress was asked to ban the manufacture and sale of cheap handguns. The President's proposal would also require a waiting period between purchase and delivery of a handgun. President Ford rejected federal measures to register guns or gun owners. Thus, the major decisions on gun control would be left to the states. This is a moderate policy, and it deserves support.

The only really new suggestion in the package is its weakest part. A $7.6 million fund would be set up to compensate victims of federal crimes. Insurance companies already offer policies that provide some compensation. And the measure would do nothing to reduce crime.

Despite its limits, the President's plan moves in the correct direction of sterner handling of criminals. But as the President noted, "the level of crime will not be substantially reduced unless state and local governments themselves enact strong measures."

Within the limits of his powers, the President has pointed the way to better crime control. It is now up to state and local governments to follow.

Pittsburgh Post-Gazette

Pittsburgh, Pa., June 24, 1975

IN HIS first major pronouncement on what used to be called the "law-and-order" issue, President Ford has endorsed a popular as well as correct view — that the main emphasis in the fight against crime in the streets is to get criminals off the streets.

To the credit of the President and Atty. Gen. Edward Levi, however, the Ford administration's first proposals on street crime eschew confident rhetoric for a recognition that the crime problem isn't succeptible to speedy solution.

This realism is evident, first of all, in Mr. Ford's emphasis on the fact — conveniently ignored by his predecessor in anticrime stump speeches — that the federal government has a frustratingly limited role to play in controlling street crime, the greatest threat to "domestic tranquility."

Realism also marks the cornerstone of Mr. Ford's anticrime proposals — mandatory jail sentences for those convicted of violent crimes. Messrs. Ford and Levi have rightly concluded that perpetrators of such crimes must be convinced that, if convicted, they will see the inside of a jail.

But both men also realize that such a policy can become counterproductive. Mandatory sentences that are too severe or too specific — such as the life sentences for drug pushers contained in an ineffective New York law — can lead to an increase in acquittals (because jurors know the judge cannot be lenient) and in more frequent plea bargaining, which allows the criminal to escape a mandatory jail sentence by pleading guilty to a lesser crime and saving the court system the expense of a trial.

The mandatory jail-sentence proposal of the President — which will soon be incorporated in specific legislation — recognizes this delicate balance by leaving to the judge the length of the mandatory sentence.

The other proposals made by the President have in common with the mandatory-sentencing suggestion lack of drama and moderate — but credible — expectations of success. Legislation to provide written guidance to federal judges on sentencing might well end some of the more outrageous inequities. So might another Ford proposal well worth implementing — giving appeals court judges limited power to review sentences made by trial judges. The President's suggestion that some first offenders — notably young defendants — be diverted into rehabilitation before standing trial would relieve the overburdened judicial system without seriously jeopardizing society.

"Law and order" disappeared as a success-guaranteed political issue not only because its chief beneficiary, Richard Nixon, himself broke the law but because politicians learned that one administration is not time enough to establish either law or order where lawlessness is a way of life. The Ford proposals reflect that sober perspective but also propose valuable new initiatives.

CHICAGO Sun-Times

Chicago, Ill., June 22, 1975

Aside from some new phrase-making with his call for "domestic tranquility," President Ford's much-awaited crime package was surprisingly sparse. Few could find fault with some parts of the proposed legislation. We support his call for compensation of crime victims, improving prison facilities and more funds for justice programs and increasing the number of federal judges. But the rest of his package was designed more for publicity than for any real effect on crime.

Ford has asked Congress for new laws that will place mandatory minimum sentences on some federal crimes. Such measures will have virtually no impact on crime anywhere in America.

First, those crimes that concern us most—murder, rape and armed robbery —do not come under federal law in all but the most extraordinary circumstances. The number of crimes prosecuted in all federal courts in 1973 accounted for only 2 per cent of the entire criminal prosecutions in the country.

Second, mandatory minimum sentences merely shift the focus of sentencing from the judge to the prosecutor. With the judge obliged to abide by mandatory sentences, the kind of crime a defendant is charged with becomes all-important in the defendant's fate. That is up to the prosecutor, who, faced with staggering backlogs, needs quick pleas of guilty in order to survive. So Ford's proposal will merely encourage what is already going on: prosecutors lowering charges in exchange for pleas of guilty.

Third, Atty. Gen. Edward H. Levi already is hinting that the mandatory minimums will only be six months to a year in length. We suspect that Levi, a legal scholar of repute, knows the relative worthlessness of the whole concept and is trying to make the measure as harmless as possible.

But Ford's gun-control proposals are even more of a deception. Ford will ask Congress for legislation that will ban the manufacture of cheap handguns—the so-called Saturday-night specials—in this country. Congress has not exactly been waiting for Ford to act; more than 40 bills aimed at such a ban are under consideration. But while such a ban may reduce the 1.5 million guns made annually in America by 20 to 50 per cent, many experts believe that criminals will merely purchase a more expensive gun when the cheaper ones are banned.

Further, as Norval Morris, dean-designate of the University of Chicago Law School, has said, the only solution to the gun problem is to ban the possession, not the manufacture, of guns. But such a ban on possession is what Ford has avoided.

The public should not expect too much from the federal government in controlling crime. Federal policy is a limited tool in the struggle. But a measure like banning the possession of handguns, which the President could have asked for, is precisely where federal policy could be most effective.

If Ford really wants to ensure domestic tranquility, he should do so with effective proposals. The brave words and bombast that we have seen so far won't do the job.

St. Petersburg Times

St. Petersburg, Fla., June 23, 1975

Crime is a proper topic for a president to address, even though crimes which worry people most — rape, muggings, burglary, murder — usually fall outside federal law enforcement jurisdictions. Thus, much of Richard Nixon's "law and order" talk was to win votes, not curb wrongdoing.

YET, A courageous White House can promote "domestic tranquility," a term used often last week in President Ford's message to Congress on crime. That Mr. Ford, too, dodged courageous proposals and wooed votes indicates the weakness, and danger, in his message.

It makes no sense for the President to urge Congress to ban the domestic manufacture, assembly or sale of cheap handguns known as "Saturday Night Specials," but not oppose possession of them or suggest handgun registration. Required registration would help keep such weapons from those who use them most — criminals.

It makes no sense to call for new mandatory jail terms when experience shows that is a tactic more likely to overcrowd jails even further than to reduce crime.

It makes no sense to claim that "for too long, the law has centered its attention more on the rights of the criminal than on the victim of the crime," as Mr. Ford did, when that is a distortion of intent. The attention the law pays to such rights is aimed at protecting all people — everyone — from abuses by the state. Power corrupts, including, in some places, police power. With that knowledge instilled in them by experience, the Founding Fathers provided the Bill of Rights. Its protections, however, have been eroded, a fact which requires the law's attention to such rights.

INSTEAD OF inflaming the passions of those who think only superficially about crime, Mr. Ford could have served the country better by speaking more of ways to end the kinds of high-level, white-collar crime which cause broad disrespect for law and which tend to encourage the kinds of crime that show up in the official statistics.

He could have called for a new national assault on the conditions that breed crime, for national "government in the sunshine" so that people can see officials serving the general — not the special — interest, for a voluntary reduction of the glorification of violence in films and on television, and for an array of other positive anti-crime steps.

Crime is a problem in the United States; however, bigger police forces and bigger jails have done little so far to reduce it. New ideas and new attitudes are needed to help individuals understand their responsibility not to commit unsocial acts against others. Pressures can force even the well-educated and financially well-to-do into criminal acts — as many caught in Watergate's web confessed. Pressures on the poorly educated and the desperate are far greater.

THE PRESIDENT'S message contained some positive aspects, particularly his call for aid to the victims of crimes. But its dominant tone and principal proposals were sadly distorted by political concerns. The country has heard all that before; it needed no more, especially from President Ford.

CHICAGO Daily Defender

Chicago, Ill., June 24, 1975

The long-awaited Ford anti-crime message to Congress contains a few encouraging features; but it is overweighted with some disturbing recommendations that can only be classed as political demagoguery. He has ordered the Law Enforcement Assistance Administration to deemphasize its funding of police hardware programs and to concentrate on combating crime in heavily populated urban areas. The agency would have its life renewed until 1981.

The proposal shifts the emphasis from protecting the rights of criminals to insuring those of their victims. The bill would provide compensation for victims of violent crime that come within the Federal purview, thus establishing a model for states and local agencies. The President calls for developing programs for youthful offenders and pretrial diversion programs for first offenders. We find the above-mentioned provisions satisfactory; even though we recognize the possible danger of coming down too hard on innocent inner city residents while giving a lighter touch to crime in the suburbs which is certainly on the rise also.

What we find wholly objectionable about the Ford package is the obvious catering to the die-hard opponents of gun control legislation. The President says he is unalterable opposed to Federal registration of guns or gun owner." He wants Congress to enact legislation with those who use handguns for criminal purposes. Mr. Ford stopped just short of the language previously used by Atty. Gen. Edward Levi who a few months ago proposed banning handguns in urban areas of high crime incidence. Once again, we say that there must be a total ban across the board for country, suburbia, town or city in the manufacture, sale, possession and distribution of handguns and handgun ammunition, with the exception of legitimate representatives of law enforcement and security forces.

At no point in the President's message did he touch upon the contributing causes of crime, poverty, discrimination and lack of educational opportunities; neither did he recognize the important component of any anti-crime campaign, citizen action. Our disappointment in the proposal is exceeded only by the grim fact that such political posturing as the 1976 election looms ahead will do little to cure the cancer of crime in our society.

Chicago Daily News

Chicago, Ill., April 7, 1977

Cracking down on criminals

Not surprisingly, Gov. Thompson's outline for a tough new anticrime program already has attracted vehement denunciations, even before the necessary legislation has been introduced in Springfield.

It is not surprising because although details remain to be spelled out, Thompson's direction is clear: He wants to fortify society's right to protection from criminals. That rankles some defense lawyers and civil libertarians who favor the trend over the last decade in which the zealous defense of criminals' rights has held top priority in the justice system, leaving victimized citizens frustrated, embittered and confused.

At the heart of Thompson's program is a new category of crimes — appropriately named Class X — that includes rape, kidnap, arson, possession of a dangerous weapon while committing a felony, taking indecent liberties with a child and the sale of hard drugs. Stiff and definite sentences — from six years to life without parole or probation — would be mandated by law upon conviction of a Class X crime, a murder conviction would carry a minimum mandatory 14-year sentence, and three Class X convictions would require automatic life imprisonment without parole. Indefinite sentences,

like 6 to 12 years, would be abolished.

Three convictions of felonies not in Class X also would carry specific sentences, again without parole or probation. In all criminal cases, judges would be bound to limit continuances and ensure speedy trials.

With sentences mandated and parole abolished in many cases, judges and parole boards would have only limited discretion in punishing criminals, and the ideal of rehabilitation would suffer.

But the fact remains that too often in the past, discretion in sentencing and parole has had the effect of exposing more innocent victims to a hardened criminal who has proved himself to be beyond rehabilitation.

Thompson bluntly states the thinking behind his recommendations: "Sooner or later we have to tell criminals that we are not going to fool around with them any longer."

To be sure, the governor's program must be debated openly and fully, and the constitutional rights of the accused must be protected assiduously. But as our series on the future of the Chicago area has shown, society's well of sympathy for criminals has, at long last, run dry.

The Washington Star
and Daily News

Washington, D.C., November 28, 1977

Reforming criminal sentences

Illinois Gov. James R. Thompson is expected to sign into law a criminal-sentencing bill that, we hope, heralds a legislative trend in other states. The measure, which received final General Assembly approval Wednesday, is a sensible reaction against the devoutly held notion of penal rehabilitation and the idealistic but increasingly discredited attempt to tailor criminal sentences to the particular individual.

The bill creates a "Class X" category of felonies for 10 specific crimes, such as robbery, rape, kidnapping and deviant sexual assault (murder is a separate category with sentences of 20 to 40 years — and twice that time in certain circumstances — life or the death penalty). "Three time losers," convicted of three serious crimes including murder and most Class X crimes — would automatically receive life sentences. The bill also does away with parole boards and restricts judges' sentencing discretion by requiring determinate sentences — X years for conviction of crime Y — rather than the minimum-maximum prison sentences now usual, which often result in the minimum term being served.

The infatuation with rehabilitation and parole is beginning to wane under the dismal weight of recidivism rates. And not a moment too soon. The basic vulnerability of both ideas is that they assume an ability to predict human behavior with a precision beyond present skills.

The determinate sentence as a general replacement for minimum-maximum sentences conforms to a fundamental principle of criminal justice: swift and sure punishment. A stickup man, whether novice or journeyman, must know that he will serve a specific amount of time if he is nabbed and convicted. Street-wise cons, canny lawyers and judges of unfocused compassion not infrequently can make a mockery of

that axiom, reducing deterrence to a joke.

The Illinois bill is, we gather, one of the first major state initiatives to reflect the fresh thinking about sentencing. We note that the pending recodification of federal criminal laws also would move somewhat in this direction (the measure, S.1437, has been approved by the Senate Judiciary Committee and is expected to be considered by the full body early next year).

Under this bill — a heavily re-worked version of last year's hotly disputed S.1 — a sentencing commission would develop guidelines to provide a general direction for federal judges. The bill would also sharply curtail rehabilitation as a factor in criminal sentencing and would also limit the use of early releases on parole. The laudable intent of these provisions would be to insure more uniform and realistic sentences, sentences more consonant with time actually being served by convicted felons as opposed to the long maximum, and rarely served, sentences on the books.

There is a growing mood of pragmatism — rather desperately arrived at — in criminal sentencing. While the debate and the research continue, those with responsibility for containing criminality are more and more inclined to endorse such procedures as the determinate sentence and junking of parole. Our knowledge, for practical purposes, now is largely limited to the obvious: That an imprisoned felon is hampered in the commission of new crimes.

A society that concedes an inability to deal with criminality is a society in an advanced stage of atrophy. Perhaps one day we can be more confident of how criminal behavior develops and how it may be changed. Until then, however, those who commit serious crimes must know they will be held to account — as responsible agents of their own actions.

Post-Tribune

Guarding Your Interests Daily

Gary, Ind., April 7, 1977

Getting tough on crime strikes a popular chord

Illinois Gov. James Thompson's plea for getting much tougher on crime is certain to generate an immediate popular response not only in his own state, but across the country.

The cynical may say that that is exactly what Thompson wants in view of his scarcely veiled ultimate presidential ambitions.

Students of his past will relate, no doubt accurately, the Thompson message to his experience as Unit-

ed States District Attorney for the Chicago area.

There will be theorists and sincere students of crime problems who will argue with his tough mandatory sentences and banning of clemency for certain types of crimes including rape, arson, kidnaping for ransom, indecent liberties with a child, dealing in hard drugs and committing a felony with a dangerous weapon.

Some judges already are arguing that treating first offenders — even when the most heinous crimes are involved — the same way as hardened criminals can turn many who could be saved beyond redemption. Students of government may point to former Gov. Nelson Rockefeller's tough narcotics crime program in New York and demonstrate it has not solved the problem. Even many citizens who welcome the toughness may balk as

taxpayers at the additional cost of keeping so many more in prison.

But as long as the crime scene remains as menacing as it is for most, Thompson's plan is certain to have wide appeal. Only time can tell if it would work, and then only if the Illinois legislature goes along, but there can be no doubt that the public is looking for crime answers and this is a package most will want to buy.

Chicago Tribune

Chicago, Ill., April 7, 1977

Gov. Thompson fights crime

Gov. Thompson's current crime-fighting proposals thoughtfully address a major unsolved social problem. "We are going to get tough on crime," he says, to certain popular applause.

The governor has not simply made a speech or issued a press release. He is proposing legislation and a couple of new agencies—a Criminal Sentencing Commission and a statewide public defender agency. His proposals can be modified in the course of legislation where needful. As it stands, the plans call for both new statutory directives and some new personnel.

Though "toughness" is a popular term in talking about crime, there is an even better one—justice. Toughness and leniency both function best in the service of justice, the primary objective. The best deterrent to crime is certain and swift punishment, rather than severe punishment unevenly applied. But to improve our criminal justice systems, a little more toughness at a number of points will be required.

One of the governor's major proposals is the designation of Class X felonies, a group of especially heinous offenses. Here he would require by law stiff minimum sentences, fixed sentences, and parole ineligibility. Three convictions for Class X offenses would constitute being a habitual offender subject to life imprisonment without parole. This is the toughest of Gov. Thompson's tough proposals. In practice, it could prove less ironclad than may appear. Prosecutors' discretion in bringing charges and in plea bargaining after charges are brought can have an incalculable impact, and go far toward frustrating his draconian intent.

Gov. Thompson addresses plea bargaining, too; he calls for written state-

ments giving the reasons for reducing or withdrawing a serious charge. He would speed trials by requiring prompt disclosure of pre-trial motions planned, and by restricting continuances to those necessary to prevent miscarriage of justice. He would improve the information available when bail is set. These changes, if put into effect, would reduce the roles of ignorance and technical ingenuity as impediments to justice.

In addition, Gov. Thompson would give the prosecution as well as the defense a voice in choosing a judge, and would move the public defender function from the counties to the state. The side effects of these well intentioned proposals will require study—as will, of course, the whole package.

Gov. Thompson shows a continuing sense of responsibility for the treatment of convicts after sentencing. His proposals to convert some underutilized downstate mental facilities to penal institutions could mitigate several problems at once. True, sites away from centers of population are less desirable for penal purposes than ones in cities. But overcrowding and vast size are worse evils than a downstate location.

The main point is that Gov. Thompson is fulfilling his campaign promises to do s o m e t h i n g about crime. Vigorous, thoughtful executive attention to crimes, courts, and prisons is vastly more productive than the executive neglect of such subjects characteristic of too many governors. The pursuit of justice in dealing with crimes and offenders is troublesome, but it can be rewarding. It can be rewarding both to a governor brave enough to attempt it and to a public frightened and exasperated by the epidemic failures of our criminal justice systems to produce wanted results.

Register-Republic

Rockford, Ill., April 8, 1977

'Big Jim' and crime

"No probation. No suspension of sentence. And no parole."

With these words, Gov. James R. Thompson has unveiled his program "to get tough on crime" in Illinois.

What he proposes could serve to comfort society and, at the same time, alert criminals that a day of reckoning is soon to arrive.

Under the plan Thompson is sending to the state legislature, a category of "Class X" felonies would be created as the heart of this "get-tough" program.

The person who rapes, commits arson, kidnaps for ransom, takes indecent liberties with a child, deals in hard drugs or uses a dangerous weapon to commit a felony would be guilty of a "Class X" crime.

When convicted, the felon would automatically be sentenced to at least six years in prison—never less. The sentence could be up to life imprisonment.

Once sentenced, there would be no probation, no suspension of sentence, no parole.

The potential criminal even considering one of these crimes would know beyond doubt that if caught and convicted he would spend at least the next six years of his life behind bars.

And, if this same offender

should be convicted three times of a "Class X" felony, the automatic sentence would be life imprisonment.

Those are harsh terms.

But Governor Thompson is reflecting a growing school of thought that holds punishment can be a deterrent if the consequences are well understood in advance.

Meantime, the Thompson crime-fighting package also contains some surprises for defense attorneys.

Traditionally, an attorney defending the accused can demand—and get—a jury trial. The same attorney also can demand to know what evidence and which witnesses the prosecutor intends to present during the course of a trial.

Thompson proposes to give the prosecutor a more balanced position with this defense attorney. Thus, under his proposals, the prosecutor also could ask for a jury trial, could also demand to know what witnesses the defense intends to call, and could ask for a different judge if he thinks the presiding judge is "soft" on crime.

We think Thompson's approach is a start toward vindicating a campaign pledge to contain crime in Illinois. It is a start toward giving criminals the tough treatment which they unlawfully mete out to others.

Los Angeles Times

Los Angeles, Calif., February 8, 1977

A Reform, Not a Cure-All

The Uniform Determinate Sentencing Act, scheduled to become effective July 1, is a significant reform of the criminal-justice system in California.

Supported last year by most law-enforcement officials, including Atty. Gen. Evelle J. Younger, the act (Senate Bill 42) replaces the present indeterminate sentencing law, adopted in 1917.

The theory behind penal reform 60 years ago was an ideal cherished by the reformers of that era: Punishment would be tailored to fit the offender, not the offense. That seemed to make sense. The law held out the promise of early release for those who could demonstrate evidence of rehabilitation.

Convicts received elastic prison terms—for example, six months to life for assault with a deadly weapon—and the decision about release was put into the hands of the Adult Authority or the Women's Board of Terms and Parole.

The system proved to be capricious. In 1975, a minority report of a State Bar study said the law was "no better than random selection" among the prison population, and imposed "a great inequality of justice."

The new law, which excludes from its provisions certain offenses like first-degree murder, kidnaping for ransom, or assault by a prison inmate, is also based on theory—one that reverses the philosophy of the indeterminate sentence. SB 42 tailors punishment to the crime, and requires a uniform system of fixed sentences based on the severity of the offense and the criminal record of the convict.

This procedure rests on factual data, not on a prediction of future behavior, and removes the uncertainty of the present law that a federal judge criticized last year as "a hit-and-miss thing."

But since last September, when Gov. Brown signed into law the Uniform Determinate Sentencing Act, it has come under steady criticism, and a move is under way to amend it out of existence.

The principal criticisms are these:

—The law, which applies retroactively to present prison inmates, will on July 1 suddenly release an extraordinary number of prisoners, many dangerous, and thus constitutes a serious threat to public safety.

—Sentences under the determinate statute are not sufficiently severe.

—Judges are not permitted sufficient discretion.

—And, finally, the 90-day period to apply SB 42 to present prisoners is too short a period to complete the required procedure.

The Department of Corrections estimates that 1,000 to 1,500 more prisoners will be released during the first year that the new law is in effect than would have been released under the old system—not 7,000 to 8,000, figures used by some critics of the new law.

Sen. John A. Nejedly (R-Walnut Creek), the author of the act, says that under its provisions dangerous inmates can be kept in prison.

Nejedly and other supporters of the reform say that sentences under SB 42 will correspond roughly to their present length, and, furthermore, that terms provided by SB 42 are longer than the national average.

The new law, according to Nejedly, does give judges sufficient discretion based on the record of the defendant before the court. Michael Snedeker, chief counsel for the Prisoner Union, agrees, and adds that the wide discretion allowed judges under the indeterminate sentencing procedure was "a poisonous part of the system" because it resulted in wholesale inequity.

Referring to the three-month period allowed for application of SB 42 to present inmates, Nejedly says he would favor an extension if that is necessary, and would agree to any other changes if they are needed to implement the law properly, but he maintains that essentially the law is sound, and that, significantly, "it clarifies the sentencing process so that the public can understand what is being done and why."

Further illumination of this process can be expected when the Judicial Council of California holds public hearings on rules it has adopted tentatively for felony sentencing under the new statute. One hearing will be held in March and two in April.

Several conclusions can be drawn from the sharp debate over SB 42. The indeterminate sentence has failed, and had to be replaced. Many criticisms of the new law are overdrawn and premature. The law, shaped by legislators seriously concerned with the improvement of the criminal-justice system, deserves an opportunity to prove its worth.

Brown, an advocate of the reform, went to the heart of the issue when he said that the differences between opponents and proponents of fixed-term sentencing are "really a philosophical" dispute over crime and punishment.

All agree that the public must be protected against crime and criminals, but the debate has been posed in terms that suggest that the entire answer lies in the reform of the criminal-justice system. Reforms should be made when necessary, but more basic solutions to crime lie outside the justice system, in the hard reality of social conditions.

Justice Oliver Wendell Holmes pointed to this when he said many years ago that if the law "stood on the moral grounds proposed for it," the law would have to consider the criminal's "abnormal instincts, want of education, lack of intelligence, and all the other defects which are most marked in the criminal classes."

Only recently, Robert Di Grazia, then police commissioner in Boston, observed "that those who commit crimes that worry citizens most—violent street crimes—are, for the most part, the products of poverty, unemployment, broken homes, rotten education, drug addiction and alcoholism, and other social and economic ills . . ."

We should not be under the illusion that the criminal-justice system can reach these problems.

THE SACRAMENTO BEE

Sacramento, Calif., January 16, 1977

An Unjust System

There is compelling evidence of the need for congressional attention to the serious disparity in the sentencing of criminals in federal courts throughout the country. The wide variance in penalties under the loose "different judge, different sentence" system calls for basic reforms.

The problem is one that California has wrestled with for many years and finally done something about. Although some controversial changes may be sought by Gov. Edmund G. Brown Jr., the essential fact is that in July, most of the state's 60-year-old system of indeterminate prison sentences will be abolished.

Sen. Edward M. Kennedy, D-Mass., has introduced a bill in Congress which would have the effect of eliminating the open-ended sentencing in federal courts. Chief Justice Warren Burger has not endorsed the measure but he does say the discretionary power of judges needs to be reviewed.

Neither Kennedy nor Burger blames the judges themselves. Kennedy says the jurists must act without any guidelines because Congress has never built standards or safeguards into the sentencing process.

The result has led to a game of chance for those who stand before the law. Different judges often mete out different sentences to similar defendants convicted of similar crimes, depending on the sentencing attitudes of the particular judge.

Examples: In 1974, the average federal sentence of imprisonment was 42.2 months. But in the Southern District of Georgia the average was only 18.4 months. In the Western District of Michigan, it was 94.9 months.

In one year, the average length of prison sentences for perjury in the Southern District of New York was 5.2 months, for all federal courts 28 months; bail jumping, 10 months for New York, 25.6 months for all; bank robbery, for New York, 69.6 months, 124.1 months for all.

It is such inconstancy that prompts Kennedy to derogate what happens as a national scandal — arbitrary and unjust. His bill would impose uniform standards not only to determine how long to put offenders behind bars but also whether those persons should be imprisoned at all. It adopts the concept of imprisonment as punishment and not rehabilitation.

Several key provisions of the measure should have further study, such as requiring already overburdened U.S. circuit courts to review every federal sentence. But, in the light of the evidence, the overall merit of the idea behind the proposed reform is one we unhesitatingly endorse.

The Salt Lake Tribune

Salt Lake City, Utah, May 25, 1977

Sentencing Disarray

One factor that distinguishes the latest attempt to reform and recodify federal criminal laws is introduction of guidelines designed to reduce gross sentencing disparity.

A new bill bringing together the grab bag of federal criminal laws in one overall criminal code has been introduced in the Senate by Sen. John L. McClellan, D-Ark., and Sen. Edward M. Kennedy, D-Mass.

In addition to establishing sentencing guidelines for federal judges, the bill would require that variation from the standards be justified in written opinions. The bill also provides for appellate review of sentences, a proposal certain to receive a cool reception from both trial judges and those on the appeals courts, too.

Sentencing disparity is now recognized as one cause of widespread failure of the corrections system to correct. But remedies necessarily involve limitations on the hallowed concept of judicial discretion.

Sentencing is a complex exercise of judgment that blends such variables as the law, the judge's perception, the defendant's record and attitude, feeling in the community, and even whether "his honor" had a good night's sleep. An enormous range of results is thus assured.

This was documented by a recent test conducted by the Federal Judicial Center in which 50 judges read presentence reports on 20 cases. In 16 of the 20 the judges disagreed on the basic question of whether a prison sentence was even appropriate. A similar group of judges recommended sentences in a hypothetical tax evasion case ranging from a six months suspended prison sentence to five years and a $20,000 fine.

Robert B. McKay, former chairman of the New York State Special Commission on Attica, summed up the problem in an address to western appellate judges last summer at Coeur d'Alene, Idaho. "Society," he said, "has generally failed to determine on a rational and defensible basis what punishment is appropriate to the severity of the offense and for the individual offender. That failure is the most serious injustice inherent in the criminal justice system of the United States."

The McClellan-Kennedy criminal code bill's sentencing guidelines and provision for appellate review of sentence are urgently needed intitial moves toward overdue reform.

Although the guidelines impose curbs on judicial discretion, they permit sufficient flexibility to allow exceptions where circumstances dictate. No sentencing "formula" is going to produce perfect, uniform justice. But the guidelines will narrow the margin for outlandish variation now commonplace.

THE BLADE
Toledo, Ohio, June 28, 1977

Let Punishment Fit The Crime

LEGISLATION tightening up criminal codes in California specifically takes note that incarceration is for punishment only and not rehabilitation. This firm view, as applied to so-called career criminals with multiple felony records, appears to reflect a trend in many states. Some now call for mandatory minimum sentences along with sharp reductions in the discretionary powers of judges and parole boards.

These and other steps indicating a tougher attitude toward such criminals are an outgrowth of questioning of many of the basic assumptions about prisoner rehabilitation. A conference of law-enforcement officials and judges at Bowling Green State University the other day produced the unsurprising report that experts in sociology say the only solution to handling a person with two to four felony convictions "is to put him behind bars where he can't repeat." The sociologists are saying, in effect, that correctional treatment has failed to reform hardened criminals or reduce crime.

Such admissions have come after a prolonged succession of penal reforms premised on letting the sentence fit the individual rather than fit the crime. The outgrowth of all this has been, if anything, to encourage crime because of the sympathic treatment accorded offenders.

Some criminologists are convinced that another way to reverse the rise in crime is to abolish all probation for anyone convicted of a serious crime. The certainty of having to spend some time in prison, they maintain, would deter many would-be offenders. The same assurance of a mandatory minimum sentence for first offenders might also break the endless revolving-door cycle that probation, parole, and ineffective rehabilitation have spawned.

The Pittsburgh Press
Pittsburgh, Pa., June 21, 1977

Equal Sentencing

The problem of widely varying sentences for similar crimes has long plagued the criminal-justice system and puzzled the public. It contributes, sometimes wrongly, to the popular image of "soft" and "tough" judges.

To end the disparities, several states have adopted uniform-sentencing laws.

Now, a similar law for Pennsylvania is awaiting action by the House Judiciary Committee and, importantly, has won the endorsement of Allegheny County District Attorney Bob Colville.

It deserves sympathetic consideration.

★ ★ ★

The proposal before the legislators calls for establishing a State Commission on Sentencing, which would draw up recommended prison terms for various crimes, with harsher penalties for repeaters.

Judges would not be absolutely bound to impose those sentences, but when they don't they would be required to explain why in written opinions.

This approach is viewed as a compromise between the every-judge-for-himself sentencing system (as in Pennsylvania) and the one which mandates penalties and allows judges no leeway at all.

The courts generally have resisted outside efforts to curb judicial discretion. However, with many judges misusing if not abusing that discretion, it's hard to fault the idea of setting some limitations.

★ ★ ★

The goal should be fairness and uniformity in the handling of criminal offenders. The public expects as much.

Indeed, common-sense justice will not prevail until we reach the point where a lawbreaker can expect the same punishment no matter which courtroom, or which county, he may appear in for sentencing.

The Des Moines Register
Des Moines, Iowa, June 13, 1977

Unequal sentences

What is a fair penalty for failure to file and pay state income taxes? Iowa Revenue Director Gerald Bair thinks that judges in Polk County have been too lenient. That seems to be true. But it also seems that few Iowa judges agree on a "fair" penalty.

Bair provided data showing that 30 out of 40 cases prosecuted outside Polk County since 1973 resulted in fines. In the same period, six of 20 offenders in Polk County were fined. The others were given either suspended or deferred sentences or probation.

The maximum penalty is one year in jail or a $2,500 fine on each count. Failure to file and failure to pay in one year would constitute two counts.

No pattern in the sentencing is evident. A Carroll County man was fined $2,000, placed on probation for 18 months and sentenced to six months in jail (suspended) for failure to file and pay for one year. A Dubuque County man got a one-year deferred sentence for failure to file and pay for four years. A Polk County man got 90 days suspended and 180 days probation for failure to file for seven years. A Washington County man got a $4,000 fine for failure to file and pay for four years.

Those who violate tax laws are usually white-collar or professional workers, not the types who usually are sent to jail (some judges evidently have too much empathy with tax offenders).

Disparity in sentencing isn't as important in tax cases as in more severe criminal cases, because in just one of 61 cases studied was anyone sentenced to spend time in jail. Nonetheless, justice ought not to vary on the basis of the county in which the defendant lives. Bair's data is an argument for requiring judges to explain their sentences.

The Dispatch
Columbus, Ohio, June 15, 1977

Disparities In Justice

DISPARITIES in sentencing practices as well as abuses of the parole system have played major roles in the sharp erosion of public confidence in this nation's criminal justice mechanism.

Thus far, leaders of the justice system have been unable to explain to the public why a convicted criminal is sentenced to 12 to 15 years, but is paroled in five years. Or why another criminal in an identical situation is granted shock parole or shock probation.

A measure before a U.S. Senate judicial subcommittee is worthy of intense study and consideration.

Part of a new federal criminal code bill, the measure would virtually abolish the parole system. Convicted prisoners would serve the time to which they were sentenced. And the sentencing would be uniform nationwide.

U.S. Atty. Gen. Griffin Bell testified before the subcommittee he thought such a measure would be a monumental step forward in providing a penalty system which would be fair to both the defendant and the public.

That the public currently is short-changed is obvious.

There is merit in the contention that judges should be granted some jurisdiction in determining the degree of the sentence. But that contingency is covered by the proposal.

A judge could deviate from the range of sentences stipulated for a specific crime. But any deviation must be accompanied by a written explanation.

Too, either the prosecution or the defendant could appeal the degree of the sentence imposed.

In all cases, however, a sentence would be positive.

The public deserves to be assured that once a criminal is found guilty and is sentenced he will indeed serve that sentence.

The Philadelphia Inquirer
Philadelphia, Pa., June 21, 1977

A sensible sentencing plan

Few aspects of the criminal justice system have received as much attention in recent years as the wide disparity — intentional and unintentional — in sentencing. Study after study demonstrate that the length of a defendant's sentence depends as much, if not more so, on the personality and philosophy of the sentencing judge as on anything else.

There is virtual unanimity on the seriousness of the problem, yet little agreement on the best solution. One approach which deserves serious attention is the so-called presumptive sentencing concept, which is before the Pennsylvania legislature in House Bill 953. The bill would lead to the establishment of non-binding sentence recommendations and permit appellate review.

It is a more sensible approach than mandatory sentencing, which the legislature narrowly avoided adopting several months ago. Mandatory sentencing would strip judges of any discretion by requiring them to impose a predetermined sentence for a particular offense.

Despite its wide appeal, opponents of mandatory sentencing were able to prevent its passage by convincing legislators that it would be an expensive proposition. Since more defendants would be sent to prison, more prisons would have to be built, more guards hired and other costly expenses incurred.

Mandatory sentencing, however, is defective for reasons other than just its financial consequences. It refuses to recognize that no two crimes and no two criminals are alike. It would replace one problem — too much discretion—with another—too much inflexibility.

As one court official properly has observed, "There should be disparity. What you don't want is undue disparity."

The presumptive sentencing concept helps to avoid just that. A statewide sentencing commission would be established. After research and study it would develop a set of sentencing guidelines for trial judges. While it is presumed that the sentencing commission's recommendation will be followed, a judge would not be barred from imposing another sentence if circumstances warranted. In that event, however, he must state his reasons in open court and in writing.

Moreover, a sentence could be appealed to the state Superior Court, which could modify it if it is out-of-line with the crime, the defendant's background or what other defendants have received. Presently, no such appeals are permitted, and a trial judge's sentencing is final.

Questions have been raised about HB 953 concerning the composition of the commission and whether the commonwealth should be permitted to appeal what it considers too lenient a sentence.

However, HB 953 is a step in the right direction, and the legislature would be far wiser in pursuing it than in opting for mandatory sentences, which would create as many, if not more, injustices than the present system.

Democrat and Chronicle
Rochester, N.Y., December 7, 1977

See sentencing as the failure it often is

ONE of the best things about the recent annual conference here of the New York State Association for Human Services Inc. (AHS) was the simple fact of its occurrence.

For in the broad domain of human affairs, there are public attitudes that need to be changed, and AHS serves as a useful educational forum and tool.

In the area of criminal justice, U.S. District Judge Marvin Frankel spoke of the ignorance of what goes on in the criminal system, and of the misunderstanding of what the system can and cannot do.

Indeterminate court sentencing, it was fairly well agreed at two of the sessions, does little for justice — whether justice is measured by prisoner welfare or the public welfare.

BUT the public, emphasized several of the speakers, isn't about to stand for shorter, more definite prison terms.

DA John Finnerty, president of the State District Attorneys' Association, told one of the seminars that if the issue were put to a referendum, it would fail.

"When people read that John Smith has been sentenced to an indeterminate period of 10 years, they think it's a good thing. They don't appreciate that he may be out in a few months."

". . . The public wants harsher sentences, but it's not prepared to give support to the after-care of inmates."

State Correctional Services Commissioner Benjamin Ward said bluntly that "any scheme that talks about less time for inmates won't fly . . . The sentiment is not there.

"The public is getting and accepting the fiction that criminals are being put away for a long time. They're not."

Such attitudes—and Ward called on newspapers to help correct them—persist in the face of mounting evidence that the present prison sentencing system isn't working.

There are two kinds of inequalities.

One is the result of mandatory sentencing that puts people away for fixed terms regardless of even profound differences in circumstances.

The other injustice comes from the excessive discretion permitted judges in many other cases, so that wildly varying sentences are handed out around the nation.

Said Frankel: "The great inequality and disparity of sentencing has begun to upset the lawyers, the judges, the community . . . That disquietude combines with other uneasiness to produce a ferment and a challenge."

THE FERMENT and the challenge involve these emerging convictions:

• Prisons do little to rehabilitate people.

• Long sentences, actually served, only harden the offender, so that the public is not really protected in the long run.

• The public must be made aware that indeterminate sentences are usually not what they may seem to be.

• Offenders need to know from the start how long they'll be in prison.

• Short, fixed, flat-time sentences hold out the best hope for justice.

• The focus of the prison system should be on the repeater, the professional criminal.

NOW the task is to persuade the people who pay the taxes and elect the legislators and set the climate for change that these are goals worth achieving.

The Providence Journal

Providence, R.I., June 18, 1977

Fair and equitable sentences for white collar crimes

The U.S. Justice Department, apparently seized with the trend in national sentiment against inequity in sentencing criminals, is beginning to talk tough and with good reason. "There is a growing sense in our country," said Barbara A. Reeves, an attorney in the anti-trust division, "that justice is not fair and equal, and that white collar criminals, such as price fixers, get preferential treatment in our criminal justice system."

Denying any desire to fill the jails with businessmen, Miss Reeves said, "But there are hundreds of thousands of businesses in this country. We can't watch all of them. So we want to be able to say, 'If we catch you, you will certainly go to jail."

Prison sentences for collusion, embezzlement, bribery and a variety of other crimes committed by middle-class, otherwise solid members of the community are the exception rather than the rule. Six years ago 29 Rhode Island plumbing contractors were convicted of conspiring to fix prices in $6-million worth of building contracts, but U.S. District Court declined to hand down prison sentences. A paper box executive got 60 days for price fixing but the penalty was reduced to 15 days in a work release program.

One view is that the reputable businessman who violates the criminal statutes is punished sufficiently by the notoriety of a conviction, though he may have misappropriated thousands of dollars to his own use or for the benefit of others. Contrast that with the petty criminal who takes $50 in a holdup and goes to prison for five years or the youth seized with a marijuana cigarette who the judge says must serve a year behind bars.

Judges as well as prosecutors are to blame for maintaining this double standard. Miss Reeves puts it this way: "I think the judges still look at (white collar criminals) and see reflections of themselves — responsible people who belong to the right clubs and support civic projects." The Justice Department, she said, is urging judges to see criminals.

Perhaps this shift in emphasis at the federal level will have a positive effect where it counts. The most desirable result would be to deter the individual bent on "sophisticated" lawbreaking. Prosecutors vulnerable to political and community pressures may begin to realize it is no longer respectable to judge criminals by their station in life. And judges who feel the sting of public criticism often enough may conclude that leniency for the influential citizen is not justice when meted out on the basis of who the defendant is and where he comes from.

As Miss Reeves says, there is no conclusive evidence that prison terms are an effective deterrent, but they're worth trying, particularly since fines don't work.

The Boston Globe

Boston, Mass., June 12, 1977

Crimes and punishment

The responsibility of the nation's courts is not only to render just decisions but to act in a fashion that reenforces public confidence in the judiciary. Regrettably, that test is failed almost daily by the imposition of widely divergent sentences on defendants in what to all outward appearances seem to be comparable criminal cases. The proposal by Sen. Kennedy to establish standardized sentencing criteria for the Federal judiciary — a plan heartily endorsed by the Carter Administration — would take the first step toward restoring legitimacy of sentencing procedures.

The proposal, contained in massive legislation rewriting the Federal criminal code, is a compromise between the present almost indeterminate system of sentencing and a system of absolutely mandatory sentences. Hearings on the legislation began in the US Senate last week.

Under the fixed-sentencing plan, a narrower range of possible sentences for a particular crime — say, four to eight years in jail — would be established and a set of criteria would be drafted to guide the presiding judge in determining where along the range he should set the sentence. The criteria would include such factors as the defendant's age, criminal record and specific involvement in the crime.

Only in exceptional circumstances could the judge impose a sentence either more lenient or more harsh than the recommended range. And in these cases, the judge, for the first time in the Federal system, would have to give a written opinion justifying his sentencing decision and it could be appealed, either by the defendant or the prosecutor. The Kennedy plan would have the added salutory benefit of gradually phasing out the Federal Parole Board and its arbitrary power over convicts's lives.

Embodied in the proposal is a major retreat fro the idea, respectable until recently, that prisons ca rehabilitate inmates. It embraces, instead, the ol fashioned but still popular notion that the primar purpose of prison terms is to punish offenders.

Few would dispute that prisons have failed a rehabilitative institutions. Yet, fixed-sentenc procedures must not foreclose totally the opportunit for a truly rehabilitated prisoner to seek judici review of his sentence. Further, it must not be used a an excuse to abandon all rehabilitative programs i the penal system.

Most important to the implementation of th Kennedy proposal would be the development sound, reasonable and publicly acceptable sentencin criteria. The job would be given to a Feder Sentencing Commission. As now drafted, the propos would have that commission appointed by the Feder Judicial Conference; and it could be composed only judges or lawyers. The bill should be amended to giv the President appointing authority and membershi should include prison officials, parole officials an persons outside the criminal-justice system.

The primary beneficiaries of the propose Kennedy plan would be the convicts themselves. The no longer would face indeterminate and embitterin sentences, their futures subject to the whims correctional officials. But there are broader potenti benefits for society as well.

Fixed sentences might secure "sure justice" an end the system under which criminals can gambl that a lenient judge or an automatic early parole wi have them back on the streets in short time. And tha in turn, may serve as a deterrent to criminal activit No one knows for sure, of course. We've never tried before.

The Times-Picayune
New Orleans, La., February 26, 1977
Sentences

A local doctor who pleaded guilty in U.S. District Court to submitting false claims for medical services in the waterfront union welfare scandal was given on Feb. 18 what the public doubtless considers punishment that was both just and exemplary. He had to pay back the $3,731 he admitted taking, he was fined $5,000, and he was put on probation for three years, a condition being that he give two days a week for 90 days to volunteer-type civic work.

The sentence, in sum, combined restitution, punishment, an introduction to rehabilitation, and surveillance for a substantial period.

Ten days earlier, also in U.S. District Court, four companies that operate the New Orleans public grain elevator were allowed to plead nolo contendere after indictment on charges of conspiracy involving alleged false weighing of grain. No dollar figure was given, but the indictment alleged that the companies, by shortweighing shipments, acquired an unearned accumulation of some 1.4 million bushes of salable grain.

Their sentence was the maximum for the offense — $10,000 per company. So much for punishment. Of restitution, nothing. Of surveillance (as, perhaps, a form of enforced rehabilitation), an affirmative action program approved by the Departments of Agriculture and Justice to assure the irregularities do not reoccur.

We are not criticizing the judge in the second case, for judicial discretion is often circumscribed by the law. But when one person is fined $5,000 for taking $3,731 and made to give the $3,731 back, and four corporations are fined $10,000 apiece for taking the commodity equivalent of millions and not made to give the millions back, something seems out of kilter. Nonviolent, "white-collar" crime, unlike much violent, anti-person crime, seems especially adapted to restitution as part of the punishment, and our lawmakers should make the laws that way.

THE ARIZONA REPUBLIC
Phoenix, Ariz., February 12, 1977
Evaluating judges

Question: Who is the best judge — the one who sentences a thief to five years, or one who sentences a thief to probation for one year?

Answer: Neither is better than the other.

Because, if two such separate cases were scrutinized more thoroughly than just the sentencing, the observer might find, for example, that one thief stole a loaf of bread, and the other stole an automobile. Thus, sentences would and should vary.

But under a bill introduced by Rep. Donna Carlson, R-Mesa, no such distinctions would be drawn in a set of new reports which she would require of all courts.

In essence, Rep. Carlson would have judges keep a scorecard of all criminal cases, showing what kind of sentences judges mete out.

There is no question that some judges are softer on criminals than others. Some are more concerned about defendants in criminal cases, than the victims.

The Carlson approach, however, is too simplified and too superficial in its approach to stir reform in the courts.

But the bill does have some virtues — it already has drawn the subject of sentencing practices into the open where they should be discussed.

Of all components in the criminal justice system, the courts are the least understood and the least visible — but, by far, the most important. The wide latitude of discretionary powers held by a judge are enormous — he can delay a case, throw out charges, issue directed verdicts, speed up or slow down a trial, disqualify jurors, allow or prohibit certain testimony, and fix virtually whatever sentence he chooses on conviction.

Yet, while most citizens have some comprehension of their police and their prosecutors and their prisons, judges and the workings of their courts remain a mystery to most persons. Consequently, when Superior Court judges stand for public vote, most citizens have scant opinion of their effectiveness.

Perhaps Rep. Carlson's bill will stir the judiciary and the Bar to design its own system of performance evaluation. The attorneys and judges of the state certainly owe it to the public to provide some measurement, other than opinion polls, of how well the system is working.

If they don't believe they have that responsibility, then it is only a matter of time until Rep. Carlson will find ample support for her type of legislation.

THE SAGINAW NEWS
Saginaw, Mich., February 2, 1977
Sentencing reform no topic for simplistics

The subjects of crime and punishment are going to get legislative attention this year — and that is precisely where the wrinkles in state court sentencing practices should be ironed out.

Certainly they are not subjects to be ironed in voting booths, as Oakland County Prosecutor L. Brooks Patterson would have it. Mr. Patterson is properly concerned about the state of crime and punishment in this state. So is just about everybody. The public is demanding sterner handling of criminals and will likely get it.

But crime and punishment are more than emotional topics. They are complex ones to be dealt with thoughtfully and rationally.

Thus we are somewhat distressed that Patterson and others are traveling about the state playing upon emotion, some, including Mr. Patterson, possibly hoping to build political careers by passing petitions and bringing pressure to bear in Lansing.

This newspaper is just as concerned as Patterson about crime's impact on the public and the need to reform the prison sentencing structure.

Moreover, any reform worth the effort, should be codified law embodying the certainty of punishment for crime and equal punishment for equal crime. Just about everybody is agreed on that, too.

But we shudder to think this problem can be simplified by abandoning parole boards, setting flat minimum sentences across the board; in effect throwing away the book on judicial discretion — along with the keys to the cell.

That could bring more fracturing of justice. And, as we have already been reminded, the same public that would demand that would also have to accommodate the cost of larger prisons and more prisons. We may have to, anyway, before we're through.

A considerable amount of study has already gone into this subject in Lansing. And it is from that body of opinion we would would prefer to see drafted judicial sentencing reform.

Excellent work has been done on this by State Corrections Director Perry Johnson and Sens. Anthony Derezinski, D-Muskegon, and Dennis Cawthorne, also of Manistee, a Republican.

They have not only been reading up on the subject but have been working with a State Bar subcommittee.

Johnson would like to see all crimes, below first degree murder, classified by degree of seriousness — each bracket carrying maximum sentences. Judges would be allowed the discretion of setting minimum sentences of up to half the maximum with mitigating circumstances. Rules covering "good time" deductions from sentences would be revised and stiffened. Parole boards would retain decision between minimum and maximum terms. And first degree murder would remain automatic life without parole unless commuted by the governor.

Derezinski is advancing the presumptive sentencing concept in which specific sentences would be established for serious crimes. Judges would be able to alter the penalties only under specific circumstances spelled out by the law.

These are the highlights of two current proposals for prison sentencing reform. Each carries the thrust of certain sentencing while preserving the right of the judiciary to function as something besides a clerkship. And keeping it away from a return to the age of the "hanging judge."

Either way, they represent the proper approach.

The Kansas City Times

Kansas City, Mo., April 25, 1977

Criminals' Terms Can Create Climate for Crime

The sentencing of convicted criminals, which has a direct bearing on whether they are sent to prison or remain in the community, has been undergoing rather stringent scrutiny in recent years. Legal scholars and special commissions who have examined this issue seem to agree that the sentencing process is one of the weakest links in the criminal justice system.

Much of the concern centers on the disparities. One individual convicted of robbery is assessed a 5-year term while another defendant found guilty of the same crime is placed on probation. The difference here may be proper but in too many cases it appears that judges lack standards and guidelines that could bring more consistency to the fixing of penalties.

The special group that investigated the uprising at Attica prison in New York found that the most urgent inmate grievances were the result of what many prisoners considered inequitable treatment in sentencing. The convicts were embittered about the variances, which included some defendants not being sent to prison at all.

One practical effect of the shortcomings in sentencing procedures is the potential for more crime. Individuals with a criminal bent are tempted to try to "beat the system" because they think the disparities could work to their benefit. They are willing to commit a crime on the chance that they will be placed on probation or receive a light sentence rather than a substantial term. This playing of odds can make the public vulnerable to the vagaries of the criminal mind.

Complicating the matter is the inherent nature of sentencing. Judges often base their decisions on different purposes and objectives. A sentence may be assessed in an attempt to rehabilitate an offender. Or to deter that offender and others from committing crime. Another objective is to incapacitate criminals. Still another is to punish lawbreakers for violating society's rules. When the diversity of attitudes among judges is added to this mix, it is easy to understand why criminal sentencing often is viewed as a lottery.

Consider a few comparisons. In the federal courts system the national average for bank robbers earlier in this decade was about 11 years. In the northern district of Georgia the average was 17 years, while it was five and one-half years in the northern district of Illinois. Sentences for the same crime vary widely among the states. Within states the terms can also have a broad range because of discretions granted by law to the courts. Complaints are also voiced that persons convicted of so-called white-collar crimes fare better than those found guilty of so-called street crimes. Indeterminate sentences are also blamed for resentment among prisoners because they think too much power is placed in probation and parole boards.

Efforts to change sentencing practices are under way or have been successful in several states.

In Missouri a proposed criminal code, the first revision of that body of law since 1835, is under consideration in the General Assembly. One of its more important provisions involves uniformity in sentencing. A measure to make the federal system more consistent has been introduced in Congress. That legislation would create a special sentencing commission and a procedure for appellate review of terms assessed by judges. The commission would be responsible for fixing ranges of sentences. A judge would have to justify in writing any penalty that did not fall within the prescribed range.

Emphasis would be placed on consideration of the nature and circumstances of the crime, background of the defendant, seriousness of the offense and how the sentence would effect respect for the law and deter crime.

Sentiment has developed in recent years for mandatory sentences instead of indeterminate terms. Mandatory sentences require a convicted criminal to serve time in prison without regard to the circumstances of the crime or background of the individual who committed it. Indeterminate terms allow more flexibility. Missouri and Kansas have mandatory laws; a bill pending in Congress would add that alternative to the federal system.

As matters now stand, sentencing, or much of it, is too arbitrary. The inconsistency is also considered an erosive agent. Sentencing should be designed to curb crime, not encourage it.

THE PLAIN DEALER

Cleveland, Ohio, October 22, 1977

Crime and punishment

For decades, if not generations, criminologists have befuddled themselves and the public with a variety of muddled theories on crime and criminal justice. These theories, put into practice, have added up to a generally perceived failure to deter crime and to deal properly with the criminal.

Fortunately, new voices are now being raised in defense of some disarmingly simple and sensible ideas on the subject.

Simply put, these new concepts center on the deterrent effect of mandatory and predictable prison sentences for crimes of violence.

Lengths of prison sentences would be determined by the crime committed and not by speculative projections of a convicted criminal's future behavior. Thus, parole, shock parole, time off for good behavior and rehabilitative considerations would have a minimal role in determining the length of a criminal's stay behind bars.

Those who committed serious and/or violent crimes and those who contemplated the commission of such crimes would know exactly what awaited them if they were apprehended and convicted.

Existing statistics showing actual prison time served for a wide range of major crimes are strong indications that current sentencing and parole practices provide inadequate deterrents for all too many criminals.

One recent survey conducted by Ohio's Bureau of Criminal Identification revealed that while 43,000 serious offenses were reported in this state in 1975, only 5,084 violent offenders were convicted and nearly 2,500 of these offenders either served no jail time or were incarcerated for only a few months.

When considered together with statistics that show 87% of all serious crimes are committed by repeat offenders, these figures argue powerfully for a system of tough, mandatory sentences for violent offenders and particularly for second-time and third-time offenders, the so-called career criminals.

Following an in-depth study by a special task force, Ohio Atty. Gen. William J. Brown drafted comprehensive legislation providing mandatory minimum sentences for violent offenders, abolition of bail for repeat offenders appealing convictions for crimes of violence, and the addition of 15 appellate court judges to speed up consideration of appeals.

The bill was introduced in the Ohio House in August by State Rep. Dennis E. Eckart, D-18, and hearings are expected to begin next month in the Ohio House Judiciary Committee.

The Plain Dealer believes this bill, and the concepts it incorporates, merit very serious consideration. We urge the Judiciary Committee and its chairman, State Rep. Harry J. Lehman, D-16, to conduct extensive hearings.

The Plain Dealer plans to monitor these hearings and to publish future editorials on this legislation, which we believe may hold the promise for significant improvements in the criminal justice system and in efforts to safeguard a society both frightened and deeply troubled by violent crime.

The Miami Herald

Miami, Fla., February 26, 1977

Mandatory 3 Years Is Little Enough

"THREE years to Life." That's what the billboards on the Florida landscape said in bold type, right next to a stark silhouette of a handgun.

The signs were put up to publicize a 1975 state law requiring a mandatory minimum sentence of three years in prison for persons carrying a firearm during the commission of a felony.

According to the law, there was to be no probation, no parole, no "withholding of adjudication of guilt." In short, no loopholes for the criminals to wriggle through.

Some Florida judges could not believe that the Legislature's act meant what it said, so the law was tested — and the law won. Florida's Supreme Court recently upheld it. Unanimously.

We have no illusions that this statute or any other one will necessarily discourage armed robbers from plying their trade. It's a profitable endeavor, and most of those doing the robbing are not noted for having much concern over the consequences of their acts.

But at least those thugs who do get caught and convicted will be kept out of action for a minimum of three years instead of resuming business as usual after a few hours in the county jail.

Of course, the punishment provides slight consolation for the families of the dead filling-station attendants and convenience-store clerks gunned down by armed robbers.

The bereaved must wish Florida had a law that would put away some of the gun-wielding goons for "three years to life" before they use their guns rather than afterwards.

The Salt Lake Tribune
Salt Lake City, Utah, April 7, 1977

Lift Presence Curtain

In almost every case a judge must have more information than was disclosed during a criminal trial if he is to impose a fair and meaningful sentence.

This essential link between determination of guilt and disposition of the convicted defendant is called a presentence report.

Although value of presentence reports is widely recognized, the manner in which they are utilized is the subject of sometimes heated controversy. Argument stems mainly from differing views on whether the defendant should be allowed to see and contest a report's accuracy.

In Utah it is the judge's decision whether to make ordinary presentence reports available to defendants. Many do. Some reportedly do not.

The other day the Supreme Court of the United States overturned a death penalty imposed on a Florida murderer who had been denied access to the presentence report used by the sentencing judge. The defendant, the court said, must be given a chance to explain or deny contents of such reports.

There are a number of reasons why some judges feel they must keep presentence reports confidential. They believe that disclosure would dry up sources of information, especially information of an intimate sort. It is also felt that disclosure would — or could — unduly delay final disposition of the case. Further, some think disclosure could prove harmful to the rehabilitative efforts of the defendant.

These and other reasons are bolstered by the contention that it is not unfair to the convicted individual to deny access to the report because after conviction his case is no longer a matter of law but a social problem instead.

Adult Probation and Parole officials of the Corrections Division, who prepare presentence reports for Utah courts, flatly reject these arguments.

In light of the Utah probation and parole workers' experience it is difficult to see why any convicted defendant is denied the opportunity to examine his report.

The Utah evidence is significant because it involves a sort of "born again" attitude by probation and parole officials. And the new attitudes are buttressed by events.

Prior to passage of Utah's 90-day diagnostic sentence statute a few years ago, many probation and parole people were adamantly opposed to any form of disclosure of presentence reports. But the new law mandated that the defendant must be allowed to examine the report filed after the 90-day period. None of the feared consequences occurred. Neither, say probation and parole officials, have there been adverse results where ordinary reports were made available to defendants awaiting sentence.

In light of what happened — or failed to happen — when presentence reports were shown defendants and in view of the Supreme Court decision in the Florida murder case, sharing of presentence reports with interested parties should become universal in Utah.

The Evening Bulletin
Philadelphia, Pa., October 9, 1977

Good compromise in sentencing

In a recent study, 50 federal judges were given 20 identical files of actual cases and asked what sentences they would impose on the defendants. In an extortion case one judge sentenced the defendant to 20 years in prison while another sentenced him to only three years. There were other striking differences.

Similar disparities in sentencing exist among state judges. This variation fosters disrespect for the criminal justice system. It creates discontent in prison among inmates serving different sentences for similar crimes. It diminishes the deterrent impact on criminals because it promotes their belief that if they're caught, they could be lucky and get off light.

So uniform sentencing is a worthy goal for all court systems to work toward. Some states like Maine and California have attempted to achieve it by stripping judges of all discretion and substituting fixed sentences for specific crimes. Such a rigid approach creates new problems. No two crimes are exactly the same. Neither are any two criminals. Forcing them into an inflexible formula might result in worse inequities than the disparities of existing discretionary systems.

Pennsylvania's Legislature rejected this compulsory route when it voted down mandatory sentencing during its last session. House Bill 953, currently awaiting action, would set voluntary guidelines for judges in their sentencing. Rather than a specific sentence, it would recommend a range, for example, of from two to four years for burglary.

This bill would provide help particularly useful for judges throughout Pennsylvania who might be unfamiliar with standards for sentencing on crimes that rarely come before their bench. Under the bill's provisions, judges would not have to conform to the bill's guidelines. But their sentences would be subject to appeal to Superior Court. The state's Supreme Court has already required judges to issue written explanations of their sentences.

Moreover, the bill's guidelines would provide for exceptions by defining circumstances that could mitigate or aggravate a crime and reduce or increase the sentence.

The guidelines would be drawn up by a special committee. Its members would be chosen by judges, the Legislature and the Governor — the largest number by the judges.

House Bill 953 was introduced by Rep. Anthony Scirica (R-Montgomery), who has pushed improvements in Pennsylvania's criminal justice system. It seems an excellent compromise.

The Sun Reporter
San Francisco, Calif., February 20, 1977

Mandatory jail not realistic

Proposals of mandatory jail sentences for people who commit serious crimes are receiving strong support from state legislators and law enforcement personnel. Unquestionably, such crimes call for imprisonment rather than today's revolving-door treatment that sends many criminals back onto the streets.

But are the legislators who ask for minimum mandatory sentences also seeking court reforms of the kind proposed by Archibald Cox and supported by Gov. Dukakis? Jammed court dockets are one reason sentencing is either delayed or dispensed with in many cases. Speeding the court process is one objective of the Cox proposals.

Another reason is that the state's prison system does not have the capacity to accommodate everyone convicted of serious crime. The prison system is already overcrowded, and additional capacity is being delayed by the present hassle over prison locations. Catching up with the need will require several years, at least.

Public support for mandatory sentencing may be strong, but it won't be a realistic goal without more cooperation from both the legislature and the public.

JUDGE SENTENCES HEARST TO FIVE YEARS' PROBATION

Superior Court Judge E. Talbot Callister May 9, 1977 sentenced Patricia Hearst to five years' probation on charges stemming from an incident in May 1974 when Hearst sprayed a Los Angeles storefront with gunfire and then, in an overnight escape with two other members of the Symbionese Liberation Army, held two individuals captive. Hearst April 18 had pleaded no contest to two charges in the case—armed robbery and assault with a deadly weapon. Nine other felony charges had been dropped.

In passing sentence, Callister said he did not think there was "a heart in America that isn't full of compassion for the parents [of Hearst]." The prosecuting attorney had unexpectedly joined the defense attorney in recommending leniency for Hearst, saying that the former revolutionary did not appear to present "any threat to the community any longer." Callister did order Hearst to make financial restitution to the owner of the sporting goods store she had shot up in 1974. Hearst was currently free pending appeal of her federal conviction for bank robbery. She had been sentenced to seven years in prison for that conviction.

THE BLADE

Toledo, Ohio, May 12, 1977

THE judge, the defense attorney, even—peculiarly—the prosecutor all were at great pains to rationalize the five years' probation awarded Patty Hearst for her role in a notorious shooting spree. But the wrist-tap "penalty" is one more piece of evidence in a case that to a lot of Americans constitutes classic proof that wealth and position really do make a difference in the halls of justice.

The judge explained his leniency on grounds that Miss Hearst is not a threat to society. Perhaps no longer. But the defendant did, after all, plead no contest — in effect, guilty — to charges of armed robbery and assault with a deadly weapon in a shoot-out in which one of her bullets wounded the robbery victim. So is there not something to be said for meting out a semblance of punishment for commission of crimes of violence which under California law could result in a sentence of 15½ years to life in prison?

Not according to the deputy district attorney, who contended that "it would be wrong to satisfy those who say there is a special treatment for the rich by punishing this defendant disproportionately." But to many citizens it is hardly right to treat the defendant disproportionately to her benefit. How many other persons who commit such crimes as Miss Hearst for all intents and purposes admitted are suffering no greater penalty than probation? Is this really the standard treatment recommended by this prosecutor for offenses involving robbery with firearms and actual wounding?

But then, to hear one of Miss Hearst's attorneys tell it, the "consideration of her wealth and the name of her family worked against her every step of the way." It is one of his favorite lines, and he cannot be blamed for using it in his role for the defense. But it does not fit the impression left on the public by such facts as the continual delays Miss Hearst was able to get in court proceedings, the particularly considerate treatment she received during the relatively short time she spent in jail, and her family's ability to provide the bail to free her pending appeal of a bank-robbery conviction.

No, the handling of Miss Hearst's case — despite the "compassion for her parents" which the judge, in a comment totally irrelevant to the issue before him, professed to detect in every American heart — has not enhanced the image of justice across the land.

SAN JOSE NEWS

San Jose, Calif., May 12, 1977

Patricia Hearst, having received probation for the same crime for which two Symbionese Liberation Army companions were sentenced to prison, finds herself the central figure in a new storm of controversy. At issue is the equality of justice.

Retired Los Angeles Superior Court Judge Mark Brandler, who sentenced Emily and William Harris to 11 years to life in prison after their convictions in a robbery and shootout at an Inglewood sporting goods store, was quick to object.

Many who compare his sentencing of the Harrises to the probation granted Miss Hearst, he said, may " conclude there is unequal justice and punishment in our courts."

The judge is right. This already is happening.

It is difficult to approach the Hearst case without mixed thoughts and emotions. Among those firmly convinced that the sentences should have been the same, the background of Miss Hearst's original abduction and her apparently fear-filled conversion to terrorism are dismissed as irrelevant. "She got off because she was rich," is a common conclusion.

Of course, it also was because she was rich that Miss Hearst was an SLA victim in the first place. And last year when she stood trial for bank robbery, being rich didn't keep her from being convicted. The conviction and a seven-year sentence is under appeal.

The Hearst case is a bad one to use in an argument over equality of justice. There are too many complications.

But the controversy it has evoked may illustrate the wisdom of California's pending switch to a system of determinate sentences. The result will be a sharp limit on the discretion of judges. Their options will be narrowed. No longer will one party receive 11 years to life and another probation for the same crime.

The uncertainty of today's justice, in particular the wide variances in sentences for the same offenses, found the public speculating about "unequal justice and punishment" long before Patricia Hearst was heard of.

It is significant that the commitment to more uniform sentences does not end in Sacramento. The newest legislation to reform and recodify federal criminal laws (S-1437) includes guidelines for sentencing by federal judges.

Only experience will prove the wisdom or folly of determinate sentencing. But its potential for eliminating suspicions of unequal justice has taken on added significance.

THE STATES-ITEM

New Orleans, La., May 12, 1977

Los Angeles Superior Court Judge E. Talbot Callister faced a difficult job in reaching a decision in the Patricia Hearst case.

She had pleaded no contest to charges of assault and robbery in a 1974 shootout at a sporting goods store, and the judge could have given her up to life in prison, adding that sentence to the seven years she has received in a San Francisco robbery. By doing so, Judge Callister could have run the risk of criticism for ruining a young woman's life, and he would have gone against the wishes of both sides in the case.

Or he could put the 23-year-old heiress on probation, which would virtually free her and leave the judge vulnerable to the charge that those with access to money and power — Miss Hearst fits both categories — can avoid justice.

He chose the latter route after hearing prosecution and defense attorneys ask that Miss Hearst spend no more time in jail because, they said, she poses no threat to society.

There were also kind references to Miss Hearst's parents, who have assumed responsibility for her behavior.

This decision was wrong — not because the judge exercised compassion but because the ruling can only serve to erode Americans' flagging faith in "equal justice under law." This tenet, which is carved on the U.S. Supreme Court building, was severely damaged by former President Nixon's pardon, and Judge Callister's decision was not reassuring.

Some of Miss Hearst's sympathizers argue that she has already suffered enough for the incidents that occurred during her life underground with the ragtag Symbionese Liberation Army. This is an appeal to the heart, not to reason, and it has not kept others out of jail.

THE SAGINAW NEWS

Saginaw, Mich., May 11, 1977

Second-guessing a criminal sentence is chancy business, especially in one of the most bizarre cases of the century.

In our view, however, the judge who lightly slapped Patty Hearst on the wrist richly deserves some second-guessing.

The fact that her parents are "good people who love their daughter" hardly seems to justify probation for admittedly spraying machine-gun fire into a sporting goods store during a robbery.

Any way one looks at it, Patty Hearst without her parents' millions would simply be another young criminal going to prison. The lesson that we have a double standard of justice will not be lost on less-privileged young people who turn to violence for whatever purpose and lose their freedom behind bars.

Patty can now return peacefully to her embroidering and horseback-riding, while her parents' attorneys fight her appeal in her bank-robbery conviction.

We can hear the groans from the blindfolded lady holding the scales of justice.

The Des Moines Register

Des Moines, Iowa, May 12, 1977

It would be easy, and wrong, to jump to conclusions about the dispensation of justice with respect to Patricia Hearst. But those inclined to think that her family's money is getting her off easy ignore the unique circumstances of her case.

She was kidnaped by a lunatic band, the Symbionese Liberation Army (SLA), and physically and psychologically abused. Her criminal acts took place when she was under the influence, if not control, of the SLA.

So placing Hearst on five years probation, as a California judge has just done, is an appropriate penalty for her part in the armed robbery of a sporting goods store in 1974 (she also is required to make restitution for damages). Hearst could have been sentenced to a 15½-year-to-life prison term for assault and robbery, charges to which she pleaded "no contest."

Defense and prosecution alike recommended probation. They described Hearst as no threat to society and as a victim of authorities who may have gone too far in their determination to avoid charges of favoritism on behalf of the heiress.

However that may be, Patricia Hearst already has been so profoundly affected, her life so disrupted and complicated (by another prison sentence, for one thing), that further substantive state-imposed penalties would be vindictive.

THE PLAIN DEALER

Cleveland, Ohio, May 12, 1977

At first blush, the absence of jail time in the five-year probation sentence handed down to Patricia Hearst on armed robbery and assault charges must seem a classic case of leniency for a wealthy and prominent felon. But on reflection, we suggest the sentence fits the crimes considered in the context in which they were committed.

Miss Hearst simply does not fit the usual profile of the armed robber. As Los Angeles Superior Court Judge E. Talbot Callister noted, it is impossible to believe that Miss Hearst would have played her role in the robbery of Mel's Sporting Goods Store had she not first been kidnaped by the brutal and bizarre Symbionese Liberation Army.

Judge Callister's conclusion was sensibly drawn.

Parenthetically, although it did not succeed as a defense in her earlier trial on federal bank robbery charges, there is credible evidence that many kidnap and hostage victims undergo a psychological transformation that leads them to involuntarily identify with and aid their kidnapers. Miss Hearst's youthfulness and insecurity would seem to have made her particularly vulnerable to this reaction.

Certainly this case could not have been fairly judged without reference to the mitigating circumstances, including the fact that Miss Hearst pleaded no contest to the charges.

Finally, the pre-sentencing probation report indicated that Miss Hearst is not likely to pose a future threat to society. The report's recommendation — probation for Miss Hearst — was rejected by the Los Angeles County Probation Department. Nevertheless, the tenor of the report rings true. It is difficult to foresee a circumstance in which Miss Hearst might again become an armed robber.

Patricia Hearst remains free on $1.2 million bail pending appeal of her conviction on the federal bank robbery charge. She faces a seven-year prison sentence for that conviction. She is far from out of the woods.

We cannot judge whether her appeal will or should succeed. But we can say that the character of the defendant and of her crimes in the sporting goods store incident justify her five-year probation sentence.

Chicago Tribune

Chicago, Ill., May 11, 1977

The judge called it the most difficult of the thousands of cases he has heard. The prosecuting attorney concurred, "There has never been a case like this." And with that, they agreed to nudge the bizarre and painful story of Patty Hearst another step nearer what seems, in view of all that has happened, to be a sensible ending.

Miss Hearst pleaded nolo contendre to charges of participating in a robbery and shooting at a Los Angeles sports shop in 1974, and could have been sentenced to as much as life in prison. Instead, she drew five years' probation and must pay $6,000 to the store owner.

Miss Hearst's troubles aren't over, of course. She is still out on $1 million bail pending appeal of a seven year sentence for her role in a San Francisco bank robbery staged by her captors, the self-styled Symbionese Liberation Army.

Justice is difficult in this unprecedented case. Public opinion toward her has swung wildly from sympathy to confusion and to condemnation. But the machine-gunning, obscenity-spouting Tania seems to have been replaced by a more contrite Patty, and the fragile, troubled, vulnerable young woman has once again caught the nation's sympathy. Fears that a Hearst heiress would get off lightly because of her wealth and family position have gradually shifted to a feeling she has perhaps been treated more harshly for these very reasons.

So we concur with the decision by Judge E. Talbot Callister to give Miss Hearst probation—not so much because of his reasoning that she is not a "present or future" threat to society, but because of factors inherent in the case itself. Not even psychologists can agree with the effects of the violent kidnapping and weeks of physical and emotional torment the SLA inflicted on Miss Hearst. But these are beyond doubt powerful extenuating circumstances. And Miss Hearst has already served 14 months in jail without bond.

We welcome, too, the removal of one more burden from the Hearst family. Millions of other parents, who may also feel rejected by their grown children, have watched the Hearsts trying to pay the $2 million ransom demand in food for the poor, to rescue their daughter from the radical underground, to pay her enormous legal fees, and to find some ground of reconciliation, can only sigh in relief that part of the long nightmare is over.

THE ARIZONA REPUBLIC

Phoenix, Ariz., May 16, 1977

MEMBERS of the legal community are in debate, the public is disturbed, and the criminal justice system has a new basis for criminal leniency.

All this because of a single decision by Los Angeles Superior Court Judge E. Talbott Callister.

He is the jurist who gave five years probation to newspaper heiress Patty Hearst, rather than prison time, for her part in a 21-hour crime rampage two years ago.

The sentence of probation is even more strange when one considers that Miss Hearst's co-defendants — Symbionese Liberation Army members Emily and Bill Harris — were given 11 years in the slammer for less violence.

Although all three were charged with kidnapping two men and theft of four vehicles, Miss Hearst did the Harrises one better by spraying the front of a sports shop with a fusillade of 30 submachine gun bullets.

Judge Callister gave two reasons for letting off Miss Hearst:

✔ That she had no record of criminality prior to the 1974 episode.

✔ That she probably is no "present or future" threat to society.

Several judges, including the one who presided over the Harris trial, have been critical of Judge Callister's decision. And properly so.

For what Judge Callister has done is to take a gigantic leap in the criminal justice philosophy that punishment should fit the individual, and not the crime.

The fact that (a) Miss Hearst was not a crime-prone person before her first crime and (b) that her menacing behavior is a thing of the past is specious in the extreme.

The same could be said of probably half the defendants in criminal cases in this country. How many felons are first-timers who are not likely to repeat their acts?

Can the courts excuse criminals in the hope they have learned their lesson?

Miss Hearst did not deny she machine gunned the sports shop. She didn't claim she was under duress. She simply, and wantonly, opened fire without regard to where the flying bullets would strike.

The system, which Miss Hearst branded as being filled with "pigs," has not learned that leniency historically has led to even higher levels of crime and violence.

ARKANSAS DEMOCRAT

Little Rock, Ark., May 12, 1977

While we're trying to forget Watergate, let's all of us try really hard to forget Patricia Hearst, too. If there's no question about Richard Nixon's guilt (and there isn't) what are we to say about Hearst's probationary five year sentence for machine gunning a sporting goods store as a cover action for a robbery?

Let's see. What all did Hearst do? She robbed a bank (7 years) and pleaded no contest to the assault-and-robbery charges growing out of the machine-gunning incident. She is out of prison (she isn't "safe" there) while on appeal from the first conviction — and Superior Court Judge E. Talbott Callister says she's no threat to society.

Deputy District Atty. Sam Mayerson says moreover that law enforcement was so intent on not showing favoritism that there was danger of Hearst's "being punished too harshly." We suppose the judge felt that way, too; for he remarked on how all American hearts were with the defendant's parents. He could have given Hearst life in prison.

So ends — we're tempted to say — the case of Patricia Hearst, whose tale was that she did all these things while a kidnap victim. One jury didn't buy the story and her plea of no contest in the sporting store case was probably a wise one, considering how both judge and prosecution were moved to the heart by her plight.

Oh, yes, Mayerson had this final remark. "There has never been another case like this and I sincerely hope there will not be again." So do we, Sam.

DAILY NEWS

New York, N.Y., May 11, 1977

California Judge E. Talbot Callister's emotional drivel about Patty Hearst's poor, distraught parents really sticks in our craw.

Under the circumstances, the judge's sentence of probation for the newspaper heiress' part in the sporting-goods store shootup may have been the proper mix of justice and compassion.

But his speech about how the Hearsts are "good people who love their daughter," and how hearts in America are "full of compassion for her parents" makes it look as if his decision was based on what family Patty came from—not what crime she committed.

Most parents are heartbroken when their children get in trouble. Is their grief less genuine, or less deserving of judicial pity, than the Hearsts'?

The Hartford Courant

Hartford, Conn., May 30, 1977

The relatively light sentences given Patricia Hearst and Claudine Longet are grounds for legitimate claims that rich folks and other folks face different standards of justice.

These widely-publicized cases, though, are being used improperly by judges who seem unwilling to think for themselves when they reduce the sentences of more ordinary defendants.

Courts at all levels face the problem of sharply different sentences given for similar crimes. But in their search for a common denominator, the courts should not settle for the lowest.

By any standard, Miss Hearst's case is a unique episode in the history of criminal law. Miss Longet's case was not as unusual, but it received extraordinary publicity.

There is at least one recorded instance in which a judge sharply reduced a sentence, citing the probation given Miss Hearst by a state court in California (she also faces a seven-year term on federal charges). It is widely believed that other judges have done the same without openly stating the reason. The Hearst and Longet cases have become precedents not because they provide enlightened new insight into the law but because they have been widely publicized.

The immediate solution is for judges to make best use of what is supposed to be their leading quality: Their judgment. Judges often show concern about the influence of publicity on jurors; they should also check up on themselves.

A longer-range answer might be found in the most recent proposal to revise the federal criminal code. Standard sentences would be established for various offenses, and judges could use these as basing points from which to allow for the circumstances of specific cases.

To observe such standards would establish a degree of equity and uniformity. The standards, though, should not merely be adopted from the most widely-publicized cases.

DAYTON DAILY NEWS

Dayton, Ohio, May 11, 1977

In the decision to place Patty Hearst on five years' probation for shooting up a sporting goods store during a hold-up, the criminal justice system finally has managed to take a clear-eyed look at her case.

Los Angeles Judge Talbot Callister neatly checked off the reasons for not adding another prison sentence to the one Miss Hearst already faces if her appeal fails.

To protect society? The chance of Miss Hearst becoming a desperado again are so small you'd have to range far right of the decimal to find it. To rehabilitate the defendant? There's nothing about Miss Hearst to suggest she's the least "criminal" in ordinary circumstances. To deter other crime? Only in the unlikely event any criminal identifies with Miss Hearst personally or with her situation. To prove the rich don't get off easy? That would mistreat her because she is rich.

Further, and properly, the judge took into account the fact that Miss Hearst already has spent nearly a year in jail and that she took up law-breaking after "57 days of horrible torture by her abductors," as he put it.

The judicial proceedings through which Miss Hearst is being sprocketed have excited a lynching mood in an appalling number of us, inspiring cynicism and vindictiveness in about equal measure.

Yet the abiding feature of the case is that Miss Hearst is at least as much a victim as is anyone else — an accident victim, say, of the collision of her own personality with a band of crazies, at an intersection that she not only didn't seek but to which in fact she was forcibly taken.

This does not, of course, utterly wash her of responsibility for her reactions, as the consequent indictments alone emphasize. But it is interesting how self-righteous many folks are — a claimed sanguinity about themselves serviced, at least in part, by the fact that they never are likely to be tested comparably.

Question: How much of this prison-mongering is a kind of whistling past the graveyard by persons really uncertain about the strengths of their own personalities?

Capital Punishment: Is it cruel or unusual?

In 1972 the Supreme Court in the case of *Furman v. Georgia,* struck down as unconstitutional the existing laws permitting capital punishment, that is, the imposition of the death penalty as a form of punishment.[1] Proponents of capital punishment feared that after 200 years the death penalty was soon to be extinct in the United States. Seasoned readers realized that the *Furman* decision (unique in itself in that each of nine justices wrote a separate opinion) focused the Court's concern on how the death sentence was applied, not on the death sentence itself. Only two justices firmly rejected the death penalty as an unconstitutional measure.

Any understanding of the principles underpinning the rationale of the death penalty cases requires an analysis of the Supreme Court's definition of the "cruel and unusual" clause of the Eighth Amendment. "Cruel and unusual punishment" draws its meaning from the "evolving standards of decency that mark the progress of a maturing society."[2] When the Eighth Amendment was adopted in 1791, capital punishment was applied in about a dozen criminal classifications. It was not as widely used as in England, where more than 200 crimes, including breach of the peace, were subject to the death penalty. The number of crimes subject to the penalty of death was progressively reduced so that most states only employed capital punishment in cases of pre-meditated murder. This was achieved because of the pressure of the Quakers and others influenced by the theories of Cesare Beccaria, who believed that capital punishment was not an effective deterrent since it was applied so randomly.[3] William Bradford, first an attorney general of Pennsylvania and then of the United States, was a powerful exponent of imposing the death penalty only in instances of murder. The religious revival of the 1830's and 1840's and the anti-slavery movement, also deeply opposed to capital punishment, helped spread the crusade for abolition. The movement had the greatest success in the New England and Mid-Atlantic states, though Michigan in 1846 was the first state to eliminate the gallows except for treason. By the start of the Civil War, three-quarters of the states had made robbery and burglary non-capital offenses. The South lagged in the abolition movement, particularly North Carolina which listed 20 capital crimes up until the Civil War. Slaves were subject to execution for any number of trivial reasons. By the time the Supreme Court decided *Furman,* approximately one-quarter of the states had eliminated the practice altogether.

The constitutional standards of "cruel and unusual" are thus defined by the prevailing sentiment of the populace and the history of capital punishment. Justice Byron White, who has held that execution is not a constitutionally impermissible form of punishment, believes that a dictionary would define it as cruel.[4] Opinion polls have revealed a dramatic shift in support for the death penalty; in 1966 40% favored it, but in 1976 the figure was 60%.[5]

Justice Thurgood Marshall, one of the two members of the Court who finds the death penalty, no matter how applied, to be cruel and unusual, has cautioned against the use of raw opinion polls: the question is not whether a substantial proportion of Americans would find "that capital punishment is barbarously cruel but whether they would find it to be so in the light of all information presently available."[6] A survey conducted after Justice Marshall's opinion seemed to bolster the hypothesis that many Americans support the death penalty based on false assumptions.[7] The pollsters provided the interview sample with some salient facts about murder statistics: alcohol is associated with two-thirds of criminal homicides;[8] most murders are the result of arguments between acquaintances;[9] and first degree murder parolees have the lowest rate of recidivism for any group of convicts.[10] In one study, out of 1293 parolees convicted of murder, only one was convicted of a second murder.[11] After exposure to this information, support for the death penalty plummeted. If most murders are a result of alcoholism and momentary anger, a highly combustible mix not easily regulated by threat of sanctions, it is questionable if capital punishment would serve as a deterrent. The old adage of an eighteenth century British judge to a convicted defendant seems to have worn thin: "Young man, you are to be hanged not because you have stolen a sheep, but in order that others shall not steal sheep."

Public opinion aside, it is the behavior of the legislatures to which the majority of the Court looks for guidance in determining its definitions. Thus, in *Coker v. Georgia,* the Supreme Court struck down as unconstitutional the death penalty in rape cases.[12] In part, this decision was based on the fact that the vast majority of the states had eliminated the death penalty for rape. In *Gregg v. Georgia* the Court noted that since *Furman* 35 states had enacted statutes providing for the death penalty in crimes resulting in the death of a person;[13] that Congress passed a death penalty for air piracy resulting in death; and that the voters of California passed a constitutional amendment authorizing capital punishment after the State Supreme Court ruled it unconstitutional. The willingness of the jury at times to impose the death penalty also signaled to the Court that contemporary values still supported use of capital punishment.

By itself, support of the community is still inadequate to satisfy the constitutional requirements of the Eighth Amendment, "the sanction imposed can not be so totally without penological justification that it results in the gratuitous infliction of suffering."[14] The legitimate bases for inflicting the punishment of death are retribution and deterrence. The fact that retribution had earlier been declared as "no longer the dominant objective of the criminal law,"[15] did not forbid its application in cases that are "so grievous an affront to humanity." Total rejection of the biblical concept of retribution, the Court feared, would result in a threat to the stability of government.

"When people begin to believe that organized society is unwilling or unable to impose upon criminal offenders the punishment they 'deserve' then there are sown the seeds of anarchy, of self-help, vigilante justice, and lynch law."[16]

On the crucial question of deterrence, the Court did not dispute the fact that there has been no convincing proof[17] that the death penalty has had any effect on homicide rates. Rather, in the absence of hard statistics, the Court reasoned that it would not be constitutionally impermissible for a legislature to make a reasoned judgment that for certain classifications of murder the death penalty would serve as a deterrent.

Finally, the Court asked itself if the penalty of death is disproportionate in relation to the crime for which it is imposed. In the question of rape, where the physical harm is usually not permanent, the Court answered in the affirmative, stating that it was grossly out of proportion to the seriousness of the crime. In the case of murder, however, the Court reasoned otherwise: "It is an extreme sanction, suitable to the most extreme of crimes."[18]

The Court's conclusive rejection of the argument that the death penalty was an unacceptable mode of punishment was not reached until 1976. The *Furman* decision of 1972 sidetracked the fundamental issue and rejected the existing capital punishment statutes as unconstitutional because of the arbitrary and capricious manner in which they were applied. The infrequent imposition of the death penalty in the preceding ten years had created a situation where it was highly unlikely that a defendant convicted of murder would actually be executed. The deterrent justification of capital punishment would be eroded if there was no certainty that murder would be punished by death. A review of past executions demonstrated no clear standards in the imposition of the sentence: a depraved killer might receive a life sentence while a one-time murderer might experience the gallows. In view of the penalty's uniqueness in its total irrevocability, its unabashed rejection of rehabilitation, and "its absolute renunciation of all that is embodied in our concept of humanity" the Court insisted that specific due process safeguards be established to prevent the death penalty from being imposed "so wantonly and freakishly."[19] It is interesting to note that Edmund Burke, the eighteenth century conservative English philosopher, presented a contrary argument in fearing that the impact of sentencing and hanging would only be diminished if it became too common:

> "It is certain that a great havock among criminals hardens, rather than subdues, the minds of people inclined to the same crimes; and therefore fails of answering its purpose as an example."[20]

Justice Potter Stewart mentioned that if there was a discernible thread visible throughout death row, it was the color black. Of all the persons executed since 1930, 53.5% have been black.[21] This frequency is far higher than the proportion of blacks in the general population or among those convicted of crimes. If only execution statistics for burglary and rape are examined, the discriminatory nature of the death penalty is placed in sharper focus: 100% of all those executed for burglary and 95% for rape were black.[22]

The response of the state legislatures to conform to the Supreme Court decision requiring due process standards in imposing the death penalty was uneven. The 1976 term of the Supreme Court rejected the death penalty statutes of Louisiana[23] and North Carolina,[24] but approved the statutes of Texas,[25] Georgia[26] and Florida.[27] The Louisiana and North Carolina state legislatures attempted to eliminate the arbitrary nature of executions by simply making the death penalty mandatory in all murder convictions. The Supreme Court made it clear that mandatory death sentences were as constitutionally abhorrent as capricious death sentences and countered the general historical trend of applying capital punishment sparingly.[28] The state statutes that were approved generally contained an individualized sentencing determination that provided the jury with specific guidelines in deciding whether to invoke the death penalty. After a decision of guilt, the jury would have to consider not only why the death penalty should be imposed but why it should not. The jury should take into consideration the circumstances of the crime, the attributes of the defendant and any mitigating factors. The defendant also should be entitled to an expedited appeal, allowing an appellate court to review the comparability of each death sentence with the sentence imposed on similarly situated defendants to insure that the sentence of death would not be disproportionate. All of these requirements are necessary to avoid the arbitrary and capricious imposition of the death sentence.

The procedural barriers constructed by a Supreme Court, desirous of all but outlawing the death penalty, have not impeded the prosecutors; several hundred people now wait on death row. Nor has it seemed to eliminate the criterion of race in determining who shall die; more than half of those sentenced to die belong to racial minorities. However, it has confronted Americans with the specter of state executions for the first time since 1967.

The Gary Gilmore spectacle and the debate over whether executions should be publicized serve as a clear warning that the operation of the electric chair, the gallows, the firing squad and the gas chamber may soon be as impressed upon the American consciousness as the hanging tree of Tyburn, the three-legged gallows once used to execute London's condemned, was on the English of the eighteenth century.[29] In a world where over 70 countries have ended capital punishment,[30] the United States faces the dubious distinction, like London of yore, of becoming the citadel of the gallows.[31]

Whether public executions will have any deterrent value is of some doubt. It is frequently remarked that the surest place to have had one's pockets picked in eighteenth century England was at a public hanging. Charles Dickens in *Oliver Twist* reminds us that pickpockets also faced the gallows. However, one survey reveals another equation: as the frequency of executions rise so does the opposition to them.[32]

Notes

1. *Furman v. Georgia,* 408 U.S. 238 (1972).
2. *Trop v. Dulles,* 356 U.S. 86, 101 (1958).
3. See Michael Meltsner, *Cruel and Unusual: The Supreme Court and Capital Punishment* (New York: Randon House, 1973) pp. 47–51; Hugo Bedau, ed., *The Death Penalty in America* (Garden City, N.Y.: Anchor, 1967).
4. *Furman, supra* 312 (White, J., concurring).
5. Austin Sarat & Neil Vidmar, "Public Opinion and the Death Penalty," 1976 *University of Wisconsin Law Review* 171, 175.
6. *Furman, supra* at 362 (Marshall, J., concurring).
7. See especially Sarat & Vidmar *supra,* pp. 187–191.
8. Marvin E. Wolfgang, "A Sociological Analysis of Criminal Homicide," in *The Death Penalty in America, supra,* pp. 74–89.
9. *Ibid.*
10. Sarat & Vidmar, *supra,* p. 202.
11. Ibid.
12. *Coker v. Georgia,* 45 U.S.L.W. 4961 (June 29, 1977).
13. *Gregg v. Georgia,* 428 U.S. 153, 179–181 (1976).
14. *Gregg, supra,* 183.
15. *Williams v. New York,* 337 U.S. 241, 248 (1949).
16. *Furman, supra,* 308 (Stewart, J., concurring).
17. See Thorsten Sellin, "Execution in the U.S.," in *Capital Punishment,* ed. by Thorsten Sellin (New York: Harper & Row, 1967) p. 35.
18. *Gregg, supra,* 187.
19. *Furman, supra,* 310 (Stewart, J., concurring).
20. Quoted in Douglas Hay, "Property, Authority and the Criminal Law," in *Albions Fatal Tree* (New York: Pantheon, 1975), p. 56.
21. *Prison Statistics,* No. 45 "Capital Punishment 1930–1968" (August, 1969) p. 7.
22. *Ibid.*
23. *Roberts v. Louisiana,* 428 U.S. 325 (1976).
24. *Woodson v. North Carolina,* 428 U.S. 280 (1976).
25. *Jurek v. Texas,* 428 U.S. 262 (1976).
26. *Gregg, supra.*
27. *Proffitt v. Florida,* 428 U.S. 242 (1976).
28. *Woodson, supra,* pp. 291–296.
29. Peter Linebaugh, "The Tyburn Riot Against the Surgeons," in *Albion's Fatal Tree, supra* at pp. 65–117.
30. Some of these nations have ended capital punishment by actual abolition (*de jure*), others by practice (*de facto*). See *United Nations Department of Economical and Social Affairs, Capital Punishment* (1968). Pt. II pp. 83–85, 96–97.
31. Peter Linebaugh, *supra,* p. 66.
32. See *Furman, supra,* p. 340 (Marshall, J., concurring).

SUPREME COURT BARS DEATH PENALTY AS 'CRUEL & UNUSUAL' PUNISHMENT

The U.S. Supreme Court ruled 5–4 June 29 that the death penalty as it was currently applied in the U.S. violated the Eighth Amendment's prohibition against cruel and unusual punishment. The court's majority opinion did not, however, irrevocably abolish capital punishment; three of the five justices wrote opinions indicating that new laws eliminating the discretionary manner in which the death sentence was applied might be viewed as constitutional by the court. The decision granted an immediate reprieve to the estimated 600 inmates in prison death rows across the country. The last execution took place in 1967.

Voting with the majority, Justice Potter Stewart concluded that the death sentence was unconstitutional "under legal systems which permit this unique penalty to be so wantonly and so freakishly imposed." Justice Byron R. White, in a concurring opinion, added that the deterrent factor "would not be substantially served where the penalty is so seldom invoked that it ceases to be the credible threat essential to influence the conduct of others." Justice William O. Douglas objected to the way the death penalty was "selectively applied, feeding prejudices against the accused if he is poor and despised . . . lacking political clout, or if he is a member of an unpopular minority." Justices Thurgood Marshall and William J. Brennan Jr. said the imposition of the death penalty was inconsistent with twentieth century moral principles. Brennan noted that the death penalty "must inevitably be inflicted upon innocent men" and that "death has been the lot of men whose convictions were unconstitutionally secured in view of later, retroactively applied, holdings of this Court."

Chief Justice Warren E. Burger led the four Nixon appointees in dissent, charging that the effective banning of the death penalty violated the principles of federalism and separation of powers incorporated in the Constitution. Burger suggested that state legislatures could remedy the arbitrary and selective way in which the death penalty is administered by setting "standards for juries and judges to follow in determining the sentence in capital cases or by more narrowly defining the crimes for which the penalty is to be imposed."

The Afro American
Baltimore, Md., July 15, 1972

The Supreme Court by the closest of margins, 5 to 4, has abolished the death penalty as "cruel and unusual punishment."

At long last the United States has lifted its head from the dark ages and joined more enlightened nations of the world in discarding this barbaric practice of legalized killing.

The fact that 600 men were on death row at the time of the ruling adds credence to the argument that executions have not been an ultimate in detering crime.

There are no indications in other countries nor in states that abolished the death penalty earlier that moving away from executions caused any dramatic increase in capital crimes.

But there is plenty of evidence to show that executions sometimes resulted in the legal murder of the wrong man and that they discriminated against the poor, particularly the black.

Justice William O. Douglas, Thurgood Marshall, William J. Brennan Jr., Potter Stewart and Byron R. White turned in the majority decision while President Nixon's four appointees disagreed. All nine justices filed separate opinions.

Unless we are a lot worse as a society than other countries, the abolishing of the death penalty will prove a healthy thing.

Los Angeles Times
Los Angeles, Calif., June 30, 1972

The Supreme Court has decided that the death penalty, as generally applied in the United States, is in violation of the Constitution.

The court decision, by its length, by the variety and occasional contradiction of its opinions, by the diversity of its reservations and dissents, reflects the uncertainty of the nation itself on this question. For the moral and legal aspects have become overwhelmed in the minds of many by questions of personal security in a time of increasing violence in the American society. And fact is not easily separated from opinion, nor reason from emotion.

We are convinced that the death penalty is no longer appropriate, if it ever was, in the American system of justice. We would have preferred to see it eliminated by legislative action and constitutional amendment. But in this, as in some other sensitive issues, legislative determination has not matched need. Confronted with the issue, the courts, both state and federal, have had no choice but to act. And in their actions, they have frequently disagreed.

It would have been more satisfactory, if the federal court could have acted with the near unanimity of the decision of the California Supreme Court last February. We welcomed that decision as a wise application of judicial power in the contemporary interpretation of the state constitution. If the federal decision is less clear, it is no less welcome.

The decision appears to leave standing those laws that make mandatory the death penalty and to leave with the Congress and the legislatures of the states discretion to provide mandatory capital punishment if it is found essential to controlling certain heinous crimes. This was implicit, at least, in the opinions of two of the five justices who found the death penalty generally unconstitutional, and it can be assumed that the four justices in dissent would uphold such laws. If the death penalty is to be tolerated at all, it is reasonable to apply it only where it is mandatory, for this would eliminate the broad abuse and discrimination which has seen, according to some studies, a disproportionate number of the poor on Death Row.

There is no certainty whether this decision will disqualify the constitutional amendment on the November ballot in California. This amendment was designed to overcome the decision of the California court and restore the death penalty to the state constitution. At first glance, its provisions would appear to violate the principles supported Thursday by the federal court.

Some proponents of the death penalty have argued that it is essential to law and order. The Supreme Court, like the California court before it, found no persuasive evidence that the death penalty is a deterrent to crime. It is apparent that law and order depend on other things, a broad balance between law enforcement, swift and sure justice, progressive corrections.

The sweep of the decision appears to us just, consistent with the value placed on individual life in America today.

THE ROANOKE TIMES
Roanoke, Va., July 1, 1972

Traditionally this newspaper has supported at l e a s t tentatively the idea that c a p i t a l punishment, as practiced in the United States, is wrong according to the best ethics. Another view has been expressed less forcefully: It is hard to support the belief that society should provide lifetime maintenance for a certain level of criminals: men like Sirhan Sirhan, killer of the late Sen. Robert Kennedy; James Earl Ray, killer of the Rev. Martin Luther King; and Arthur Bremer if he is convicted of the attempt to murder Gov. George Wallace.

The rule of an eye for an eye, a tooth for tooth, has receded in the slow growth of civilization. Belief in the death penalty as a deterrent to murder also has eroded in the face of some hard statistics to the contrary. Nevertheless there are c r i m e s of such outrageous intent and consequences as to merit capital punishment with some hope of it being a deterrent. Kidnapping, sky-jacking, political assassinations, killings of prisoners by prisoners, killings of guards in a prison, killings of police and court officials would be among them.

Upon those convicted of such outrageous capital crimes we wish no cruel and u n u s u a l punishment; a swift and painless death will do. Those who perform such crimes do not have a due bill for lifetime support. Their tortured past histories, suggesting childhood surroundings or society in general are to blame and not them individually, are regrettable but dispensable. Life must become more tolerable for the law-abiding citizens who ride airplanes, run for political office, obey the law and defend the defenders of the law.

The opinion expressed above is not unanimously supported by the editorial staff, but it prevails. Its greatest weakness is the always horrible possibility that the *wrong* person be condemned to a swift, painless death. Another weakness is that even when guilt is sure and the level of crime worthy of death, years of delay can intervene and make a mockery of a solemn proceeding. American justice has not yet suitably met the demands for both certainty of guilt and swiftness of execution.

S i n c e there are five different opinions in the five-man majority, these must be studied in detail to see if there is a sufficient uniformity of opinion on which state officials can act and private citizens deliberate. The four-man minority opinions need also to be searched. While many concessions must be made to the higher ethic and some demonstrated fact, there should not be a complete abandonment of capital punishment. For capital crimes punishment is not society's revenge but society's attempt to maintain itself peaceably.

THE KANSAS CITY STAR
Kansas City, Mo., July 1, 1972

With the death penalty lifted from more than 600 individuals awaiting execution in the United States, a heavy burden also is lifted from the spirit of the country.

The decision this week by the Supreme Court was 5-4 against legal killing. Nine separate opinions were given. There is the possibility that, in the future, capital punishment might be permissible in a state under mandatory and narrow law for very specific offenses and that the court might uphold such a law. But that does not seem likely. There has been no execution in the United States for nearly six years. What state would like to be first to resume the practice? There was a story out of Topeka many years ago that when Kansas decided to reinstate the death penalty after an absence of years, the legislators could not determine the method. It was resolved when somebody stood up and said:

"Hangin's cheaper."

And so Kansas decided to suffocate its major felons by means of a rope. Other states have suffocated them by gas. Some have burned them to death with electricity. Even in the states with long traditions of putting criminals to death there may be a reluctance to return to suffocation (and sometimes decapitation) or burning or any other means of ending a life.

That said, the public has a right to expect protection from people who maim and kill other people. The public has a right to expect protection from the type of mind that can bring on the indescribable anguish that comes with the kidnaping of a child or that places an airplane full of people on the edge of extinction. Whether the death penalty is a deterrent in these matters, as the President suggested the other night, is open for debate. But a life sentence ought to mean a life sentence—not parole after a few years. Many can agree with the essential court philosophy that the death sentence has been "wantonly and freakishly" applied in violation of the 14th Amendment and that it is "cruel and unusual" to kill a person and in violation of the 8th Amendment.

But a shudder goes through the nation at the thought of the eventual release of mass killers or individuals who killed slowly and deliberately with forethought. No matter what reasons are given concerning insanity or what evidence is given of cure, the public simply does not want such people on the loose.

The death penalty ought to go and go forever with no exceptions. Justice Thurgood Marshall is right in his view that it is a milestone on the long road up from barbarism. But barbarism still exists in individuals and it must be contained. Imprisonment is a means of isolation and, we hope, increasingly of rehabilitation. With the death penalty now gone, imprisonment, in certain specified cases, must be until death.

The Chattanooga Times
Chattanooga, Tenn., July 2, 1972

The death penalty is unconstitutional, less because of the assault it represents upon the sanctity of human life than of the infrequency and unfairness with which it is presently imposed.

If five separate opinions, concurring in the decision of a ruling majority, can be briefly summarized, that is the major thrust of reasoning of the Supreme Court in invalidating capital sentences by the states.

We find no justification for capital crimes and harbor no maudlin sense of pity for those who commit them, but we find the Court's conclusion persuasive.

The concept was most succinctly stated by Mr. Justice Brennan in his concluding sentences:

"Death is an unusually severe and degrading punishment; there is a strong probability that it is inflicted arbitrarily; its rejection by contemporary society is virtually total; and there is no reason to believe that it serves any penal purpose more effectively than the less severe punishment of imprisonment."

The punishment of death "is therefore 'cruel and unusual'," and thus prohibited by the 8th Amendment, he found.

He bolstered the rationale of finding the death penalty unacceptable because of its diminishing role in today's treatment of crime and punishment in these words:

"The outstanding characteristic of our present practice of punishing criminals by death is the infrequency with which we resort to it. The evidence is conclusive that death is not the ordinary punishment for any crime.

"When a country of over 200 million people inflicts an unusually severe punishment no more than 50 times a year, the inference is strong that the punishment is not being regularly and fairly applied."

Using the same reasoning, Mr. Justice Stewart found that the petitioners in the cases before the courts "are among a capriciously selected random handful upon whom the sentence of death has in fact been imposed." The Constitution, he went on, simply "cannot tolerate the infliction of a sentence of death under legal systems that permit this unique penalty to be so wantonly and so freakishly imposed."

Mr. Justice Marshall hit upon the one aspect most disturbing to us—the chance of an error in convicting an innocent person, coupled with the absolute finality of the penalty:

"Just as few Americans know little about who is executed and why, they are unaware of the potential dangers of executing an innocent man. Our 'beyond-a-reasonable-doubt' burden of proof in criminal cases is intended to protect the innocent, but we know it is not foolproof."

Mr. Chief Justice Burger, dissenting, pointed out the legal uncertainties caused by the divided opinions of the Court's ruling view. It is high time, he said, for the states to take a new view of the whole problem of punishment for heinous crimes. Indeed it is. If murderers and rapists are to face at most long terms of imprisonment, laws must be written to assure their serving out the full sentences behind bars. Beyond that, of course, there is the border question of penal reforms which the Court all but ordered in its discussions of the inequities of the present system.

CHICAGO Sun-Times
Chicago, Ill., June 30, 1972

The U.S. Supreme Court has declared the death penalty unconstitutional, and the decision is one for which this newspaper long has argued. It is a decision that will have the immediate effect of sparing the lives of 600 condemned persons — 31 of them on death row in Illinois — and it could begin to erase the stigma that results from revengeful taking of human life in the name of a relentless state.

The matter was decided on the constitutional ground that the death penalty violates the 8th Amendment prohibition against c r u e l and unusual punishment. Yet, capital punishment, whether by hanging, or electrocution, or gas, or by some even more horrible means, historically has been a divisive and emotional and highly personal issue. The court's uncomfortably narrow 5-to-4 ruling reflected the divisions and varying rationales that have become common in legalistic debate over the death penalty. In fact, the nine justices issued 11 separate opinions in the test cases before them.

Unfortunately, the opinion which could spark the most discussion is the dissent of Chief Justice Warren E. Burger. Burger interpreted the majority opinions written by Justices Potter Stewart and Byron White as being pivotal and said each assumed that the "punishment of death now is meted out in a random and unpredictable manner." In what appears to be a not-too-veiled invitation for state action that could revive the death penalty issue in the courts, Burger said the Stewart and White decisions give state legislatures ground to establish capital-case standards for judges and juries and even to reinstate capital punishment on a selective basis.

Such further state action appears to us as profitless from either a legal or a humane point of view. There has not been an execution in the United States since 1967, and the court's majority decision of Wednesday thus upholds what has become the dominant American point of view. The death penalty is nationally degrading, does not deter criminals and does not assist in rehabilitation of prisoners. It is very difficult to rehabilitate a dead man, or to free a dead man ultimately found to have been innocent.

There may, of course, be state efforts to defy common sense and to reinstitute the death penalty. Such a spasm would not be out of character for the Illinois General Assembly. However, we hope that the gut desire for retribution will be subordinated to a civilized desire for morally acceptable punishment in conformity with the 8th Amendment as interpreted by the court's majority.

The New York Times
New York, N.Y., July 3, 1972

"The death penalty is to the body politic what cancer is to the individual body," Albert Camus once wrote, "with the single difference that no one has ever spoken of the necessity of cancer."

The Supreme Court has finally checked, if not cured, the cancer of capital punishment that has continued to corrode the American system of justice long after its abolition by most European democracies and by more than a dozen American states. Although the decision of a divided Court, as reflected in nine separate opinions, leaves disturbing ambiguities, the majority has affirmed that the death penalty—at least in the three cases directly involved—"constitutes cruel and unusual punishment in violation of the Eighth and Fourteenth Amendments."

The views of a growing number of citizens and lawmakers are reflected in Justice Marshall's finding that capital punishment is "morally unacceptable" and Justice Brennan's judgment that the death penalty "does not comport with human dignity."

In his dissent, Chief Justice Burger has suggested that the Court's historic ruling leaves the state and Federal legislatures free to reconsider the whole question. It is fitting that they do so—not, as the Chief Justice implies, to try to revive the cancer under some strained constitutional loophole but to abolish once and for all a barbaric punishment that infects the state with the sickness of the criminal without significantly contributing to the cure of crime.

© 1972 by The New York Times Company. Reprinted by permission.

ST. LOUIS POST-DISPATCH
St. Louis, Mo., June 30, 1972

The Supreme Court's decision restricting capital punishment is a historic one, narrow and inconclusive as it may appear. And it is not so inconclusive for about 600 men now on death row in this country.

Its first impact should be to spare the lives of these prisoners. Indeed, a contradictory decision that would have permitted mass bloodletting (in Missouri and Illinois among other states) would have been shocking; we suspect the possible results had more than a little to do with the court's conclusion.

The four Nixon appointees to the court object to that conclusion for various reasons. Since every single justice issued his own opinion, Chief Justice Burger can complain that there was no clear-cut majority and that the future of capital punishment is left in limbo. Justice Powell says none of the five majority opinions provided an adequate constitutional basis for abolishing the death penalty and Justice Rehnquist accuses the majority of disregarding judicial self-restraint.

That is the rhetoric to be expected of so-called strict constructionist judges, but it does not answer one question. What would the four Nixon appointees have done? Would they have agreed that capital punishment is acceptable simply because it always has been, and therefore have allowed hundreds of executions across the country?

In fact the death penalty is no longer so acceptable; recent polls indicate more Americans oppose than favor it. The penalty has not been exacted for five years and was put to declining use for 30 years before that. Most of the Western world has abandoned it.

These points might not interest those who hold to a narrow interpretation of the Constitution, but they go to the heart of the question of whether that document was written so as to apply to changing times. We believe it was. After all, when the Eighth Amendment against "cruel and unusual punishment" was adopted, lopping off ears and hands was no longer considered appropriate punishment. Can it really be considered appropriate today for the state, created partly to protect life, to take life deliberately? Not even the "eye for an eye" justification upholds the idea; one of the three cases overturned by the Supreme Court involved an assault in Georgia in which no life was taken.

Justices Brennan, Douglas and Marshall dealt considerably with what might be called the moral question of execution in this day and age. Justices Stewart and White emphasized the reluctance of judges and juries actually to impose the death penalty. Justice Stewart felt that neither the Eighth nor Fourteenth Amendments could allow "this unique penalty to be so wantonly and so freakishly imposed."

That is anther matter. Inequities in punishment for crime may be almost inevitable, but where the death sentence is involved the inequities are a matter of life and death. Death row statistics show that the sentence falls most often on the poor, the ignorant and members of minority groups. Even if capital punishment is not considered degrading and dehumanizing, it represents unequal justice.

Chief Justice Burger interprets the court decision as one leaving state legislatures with freedom or duty either to eliminate the death penalty or to revive it for certain crimes and, in any event, to review the subject. An objective review, devoid of the emotion of vengenance, would find with Justice White that the penalty does not meet "any existing general need for retribution." It does no good. What it does do is to diminish the moral authority of law. It should be totally abandoned.

The Evening Gazette
Worcester, Mass., July 1, 1972

The scope of the Supreme Court's decision on the death penalty "is not entirely clear," says Chief Justice Warren E. Burger. He understated the case.

The five justices who ruled against the death penalty as presently constituted issued five separate, often different opinions. Three of them seemed to say that capital sentences in any instance violated the Eighth Amendment prohibition against "cruel and unusual punishment." Two of the others indicated that the lack of uniform imposition of the penalty was the reason it could be considered cruel and unusual.

The four Nixon appointees all wrote separate dissenting opinions. Generally they agreed that the future of the death penalty was more a matter for legislators than judges to decide.

For the 600 persons living on death row, the narrow, confusing ruling appears to mean a lease on life. But it may also mean more mandatory life sentences without hope of parole. Many states probably now will rewrite portions of their criminal laws.

On balance the decision was a welcome one. The death penalty has proved to have more liabilities in its uneven and sometimes unjust applications than it has advantages as a deterrent to serious crime.

But everyone concerned with the law would feel more comfortable if the high court had been better able to define the issues and provide clear answers.

The Washington Post

Times Herald

Washington, D.C., June 30, 1972

It is impossible to read even a part of the outpouring of words from the Supreme Court in the death penalty cases without recognizing the momentous nature of the question it faced and the prolonged deliberations that led to its resolution. Perhaps never before has the question of death as a legitimate punishment been so thoroughly canvassed as it is in the nine opinions encompassing more than 50,000 words. The effective holding of the Court—that death penalties may no longer be imposed unless they are automatically imposed on all those convicted of a particular crime—is not the result we would have preferred. We would have joined those two Justices, Brennan and Marshall, who voted to bar death outright as a cruel and unusual punishment. But this intermediate step should be just as effective in closing down the death chambers of the Nation. No legislature is likely to decide that all rapists and/or murderers must be executed.

The differences between the Justices on this issue are fundamental, not just on the matter of death as a punishment but on the place of the Court itself in the American system of government. It is easy to make the argument, as the four dissenting Justices do, that the Court has overreached itself and stepped into an arena more appropriately reserved for Congress and the state legislatures. It is an argument based on strong underpinnings and substantial precedents but one that materially weakens both the power of the Court and the strength of the protections the Bill of Rights provides to all Americans.

It is true, no doubt, that at the time the Constitution was written the bar against "cruel and unusual punishments" was not regarded as abolishing the death penalty. But neither did it bar flogging, expatriation, sentences to be served in chains, or imprisonment for illness as punishments. These have become recognized over the years as penalties which must fall as "cruel and unusual" because of changes in the temper and the conduct of American society. So it is, it seems to us, with the death penalty. The use of it has grown increasingly repugnant and it quite appropriately should join disemboweling and drawing and quartering as a remnant of an uncivilized past.

By almost any contemporary definition, the death penalty is both cruel and unusual. It is the only punishment imposed in American law which inflicts pain. It is the only punishment that is used so rarely as to be unusual. Indeed, it is that latter point which provides much of the evidence of the nation's changing standards. Among the thousands of cases tried each year in which juries could impose the death penalty, it is actually imposed in only a hundred or so. Of these, governors regularly commute many. Of the others, many more are never carried out because of the unusual care and scrutiny every appellate court gives to them in the name of due process. No one has been executed anywhere in the country in the last six years and only 93 in the last 10—a figure smaller than that for any single year for which records were kept prior to 1950. There is much truth in Justice Brennan's observation that "the likelihood is great that the punishment is tolerated only because of its disuse."

There is another point about the death penalty which should not be overlooked. Justice Douglas put it this way:

Former Attorney General Ramsey Clark has said, "It is the poor, the sick, the ignorant, the powerless and the hated who are executed." One searches our chronicles in vain for the execution of any member of the affluent strata of this society. The Leopolds and Loebs are given prison terms, not sentenced to death.

Given evidence of this kind, and there is much more of it, about the impact of death sentences in practice, we are driven inevitably to the conclusion that the distaste of it is so widespread as to justify fully the Court's decision. To hold otherwise, to rely primarily or exclusively on past history, as some of the dissenters would, is to read the cruel and unusual punishment clause out of the Bill of Rights. That clause, at the very least and in the words of Justice Stewart, "cannot tolerate the infliction of a sentence of death under legal systems that permit this unique penalty to be so wantonly and so freakishly imposed."

We trust that the death chambers will now be dismantled.

St. Petersburg Times

St. Petersburg, Fla., July 2, 1972

The American civilization reached a new height of respect for human life this past week when the U.S. Supreme Court declared the death penalty unconstitutional.

THE PROCESS by which civilization advances to such landmarks was well described by Justice Lewis F. Powell. Even though he was among the dissenters, Powell recognized the majority viewpoint that the constitutional standard of prohibited "cruel and unusual punishment" does evolve.

Branding or nailing of the ears, accepted punishments in colonial America, are universally considered outrageous in 1972.

Capital punishment as practiced until 1967 is today unconstitutional. Now that the high court has spoken, it is doubtful that the penalty will be revived, despite Chief Justice Warren Burger's attempt to make a place for it.

This decision has an importance beyond the immediate issues. More clearly than before, this court forecast its own future. The four justices appointed by President Nixon who comprised the dissenting minority — Justices Burger, Powell, Harry A. Blackmun and William H. Rehnquist — wrote in separate opinions along a common theme. They were concerned that the majority was not exercising judicial restraint. A legislative, not judicial, remedy was proper.

WHAT IS judicial restraint? Each justice has his own answer. Rehnquist strongly condemned the majority for "imposing upon the nation the judicial fiat of a majority of a court of judges whose connection with the popular will is remote at best." Is judicial restraint merely following "the popular will"?

Kindly Justice Blackmun's is more interesting. Almost in a confessional tone, he says the case gives him "an excruciating agony of the spirit." He yields to no one in abhorring the death penalty. It violates childhood training and life's experiences. "It is antagonistic to any sense of 'reverence for life.'" Abolishing the penalty is the right and moral thing to do, says Justice Blackmun. Then he adds: "But . . . it (abolition) makes sense only in a legislative and executive way and not as a judicial expedient."

IN OTHER words, Blackmun thinks the death penalty is unconstitutional, but he wants somebody else to say so.

It is judicial restraint for a justice to vote to continue to put people to death by what he feels is an unconstitutional means? Blackmun's agony almost suggests that he feels constrained not to vote his own honest interpretations of the evolving language and standards of the Constitution.

The doctrine of judicial review in the American system was established largely through the bold leadership of the great Chief Justice John Marshall, particularly in the Marbury v. Madison case of 1803.

If the four latest appointees continue their narrow interpretation of their powers, the Supreme Court seems headed into eclipse as an institution to defend the American liberties guaranteed in the Bill of Rights. That causes a national agony of the spirit, as it did when the unresponsive court of the 1930s blocked economic reforms desperately needed by the country.

The future of the court could be one of the most significant long range issues in the upcoming presidential campaign.

The Birmingham News

Birmingham, Ala., June 30, 1972

In dissenting against the U.S. Supreme Court's five-member majority which yesterday ruled the death penalty unconstitutional, Justice Harry A. Blackmun wrote, "I fear the court has overstepped."

Blackmun's dissent is succinctly and aptly put.

The court has overstepped. It has sweepingly set aside a form of punishment which has been meted by courts since this nation was founded.

The grounds given for their opinions by the majority varied, but were close to Justice Thurgood Marshall's view that capital punishment is "morally unacceptable." This view was practically echoed by Justice William J. Brennan Jr., who had decided that the penalty "does not comport with human dignity."

These are subjective opinions which the court ought not to impose on the nation as a whole. True, many people may share these opinions. But the legislatures of the states and the lawmaking branch of Congress exist to translate changing values into law.

The court should not have taken this function upon itself.

Because the court has deprived the states of all but a residue of latitude regarding the death penalty (it ruled that the punishment could be reinstated by legislatures in certain limited circumstances) the ruling represents another blow against the doctrine of federalism.

Justice William H. Rehnquist, who dissented also, said the ruling completely disregarded "judicial self-restraint." We could not agree more heartily.

It is not necessary to favor capital punishment per se to agree that the court, on shaky grounds, has chosen again to usurp legislative prerogatives.

The sweeping ruling is more evidence that our system of government lacks an effective check on the growing tendency of the court to extend its domain beyond the interpretation of the law into the realm of transmuting personal moral views into the law of the land.

St. Louis Globe-Democrat

St. Louis, Mo., June 30, 1972

In what is probably the most amazing, utterly confusing decision in generations, the United States Supreme Court declared yesterday the death penalty—as now used in the United States—violates the Constitution and so is outlawed.

But even the justices, who issued nine opinions, did not know the full meaning and scope of the muddled decree. They were sharply divided. The decision was 5 to 4, all members appointed by President Nixon dissenting.

The opinions furnished a startlingly ambiguous array of views.

About the only thing clear was that in the three cases on which they passed, one for murder and two for rapes, the death penalty was barred.

Apparently the door remains ajar for state legislatures to reinstate capital punishment under certain circumstances.

☆ ☆ ☆

Chief Justice Warren Burger, one of the dissenters, emphasized that the court majority in setting aside the death penalty as "cruel and unusual punishment," gave state legislatures the "opportunity and indeed the responsibility to make a thorough re-evaluation of the entire subject of capital punishment."

Burger declared he found it hard to understand how the Supreme Court could overturn the death penalty now, when it has been accepted since the founding of the nation. So do most Americans. He expressed great uncertainty over the significance of the ruling.

It is as obvious as any reading of the federal Constitution on any subject, that framers did not intend by the Eighth Amendment to ban the death penalty, as legislated by states or federal government. Capital punishment existed when the Constitution was written and has existed ever since.

Only in the last five years—during the worst crime scourge the nation has ever suffered—has the death penalty been withheld while some 560 convicted felons, including 501 murderers, have not been executed awaiting a high court ruling.

What will happen now to these death-row prisoners isn't remotely clear from the new court holding. Will they be retried? Resentenced if possible? Or freed? The court gave no indication. Probably justices haven't any idea?

One of the dissenters, Justice Harry Blackmun said he "suspected," the decree would even knock out the death penalty for treason or assassination of a President.

☆ ☆ ☆

It is significant that only two of the justices who rendered the majority opinion, Thurgood Marshall and William Brennan, held that the Eighth Amendment bans capital punishment for all crimes in all circumstances.

Justice William O. Douglas, one of the most liberal members of the bench, observed in his majority opinion, it might be constitutional to make the death penalty mandatory for certain crimes if applicable to all subjects equally.

Justice Byron White, also one of the majority in the presumptive outlawing of capital punishment, said, "I do not intimate that the death penalty is unconstitutional per se, or that there's no system of capital punishment that would comport with the Eighth Amendment."

Obviously at least two, possibly more, of the majority did not intend to rule on the use of capital punishment under all conditions.

They did not decide deliberately, certainly not lucidly on the issue of constitutionality under the injunction of "cruel and inhuman punishment."

☆ ☆ ☆

Were the court or the nation to accept the Marshall-Brennan construction that all capital punishment is unconstitutional, the gates against wanton murder would be thrown wide.

The worst criminals would chance capture, even imprisonment from which they might be released reasonably soon on parole.

The penitentiaries would be a slaughterhouse for guards, especially when life-termers are involved. Police could become clay pigeons. Treason would become a civil offense. The military would have to banish articles of war embracing death for traitorism during war.

Organized crime would feel it had won another victory.

Justice Burger said of the majority decision, "The future of capital punishment in the country has been left in an uncertain limbo." The Supreme Court has an obligation to remedy this chaotic decision and do it quickly.

THE INDIANAPOLIS STAR

Indianapolis, Ind., July 3, 1972

As might have been expected on the basis of past performance, the liberal majority of the United States Supreme Court, seemingly swayed more by ideology and sentimentalism than by principles of law and common sense, has ruled the death penalty unconstitutional.

The ruling offers mercy to murderers but is blind to the rights of potential murder victims.

In one of the four dissenting opinions, Chief Justice Warren E. Burger wrote that the court had gone "beyond the limits of judicial power." Justice Harry A. Blackmun wrote, "I fear the court has overstepped." Justice Lewis F. Powell Jr. wrote that none of the five majority opinions "provides a constitutionally adequate foundation for the court's decision." Justice William H. Rehnquist said the ruling had completely disregarded "judicial self-restraint."

The point that the court had wandered off-course was the consensus of the dissenters. It is based upon the idea that the function of the court is to discover the genuine meaning of law on the basis of intent, that it is to interpret law honestly and skillfully, and not to encroach upon the legislative function.

For it should be plain that there is a considerable difference between what the authors of the Constitution truly intended and what a clique of left-leaning ideologues wish the founding fathers had intended. If basic American law is to be built upon current emotions rather than historical realities, the Constitution might as well be thrown in the wastebasket. In essence, that is what the liberal majority has done.

All five justices cited the Eighth Amendment prohibition of "cruel and unusual punishment." But by stretching it to cover the death penalty they injected their own emotional viewpoints into it instead of extracting the meaning conveyed by the Bill of Rights as a whole.

The meaning of the whole document with respect to the death penalty is found in the Fifth Amendment admonition that no person shall be "deprived of life, liberty or property without due process of law." That certainly says that deprivation of life by due process of law is permissible.

Most of the majority opinions delved into the kind of thing heard on panel shows: executions are "excessive," "morally unacceptable," "undignified," "distasteful" and so forth.

So, it must be emphasized, is murder. Homicides now total more than 16,000 a year in the United States and the rate is going up approximately 8 per cent annually — much faster in some urban areas. The softer the penalties, the more gutless the courts, the bloodier the slaughter.

The ultimate legal effect of the new decision is uncertain. Chief Justice Burger was no doubt right in saying: "The future of capital punishment in this country has been left in an uncertain limbo."

But that of murder has not.

Future crime statistics will show the size of the harvest in innocent human lives.

DAILY NEWS
New York, N.Y., June 30, 1972

In a 5-4 decision, the U.S. Supreme Court held yesterday that the death penalty as handled under present laws is unconstitutional.

It seems that electrocution, hanging, the gas chamber, the firing squad, etc., violate the 8th Amendment's ban on cruel and unusual punishments.

Victims of murderers, rapists, kidnapers et al., far oftener than not, suffer very cruelly and unusually. But the court's reaction to that gruesome fact appears to be: "So what?"

Each of the nine justices filed a separate written opinion. They ran all around Robin Hood's barn in a wild and confused race, with conflicting views flying hither and yon and back to hither, and with the court, we fear, losing considerable public respect in the process.

Chief Justice Warren E. Burger—a wild day in his court.

In the process, too, they annulled death sentences already passed on some 600 deserving criminals all over America the beautiful.

Unless we err (as well we may in this swirling dust storm of judicial prose), the court left a loophole or two, so that state legislatures may adopt the death penalty in carefully circumscribed and strictly limited ways.

So how about the New York Legislature readopting the death penalty in its oldtime inclusiveness and seeing what the Supreme Court does about that? And wouldn't it be an idea—a most constructive idea—for believers in vigorous law enforcement to start the ball rolling toward a federal law or constitutional amendment reversing yesterday's Supreme Court decision and ordering the court to keep its hands completely off said law or amendment forevermore?

THE RICHMOND NEWS LEADER
Richmond, Va., July 5, 1972

In voting to strike down the death penalty in 39 States and the District of Columbia, a five-man majority of the U.S. Supreme Court ambled all over the landscape to find justification for its decision. The result, as Justice Lewis F. Powell, Jr., observed, was that none of the Court majority "provides a constitutionally adequate foundation for the court's decision."

Here was the court majority, acting not from sound constitutional principle, but from vague sociological sentimentalism: Justice William Brennan found the death penalty an infringement of "human dignity." Justice Thurgood Marshall decided capital punishment is "morally unacceptable" and "excessive." Justice Byron White determined that the death penalty has been used so infrequently of late that he no longer saw any need for it. Justice Potter Stewart decided that the death penalty had been applied in a "wanton and freakish manner." Justice William Douglas found the death penalty to be a denial of equal protection.

Only three of the five Justices cited the Eighth Amendment's prohibition against cruel and unusual punishment in their opinions. None of the five referred at all to the Fifth Amendment which cites restrictions to be placed on anyone "held to answer for a capital" crime, or this amendment's prohibition against depriving anyone of life without due process of law. From this amendment, anybody who can read a word of English can determine that the Constitution permits the death penalty. The fact that five justices could agree that their job was not to interpret the Constitution, but rather to enact social legislation best left to State legislatures, reminds the nation once again that the law of the land is grounded not in the Constitution, but in the opinions of only five men.

Chicago Tribune
Chicago, Ill., July 3, 1972

Those who say that the Supreme Court has ruled out the death penalty are wrong in fact: it will be a shame if they turn out to be right in effect.

Each of the nine justices wrote his own opinion, and six of them made it clear that they were not declaring the death penalty in itself to be unconstitutional. The two pivotal opinions in the 5 to 4 decision, those of Justices White and Stewart, held somewhat ambiguously that the death penalty is cruel and unusual and therefore unconstitutional simply by virtue of the rare and "freakish" manner in which it has been carried out.

In his dissent, Chief Justice Burger said that the decision had put the country in "an uncertain limbo" and interpreted it as meaning that states may continue to impose the death penalty "by providing standards for juries and judges to follow . . . or by more narrowly defining the crimes for which the penalty is to be imposed."

He said states might also avert the appearance of caprice and discrimination by making the death sentence mandatory on certain charges, but he quite properly opposed this as worse than abolishing the death sentence. It would deny the flexibility which is a major virtue of our judicial system.

President Nixon reiterated his belief that capital punishment is a "necessary deterrent" of last resort, and said he hoped that the court's decision would not apply to the federal crimes of hijacking and kidnaping.

Nobody in his right mind relishes the thought of capital punishment; but in an era of increasing violence and terrorism, it would be a shame to remove the death penalty entirely as a deterrent and to make it unavailable to all of our courts even in extreme cases. The movement against the death penalty [and it is already being reversed in some countries] has been based more on emotion than legality, and this is nowhere clearer than in the present decision. It took five different opinions to explain the reasoning of the five-man majority. And about the only point on which they could agree was the most vulnerable, namely that there have been no executions in the United States since 1967; hence the punishment is unusual.

The main reason there have been none is that the states have been waiting to see what the Supreme Court would say about the death penalty; nobody, understandably, wanted to be responsible for taking a human life if the act of doing so was about to be declared unconstitutional. What the majority has now held, in effect, is that the present manner of imposing the death penalty is unconstitutional because the states thought the court might rule it constitutional. This merry-go-round logic is unworthy of the court. And it was hardly enhanced by the subsequent pictures and reports of convicted rapists and murderers gleefully toasting the Supreme Court for its decision. Where, in all this rejoicing, is any concern for the victims of these murders and rapes?

The people of Illinois have voted two to one in favor of retaining the death penalty. The people of most other states evidently feel the same. We hope that the ill-considered rejoicing will subside and that the courts and the states and the federal government will get together on a solution—perhaps along the lines suggested by the Chief Justice—which will protect the poor from discrimination and at the same time protect all of us from the depredations of criminals and terrorists who think the worst that can happen to them is a few years in jail.

BUFFALO EVENING NEWS
Buffalo, N.Y., June 30, 1972

The U. S. Supreme Court, by its 5-to-4 decision holding the death penalty as applied under all present statutes unconstitutional, has read something into the Eighth Amendment's ban on "cruel and unusual punishments" that was certainly not put there by the Founding Fathers, nor by any subsequent amendment, nor by Congress, nor so far as we can judge by modern public opinion.

And yet this judicial decree now confronts us with a sweeping new constraint on our criminal law which we greatly fear this nation may live to regret.

It is one thing to restrict the death penalty by statute, as we have favored and as New York State has done by limiting its application to the most exceptional of circumstances. This state's law, for example, no longer applies capital punishment in any ordinary murder case but very properly limits it to the killing of an on-duty peace officer or a nothing-to-lose killing by a life-term prisoner. But it is something very different to lift it out of the legislative arena entirely, as this decision appears to do, by hardening it into a constitutional doctrine that neither admits of carefully pondered exceptions nor permits any subsequent legislative reconsideration.

The very closeness of the court's division cloaks the decision with elements of uncertainty that are particularly regrettable on such a fundamental — literally a life-or-death — issue. For the 5-to-4 vote itself splits the court sharply between the five Warren Court holdovers and the four Nixon newcomers. This suggests that, with just one more Nixon appointment, the nation's fundamental law on capital punishment could be reversed again.

And even among the five who voted to outlaw the death penalty, there was considerable wobbling. Justice Stewart, for example, generally agreed that this form of punishment has become "cruel and unusual" in that it is almost as "freakishly" imposed as is death by lightning, but he indicated he might take a different view if any state made the death penalty mandatory for everyone who committed certain crimes. Justices Douglas and White added similar reservations.

Meanwhile, in California, where death sentences for Sirhan Sirhan and Charles Manson, among others, have been commuted by a state Supreme Court ruling that capital punishment violates that state's constitution, a campaign to restore the death penalty, led by Gov. Reagan, has succeeded in putting an initiative proposition to that effect on this November's ballot.

A Yes vote in California, to be sure, might not restore capital punishment there in the face of yesterday's decision outlawing it nationally. But if it is approved there, it would undoubtedly spur a movement for a comparable federal amendment. That, on a matter that has always before been regarded as within the discretionary legislative jurisdiction of the states and Congress, is no proper way to legislate. But neither, in our opinion, is legislation-by-judicial-decree.

THE BLADE
Toledo, Ohio, July 3, 1972

THE DOOR may still be open a crack, but the Supreme Court apparently has decided that the Eighth Amendment takes precedence over the biblical injunction, "an eye for an eye." In its decision that capital punishment, in three specific cases, would violate the constitutional injunction against cruel and unusual punishment, it has made difficult if not impossible the use of the death penalty.

True, it was a divided decision, 5-4. True, only two of the majority appeared to feel that death is cruel and unusual punishment for all crimes and under all circumstances. The only solution which the justices, in a variety of divergent opinions, left open is for state legislatures to somehow write new statutes which would be constitutional.

Chief Justice Burger, a member of the minority, phrased it thus: "Legislative bodies may seek to bring their laws into compliance with the court's ruling by providing standards for juries and judges to follow in determining the sentence in capital cases or by more narrowly defining the crimes for which the penalty is to be imposed." In other words, make the penalty the same for specific crimes under similar circumstances.

The court did not say so, but it apparently was reflecting the nation's changing views toward humanity. Millions of people now feel that it is uncivilized to take a human life, even if the individual has taken a life himself. To some extent, this feeling has influenced juries, which increasingly have declined to impose the ultimate penalty. Many governors of states which provide for capital punishment have said they will not approve such a penalty even if a jury does order it, a privilege given governors under executive clemency. Yet the court's decision leaves some serious questions unanswered.

There are some signs of wider recognition that death should not be exacted for crimes of passion, specifically those committed without premeditation in the heat of emotion. But what of the professional killer? Or the police killer? Or the one who kills for the thrill of it? What of the robber who holds up a service station, or a grocery, knowing that at the first sign of trouble he will rely upon his gun?

Is not the court's decision an open invitation at a time when the crime rate is rising with deadly mathematical precision? Are not criminals being encouraged to indulge that strange quirk to gun down other human beings, knowing that the worst they can expect is life imprisonment, always with the possibility of parole or escape? This decision seems disturbingly to do just that. Legislatures should undertake the task—difficult as it may be— of writing a set of statutes which will give the citizens and their law enforcement personnel some sense of deterrent protection against the kooks and criminals who put such a cheap price tag on the lives of other humans.

The Topeka Daily Capital
Topeka, Kans., July 2, 1972

To the chagrin of many law enforcement officers, lives of about 600 criminals, convicted and waiting on death rows, now hang safe and secure from a 5-4 decision by the U.S. Supreme Court.

By that narrow margin Thursday, the court held the laws imposing death penalties were in violation of the Fourth and Eighth amendments to the U.S. Constitution.

The Fourth Amendment guarantees equal protection under the law for all citizens while the Eighth Amendment prohibits cruel and inhuman punishment for any crime.

So divided was the court that each of the nine members wrote separate opinions to supplement its finding the death penalty was unlawful in certain instances.

President Nixon, in his televised press conference Thursday night, hinted personal disagreement with the court's decision in two comments. One was that he considered capital punishment a deterrent to certain crimes, particularly kidnaping.

He referred specifically to the Lindbergh Law which made kidnaping and transporting a victim across a state line a capital offense, punishable by death. It reduced, he said, the rampant threat that once faced every wealthy family in the land.

The President's second reference was more oblique. He said the narrow margin by which the decision was reached was an indication that he had restored as much "balance" as he had been able since taking office.

Atty. Gen. Vern Miller of Kansas decried the court's decision. He said conversations with prisoners in Kansas made it clear the death penalty was a positive deterrent to murders in prisons.

He said he had questioned prisoners in Kansas who told him they would have killed someone in the commission of a crime if Kansas had not had the death penalty.

Prisoners also have told Miller, he said, that they would have killed the guard or a prisoner at one time or another in the penitentiary if it had not been for the death penalty.

Miller saw the need for imposing the death penalty in cases where a law officer, performing his duty, was killed, killing of a victim in commission of a crime, killing of a witness to prevent his testimony, and the slaying of one prisoner by another in a penal institution.

If the most severe penalty possible to impose is life imprisonment, what could a prisoner serving the maximum sentence possibly lose by killing one or more inmates in the prison?

It seems unusual the high court would consider the death penalty to be cruel and inhuman punishment as defined by the U.S. Constitution. Nothing is more inhuman than the taking of a life by premeditated murder, whether the killing were accomplished by a gunshot, a knife, a hatchet or an axe.

Chief Justice Warren E. Burger, in his dissent, said the court had left the door open for state legislatures to re-enact the death penalty statutes covering specially designated offenses.

He said the court had gone beyond the limits of judicial power, but fortunately left some room for legislative judgment. Justices Harry A. Blackmun, Lewis F. Powell Jr., and William H. Rehnquist, all Nixon appointees to the court, joined with Chief Justice Burger.

The court's decision emphasized once more its willingness to come down on the side of the criminal rather than that of victims or members of the public who consider laws something to obey and law enforcement officers men to respect and assist.

Surely, state legislatures will direct immediate attention to the subject and reinstate the death penalty in certain cases. It is a deterrent to the commission of capital crimes, particularly to those upon whom the death penalty has been imposed and executed.

THE ARIZONA REPUBLIC
Phoenix, Ariz., July 1, 1972

The Supreme Court's landmark 5-to-4 decision against capital punishment, with its majority and minority opinions almost hopelessly confused by nine separate opinions outlining views of the individual justices, was certainly a disappointingly muddled example of judicial lawmaking.

All nine justices expressed personal revulsion for the death penalty. But only the four justices appointed by President Nixon, who upheld its constitutionality in their minority opinion, had the courage outspokenly to abjure their personal views and render a truly judicial verdict. The rest assumed the role of legislator in a familiar pattern of decision-making that Chief Justice Warren Burger correctly noted does "little to inspire confidence in the stability of the law."

This verdict against the death penalty, based mainly on the sentimental notion that it constitutes "cruel and unusual punishment," was a partial return to the softness that permeated judicial renderings of the Warren era.

We say partial, because reservations in favor of capital punishment for certain heinous crimes in the majority concurring opinions of Justices Potter Stewart and Byron White give us at least some hope that the death penalty might still be invoked in special cases.

And we must retain limited but certain application of the death penalty for mass killing, kidnaping, hijacking, and other wicked crimes. For if as the result of this decision we are hereafter prevented from imposing rightful penalties for capital offenses, we will have announced to criminals everywhere a fundamental lack of conviction in the ultimate foundations of the criminal law that they will be quick to detect and exploit.

A criminal justice system without the death penalty would have dire consequences in our prisons, where convicts serving life sentences with no chance of parole would likely murder guards and other prisoners with impunity if they had a mind to do so. And it would be open season for criminals generally, who, if caught committing second or third felonies that carry an automatic penalty of life imprisonment upon conviction anyway, would also likely kill innocent citizens and police to avoid capture.

Another possible consequence of complete elimination of the death penalty is a revival of widespread vigilante justice. Irate citizens might take it upon themselves to execute criminals illegally, with or without benefit of trial, to exact a measure of justice they believe has been denied them.

Judges and legislators in every state must now carefully study all the possible ramifications of this confusing Supreme Court decision, with an eye to establishing concrete, uniform application of the death penalty on a limited basis for certain heinous crimes.

The Detroit News
Detroit, Mich., July 2, 1972

Law is made by the U.S. Supreme Court the way stalagmites are formed on the floor of a cave—slowly, drop by drop. Last week, the court added another drop to its structure of opinion on capital punishment but left the stalagmite not quite complete.

The court had been expected to say unequivocally whether capital punishment is constitutional. It ended up saying, however, that capital punishment, as presently applied, is unconstitutional but hinting that the death penalty might be constitutional if applied in a less wanton and more uniform manner.

Justices Thurgood Marshall and William Brennan Jr. left no doubt that they think capital punishment for any crime and under any circumstance violates the Eighth Amendment. Justice William O. Douglas explained his position less sharply but his philosophical home is with Marshall and Brennan.

Justices Byron White and Potter Stewart, who joined in the majority opinion, left the door ajar for possible reversal of opinion should the issue of capital punishment come before the court later in different context.

As Justice White sees it, death may be a fit penalty for rape or murder but infrequent use casts doubt on whether such punishment is needed to satisfy any existing general need for retribution. Stewart finds the penalty invalid because of loose and inconsistent application; it is cruel and unusual "in the same way that being struck by lightning is cruel and unusual."

As Chief Justice Warren Burger observed in a dissenting opinion, the pivotal concurring opinions of White and Stewart may encourage the states to write laws that mete the death penalty in a less random and more predictable way. The assumption is that the Supreme Court might under those circumstances declare capital punishment constitutional.

Some states surely will take advantage of this opening. There remains a strong public feeling that certain categories of crime such as forcible rape and murder require the ultimate penalty.

If President Nixon is correct, the court's ruling does not necessarily apply to such federal crimes as kidnaping and hijacking. Can it persuasively be argued that rape and murder are less objectionable than kidnaping and hijacking?

As the states react to the court's decision, the whole question of capital punishment and its deterrent value will probably be debated anew. We have no doubt that the death penalty deters crime. Obviously, an executed criminal will not commit another crime. Others who might commit crimes are prevented from doing so by the prospect of the supreme punishment.

However, the very thing that gives the death penalty deterrent value — its finality — also raises the most persuasive argument against its use. It gives society no margin for error. If an executed person is later found to have been innocent, the state has no way of correcting the mistake.

Such agonizing questions are with us still, for the Supreme Court apparently has left full determination for another day.

The Dallas Morning News
Dallas, Tex., July 1, 1972

THE SUPREME COURT, by a 5-4 majority, has set aside the death penalty, as it is presently administered in this country.

The five justices who were named to the court by previous administrations opined that the death sentence is "wantonly and freakishly imposed" and also that it is applied selectively to "unpopular groups."

One member declared that the death sentence is "cruel and unusual punishment" because "punishment must not be so severe as to be degrading to the dignity of human beings."

It is significant that the five men whose act of will carried the day in this decision are the survivors of the old Warren court. This is very much a Warren court decision in its style, in its adherence to currently popular intellectual fashions among the elite and in its casual contempt for both the legislative prerogative and the democratic process.

TWO OF THE four Nixon appointees declared in their dissenting opinions that they have a personal distaste for the death sentence. Both Chief Justice Burger and Justice Blackmun asserted that if they were legislators, they would vote against it. However, the vital difference between the strict constructionists and the Warren court justices is precisely that they realize they are not legislators. They know that they do not have the right to seize the legislative function from officials elected and constitutionally empowered to carry out that function.

As Justice Rehnquist pointed out, the Warren court holdovers have, in one stroke, invalidated laws passed by Congress and 40 of the 50 state legislatures. They have, furthermore, denied the jurisdictions the power to legislate on this subject in future, except as detailed in rather obscure guidelines laid down by the 5-man majority.

However, this constitutional issue, as meaningful as it is for the future, is somewhat overshadowed by the immediate effects. In prisons all over the country, cheers, shouts and jubilation were the order of the day, as convicted murderers and rapists joyfully contemplated the prospects of returning to the streets.

JUST AS THE death sentence has been for years an empty threat, because the courts kept it from being carried out, so the life sentence is equally misnamed, amounting not to life but to a few years of incarceration. Already a defense attorney for the murderer of a policeman has begun the familiar argument that the high court's recent ruling means that his client, convicted last week, can be "rehabilitated."

Under the current conditions, the court's ruling probably means that the individuals convicted of the most horrible crimes will not only live but will in time be returned to circulation.

The court's Warren majority decided that the state must not degrade the dignity or take the life of those who have degraded the dignity and taken the lives of their victims.

Now the armed robber, the rapist, the hijacker and others who commit violent crimes have been given an enormous incentive to protect themselves by murdering their victims and others who might be witnesses against them. With no truly severe penalty facing them for the additional crime of murder, they can be expected to repeat the numerous instances in which criminals have murdered witnesses singly or, as in the murder of the deputies here, in wholesale groups in order to cover comparatively minor crimes against property.

It is fair to ask: In the court's decision to save convicted criminals from the "cruel and unusual punishment" of execution, how many innocent citizens have been thereby condemned to the cruel and unusual punishment of murder?

The Cincinnati Post
TIMES ⋆ STAR
Cincinnati, Ohio, July 1, 1972

The Supreme Court's 5-4 decision declaring the death penalty unconstitutional in almost all criminal cases is more confusing than clear-cut.

All nine justices wrote separate opinions on the subject, which centered on the question, Is such a penalty "cruel and unusual" punishment?

Two justices, William J. Brennan Jr. and Thurgood Marshall, said flatly the death penalty is unconstitutional. Three others, William O. Douglas, Potter Stewart and Bryon R. White, objected to the uneven, random way the death penalty has been applied.

"These death sentences," wrote Justice Stewart, of Cincinnati, "are cruel and unusual in the same way that being struck by lightning is cruel and unusual." Under our legal systems, he wrote, this "irrevocable" penalty is "instantly" and "freakishly" imposed.

Though he was in the minority in Thursday's ruling, Chief Justice Burger put his finger on the key question, What next? In effect, he pointed to the various states to review their laws on the death penalty, with an eye to defining more narrowly, if they wish, the standards that judges and juries should follow in determining sentences in capital cases.

WHAT THIS MEANS, apparently, is that the 34 states where capital punishment is permitted (including Ohio), will have to eliminate executions entirely or redraw their statutes so that judges and juries will be specifically directed as to when the death penalty would apply.

The death penalty has been outlawed, or restricted to such crimes as killing a policeman or a prison guard, in 16 states.

Arguments for and against capital punishment are difficult to prove and equally difficult to refute.

THE USE OF the death penalty in rape cases sometimes has been highly questionable, often with racial overtones. Yet is it really "cruel and unusual" to execute a criminal convicted of raping and murdering a child, or gunning down a police officer in cold blood?

And if capital punishment is an excessive penalty, what about life imprisonment? Where do you draw the line?

The answer to these questions, it seems to us, is that some crimes are so odious, and some criminals so incorrigible, that only life imprisonment, with no provision for parole, could be a suitable substitute for the death penalty.

This is a challenge the states must accept—either by retaining the death penalty on a limited basis, or by permanently separating vicious criminals from a society that needs all the protection it can get.

The Salt Lake Tribune
Salt Lake City, Utah, July 3, 1972

Five Supreme Court justices found that capital punishment as now administered in the United States is "cruel and unusual" punishment forbidden by the Eighth Amendment. But the four dissenting justices, some of whom personally oppose the death penalty, may have greater effect on shaping reaction to the ruling.

The five-member majority arrived at its conclusion by different legalistic routes Three of them, Justices William O. Douglas, William J. Brennen Jr., and Thurgood Marshall, held that capital punishment in modern America necessarily violates the cruel and unusual punishments prohibition. The two "swing men," Justices Potter Stewart and Byron R. White, found that the present system operates in a cruel and unusual way, because it gives judges and juries the discretion to decree life or death and they impose it erractically

This alignment seems to mean that no future law imposing the death sentence can pass muster before the present court unless it satisfies the objections of Justices Stewart and White. Chief Justice Burger indicated how this might be accomplished, thereby raising the possibility that the death penalty is not forever banished.

Since it was a bare majority decision on a highly emotional issue, the capital punishment ruling is likely to provoke a vindictive backlash. The forces of retaliation would do well to heed the dissents of the chief justice and Justice Harry Blackmun before rushing into action. And they should realize that the Supreme Court only confirmed what legislatures in nine states and supreme courts in two others have already decreed — that the death penalty is not necessary.

In suggesting ways legislatures might pass the Stewart-White "test" the chief justice said lawmakers could state in statute books in detail the conditions under which a judge or jury can impose the death penalty or the legislatures could revert to the practice of more than a century ago and impose mandatory death sentences for those convicted of certain crimes. Accompanying these guidelines was a qualifying admonition, that Congress and state legislatures "make a thorough re-evaluation of the entire subject of capital punishment," including a serious inquiry into whether it actually serves as a deterrent.

Putting himself in the position of a legislator who, in light of the court's ruling must now reconsider his state's laws on capital punishment, Justice Blackmun said "Were I a legislator, I would vote against the death penalty. . ." And Chief Justice Burger noted that "if we were possessed of legislative power, I would join with Mr. Justice Brennen or Mr. Justice Marshall or, at the very least, restrict the use of capital punishment to a small category of the most heinous crimes . . ."

Putting aside all the legal technicalities, the constitutional arguments and the questions of the court's authority, it seems clear that given an opportunity to weigh alone the merits of capital punishment, the court would have ruled at least seven to two against. That is something legislators, who will be considering the merits alone, should bear in mind, too.

The Boston Globe
Boston, Mass., June 30, 1972

The 600 persons, including two women, who have been awaiting their date with the executioner, are commonly viewed as the chief, though perhaps only temporary, beneficiaries of the United States Supreme Court's 5 to 4 and curiously ambivalent decision that capital punishment is cruel and unusual and hence unconstitutional under the Eighth Amendment

Argument could be made, however, that society itself, the society of the law-abiding, benefits even more, for it now, and unless the Court changes its mind, could be spared the subtle brutalizing that was its own fate every time it condemned another human being and took away his life in the gas chamber, on the gallows, in the electric chair, before a firing squad or however.

The decision, if something so hedged in ambiguities can in fact be called a decision, is one of the most curious in judicial history. The dissent by the four Nixon appointees is no surprise. It is now almost the custom for Chief Justice Warren E. Burger and Associate Justices Lewis F. Powell Jr., Harry A. Blackmun and William H. Rehnquist to stand together in opposition to Associate Justices William O. Douglas, Thurgood Marshall, Potter Stewart and William J. Brennan Jr., with Associate Justice Byron R. White the swing man. One gets the impression that what might almost be called the two courts are interpreting different Constitutions. It is what results when politics is a factor in the selection of justices.

In this case every one of the justices filed his own opinion. The resulting confusion is in no way lessened by the opinion of Chief Justice Burger which practically invites the state legislatures to ignore the decision by writing new death legislation if they so desire.

"The future of capital punishment in this country," he wrote, "has been left in an uncertain limbo." He might have added, "And how!"

Under today's decision, he wrote, the legislatures are free "to eliminate capital punishment for specific crimes or to carve out limited exceptions to a general abolition of the penalty without adherence to the conceptual strictures of the Eighth Amendment."

But since the three cases decided all turned on the argument that capital punishment is cruel and unusual, one would think the Court might have stuck to the question. Only Justice Brennan and Marshall faced the issue squarely, holding that capital punishment for all crimes and under all circumstances is unconstitutional under the Eighth Amendment.

The waffling of the justices, it might respectfully be suggested to Chief Justice Burger, seems to indicate that he should have held them in conference at least until they more adequately had explored each others' minds. Mr. Burger said he would not attempt "a definitive statement" as to the extent of the Court's ruling.

But if the Chief Justice is himself so baffled by the Court's decision, pity all others who are required to make the effort to understand it.

THE ATLANTA CONSTITUTION
Atlanta, Ga., June 30, 1972

In what is clearly destined to be one of its most controversial and emotional decisions ever, the U.S. Supreme Court yesterday ruled against the death penalty in a narrow 5-4 decision.

This decision is, in its way, so monumental and far reaching that each of the nine justices of the high court chose to write a separate opinion explaining exactly what reasoning led him to his final opinion.

The ruling has been denounced by some as an endorsement of murders and rapists. We think that is foolishness. Yet, at the same time, the decision cuts deeply into the fabric of our system and even theory of justice in this country. We suspect that most of us have somewhat of a mixed feeling about the decision itself. Moreover, the implications are so complex and varied it may take a period of time, of viewing the apparent result of this decision, before anyone can fully appreciate its effect.

This newspaper has never stood among those calling for the abolition of capital punishment. We have believed that some crimes justified the death penalty, that society has a right to protect itself, that there exist sometimes on the record examples of such unusual cruelty and violence that the individuals involved seem beyond the pale of any rehabilitation, that the death penalty may be warranted in such cases simply to prevent future evil. The Charles Manson case comes to mind.

Yet, we are not willing to condemn the Supreme Court decision throwing out capital punishment. Values and beliefs of a society change. Up until just a few years ago, a good many people were tried and convicted and executed for murder and for other capital crimes. That has changed, as the attitudes of the public and law enforcement officials and interpretations of the law have changed. As a practical matter, no one has actually been executed for any crime in the United States since 1967, and not in Georgia since 1964. In a way, the high court decision amounts only to an acknowledgement of existing practice.

There is an unhappy political side to the court's decision. We wish frankly that this were not so, and we hope no one attempts to make it a partisan issue. But the fact — and it should be noted — is that the four dissenting justices in the 5-4 decision are the four justices appointed by President Nixon.

We would suggest three questions that might play a part in any reasonable discussion of the court's decision. Is revenge a proper motive for executing anyone? Our answer would be no, that to the extent that capital punishment has served as the revenge of society, that this taking of life is hard to justify on religious or moral or ethical grounds. Two further questions: Has capital punishment served to deter would-be murderers (or other capital criminals) in the past? And, what punishment and-or rehabilitation approach should now take the place of capital punishment?

The matter of whether the idea of capital punishment has served as a deterrent to crime has been amply debated. But now, in light of the Supreme Court decision, it will be significant to observe carefully what actually seems to happen. The last question may be the critical one, because courts and legislators and law enforcement officials in Georgia and other states must now consider it carefully. We have one immediate specific suggestion: a life imprisonment sentence has often meant, in fact, the possibility of parole in as little as seven years. A longer guaranteed sentence ought to be considered in the absence of capital punishment.

FORT WORTH STAR-TELEGRAM
Ft. Worth, Tex., July 1, 1972

In the words of Chief Justice Warren Burger, "the future of capital punishment in this country has been left in an uncertain limbo." Strictly speaking, the Supreme Court Thursday did not "abolish" the death penalty, although that certainly will be the practical effect for the time being.

The justices by 5-4 vote threw out capital punishment because the death penalty, to quote from the opinions, has been freakishly imposed, capriciously selective, "pregnant with discrimination."

Anyone who has spent much time observing the outcome of capital cases in Texas or elsewhere knows that the Supreme Court was stating only simple fact in its excoriation of the "caste" aspects of law enforcement in this country. The well-to-do defendant has got the most resourceful legal talent; the impecunious defendant has got the chair. It was once the case in India that Brahmins were not subject to the death penalty. Americans would never write any such thing into their lawbooks; they have just followed it as a matter of unwritten custom.

It is wrong to administer the death penalty in this way, said the justices, and they were right. Whether it is so clearly right that the death penalty itself should be forever banished from our kindly shores is another and very different matter.

Our own thinking aligns itself very closely to that of Dr. George Beto, the clergyman-penologist who has served so capably and humanely the last 10 years as director of the Texas Department of Corrections.

"Philosophically," said Dr. Beto, "I have always been committed to the death penalty. I recognize and am disturbed by the inequities involved in its administration."

It must be noted that only two justices — Brennan and Marshall — wrote that the Eighth Amendment bars capital punishment for all crimes under all circumstances. Several of the dissenting opinions speculated that federal and state governments might be able to write new and more narrowly drawn death penalty statutes that would win the approval of a Supreme Court majority. Whether or not this will be the case must await further decisions.

Meanwhile, it is still our opinion, previously expressed many times, that the death penalty must be available to society as a means of dealing with heinous crimes. We do not agree for one moment with those justices who on Thursday opined that the death penalty is some sort of barbarous relic in an enlightened and progressive society. Its selective administration may have been barbarous; the penalty itself, no.

It is the duty of the community to defend its citizens. The community is gravely obligated—by the very purpose of its existence—to see to their protection. Sure and swift punishment, not excluding the ultimate punishment, helps guarantee that protection.

The community, while exerting care not to violate the rights of any individual, must show more regard for its citizens in general than for any one member. It would be misdirecting its concern if, in trying overzealously to protect or reform a criminal, it allowed law and order to fall by the wayside and the citizens to suffer the consequences.

The community need not and should not execute criminals if another punishment will be as effective. Whether any other punishment will be as effective we do not know.

What we do know is that a great many citizens, probably a majority, believe the death penalty is necessary. If, as a consequence of the Supreme Court ruling, it is reinstituted but applied more surely, more swiftly and more equitably, society could be the eventual gainer.

THE DAILY OKLAHOMAN
Oklahoma City, Okla., June 30, 1972

THERE are only nine justices of the Supreme Court of the United States. Yet those nine men found it necessary to issue 11 separate opinions in the process of reversing two death sentences meted out in the courts of Georgia, and a third from the courts of Texas.

The effect of these rulings is to outlaw the death penalty in all of the United States for the present. The justification for this radical step is that the Constitution says that "cruel and unusual" punishments will not be inflicted (by the courts).

In thus citing the provisions of the Eighth Amendment, the high court seems to ignore the Tenth Amendment again. Yet only recently it cited that amendment in another landmark decision. The Tenth is the one which says that "the powers not delegated to the United States by the Constitution, nor prohibited by it to the States, are reserved to the States respectively, or to the people." Up to now, the federal government has left the question of whether to establish capital punishment or not up to the individual states.

In his dissenting opinion, Chief Justice Warren E. Burger stressed that while the court was setting aside the death penalty, it was also giving the state legislatures "the opportunity and indeed unavoidable responsibility to make a thorough re-evaluation of the entire subject of capital punishment."

In one respect, at least, the decision is no surprise. The court had to recognize the fact that judicial processes leading to a ruling on the constitutionality of capital punishment during the past five years have resulted in a moratorium on all executions. At present, more than 580 persons, including two women, are under sentence of death in this country. A ruling which released all those stays of execution at once would have resulted in a cry of "bloodbath" from the foes of capital punishment.

Yet each of these convicted felons was found guilty and sentenced for a horrible crime. Each has been found unfit to live among decent people, or to put it another way, society has found in each case that the individual convict threatened the safety of his fellow men.

So in most cases, at least, there will have to be some kind of individual action taken to change or commute the sentence lawfully imposed, to comply with the latest ruling of the Supreme Court.

But that is quite apart from the obligation to review the whole subject of capital punishment which the Chief Justice says is the unavoidable responsibility of the state legislatures.

In that review, each state will have to face the real constitutional issue which the courts have avoided: is the penalty of death itself cruel and unusual punishment? Or does the cruelty exist only in the form of execution prescribed by present laws?

All law must be interpreted in terms of current tools, concepts, and customs. Thus a law which restricts the operation of a "vehicle" that was written in the horse-and-buggy days may have been practical at one time, and be found unenforceable in the day of the high speed automobile. In the same way, the prescribing of death by hanging, gas chamber, or electric chair is an anomaly in the era of quick and effective anesthetics, which can be quickly and painlessly lethal in certain known dosage.

And this may be the course open to the legislatures. The hue and cry of protest which began as soon as the court's decision outlawing the death penalty became known will quiet down some as the details of the opinions are published in full. But the fear that it ushers in an era of extreme permissiveness for criminals, and especially for those given to violent crime, will persist. It will force the states to enact some form of capital punishment, if only as a standby law to be imposed in times of severe crisis.

CAPITAL PUNISHMENT UPHELD 7-2 IN CASES OF MURDER CONVICTIONS

The Supreme Court July 2 affirmed, in a landmark 7-2 ruling, that the death penalty did not violate the Constitution's ban on "cruel and unusual" punishment. The holding was confined to the legitimacy of capital punishment for murder convictions. The decision upheld the sentence of a man convicted for murder under a 1972 Georgia statute. With identical 7-2 votes, the court approved Texas and Florida laws providing for the imposition of the death penalty. However, the court voted 5-4 to strike down capital punishment laws in North Carolina and Louisiana. The court objected to provisions of the laws that made capital punishment mandatory upon conviction for certain crimes.

In 1972, the court had, by a 5-4 vote, barred capital punishment as then practiced in the U.S. The justices in the majority then had advanced several different arguments against capital punishment: Justices William J. Brennan Jr. and Thurgood Marshall held that death was, under current moral standards, unconstitutionally harsh; Justice William O. Douglas reasoned that the punishment was unconstitutionally discriminatory because of its disproportionate impact on minority and lower-class individuals, and Justices Potter Stewart and Byron R. White cited the "freakish" and arbitrary manner in which the death penalty was imposed.

The judgment of the court was expressed in two opinions written by Justice Stewart and subscribed to by Justices Lewis F. Powell Jr. and John Paul Stevens. In the Georgia case, (*Gregg v. Georgia*), Stewart noted that the fact that 35 state legislatures had reenacted death-penalty laws since the 1972 Supreme Court ruling tended to undercut the argument that "standards of decency had evolved to the point where capital punishment no longer could be tolerated." Capital punishment, Stewart said, was "an expression of society's moral outrage at particularly offensive conduct"; as such, he maintained, it was "essential" to a society that asked its citizens "to rely on legal processes rather than self-help to vindicate their wrongs." Stewart also held that the death penalty served as a deterrent to certain kinds of murders.

Moving from a consideration of the death penalty in the abstract, Stewart argued that the particular sentencing procedures contained in some of the states' new laws adequately answered the objections of the 1972 Supreme Court ruling. In the case of Georgia, Stewart said that the new procedures "focus the jury's attention on the particularized nature of the crime and the particularized characteristics of the individual defendant." The jury, Stewart noted, must determine "at least one statutory aggravating factor before it may impose a penalty of death, and thus could not "wantonly" or arbitrarily impose death sentences.

Concurring in *Profitt v. Florida, Jurek v. Texas,* and the Georgia decision were Chief Justice Warren E. Burger, Justices William H. Rehnquist, Harry A. Blackmun, and White. Dissenting were Justices Marshall and Brennan. The majority in *Roberts v. Louisiana* and *Woodson v. North Carolina* consisted of Justices Stewart, Powell, Stevens, Marshall and Brennan. Dissenting were Burger, White, Blackmun, and Rehnquist.

Rocky Mountain News
Denver, Colo., July 5, 1976

THE SUPREME COURT showed a proper regard for history, law and public sentiment the other day when it ruled that capital punishment — the execution of dangerous criminals — is not in itself a violation of the Bill of Rights.

The upholding of the death penalty may seem stark and uncharitable, especially at a time when the nation is celebrating its 200th birthday.

But there is nothing in English or colonial history, or in the "contemporary standards" of modern-day Americans, to indicate that putting a man or woman to death for murder or some other vicious crime is "cruel and unusual punishment" in a constitutional sense.

"Capital punishment," wrote Justice Potter Stewart in the court's 7-to-2 decision, "is an expression of society's moral outrage at particularly offensive conduct. This function may be unappealing to many, but it is essential in an ordered society . . ."

At least 35 states have enacted new death penalty statutes since the Supreme Court ruled four years ago that most capital punishment laws around the country were arbitrary and unfair, resulting in random executions that seemed to have no consistency or justification.

The court agreed to review five of the new laws. Three of them — in Georgia, Florida and Texas — were ruled constitutional because they gave judges and juries detailed guidelines which permit some discretion on when the death penalty should or should not be imposed.

Two other state laws — in North Carolina and Louisiana — were struck down by the court because they imposed the death penalty automatically on first-degree murderers. Judges and juries were given no standards to use in determining who shall die.

This apparently means that states like Tennessee, New Mexico, Indiana, Kentucky and Mississippi, which have relatively rigid execution laws, may have to revise them.

States like Colorado, California, Ohio, Pennsylvania, Alabama, Arkansas and Wyoming, which have more carefully defined standards, may be in compliance with the new ruling.

Opponents of the death penalty argue that justice is uneven in murder cases — that poor blacks, for example, are more likely to be executed than whites who can afford fancy lawyers.

But it seems to us that some crimes are so heinous — the rape and murder of a child, the gunning down of a police officer, the mass slaying of a family, the assassination of a political leader, the slaughter of passengers during a skyjacking — that affluence or skin color should have little to do with the verdict.

The Supreme Court is not saying that capital punishment is an effective deterrent to crime. It may or may not be.

The court simply is saying that the death penalty is one option a state may consider in trying to protect its citizens and cope with violent crime.

The Saturday
OKLAHOMAN & TIMES
Oklahoma City, Okla., July 10, 1976

DESPITE some misgivings about acting too hastily, there is an overriding urgency that supports Gov. David Boren's call for a special legislative session to write a new death penalty law.

Literally, human lives could be at stake. The hiatus in capital punishment produced by the U. S. Supreme Court's recent voiding of the Oklahoma statute means the perpetrators of murder in that period will not have to pay the supreme penalty if caught. In effect, they're being given a license to kill; so the gap must be closed quickly.

The proposed timetable of legislative action outlined by the governor indicates there is no reason a new law cannot be adopted within a week after the session is convened July 19. But the legislators will have to stick to their guns and avoid being diverted by extraneous matters or side issues.

The philosophical justification for capital punishment in Oklahoma need not be debated. That question was already decided by passage of the 1973 law that was presumed to cure the constitutional shortcomings exposed by the Supreme Court's 1972 ruling.

Obviously, it represented the majority viewpoint in Oklahoma. The only question now is how to make the law conform to the high court's present thinking.

Even with the decision to proceed without delay, the legislature must be sure the new law is carefully and correctly written. Bill-drafting errors that plagued the last two sessions cannot be tolerated. Preliminary work is being done by the staffs of the governor and the attorney general. But it would be wise also to solicit the help and advice of seasoned members of the legal fraternity as well as veteran prosecutors and defense lawyers. This time, let's have a law that will stand the test.

The San Diego Union
San Diego, Calif., July 6, 1976

The United States appears to be coming full circle on the issue of capital punishment. The U.S. Supreme Court has now reaffirmed one of the oldest rules of human society— that some crimes are grievous enough to demand the life of the criminal.

No death sentences have been carried out in this country since 1967, when challenges of the constitutionality of capital punishment began staying the hand of the executioner. The Supreme Court in 1972 upheld those challenges in a 5-4 decision but left the way open for states to revise their statutes covering capital crimes in an effort to meet constitutional objections.

Most states have done so, and the effect of last Friday's decision in five new cases brought before the court was to sort out the features of new state laws which pass the constitutional test and those which do not. California is among 16 states whose newly-enacted death penalty laws appear to satisfy the test. Laws in 18 other states apparently fail.

The overriding significance of the opinions handed down last week, however, is that a majority of the court has reached a consensus on the fundamental question of capital punishment. Only two justices—Thurgood Marshall and William J. Brenna Jr. — remain convinced that the death penalty is wrong in principle. And eight of the nine justices who participated in the 1972 decision are still on the court.

The fact that so many states have sought to restore capital punishment since 1972 impressed the court. "It is now evident," wrote Justice Potter Stewart in the key opinion, "that a large proportion of American society continues to regard it (the death penalty) as an appropriate and necessary criminal sanction." The task of assuring that the penalty is not applied in an "arbitrary and capricious manner," which was the main objection made by the court in 1972, has been found to be not insurmountable.

This ruling from the nation's highest court of appeal will clarify the fate of persons sentenced to death under new state laws but it is not likely to end the philosophical arguments about capital punishment. Justice Stewart acknowledged that the court had seen no evidence proving that the death penalty is a deterrent to crime. What it has seen is the overwhelming judgment of legislators that it does, and the Supreme Court cannot overturn that judgment.

Nor is the court insensitive to the argument that demanding a human life in retribution for a crime is inhumane. Again, Justice Stewart points to enactment of capital punishment laws as "an expression of the community's belief that certain crimes are themselves so grievous an affront to humanity that the only adequate response may be the death penalty."

A period of great agonizing and deliberation for lawmakers and jurists in America may now be coming to an end. The pronouncements from the Supreme Court in answering the constitutional questions arising about the death penalty have been logical and responsible. The moral law which has always stood behind various death penalty statutes, as imperfect as the application of those statutes might have been, remains the ultimate guide.

THE ATLANTA CONSTITUTION
Atlanta, Ga., July 3, 1976

In 1972 the U.S. Supreme Court ruled that the death penalty as then administered was cruel and unusual punishment and therefore unconstitutional.

It was not a popular ruling. The sharply rising crime rate, continuing over a decade, had severely eroded support for the abolishment of capital punishment. But the court held, and justly, that the death penalty was almost invariably inflicted on the poor and on blacks to an extent that made its administration obviously unfair.

Immediately after that ruling many states, including Georgia, began preparing new laws on the death penalty that would meet the court's objections to the laws overruled. On this historic weekend, the Bicentennial celebration of the nation's 200 years of existence, the Supreme Court has again spoken on the subject of death for criminals. And this time, by a 7-2 majority, the death penalty is upheld as constitutional. Georgia's new laws were among those approved.

Most citizens in this nation will probably agree with the court's ruling. The crime rate has hardened us on the question of what to do with the violent and murderous among us. While the effectiveness of the death penalty as a deterrent has long been questioned and no doubt will continue to be questioned, the majority of citizens are convinced that other methods of dealing with crime and criminals are not working. The ruling idea today is that punishment for criminals at all levels should be swift and certain and fair. If the death penalty is administered by those standards, perhaps it will be effective as a deterrent.

One consideration has troubled thoughtful people since the court's 1972 ruling. Since then the death row population has increased to 576 men and 10 women (mostly young, poor, black) —these are people whose convictions have been upheld after appeal; many, many more are under sentence but still appealing. Are we to be faced with the spectacle of that many executions in a short space of time? Hardened though we are and perhaps must be, that is not likely. If we are to have the death penalty, it should be reserved for the most serious crimes and offenders and applied with scrupulous care to make sure we are punishing an offender for what he has done, not for what he is.

TULSA DAILY WORLD
Tulsa, Okla., July 3, 1976

THE U.S. SUPREME COURT'S 7-2 approval of capital punishment laws in three States does much more than restore the death penalty. Together with other recent common sense decisions, it restores confidence in the Court itself.

The new ruling is the most persuasive evidence to date that the SUPREME COURT has abandoned the "activist" policy of recent years. It indicates again that the practice of revising the CONSTITUTION to meet the individual tastes and social views of Justices has come to an end.

A majority of the SUPREME COURT has expressed personal opposition to capital punishment. But in its official action, the majority recognized that the issue was the Constitutionality of supreme penalty and not whether they thought it was right or wrong.

"The existence of capital punishment was accepted by the framers of the CONSTITUTION, and for nearly two centuries this Court has recognized that capital punishment for the crime of murder is not invalid per se," Justice POTTER STEWART wrote in the majority opinion.

The new ruling clarifies a muddled 1972 decision that had effectively left the capital punishment question up in the air. The earlier decision had ruled out the death penalty under then existing statutes. The Court said that the punishment had been meted out inconsistently. Laws must be specific and applied with an even hand. That was reasonable enough, but not very clear.

Lawmakers attempted to revise statutes to conform to the 1972 ruling, and most of them missed the mark. The new decision approves laws in Georgia, Texas and Florida, and other States with specific guidelines for sentencing defendants to death. But it struck down laws in other States including Oklahoma, where legislators had ordered mandatory death for all persons convicted of the same capital crime. That, it turned out, was more consistency than the Court wanted.

The confusion of the 1972 ruling has now been cleared up.

Herald ✦ News
Fall River, Mass., July 7, 1976

The Supreme Court has now ruled that capital punishment, under very limited circumstances, is constitutional and that states can legislate the death penalty. The long awaited ruling reverses a previous one in which the nation's highest tribunal declared capital punishment unconstitutional but left the way open for states to decide the issue for themselves.

There can be no question that the new ruling will be well received by the public as a whole, and the reason why it will be is obvious. The public is convinced that the death penalty is a real deterrent to persons contemplating murder; it believes that the fact that would-be murderers no longer feared for their own lives contributed to the massive increase in crimes of violence in recent years.

Had the virtual end to capital punishment not been followed by a frightening escalation in the crime rate, it is improbable that the public would have wished the death penalty reinstated. But the escalation did occur, even though experts still dispute its connection with the earlier Supreme Court ruling. Even many criminologists now believe that only fear of punishment keeps many criminals from obeying their anti-social impulses, and this, they claim, is especially true of would-be killers.

The issue of capital punishment is not settled by the new ruling, and its opponents will continue to fight against it. But the Supreme Court decision does mean that those who take a human life at least run the risk of losing theirs. That risk is what the court and the public hope will help keep the crime rate down.

DAILY ✦ NEWS
New York, N.Y., July 3, 1976
CAPITAL PUNISHMENT

—was endorsed as constitutional by the U.S. Supreme Court yesterday, even though two of the five state death-penalty statutes the tribunal reviewed were knocked down for technical reasons.

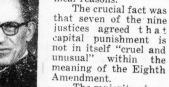

Stewart   White

The crucial fact was that seven of the nine justices agreed that capital punishment is not in itself "cruel and unusual" within the meaning of the Eighth Amendment.

The majority views were expressed in two separate opinions, one written by Justice Potter Stewart, the other by Justice Byron White.

Stewart cut straight to the heart of the Eighth Amendment issue by pointing out that the death penalty was in common use and was widely accepted at the time the Constitution was written and adopted.

As for the more widely used argument that capital punishment offends modern sensibilities, Stewart noted that 23 states had enacted legislation prescribing execution for certain crimes since a 1972 high court ruling which outlawed the death penalty as then applied.

Since the legislative branch embodies the public will, the jurist concluded that the passage of the new statutes was "a marked indication of society's endorsement of the death penalty."

Now that the fundamental question has been resolved, it should be a simple matter for the states to pass or revise capital-punishment laws conforming to the specific standards set by the Supreme Court.

With homicides rising alarmingly, the sooner they do so the better.

The Dallas Morning News
Dallas, Tex., July 8, 1976

IN TWO landmark decisions within the past week, the Supreme Court has gone a long way toward making the justice system respectable again.

We use the word in its literal sense, "having claims on respect," for many of the court decisions that have twisted the system in recent years have cost it dearly in the respect of the people.

Too often, the courts have set free criminals who are clearly guilty simply because of some minor technicality, some slip in police procedures. Too often, 2-legged predators who have committed brutal murders have been let off with nothing more severe than a few years in prison, after which they are put back on the streets.

The court acted Tuesday to stop the first juridical offense against common sense, by barring federal courts from freeing criminals because of technical violations by the police or lower courts.

But its finding of last week, in which it accepted the death penalty as constitutional, is one that a great majority of Americans has demanded. According to the latest Gallup Poll, 65 per cent of the citizenry favor the death penalty for the crime of murder, with only 28 per cent opposed. The majority in favor is the largest in nearly a quarter of a century.

The high court had held in 1972 that the death penalty laws then in force were too often subject to "arbitrariness and caprice." But this decision was followed by legislation in 35 states and in Congress to reinstate the death penalty under conditions conforming to the court's wishes.

All of this, said the court in its latest finding, is a "marked indication of society's endorsement of the death penalty for murder."

"In a democratic society, legislatures—not courts—are constituted to respond to the will and consequently the moral values of the people," the court concluded.

Two of the most consistently liberal justices voted against the decision, objecting to capital punishment as excessive.

This has long been a tenet of liberal philosophy, but it is one with which the public is thoroughly fed up. The practical result of this philosophy has been a system that zealously protects criminals from death, but seems incapable of sparing any public concern for the deaths these criminals inflict.

The philosophy that excuses and alibis the criminal for his crimes against the law-abiding has made our system of justice a joke. It has played a major part in making many of our cities nearly untenable for the decent citizens. It has had its day and it has failed utterly.

The court has taken two giant steps toward restoring justice that punishes the lawbreaker and protects the law-abiding. We have seen enough of the reasoning that forgives the criminal and forgets his victim.

The Seattle Times
Seattle, Wash., July 5, 1976

THE United States Supreme Court's welcome finding that capital-punishment laws can pass constitutional muster now makes clear a priority obligation of this state's Legislature.

Olympia's lawmakers must act at the first available opportunity to refine the death-penalty statute approved overwhelmingly last November when it was presented to the voters as Initiative 316.

That measure, which became effective as a state law only two days before last week's high-court ruling, prescribes mandatory capital punishment for murder in especially aggravated situations.

Because of the conditions attached by the court to death-penalty laws, this state's voter-approved initiative appears to have been invalidated.

During last year's debate on Initiative 316, sponsors conceded that the measure faced an uncertain future in the courts. But they advocated passage as one means of making a strong public expression against the criminal-justice system's failures to curb crimes of violence.

And speak they did — the voters gave the initiative a better than 2-to-1 favorable vote, sending Olympia a clear message that the public wants some sort of capital-punishment law included in this state's criminal codes.

Four years ago, the Supreme Court created considerable confusion with a ruling invalidating death-penalty laws enacted over the years by 36 states and the federal government.

Most of the states scrambled to re-enact laws to meet objections cited by the court in 1972. But a larger question — whether the death penalty is "cruel and unusual" and thus forbidden under the federal Constitution — remained unanswered.

Last week, that question finally was resolved. Citing a long history of public acceptance in this country and Britain, the court majority held that death "is not a form of punishment that may never be imposed."

The majority indicated that state laws like one enacted in Georgia are acceptable when they provide adequate restraints against the arbitrary or capricious imposition of capital punishment — court reviews, specific jury findings which take into account the circumstances of a capital crime and the character of the defendant, and so on.

Such restraints plainly are in order, since statistics show that the majority of inmates already on state-prison death rows are young, black and poor.

With the high court's guidelines now spelled out more clearly, this state's Legislature can act with greater confidence in meeting both constitutional requirements and the sentiments of the voting public.

The Salt Lake Tribune
Salt Lake City, Utah, July 5, 1976

Some murders are so outrageous that even persons ordinarily opposed to capital punishment are hard put to reconcile their ideals with revulsion the crimes generate.

Some murders, though tragic and legally impermissible, are nevertheless the result of conditions that mitigate against exacting the extreme penalty.

The latest U.S. Supreme Court rulings on the capital punishment laws of several states seek to restore the death penalty for the worst type murders while permitting judges and juries to opt for lesser penalties where circumstances so indicate. In either instance precise statutory guidelines must be followed in deciding for or against execution once a guilty verdict has been returned.

In so ruling, the court majority in a variety of separate opinions, has maintained a somewhat tortured consistency with the 1972 decision which outlawed the death penalty as then administered.

In the 1972 opinion a divided court held that capital punishment was unconstitutional because judges and juries were applying it capriciously and in "a wanton and freakish" manner. Statistics showed that the death penalty was applied most often to members of minority races.

Reaction by the states was two-pronged. Some, such as North Carolina and Louisiana, attempted to meet the court's 1972 objections by imposing mandatory death sentences for everyone convicted of certain crimes, thus ending alleged discrimination. Other states, such as Georgia, Florida, Texas (and Utah) took a different approach. They set precise standards and procedures designed to attain consistent application while at the same time recognizing special circumstances of each case.

The Supreme Court struck down the North Carolina and Louisiana laws because they violated standards of "human decency" and accorded "no significance" to the character of the defendant. The court upheld the Florida, Texas and Georgia laws which do what the voided laws do not.

It has taken four years but the states now have a fairly clear directive. They may impose the death penalty under conditions which permit consideration of individual aggravating or mitigating circumstances under precise statutory standards.

The challenge is obvious. Unless the states follow the spirit as well as the letter of the guiding standards they will slip back into the capricious sentencing that brought on the 1972 ruling. It's a legal tightrope and time alone will determine if the states can walk it.

For the present, however, the court's sanction of capital punishment for the "worst" cases of murder is an accurate reflection of popular sentiment.

That sentiment has changed in recent years. Support for return of capital punishment, though general, is also discriminating. It is not a call for broad, mandatory application against all killers. It is instead a cry from a harried people for positive, measured retribution for heinous murders.

A legal, tempered means of satisfying this demand is set forth in the new Supreme Court rulings. As for questions treating the morality of capital punishment, its deterrent value and its sociological sidelights, the justices properly left them for other forums.

THE INDIANAPOLIS STAR
Indianapolis, Ind., July 8, 1976

The United States Supreme Court has spoken again on the constitutionality of the death penalty, and one part of the gist of its new set of pronouncements is that its 1972 decisions striking down death penalty laws have been widely misinterpreted.

A great many state legislatures, including the Indiana General Assembly, construed the 1972 decisions to mean that the death penalty, to be constitutional, should be automatic on conviction of murder under certain conditions. The court had ruled that the death penalty as then imposed in Georgia and Texas, and by implication in other states, was "cruel and unusual punishment" because it was "wantonly and freakishly imposed" under the discretion allowed to juries or judges.

Then last week the court struck down North Carolina and Louisiana laws requiring the death penalty for a convicted killer without regard to the characteristics of the individual defendant or the heinousness of the crime. These laws were too rigid, the court said.

This week, on the final day of the current term, the court overturned Oklahoma's mandatory death penalty.

But also last week the court upheld new death penalty laws in Georgia, Texas and Florida. The saving feature of these laws is that they provide specific guidelines to be followed by jury or judge in deciding whether or not a convicted murderer should be sentenced to die.

Since the 1972 decisions there had been apprehension or anticipation, depending on the point of view, that the court might go in the other direction — might rule that the death penalty by its nature is unconstitutional.

The court has now said squarely, on a 7-2 vote, that the death penalty can stand up against the constitutional prohibition of "cruel and unusual punishments." It is plain, however, that a capital punishment law must be carefully drawn to allow for mercy to an individual defendant under a systematic and nondiscriminatory procedure for determining in each case whether the death penalty should be imposed.

When the full texts of last week's decisions are available the Indiana Law Study Commission will study the question whether this state's capital punishment statute needs revision. In any event the ground upon which such a statute can rest now seems more firm.

This fact is reassuring to those who believe, as we do, that the death penalty is a necessary aid to the deterrence of murder.

The Oregonian
Portland, Ore., July 3, 1976

The Supreme Court reversed itself Friday in upholding the death penalty in three states — Florida, Georgia and Texas — while invalidating it in Louisiana and North Carolina.

Four years ago, the court overturned all capital punishment legislation on the books then because such laws, the court said, gave too much discretion to judges and juries. Friday's rulings took the opposite tack. The 7-to-2 majority of the court upheld those laws that provided for such discretion, within certain guidelines. A separate 5-to-4 ruling rejected laws that made the supreme penalty mandatory for certain crimes.

A Washington state law, passed by the people last fall, makes the death sentence mandatory for aggravated first-degree murder. Most of the other 35 states that passed capital punishment legislation after the 1972 Supreme Court decision also mandated the penalty for certain crimes. Following Friday's decision, it is questionable whether such laws would pass the high court's test. Washington state's law became effective July 1, and no one has yet been convicted under its terms. But it is possible that the Supreme Court ruling endorses some leeway to judges and juries in the determination of what constitutes aggravation in a killing.

In any event, Washington state officials have been preparing at Walla Walla state prison a scaffold for hanging any one convicted under the law. The hangman's identity is to be secret, and it is to be hoped that no one need assume that revolting task.

There are 572 men and 10 women imprisoned under sentence to death in 30 states, 116 of them in North Carolina.

Justice Stewart, who wrote the court's majority opinion, said that mandatory death laws — perhaps such as that in Washington — "simply papered over the problem of unguided and unchecked jury discretion." He observed that widespread reenactment of the death penalty by the states was "indication of society's endorsement of the death penalty for murder." In striking down the North Carolina law, Justice Stewart said that it "treats all persons convicted of a designated offense not as uniquely individual human beings, but as members of a faceless, undifferentiated mass to be subjected to the blind infliction of the penalty of death."

Fundamentally, the court's ruling was that death inflicted by the state is not a cruel and unusual punishment such as forbidden by the Constitution.

The federal government has a law providing capital punishment for aggravated cases of air piracy resulting in death. Such a penalty has not been imposed under the law, and the law's validity now is not clear.

Oregon voters several years ago decisively rejected the death penalty. An initiative petition effort to reinstall it has just failed. The 1977 Legislature will certainly have the issue before it. Its potential members should give close study to the Supreme Court decisions, bearing in mind the questionable nature of a public policy that, as in Washington, keeps the executioner's identity secret. Obviously, it is dirty work.

THE SAGINAW NEWS
Saginaw, Mich., July 7, 1976

Advocates of the return of the death penalty for convicted murderers are considerably cheered by the U.S. Supreme Court's ruling upholding such laws in three states, striking down capital punishment laws in three others.

We are not. Because this is another bewildering opinion about as confusing as to what the court's true intentions are as that delivered by the high court in 1972. And because too many moral and philosophical arguments make it impossible to persuade ourselves that the state's taking of one life for another accomplishes anything.

At a more fundamental line what really frightens is that with capital punishment there is always a chance that the wrong party can get executed. Life in prison at least leaves a chance for reversal on proof.

It must be acknowledged that there is considerable public clamor for a return to capital punishment. That clamor has been satisfied by the high court with its 7-2 ruling reversing the 1972 decision declaring the death penalty cruel and unusual punishment.

The court's latest ruling — on a subject of which there is a body of law as old as civilization — is therefore another monumental direction change. But are states that haven't executed anybody since 1967 going to feel better about it? We're not that sure.

It is bound to touch off a flurry of activity by legislators and petitioners who are interested in the death penalty.

In this state, within hours of its announcement, it has already done that. Rep. Kirby Holmes, R-Utica, has signified his intention to push the death penalty back onto the books in Michigan. Somehow, we're not cheered by that, either — and it just seems Mr. Holmes ought to find something more wholesome and constructive to do with his time.

If this makes us soft-headed, then we, too, stand convicted along with the governor. This state erased the death penalty from its law 130 years ago, reinstated it once or twice and then got rid of it for good in the early 1930s.

We think it important, however, that enthusiasts for capital punishment read carefully what the Supreme Court has said.

Initially in 1972, in a vague and decidedly split 5-4 decision, it left the door open for the latest order.

What it really said then was that capital punishment as practiced was "cruel and unusual punishment" — indiscriminate in its applications state-by-state and totally lacking in judicial standards in its various locales, some death laws leaving no discretion to judges or juries, but in actuality too discriminate as it applied to rich and poor.

What it has said now is something else. Basically it has concluded that capital punishment per se is not unconstitutional. It has gone to say that states may institute and carry out the death penalty for certain crimes considered to be capital offenses so long as such laws provide that courts weigh carefully mitigating and aggravating circumstances before ever pronouncing a death sentence.

In short, capital punishment laws must not mandate death. Here, we think, the high court has taken all states into deep water and told them to sink or swim with death sentences.

We wonder if the court hasn't really opened a new can of worms in its meticulous effort to sanction capital punishment and justify it so long as it has no mandates.

Whereas the 1972 Warren court found the death penalty too indiscriminately used, it now calls upon the states for great discretion. Given such insight as we have, we're not sure what the 1976 court has said. In 1972 when the states were found guilty themselves of applying the death penalty much too casually — most often to the poor and the minority defendant — some states rushed to slap on mandatory death sentences for anybody judged guilty of murder.

Now the court has, in effect, struck that down and told the states to again use di_ etion with death penalties.

We can hear the distant drumming once again of hundreds of appeals. They will begin the first time a white defendant is given life for murder of one sort or another and a minority one sentenced to death for a similar crime. We must now depend greatly on any court's judgment of extenuating circumstances.

And there is nothing which suggests to the many states just what crimes may be punishable by death. Some states may institute capital punishment for three types of murders, others perhaps for as many as 10 — or all. What happens to standardization then nationwide?

We think the 1976 high court has stumbled on this as badly as the 1972 court. Has it simply told the states to find their own ways' of killing convicted murderers — with care? Certainly the wheel of social behavior has been given a hard turn backwards with the high court's renewed sanction of death at the hands of the state.

The Sun Reporter
San Francisco, Calif., July 10, 1976

The bicentennial gift of the United States Supreme Court to over 550 condemned prisoners on death row was a ruthless decision which in essence upheld capital punishment indicating that society's retaliation by death of felons at the hands of the states does not violate the Bill of Rights provisions against cruel and unusual punishment.

A brief survey of the inhabitants of death row reveals that approximately 50 percent are Black Americans, more than 20 percent are Chicanos and the rest are white.

The death penalty has always been an instrument of a racist society in which second class citizens who jump over the bounds of pre-prescribed propriety are punished by the ultimate weapon. Between 25 and 30 of the prisoners have been convicted of rape.

The NAACP and Professor Anthony Amsterdam of Stanford University are pledged to continue the struggle. The California Supreme Court must now act on a number of cases which have been held in abeyance until the U.S. Supreme Court ruled on this important question.

Not withstanding the propaganda of supporters of the death penalty, statistics have shown that in these states which have eliminated capital punishment, hideous crimes and murders are no more numerous than those states which still impose the death penalty.

The taking of a human life, even those guilty of heinous crimes, is destructive of the moral fibre of the society which wreaks its vengeance upon the perpetrators of a crime. Any individual who takes a human life suffers from some degree of psychotic behavior.

Can a society back away from organized murder in the name of law and order without having the blood of the victim of society's pontification upon its hands?

PORTLAND EVENING EXPRESS
Portland, Me., July 8, 1976

The United States Supreme Court decision declaring that capital punishment may be constitutional within specifically defined limits ought to be no excuse to revive the death penalty in Maine.

Maine wisely abolished the death penalty here almost 90 years ago and has survived comfortably without it since. The fact that the Supreme Court finds that there may be no constitutional barrier to snuffing out a human life does not alter our position of opposition to the ultimate penalty.

Execution by the state has never proven to be a significant deterrant to the commission of major crimes. And, precisely because of the nature of capital punishment, any error by the state cannot be remedied.

Capital punishment has a primative viseral appeal as an act of revenge by society to the violent misdeeds of the individual. But it must be possible, short of returning to the jungle, for society to exact a penalty as meaningful without resorting to dropping a man or woman through the gallows' trap or frying them to death in an electric chair.

An alternative to the death penalty exists in the form of life imprisonment. Unhappily, in Maine and elsewhere, a sentence of life imprisonment may mean a jail sentence of as little as a dozen years. The courts and the parole boards have it within their power to stifle agitation for the reintroduction of the death penalty by assuring that a life sentence becomes precisely that.

In short, the death penalty may be constitutional. But it remains unconscionable.

The Kansas City Times

Kansas City, Mo., July 8, 1976

It is difficult to determine exactly what the Supreme Court has done in regard to the death penalty except to say that it "is not a form of punishment that may never be imposed. . ." That would seem to take care of the proposition that execution by the state is in itself cruel and unusual punishment and therefore unconstitutional.

But the situation remains muddled, full of exceptions and figurative whereases, and apparently there is nothing like a national standard that can be applied across the land. The convoluted double negatives in so much of the court's language, as in the example above, surely is evidence of the second thoughts and strained reasoning that must have gone on in reaching the multiple decisions. Obviously a large part of the general conclusion was based on the belief that capital punishment is a "popular" remedy. At least the court noted a "marked indication of society's endorsement of the death penalty for murder"—establishing this thesis on recent acts by legislatures. That is not really a very good foundation upon which to build constitutional interpretation. The legislatures of the various states have done wondrous things in the past—some of which the United States Supreme Court has had to countervail.

No one is certain how many of the 600-plus individuals on death rows of American prisons can or will be put to death. Governors still are in the picture, and despite the court's reading of the popular desire for bloodshed, we wonder which state wants to be the first to legally kill a human since 1967 when Luis Monge died in the gas chamber in Colorado for killing his wife and three of their 10 children. Of course the state of Colorado killed a crazy man.

Maybe that is what our civilization wants to do with its criminally insane—kill and forget about them. If society demands a ritual cleansing, if we will all feel better when the life of the criminal is blotted out in reality and in the public consciousness, then let us admit that is why the executions should resume.

If, however, the point of the scaffold is deterrence and example, then the executions should be public—perhaps on television—and with as much fanfare and publicity as possible. A legal killing hidden away in the dark of night behind prison walls is no deterrent. Some might say that this would be barbaric. But we can't have it both ways. State executions are either for public example or they are acts of public revenge. Either way, when the life is snuffed out, the state is acting on behalf of all of us.

Detroit Free Press

Detroit, Mich., July 9, 1976

THE U.S. Supreme Court's ruling last week that capital punishment is not inherently unconstitutional brings to a close, at least for now, the legal aspect of this age-old controversy. The issue now becomes a political question, to be settled in the various state legislatures of the nation.

In its ruling, the high court rejected the contention that the death penalty violated the Eighth Amendment's prohibition of "cruel and unusual punishments." The 7-to-2 ruling held that the states could constitutionally impose capital punishment, so long as the death penalty was not applied automatically to all persons convicted of certain crimes.

In so doing, the court validated approximately half of the 34 individual state laws mandating capital punishment that have been enacted since 1972, when the court knocked down all existing death statutes as too arbitrary. Those states with laws imposing mandatory capital punishment upon conviction for certain crimes must now rewrite their statutes in accordance with last week's decision.

We find this latest Supreme Court ruling on capital punishment to be troubling and disappointing. The death sentence remains today what it always has been: a lingering echo of our darker instincts, a throwback to a time when human beings meted out "justice" quickly and brutally.

Reformers have fought for centuries to end this dark practice once and for all. In the 1960s, changing public values gave new impetus to the drive for abolition. No one has been executed in this country since 1967; and, despite increased public support for capital punishment in recent years, opponents of the death penalty had strong hopes that the Supreme Court would resolve the issue on constitutional grounds.

Those hopes have now been dashed. Curiously, the high court validated the use of the death penalty while simultaneously admitting that no real evidence of its deterrent value existed. The seven justices in the majority simply ducked this important issue, saying it was best left to the states to decide.

Even more troubling, the court seemed to approve of the concept of retribution as a legitimate function of the legal system. Capital punishment, the majority held, was in part "an expression of society's moral outrage at particularly offensive conduct." This argument is little more than a euphemism for the actual, if unspoken, appeal of capital punishment: revenge. Society has ample means to protect itself from violent offenders, short of executions. The urge to exact the ultimate punishment serves no protective function whatsoever; it serves only to satisfy the dark instinct for vengeance.

Finally, the court's reliance on the popularity of the death penalty in recent public opinion polls strikes us as an inappropriate basis for rendering a decision. The issue before the court was whether capital punishment could be squared with the principles and requirements of the Constitution. The views of a statistical majority hardly bear upon the constitutionality of the practice.

In ruling as it did, the high court has not ended the controversy over capital punishment. It has simply moved the dispute into a different arena; the legislatures of the various states. And despite the current groundswell of support for a quick, easy "deterrent," it remains to be seen how legislators and their constituents will react, once some states again begin to put people to death. The political process is unpredictable; and Americans may find it far more difficult to countenance the actual fact of an execution, than to support the general concept.

The Boston Globe

Boston, Mass., July 11, 1976

Four years ago the US Supreme Court ruled that the death penalty as imposed in this country violated the Eighth Amendment of the Constitution prohibiting "cruel and unusual punishment." The Furman decision, as it has been called, raised the hopes of those who believe that capital punishment should be abolished.

But Furman was hardly more than a respite. Only two justices, Brennan and Marshall, held then (as they do now), that the death penalty per se is unconstitutional. The opinions of other members of the court suggested that states which chose to do so could design acceptable laws. Thirty-five states responded by passing either mandatory laws, in which death was to be the automatic penalty for murder and several other offenses, or laws which permitted use of the death penalty when controlled by legislative guidelines.

Last week the court again took up the death penalty, but where it took it is not altogether clear. Although Chief Justice Burger in particular had encouraged the passage of mandatory death-penalty laws in 1972, the Court this time ruled against a mandatory North Carolina law and thereby voided the laws which most of the 35 states had passed. In another case it endorsed Georgia's death-penalty statute, which has guidelines. It is likely that the states which want to reinstitute the death penalty will follow the Georgia model.

The effect of the Georgia case on the use of mandatory penalties in general is uncertain. In the case of the death penalty, which is unique in its finality, the court's refusal to allow mandatory sentences is an improvement. Life and death are too important to be controlled entirely by the cold words of a statute.

The court wades into muddy water when it discusses what it sees as the two social purposes of the death penalty, deterrence and retribution. First, it admits that there is no conclusive proof of the death penalty's deterrent effect. Then it goes on to say, that for many it "undoubtedly is a significant deterrent." Dissenting, Justice Brennan held more logically that the death penalty "serves no penal purpose more effectively than a less severe punishment." That leaves retribution. "In part," the court said, "capital punishment is an expression of society's moral outrage at particularly offensive conduct." That may be so, but in this supposedly enlightened, scientific age, there must be suitable alternatives to cruel revenge.

In Massachusetts, where capital punishment has been unconstitutional since the Supreme Judicial Court ruled against it last December, a death penalty revival would take a constitutional amendment. This would require two favorable votes by the Legislature, sitting in constitutional convention, and a state-wide referendum. Let us hope that, in the three years that would take, the public will recognize the horror of this excessive punishment and abolish it once and for all.

TEXAS JUDGE AFFIRMS PRESS' RIGHT TO WITNESS EXECUTIONS IN STATE

A federal judge Jan. 3 ordered the Texas Department of Corrections to allow reporters to witness any future executions and to interview prisoners awaiting execution. The department's director, W. J. Estelle, had issued a directive in December stopping reporters' access to death row prisoners. Judge William Taylor Jr. called Estelle's ban unconstitutional, claiming that newsmen had a constitutional right to witness all executions held in Texas.

Judge Taylor's ruling was challenged by the attorney for Jerry Jurek, who was scheduled to die in the electric chair in Texas Jan. 19. Included in the petition for a postponement of the execution was a legal objection to its televised filming. Jurek's lawyer, Jay Topkis, said the order was not "consistent with evolving standards of decency." The suit against Estelle's ban had been filed by a Dallas television newsman and the American Civil Liberties Union.

FORT WORTH STAR-TELEGRAM

Fort Worth, Tex., January 10, 1977

Most people are reacting vociferously to a federal judge's ruling to allow television stations to film executions in the state prison at Huntsville.

That's understandable. Few subjects stir such volatile emotions as the death penalty—as death itself, for that matter.

And it's understandable that many people, including State Atty. Gen. John Hill, who says he is appealing the ruling, express revulsion at the idea of having the grisly scenes from the death chamber flashed electronically into their living rooms.

However, the primary concerns dealt with in Judge William Taylor's ruling had to be fact and law, not emotions or public preferences in the area of TV viewing.

The fact is that the State of Texas does have a capital punishment law.

Given that fact, certain other points follow in order, namely:

• The death penalty law is part of the criminal justice system in Texas—part of what the Constitution calls "due process."

• As such, an execution carried out under the law is an official action to which public access, under the Constitution, cannot be denied.

Thus, Dallas television newsman Tony Garrett acted properly in seeking the intervention of a federal court to assure his right of access, and that of other TV as well as print media representatives, to executions.

And Judge Taylor was correct in the ruling he issued, allowing representatives of the television medium to cover executions on the same basis as print media representatives

have covered them in the past—that is, through "pool reporters" who share their reports with others.

This ruling was most important from the standpoint of the public's right to know, which is actually what the First Amendment freedom of the press guarantee is all about.

It should be the prerogative of the public, not the state, to decide who witnesses an execution.

The ruling staunchly reaffirms that point.

The right to witness an execution and the actual witnessing of one, however, are too entirely different questions. And on that point hangs the issue of whether or not executions will ever actually be shown on television or displayed pictorially in the print media.

If the public overwhelmingly opposes such display of the execution scenes, it is doubtful that many TV stations or newspapers will offer it.

Those who present it once might be so inundated with protests that they would never try a repeat performance.

Signs of public protest already are becoming evident. Although some TV newsmen seem to feel that executions would draw a huge audience, most stations, according to one poll, indicate that they would be reluctant to carry them.

Whatever the ultimate decisions on the showing of execution scenes, however, Judge Taylor's ruling left the switch in the hands of the people, and that's a development to applaud.

Where the power to make such decisions have been allowed to pass to the hands of the state, the people often have regretted it—and have usually been a long time getting it back.

ST. LOUIS POST-DISPATCH

St. Louis, Mo., January 10, 1977

There are two ways of viewing a ruling by U.S. District Judge William Taylor Jr. of Dallas to the effect that television reporters have a constitutional right to film executions and to broadcast the film to the public. One way is to consider the decision in the light of the public's right to be informed visually, as well as in print, of what is undeniably a public function. As Judge Taylor said, it would be "unthinkable to conduct an execution in private." Another way to look at the decision is to consider its result in terms of the revolting impact it may produce on viewers of home screens.

Although many Americans may recoil at the prospect of seeing a hanging or an electrocution on home television, is that a reason for government to step in to bar television cameras from an event being carried out by authority of the state as a part of its law enforcement function? Television should have the right to convey, and the public receive, visual reports of an execution under the same rationale that television may convey, and the public receive, visual reports of the sometimes abhorrent conditions inside prisons or the loathsome scenes of killing in war.

The question of the impact on home viewers is one to be considered by television editors and by individuals concerned. Editors can control the time of the broadcast, bearing in mind the potential viewing audience. And they can put viewers on notice of what is to come — as they do now with respect to scenes of carnage — so that prospective viewers may choose not to watch. But government should not seek to bar the public from viewing what is being done in its name.

THE DALLAS TIMES HERALD

Dallas, Tex., January 5, 1977

THERE ARE constitutional guarantees, as emphasized by U.S. Dist. Judge William Taylor Jr., in news media access to prisoners, trials and executions.

Judge Taylor ruled Monday the news media cannot be barred by the State of Texas from interviewing prisoners on death row in the state penitentiary or from witnessing their execution.

What at first glance may seem to some persons as a macabre interest of the news media, is in substance a matter of continued protection of the public's right to information without far-reaching prior restraints of government.

Judge Taylor's ruling is consistent with the traditional recognition of First Amendment protection.

What makes Judge Taylor's ruling unprecedented in legal history, and likely to create an additional issue in the current national debate over the death penalty, is the explicit conclusion that television news media have the same constitutional protection as the print news media.

In the lawsuit filed by Dallas television newsman Tony Garrett of KERA-TV against W. J. Estelle Jr., chief of the Texas Department of Corrections, and other parties, Judge Taylor ruled executions may be filmed for broadcast as news reports.

Never have state executions been filmed for television news broadcast in the United States.

However, photographs have been taken and widely published in past years when executions were public events in the broadest sense.

Newspaper reporters have always witnessed executions in Texas and elsewhere, but the television news media, being a relatively new communications technology, has only recently come to full acceptance and participation as an integral element of the American press.

In *Garrett vs. Estelle, et al*, there were three primary points involving the news media and the First Amendment to the U.S. Constitution.

First, Judge Taylor ruled that Mr. Estelle's interpretation of state law on who may witness an execution was too narrow. Mr. Estelle recently banned all representatives of the news media on the basis of his reading of a state law enacted in 1965.

Second, Judge Taylor ruled that the Texas law upon which Mr. Estelle based his recent ban of death row prisoner interviews by the news media is an unconstitutional prior restraint of the public's right to information via the news media. Dallas attorney Fred Time on behalf of Mr. Garrett argued that any ban on prisoner interviews by the state must be on a case basis when security risks or other serious concerns of the state can be shown.

Third, Judge Taylor ruled that the constitution could not be interpreted "to distinguish between the print media and the television media."

Judge Taylor ruled on the constitutional issues, not on whether a television station should or should not televise an execution.

Station KERA-TV has not determined if it will televise an execution. That is not the issue involved in the lawsuit or Judge Taylor's ruling.

The basic question involved was whether Mr. Estelle or the state could bar the news media from witnessing and reporting on such an event.

Judge Taylor properly ruled that the restraints were illegal and reaffirmed the public's right to have a free press.

The Dallas Morning News

Dallas, Tex., January 5, 1977

FEDERAL JUDGE William Taylor's ruling to allow filming of executions in Huntsville was not a victory for the ghoulish as some might contend.

Judge Taylor simply said that an execution was an act of state, therefore it would be unthinkable for the media to be excluded. The state, he implied, does not have the right of prior restraint to determine what the news media may publish. And on this point, the judge is on sound constitutional ground.

Tony Garrett, a reporter for KERA-TV, challenged, with the assistance of the American Civil Liberties Union, new rules set down by W. J. Estelle Jr., director of the Texas Department of Corrections, prohibiting interviews with death-row inmates, prohibiting a news media representative from the execution chamber and banning cameras in the chamber.

Estelle, who has a commendable record in his relations with the news media, contended that the state's criminal procedures do not specifically allow interviews with the condemned and do not specifically name media representatives among the persons required or allowed to be present in the execution chamber.

If Taylor's ruling is upheld, the decision on whether the execution should appear on television or whether still photographs of it should appear in newspapers properly will rest on the shoulders of the news directors and editors of these institutions, as it should in a free society.

And the question of taste, no doubt, will be a subject of heated debates across the nation.

There is ample precedent for showing mortal violence on television. How many times, for example, have Americans seen the assassination of John F. Kennedy? Or Lee Harvey Oswald's death? And the Vietnam War, including executions of citizens, has been televised repeatedly.

If the death penalty is to be a deterrent to would-be criminals—and The News believes it is—a strong argument can be made for publicizing the actual execution through all media.

Prison officials have expressed concern that filming of the execution could make the act a circus. And it shouldn't. But that responsibility rests, too, with the media to approach an execution with professionalism and good taste.

The U.S. Constitution assures this nation not a responsible press but a free one. The media must provide the responsibility themselves, and they can be controlled through public attitudes toward their actions.

So Judge Taylor came down firmly on the side of the free press. It is up to the media to exercise restraint in this reaffirmed freedom. Death is never a game, and in covering executions, the dignity of the victims of the criminals should be preserved by making society's retribution the solemn act it is intended to be.

DAYTON DAILY NEWS

Dayton, Ohio, January 6, 1977

Now that a federal court has said a television stations can film an electric chair execution in Texas, Americans are faced with some peculiar questions.

For instance, should televised executions be encouraged in the hope that the repulsiveness would stop the killing, or should they be discouraged because they would burst the lid off the Nielsen ratings and heat up blood lust coast-to-coast?

There is something to be said for bringing Americans face to face with the violence they are accepting in capital punishment, just as the Vietnam war came to be resisted because it was occuring at 6:30 p.m. daily in our living rooms.

The media violence in America, though pervasive, also is sanitary: the routine killings on the westerns and cop shows are perhaps a bit bloody but rarely gory. Violence is portrayed as a clean, rather decisive solution, like the excision of a wart.

People who have witnessed car wrecks, shootings and stabbings know that death and pain are not usually so pretty. Even newspaper reports cannot convey the horror the way the visual media can; most newspapers forego most of the photo "opportunities" and descriptions available to them. It is a game society plays to keep some sense of its own tenuous civility.

But it seems marginally better for Americans to have illusions about the reality of their policies than to indulge the worst of them as prime time entertainment. Television should be free to get the news, but careful in what it presents.

Admittedly, it seems hypocritical to recommend good taste in presenting something that is inherently tasteless. And that, really, is what the issue boils down to: capital punishment itself. It is the killing that is wrong, whether it is some kid stabbing an old person in the Bronx or Texas pulling the switch after the pretty couple oozes through the Geritol commercial.

Should we, as a people, do anything as a public policy that we aren't proud to have our children watch us do?

ARKANSAS DEMOCRAT
Little Rock, Ark., January 8, 1977

A Texas state judge has ruled that electronic media (TV) may no more be excluded from filming an execution than the print media may be barred from reporting it — even if the filming means that an electrocution (one of which could occur Jan. 14) might be broadcast into homes soon after it occurs.

There's been no execution in the United States for almost a decade. During that time, the immediacy of TV newscasts has improved markedly. So the question of televising executions is a new one. And it has more than a little significance, since the Parent-Teacher Association, Action for Children's Television and like groups already are battling the TV violence that now exists.

Live violence on television is not unprecedented. Millions watched aghast when Jack Ruby fatally shot Lee Harvey Oswald in front of the cameras in 1963. And about that time networks began using satellites to beam back grisly filmed violence from Vietnam battlefields, all to be served up at suppertime on national newscasts.

Vivid, lurid accounts of men injured in combat, of civilians victimized by crossfire, were tremedously influential in molding public opinion and causing President Nixon to wind down the war. So the power of television with its graphic depiction and impact of immediacy, no longer may be denied as a powerful factor in pricking the social conscience of Americans.

It's difficult to imagine the impact on us all if, in effect, television returns us to the days of "public" executions, when throngs of curious persons flocked to witness well-orchestrated "events" — hangings, shootings, decapitations and quarterings.

Shocking as the Oswald slaying was to see, televised executions would be more so because TV viewers must know it is they who sanction the killing of the culprit by the state of which they are citizens. An executioner is but their agent, the one who detonates the gas pellet or pulls the switch on the behalf of society.

Perceptive viewers in the 1960s realized this about the Vietnam films, too — that the death and mutilation they were seeing from Vietnam was perpetrated in their names and that of their fellow Americans. Never before had a war been so realistically and instantaneously brought home to us — certainly not in the newsreels of the 1940s, or in the days-old film clips from Korea.

If the Texas judge's ruling holds, and if capital punishment is to resume in earnest, it seems we all may have the chance to witness the moment of truth, the ultimate in televised violence — an execution — from the comfort of our favorite easy chairs. Like the old public executions, the TV version may or may not deter crime.

What's more certain, television viewers will no longer be removed from the reality of imposed death. It will all be there on the 6 o'clock news. Rated "PG" for parental guidance.

New York Post
New York, N.Y., January 10, 1977

In upholding a Texas TV newsman's fight for the right to televise executions at the state's penitentiary, Federal District Judge William M. Taylor Jr. ruled that the event was "an act of the state" subject to full exposure. He stipulated only that the coverage be restricted to one TV cameraman who would pool his film with others.

Judge Taylor found a clear constitutional question at stake, and his view may well be sustained. Perhaps there is logic as well as law on his side. If the electric chair is to be reinstated as an American institution, there may be some redeeming social value in letting the country witness the gruesome scenes.

Former Texas Governor John Connally argued not long ago that such TV productions could serve as a deterrent to crime. The matter may not be quite that simple. A preponderance of public sentiment in Texas (and other states) has long favored restoration of capital punishment. Yet recent opinion polls show strong majorities in Texas itself — from 65 to 70 per cent — opposing TV airing of the spectacles.

This at least raises the possibility that many who profess to favor the death penalty would prefer not to (literally) see it being carried out. Should they be spared the sight?

* * *

Conceivably, TV airing of "the last mile," with instant replays, could impart a new dimension to the debate over capital punishment.

We are hardly advocating the idea. But some of its sponsors might be curiously confounded by the echoes of such macabre "specials."

THE ATLANTA CONSTITUTION
Atlanta, Ga., January 8, 1977

Televised executions?

The idea has been seriously proposed and a federal judge in Texas has signed an order that would allow it.

With capital punishment now revived by the Supreme Court, and with execution dates definitely set for many, including Gary Gilmore on Jan. 17, the possibility of televised hangings, shootings, gassings or electrocutions is not mere talk.

You—and the children—may soon have the opportunity to view the ultimate in television violence as the states begin executing the several hundred prisoners now on death rows. Parental guidance is advised.

Since the purpose of executions supposedly is to deter, there is a grim but undeniable logic in this proposal. Watching another human being put to death should certainly convey a message to all but the most obtuse. Don't do what this person did—or, perhaps, don't get caught as he did.

Those who may favor capital punishment, but feel a little squeamish about featuring it on the 7 o'clock news, should consider the fact that we are all used to seeing people killed by the scores on television. Mostly, of course, it is just play acting; but sometimes it is for real. Jack Ruby killed Lee Harvey Oswald on camera. The Saigon police chief executed a Viet Cong prisoner on TV during the late war.

Probably most Americans favor capital punishment (over 60 per cent in some recent polls) but prefer that it be carried out discreetly removed from public view. We want it done but we don't care to watch it. The proposal to make a spectacle of executions has the merit of testing whether we really believe in capital punishment. Opposition to the Vietnam War intensified rapidly as the reality of that war was presented on our television screens. It could be that televised executions, instead of having a salutary effect, would disgust most people, brutalize others, and change quite a few minds.

There hasn't been an execution in this country in almost a decade. There hasn't been a *public* execution in 40 years, and these have been rare in our century. Rising crime and an intensified public reaction against it have brought us back around to this extreme form of punishment. But putting it on television—that will challenge our commitment to it.

AKRON BEACON JOURNAL
Akron, Ohio, January 12, 1977

WE FIND no fault in principle in the ruling of a judge in Texas that it is legally proper for television newscasters to film and broadcast an execution.

The television camera is a new and powerful instrument of journalism, and this seems a logical extension of long-established free press rights that had to come sometime.

Even so, it's hard to restrain a shudder.

Maybe a nice film sequence on finishing off a malefactor with a firing squad or a whiff in the gas chamber or a jolt or two in the electric chair is just what America needs to liven up the evening TV news.

You don't have to go back very far in the history of American newspapers to find essentially the same thing, in lurid pictures and stories, jazzing up the lead pages of tabloids and a lot of other papers.

And maybe it will be good for us to watch the real thing. Toughening us up, you might say, for a return to the good old days.

The good old days . . .

The Romans, after all, came in droves to watch the lions polish off the dirty Christians, the cheers filling the Colosseum like the "oles" saluting the matador as he slaughters the bull with style.

Crowds of the French watched happily, munching their lunches, as the guillotine of the Terror did its efficient work.

And in our own country the good, popular hanging was once a bigger crowd-pleaser than a Sunday church social.

How this new access will affect views on capital punishment is impossible to say. It will almost certainly increase discussion of it, but may do no more than reinforce already existing attitudes.

In any case, the thought of it makes us uneasy.

The Philadelphia Inquirer
Philadelphia, Pa., January 12, 1977

The premise, however, is false. There is simply no evidence, none whatsoever, proving that the death penalty does deter. Indeed, as Dr. Samuel Johnson observed a couple of centuries ago, the best place to find pickpockets plying their trade in London was among the crowds assembled to watch pickpockets and other malefactors being hanged.

As representatives of what people sometimes call the print media, we want no advantages over the electronic media. But then we don't want ever to see another execution, because we hold, with Justice William Brennan, that "the punishment of death, like punishments on the rack, the screw and the wheel, is no longer morally tolerable in our civilized society."

If you have a taste for gallows humor, or, in this instance, electric-chair humor, consider the recent ruling of a federal judge in Dallas.

Judge William M. Taylor, in a suit filed by a television newsman, has ruled that Texas prison officials could not prohibit filming an execution in the Texas electric chair. The judge declared that such an execution is an "act of state" and that it is "inconceivable" as well as "unthinkable" to conduct it in secret.

Well, if you start on the premise that the death penalty is a deterrent, the judge's ruling makes a kind of macabre sense. Why not show executions on TV? Why not broadcast them on prime time and encourage the kiddies to watch as a human being is fried or gassed or shot or hanged?

THE SACRAMENTO BEE
Sacramento, Calif., January 7, 1977

A Texas television station that recently won a court decision permitting it to televise executions in the state's electric chair at Huntsville is now pondering whether or not to do it.

There is no question in our mind about this abhorrent prospect. It shouldn't be done.

The death of a human being at the hands of the state, no matter how reprehensible the crime for which the ultimate penalty is demanded, should be treated with gravity and common decency.

Turning it into a TV spectacular would create a carnival atmosphere. Inevitably, it would be exploited to pander to morbid curiosity. And we see no countervailing good purpose to be served by giving viewers the opportunity to watch a person die on camera.

The very idea of it runs against the grain of Americans' traditional sensibilities. Even during the years when capital punishment was commonplace in this country, public executions were prohibited largely because of the people's innate revulsion and a general sense that even the worst criminal deserves respect as a human being at the moment of death.

There are many things television and other news media have a legal right to present to the public but don't, largely as a matter of decency. Execution of a criminal by the state surely should be one of them.

BUFFALO EVENING NEWS
Buffalo, N.Y., January 5, 1977

Casting discreet restraint and human sensitivity to the winds, a federal judge in Texas has ruled that the television media have as much right as print reporters to record every last-gasp detail of a prison execution — not, mind you, just as reporters taking notes and reporting what they saw, but on film for broadcast into everyone's living-room.

"How," asked District Judge William Taylor Jr., "can you say we will let someone in with a pencil and notebook but not a camera or tape recorder?"

The answer, of course, is that the long-standing distinction between a reporter's account and camera coverage in the case of executions is as valid as the well-established and respected court tradition prohibiting the intrusion of cameras in public trials. For there is, after all, a vast difference between a reporter's description or artist's sketch of court proceedings, and the distracting hippodrome effect of opening these to massive multi-media coverage by camera and live TV.

Thus the issue, contrary to Judge Taylor's reasoning, is not whether all media should have the same right to be represented at executions. Rather, it is whether such events should be turned into media-event circuses or, as we believe, governed by coverage rules similar to those which protect the dignity and decorum of the courts.

Surely the television tube is saturated enough already with fictional mayhem without letting the revival of capital punishment become a signal for a luridly tasteless and dehumanizing exploitation of that ultimate penalty of criminal justice for its dramatic effect. The arousal of morbid fascination in such media-smotherage could mark a sad retrogression to Wild West lynch-mob days.

DESERET NEWS
Salt Lake City, Utah, January 5, 1977

Executions should not be turned into a distasteful publicity circus — a point this page made recently in citing a 1961 Utah law which seeks to curb such excesses.

The Utah example needs to be kept in mind in view of a federal judge's ruling in Texas this week that executions at the Texas state prison could be filmed and later televised.

Such a decision stirs the sensitivities not only of many ordinary citizens, but even of hardened newsmen. The news director of one San Antonio TV station said flatly that "We will not put it on." And the news director of WFAA-TV in Dallas commented: "I fear that a circus could be made" out of the scheduled Jan. 14 execution of Mark Milton Moore, 25, convicted of a 1973 murder in Dallas.

The question of propriety is of profound interest in Utah because of the Jan. 17 execution date of Gary Mark Gilmore.

Utah law specifically spells out who may be present at an execution. The sheriff must invite a physician, the county attorney, and "such peace officers as he may think expedient to witness the execution." Also permitted to be present are up to two ministers of the gospel "and any persons, relatives or friends, not to exceed five" whom the defendant wishes present.

"But no other persons than those mentioned," reads the law, "shall be present at the execution, nor shall any person under age be permitted to witness the same."

That, of course, excludes the news media altogether. There are cogent reasons, however, for permitting the unobtrusive presence of a pool reporter equipped only with a pencil and notebook, whose report could be shared with the rest of the media. Some executions in the past have been botched — a fact the public deserves to know if it happens again.

But certainly, in the name of human decency, execution scenes should not be lighted up with TV lights and splashed over living room screens to add their brutalizing effect to the human spirit.

The Detroit News
Detroit, Mich., January 10, 1977

The ruling of a federal judge and the words of a prominent politician have recently turned back the pages of history to those bloody times when supposedly civilized countries staged hangings in public.

U.S. District Judge William M. Taylor Jr. ruled last week in Dallas, Tex., that television reporters should be permitted to film and later televise executions. This ruling followed close upon a remark by former Texas Gov. John Connally that if capital punishment returns, he favors televising executions as an "impressive deterrent" to crime.

The ghouls are obviously on the loose once more.

During the Middle Ages and at certain later times, executions were treated in Great Britain as public holidays. A British clergymen of the early 19th century described the festive mood that surrounded the hanging of Josiah Misters in 1841:

"The town was converted for the day into a fair. The country people flocked in their holiday dresses, and the whole town was a scene of drunkenness and debauchery of every kind...A very large number of children were present: children and females constituted the larger proportion of the attendance."

While local citizens would flock in great numbers to see the corpses twisting on the gibbets, attendance from any great distance was naturally prevented by lack of speedy transportation. Today, however, millions of persons sitting in their own homes could attend the picnic — or at least a rerun of it — by merely turning on their TV sets. Perhaps in the case of multiple executions, the good judge could also provide for brass bands and baton twirlers to relieve the monotony of half-time.

However, we're glad to find that not everybody in Texas is mad. Remarking that "There are some things we just don't do," Texas Atty. Gen. John L. Hill last week announced he will appeal Judge Taylor's ruling. If allowed to stand, the ruling would open the way for the ultimate in violence on a medium already soaked in blood. And in this case, the blood would be not fictional but real.

THE ☀ SUN
Baltimore, Md., January 5, 1977

The decision of a Texas judge to permit the televising of executions opens great vistas for the toy manufacturers. Anyone who spent any time shopping for wee ones before Christmas would have noted how close a tie there is between the top TV shows and the dolls and games and other assorted playthings on the retail shelves. If the death penalty makes it to the ubiquitous screen, an instant market should develop for toy guillotines, battery-operated electric chairs and pop guns or darts with appropriate targets. But back to the judge. A fastitious gent, he decreed that the executions have to be taped. None will be broadcast "live."

THE ARIZONA REPUBLIC
Phoenix, Ariz., January 11, 1977

Federal Judge William Taylor Jr. ruled in Dallas the other day that the press could not be barred from a legal execution, if the death sentence is re-established.

Nor, said the judge, could the press be denied the right to interview prisoners on death row if the prisoners were willing to talk.

We think the judge is right. There would be an instinctive public suspicion of an execution which was not witnessed by at least some members of the public and of the press. And certainly a condemned person should be allowed to tell the public what he thinks and feels.

But the judge went too far in holding that television reporters could take and broadcast pictures of the gassing or of the electrocution of a condemned criminal.

Judge Taylor compared a newspaper reporter's pencil and notebook to a television reporter's camera.

That's a bad comparison.

Print media people don't need to throw an intense light on the subject they are writing about. Frequently they don't even need a notebook. But the TV reporter has to lug 30 or 40 pounds of equipment around with him. He has to tell his subject when to start talking (or acting) and when to stop.

He and his camera have their place in the collection and dispersal of news. But that place is not inside an execution chamber in an American prison.

THE MILWAUKEE JOURNAL
Milwaukee, Wisc., January 16, 1977

The impending revival of executions in the United States raises a nauseating question: Will the killing be televised? Already a federal judge in Texas has ruled that the frying of persons in the state's electric chair can be filmed and broadcast.

TV stations might shun the opportunity, concluding that the scene would be too offensive to beam into living rooms. However, a reasonable argument for televising can be made by both the supporters and foes of capital punishment.

A supporter, believing that the death penalty deters violent crime, could argue that the horror of televised executions would heighten deterrence. A foe of the death penalty, believing it cruel and unusual punishment, could contend that executions in dying color would drive home the barbarity of the practice and end it.

Of course, one could also argue that when hangings were public they did not seem to deter crime; it is said that the surest place to find pickpockets at work in 18th century London was in a crowd assembled to witness one of their own being hanged. Or one might speculate that televised executions could steadily desensitize, inuring the public to killing in cold blood.

Appalling argumentation? Sickening speculation? So it is with the capital punishment controversy; the stink in the nostrils simply gets stronger as death rows again fill and states move from abstract debate to grisly reality in the video age. The best option, still available in states reviving the death penalty, is to abandon the degrading policy of official killing before the first person is methodically roasted, gassed, hanged or shot — on cue and perhaps on camera.

Arkansas Gazette.
Little Rock, Ark., January 17, 1977

From our point of view the notion of televising executions is abhorrent, and if this comes to pass it will be one more sign of the descent of American society in matters of decency, which is to say, matters of civilization.

We're glad to note that this view seems to be shared by the CBS and NBC networks. Spokesmen for both of these have said their news organizations will cover executions of condemned criminals but will not show the death penalty being carried out, either live or on their national news programs. It's regrettable, however, that ABC remains indecisive, its news president saying "I would not rule out * * * pictures on a news broadcast." He seems preoccupied with the legalities: "If the print press has access to an execution, we believe we have the same rights * * *."

Hence the First Amendment is called into this morbid picture, and indeed a federal judge down in Texas has ruled that television does have an equal right to project official killings, the first of which in many years is tentatively scheduled in that state next Wednesday. Still, we expect that this is not the final word of law; higher judges eventually may or may not decide there is a legal difference between telling of an execution in print and bringing it into our living rooms with all its writhings and twitches. The licensed public-domain status of television may bear upon the outcome, as well as the plea that a person has a right to die with at least a minimum of dignity, without his final contortions being made a public spectacle.

These are sticky and unpleasant questions of law. No one likes to place restrictions on television news coverage. But there is news, and there is show business, and sometimes it's difficult to tell where one ends and the other begins on The Tube. Nor is the freedom to televise unrestricted even now under law—it's denied in most courtrooms of the nation. The question there is fair trial, while this proposition related to official killings raises mainly ethical and social questions, and the point that even a condemned person may have entitlement to at least a fragment of privacy in accord with civilized standards: Not to be made the authentic sideshow to all the violent drama on TV.

The official shooting to death of Gary Gilmore in Utah will be news, all right, but who can say it would not also be entertainment for a great many viewers, in the perverse definition of the term which has become all too largely a reality in our time? Who can say it would not be one more factor in desensitizing us to violence? According to one expert estimate, the average American child upon reaching age 14 has seen 11,000 murders on TV. If these do not reflect the real thing, in many cases it's not for lack of trying by the producers. Some observers say that to bring the real thing to us, undiluted, might be a shock which would instill more regard for human life and less regard for capital punishment. But the possibility also exists that it might only cheapen human life a bit more.

This isn't to say that executions for entertainment are anything new. The Romans popularized this, and the great lawyer and psychologist Clarence Darrow clearly defined its troubling import for modern society. Years past, in Arkansas, people sometimes traveled 50 miles by wagon to see a public execution, assembling in crowds of hundreds and having dinners on the grounds. But there is something even more obscene about the thought of all of us seeing them idly in our recliners in the evenings while sipping refreshment. Is it possible that someday we may have commercial sponsors clamoring to get their spots on the Execution of the Month?

Maybe not, but we think the judge in Texas went somewhat too far, too fast, in considering this, and that Utah has gone too far the other way in prohibiting any of the press from even witnessing Gary Gilmore's execution, so as to relay back to the public even the bare news that he actually was shot.

Extremism in either direction often makes for the emergence of bad law and poor policy in the end. We must hope, finally, that the television industry exercises decent discretion—that ABC will not be a hold-out for giving us "living" death, which might make the other networks decide their present admirable policy is untenable from the standpoint of competition. The competition in televised violence already has exceeded civilized limits.

CAPITAL PUNISHMENT RESUMES IN U.S. AFTER DECADE AS GILMORE EXECUTED

Convicted murderer Gary Mark Gilmore, 36, Jan. 17 was shot to death by a firing squad at the Utah State Prison at Point of the Mountain. Gilmore was the first person to suffer the death penalty in the United States since 1967.

Gilmore had been convicted of the July 20, 1976 slaying of a Provo, Utah motel clerk, Bennie Bushnell, 26, and had admitted killing Max Jensen, 24, a law student working as a service station attendant in nearby Orem, the previous night. Gilmore had been sentenced to death for the Bushnell murder. He had demanded that the state carry out the sentence and had disparaged those individuals and groups who had attempted to block his execution. He had emphasized his wish to die by twice attempting suicide in 1976. Gilmore's actions, and the struggle to keep him alive, had been heavily publicized by the news media.

Opponents of the death penalty made several futile efforts to delay the execution. The Supreme Court Jan. 11 rejected one such request from Douglas A. Wallace, a Vancouver, Wash. lawyer, on the ground that he lacked standing, or the legal right to bring a court action. Attorneys representing two convicted Utah killers Jan. 14 unsuccessfully sought orders to stay the Gilmore execution from U.S. District Court Judge Aldon J. Anderson and Utah District Court Judge Dean E. Condor. Utah Gov. Scott Matheson Jan. 14 also denied a request for an executive stay, citing a stay order granted by his predecessor in 1976. (The state parole board had refused to commute Gilmore's death sentence after the temporary stay had been granted.) A petition from the convicts on Utah's Death Row was presented Jan. 16 to Supreme Court Justice Byron R. White, who rejected it. Although White said he spoke for the majority, the same petition was brought before Justice Harry A. Blackmun the same day. Blackmun also rejected it.

THE ROANOKE TIMES
Roanoke, Va., January 26, 1977

On the eve of a legislative vote on capital punishment the General Assembly has received an impressive, eloquent appeal against capital punishment signed by bishops and ministers representing a broad range of churches and denominations. The document should be treated with great respect; it is a reminder of the source of life and the circumspection that should accompany any governmental taking of it.

The legislators need not feel overawed, however. A degree in divinity or a place in a pulpit does not preclude other ways of reaching a conclusion on the question: How to punish the violation of a commandment of all established religions: Thou Shall Not Kill.

We hold to the premise that respect for life diminishes when the penalty is diminished for the wanton taking of life. When the penalty for the taking of life is no more than the penalty for a particularly outrageous theft or series of lesser crimes, society has lost its nerve. It has lost the capacity to provide a scale of punishments equal to the offenses.

There is admittedly a practical frustration in applying the rule. The American Civil Liberties Union (ACLU) and other opponents of capital punishments will interfere even in cases where they are not invited to participate. They will stage such a cat-and-mouse spectacle of delay as to inflict a punishment more "cruel and unusual" than the swift one imposed by the courts as directed by the legislature.

Also the opponents of the law (with the aid of the media) will cause the public to think of Gary Gilmore when the public ought to see the two college boys killed by Gary Gilmore, one of them killed while he lay helpless and unthreatening on the floor. Soon attention will be centered on some apparently clean-cut Texan when what should be remembered is a 10-year-old girl first raped, then killed, then thrown into a river.

The distractions are great; the possibilities of deterrent are lost during the distraction. The practical reasons for giving up on the death sentence are more visible than the reasons for not having one. Nonetheless the principle is sound that the greatest crime should have the greatest punishment. Legislators who believe that principle need not be deterred from voting for capital punishment in those cases clearly deserving it. If they hold to the principle, the sense of the people generally may yet prevail.

DESERET NEWS
Salt Lake City, Utah, January 18, 1977

It isn't an easy task for a state to be the first in nearly 10 years to execute a condemned criminal. Not even when the criminal has vigorously fought for the right to die for his murders.

For most Utahns, along with sorrow for the loss of human life — any life — there is a profound sense of relief that the tension and the glare of worldwide publicity are about over, now that Gary Gilmore is dead.

It has been a long ordeal, for Gilmore most of all, but also for every person sensitive to problems of justice, of law, and of human suffering. The anguish of indecision and uncertainty lasted to the very end, due to the ill-considered midnight stay of execution by Judge Willis Ritter after all other courts, both lower and higher, had made their firm decisions. America's long, sad history of legal executions has seen many last-hour reprieves, but the 10th Circuit Court's overturn of Ritter's stay may be the first last-hour — indeed, last-minute — death order on record.

No one can be happy or satisfied with the record of this bizarre case. But sober reflection will show it is hard to fault any Utah official, agency, or court. Governor Rampton acted properly in granting the first stay; to do otherwise would have been an unseemly rush to death. The Board of Pardons acted conscientiously and with dignity. So did the various Utah courts. The Attorney General's office properly and effectively fulfilled its role in seeking Gilmore's execution. Warden Sam Smith did his job as well as a man could do under these difficult, tension-packed circumstances.

As this page has previously noted, putting a human being to death is a grisly business and should be carried out only under the most stringent legal safeguards.

As the Gilmore case has so dramatically exemplified, the first order of business must be to write into Utah law a provision for mandatory court review of all death sentences. That would help safeguard the rights of the defendant in capital cases, while still satisfying the demands of justice. Had Utah had such a provision, much of the circus aspects of this case would have been avoided.

Mandatory review would assure that no Utah prisoner in the future will be legally executed on the basis of one set of testimony heard by one group of men and women. Surely human life, even that of an accused killer, is worth more than that. But, on the other side of the coin, the courts should speed up the review process as much as legally and morally possible.

Utah's execution this week has, in effect, reopened the door to the legal taking of human life. The state now has an obligation to do what it can to make that taking of life as carefully considered, as orderly, and as humane as possible.

The Salt Lake Tribune
Salt Lake City, Utah, January 18, 1977

Capital punishment, by its grim and final nature, inspires extraordinary efforts to stay its imposition. So there is no way the condemned or those opposed to the death penalty can be prevented from pushing last minute, longshot appeals in the courts and otherwise. Nor should there be.

Because of unique aspects of the Gary Mark Gilmore case, down-to-the-wire legal maneuvers sometimes bordered on the theatrical. They tested many a layman's patience with the judicial system. And all of them failed.

Unlike Gilmore, few persons sentenced to death seek to hasten their departures. His eagerness to die was a critical element that set this bizarre case apart.

Public attention was further generated by the fact that Gilmore figured to be, and indeed was, the first person executed in the United States in almost a decade. Now that he has been shot by a Utah firing squad and capital punishment, for better or worse, is again in force, other executions will lack the novelty of the first one.

These factors and Gilmore's flair for the sensational, gave impetus to last-ditch efforts to block his execution. And a previously unnoticed flaw in Utah's death penalty statute produced a ready vehicle.

Focus of the final legal jousting was the fact that Utah law does not provide for automatic review of all death sentences.

Lawyers opposing the Gilmore execution, but not Gilmore himself, maintained that lack of review would cause the appellate courts to declare the Utah death law unconstitutional. It was noted that the United States Supreme Court's latest decisions seemed to hold that automatic review was necessary if state capital punishment laws were to pass muster.

The United States Supreme Court may or may not have agreed with this position. It did not get the opportunity because Gilmore refused to raise the question and the court would not hear it from others.

Never mind. Utah law should provide for mandatory review in capital cases as a matter of simple justice and orderly procedure.

A bill to provide this additional safeguard is before the Legislature. Its passage will remove one cause for attacking future death sentences.

Automatic review would go far to assure society that in taking a killer's life it had acted well within society's laws. It could have prevented some of the highly publicized legal sparring that marked the Gilmore case and in future death penalty dramas as well.

Mandatory review would not mean an end to 11th hour appeals which, despite their sometimes exasperating aspects, constitute a final chance to prevent a possibly tragic miscarriage of justice.

THE DAILY HERALD
Biloxi, Miss., January 18, 1977

Gary Mark Gilmore has brought capital punishment back into American society after an absence of nearly ten years. Our society needs it.

His death yesterday by firing squad gives concrete meaning to the Supreme Court's finding that the death penalty does not constitute cruel and unusual punishment.

There's another execution scheduled in Texas where Jerry Lane Jurek, a convicted child-killer, is to die in the electric chair, barring intervention by the government or the Supreme Court.

For a decade, arguments about the death penalty have swirled about in the courts, in the press, in magazines and in legislatures. In that interim of remission, the deterrent effect of the ultimate sentence has been effectively reduced, not only in the minds of those who would break the laws covered by the death penalty, but also in the minds of those citizens with no intentions of breaking those, or any other, laws.

Gilmore's death has changed that. If Texas does execute Jurek, with news and television cameras recording the deed, there is every possibility that visions of capital punishment may appear on television screens in millions of American homes. Remembering the impact upon America from watching the first war televised in bits and pieces nightly, it is impossible to assess the changes that might be stimulated from the televising of a rash of executions.

Capital punishment has had an inconsistent history in America. The movement to abolish it peaked in the years before World War I when, in a 10-year period, nine states and Puerto Rico outlawed the death penalty for most crimes. After that, a number of states abolished the death penalty only to reinstate it later. After 1917, no state succeeded in abolishing capital punishment for 40 years.

There are no accurate statistics on the total number of Americans who have been executed because of the lack of an accurate accounting in the years prior to 1930. But testimony before a Congressional subcommittee in 1972 contains an estimate that the total has been "something on the order of 7,000 executions in this century under state and federal law."

Abolitionists will argue that the rising crime statistics refute any contention that the death penalty has been effective as a deterrent. Others will reply that each execution has effectively deterred any repetition by the criminals so dispatched.

Opinion polls show that the public favors the death penalty, but by a vacillating margin over recent years. Those poll results can be expected to swing to disfavor should the televising of executions become anywhere near as common as the Vietnam war reports once were.

Until that happens, if it does, the death penalty has returned.

It is necessary if this country is to be a nation of laws that include a system of of justice wherein a variety of punishments are meted out, increasing in severity as the crimes increase in heinousness. There must be a maximum punishment for the most heinous of crimes.

THE DALLAS TIMES HERALD
Dallas, Tex., January 18, 1977

GARY MARK GILMORE is dead at last. His body is still. He is gone.

He kept saying that he wanted to go, and he will not be missed by many for long. He is dead because the deeds that he did were so terrible that society said he had to go, and he apparently agreed. At least he did not want to stay where he was.

Society thought long and hard before it did to Gilmore what Gilmore did to others, but for some the decision was easy and right. "An eye for an eye" has been in the human mind for a long time, and its simple fairness is hard to refute.

But many even among those who wanted Gilmore's death — and the death of hundreds more on the nation's death rows — were not motivated by revenge. The deed must be done, legislatures and juries and judges have said, to protect society itself, to save that fragile thing we call civilization from those who would carry us back to the animal past. To deter others who are tempted to go Gilmore's way. The death penalty may not be a perfect antidote to crime, their reasoning goes, but this is an imperfect world, and at least we will not have to be afraid of this *one* criminal anymore.

Others say that to do to Gilmore what Gilmore did to others is to pull all of us down to his level; that for society to take Gilmore's life is to make Gilmores of us all. It is this doubt which kept alive for months a man who said he wished to die. No defense lawyer wanted to believe that he could have saved a man's life and did not. No judge wanted to say the final, irrevocable yes. No state was eager to be the first in a decade to officially and deliberately snuff out a human life.

During the long months of hesitation, Gilmore became something more than a man, more than a murderer. He became a cause, the vehicle for renewal of an old, old debate: What is justice? To whom should the state show mercy?

The debate will begin anew, again and again, as each of the hundreds sitting in cages on our death rows moves along his own Last Mile. We shall have new flurries of legal briefs and arguments, more news accounts of last meals and last words, perhaps even television film of the death throes. Although others will go out with less fanfare and senationalism than Gilmore, who had the fortune or misfortune to be first, none of it will be nice to see.

But the Supreme Court has said that to kill a criminal is not cruel or unusual if the killing is done without bias. And by so ruling, the Court has refused to force us to be merciful.

If we wish to be merciful, we can, of course. We could order our legislatures to allow no more firing squads, no more electric chairs, no more gas chambers, no more hangmen's ropes. We could even amend the Constitution.

But for now, the people of Utah and Texas and other states say, "An eye for an eye." And we shall see whether any good comes of that exchange.

ARGUS-LEADER
Sioux Falls, S.D., January 18, 1977

It is a matter of note that the first execution to take place in the United States in almost 10 years occurred because the condemned man conducted a lengthy fight to have the sentence carried out.

A last-minute effort by opponents of capital punishment to have Gary Gilmore's sentence stayed was unsuccessful when a federal appeals court lifted the stay order of another federal judge.

The last previous execution in this country occurred in Colorado's gas chamber.

Gilmore's execution likely will mean that other executions in other states will follow.

There are situations in which the imposition of the death penalty is appropriate. The crimes of hijacking, kidnaping and murder of the kind committed by Gilmore are justifiable reasons for exacting the death penalty.

Gilmore was sentenced for killing Bennie Bushnell, 26, a Provo, Utah motel clerk last July. He also admitted killing Max David Jensen, 24, the night before. Mr. Jensen was a service station attendant. Both murders were during robberies and each victim left a young widow and child.

Executing Gilmore won't bring back the two young men he murdered, but it may deter some other hood in Utah from killing a victim during a robbery. The state of Utah will also be spared the problem and expense of looking after Gilmore for what would have been the rest of his life.

The arguments, pro and con, about capital punishment in this country during the last 10 years have served a good purpose. State and federal laws have been changed to protect the accused, and to attempt to get a more even application of the extreme penalty.

This country faces a real problem in combating crime. The application of the death penalty in a number of states may make wouldbe murderers think twice before they take somebody else's life. An effort by local governments to prosecute more criminal cases, whether or not they're capital offenses, to the end that punishment is virtually certain, would do much to counter the crime problems confronting this country.

The Birmingham News
Birmingham, Ala., January 18, 1977

After 10 years in which there were no executions in America, the nation still is divided over the issue even though the suspension has been broken by a firing squad in Utah.

Gary Mark Gilmore, who died yesterday, was a curious candidate for the death penalty. He freely admitted he was a killer and wanted death rather than a life sentence.

But what Gilmore wanted or didn't want is not the yardstick by which the nation should measure the pros and cons of capital punishment. The principles are of a general nature; they must be determined on the basis of what is just for society and most effective in protecting the innocent from hardened criminals such as Gilmore.

A number of arguments can be made against the death penalty. Other arguments can be made in favor of the death penalty. Many earnest people these days find themselves morally torn over the question, and now, with the execution of Gilmore, that question has been made very real.

It is argued that capital punishment is not a deterrent to the heinous crimes it is meant to punish. Possibly other would-be murderers will not be deterred by the death of Gilmore. Certainly Gilmore was deterred neither by death nor life in prison, and he killed in cold blood.

The fact is, no punishment has proven effective as a deterrent against heinous crimes. If the death penalty must be abolished because it does not deter, then imprisonment must also be abolished, because it doesn't deter, either. But, of course, that would be absurd.

What is certain now is that Gilmore will never harm another soul. If his execution does not cause even one other person to relent from murder in cold blood, we all may rest assured that Gilmore has claimed his last victim. To some individual who might otherwise have been killed by Gilmore, that is a blessing of the highest order.

Even a life sentence does not effectively isolate a hardened killer from potential victims. Prison officers and other inmates come in contact with the killer every day. The only weapon the killer needs is a sharpened screw driver or any honed piece of metal if he wants to kill someone else in that micro-society behind bars. Killings in prisons are not rare.

The argument can be made that society places a lower value on human life if it kills someone in the name of justice. But to whom would society be communicating this value system except to those whose respect for life already deters them from violence? It is a nuance which is lost upon the killers and would-be killers in society. If such a value system prevailed in the law, the only persons to be executed would be the victims of crime.

The best argument, perhaps, against capital punishment is that there is always the potential for error—that an innocent person might be forced to die. No one can guarantee that any particular judgment of the criminal justice system is accurate and fair. It is not unusual for the system to malfunction because it, as any other human activity, is subject to human error.

But behind this argument is the tendency to want to err in favor of the accused rather than in favor of potential victims. It is not impossible for innocent persons to be convicted, but it is rare that a guilty verdict is maintained after the usual appeals and after all legal safeguards have been observed. However, it is not unusual for innocent persons to be killed every day behind grocery counters, on the streets and so on.

The death penalty is not so valuable for the last victim of crime as it is for the next potential victim of crime. There is no lack of certainty that Gilmore was guilty, and he will never kill again.

In executing Gilmore, the state of Utah has acted with justice and resolve. If criminal justice were carried out with equal resolve in every jurisdiction, the public safety would be immeasurably enhanced.

Richmond Times-Dispatch
Richmond, Va., January 18, 1977

How many people, we wonder, can readily identify Max David Jensen or Bennie Bushnell? Not many, we suspect. How many can readily identify Gary Mark Gilmore? Nearly everyone, for his name has been on the front pages of the nation's newspapers for the past two days and had been there several times before.

Max David Jensen, who died violently last year at the age of 24, was a young law student with a wife and infant daughter. He worked at an automobile service station to make ends meet. Bennie Bushnell also died violently last year, the very day after Max David Jensen's death, at the age of 25. Bennie Bushnell worked at a service station too, supporting a wife and child and trying to make enough money to return to college.

Cause of both deaths? Gary Mark Gilmore, who robbed and mercilessly shot both men last summer. Yesterday he was executed by a Utah firing squad. He was 36.

Gary Gilmore's victims were decent and law-abiding citizens who posed no threat to society, but he had been a menace since he was 14, robbing, mugging, raping and shooting his way through life. He displayed his sociopathic tendencies even in prison, where he once permanently paralyzed an inmate by hitting him with a hammer. His callous attitude toward life he expressed in a letter he wrote to a girl friend soon after killing the two men last year:

"If I feel like murder, it doesn't necessarily matter who gets murdered. Murder is just a thing of itself, a rage, and rage is not reason, so what does it matter who? It vents a rage."

Opponents of capital punishment treated the man who expressed these views as a martyr and fought hard to save him from execution. Their efforts made him a celebrity whose life will be remembered in a book and a movie.

After his execution yesterday, a spokesman for the American Civil Liberties Union, which led the fight against it, tearfully accused Utah of being barbaric. But might it not have been more barbaric to allow the man to live and endanger the lives of even more human beings? Considering his willingness to kill anyone simply to vent a rage, no one within his reach, in prison or on the streets, would have been safe.

If ever a man deserved to die at the hands of the state, Gary Mark Gilmore did. We are sorry that his life was such a bloody tragedy, but we shall shed our tears for Max David Jensen and Bennie Bushnell.

The ❦ State

Columbia, S.C., January 19, 1977

THE American news media are taking their lumps from some critics for the coverage given to the legal maneuvers involving convicted murderer Gary Mark Gilmore — and for the coverage of his execution by firing squad.

The thrust of the criticism is that the news media have whipped up the morbid interests of too many Americans, that too much attention was focused on Gilmore.

Perhaps the criticism is justified in some specifics, but as a matter of news the Gilmore case was more than just a run-of-the-mill one in that he was the first person to be executed in all of the United States since 1967. And with that fact rode all of the controversy over capital punishment, and the rising concern for victims of crime.

There were other elements in the Gilmore story which set it apart — his own wish to die and the efforts of lawyers to keep him alive; his own suicide attempts, and that of his girl friend. And finally, the commercial overtones that involved one of his attorneys.

If Americans seize on the Gilmore stories to whet a morbid thirst, we are persuaded they would have found what they were seeking in other news stories or events even if Gilmore had not existed.

It is possible the news media may have told many Americans more than they really wanted to know about Gary Gilmore. But the telling of his story could no more be avoided by the news media than Gilmore could have escaped his own destiny before the firing squad Monday morning.

The Seattle Times

Seattle, Wash., January 18, 1977

GARY Gilmore and the State of Utah both got what they wanted yesterday — America's first legal execution in 10 years.

Befitting the circus nature of the event, the only witnesses to Gilmore's execution, other than his uncle and prison officials, were a Hollywood literary agent and two lawyers involved in arranging book and movie rights to the story of Gilmore's ignoble life and death.

Given the bizarre nature of that moddern tale of crime and punishment, those rights no doubt will be among the most profitable "literary" investments of the decade.

The noxious ballyhoo of the "Gilmore legend" has yet to reach its peak.

Grotesqueries aside, Gilmore's execution is a historic event that opens a new chapter in the long and tortuous debate over capital punishment in the United States and each of the 50 states.

One category of participants in the debate opposes capital punishment, on principle, in any and all circumstances.

But for a larger number of people, the question boils down to whether or not the death penalty is an effective deterrent to murder and other heinous crimes such as kidnaping and treason.

There are well-qualified criminologists on both sides of that question.

The United States Supreme Court opened the door to Gilmore's execution and that of others on "death rows" elsewhere around the country with a finding last summer that capital punishment does not constitute "cruel and unusual punishment" as forbidden by the Constitution.

The high court held further, however, that state capital-punishment laws are acceptable only when they provide adequate restraints against arbitrary or capricious imposition.

In November, 1975, Washington State voters, by a better than 2-to-1 margin, approved an initiative providing mandatory capital punishment for murder in especially aggravated situations.

Since the compulsory feature of the initiative does not meet the ground rules subsequently set forth by the Supreme Court, this state's legislators are left with the responsibility to modify the law both to meet the federal requirements and the overwhelmingly voiced sentiments of voters in this state.

The lawmakers now in session in Olympia ought to act without delay.

Meanwhile, it can be said that the fates chose well in determining which convicted killer should be the one to open a new era in the history of capital punishment. Relatives of the two young men whom Gilmore senselessly gunned down while commiting robberies will testify to that.

FORT WORTH STAR-TELEGRAM

Fort Worth, Tex., January 19, 1977

Gary Mark Gilmore is dead. There was little rejoicing at his passing that we can detect.

The news that a rifle squad had, after exercise of every avenue of judicial appeal, finally taken his life came with shocking impact.

Though we have editorially supported resumption of the death penalty as a deterrent to crime, we join all who are sorrowed by the seemingly unnecessary death of another human.

Gilmore's execution came only after every possibility of delay or reversal was at last denied through due process.

Here was a man who had capriciously killed two persons, and who admitted if he hadn't been caught, he would have killed others.

Yet emotions run high on the subject of capital punishment. The Supreme Court by a 5-4 vote in 1972 declared the death penalty unconstitutional as it was at that time imposed. But the justices found it necessary to write nine separate opinions.

The emotions cloud the issue.

That Gilmore was guilty of murder was never in doubt. His crime was so heinous as to deserve the maximum penalty legally permissible. Few would argue that point.

The significance of Gilmore's execution, then, is not that he was wrongly punished, but that he was the first to legally die for a crime in almost 10 years, and that his execution might lead to a resumption of capital punishment.

We join all who regret that this human chose to misuse his life and, in so doing, sacrificed it. We join all those, also, who mourn his victims. We find satisfaction only in that he had no further opportunity to kill.

On capital punishment, the Star-Telegram noted editorially Jan. 19, 1972:

"The swift and certain execution of the law — punishment by a means bearing a just proportion to the enormity of the crime — is the best deterrent known."

That reasoning, regrettably, still stands.

The Topeka Daily Capital

Topeka, Kans., January 20, 1977

The long ordeal of the Gary Mark Gilmore case is over.

Gilmore, who committed a cruel murder in a motel robbery and who wanted to die for it, was executed Monday by a Utah firing squad.

For the first time in nearly 10 years, a state executed a criminal.

Though courts approve capital punishment in certain cases, many Americans oppose it. They argue it is wrong to kill under any circumstances and that executions by the state involve all citizens in killing. That argument is wrong.

Many other Americans favor the death penalty, arguing that it is needed to prevent the worst of crimes. It can save lives, they maintain.

Gilmore's case was unusual. He wanted to die; others fought to keep him alive. His mother's efforts for him were understandable.

However, the American Civil Liberties Union and other liberals took up the cause. Determined to stop capital punishment at all costs, they ignored what Gilmore wanted, being more interested in protecting others on death row. Their appeals delayed the case unnecessarily.

It is appalling to think there may be similar long wrangles about every murderer on death row. There may be valid issues in some of these cases; if there are, courts should decide on them.

But since the Supreme Court has declared the death penalty constitutional under certain circumstances, the struggle over it should be transferred to state legislatures.

Let those favoring capital punishment seek laws that comply with Supreme Court rulings. Kansas' lawmakers should pass such a statute.

Groups opposing it should fight in legislatures. not in courts. Let's have no more Gary Gilmore cases.

THE INDIANAPOLIS STAR
Indianapolis, Ind., January 19, 1977

Gary Gilmore has been executed for the murder, during a crime spree, of a young part-time gasoline station attendant who was trying to work his way through law school.

Gilmore, during the same crime spree, murdered another young man, a motel manager, who had quit school, where he was studying accounting, to work for a year.

Both were decent young men, married. Both had small children, and the motel manager's wife was expecting a second. Both men had every right to live.

The murders were wanton, cold-blooded and pointless. They were among more than 20,000 homicides that took place in 1976, the ninth year of the nation's moratorium, in effect, on capital punishment.

The "moratorium" began in 1968. During the first six years of the decade, the number of homicides rose slightly — from 9,100 to 9,900. During the first five years of the decade there were 181 executions for murder, an average of 36 a year. The threat of the death penalty hung over the potential murderer.

Under the impact of a concerted campaign against capital punishment, based on ideological and sentimental reasons, the number of executions dropped in 1965 to seven, in 1966 to one and in 1967 to two. For a decade there would be no executions.

In 1968 the number of homicides surged to 13,700. From then on the total of murders rose by 1,000 or more each year until by 1974 the toll was 20,600 and still rising.

If the number of murders had stayed below the level that prevailed before the sudden drastic drop and then halt in capital punishment, more than 70,000 murder victims would be alive today.

There are those who continue to insist that the death penalty does not deter murder, even though murder grew like a plague as soon as the executions stopped. From then on, what had the murderer to fear? He stood little more risk, if any, for this ugly crime than for stealing a truckload of hogs.

The first execution in the United States in a decade may mark a turning point in American society's dealing with the most vicious of crimes. Certainly there should be no decline in the most scrupulous safeguarding of the rights of the accused and observance of due process of law in dealing with the convicted.

But there should be a return to the time-tested and awesome principles of justice that are fundamental if our society is to protect the innocent.

The Kansas City Times
Kansas City, Mo., January 18, 1977

Gary Gilmore has been killed by the state of Utah. He is no loss to mankind. Gilmore was an egocentric murderer who learned how to manipulate the press with a low cunning. The spotlight and his own alleged wish for death that came with it were all that counted for him; the fact that his execution could start a chain reaction of legal killings around the country was a minor matter to Gilmore.

He is important only because he may be the trigger for these other deaths and a return to wholesale executions in the United States. Until Gilmore, no one had been legally slain under American justice for almost 10 years. Now the stigma of being first has been accepted by the strange state of Utah and others may follow more easily.

Gilmore had become such a chattering bore that his departure almost is an excuse to feel relief. Unfortunately the real victim is not Gilmore but the system of justice that admits helpless failure and kills in frustration.

There was no dignity in Gilmore's death, either for him or for society; there should be no sense of a job finished or vindication. In the last analysis Gilmore made it easier for the state to kill him because of his unholy racket about wanting to die. Thus a system that wouldn't have taken Gilmore's advice on how to change a tire follows his line on a matter of life and death—not only for Gilmore but for hundreds of others.

Already a sickening panoply of autobiography, film and song is being prepared by promoters who circle like vultures. He will be with us for a long time to come. The Gilmore story did not come to a bloody end on that cold January day in 1977. His sordid monument is in the deaths to come and a diminished American civilization.

The Idaho STATESMAN
Boise, Idaho, January 18, 1977

Gary Gilmore's execution provided the final scene in a minor drama that became a major national happening. The question of capital punishment, an issue that has been argued and reargued for the last decade, became enshrouded in one man's wish to die.

Those who oppose capital punishment point out quite properly that crime statistics do not indicate that executions prevent murders. The critics also argue that capital punishment requires the state do do the very thing that our society says is wrong — deliberately take a human life

But our society deplores the mindless violence of its Gilmores. The passion for vengeance is strong and national polls inevitably show that a majority of Americans supports the death penalty as the final answer.

Yet the Gary Gilmore case must not be considered a benchmark in this continuing debate. He received more attention than he deserved. And how can his death be considered punishment of any type, when he begged to die?

The crackle of gunfire shortly after dawn Monday morning should bring at least tacit approval and, in some cases, pleasure to those who want the state to seek revenge. Unfortunately, it does not provide any clear answers to many of the rest of us.

All that was proven in Utah was that one warped, violent man was granted his wish — death — in a society that continues to be one of the most violent on earth.

Our only hope now can be that the name of Gary Gilmore disappears from the minds of most Americans as quickly as it appeared. Neither he nor the event in Utah on Monday morning merits remembering in the inevitable TV specials.

THE ATLANTA CONSTITUTION
Atlanta, Ga., January 18, 1977

The execution of Gary Gilmore ends almost a decade in which the death penalty was suspended.

Those who opposed that extreme punishment had long argued, and with justice, that it was inflicted mostly on the poor, on blacks and other minorities. And for a few years the death penalty was in effect outlawed by a Supreme Court ruling recognizing this fact. The court never ruled out death as a punishment, but it required the states to rewrite their laws so that the death penalty would not be inflicted in an arbitrary, discriminatory way.

Last year the Supreme Court was satisfied that the laws in many states, Georgia included, met its standards. Several hundred condemned prisoners on the nation's death rows are confronted now with the probability that they will eventually suffer the extreme penalty.

Gilmore, a murderer, was unusual but not unique in actively desiring and even demanding that he be executed. None of us can know what was in his heart—we can only judge by externals. But those externals—his behavior, his taunting of judges and others in the criminal justice system, his suicide attempts, his skillful manipulation of the media, his assignment of his life story to be published —all argue that he meant what he said: he wanted to die.

Given that wish on Gilmore's part, given the slow but inexorable legal process with its full quota of delays, including a final-hours stay and an overturning of that stay, it is best that this episode is now ended. Frantic maneuverings by those determined to prevent the execution contrast with Gilmore's apparently cool acceptance. No one's death is occasion for celebration—even this one. But when the Utah firing squad did its work yesterday morning, it not only ended Gilmore's life but also ended a long period of doubt about whether the death penalty would actually be revived. He had dared society to do what its law requires. And for a while there was doubt that society would revive a penalty so long unused.

Now that the question is answered we need not expect a quieting of the debate. The death penalty is an emotional and profound matter both for those against it and those for it. But its opponents, in a nation plagued by violent crime beyond almost any other in the civilized world, are challenged now as they haven't been in almost a generation. Sixty per cent or more of our people favor capital punishment in extreme cases. On the other hand, those charged with inflicting that punishment—judges, juries and all the others—are challenged, too. If we must have the death penalty restored, let it be administered with scrupulous care and justice.

Detroit Free Press

Detroit, Mich., January 18, 1977

WITH A black hood over his head and tennis shoes on his feet, Gary Gilmore succeeded in an ambition Monday. He made himself the center of a drama watched by the whole world.

Many another sociopathic criminal must have been envious. After all, Gilmore not only had achieved what some criminals would view as the status of a star, with promoters standing by to portray his life and put him on movie screens. He also had succeeded in getting himself killed, something he recently had failed at in two attempts at suicide.

The real question is not whether Gilmore's execution by a Utah firing squad will deter anyone from commiting a capital offense. Generations of experience with the death penalty have failed to yield proof that it is more a deterrent than a lifetime sentence.

The real question, instead, is whether this execution and others soon to come will encourage other sociopaths and psycho-paths to gain their warped pieces of glory by killing or ruining the lives of others.

By resuming executions after a 10-year lapse, the country has adopted the view that the ultimate kind of brutalization will stop brutalization.

It is true that a kind of order has been maintained in places that frequently resorted to killing people to keep order: the Soviet Union in Joseph Stalin's day, for instance, and the American South during decades of lynchings followed by decades of frequent state executions.

But it also is true that American states that have had the most executions also have had the highest, or very high, capital crime rates. We are not sure about the argument that brutalization by the state encourages private brutalization, but we suspect that is right. Certainly the country makes a bad mistake in assuming that its murderers, rap-ists and armed robbers have minds that work like everyone else's, that they will be chastened by the possibility of execution; that, in fact, they usually are fully rational.

The Supreme Court, by ruling last July that the death penalty does not violate the Constitution's prohibition against cruel and unusual punishment, has opened the way for many more executions following Gilmore's. But the Supreme Court has not required that. Some 35 states have required it by adopting the death penalty.

The most spurious part of the Supreme Court's reasoning in that decision was its declaration that, though capital punishment may be applied, it cannot be applied capriciously. It must be applied with an even hand. Yet hundreds of criminals who committed crimes as bad as Gilmore's will not face execution, in many cases because the Supreme Court itself has found fault with state capital punishment laws.

Where is there any evenhandedness when more than 100 North Carolina prisoners given the death penalty will escape it because the Supreme Court threw out that state's capital punishment law? Where is there even-handedness when middle-class killers escape death because of strong legal representation and the money to fight their cases, while others with less means pay the price?

The Gilmore execution is only the beginning of a chain of state killings that rest upon legal disparities, arbitrary judicial decisions and class distinctions. That, as much as the moral question of whether the state should take a life, is the crux of the matter.

ST. LOUIS POST-DISPATCH

St. Louis, Mo., January 18, 1977

The execution of convicted murderer Gary Gilmore by a firing squad at Utah State Prison was a legal barbarism that has diminished every person in that state, and, by extension, every American as well. For the killing was carried out under color of law in the name of the people who have said in effect that this dreadful devaluation of human life was an acceptable punishment. And it may be only the beginning of an unprecedented legalized bloodbath. The nation's death rows house 432 prisoners for whom Gilmore's execution may bring their own a step closer.

Utah's death penalty strikingly failed to deter Gary Gilmore's crime, as capital punishment statutes elsewhere have similarly failed to deter crime. How then can the Gilmore execution be considered an effective deterrent to others? It can be argued of course that Utah had to take Gilmore's life as a simple retribution for the life he took. But those who take that view surely should be prepared to show that a valuable social purpose other than pure mindless vengeance is served thereby. What social purpose did Gary Gilmore's death accomplish? None that we can see. One horrible crime was followed by a punishment that cannot be undone. What if Utah's death penalty is ultimately held to be unconstitutional?

Dostoevsky wrote in *The Idiot* that "To kill for murder is a punishment incomparably worse than the crime itself." Albert Camus held that capital punishment was the most premeditated of murders. No state — not Utah, not Missouri, not Illinois — should have the right to shoot, suffocate, electrocute or otherwise kill any human being. Crime merits punishment. But capital punishment should be unacceptable to a civilized society.

The Evening Bulletin

Philadelphia, Pa., January 18, 1977

Gary Gilmore is dead and his execution yesterday on the frozen fields of a Utah prison has set off even stronger waves of debate over both the legality and the morality of capital punishment.

There is a great irony in this since Gary Gilmore is an unlikely symbol around which to argue things moral, legal or philosophic. His life of crime, the cold blooded murders he committed, his refusal to show remorse or concern for his victims or for their families can, in fact, be used as an argument on behalf of execution as the ultimate weapon of the state against crime.

But were the bullets from a firing squad punishment for Gary Gilmore? He insisted he wanted to die. He cursed and abused those who attempted to prevent his execution. Would it not have been punishment more severe to have kept him alive and in prison? Or was this stance a ruse on the part of the man who manipulated everyone and everything and, in his final days, caused a nation to writhe and an important sector of our court system to appear vacillating — and worse.

As we are all aware, the execution of Gary Gilmore yesterday was the first in the United States in nearly 10 years. In prisons throughout the United States the condemned await the hangman's noose or the electric chair.

A man awaits in Delaware.

Legislation to reinstitute capital punishment is moving in both the Pennsylvania and New Jersey legislatures. And so the issue is going to be with us even more prominently in the weeks and months to come.

What can be made of the execution of Gary Mark Gilmore that will benefit a society for which he showed such contempt for most of his life? Well, probably the best thing is to have the United State Supreme Court issue, at least to the other level of federal courts, an order setting out very precisely the grounds for appeal in capital punishment cases and the procedure to be followed in pressing such actions. This could at least prevent what Gary Gilmore himself complained of as being made to feel "like a yo-yo" between life and death. No one deserves this.

And since the United States Supreme Court has found that capital punishment is indeed permissible, it should also travel the extra distance — in responding to cases already before it — to clear up the confusion that still exists as to when it may be imposed.

The Toronto Star

Toronto, Ont., January 18, 1977

And so the macabre Gary Gilmore freak show is over.

It has been one of the most revolting reversions to barbarism in recent years. Ugly savage instincts, dormant but obviously not done away with, surfaced with a passion as supposedly civilized people toyed with a human life in this on-again, off-again execution.

And what has it accomplished, this first official state killing in the U.S. in 10 years?

It has hardly been a tribute to the judicial system, which in its jurisdictional feuding merely offered new ways for publicity seekers to try to climb aboard the bandwagon.

Nor has it brought credit to legislators, who have been unable to clearly stamp out the barbaric practice of state killing even though Americans thought it had been done away with.

And in the ultimate, it has not even done anything to make Americans safer. There might at least be an argument for capital punishment if it could be shown that it deterred potential murderers, but there is no such evidence.

So in the end, everyone is diminished by Gary Gilmore's death.

It doesn't matter that the killer himself wanted to die. What matters is that the state, deliberately, killed him.

The five rifles that finally punctured the mounting circus balloon finally gave Gilmore the peace he had sought.

It will not be so easy for the conscience of the society that sanctioned the execution.

Newsday

Garden City, N.Y., January 18, 1977

If the purpose was retribution, society got its due yesterday when it put a merciless killer to death. But retribution is a bad reason for breaking a 10-year moratorium on legal killings in this country. And more executions will follow even though the man who was scheduled to die tomorrow won a late reprieve from the Supreme Court.

For every day remaining in 1977 there's a condemned murderer awaiting death in America. For most, the legal process takes longer than it did for Gary Gilmore, who refused all appeals. Jerry Lane Jurek, who was to have been executed shortly after midnight tonight, is one of them. His appeal was based in part on a court order allowing television cameras to record the event. That would be about the only way to outdo the grisly circus provided by Gilmore's fight for death.

The concept of capital punishment is simply not compatible with a society that prides itself on being just. If the crimes of the 345 men and five women sentenced to death were to be compared to those of murderers who were merely sent to prison instead, we doubt if there would be much difference. There *is* a difference in the people, though; the murderers who inhabit our death rows are more likely to be poor and black.

Given the amount of violent crime in our society, the search for a deterrent is understandable. But study after study has concluded that capital punishment does not bring the murder rate down. In Gilmore's case, there was obviously no deterrent value; he said repeatedly he preferred death to life in prison. And it's hard to believe that fear of death would have kept a borderline retardate like Jurek from killing.

Most murders are acts of anger or passion, committed with little regard for the consequences. Not so when the state kills deliberately in the name of us, the people.

Wisconsin ⚖ State Journal

Madison, Wisc., January 19, 1977

The State of Utah killed Gary Gilmore Monday after a grotesque tug-of-war.

The spectacle saw Gilmore, a jail-prone, suicidal loser insisting on being put to death while those opposing the death penalty fought the execution through a legal maze of court actions resulting in a series of delays and contradictory decisions.

We oppose the death penalty because we know of no proof that it serves as a deterrent to those who would commit capital crimes, because there is always a chance of mistake and because even in years when death sentences have been legal there was a revulsion to carrying them out.

We agree with Robert A. Pugsley, a fellow at New York University Law School's criminal law education and research center, who wrote:

"The argument . . . is not that a particular murderer might not justly deserve to die. Rather, the question must be: Can our society impose such a punishment without thereby corroding the very bases of human dignity and respect for life which it is part purpose of a retributivist punishment scheme to preserve? . . . Still more basic: Can a punishment which takes life be truly just?"

Also, there is the inevitability of Gilmore, a brutal murderer, becoming something of a folk hero. Already the magazine interviews are being published, the books are in the process of being written. No doubt there will be ballads and poems and songs distorting facts and values.

There can be no good to come out of the Gilmore execution, except perhaps the lesson that while the death penalty seems to be popular in the abstract, that popularity turns to a taste of ashes when the time for state-imposed death arrives.

Citizens of states such as Wisconsin, which do not impose the death penalty, can be relieved that the agony of responsibility for the official taking of human lives will be spared them.

Citizens of states which do condone execution can look forward to the Utah experience when it becomes time for the hundreds of Gary Gilmores on death rows throughout the nation to be killed.

St. Petersburg Times

St. Petersburg, Fla., January 19, 1977

Of all the postmortem commentary on Gary Gilmore, one of the more thoughtful reactions came in the form of a question from a San Francisco high school student. "I wonder why we did it?" he said.

WAS IT because the four steel-jacketed bullets that ripped through Gilmore's heart are likely to deter others from becoming cold-blooded killers? In upholding capital punishment last July, the Supreme Court conceded there is no real evidence that it serves as a deterrent. Former prison wardens, who questioned condemned men on earlier death rows, say none of them thought of the death penalty when murdering others.

Retribution? Undoubtedly many folks in this nation still ascribe to the frontier standard of an eye for an eye, a death for a death. But few states would claim such a standard sufficient for giving official sanction to the taking of human life.

IN LARGE PART the Supreme Court based its ruling on capital punishment's "long history of acceptance both in the United States and England." It noted the 34 states, including Florida, that in one form or another had reenacted the death penalty since older laws were struck down in 1972.

And, indeed, the late Justice Earl Warren once said the Eighth Amendment's ban on cruel and unusual punishment "must draw its meaning from the evolving standards of decency that mark the progress of a maturing society."

Neither legislative actions, opinion polls, nor the granting of Gary Gilmore's death wish offers a true measure of the standards of decency in America today.

Despite all the notoriety that placed a life-long loser in the international spotlight, only a few witnesses looked on as Gilmore, strapped in a chair at the Utah state prison, said, "Let's do it," and stoically accepted his fate from a hidden firing squad.

A HERO? Of course not! Gilmore's own brother said he was a dangerously deranged man who should never again be turned loose in society. He brutally murdered two young men who were married and had small children. The long ordeal of his on-again, off-again execution angered a nation, just as it did the condemned man himself.

Weary of the attempted suicides, the appeals and hearings, most Americans longed for an end to the circus of death in Point of the Mountain, Utah. Some were relieved when the it finally came, the first execution in the United States in 10 years. But Gilmore's death, and society's role in it, apparently only ensured that exploitation of the Utah case will continue — in magazine articles, a book and movie.

As the nation turns its attention to other death rows, including Florida's, the possibility of television and other visual coverage threatens to make even more of a spectacle of future executions. That prospect bothers a lot of people, including members of the media. "It's something a genteel society doesn't want to see," said a local circuit judge the other day.

WHICH IS exactly why this genteel and maturing society ought to see it. At the very least it would cause more of us to ask why we did it.

Democrat and Chronicle
Rochester, N.Y., January 20, 1977

THE EXECUTION of confessed murderer ary Gilmore makes uncomfortable both those ho approve the death penalty and those who ppose it.

Gilmore was not deterred from killing by the apital punishment law and that's hard to accept r those who favor the penalty.

But those who want to abolish it also have to eal with the fact that Gilmore wanted to die nd mocked their arguments to boot.

The confusion created in many minds by the ilmore case was evident at the Utah prison here the sentence was carried out by a firing quad.

Provo lawyer Robert Moody, hired to protect ilmore's posthumous literary rights, denounced e cruelty of those "people with their causes" ho tried to interfere. But after seeing his client ot, he was obliged to add: "It's a very brutal nd of thing and I would only hope we can take look at ourselves and our system."

The prison warden has been quoted as ying: "It's one thing to believe in it (capital nishment). It's another thing to be put in the sition of having to carry it out."

When all the arguments are in, the fact remains that capital punishment is a brutalizing experience, not just for those who must do the executing but for the broader society as well.

There are many who say that Gilmore got exactly what he asked for and what he deserved and that society is well rid of him.

But there are also those who were appalled by the revolting manner in which the whole on-again-off-again affair was handled.

Shana Alexander put it as well as anyone when she said before the execution: "Look at the blood-lust this case has stirred up already with its promise of legal ritual murder: the disgusting scramble to get onto the Utah firing squad . . . the deadly duckblind where the lucky shooters sit. These bizarre arrangements make a mockery of justice."

The death penalty, no matter how it is carried out, is a barbarous affront to human dignity.

And the debate about it focuses attention once again on the questions that Clarence Darrow asked: Why is it mostly the poor who are executed? Who knows why men kill? Why do so many who read about the executions get a little thrill of pleasure in their hearts?

OREGON Journal AN INDEPENDENT NEWSPAPER
Portland, Ore., January 19, 1977

The Gary Gilmore case helps to illustrate one of e things that is wrong with the death penalty.

Gilmore, who was executed by a Utah firing uad early Monday, may in death be turned into a lk hero when he is anything but that.

An inordinate amount of attention has been fo-sed on him because he had asked to be allowed to e, because his was the first life taken by a state in arly 10 years, because innumerable legal maneuv-ings have intensified the drama and because the ople of this nation are sharply divided, from a ilosophical point of view, over capital punishment.

We find it revolting that a producer has paid 00,000 for the rights to the Gilmore life story and at another execution scheduled in Texas, now layed, may be filmed for television.

The Gilmore life story is terribly sordid, and if is man faced a life sentence instead of standing up efore a firing squad with a spirit of bravado, that ory would not be glorified.

Sentiment in this country toward capital punish-ent has swung from one side to another like a endulum. The U.S. Supreme Court has been am-ivalent. Its latest decision, in July 1976, partly versed a 1972 decision in which it had struck down laws it said were too inflexible. Last year it upheld laws in three states but nullified laws in two others which it said were too broad in scope.

Even when there has been no question about constitutionality, convicted killers have been kept on death rows for interminable lengths of time because important segments of society have inherent objec-tions to the state being in the "death business."

Right now a probable majority of Americans favors capital punishment in theory. That might change if we have a rash of executions.

The attitude of Utah prison warden Sam Smith illustrates the state of mind of many people. Smith believes in capital punishment but hated to carry out the Gilmore execution.

Most people in the corrections field oppose the death penalty. They believe that it does not deter, that it is demeaning to society and all those who have to be involved in carrying out executions and that it falls most heavily on those least able financially to defend themselves.

Despite our feelings against the death penalty, it is in a sense a relief to have the Gilmore case over with. But it will be tragic if the Gilmore story is exploited in book and film in a way that it would not have been if he had been locked up for life.

The Globe and Mail
Toronto, Ont., January 18, 1977

Among all the frantic confusion, all the seamy sideshows and the grotesque circus that led up to the execution of Gary Mark Gilmore, there is one thing, and only one, that matters:

What has happened in the United States after a hiatus of almost 10 years has put the hand of the state, and of the people, back on the rope, the switch or the trigger. It has taken the community back to the retrograde and discredited delusion that things can be changed for the better, that problems can be solved, that wrongs can be righted, by killing people.

Capital punishment is no deterrent. There is not a scrap of evidence to ex-cuse it on that ground. The evidence is rather that the penalty is the farthest thing from the murderer's mind when he commits his crime. Capital punishment is a confession of failure to find a ra-tional means of protecting society, pun-ishing crime and upholding the law. It is in fact a monstrous means of diverting public attention, by a primitive act of vengeance, from society's failure to achieve any real progress toward a more law-abiding, less violent society.

"He died in dignity," said an uncle. Dignity? The last weeks and months of his life were sick and sordid. A scramble of appeals and counter-appeals, at-tempts at suicide, a convicted killer sen-timentalized and lionized for having cursed the American Civil Liberties Un-ion when it fought to prevent the state from embracing the morals and the methods of the killer.

His case became a freak show. On the weekend of his death the approaching execution served as fodder for comedy writers on American network television. After the surprise midnight order for a stay of execution the Appeals Court was called together before the light of day to review and reverse the order. In the last hours of his life Gilmore telephoned a country music radio station in Salt Lake City to ask for the playing of a song written to celebrate his suicide pact with his fiancee last November. The song is a local hit. Among the wit-nesses at the execution, in an old, un-used prison tannery, was a promoter, Laurence Schiller, who owns the rights to the story of Gilmore's life and death.

That Gilmore wanted execution is irre-levant. Civilized society does not leave the choice of penalty up to the convicted criminal. Civilized society does not em-brace the morals of the murderer or ask his advice on questions of life or death. It does not believe one killing can atone for another. It knows vengeance cannot raise the dead.

DAYTON DAILY NEWS
Dayton, Ohio, January 18, 1977

So we have, in fact, killed Gary Gilmore and now what amounts to a national blood-bath can begin. There are about 350 men and women under sentence of death in the United States — 64 in Ohio alone. If we kill one a day, regularly working at the slaughter like a good butcher, it would be next December be-fore they would all have been shot, hung, gassed or electrocuted. But, of course, more are being added to the list all along. So the list really is endless.

Capital punishment is wrong. It is wrong because it is pointless. If executions deterred crime — the reason usually cited for conduct-ing them — at least a pragmatic case could be made for the death penalty.

But executions do not deter crime. Many West European nations have quit this barbar-ism, without any worsening of crime. Many American states abolished it decades ago; crime in those rose no more than in the states that keep killing.

It has been nearly 10 years since the United States last took the lives of its own citizens. Ironically — if something this seri-ous can fit under that indulgent word — we have begun killing again, in the supposed cause of deterring crime, at a time when the rates of serious crime have been falling.

No, the reason for the death penalty is not to deter crime. That is the excuse, the socially respectable lie into which mass hypocrisy gulls us, so as to give us a little splinter of self-respect to hang onto in this killing busi-ness.

The reason is revenge. That is all that executions accomplish. They act out one of society's grimmest strains. They give all of us, vicariously, license to do just what Gil-more did: To kill either wantonly or for mere self-gratifying reasons.

Gilmore understood that better than most. The evidence is clear that he was a would-be suicide — like many such, one who never could quite bring off his own death. But he could murder and he did, so that the state — the public: we — would complete his suicide for him. This has now been done, with a lot of distracting legal rigamarole.

Gilmore played on the public revenge lust and implicated us as accomplices, not merely in his own death but in those of his victims. By dutifully and, according to some indica-tions, even gleefully shooting him, the society has confirmed the practicality of his murders. The act was little better than his and it could even be argued that it was worse. His mur-ders at least got Gilmore something — the death he wanted and couldn't manage on his own. Ours will get us nothing.

Gilmore trusted himself to the nation's worst impulses and was not disappointed.

DEATH PENALTY IS NOT MANDATORY FOR KILLING OF POLICE OFFICERS

The Supreme Court June 6 ruled that states could not impose an automatic death penalty for the killing of police officers. However, the court left undecided the circumstances under which a death sentence could be constitutionally mandated.

In *Roberts v. Louisiana*, Harry Roberts, convicted of the 1974 slaying of a New Orleans police officer, had been sentenced to death under the same Louisiana law that the Supreme Court subsequently struck down in July 1976. Although the 1976 ruling had involved another convicted killer, Louisiana had indicated it would not carry out the Roberts execution because of the decision. The high court gave no reason why it chose to review the Roberts case.

Justices Thurgood Marshall, William J. Brennan Jr., Lewis F. Powell Jr., John Paul Stevens and Potter Stewart formed the majority in the 5–4 ruling. The majority opinion was unsigned, but Marshall and Brennan issued a statement reiterating their opposition to the death penalty. Chief Justice Warren E. Burger and Justices Harry A. Blackmun, Byron R. White and William H. Rehnquist dissented for a variety of reasons.

The majority affirmed the 1976 decision and, while acknowledging society's duty to protect its law enforcement officials, said it was "incorrect to suppose that no mitigating circumstances can exist" in the killing of police officer. Those mitigating circumstances might include, the court said, "the absence of any prior convictions, the influence of drugs, alcohol or extreme emotional disturbance" and circumstances believed by the defendant to provide a "moral justification" for his action.

Pittsburgh Post-Gazette

Pittsburgh, Pa., June 9, 1977

AS SURE as God made little, mean capitals outside of Indianapolis, legislators and others throughout the nation are going to deplore Monday's Supreme Court decision on capital punishment as a further judicial license for crime and mayhem, specifically a ticket to kill policemen.

The decision is no such thing. The court merely reaffirmed its ruling of last year that capital punishment is permissible as long as laws requiring it include a provision for discretion by judge and jury, as circumstances warrant, in sentencing a criminal to death. The justices in a 5-4 decision said that this rule covered all cases, including laws against the murder of law enforcement officers.

The particular case in question involved a Louisiana man sentenced to death for killing a policeman under the mandatory death penalty law in effect in that state. The problem the court had with the law was not that it ordered death for killing a policeman but that the sentence was mandatory.

Only two states, Louisiana and New York, appear directly affected by the decision, but all 50 in the Union now have clear guidelines from the court on the capital punishment question. It is *not* cruel and unusual punishment and it *is* permissible under the Constitution as long as laws ordering it do not make the sentence mandatory. No matter what else one may think of that, there is no longer any doubt about what the law of the land is on public executions.

The Detroit News

Detroit, Mich., June 8, 1977

When the U.S. Supreme Court upheld the death penalty in a landmark decision last July, foes of capital punishment cried that the door had been opened to reckless and wholesale slaughter by the state.

A careful reading of the ruling did not support that fear. This week, the justices handed down a decision which further illustrates their restraint and caution. Under the guidelines established by the court, no citizen can be railroaded to the electric chair or the firing squad.

Echoing its previous words on the subject, the court asserted this week that a state may not impose a mandatory death penalty on persons convicted of killing police officers. Specifically, it held that the law under which Louisiana sentenced Harry Roberts to death for the fatal shooting of a New Orleans police officer constitutes "cruel and unusual punishment."

The decision does not preclude death sentences for the murderers of policemen. It forbids the automatic application of the death penalty. The distinction is a sensible and humane one; justice should never become a knee-jerk reaction.

Like any other crime, the killing of a policeman may involve mitigating factors such as the youthfulness of the offender, absence of prior conviction, the influence of drugs, or extreme emotional stress. The Supreme Court says the jury should have the authority to consider such factors. We agree.

This concurrence does not signify retreat from our position on capital punishment. For certain kinds of crime — depending upon the circumstances — death may be the only adequate penalty with which to express society's moral outrage.

Without placing a higher value on the life of an individual policeman than on the life of any other citizen, most people recognize the symbolic importance of the policeman as an enforcer of the law. Anybody who guns down a policeman takes a shot at the whole of society; in that sense, the crime becomes a very special one.

We oppose the wholesale application of capital punishment but consider the death penalty appropriate, provided judges and juries are allowed to weigh mitigating factors, for the murderers of law officers. Likewise, we think it should be applied to terrorists who commit murder and to the rapers and murderers of children.

As one of the minority of states not using the death penalty, Michigan denies itself an important and justifiable weapon against crime. The Supreme Court's cautious standards, striking a balance between the rights of suspects and the needs of society, provide a sensible framework for the writing of a capital punishment law which Michigan citizens could accept in good conscience.

Alternative Sentences: Is true restitution possible?

Opponents of crime compensation argue that it will result in a costly bureaucracy that will become prohibitively expensive. They also believe the system will encourage the filing of fraudulent claims. Supporters, however, argue that controls will be effective and the system will induce more victims to report violent crimes.

The expense and disappointing results of the prison system have encouraged the search for non-incarcerative punishments. In Sweden 97% of all sentences for criminal conviction are in the form of fines.[1] In this country the concept of restitution, that the victim should be compensated by the offender, has been gaining increasing acceptance. Apprehended offenders have always faced the possibility that their victims would sue them in civil court for damages suffered. However, the expense of obtaining a private attorney and the probability that the criminal has no funds has made recourse to this remedy rare. The use of restitution in criminal proceedings has not been unknown; juvenile courts have often required delinquents to make compensation for their criminal acts in lieu of imprisonment or prosecution or as a condition for probation. In the criminal courts, an informal system of restitution exists: prosecutors will sometimes agree to dismiss criminal charges if the defendant makes amends for the damage caused the complainant. Several jurisdictions also require that defendants be charged with the costs of the criminal proceeding if they are convicted.[2] This restitution to the state may include the expense of transcripts, jury fees and public defender representation.

There are limits to the value of restitution as an alternative to prison. It does not resolve the problem that the vast majority of criminals are never apprehended. Nor does it seem a practical solution to the violent offender. The scheme of requiring the offender to obtain a job in order to recompense the victim may be fanciful in view of the high unemployment rate and the job discrimination faced by ex-offenders. One must ask if the system is not successful in obtaining jobs for the unemployed before they commit crime, why should it be afterwards?

Restitution statutes may raise some serious constitutional objections if they mandate a jail term for failure to recompense the victim. The Supreme Court in *Williams v. Illinois* has held that the equal protection clause of the Fourteenth Amendment is violated if the law subjects a certain class of convicted defendants to a period of imprisonment because of indigency.[3] In *Williams*, restitution was not directly in issue. The challenge was to the Illinois practice of requiring prisoners to remain incarcerated after the expiration of their prison term if they were unable to satisfy the fine imposed by the court. A companion case to *Williams, Morris v. Schoonfield,* seemed to anticipate the restitution/fine alternative in a concurring opinion by four of the justices. "The constitution prohibits the state from imposing a fine as a sentence and then automatically converting it into a jail term solely because the defendant is indigent."[4] The opinion suggested that in order to overcome the constitutional infirmities, the state must take care to offer alternatives, such as obtaining jobs for indigents. *Tate v. Short,* a decision handed down a year later, rejected the practice of jailing traffic offenders unable to pay their fines, who otherwise would not be subject to a prison sentence.[5] The Court did not rule out imprisoning defendants who were unable to satisfy payment of fines through alternative methods. Unless all classes of offenders are allowed to partake in a restitution alternative to imprisonment, an acceleration of discretionary justice will result; the poor offender will be jailed for inability to pay, while the wealthy one will be continued at liberty.

Closely connected to restitution is crime compensation. State crime compensation boards would aid crime victims who suffer monetarily from medical expenses and loss of income. The House of Representatives is considering in the 1978 legislative session a national crime compensation act that would provide grants to state compensation boards. Twenty-two states presently have some form of crime compensation systems. New York recently perfected its compensation provision to entitle crime victims to recover any of the profits offenders earned through media exploitation of their misdeeds. This provision might be prone to constitutional attack since it provides for a taking of a person's property without a due process hearing. A 1975 survey of crime compensation programs in five states and three foreign countries concluded that at present the most pressing problem is publicizing the existence of the compensation boards and informing victims of the benefit and eligibility rules.[6] The results also seemed to demonstrate that the cooperation of victims with the police and prosecution increased. The New York statute makes such cooperation a requirement for compensation relief.

Notes

1. David F. Greenberg, "Alternative to Prison," in *Prisoners' Rights Sourcebook* ed. by Marilyn G. Haft & Michelle G. Hermann (New York: Clark Boardman, 1973) p. 602.
2. On the constitutionality of such statutes see, e.g. *Fuller v. Oregon,* 417 U.S. 40 (1974); *James v. Strange,* 407 U.S. 128 (1972).
3. *Williams v. Illinois,* 399 U.S. 235 (1970).
4. *Morris v. Schoonfield,* 399 U.S. 508 (1970) (White, J., concurring).
5. *Tate v. Short,* 401 U.S. 395 (1971).
6. James Brooks, "How Well are Criminal Injury Programs Performing," 21 *Crime & Delinquency* 50 (1975).

THE DAILY HERALD
Biloxi, Miss., October 5, 1977

Aid to victims of violent crime

The crime victim bill which passed the House last week is one we would heartily endorse, save for a serious omission.

It would establish a program of federal compensation for injuries received by victims of muggings, rapes and other violent crimes.

The serious omission, in our view, is that it contains no provision that places some responsibility on the offender to compensate his victim.

Restitution by the criminal should be part and parcel of any victim compensation plan, when the criminal has been apprehended.

Otherwise, the plan will be void of any aspect of crime prevention. And we fear that the plan would be more susceptible to ripoffs by the unscrupulous should the only payouts come from tax funds.

The House-passed bill extends the federal sphere of influence to victims of violent crime, a segment of our society that continues to grow. The victims attract attention, but minimal relief.

There are restrictions in the bill. Federal aid would only go to the 20 states that now have programs to compensate victims of violent crimes. Those states could receive federal funding for up to 25 per cent of the cost of their programs; maximum compensation for any victim would be $25,000. Compensation for property losses, such as stolen cars, and compensation for losses covered by insurance are excluded.

Since this state has no program of compensation, Mississippians who become victimized will not share in the federal assistance. Perhaps enactment of the federal program would be an incentive for Mississippi to adopt a state program.

One opponent of the bill argued that its passage would be tantamount to a dire and unfortunate confession that "...we are not able to handle the criminal problem." It is a truthful confession, adequately supported by crime statistics.

There is another danger that the program, if instituted, will one day be expanded beyond compensation for medical costs and work-loss expenses arising from violent crimes. Such an expansion would play havoc with the proposed funding allowance of $30 million per year for three years, which is what the current bill projects.

But the most important flaw is the failure to affix restitution responsibility upon the perpetrators of crime. We hope that the Senate takes note of and corrects this deficiency, then votes passage.

The Seattle Times
Seattle, Wash., November 21, 1977

Federal duty to aid victims of crime

ALTHOUGH disagreement persists on some of the detailed mechanics, Congress appears to be closer to paying federal dollars to victims of certain crimes than at any time since 1972.

The Senate has voted victim-compensation bills at least five times in as many years. But the House, worried about costs and federal involvement in a state-government responsibility, has tended to drag its feet.

Fortunately, House resistance has begun to crumble. While the vote was close (192 to 173), members for the first time approved a bill the other day to help reimburse crime victims for uninsured medical expenses and for lost wages.

Nearly half the states, including Washington, are far ahead of the federal government in providing at least token relief to victims of violent crimes, through a system of payments not unlike those disbursed for on-the-job deaths and injuries.

(Neither the existing state programs nor the proposed federal measure reimburse victims for property losses or intangible "pain and suffering.")

The House version would have the federal government contribute 25 per cent of a state's payment of a victim claim not to exceed $25,000 for medical costs and work-loss expenses, only half of what the Senate had voted earlier.

Estimated costs (perhaps $50 million a year) are not inconsequential, but still are far below what the federal government spends for a variety of far less essential purposes.

Among the opponents, Illinois Representative Robert McClory said the bill should be rejected because it amounts to a "confession that we are not able to handle the crime problem."

Perhaps so. Yet refusing to concede government's inability to get crime under control — especially violent criminals who prey on the poor and the elderly — would do nothing to discharge a responsibility for gaps in public-safety services.

The principle underlying such legislation is entirely valid. Federal participation in the victim-compensation effort should be a catalyst to new programs in states now without them, and should undergird and improve those already in existence.

THE COMMERCIAL APPEAL
Memphis, Tenn., October 22, 1977

Aiding Crime's Victims

TENNESSEE IS 1 of 20 states to establish a fund to help compensate the victims of violent crimes for medical expenses and lost work time. It is also 1 of 19 states with compensation programs that would be denied federal funds if a bill passed recently by the U.S. House of Representatives is enacted in its current form.

The House-passed version pledges that the federal government would reimburse up to 25 per cent of state awards to crime victims. Its sponsors saw federal participation as a way to encourage states to form or continue these needed programs. But instead of allowing states the flexibility of direct grants, House members wrote such restrictive criteria into the pledge that only one state — New York — could possibly qualify for federal help under the House rules.

TENNESSEE'S PROGRAM, now scheduled to take effect July 1, 1978, falls well within most limits set by the House. It allows injured persons or surviving dependents to be compensated by awards of up to $10,000. It requires they cooperate with law enforcement authorities investigating and prosecuting the crime. All claims must be heard and awards set by the state's courts, and any award made must be reduced by the amount of any outside compensations. And it calls for those convicted of crimes to help victims through payments into a state compensation fund established under the 1976 law.

That fund was too low to provide adequate compensation when the law originally was slated to go into effect on July 1, 1977, so the General Assembly this past session voted to postpone the program a year. State legislators also made some minor housekeeping changes as well as extended a criminal's liability beyond $21 upon conviction to also include the possible payment of up to 10 per cent of any earnings while under court jurisdiction.

BUT TENNESSEE and other states fall short when it comes to two controversial House provisions: that victims be "blameless" in the crimes and that states require anyone who agrees to pay a person accused or convicted of a crime for an interview, article, or other account related to the crime instead pay that money into an escrow account to be held for the victim.

Tennessee leaves it to the courts to decide whether an award should be limited or denied because of a victim's behavior before, during or after the crime. It has no automatic "blameless" clause but vests this discretionary power where it belongs: in a court of law.

While no state wants criminals to profit from their crimes, Tennessee along with 18 other states has no provision to attach the earnings of anyone accused of a crime. New York is the only one that possibly could qualify here. And though House sponsors questioned the constitutionality of a provision that would tie up the assets of those accused but not convicted of crimes, House members passed this amendment by a vote of 245-113.

Tennessee has a good law that should go far toward cushioning at least the financial losses that victims of violent crime and their families have had to suffer alone for too long. It and the 19 other states have recognized this responsibility, and they should find encouragement, not senseless manipulation, when Washington decides to help. We hope the Senate provides that encouragement when it considers this bill early next year.

DAILY NEWS

New York, N.Y., May 7, 1977

RESTORING SOME BALANCE

A bill to provide federal compensation to victims of violent crimes is forging its way through the congressional maze, and chances are good for its success.

Such a program makes sense, in our judgment, as long as strong safeguards against fraud are built in. We've done plenty in recent years to protect the rights of criminals. Help for their injured victims is overdue.

To forestall the program's becoming yet another gigantic federal bureaucracy, all funds should be channeled through local crime victims' compensation organizations on a matching basis. New York City and State already have such operations, and the infusion of federal money should strengthen and expand the services they offer.

HERALD EXAMINER

Los Angeles, Calif., May 22, 1977

Victim Compensation

In the past 12 years, 19 states have initiated programs to provide some measure of compensation to victims of crimes.

Congress is considering (H.R. 3686) which recognizes that direct federal assistance might be warranted to compensate both crime victims and witnesses.

The resolution would encourage states to enact legislation setting up their own programs to compensate federal and state victims.

In general, HR 3686 would provide for payment by the federal government of 100 per cent of certain costs of compensating victims of federal offenses and half of the costs to victims of state offenses.

We endorse the bill's general concepts, and its intended goal of reducing the financial burdens of violent crime victims.

California's victim compensation plan is somewhat of a mixed blessing. On the one hand, it has paid out $9.7 million since 1967 to victims of violent crimes. However, the state, not the perpetrators of the crimes, is stuck with the costs involved.

In 10 years the state has collected only $80,145 from the criminals involved in the $9.7 million expenditure. Collection and enforcement problems complicate the matter, but more often than not the defendants are unable to pay the fine.

Under the California program, the state is empowered to pay up to $23,500 to a crime victim for medical expenses, loss of wages or support, job training and attorney fees.

The program is never likely to be self-supporting. Nor is it necessary that it meets that condition. But laws can be changed to bring the program more in balance.

The Joint Audit Committee, commenting on the program, recommended that the courts' ability to impose mandatory but nominal fines for certain criminal offenses be expanded.

Assemblyman Mike Cullen (D-Long Beach), committee chairman, sees the state receiving an additional several thousand to several million dollars a year under such a system.

Victim compensation programs are designed to assure that no single person has to bear the full costs of a serious violent crime committed against him. Whether in California or any of the other 18 states, this is an admirable goal.

Having the state taxpayers pick up the bill, however, rather than require direct restitution from the perpetrator of the crime is only a partially just solution.

The Philadelphia Inquirer

Philadelphia, Pa., October 14, 1977

Help for victims gets closer

The U. S. House of Representatives last week approved a bill that would provide financial assistance to innocent victims of crime. It is the first time the House approved the concept, though it has lingered in House committees for years.

Thus, with the bill now going to the Senate, which has passed similar versions in the past, the House action is an encouraging sign that the financial needs of the crime victims will soon be recognized by the federal government.

Of all the participants in the criminal justice system, the victim is the most neglected. It is estimated that of the $15 billion spent on criminal justice last year, only 1 percent went to the victim.

Bitter at being neglected, crime victims frequently turn their backs on the system by failing to report crimes or by refusing to testify against defendants. Thus, society ends up paying the cost of their neglect.

There have been positive developments in recent years, however. About 20 states, including Pennsylvania and New Jersey, have established programs to compensate victims for medical costs and loss of earnings. But with crime soaring along with medical costs, the financial strain on the states has been enormous.

In New Jersey, for example, there is a backlog of 2,300 cases because of insufficient funds. And the $900,-000 appropriated by the state legislature last year covered the costs of only 87 percent of the claims.

The federal government can help ease the financial burden by becoming a partner with the states in assisting victims. The bill passed by the House does just that by requiring the federal government to reimburse each state 25 percent of the awards granted to victims. Its passage would not only help existing state programs. It would give new impetus to others to establish their own.

Victim compensation is not, as some critics charge, an unwarranted intrusion into the insurance business or one more government giveaway. It is instead a fundamental recognition that government's responsibility toward fighting crime extends beyond more deterence and apprehension. It includes taking care of persons who, through no fault of their own, have been victimized.

The House action is a big step towards the federal government's meeting the responsibility.

Rocky Mountain News

A Scripps-Howard Newspaper   Reg. U.S. Pat. Off.   Colorado's First Newspaper—Founded in 1859

Denver, Colo., October 25, 1977

Aiding crime victims

HAVING WAGED WAR for years against criminals, the country now seems equally determined to do something for the victims of violent crime.

At least 20 states, including California, Kentucky, Ohio, Pennsylvania and Tennessee, compensate crime victims for the injuries they suffer or the income they lose.

More than 20 states – with Colorado being the prime example – operate restitution programs in which convicted criminals are required to pay the people they've robbed or cheated along the way.

Just last month, the U.S. House of Representatives passed a bill that would reimburse states for up to 25 percent of the first $25,000 they pay to victims of violent crime.

Given a choice, we'd prefer that the federal government stay out of the crime compensation business except when federal crimes are involved. Most crimes, after all, are covered by state rather than federal law.

It also would be wiser, when possible, to require restitution by the criminal himself rather than shift the financial burden to the taxpayers, who have plenty of other bills to pay.

However they're carried out, though, programs for aiding crime victims have obvious merit and should be encouraged. Many victims are elderly people on limited incomes. Others are so badly hurt they're unable to work for long periods of time.

One of the more effective restitution programs is operating in Hamilton County, Ohio, which includes the city of Cincinnati. In that program, young criminals work (under close supervision) in parks and other public facilities and repay their victims with the money they earn.

This approach makes more sense than simply tossing youthful lawbreakers in jail, where they can do little or nothing to learn a trade or repair the damage they've done.

The Salt Lake Tribune

Salt Lake City, Utah, April 2, 1977

Crime Victim Compensation: Development Questionable

Crime has become such a pervasive and immense problem in the United States, a readiness to consider more than the usual response is growing. This development can be glimpsed in an increasingly accepted theory that the government should compensate crime victims.

Testifying recently before a U.S. House judiciary subcommittee, Georgetown University Law Prof. Paul F. Rothstein propounded the theory. He said, in essence, that when people are severely injured or deprived by a criminal act, it means government has defaulted on its promise of protection against such trauma. And, therefore, the government is obligated to make some restitution. It is more a revived than totally new concept.

The Babylonian Code of Hammurabi, 4,000 years old, held that "If a man practices brigandage and be c ptured, that man shall be put to death." Then it added: "If the brigand be not captured, the man who has been robbed shall, in the presence of God, make an itemized statement of his loss, and the city and the governor, in whose province and jurisdiction the robbery was committed, shall compensate him for whatever was lost." Equivalent stress on compensation can be found in Mosaic law and in the penal codes of Athens and Rome.

Currently, it is increasingly common for local laws in this country to require juveniles, or their parents, to make restitution in delinquency cases involving theft or vandalism. However, the trend is moving well beyond that.

The House of Representatives is considering bills which would appropriate as much as $60 million by 1980 for payments to Americans who become victims of serious, violent crime. At last report, 23 states have enacted similar programs. In this there is a definite shifting emphasis.

Hammurabi, the Athenians and Romans notwithstanding, Americans have usually met increased criminal activity with strengthened law enforcement. That is, more policemen, more crime detection and preventive methods, accelerated prosecutor diligence and ingenuity, expanded prison and prisoner rehabilitaiton efforts. In sum, the sort of "protection" Prof. Rothstein refers to. That, evidently, was for former, simpler times.

There does seem to be a basic element of fairness in adequate public aid for people who are seriously injured or who lose the breadwinner through a violent criminal act and who have no other source of financial support. But it also is necessary to ask how far such a policy should go.

If the idea extends to every mugging, burglary, hold-up and fraud case, society, though its government, would be striking a troublesome bargain with crime. It would be acknowledging the inevitability, rather than the vincibility of lawlessness.

Certainly there's reason to doubt traditional ways used to reverse constantly rising crime rates. However, there's equal cause to wonder if easing the impact, by indemnifying crime victims, government wouldn't be aggravating the problem more than alleviating it.

THE INDIANAPOLIS NEWS

Indianapolis, Ind., October 10, 1977

Compensation for crime victims

The U.S. House of Representatives last week approved legislation to provide compensation to victims of violent crime.

The action marks a long step forward in the campaign for this reform. The Senate has passed crime victim compensation bills on five occasions since 1972, but this is the first time the House has endorsed the concept.

The Carter administration, too, is on record as favoring the idea in principle while objecting to some of the potentially costly features of specific legislation. As a consequence, a modest victim compensation program is well on its way to reality.

The latest House legislation provides Federal grants to the states which, through their own compensation programs, pay the medical bills of people injured by criminals. Some 24 states have already enacted some form of compensation and would qualify.

The House bill sanctions state payment of individual claims of up to $25,000 for medical expenses and lost wages, with the Federal government contributing 25 percent of the total.

A key provision of the legislation is that the states, in order to be eligible, would have to have compensation plans which provide that a sentencing judge could require the criminal himself to make restitution payments to his victim. It thus reasserts an important principle that was once well established in Anglo-Saxon law: that a lawbreaker has direct responsibility not only to society in a general sense but also to the individual he harmed. Such sentencing would not only assist the victim but could contribute to effective rehabilitation of the offender.

The Senate is not expected to act until next year because of its entanglement with energy legislation. The issue, however, is one of some urgency and should not be allowed to get lost in the shuffle.

St. Louis Globe-Democrat
St. Louis, Mo., February 5, 1977
MAKE CRIMINALS PAY VICTIMS

In today's society the victim of crime is the loser, physically and financially. Concern for the victim has emerged here and there occasionally in recent years. But the main focus remains unchanged as liberals and bleeding hearts champion the cause of criminal defendants and stand guard over their "rights."

That's simply not right.

In the past the U.S. Justice Department has expressed support for bills that would compensate victims of federal crimes, but attempts in 1975 and 1976 to pass such legislation failed.

There are only 12 programs for victims in the entire country. Illinois has had a Crimes Victims Compensation Act since Oct. 1, 1973. Payments range up to $10,000, and nearly 2,000 victims currently are awaiting action on their claims for compensation. Several unsuccessful attempts on similar legislation have been made in the Missouri General Assembly.

But the question arises: Why should taxpayers pick up the tab for the pain, damage and loss inflicted by the criminals?

Columnist Bob Wiedrich recently pleaded the case of the victim by pointing out: "If the criminal is indigent, the victim in his role as a taxpayer helps foot the bill for the public defender who represents the crook in court. He contributes to the cost of the court trial. His tax dollars help finance the cost of incarceration and rehabilitation and whatever the price is for maintaining parole supervision of the convict once he is released.

"If there is an appeal of the conviction, the victim of the crime also assists in financing the cost of that proceeding if the criminal persuades the courts he is without funds. In short the victims of crime catch it from all sides. They usually are manhandled by the criminal justice system far worse than the criminal himself."

Why not make the criminal pay for his horrible deeds?

One approach would be the forefeiture of a criminal's assets after his conviction to compensate for hospitalization, the inability to work and other losses suffered by a victim who may be worse off financially than the attacker.

Another would be to require the criminal to pay while he is serving behind prison bars. A percentage of the salary paid to individuals convicted of violent crimes could be earmarked for compensating victims. People in honest pursuits have withholdings for income taxes and Social Security payments deducted from their paychecks. The same practice could be extended to convicts to supply money to a fund for victims.

A procedure for getting money from criminals for a victims' fund is not new. A bill in Congress two years ago provided that money from criminal fines would be used for such a purpose. Other funds would be composed of 20 per cent of the net profits of the federal prison industries.

Cutting into the prison earnings of a convict would give him further food for thought about his wayward life. There is no justification for pampering the attackers by placing an additional burden on taxpayers. The withholding method also could provide a standard for the length of sentence to be served. The greater the compensation, the longer the term. This formula would make far more sense than the widely varying punishment that is doled out at times for similar crimes.

Criminals no longer would be waiting for the day they are paroled but to the time they have paid their debt to society and its innocent victims.

ALBUQUERQUE JOURNAL
Albuquerque, N.M., October 5, 1977
Paying Crime Victims

A bill approved by the House to compensate victims of violent crimes is well intended but has major shortcomings.

Under provisions of the bill, states with programs to compensate victims of violent crimes could receive federal funding up to 25 per cent of the cost. Maximum compensation for any one victim would be $25,000.

The Republican Policy Committee of the House of Representatives raises some objections to the bill as it was approved by the House. The bill fails, the committee said, "to address the fundamental relationship between the criminal and the victim by failing to recognize the criminal's responsibility to the victim."

There is little argument that compensating victims of violent crimes is a legitimate interest of government. Victims should be treated with compassion and justice and should not be forced to bear the financial burden of their injuries by themselves.

The House bill should be amended to place a greater burden upon the criminal so that the criminal would be forced to share the victim's economic burden. The criminal's property (if any) should be attached and any earnings of the criminal while imprisoned should go to the victim.

The ideal situation would be to apply an even greater share of a community's resources to crime prevention. But even the $30 million annual appropriation for crime victim compensation and the matching amounts from participating states would not end the nation's crime problem.

The Burlington Free Press
Burlington, Vt., November 28, 1977
Federal Aid for Crime Victims

PROPOSED LEGISLATION in Congress would provide federal aid to victims of violent crimes. This proposal is certain to be the subject of extensive debate in 1978.

In fact, the debate is already in progress in the nation's media. In the current issue of U.S. News & World Report, Rep. Peter W. Rodino Jr., D-N.J., presents the case for such legislation and Rep. Charles E. Wiggins, R-Calif., gives reasons for opposing it.

Rodino says that innocent victims of violent crime have been too long ignored and that the time has come to provide compensation for them.

Under a bill passed by the House, each state would be called upon to set up a compensation program and administer it. The federal government would pay one-quarter of the awards up to $6,250 per award.

It has been estimated that the federal share of such awards might total from $10 million to $25 million the first year of operation. Each award would be based primarily on medical bills and lost wages. Property losses would not be covered in compensation.

Already 22 states have set up their own compensation systems. It is not clear whether all state systems would be required to meet standards adopted by the federal government, or if states would be allowed to determine rates of compensation.

States which have not yet adopted violent crime compensation systems are likely to resist this new undertaking, particularly if they are having difficulty in providing income to meet present needs. While it is stated that it is not intended to force states into the federal system, if they choose not to come in, it seems obvious that pressures would build up once the legislation was passed.

Wiggins opposes this legislation for several reasons. He says that victims of violent crimes already get considerable aid, including medical payments under medicare or medicaid, as well as other forms of insurance. He feels the proposed crime compensation plan would establish a new bureaucracy duplicating in many cases aid which is already available.

It is claimed by Wiggins that adoption of this legislation would open the way to fraud. "Allegations will be made that injuries resulted from criminal acts, even though no defendant or suspect is ever apprehended."

While it might be argued that no award would be made without proof of actual crime, experience with other government programs in which money is dispensed for various purposes leads to the conclusion that many claims are paid without adequate proof of eligibility.

Wiggins says he has compassion for those injured as a result of violent crime, but he also has compassion for those injured in other ways through no fault of their own. If government aid is to be provided to pay expenses of crime victims, it should be given to victims of accidents, without discrimination, he argues. He thinks such aid is being given to a considerable extent now under medicaid, when there is demonstrated need.

This is another effort of the federal government to spread its protective wings over its citizens in order to ease their burdens in time of trouble. While this compassionate goal is commendable, it again raises the question as to how far the citizens wish to be protected if their taxes are to be steadily increased in order to provide this protection. There are many who feel that in order to have freedom one must accept great risks.

Sentinel Star
Orlando, Fla., April 27, 1977
Why not make the distinction?

LONG OVERDUE legislation to compensate crime victims has passed both houses and after a conference committee makes minor adjustments should be ready for a final vote. If all goes well the state soon will have a system permitting judges to order a criminal to repay his victim or letting the state do it through a fund established by a surcharge on criminal fines.

What could be fairer than for criminals to pay for the damage they do? Those who see the justice in such an arrangement are further encouraged by the prospect of legislation on the federal level recognizing the principle.

THE AMERICAN Bar Association has asked Congress to recognize that crime victims have the same right to compassionate government action as victims of fires, floods and earthquakes.

Says Judge Eric E. Younger, chairman of the ABA Committee on Victims: "Crime is a tragedy to which society has an obligation to react humanely toward those who have been stricken. Victimization potential can be adjusted somewhat, but not eliminated, and the theoretical right of legal action against a perpetrator is worth virtually nothing."

Agreed so far, but there's a caution flag.

The ABA proposal goes beyond federal aid for federal crimes and would have Washington reimburse all victims among the 215 million U.S. citizens — state, county and municipal — with "no concern for the state-federal crime distinction."

THAT'S HARD to justify, in view of the fact that a number of states have crime victim compensation laws that would be made moot.

What's wrong with making the distinction? Why not let Washington look out for victims of federal crime and the states deal with those on their own levels?

RAPID CITY JOURNAL
Rapid City, S.D., February 21, 1977
Local program a model for crime compensation

Sen. James Abourezk is proposing to compensate victims of state and federal crimes.

Under terms of a bill he is co-sponsoring with Sen. Hubert Humphrey of Minnesota, states could apply to the federal government for grants to pay 50 per cent of the costs of compensation for state crimes and 100 per cent of the costs of compensation for federal crimes.

Crime victims would be reimbursed primarily for medical expenses, physical or occupational therapy and loss of earnings.

"While our society spends millions each year prosecuting and punishing criminals, we spend practically nothing on compensating victims of their crimes," Abourezk said. "Through no fault of their own, crime victims often find themselves jobless or deeply in debt to medical bills."

The senator is absolutely correct, in our book, except in one aspect of the proposal:

Through no fault of their own, taxpayers apparently will be slugged with the costs of the program.

We have a better idea.

In 1973 the Pennington County Victims Assistance program was initiated, funded at first by the federal Law Enforcement Assistance Administration (LEAA). In 1975 the program was taken over by the Seventh Judicial Circuit Court.

In the words of the court, "The primary goal of the victims assistance or restitution program is designed to make the offender responsible for losses he has caused and a secondary effort is that of collection of the losses for the victim."

Has the program worked? It surely has. In three years, $35,885 in restitution has been ordered and $18,483, or slightly more than half, actually has been collected. Part of the remainder is in the process of collection and part is being written off because the offender was jailed.

The federal government probably would be receptive to Pennington County's approach. It is, in fact, spending $2 million right now — through LEAA programs in seven states — "to help evaluate a concept in which criminals, instead of being sent to jail, are ordered to repay their victims through work."

Pennington County's success demonstrates that the program, if established elsewhere (on a local, not a national, level), could be beneficial to the victim, to the offender as well, and to the taxpaying public too.

Wisconsin 🏛 State Journal

Madison, Wisc., July 1, 1977

Why not restitution?

The president of the American Bar Assn. (ABA) favors forced restitution by criminals as an instrument of rehabilitation as well as repaying the victims.

Writing in the ABA Journal, Justin A. Stanley said "restitution properly broadens the objectives that underlie the imposition of criminal penalties" and reinforces the more traditional objectives of punishment, deterrence and rehabilitation.

More important, in many cases it could provide a prompt remedy for the innocent victims, who gain little from the satisfaction that lawbreakers are dealt with through fines or probation.

Resitituion programs have been successful in Illinois, Georgia, Colorado, Oklahoma, Ohio and Florida.

"When the program succeeds," Stanley said, "no one pays a fine or goes to jail, no one suffers the expense of a court trial and no one is forced to wait months for a hearing.

"In cases of minor offenses — traffic violations, juvenile vandalism or shoplifting — when the typical sentence has been a fine, restitution offers an alternative that constitutes a much greater inconvenience to the offender and hence is at once both a better punishment and a more effective deterrent."

Restitution is unrealistic in many major crimes but it would be a practical response to some minor infractions.

Stanley gave examples of speeders sentenced to a morning of picking up highway litter and juvenile vandals who, instead of being rescued by their parents'checkbooks, are forced to work in community service agencies or to repair their damage.

The Dane County court system should consider restitution as a routine policy.

OKLAHOMA CITY TIMES

Oklahoma City, Okla., June 24, 1977

Help for crime victims?

RESTITUTION to the victim as as a means of improving the criminal justice system is getting increased attention these days. Some judges individually, in Oklahoma and other states, are utilizing it as an alternative to incarceration.

The president of the American Bar Association believes that forcing criminals to repay their victims could be a powerful instrument of rehabilitation. Writing in the "President's Page" of the ABA Journal, Justin A. Stanley said restitution reinforces the more traditional objectives of punishment deterrence and rehabilitation.

He said that, with an unacceptably high crime rate, new approaches, such as restitution, are needed to safely bring lawbreakers "back into the mainstream of society."

Stanley cited restitution programs in Oklahoma, Deerfield, Ill., Georgia, Colorado, Columbus, Ohio, and an ABA-supported project in Orlando, Fla.

Oklahoma has a law giving judges the discretion of requiring restitution of damages to the victims of crimes, to be paid through the Corrections Department. Oklahoma County juvenile court has decreed restitution be made by some of the youthful offenders it handles. And the state Pardon and Parole Board has specified restitution as a condition for granting paroles for convicts.

The ABA president contends that, in minor offenses — traffic violations, juvenile vandalism or shoplifting — when the typical sentence has been a fine, restitution is a much greater inconvenience to the offender and hence is both a better punishment and a more effective deterrent.

In many criminal cases, of course, restitution would not be practical. And the concept should never be allowed to emphasize rehabilitation to the extent that punishment is forgotten.

The Kansas City Times

Kansas City, Mo., March 21, 1977

Paying the Price for Crime

Restitution in the rehabilitation of criminals is on the upswing in this country. Authorities are recognizing that many offenders are helped by being required to repay their victim with money or by working out the loss. A direct public benefit is that the offender does not necessarily have to be kept in jail or prison, thus saving tax money that would be spent for incarceration.

Restitution as a correctional tool has become widespread enough at the grass-roots level that it has captured the attention of the Law Enforcement Assistance Administration. The federal agency recently set up a $2-million program to encourage and evaluate this correctional method in seven states.

The subject was also discussed at a recent conference sponsored by the LEAA in Washington. Several examples of successful restitutive efforts were cited. One involved a young man who wrecked a car he had stolen. Instead of going to jail he went to work for the insurance company that paid damages in the accident. The offender, who paid off the loss by working for the company, is, two years later, still an employee. Now, however, he is a regular worker.

In another case an individual burglarized a mobile home sales office. He also took a job at the firm to pay off the loss. Later he became a salesman for the firm and now has been advanced to a partner. A third example cited also had a positive ending. A man apprehended breaking into a minister's home was given a chance to pay for his crime by working for the victim. The offender, who had spent more than half his life in incarceration, has not been in additional trouble in three years.

Restitution, of course, cannot be used in every case. Some offenders cannot be released from custody because they are dangerous to society. Moreover, there are important matters to be considered. The plan must be fair to both victim and offender. How the repayment is determined can be a crucial part of the program. Authorities differ on whether there should be a face-to-face meeting between the offender and the victim.

In some communities offenders can do public service work—in hospitals and for civic and charitable groups. "This gives these organizations extra assistance and gives the offender an opportunity to do something positive instead of sitting in a jail cell doing nothing," remarks one professional.

The underlying purpose of restitution is to make the offender understand the crime he or she has committed has direct impact on an individual and the community. Making payments by working is a measure that many persons can readily grasp. The LEAA project should help authorities develop and refine restitution as a useful practice in the fight against crime.

The Dallas Morning News

Dallas, Tex., May 14, 1977

Justice for Victims

A STOREKEEPER is shot during the course of a robbery. Later, the armed robber is wounded by police during apprehension. Now who pays for what?

If the storekeeper has insurance, he will be compensated for his injuries. If not, he foots the bill himself.

The criminal, on the other hand, will have his treatment paid for by the state. If he has no money, the state will furnish him an attorney. Upon conviction, the state also will spend thousands of dollars trying to rehabilitate the bandit.

As a taxpayer, the storekeeper is actually subsidizing his assailant, while at the same time, trying to care for himself. Hardly fair, is it?

State Sen. Ron Clower of Dallas doesn't think so. And he has sponsored a proposal to provide assistance to those who suffer bodily injury or death as a result of a violent crime. The bill passed the Senate Friday.

Clower's proposal includes what he considers the best portions of laws in 23 states that already provide compensation for crime victims.

Awards authorized by the bill cover medical and hospital care, funeral expenses, loss of earnings or support and child care to a maximum of $50,000. The Indus-trial Accident Board, which has expertise in determining injury and death claims, would administer the compensation system. Funding would be provided by a $5 court cost assessed for violation of certain laws in Texas.

Additional help may be forthcoming from the federal government. Congress is considering a bill introduced by Rep. Peter Rodino that would reimburse states for compensating crime victims.

Texas already has a very limited compensation program in which it pays for examinations of rape victims.

Clower's bill would not cover victims who had insurance or could otherwise finance their recovery.

In some cases, Texas law allows a judge to require restitution of victims if the offender is placed on probation. But this approach is effective only if the criminal is caught. And in three quarters of the crime in Dallas, the perpetrator is never apprehended.

The state has a responsibility to protect its citizens. And when a person is injured during a criminal act, this responsibility has not been fulfilled.

Clower's proposal is a sound idea; it would make even a better law.

ST. LOUIS POST-DISPATCH
St. Louis, Mo., February 24, 1977
Aiding Victims

Illinoisans are not as well acquainted as they should be with the Crime Victims Compensation program which went into effect in 1973, and Attorney General Scott would like to amend the law so that more people will be aware of the program. If the Legislature agrees, victims of violent crime or their survivors would be automatically advised of the state law that provides up to $10,000 for loss of earnings and medical and funeral expenses not covered by insurance.

Mr. Scott is also proposing amendments to speed up the processing of claims and,

whenever possible, to require convicted criminals to repay the state for the financial assistance paid out to their victims. When the Legislature enacted the Crime Victims Compensation law, its intention was not to confer obscurity on the new program nor to impose burdensome requirements on victims wishing to apply for help. Yet most victims are not familiar with the program and those who are have to wait an average of one year to receive assistance. Even with those shortcomings, however, the program in Illinois should serve

as an example to Missouri lawmakers who so far have rejected proposals for state help to victims of crime.

The amendments on speeding up the application process and on informing potential beneficiaries deserve favorable consideration by the Legislature. As for making restitution payments, the Attorney General will have to spell out his proposal in greater detail before the public and its lawmakers in Springfield can decide whether it is a sound and desirable course.

The Standard-Times
New Bedford, Mass., June 26, 1977

Aiding the crime victim is sound — with caution

Compensation of crime victims is and idea whose time came and went many centuries ago (it was part of the Babylonian Code of Hammurabi, more than 4,000 years old) and now is gaining currency again.

At present, about twenty states, including Massachusetts, operate victim compensation programs of various kinds. And the House Judiciary Committee approved a bill last month authoring the federal government to subsidize state programs that meet specified federal standards. Depending on circumstance, the subsidy could amount to as much as 100 per cent of the amount paid to the victim.

There is, of course, much to be said for such programs. The rationale for compensation rests on the implied governmental pledge of protection against crime: Local and state authorities maintain police forces, and carrying of concealed weapons of self-defense, without a permit, is generally forbidden. Thus, when a crime is committed, government may be said to be partly responsible.

Not long ago, in the Bay State, a self-employed shop keeper was held up in his store by a gunman. He surrendered his money as ordered, did not attempt to resist, but was struck down by the fleeing holdup man and sustained injuries thereby that forced him to undergo lengthy medical treatment during which time his one-man business remained closed. The victim thus was forced to pay a considerable sum to regain his health and simultaneously lost an appreciable amount of income because he could not operate his store, which was his principal support.

In such a case — and there are many other kinds equally compelling — some kind of compensation seems both just and reasonable. However, while the idea has understandably attracted wide interest,

there are sound reasons for proceeding with caution in writing its implementation into federal law.

Skeptics maintain that, even with safeguards, fraudulent claims of compensation often will go undetected, and this seems likely. Moreover, the victim in many criminial cases is partly responsible for the crime, as when an assault results from deliberate provocation. Critics of the bill passed by the House Judiciary Committee also argue that the federal government has no responsibility for enforcing a state's criminal laws and, therefore, little or no responsibility for compensating its victims. In a written dissent, nine committee members said the proposed federal compensation program "is essentially selective largesse."

In this latter connection, it might also be noted that the federal government cannot make a state or its subsidiaries enforce the law effectively or efficiently — which would tend to hold crime rates lower — even though the federal government, under this proposal, would have to pay for the results of ineffectiveness or inefficiency.

Finally, crime statistics consistently point to the fact that the largest category of murders, for example, are committed by people known to the victim and that one of the largest areas of crime involves situations in which the perpetrator and the victim are related. The federal government ought to proceed slowly indeed in the direction of subsidizing domestic quarrels.

What probably is one of the most interesting aspects of this situation is that crime victims — who, if they were to organize, might well constitute one of the nation's most powerful lobbies — have been essentially silent about the compensation.

San Jose Mercury
San Jose, Calif., April 11, 1977

Break For Victims

The Santa Clara County Board of Supervisors moved last week to take some of the emotional and financial sting out of being a crime victim. It's an experiment that deserves to succeed.

Specifically, the board agreed to act as sponsor for a "victim witness program" to be funded by the federal and state governments and by a $3,187 contribution from the National Conference of Christians and Jews.

Plans call for a group of 30 volunteers, under the direction of the NCCJ's Lillian Silberstein, to work with the county adult probation department in aiding victims of violent crime—the forgotten men and women of the criminal justice system. Initially the pilot program will be restricted to north-central San Jose, but if it succeeds, the board will be asked to expand it countywide. If the concept works in San Jose, a broader trial would certainly be warranted.

Mrs. Silberstein's volunteers will assist victims in filing for state compensation (a maximum of $23,000 is available) and in apprising the Superior Court of the nature and extent of damages sustained by the victims.

It is just here, of course, that the adult probation department enters the picture. In some cases, though not all by any means, it may be practical to require restitution from a convicted defendant as a condition of probation.

Some small sums, according to Mrs. Silberstein, may be available from the project's grants for immediate emergency aid to victims. These would

cover the cost of food or medical care in a crisis, she explained.

Restitution in any meaningful sense, however, has to come from the state. In 1974, the legislature established a crime victim compensation fund and charged the State Board of Control, a notoriously unsentimental body, with the duty of disbursing the cash. A knowledgeable local agency could be a big help in dealing with the Board of Control.

Legislation is already pending in Sacramento to increase the amount crime victims may recover, but for the moment $23,000 is the limit—a maximum of $10,000 for uncompensated medical expenses, $10,000 for income loss and up to $3,000 for vocational rehabilitation where required.

One of the glaring faults of the criminal justice system here and nationwide is that the victim gets short shrift. He may derive some emotional satisfaction from seeing a burglar, mugger or armed robber sentenced to prison, but all too often the victim's property is gone for good.

If the victim witness program can help ameliorate this injustice—and particularly if restitution from a convicted felon can be achieved more frequently—the project will be worth the $57,374 the federal Law Enforcement Assistance Administration has agreed to pour into it over the coming year. The state of California and the NCCJ will each contribute $3,187, and the county will provide the in-kind services of the adult probation department.

Post-Tribune
Guarding Your Interests Daily

Gary, Ind., March 12, 1977

What about restitution as a crime deterrent?

There is an effort in the current Indiana Legislature to require the state to compensate crime victims, but what about a law requiring perpetrators of crimes to make restitution?

We are indebted to Paul G. Wallace of the Anderson Co.'s general counsel's office for the underlying thought in this one.

He says that "Courts in Indiana make some effort along these lines, but without the benefit of statutory sanction or system."

However, he notes further that "In 1974 Iowa made restitution a condition of a deferred sentence or probation, and in 1976, Colorado said courts could order restitution in conjunction with fines, probation, imprisonment or parole," asking: "Couldn't such legislation be a starting point for Indiana?"

It sounds like an idea worth trying.

One of the concepts, compensation by the state, need not exclude the other, restitution by the criminal.

For one thing, the state compensation could be invoked when there was no arrest or conviction of the person who perpetrated the crime. Further, some criminals are in no financial position to make restitution and the victim still would be without recourse without state compensation.

But forcing a person caught to make or work toward restitution as a condition for possible clemency might well work as a crime deterrent. It seems worth a try, and if it is too late in this session it could be considered in the next.

The Topeka Daily Capital

Topeka, Kans., December 11, 1977

Moving toward a balance

Crime victims in America often are hit with a triple whammy — first when they are assaulted, assailed, robbed, raped, beaten or terrorized by the criminal; second when they go through the criminal "justice" system as witnesses, and third when all is over and done and they realize that they have no compensation of any kind coming. And the criminal probably will be walking the streets again soon.

More and more cities, counties and states are recognizing the treatment of crime victims and witnesses for what it is — cold, impersonal and offhand.

Victims and witnesses, we have been taught since our earliest school experiences, have a civic, almost patriotic, duty to step forward and aid the courts in convicting the criminal.

Once upon a time there was at least a philosophical reward for this stepping forward. That was the knowledge that the world may be a bit safer now that the villain is behind bars, that by testifying, the victim may have saved somebody else from becoming a victim.

That doesn't apply anymore.

And once in the dim past witnesses just did their duty, and victims gained the sympathy of the community. Today, they are the target of revenge by criminals freed on bail before their beating victims are out of the hospital.

But there are programs sprouting throughout the nation designed to reverse this trend in society. Shawnee County has launched a program to help counsel crime victims.

Other communities are going so far as to provide compensation to crime victims. Such a program works best when the criminal himself is forced to make restitution, for it does both the criminal and the victim some good.

Other programs now under way or proposed in America would allow victims a part in the sentencing of criminals. That teaches the victim a sense of fairness and may evoke a form of mercy that could inspire a criminal to quit his lowdown ways.

There are many possibilities. The greatest stride we have taken is that society finally has recognized the plight of the victim after all the energy we have expended on protecting the criminal. We may strike a balance yet.

The Hartford Courant

Hartford, Conn., October 15, 1977

Making the Criminals Pay

Victims of crimes seldom are compensated. A jail term doesn't return the savings stolen from an elderly woman. Even a fine is paid to the state, not to the victim.

Because of such injustices, a new penal program being tested in Connecticut and six other states has considerable merit. It calls for judges to put more emphasis on restitution than imprisonment when they sentence certain offenders. The program already is having an impact. In the last three months, Connecticut courts have ordered 35 convicted criminals to pay about $45,000 to their victims. The restitutions are expected to exceed $1 million in the next 18 months, with some 600 offenders making the payments.

True, the process is still very experimental, with the judges allowed wide discretion. Nor are the choices easy. The bench must decide which offenders are really capable of meeting payment schedules. There is also an option of a limited prison term combined with a partial repayment plan.

Most of the cases in which restitution already has been ordered involve property losses from such crimes as burglary, fraud and embezzlement. A restitution order has enforcement power, too. It is always accompanied by a long period of probation. Failure to make a weekly or monthly restitution payment can result in revocation of probation and jail for the offender.

Naturally, it is to be hoped jail can be avoided. For restitution offers a good chance for rehabilitation. And the state realizes a savings of the $15,000 it costs to imprison a person for one year.

The Connecticut test is supported by a two-year Law Enforcement Assistance Administration grant of $320,000 which will pay the salaries and expenses of the staff at the newly created Restitution Division of the state Judicial Department.

Obviously, the courts must be firm but fair in deciding which cases call for restitution. May that challenge be successfully met so that an admirable program still experimental can become standard practice.

The Birmingham News

Birmingham, Ala., April 12, 1977

Aid For Victim Of Crime

The system to aid victims of crime put in place by young Mobile District Atty. Charles Graddick could bear duplication in every jurisdiction in Alabama.

Being acutely aware of the ordeal most victims of burglaries, thefts, etc., undergo in terms of lost time, lost income and anxiety, Graddick last year assigned a fulltime aide to make the victims of crime the center of attention.

The aide, Mary Cox, is paid by funds from a Law Enforcement Planning Agency grant. Mrs. Cox takes charge of the victim from the time his or her name comes up from police investigations or grand jury proceedings.

At the outset, she sends a letter to the victim explaining the responsibilities of the victim, police and courts. Graddick believes that the victim is owed something by public officials such as explanations, briefings on developments in the case, if the defendant is convicted or not and in burglary cases a quick return of stolen goods as soon as they are no longer required for evidence.

The most important help is given the victim during court proceedings. He is briefed on what to expect in the courtroom as a witness and instead of waiting in a courthouse corridor, the victim leaves an "on-call" number where he can be reached quickly. This practice may save the victim several days' time.

Graddick says that he has found that most victims know little or nothing about criminal proceedings. Most have never even been in the courthouse, he says. So Graddick and Mrs. Cox personally confer with each victim at an early stage in the proceedings, giving him or her a tour of the important places in the courthouse, indicating where to go for various business.

Mrs. Cox uses the same notification system for police officers who must testify on their own time and benefit by not appearing in court when a postponement has been granted.

One would have to agree with Graddick that victims of crime should have to pay no more than is absolutely necessary in the way of lost time and pay for doing their duty. The kind of help the victim receives in Mobile and should receive in every court case can only increase his respect for the criminal justice system and democratic institutions as a whole.

By the same token, district attorneys' offices and the criminal courts are certain to receive a larger degree of cooperation from witnesses when they are made to feel that they are important and worthy of concern.

THE SACRAMENTO BEE
Sacramento, Calif., April 9, 1977

Victims Of Crime

Since 1975, California has acknowledged the state has some financial responsibility to victims of violent crime. But why just the state? It seems only fair that those who commit violent crimes should be required to make restitution if they have the means to do so.

Precisely that reasoning is followed in a bill by Sen. Jerry Smith, D-San Jose, and 43 legislators from both houses who are coauthors. It merits such wide support.

Its passage would require the courts to impose fines on persons convicted of violent crime, instead of leaving that option to the discretion of the courts, as now is the case.

Smith's bill would set the minimum mandatory fine at $10 and the maximum at $10,000, depending on the convicted person's ability to pay at the time of sentencing. In addition, the legislation would require courts to consider, as a condition of probation, that violent criminals pay direct restitution to victims injured by their crimes.

Proceeds from the fines would go into the state indemnity fund and would be used to compensate crime victims, as is done now with state funds.

And the state parole board would be required to consider ordering restitution as a condition of parole.

These provisions are a logical extension of the two-year-old law under which California compensates victims of violent crime for medical expenses not otherwise met or loss of income, depending on the individual's financial status. Smith's bill would raise the maximum compensation for these two categories from $10,000 each to $20,000. This is reasonable.

While they are at it, the legislators might consider making it more convenient for crime victims to pursue compensation claims. The claims are handled by the State Board of Control, but its claims hearings are held only twice a month in Sacramento and every other month in Los Angeles.

The Wichita Eagle
Wichita, Kans., February 8, 1977

Restitution, Not Revenge

The results are far from conclusive as yet, but there would seem to be some hope in a concept now under study that would order certain kinds of criminals to repay their victims through work rather than going to jail.

The Law Enforcement Assistance Administration (LEAA) has issued $2 million in grants to help pay for a two-year evaluation of the idea in seven states, including our neighbor, Colorado.

Typical cases are those of a burglar ordered to work for the man from whom he attempted to steal, a youth who stole and wrecked a car and was put to work for the insurance company that had to make good on the loss, a businessman caught passing bad checks who was ordered to work for the state's corrections department. In all these cases the early indications are that such work was rehabilitative and resulted in setting the miscreants on the path to rectitude.

If it should prove generally workable it might well help overcrowding in jails and save the taxpayers a considerable amount of money, for keeping people in prison works out to be more expensive than keeping them, say, in college.

There are a number of unanswered questions about such a program. One, of course, is what constitutes fair restitution. Another is whether such rehabilitation is lasting. Still another is whether the restitution should be made directly to the victim of the crime or to the community at large. One more question is whether the victim should have some say in how much and what kind of restitution is to be made.

It is the presence of such questions that justifies the evaluation that is presently underway.

Surely there is sufficient reason to think that present attempts at rehabilitation fall short, and to hope that the study will show the restitution concept to be valid.

Obviously there are some crimes for which it is impossible to make satisfactory repayment, and in any individual case it would seem likely that a great deal would have to be left to the judge and/or the jury after they had had the opportunity to study the character of the criminal.

But where appropriate restitution would seem a more sensible and rewarding solution than vengeance.

Minneapolis Tribune

Minneapolis, Minn., October 15, 1977

A resource center for victims of crime

A frequent complaint about criminal justice is that it isn't justice at all: The offender gets most of the attention, while the victim and his problems are forgotten. This year the Minnesota Legislature took another step toward correcting that injustice: It provided money for three centers in the state to help victims of crime. Just last week, with the aid of additional funds from a private foundation, the first center opened in a storefront in south Minneapolis.

Although concern for victims is on the rise, the center is the first in the country to deal with the broad range of their problems — broken locks or windows, compensation for loss, shelter, transportation, physical and emotional injuries and the like. The nearly 20 cases in the first week illustrate the kinds of need. Some victims sought reparation for loss suffered from a crime — a claim permissible under an earlier state law. One wanted performance on a court order for restitution by a burglar; the guilty party was tracked down and ordered to begin payments. Another wanted help to board up windows broken by vandals. In all cases the victims got immediate help from the center, or immediate referrals to other agencies.

But much of the damage done by crime occurs in the mind. For example, the victim of a break-in involving valuables sometimes can become so obsessed with his own "guilt" for not having stronger locks that he tends to forget to blame the criminal. There have been cases where such victims required psychiatric treatment to break out of the resulting depression. Officials in the Department of Correctional Services, which operates the center, believe that dealing with that kind of trauma will be an important function of the center. In other cases, victims may fail to report crimes for fear of reprisals. For people with such fears, the center will make use of a remarkable support service at its disposal — safe houses, where a victim can find protection when he or she needs it. With an around-the-clock staff of 18 (including interns and volunteers), the center will assure, commendably, that those who have been victimized by lawbreakers will also have their share of justice.

The Providence Journal

Providence, R.I., November 26, 1977

The innocent crime victim is much too quickly forgotten

When a crime is committed, attention focuses on the criminal — his apprehension, indictment, prosecution and sentence. Along the way, society tends to forget those most affected by the crime — the victims. Seldom do the courts use their authority to require restitution, and the innocent party is left to heal his wounds or make up his losses the best he can.

Compensation for victims, which Rhode Island Atty. Gen. Julius C. Michaelson talked about the other day, is not a new idea. It dates back to Anglo-Saxon England when a foot or an eye were valued at 50 shillings, a toenail at sixpence. But Americans in the last 10 years or so have become increasingly interested in government relieving crime victims of some of the burden. In 1966, California and New York became the first states to adopt compensation programs, providing aid for those who would suffer "serious financial hardship" as a result of a crime.

Rhode Island has some limited programs but Mr. Michaelson would like to see victim compensation adopted on a statewide basis. Under his proposal those convicted of felonies and misdemeanors would be assessed from $5 to $50 to build a fund for assisting in the payment of medical bills and for minor property damage.

"Obviously we couldn't compensate every victim 100 percent at the beginning," Mr. Michaelson said. But he maintained that partial payment for such things as psychological counseling, new eyeglasses or broken windows might encourage victims to testify in court. Who would set assessments and distribute the funds are details that would have to be worked out, the attorney general said, estimating that as much as $250,000 could be raised each year.

Certainly the concept is worth exploring. Whether forcing even partial restitution would be more successful under this plan than it has been in the courts is a question. One argument is that because government is responsible for protecting life and property, the state ought to assume some of the financial burden in compensating victims.

On this point the President's Crime Commission report in 1967 had this to say: "The commission has been impressed by the consensus among legislators and law enforcement officials that some kind of state compensation for victims of violent crime is desirable. The commission believes that the general principle of victim compensation, especially to persons who suffer injury in violent crime, is sound and that the experiments now being conducted with different types of compensation programs are valuable."

That was written 10 years ago. Still Rhode Island has not come to grips with the problem, though millions in public funds have been allocated, and properly so, for improvement of the state's correctional system.

Mr. Michaelson is on the right track. It is time to start remembering the forgotten victim.

Press Herald

Portland, Me., June 17, 1977

Aiding The Victims

Compensation for the victims of crime seems to be an idea whose time has come.

Some 20 states have victim compensation programs and others, including Maine, are contemplating them. The House Judiciary Committee has approved a bill authorizing federal subsidies for such state programs.

It is gratifying to those of us who have been preaching for some time that society should be as concerned about the victims of crimes as about the welfare of criminals. That concern seems to be manifest now perhaps because the number of victims increases along with the increase in the number of crimes. As there are more victims so are there more citizens who fear that they may become victims. So the concept receives greater consideration.

Perhaps it would be better said that it is an idea whose time has come again for the compensation of crime victims is almost as old as law itself. More than 4,000 years ago it was part of the Babylonian Code of Hammurabi.

While the principle remains attractive, legislative bodies putting the concept into law should be wary. Provision should be made so that fraudulent claims will not become a new kind of crime.

Criminal offenses must remain acts against the state and not against individuals but a system for easing the losses of the crime victims can be developed within that framework.

Behind the Prison Walls:
Is there any law or order?

Not until the turn of the nineteenth century were convicted criminals punished by incarceration.[1] Executions, whippings, stocks and banishment were the normal and usual punishments. Prisons were not part of the early American landscape. The influence of the utilitarian philosophy of Jeremy Bentham seeped into American penal treatment, and construction of penitentiaries began in the first decades of the 1800's. Bentham saw the penitentiary as a place not for the persistent violator but rather for those "of whose reform a reasonable expectation might be entertained."[2] The Quakers were shocked at the large number of crimes subject to capital punishment and also pushed hard for the establishment of penitentiaries as an alternative to the gallows.[3] The first penitentiary was established in Philadelphia. The goal of incarceration was to encourage criminals to ponder their acts, repent and reform. This result was to be achieved by incessantly locking prisoners in cells and enforcing an atmosphere of solitude.[4]

By the 1840's penitentiaries existed in every area of the country. Charles Dickens on his trip to the United States provided a picture of one such institution, "I believe that very few men are capable of estimating the immense amount of torture and agony which this dreadful punishment, prolonged for years, inflicts upon the sufferers."[5] While the long, hard work-days of unrelenting labor, the floggings and whippings, the monastic silence and the contracting out of prisoners to private employers are no longer accepted practices in the 1970's, prisoners still do not enjoy the same rights as other citizens.

The turbulence of American society in the 1960's also filtered down into the prisons. Numerous legal suits were initiated by prison inmates seeking extension of their civil rights.

The federal courts have responded by frequently intervening to correct conditions that subject prisoners to inadequate medical care, unsanitary facilities, lack of physical exercise, loss of contact with family, and overcrowding.[6] However, the intervention of the courts in establishing a detailed constitutional code of prison administration has been mainly limited to those cases brought by pre-trial detainees who are presumed innocent. The only rationale for incarcerating pre-trial detainees is to assure their presence at trial.[7] The state has no legitimate interest in attempting to punish or rehabilitate these prisoners. Only restrictions consonant with the minimum need for maintaining prison security are constitutionally permissible.

The position of prisoners convicted of crimes has a different order within the constitutional constellation. Constitutionally protected freedoms may be withdrawn or constricted as to state prisoners, so far as "justified by the considerations underlying our penal system."[8] Long periods of incarceration in solitary confinement with little exercise and minimal sanitary facilities have been found not violative of the Constitution.[9] The reluctance of federal courts to closely supervise the operations of state penitentiaries is a result of their stated opposition to becoming entangled in the professional judgment of prison administrators.[10]

Still, prisoner rights have been expanded somewhat; courts no longer describe prisoners as temporarily "a slave of the state."[11] Court definitions of "cruel and unusual punishment," prohibited by the Eighth Amendment, have halted corporal punishment with straps[12] and guards' beating of prisoners.[13] The right to receive and send reasonable amounts of mail,[14] the right to reading material that does not present "a clear and present danger" to the institution,[15] and the right to hold religious services of one's religious choice have won court recognition.[16] However, since a prisoner's behavior down to the most trivial aspects of his life is strictly controlled and supervised by wardens and guards, not federal judges, the opportunities for unconstitutional abuse remain great despite occasional court admonitions. It must also be remembered that few instances of unlawful prison conditions are ever aired in federal courtrooms; the process of prison litigation is too arduous and costly to pursue every case.

Prison inmates have made the most concrete gains in the area of the right to counsel and legal assistance. In fashioning a constitutional "right of access to the courts" from the Sixth Amendment right to counsel, the Supreme Court has traveled far in making legal material or legal services widely available to prison inmates. This principle was most recently reasserted in *Bounds v. Smith*.[17] The Supreme Court upheld a district court determination that North Carolina had to provide inmates with law libraries or alternative sources of legal knowledge. The Supreme Court rejected North Carolina's claim that this requirement was too costly: "The cost of protecting a constitutional right cannot justify its total denial."[18] *Bounds* constitutes a further articulation of the high value the court places upon opening channels of legal access to prisoners. *Younger v. Gilmore* required states to provide law libraries;[19] *Johnson v. Avery* prevented prison administrators from prohibiting inmates from assisting each other on legal research;[20] and *Griffin v. Illinois* entitled indigent inmates to receive their trial transcripts free of charge.[21] The trial transcripts are necessary for prisoners attempting to overturn their convictions through various post-conviction appeals.

The pursuit of difficult and often futile legal appeals through the court system serves as a source of distant hope for prisoners; to the prison administrators it is a safety valve and contributes to an inmate's positive experience with the legal system.[22] In response to the favorable reception of prison legal services by both the courts and prison officials, 95% of whom favor expansion of the program,[23] several states have provided funding to make lawyers accessible to inmates. In New York, 45 attorneys are employed in the state's penal institutions.

The Supreme Court's recognition that "independent legal advisors can mediate or resolve administratively many prisoner complaints that could otherwise burden courts and can convince inmates that other grievances against the prison or the legal system are ill-founded, thereby facilitating rehabilitation by assuring the inmate that he has been treated fairly" has not been extended to include the right to counsel for internal prison disciplinary hearings.[24] The *Wolff v. McDonnell* decision had raised hopes that a right to cousel in disciplinary hearings would soon evolve.[25] In *Wolff* the Court held that a prisoner subject to loss of good time because of prison discipline was entitled to a hearing with some due process safeguards. The Court underscored the notion that the concept of prisoner rights was not a static one:

"As the nature of the prison disciplinary process changes in future years, circumstances may then exist which will require further consideration and reflection of this Court"[26]

The 1975 term of the Supreme Court made it clear that the evolution of due process rights in the prisons would not be rapid. In *Baxter v. Palmigiano* the right to a limited due process hearing was limited to loss of good time and not to involuntary transfers, loss of privileges or placement in solitary confinement.[27] The Court also used the occasion to remove any doubts as to the meaning of *Wolff: Wolff* did not require full cross-examination of witnesses or confrontation of witnesses. These practices may be allowed in the discretion of the prison authorities based upon a reasonable accommodation to the needs of the institutions and the interests of the inmates. In *Clutchette v. Procunier,* a case decided the same day as *Baxter,* the Supreme Court overturned the lower court's decision to require prison officials to affirmatively prove that a wider due process hearing was impracticable.[28] Lawyers attempting implementation of the *Wolff* decree are strongly skeptical of good faith compliance by prison authorities in view of the difficulties in enforcing the more liberal court rulings in parole revocation hearings.[29]

The approach of the Burger Court to claims by prisoners is similar to its approach to the rights of criminal suspects. Both have been influenced by the impression that the public favors a harsher judicial approach towards criminal offenders. The public attitude towards prison life is mirrored in the legislatures' unwillingness to appropriate more money for improvements in prison conditions. That is why the recent report of a committee of the American Bar Association favoring full legal rights for prisoners, limited only by the needs of prison security, and standard wages to prisoners for their work is probably politically unrealistic at this time.[30]

Rather, the present trend is for placing more convicted criminals in prisons under the same conditions. In 1977 the United States prison population increased by 25,000 to a new high of 275,578.[31] This constituted the largest one-year jump in history. It represents a sharp reversal of the decline in prison population from 220,000 in 1962 to 200,000 in 1973. Not including approximately 250,000 being held for trial, 131 Americans are in prison for every 100,000 citizens.[32] Except for South Africa, no other Western developed nation has so many of its citizens in jail.[33] Comparable figures for other nations per 100,000 population are 18 in the Netherlands, 44 in Denmark, 43 in Sweden and 39 in Japan.[34]

The main cause of the growth in prison population is the accelerating tendency of judges to send convicted criminals to prison and for longer terms. Between 1962 and 1973 the crime rate skyrocketed, but, as noted previously, the prison population declined. The increasing numbers incarcerated have resulted in severe prison overcrowding throughout the nation. The desire to use prisons as a frequent tool of punishment is not equaled by a desire to underwrite the costs: construction of a single new maximum security cell ranges from $25,000 to $50,000; maintenance of a person in a maximum security setting is about $10,000 and is expected to rise to $17,305 in ten years.[35]

Crowded prisons frequently result in an increase in homosexual rape, shortage of rehabilitative programs and prison disturbances. The infringement of inmates' constitutional rights by overcrowding has forced federal courts to order reductions in the prison populations of Alabama and Louisiana. U.S. District Court Judge Frank M. Johnson has held that overcrowded conditions "create an environment that not only makes it impossible for inmates to rehabilitate themselves" but actually makes them worse.[36] Judge Johnson found that idleness due to overcrowding "destroys any job skills and work habits inmates may have, and contributes to their mental and physical degeneration."

The crisis of overcrowding has been pinpointed as one of the reasons for the Attica rebellion in the report of the New York State Special Commission on Attica. Overcrowding leads to greater use of lock-up; prisoners are required to stay in their cell because of the shortage of prison resources.

Lock-up under such conditions quickly becomes the prime feature of imprisonment:

> "The heart of the system remained the maximum security prison where prisoners were constantly supervised and locked in their cells at 5:00 or 6:00 P.M. and provided few services other than safekeeping."[37]

Despite initial declines after September, 1971, the prison population of Attica has again reached a new high.

Notes

1. For an in depth study of the origins of prisons, see especially chapters 4, 10 in David J. Rothman, *The Discovery of the Asylum* (Boston: Little Brown, 1971).
2. Edwin Powers, "Halfway Houses: A Historical Perspective," 21 *American Journal of Corrections* 2920 (1959).
3. Michael Meltsner, *Cruel and Unusual: The Supreme Court and Capital Punishment* (New York: Random House, 1973) pp. 47–51.
4. Tom Wicker, *A Time to Die* (New York: Quadrangle, 1975) p. 60.
5. Charles Dickens, *American Notes*, (Gloucester, Mass: P. Smith, 1968).
6. *Rhem v. Malcolm,* 371 F. Supp 594 (S.D.N.Y. 1974) affirmed, 507 F.2d 333 (2nd Cir. 1974).
7. *Jones v. Wittenberg,* 323 F. Supp 93, 330 F. Supp 707 (N.D. Ohio 1971), affirmed sub. nom. *Jones v. Metzger,* 456 F.2d 854 (6th Cir. 1972).
8. *Price v. Johnston,* 334 U.S. 266, 285 (1948).
9. *Sostre v. McGinnis,* 442 F.2d 178, 191–193 (2nd Cir. 1971).
10. *Knight v. Rajen,* 337 F.2d 425 (7th Cir.), cert. denied, 380 U.S. 983 (1964).
11. *Ruffin v. Commonwealth,* 62 Va. (21 Gratt.) 790, 796.
12. *Jackson v. Bishop,* 404 F.2d 571 (8th Cir. 1968).
13. *Inmates of the Attica Correctional Facility v. Rockefeller,* 453 F.2d 12, 23 (2nd Cir. 1971).
14. *Goodwin v. Oswald,* 462 F.2d 1237 (2nd Cir. 1972).
15. *Wilkonson v. Skinner,* 462 F. 670 (2nd Cir. 1972).
16. *Cruz v. Beto,* 405 U.S. 319 (1972).
17. *Bounds v. Smith,* 430 U.S. 817 (1977).
18. *Bounds, supra,* p. 825.
19. *Younger v. Gilmore,* 404 U.S. 15 (1971).
20. *Johnson v. Avery,* 393 U.S. 483 (1969).
21. *Griffin v. Illinois,* 351 U.S. 12, 20 (1956).
22. Albert Cardarelli & Marvin Finklestein, "Correctional Administrators Assess the Adequacy and Impact of Prison Legal Services Programs in the U.S.," 65 *Journal of Criminal Law & Criminology* 91, 95–98, (1974).
23. *Ibid.,* 99.
24. *Bounds, supra* at 831.
25. *Wolf v. McDonnell,* 418 U.S. 539 (1974).
26. *Wolf, supra,* 572.
27. *Baxter v. Palmigiano,* 425 U.S. 308 (1976).
28. *Clutchette v. Enomoto,* (sub nom.) 425 U.S. 308 (1978).
29. Nancy Lee & Donald Zuckerman, "Representing Parole Violators," 11 *Criminal Law Bulletin* 327–334 (1975).
30. "Legal Status of Prisoners," 14 *American Criminal Law Review* 1 (1977).
31. Rob Wilson, "U.S. Prison Population Again Hits New High," *Corrections Magazine,* March, 1977, p. 3.
32. *Ibid.,* p. 5.
33. Barry M. Hager, "No Agreement on Revising Criminal Code," *In These Times,* November 2, 1977 p. 7.
34. Robert B. McKay, "In My Opinion," *Corrections Magazine,* March, 1977 p. 1.
35. Rob Wilson, *supra,* p. 22.
36. *Pugh v. Locke,* 406 F. Supp 318 (D.C. Ala. 1976).
37. *Attica: The Official Report of the N.Y.S. Special Commission on Attica* (New York: Bantam, 1972), p. 16.

St. Louis Globe-Democrat

St. Louis, Mo., March 7, 1977

No Vacancies in U.S. Prisons

Prisons around the country are bursting at the seams, and conditions in Missouri and Illinois are no different. The prison population grows from year to year, and the cost of incarcerating the inmates increases.

As of Jan. 1 a total of 283,268 men and women are behind bars serving time on federal and state charges, an increase of 13 per cent over the previous year, according to a survey conducted by Corrections Magazine. Nearly 7,700 of the prisoners must be housed in county and local jails because state prisons are overcrowded.

Gov. Joseph P. Teasdale has asked the Missouri legislature for almost $2 million to provide temporary quarters for inmates. He also has requested more than $27,800,000 for the Division of Corrections for fiscal 1978, an increase of about $2.8 million above the current spending level.

In Illinois Gov. James R. Thompson is seeking $20 million over the present budget for fiscal 1978. The recommendation for an increase of almost 24 per cent for the corrections department comes at a time when the legislators are being asked to tighten the fiscal belt by adopting an austere $10 billion budget.

The dramatic upsurge of inmates is forcing governors of both states to press for action. Two new prisons have been delayed in Missouri for almost two years by public hostility to proposed sites and indecision by state officials. The state has an inmate capacity of 3,420. The present prison popula-

tion of 4,900 is expected to climb to 5,400 by next summer.

Illinois also has its problems. Inmates totaled 7,000 in 1975 and are expected to reach 13,000 next year. The expenditures during fiscal 1978 would be $132.6 million under Thompson's proposals. In addition the governor has recommended the sale of $25 million in bonds to renovate and construct penal facilities. The proposals to build prisons is expected to arouse opposition from communities that do not want such facilities in their areas.

The tide of prisoners is unlikely to be reversed soon in either state. In Missouri an armed criminal action provides for an additional sentence for felons who use a deadly weapon in the commission of a crime. Special units in St. Louis and St. Louis County are cracking down on career criminals, who are given speedy trials. In Illinois there has been a considerable decline in the number of paroles being granted. In addition the number of judges in Cook County will be doubled this year, with a corresponding increase in criminals headed for prisons.

The public must resign itself to the fact that new facilities must be provided to house the increasing number of prisoners. Delaying construction is no solution. It simply provides time for inflation to boost the final cost of erecting prisons. Even worse, overcrowding places pressure on the criminal justice system to prematurely release inmates to provide quarters for new prisoners.

THE INDIANAPOLIS NEWS

Indianapolis, Ind., April 1, 1977

Prison Progress

It is good news that plans to upgrade Indiana's prison system appear finally to be making progress in this legislature.

That Indiana's prisons are overcrowded and that several already fail to meet Federal minimum standards was documented last year in a study commissioned by the state. The study recommended a massive construction program to remedy deficiencies estimated to cost from $30 to $40 million in four years.

The proposal recommended by Gov. Otis Bowen and wending its way through the Legislature is considerably more modest but no less necessary. It would allow for the conversion of Norman Beatty Hospital to a maximum security prison and for transfer of that hospital population elsewhere. Estimates of the cost for converting and later expanding the Beatty facility range from $11 to $18 million.

Increased crime and tougher sentencing have combined to make Indiana's prison population grow by 37 percent in 1975. The adult inmate population, 4,880 two years ago, is projected to

peak at more than 8,800 by 1982. Indiana's facilities at Pendleton and Michigan City already fail to meet the 70 square feet of living space requirement established in recent Federal court decisions. Bowen's plan would allow for the transfer of 400 inmates from these two facilities, with eventual space for another 800 prisoners.

Indiana, which is committing increasing numbers of criminals to prison, has an obligation to alleviate the most de-humanizing aspects of incarceration when it can. The object, particularly in reformatories, is to rehabilitate or at least not breed more hardened criminals.

Yet the Bowen plan has not had an easy time in this session. Passage of the bill in both houses still would not assure its funding.

Obviously the Democrats and the Republicans play politics during the session. Prison improvements make an ideal subject because there is no special interest constituency to lobby on their behalf—no lobby except for the threat of a Justice Department civil rights suit and a moral obligation on the part of the state.

TULSA WORLD

Tulsa, Okla., May 27, 1977

Hiding Prison Problems

A FEDERAL Judge's order aimed at reducing the number of inmates in two overcrowded State prison facilities has, predictably, stirred a storm of protest and political reaction. And much of that reaction misses the point.

The fact that seems to get lost is this: Whether you agree with Judge LUTHER BOHANON's action or not, Oklahoma has a serious and growing problem of overcrowding in its corrections system.

It is a simple matter of numbers —too many convicts being sent into the prisons and not enough coming out. Ultimately, we are going to have to limit the number of prisoners we accommodate or build a lot of new accommodations and at a considerable cost.

But let us clearly understand the arithmetic.

The average Oklahoma prisoner now stays behind bars for only 21 months. That is a very short time, but even so much longer than the average in most other States. We could build several thousand more cells and we could double that average to 42 months. But would the average prisoner be any better off or less dangerous to society after 42 months than after 21 months?

We have no exact figures on how many "repeaters" go through the Oklahoma prison system, but au-

thorities say the recidivism rate is approximately 25 per cent.

Ideally, if you could lock up the 25 per cent repeaters more or less permanently and release the rest, you would make a tremendous dent in the crime rate. Of course, no one can predict with fine accuracy whether a convict will succeed on the outside or will return to crime. But we could do better than we are doing.

And we could concentrate on robbers, burglars and other professionals who are the most frequent repeaters. Punish the non-violent, non-professional offenders with lighter sentences or probation.

But something is going to have to give.

In 1976, Oklahoma sent 2,447 convicts into the system and released only 826. At that rate, the existing facilities and those now in the planning stages will all be overrun in a very short time.

Should we keep building more prisons and keep locking up a bigger and bigger number of people? Or should we start making some greater distinction between dangerous and non-dangerous offenders in our sentencing and parole policies?

These are questions that Oklahomans are going to have to answer —with or without the prodding of the Federal Courts.

The Topeka Daily Capital

Topeka, Kans., May 26, 1977

New prison a must

The governor's legislative liaison representative criticizes legislators for killing funds for a medium security prison.

You may or may not agree with Jim Maag's alliterative charge that the prison is a victim of "petty provincialism and pet political projects." Certainly, however, the proposed prison is needed by Kansas.

Maag correctly pointed out that adequate housing for convicted felons is necessary for public safety and personal safety of Kansans. A certain percentage of convicts cannot be "reformed," and society is imperiled if they must be freed.

Maag also pointed out Kansas' prison population has increased by 608 in two years.

Federal courts have forced some states to release prisoners because of overcrowding. In Oklahoma Tuesday, a judge ordered the state to cut population of its two main prisons in half, saying current overcrowded conditions "constitute cruel and unusual punishment." That must not happen in Kansas.

Yet Kansas' House cut out $375,000 the governor asked for final prison plans. The Senate, at

the behest of an Augusta member, amended the bill to move the site of the proposed 400-bed facility from Osawatomie to Topeka. Finally, senators deleted $125,000 for preliminary planning.

Instead, a "blue-ribbon panel" was proposed to study the penal system and a community correctional plan used in Minnesota. Opponents of the new prison contend this would eliminate need for this building. But those favoring the governor's plan point out that Minnesota now is building $22 million worth of prison facilities.

The Legislature appropriated $94,000 for a preliminary study for a new historical museum to be financed probably entirely from state funds. Yet that same body turned down a proposal for a preliminary study of a new medium security prison which would be financed at least partially by federal revenue sharing funds.

One of government's most important functions is protecting citizens from criminals. To do this, proper punishment must be provided as a deterrent. An adequate prison system is needed.

ALBUQUERQUE JOURNAL

Albuquerque, N.M., May 20, 1977

Prison Time Running Out

New Mexico has less than eight years to prepare its corrections system for a prison population four times larger than the present number.

Projections revealed by Corrections Secretary Ed Mahr indicate a 1985 prison population in New Mexico of 4,957 inmates if judges are lenient and 5,897 if they hand out the strictest sentences permitted by law. The present population is 1,140 inmates.

The projections take into account both the state's growing population and the recently passed law which narrows the sentencing options available to the judiciary.

Obviously, more facilities will be needed soon. Obviously, judges are not going to send anyone to prison if adequate facilities are unavailable.

Mahr foresees the need for additional minimum and medium security facilities. He believes the present penitentiary is large enough to accommodate maximum security prisoners.

The Law Enforcement Assistance Administration recommends that prisons have populations no greater than 500 inmates. Such limits imply the need for seven more prisons in the state by 1985. One, a minimum security facility, is being planned for Los Lunas and already has legislative funding.

Rather than a central location, the state's new prisons probably would be more useful if they were located in various parts of the state.

If the state is to be prepared to handle its rapidly growing prison population, planning and construction must move ahead rapidly. Eight years allows little time for planning, financing, constructing and staffing seven more prisons.

New Mexicans insisted upon tougher sentencing laws for persons convicted of crimes. They now have such laws. Now, they must insist upon development of the facilities necessary to accommodate a growing prison population.

THE DENVER POST

Denver, Colo., February 18, 1977

Jammed Jeffco Jail Mandates New Structure

When the Jefferson County Jail in Golden was built 19 years ago, its planners believed that it would adequately serve the county's needs for the forseeable future.

They were wrong. Population projections for Jefferson County were far off the mark, and so were the predictions for the day-in, day-out population of the jail. The county's population unexpectedly has surged to about 350,000 from 127,500 back in 1960, and paralleling that the jail is now so overcrowded that Sheriff Harold Bray has had to make arrangements to send prisoners to the Denver County Jail.

The Jefferson County Jail has bed space for 106 persons, but if State Health Department standards are strictly adhered to the jail should not house more than 53 persons. During a recent 40-day period, the jail had as many as 141 inmates and not less than 103.

What can be done to ease the situation?

Sheriff Bray has received approval from the county commissioners to board out as many as 25 persons at a time to the Denver County Jail at a cost of $13 a person per day. Similar cooperation is being sought from Lakewood and other municipalities in Jefferson County.

A program using college students to process the bonding of first-time offenders has been helpful in reducing some of the overcrowding pressure.

And additionally, the courts, mindful of the jail's problems, have tried to shorten pre-trial imprisonment and reduced sentences, but in doing so may have contributed to a rise in rearrest cases.

The ultimate solution facing the county commissioners is a new jail.

Adding on a new floor to the existing jail is not feasible, since for reasons of economy the jail was built with insufficient footings for additional floors to the one-story structure.

Further, the prevailing correctional philosophy in the 1950s when the jail was built was "lock 'em up." The facility was thus designed principally for the more hardened offenders, rather than those charged with first-time or lesser offenses. Sheriff Bray, an advocate of work-release programs for certain offenders, has had difficulty implementing such programs because of the overcrowding at the jail.

Construction of a new jail would allow the present facility, with some remodeling, to be used for the work-release and other similar programs.

Before the situation gets completely out of hand at the Jefferson County Jail — with tragic results — the county commissioners ought to give priority attention to funding and planning for a new jail.

THE COMMERCIAL APPEAL

Memphis, Tenn., February 22, 1977

Prison Problems Multiply

NO MATTER HOW TIGHT the state budget is in the coming fiscal year, the pressing need for prison reform and new facilities cannot be brushed out of sight.

Gov. Ray Blanton's proposed no-frills budget for Tennessee in fiscal 1978 includes $68.8 million for the Department of Corrections. That is up from the $59.9 million allocated this year. Blanton also has said he endorses the idea of building more regional prisons like the new one in Shelby County.

Nice as that sounds, it does not face up to the prison problem.

CORRECTIONS COMMISSIONER C. Murray Henderson says the present state prison system is taking care of 5,245 adult inmates. That is an increase of 1,300 over the previous year. Henderson has told the state Senate-House finance and government committees that within five years the prison total will top 7,000.

Where will they be put? How will

they be cared for? What efforts will be made to rehabilitate those who might be helped but who are squeezed into inadequate facilities and forgotten? What will be done to care for their health and safety?

Right now many county jails are housing an overflow of state prisoners. In many cases that puts a big part of the cost back on the local community. Shelby County Mayor Roy Nixon and members of the County Court have demanded that the state increase the allowance for county care of state prisoners from $5 a day to $9. Even $9 isn't enough according to Nixon, who says that the regional prison farm here is paid $12 a day by the state just to feed each prisoner.

What happens if there is not room enough for 7,000 prisoners five years from now? Ramon Sanchez, who has supervised a five-year plan for state prisons, predicts that the legislature is going to have to spend $249 million on

new prison facilities and $87 million a year to operate them within five years — unless something changes the situation.

Nothing seems likely to change. And $87 million may not be enough to operate even the present system, much less an expanded one, five inflationary years from now.

Is early release of prisoners going to be the answer, then?

That might cut down the prison budget but it's not going to save money in the long run. The Shelby County attorney general's office reported last December that 42 per cent of the major violators handled since the previous July involved convicts released early, by parole or extended furlough. The cost of crime by repeaters doesn't show in the state budget. And society is just transferring costs from one place to another when it ties up police, prosecutors and courts in handling the repeaters who, if they were still serv-

ing their original prison terms, would not be out breaking the law again.

TENNESSEE HAS TO come to grips with the problem of inadequate prisons eventually. The main prison in Nashville is a disgrace. Brushy Mountain is no model. And county jails cannot forever hold the surplus.

The danger signs have been made clear. But the need to expand regional prisons, to create more work-release programs for prisoners not yet locked in a life of crime, and to develop training programs for usable skills that will lead to jobs is not being met.

Competition for state tax dollars is intense, and there are few to lobby for better prisons. Nonetheless, the responsibility for coming to grips with this serious problem rests heavily on the shoulders of both the governor and the legislature.

Just getting by in fiscal 1978 is obviously not enough.

The Burlington Free Press
Burlington, Vt., April 5, 1977
Overcrowded Correctional Centers

WHEN THE STATE PRISON in Windsor closed in 1975, many corrections officials in the state breathed a sigh of relief, for they believed the ancient institution had long since outlived its usefulness and the time also had come for new directions in penal policy.

Hard-core felons were shipped off to federal prisons and those who had been convicted of lesser offenses were transferred to correctional centers. More emphasis was placed on work-release programs and a liberal furlough policy was adopted, much to the dismay of those who felt it took some of the sting out of prison sentences and allowed inmates too much freedom. The thrust toward leniency in Vermont reflected national trends toward liberalizing penal philosophy where greater stress was placed on rehabilitation than on mere punishment.

Two years later, the short-lived "new look" is being abandoned on both the state and national level. Whether it really was given an adequate chance to prove itself is a question which may be the subject of much heated discussion. But many persons feel that rising crime rates justify a reversal of the trend. Offenders, they say, must be punished not rehabilitated. While such a view may reek of 19th century thinking, there are indications of widespread public acceptance of the idea.

In Vermont, corrections officials say three of the four community correctional centers "face severe overcrowding." Supt. Richard Bashaw says the staff of the South Burlington facility is overworked while morale is low. Counsellors are unable to deal effectively with the problems of the individual inmates, he says. Plans are being prepared for a new $3 million correctional center in Rutland to replace an antiquated facility that offers inmates nothing at all in the way of suitable living conditions. The St. Johnsbury center, which is only a slight improvement over Rutland's, is scheduled to be replaced some time in the future. The only center that offers inmates any productive activities is in St. Albans. The others are merely places to serve time.

Under such conditions, it is little wonder that some judges hand out suspended sentences while corrections officials are forced to give furloughs to more inmates.

Given these facts, Vermonters must honestly ask themselves whether any innovative rehabilitation program, no matter how enlightened it might be, really has been given a chance to work. They should support efforts to upgrade those institutions which are inadequate and understaffed.

Corrections officials might then seek the middle ground between punishment and rehabilitation which will better serve the people of the state and those prisoners who could be persuaded to change their ways once their terms are served.

The Boston Globe
Boston, Mass., October 2, 1977
Reviewing the prison 'crisis'

The overcrowding "crisis" in the state's prisons proclaimed nine months ago by Gov. Dukakis and corrections officials seems now to be more a problem than a crisis. And with the sense of impending disaster removed, it would be appropriate for both the executive branch and the Legislature to re-examine the Corrections Department's building plans and to consider the most appropriate strategy for the department to pursue.

At the heart of the Corrections Department's cries of crisis last January were projections that by the end of this year the state's prisons would be woefully overcrowded.

The fact is that the population has not increased to the levels predicted. In mid-1976, when the population was 2500, the department projected it would rise to 3300 by June of this year. Then, last January, the estimate was refined downward and the projections were that the 3300 figure would not be reached until this December. And now, with a population of 2800, the system is projecting a year-end population of about 3100.

Even if that occurs—the local affiliate of the American Civil Liberties Union is projecting the population won't exceed 2950 by Dec. 31—it would not be quite the crisis that had been projected. On the other hand, what cannot be avoided is that even today, with the population at about 2800, the state prison system is slightly above the department's evaluation of capacity and it will, by all accounts, grow.

More facilities will be needed. But there is time to reconsider exactly how the unquestioned need for more prison beds ought to be met. The House Ways and Means Committee has already cut back the department's request for 600 beds in four prisons to 250 beds in two. But the department is continuing to press its case in the Senate, and there have been suggestions that the Senate Ways and Means is interested in at least three new prisons.

Certainly there is considerable merit in the department's position that it ought to run at about 90 percent capacity to provide some flexibility. But the question is where those beds ought to be located and how expansion in one type of facility might affect other penal programs.

In every bureaucracy there is a certain institutional momentum. If new prisons are established, new prisons will almost certainly be filled near or to capacity. And with them will come all the prison superintendents, corrections officers, guards and staff needed to man them. If, as the House Ways and Means Committee believes, only 250 new beds are needed, could existing facilities such as the unrenovated cottages at Norfolk or the Gralton Hall facility at Concord be used?

Another alternative is one favored by the ACLU—the expansion of the Corrections Department's program of establishing community-based "pre-release" centers. To the department's credit, the centers have proved highly successful in helping soon-to-be-released prisoners adjust to the outside world and in reducing recidivism.

Expansion of pre-release programs might not have been a realistic solution to the "crisis" forecast last January. But, in combination with the renovation of existing, unused prison facilities, it might be the answer to today's problem. The Governor and the Legislature should at least consider that alternative.

AKRON BEACON JOURNAL
Akron, Ohio, February 15, 1977

Prison space shortage

IT'S SELDOM easy to get people interested in conditions in Ohio's prisons. The old adage, "out of sight, out of mind," still applies. The topic is all the more unappealing these days when the major concern of most of us is finding the money to pay the heating bills.

Nevertheless, the potential for some severe problems is growing daily in the state's penal institutions, primarily because of overcrowding. This month the prison population again reached an all-time high, an event duplicated so often in the past 10 months that it frequently goes unreported.

Ohio's seven prisons, including the 143-year-old Ohio Penitentiary which was reprieved from the wrecking ball and rushed back into emergency service last year, were designed to handle about 11,000 inmates. This month they held 12,914. The maximum security institution at Lucasville, built to accommodate 1,620 inmates in one-man cells, is clogged with 2,205 prisoners. The Ohio State Reformatory at Mansfield, where safe capacity is 1,800, is jammed with 2,511 occupants.

The number of prisoners has been soaring since it bottomed out at 7,698 in October 1973 — a 30-year low. State prison officials predict the total will climb to 13,600 by July 1978. George F. Denton, director of the Ohio Department of Rehabilitation and Correction, expects the rate of commitments to continue to rise until 1988 or 1990.

Overcrowding ultimately intensifies the warehouse nature of prisons and sharpens tensions and emotions. Not only is it inhumane to require inmates to live in quarters like sardine cans, it also is unreasonable to require corrections officers and other staff members to work in them.

Federal judges in other states have ordered corrective actions where they concluded conditions had deteriorated to unacceptable levels. Denton worries that the same thing might happen in Ohio.

A year ago, House members Harry J. Lehman (D-Shaker Heights) and Alan E. Norris (R-Westerville) proposed a $250 million bond issue to finance construction of new penal facilities. The bonds would have been retired with revenues from increases in cigaret and liquor taxes. However, voters never were given an opportunity to express themselves on the proposal after the legislature developed cold feet and feared asking for higher taxes of any variety.

Lehman has indicated he will reintroduce the proposal soon. The legislature should give it swift consideration. There may be many arguments over the type and location of new facilities to be constructed — and over the method of financing — but there can be little doubt that additional quarters are needed.

The Salt Lake Tribune
Salt Lake City, Utah, April 11, 1977

Utah Can't Postpone Response To Its Overcrowded Prisons

Warden Samuel W. Smith has little choice but to seek authority for telling judges not to send convicted felons to Utah State Prison. The prison is dangerously overcrowded.

There is, however, a huge hitch in the warden's hope that local jails can be utilized to confine state prisoners, thereby relieving pressure on the Point of the Mountain facility. Local jails, at least those in the larger population centers, are at or nearing capacity.

Certainly this is so in Salt Lake County. Just recently Sheriff's Lt. Gary Deland described the inmate population, then at 295, as higher than administrators would like. He predicted severe overcrowding at the Salt Lake County facility unless it is expanded soon.

Utah's plight is by no means unique. A report issued April 4 by the federal Law Enforcement Assistance Administration (LEAA) noted that there was a record number of 283,145 prisoners in state and federal custody at the end of 1976, an increase of 29,329 over the previous year.

That record total included 7,738 state prisoners "in local jails at the end of last year because of overcrowded state prisons," the LEAA said. In Alabama there were 2,160 state prisoners in local jails, the direct result of federal court findings that the crowded state penal institutions amounted to unconstitutional treatment of inmates.

It hasn't come to that stage yet in Utah but Warden Smith and the Board of Corrections have good reason to believe that the Point of the Mountain prison is headed for crisis.

Severe "sardine can" conditions were predictable several years ago. There was ample advance warning. But the Legislature, in the hallowed tradition of most such bodies, assigned the prison's pressing needs a low priority. At the same time legislators enacted tougher criminal penalties that would assure increased pressure on limited prisoner housing.

The inevitable result of this course is now plain to see.

Warden Smith is in the scary position of having to hold the lid on a potentially explosive situation while waiting out cumbersome and anything but urgent procedures for maybe acquiring additional space.

A special session of the Legislature is almost certain to be called for this summer. Gov. Scott Matheson should make speeding up construction of necessary prison facilities an item for command consideration.

In the absence of a dramatic downturn in criminal activity and in Utah's general population increase, the construction of more prison facilities is but a stopgap remedy. But providing additional space might buy time during which the overall crime and confinement dilemma could be addressed in the light of conditions which cannot be ignored.

ST. LOUIS POST-DISPATCH
St. Louis, Mo., February 21, 1977

Asking For Trouble

The potentially explosive crowding of Missouri's penal system—4900 inmates in seven facilities designed to house 3890, or 26 per cent too many—parallels a national trend produced in part by the post-World War II baby boom coupled with an overemphasis on punishment. Most of the other states, including Illinois, are suffering from the same problem, and it is unlikely to go away soon so long as the public retains its current regard for retribution as the only response to crime.

As the Missouri Division of Corrections has pointed out, more than half of the nation's prison population is between the ages of 17 and 29; which is not surprising. Historically, young persons tend to get into more difficulties with the law than do those who are more mature, and almost a quarter of the nation's population is in the 17-to-29 age group. In short, the baby boom has produced more raw material than ever in the history of the country to be processed through the criminal justice system. And if prison is society's only response to crime, then of course prisons will bulge until they burst or explode, compelling taxpayers to build still more prisons.

Little to its credit, Missouri is committed to the punishment-prison construction approach. But since new construction always lags behind needs, especially in this field, many younger first-time offenders will suffer; even now the Corrections Division is having to house some of them with hardened old-timers at the main penitentiary.

A more enlightened penal philosophy—one that most certainly would have to originate with Gov. Teasdale—would consider such alternatives as beefed up probation, early parole, work release and other rehabilitative techniques. That approach cut prison population in the 1960s and it could do so today. It would ease prison tensions—stabbings are almost commonplace in Jefferson City now—conserve millions in construction costs and perhaps even save some first-offenders from a lifetime of crime and punishment.

Arkansas Gazette.

Little Rock, Ark., March 22, 1977

A Partial Prison Answer

The legislature's appropriation of $3.9 million for construction in the state prisons represents, at best, a desperate holding action. Several millions more will have to be forthcoming, and fairly soon, if Arkansas is to keep running its prison program the way it has insisted on doing in the past.

As all Arkansans should know by now, the federal courts are not going to allow the kind of overcrowding in prison living facilities that contributed so significantly to a finding in the late '60s that conditions in the prisons were cruel and unusual punishment under the Eighth Amendment to the United States Constitution.

The Cummins Unit has a limit of 1,650 inmates; the Tucker Unit has a limit of 550. During the final week of the legislative session, the prisons reached their limits and on one day had to turn away persons who had been sentenced. Apparently room has been found for them now, but each day the prison population hovers at the cut-off point.

What to do?

Governor Pryor has indicated that he will now be turning his attention to the prison problem, as well he should, and perhaps some leadership on the issue will begin to put the situation into a perspective that makes it more manageable. In a less-than-thoughtful attempt to show the criminal who's boss, the General Assembly early in the session adopted a new parole law that will be keeping inmates in the prisons for longer periods. Mr. Pryor supported the measure. But under the circumstances obtaining in the prisons the question should not be whether felons spend more time in prison. Instead, it should be how the state is going to accommodate them in a fashion that will meet federal court standards.

It is the long-range effect of this law that is particularly important at this point. There is some reason, as we have indicated, that Arkansas may be able to limp along with the $3.9 million construction program for a couple of years. In 1979, alas, there appears to be

no hope except to undertake massive building, costing many millions of dollars, or to devise some alternatives to incarceration that would seem to run contrary to the spirit of the new parole law.

A couple of possible alternatives already have been mentioned by prison officials. One, suggested as a partial answer by Correction Commissioner Jim Mabry, is to devise a statewide probation system directed by the circuit courts. Persons placed in the program would be charged a monthly fee to offset the cost of the program. Another possible alternative is for circuit judges to reduce the length of sentences they hand down under the new parole law.

Arkansas, in any case, has only partially addressed its "prison problem" with the $3.9 million construction appropriation. Addressing the rest of it will require, for starters, a lot of soul searching as well as creative thinking. The federal courts will not let this state simply ignore the challenge.

St. Petersburg Times

St. Petersburg, Fla., March 23, 1977

Our universities of crime

The U. S. Supreme Court this week added to already mounting pressures on the 1977 Florida Legislature to reform the state's counterproductive criminal justice system. If the public will send the lawmakers the same message, perhaps this will be the year Florida will begin changing its oversized prisons from universities of crime to places where most inmates can be restored to productive lives.

The Supreme Court joined the act on a technicality. It said U. S. District Court Judge Charles R. Scott acted within his powers in 1975 when he ruled that severe overcrowding in Florida prisons violated the inmates' rights to safety, medical treatment and rehabilitation. Now the case goes back to the U. S. 5th Circuit Court of Appeals in New Orleans. When the Legislature meets April 5, the possibility will hang over it that an order similar to Scott's will be reinstated.

EVEN WITHOUT the court ruling, the Legislature is obligated to continue its work to improve the criminal justice system. As usual, its hoppers are

full of law-and-order bills, many or which would make prison conditions worse.

Florida starts in this field with a sorry record. We ranked ninth among the states in population in the last census. Yet Florida in 1975 stood fourth in the number of prisoners per 100,000 population behind North Carolina, South Carolina and Georgia, all of which count some misdemeanants in their figures, which Florida doesn't. In number of prisoners, Florida's total yesterday of 18,671 was tied with New York for third behind California and Texas. Florida and New York have the same number of prisoners, even though New York has more than twice the population.

Clearly, Florida courts send too many people to prison. Once behind bars, they stay there. Louie L. Wainwright, head of the department of prisoner rehabilitation, testified in the appeal of the Scott decision that the percentage of releases by parole has declined.

NO ONE KNOWS the cost of the present system in human terms. In

dollars, it's clearly inefficient to send too many people to prison at a cost of $15 a day each and too few to parole, which costs the taxpayers $1 a day. Gov. Reubin Askew is asking the Legislature for $71-million in prison construction and $23-million more in increased budgets, including more for probation.

The prisons need space just to catch up. More money should be spent to construct more small minimum-security prisons in places where inmates can be visited by their families and where they have a better chance to earn work release.

BUT MORE prison space isn't the whole answer. The real challenge facing Florida's criminal justice system is to do a better job separating those prisoners who can be rehabilitated from the incorrigibles; to create institutions that teach more prisoners how to change their ways and fewer how to commit bigger crimes; to transform probation from a system so overworked that creative supervision is impossible into one in which it is routine.

ATTICA PRISONERS REVOLT; MORE THAN 40 DIE IN RIOT

The killing of more than 40 prisoners and hostages at New York's Attica Prison Sept. 13 was the subject of continued controversy as three separate panels opened investigations into the tragedy. In addition, lawyers from civil rights organizations and legal groups representing 1,000 inmates began interviewing prisoners to look into charges that they were beaten following the recapture of the prison. Debate continued over the actions of Gov. Nelson Rockefeller and Russell Oswald, the state corrections commissioner, in quelling the Attica revolt, and of state officials who apparently lied to the press about events at the prison.

Within hours after the Attica rebellion had been crushed, minor uprisings broke out in Pennsylvania, Illinois and Texas prisons. Meanwhile, in New York, correctional personnel threatened to strike unless officials agreed to their demands for reform of the state's penal system. This issue—prison reform—became, in fact, the main topic of debate for editorial writers once the initial controversy over the Attica tragedy cooled.

BUFFALO EVENING NEWS

Buffalo, N.Y., September 18, 1971

The worst prison uprising in American history can be a turning point if the Attica tragedy shocks this state and the nation into a recognition of what it will take in coming to grips with the dehumanizing conditions which feed an underlying and escalating mood of revolutionary militancy.

Among the many lessons which this episode points up, in the judgment of some nationally respected corrections officials, is the need for substituting smaller and more manageable prison facilities for today's huge, isolated, fortress-style, maximum-security institutions.

This was one of the cardinal reforms aims to which State Corrections Commissioner Russell B. Oswald committed himself in assuming his new job last January. Mr. Oswald, in fact, promised to resign if he failed to move "at least 30 per cent" of the state's inmates out of maximum-security facilities where the sheer size and environment greatly restrict any constructive opportunities for meaningful training and rehabilitation programs.

For some incorrigibles, no amount of reform — education, psychiatric therapy, better food, etc. — can insure a dampening of incendiary conditions all too easily ignited by the new breed of political revolutionaries. But this, as U. S. Chief Justice Warren E. Burger has pointed out, does not excuse the widespread public tolerance for the low priority accorded penal efforts to help men change — to give them some future — while they are confined.

A measure of that low priority is the general lack of protest over the perpetual dollar pinch felt by penal authorities. If there were such protests last winter in Albany when Mr. Oswald's appropriations were cut back by about a quarter in a painful budget squeeze, they were scarcely audible. At budget time, in short, prison reform seems to have no effective constituency, no determined lobby to fight for money in competition with the glamour lobbies for schools, public employe pay raises and even welfare.

Too many of us are prone to the human temptation to put off a facing-up to critical problems until the shock therapy of tragedy evokes a hue and cry for action. Penal reform translates inescapably into more money. There is just no other way to provide more and better-trained prison guards, separate penal institutions for different levels of offenders, modernized education and medical facilities, and everything else that penal reform requires.

So we must remind any lawmakers who have reacted to Attica as a problem for somebody else — as a few have — that they have their responsibility, along with the governor and his prison administrators, to find the money needed to implement long-deferred enlightened reforms. Let us pray that state correction officials are wrong in fearing that "it's going to be a lot tougher" in the aftermath of the Attica riot to win public support for a fundamental overhauling. This would be a terribly ironic denouement after the frightful price already paid — by guards and prisoners alike — for Attica's agony.

HERALD-JOURNAL

Syracuse, N.Y., September 22, 1971

Gov. Rockefeller has moved to organize an inquiry into the Attica prison uprising.

He has asked Chief Judge Stanley H. Fuld of the Court of Appeals and the four presiding appellate judges to select citizens throughout the state to determine the facts, to examine them, to lay these facts before a skeptical public.

This inquiry goes beyond the governor's early request to Presiding Appelate Division Justice Harry D. Goldman of the Fourth Department to select a board to protect prisoners' rights.

The intent also goes beyond the governor's assignment of Robert E. Fischer, the state's "super cop", to gather evidence for follow through prosecutions.

Such an inquiry, far removed from official manipulation, is due.

For the facts of Attica are in dispute.

A team of Buffalo Evening News reporters and photographers, trying to cover the violence at Attica from the beginning, reported being thwarted as much by officialdom as the Attica walls.

Even before becoming embroiled in public contradictions about how hostages at Attica died, officials had clammed up. Only one man, a public information aide to the state's corrections commissioner, tried to brief up to 200 newsmen on the hour-by-hour progress of negotiations and, finally, the assault.

New York State is noted for its platoons of public relations specialists, many earning $25,000 to $40,000 a year who show up when a new highway is dedicated. At Attica, the one man who had the job finally gave up.

While some legislators and some civilians witnessed the storming of Cell Block D, newsmen were barred. Two days later, only a few, representing all those assigned to the story, were allowed inside the prison. No newsmen went through the hospital area.

Before Monday's action, some newsmen went into the prison, also on a pool arrangement, when requested by the inmates who wanted the press to attend the negotiations, see the hostages, tell their story to the public. The inmates seemed to have a better sense of citizens wanting to know, and having a right to know, than the officialdom of the State Department of Corrections.

The panel sought by Gov. Rockefeller through the state's court of appeals judges is promised financing "to the full extent necessary." It will have the power of subpoena. It is to report "as expeditiously as possible."

The governor, thus, has moved to assure public confidence in the inquiry. It's needed.

The New York Times

New York, N.Y., September 20, 1971

Nathaniel Hawthorne characterized it: "The black flower of civilized society, a prison."

Events of recent days have forced the people of this state and nation to contemplate that black flower. A melancholy preoccupation, it can be instructive only if public officials and private citizens—and inmates, too—break free from the prison of their own preconceptions.

The first thing needed is a scrupulously fair inquiry into the circumstances which led up to the revolt of the prisoners at Attica and the deaths of forty guards and inmates—an inquiry that now seems well on its way.

But there is risk in even the best official investigation, as previous inquiries into comparable social breakdowns have shown. Too often, the investigation serves as a pretext for delay, then the final report evokes a controversy which is a substitute for action.

The compiling of an honest record would discharge a debt of honor to the dead. It would help illuminate the murky record on everything that happened before and after the mass killings. Yet one fact is plain without any investigation: What happened at Attica could have happened almost anywhere.

Virtually every large prison for serious offenders is overcrowded. Its custodial staff is undertrained. Its doctors, psychiatrists and teachers are few in number and often weak in quality. Its food ranges from mediocre to inedible. Its racial composition is steadily changing as blacks leave the backwaters of the rural South and enter the far-riskier mainstream of city life.

The mood in prisons is tense because drug addiction, sexual frustration, antisocial resentments, racial hurts, criminal guilt and fantasies of escape create tensions. A prison is a community of defeated men.

Knowing all this, the public has to ask itself whether it is prepared to pay the price in higher taxes to provide more buildings, more professional staff, better-trained guards, better food and higher wages for work done by prison inmates. Since tax-conscious suburban residents are voting down bond issues and budgets which would provide better schools for their children, it is utopian to assume that people are eager to improve prisons for criminals whom they fear and resent.

Indeed, the public has yet to make the necessary investment of public funds in properly caring for emo-

tionally disturbed and potentially delinquent children and adolescents. Money and talent ought to be spent on saving these children first rather than waiting until they require rehabilitation as adults.

*   *   *

If conditions within prisons are not radically transformed, future prison uprisings are almost certain. Prison inmates are usually men with a sense of powerlessness, lacking in self-control. In their lives, only a gun or a knife wielded to commit a crime has given them a fleeting sense of power. In negotiating with inmates, extraordinary official patience and flexibility is required since it takes time for prisoners to learn the limits of power.

The alternative of refusing to negotiate with prisoners, especially when their grievances are as genuine as they were at Attica, also entails high risk of a loss of life. Neither course provides any guarantee of a bloodless outcome. It is easy to say in retrospect that officials could have managed a specific episode better. But the responsibility does not stop with a particular Governor or National Guard commander or prison warden.

Americans have to ask themselves whether they want every evidence of malfunction in their society—a street demonstration by political dissenters, a campus rebellion, a slum riot, a prison revolt—suppressed by official violence. The moral rationale for putting violent, undisciplined men in prison is that the larger society is observing higher standards of human behavior. If that society is violent, the power to incarcerate remains, but what becomes of the moral authority?

Throughout history, the ordeal of imprisonment has instilled toughness in some men and broken the spirit of others. Men have found religious zeal within prison walls and others, like the Wobblies or Sacco and Vanzetti, have shaped or tested political convictions there. Prisons may radicalize some of their inmates but they remain, as they have always been, extremely poor starting places from which to reform or reorganize a society. Those who encourage and romanticize prison rebels are helping to make victims, not heroes.

The upheaval in the prisons is part of the wider crisis in the nation's public institutions. Here, as elsewhere, the renewal of authority can be accomplished only if it is accompanied by the reconciling power of reform.

THE ROANOKE TIMES

Roanoke, Va., September 17, 1971

Nothing now can change what happened at Attica prison, and second-guessing is cheap; but one can wish that New York State authorities had stalled awhile rather than send in the troops, guns aflame, to mow down prisoners and hostages together in one horrible massacre. It might have turned out differently.

To speculate, though, is futile. What is demanded now is pitiless public attention to what is happening in so many of our prisons, and some hard and probably expensive decisions to change the way our society treats the people it locks up.

This is not knee-jerk, bleeding-heart stuff. It may be difficult to persaude most people they should have any sympathy for those who have broken the law, or that prisoners deserve better treatment than they get. By and large, society rejects the thought that it is responsible for individual criminality; that question will not be argued here.

The point is that our prison systems as now run do little but punish; they do not reform, they do not deter people from crime, rather they brutalize inmates and breed in them greater hostility, a stronger bent for anti-social behavior. The state has reached the stage where, if it locks some men up for the first time, it had better reserve cell space for them most of the remainder of their lives; they will keep coming back, and the longer they are behind bars the more animal-like they will become.

Does this make sense? Obviously not. By maintaining penal systems as it does now, society is only storing up more trouble for itself. Not just in terms of continued crime, but in class strife as well. Those who serve time are, for the most part, poor and black, and the clashes at Attica, San Quentin and elsewhere are evidence of a dangerous political revolt by those who are no longer disposed to accept meekly what they see not as just punishment, but as oppression.

The signs of revolt will tend to reinforce fears and harden attitudes on the part of the law-abiding majority. That will make change more difficult. But it is essential. Some reformers suggest that only a small number of the prison population — say 10-15 per cent — must be confined. Other criminals, they contend, should pay their debts to society and individual victims in other ways. Or, some claim, the state should compensate victims of crime. The idea is not to ignore the criminal act, but to concentrate on alternatives to imprisonment.

Middle and upper classes already do this with methods like private restitution, special institutional treatment, psychiatric care and the like, and they are seldom condemned for it. Society needs to provide similar means for its less well-to-do and advantaged — if not for humanity's sake, then for its own self-interest.

St. Petersburg Times

St. Petersburg, Fla., September 17, 1971

The tragedy at Attica was another of those watersheds of public opinion, seeming to divide Americans, pulling them into opposite camps.

When these divisive events occur, it is the duty of good citizens to search for and cling to the middle ground.

IN ONE respect, events at Attica were quite different from those at Kent State and My Lai. The provoking victims were not college students or Vietnamese peasants. They were convicted criminals, the worst of New York state's prisoners, men who had failed to live by the rules of a free society, cruel men who had been dehumanized by prison routine, desperate men with lessened regard for their own lives and the lives of their hostages. Many of them were political radicals. These facts should have affected every decision and action before the killings occurred.

In two important respects, the killings at Attica were like those at Kent State and My Lai. They grew out of an acceptance of violence, a belief that human behavior can be controlled by the application of force. The idea was expressed by columnist William S. White: "When all else fails, lawless force must be met with lawful force — instantly and without pietistic moralisms." Of course, all else had not failed at Attica. And the blind application of lawful, wild gunfire kills innocent persons. As we said before, we believe the storming of

the prison was a reckless, poorly planned, mistaken move. The coroner's finding that the hostages and prisoners died by gunfire grimly supports that opinion.

ATTICA WAS like the other massacres in that it brought out the worst in so many persons. In the drive to fix blame and to punish, no room is left for reconciliation. It is as if everybody feels compelled to abandon the middle ground.

When he believed the hostages were killed by prisoners, the editorial writer for the New York Daily News called for revenge: "The hostage slayings were murders which we hope will be swiftly, lawfully and completely avenged." When he learned that the same deaths were caused by the guns of those storming the prison, he said we should "suspend judgment until all the facts are in." One of our readers urged a return to "instant, permanent punishment for lawbreakers." The Atlanta Constitution wrote: "The animals at Attica, who coldbloodedly slit the throats of eight hostages, and those who stood by and allowed it to happen, left the prison authorities little choice but to use troops."

Another Times reader said he believed that in articles and editorials about prison reform we "always take the side of the prison inmate."

THAT'S THE heart of this division. It is the current political belief that on law-and-order questions Americans must choose

sides. You're either for it or against it. You must show your opinion in thoughtless, automatic ritual. Columnist Joe Kraft expressed it well in a question: "Does law-and-order politics mean that the army and police are good guys even when you don't know what they have done?"

If our society is to learn from this latest tragedy, Americans must reject this ritual of side-choosing. They must ask questions. They must insist that officials act with caution in dealing with desperate men. They must realize that in some prison riot situations quick and decisive force is proper. They must realize that in other cases, talking and stalling and reasoning is better. They must realize that right is not always on the side of the government agent.

ABOVE ALL, we must hold to the middle ground, especially on these fabric-tearing issues of law and order and race. The middle ground is where action can be based on fact instead of emotion. It is where even the worst criminal can retain his self-respect as a human being. It is where citizens recognize the need to separate law breakers from society, but in institutions where their faults are corrected and where they are prepared for returning to society. The middle ground is a place where citizens question the use of deadly force because they know it seldom accomplishes what is intended.

New York Post

New York, N.Y., September 20, 1971

Clearly there is no numerical shortage of current and pending investigations into the Attica tragedy. Perhaps there is some temporary merit in that condition: the diverse groups may serve to function as watchdogs on each other. But even as all these inquiries take shape, some obviously less inhibited than others, the extraordinary and disturbing fact remains that newsmen are still being systematically obstructed in their quest for the truth about what happened on that Bloody Monday one week ago, in the crucial preceding interval, and in the days thereafter.

They are still denied access to the inmates. At the same time, Correction officials involved in the fateful events have remained unwilling to submit themselves to full and free journalistic interrogation.

These rulings have steadily ham-

pered the efforts of the most conscientious reporters to sift truth from rumor. The blackout has steadily intensified the skepticism and distrust of the public, which now knows that so many early "official" statements—such as the claim that the dead hostages were the victims of prisoner slashing rather than trooper bullets—are conceded to have been untrue.

That some lawyers for inmates and even some Congressional emissaries have been granted limited right to talk with prisoners is no satisfactory answer to the questions raised by the restrictions imposed on the press. The testimony of both legal spokesmen and political figures will inevitably be subject to charges of partisanship. While we claim no infallibility for newsmen, we believe their continued exclusion can only reflect official fear of independent scrutiny by the media.

It is now five days since Correction Commissioner Oswald's press aide said cryptically that his own initial lurid reports of the causes of death and mutilation—subsequently repudiated—were "not meant to be a factual account as to the cause of death." Why, then, were they released? Where did they originate? These are only two of the many unanswered questions at Attica.

The strategy of silence and suppression may be based on the view that this storm will pass. We earnestly resolve that it will not; we will continue to press for answers to the questions that haunt this state and nation, no matter how long the effort entailed. Too often in the past, prison upheavals have been one-day or one-week episodes, lost in the flurry of ensuing events. But Attica was too large and ghastly a disaster to be filed and forgotten.

Minneapolis Tribune

Minneapolis, Minn., September 19, 1971

Enough facts have been brought out on New York's Attica Prison massacre to indicate that the uprising was tragically mishandled. Nine hostages were killed by the gunfire of police and sheriff's deputies sent in to free them. Twenty-eight inmates died in the same gunfire. (One guard and two inmates allegedly were killed by prisoners.)

Could this violent climax to the rebellion have been avoided? Only time could have provided an answer, and as columnist Tom Wicker wrote last week, time was cut short in the fatal decision to use the force of arms to effect a final solution.

Now, in the aftermath, there are those, including President Nixon, who give full support to the violent solution. Some of the be-tough advocates blame the uprising on "militants" or "revolutionaries." They say that only force can stop such uprisings elsewhere. And they discount prison conditions as an underlying cause of the Attica and San Quentin tragedies.

Attica itself is a convincing counter to these assertions. Regardless of whether "revolutionaries" were instigators, the bitterness and hostility among inmates were so widespread that more than 1,000 of them took part in the "do-or-die" uprising. To blame such feelings on outsiders will no more solve the prison problems than did similar blame-setting solve urban-ghetto and college-campus disorders.

Attica demonstrates both cause and effect. Consider the cause. Inmates in early July had petitioned for changes in prison conditions. Corrections Commissioner Russell Oswald delayed for two months and then told the inmates that changes were coming. But he again asked for time. So nothing changed. Prisoners complained about mistreatment from the small-town white guards hired to "control" a big-city inmate population 85 percent black and Puerto Rican. They complained about inadequate food, medical treatment and recreation. They complained of lack of respect and lack of responsiveness from prison authorities. Then consider the effect. When a brutality rumor swept through the prison, inmates attempted to boycott breakfast, guards tried to force them into the dining hall and the uprising headed toward a terrible conclusion.

Force and repression didn't work at Attica. They are not working in most prisons. Former U.S. Atty. Gen. Ramsey Clark notes that 95 percent of the corrections expenditure in the nation is for custody, while only 5 percent is for rehabilitation. Norman A. Carlson, director of the U.S. Bureau of Prisons, says flatly, "The prisons have failed. People have been getting out as hardened, if not more so, than when they went in."

So prisoners often become worse criminals in prison. So the work of prison guards becomes more difficult. So the public suffers more crime when the prisoners return to society, as most ultimately will.

Reform came too late at Attica. The reform began sooner in Minnesota under enlightened gubernatorial leadership, making this state's prison system far better than most, yet far from ideal even at that. The reform now is being pushed still more aggressively by Corrections Commissioner David Fogel, as described in the article on the next page. Those reforms are not being sought in the romantic belief that all prisoners are "nice people." After all the changes, some prisoners will remain behind bars because they are too dangerous to be let loose. But the reforms are being sought in the belief that many prisoners can benefit from new approaches that give them and the community greater responsibilities in their rehabilitation.

There can be no guarantees that the reforms will be successful in anything so volatile as human behavior. But there is strong hope in the Stillwater Prison inmates' letter supporting Fogel's efforts and promising there will be no repeat of the Attica tragedy at Stillwater. The reforms should salvage lives, improve on public safety and provide something of an answer to Sen. Muskie's plaintive statement: "In our sorrow, we can ponder how and why we have reached the point where men would rather die than live another day in America."

THE ARIZONA REPUBLIC

Phoenix, Ariz., September 29, 1971

What happened at Attica State Prison is obviously much more than a local matter. Indeed, it is intimately related to the question of whether the U.S. any longer has the capacity or the will to govern.

The Attica uprising, although it may have been planned, was clearly a local matter. That is, there is no reason to think that it was part of any concerted uprisings nationally.

But there is every reason to believe that there will be one, two, three more Atticas if we do not learn from the original rebellion. And to hear some of the post-rebellion comments, the guilt-ridden left will exert every ounce of its considerable power to see to it that society is blamed for the uprising.

There is widespread need for prison reform. We have frequently pointed out the need for retraining

and rehabilitation programs, without which we can never make a dent in our high recidivism rate.

But there are widespread needs outside prison also. And the public understandably prefers to invest its resources in assisting free men rather than convicts—in some cases for reasons of vengeance, but in most cases because of a genuine belief that free men are more deserving of help than inmates (about one-half of whom are serving terms for rape, homicide, robbery, or other violent crimes).

But the guilt-ridden left is not content merely to say that prison reforms are needed and are a worthwhile investment. Instead, it is in the process (and has been since the assault on the prison) of trying to indict everyone in sight—Attica prison officials, N.Y. Gov. Nelson Rockefeller, middle-class

America — everyone except the prisoners themselves.

With the help of the always complaisant media, the left is trying to do just exactly what Vice President Spiro Agnew said—to transform the Attica revolt into "yet another cause celebre in the pantheon of radical revolutionary propaganda."

It is this thick layer of social guilt that led not just to leftist disillusionment with the Vietnam war, but to open celebration of the Communist enemy.

It is this overlay of social guilt that rendered the left immobile in face of extremist student assaults on the academy.

And now the left wants us to derive from the Attica revolt, not the lesson that we must act to prevent politicizing of our prisons, but the

lesson that we have failed again (presumably as we failed the Vietcong and our student radicals). The implication is that we are all guilty, and therefore unfit to rule.

And we may well be unfit to rule. For each of these events— the New Left mobs in the streets protesting our Vietnam policy, the SDS mobs bombing schools and disrupting classes, and now the efforts to pamper militant inmates— represents direct challenges to our established values and institutions, to see whether we have the courage of our convictions.

The result of this leftist agitation is that for the first time in this century, ordinary Americans are beginning to wonder whether their own federal and state governments have the will to govern. And the evidence, sad to say, is by no means clear-cut.

WINSTON-SALEM JOURNAL

Winston-Salem, N.C., September 16, 1971

THE clouded aftermath of the attempted prison break at Attica, New York, has had at least one unfortunate effect on the public: One villainy seems to have canceled out another. The brutality of the rebelling inmates, particularly during the first few hours of the four-day rebellion, has now been matched — or neutralized — by the understandable recklessness of the policemen and Guardsmen w h o overwhelmed the rioters early Monday morning.

And all the official alibis now being aired only make it even more difficult for the public to grasp the crucial fact that 42 persons are dead and dozens more hospitalized because a group of hardened criminals in one of the state's "maximum security" prisons took hostages, fashioned home-made weapons and demanded their freedom.

Whatever the outcome, the convicts who planned the break were the cause. Nothing can alter this.

But what impressed o u t s i d e observers about this break was the sheer desperation of the inmates. They had nothing to lose in such a bloody confrontation; many of them, in fact, seemed to welcome death as an alternative to returning to the cells.

Prison conditions t h a t can obliterate the human instinct for survival—that literally make men suicidal—must be worse than any outsider can imagine.

And if the Atticas of the future are to be headed off, we're going to have to change these conditions, somehow.

☆ ☆ ☆

There are more than 400 prisons in this country, in addition to some 4,000 jails, lockups and workhouses. Eight out of every 10 convicts in these prisons have been in prison before, and are now serving a second or third or fourth sentence.

Most of these convicts are poor. They were poor outside and they are poor inside. Indeed, until the drug crisis came along to add thousands of middle-class Americans — mostly young—to the prison population, it was virtually a class institution.

When you lock up men who have never known success or the pride of honest achievement, who weren't sent through college by permissive middle-class parents or offered a number of well-paying jobs to choose from, there are going to be disciplinary problems.

A hundred years ago, prison officials handled this by beating the offenders half to death 1d starving them until tuberculosis or malnutrition killed them off. Today, officials are more humane. Offenders are isolated in "solitary confinement," a hold-over from the old Quaker idea of giving a felon a Bible and keeping him alone day and night. But as Thomas M.

Osborne, one of the nation's foremost prison administrators, points o u t , solitary — which sounds more humane than beatings or starvation—is nothing but "the antechamber to t h e madhouse." Solitary takes a bit longer than the knout, but it accomplishes the same purpose of destroying the offenders.

The rest of it is just as bad: Demoralized guards, s o m e t i m e s sadistic and often racist, kept in the same post for 10 or 15 years, at the same low pay ... P r i s o n administrators who don't even know the conditions of the institutions they administer ... Young, minor offenders thrown in willy-nilly with hardened c r i m i n a l s , vicious homosexuals and psychotics ... Parole systems that do not work, rehabilitation programs that do not rehabilitate — just about every indictment that can be made of prisons in general can be doubly made of American penitentiaries in particular.

And until we start using the millions of dollars we spend on prisons to reshape the nature of the institution, such violent incidents as Attica will continue to bewilder and enrage those citizens who cannot imagine what it is like to be isolated from society, at the mercy both of officials who completely control prison life and inmates who can make it a hell on earth.

THE LOUISVILLE TIMES

Louisville, Ky., September 16, 1971

Sen. Edmund Muskie assessed the tragedy of Attica prison more accurately than anyone else on the national political scene. Not only did he see in the rioting that took 42 lives "the failure of both parties' recent leadership to solve the problems of America," but he also found in those terrible days "more stark proof that something is terribly wrong in America . . . We have reached the point where men would rather die than live another day in America."

He offered a solution: "a genuine commitment of our vast resources to the human needs of people." More "invented labels'" will not suffice.

Ed Muskie, so often the fence-straddler, told this one straight. It did not sit well with many of the governors to whom he told it. It will not sit well with many Americans, who for too long have allowed their prisons to be the exclusive preserve of the keepers and the kept.

Nonetheless, it had to be said. The time has long passed for mere lip service to those eternal verities, "prison reform" and "rehabilitation." They are concepts that can never become realities until society itself is willing to make that "single, clarifying decision" Sen. Muskie advocated, and carve out the festering sores that are the breeding ground for those who populate places such as Attica.

So long as the Atticas of the world are maintained, they will be the source of violent tragedy. A society that inflicts violence upon those who

Attica Cell Blocks
. . . after the siege

do violence to its rules must expect violence in return. "It seems natural enough for those who have been victims of a great deal of violence, or simply of the constant threat of overwhelming force, to conclude that they can restore their dignity only when they use violence themselves," observed Richard Hofstadter, the historian, in his study of America violence.

Just as pertinent are the words of Eldridge Cleaver, probably the nation's most articulate prison dropout:

"A convict sees man's fangs and claws and learns quickly to bare and unsheath his own, for real and final." He put the same thought another way: "We shall have our manhood. We shall have it or the earth will be leveled by our attempts to gain it."

In these statements lie the larger lessons of Attica that Sen. Muskie was urging us to turn to. What is to be gained by the laying of blame upon militant revolutionaries among the non-whites who comprised 85 per cent of Attica's inmates? What good can come of second-guessing the decision, so agonizingly made, that overwhelming force was the only way to restore law and order? The men whose responsibility that was will be haunted until the day they die by: "Did I do the right thing?"

Nor will the answer lie in better food or improved living conditions for the men behind the walls. Such promises were not enough to bar what happened; they will not be enough to stop it from happening again.

Only with the realization that prisons are meeting none of their proclaimed goals—there are more criminals outside their walls than inside them; they breed crime rather than rehabilitate criminals—can real gains be made, permanent change brought about. Until then, we are all victims of what psychiatrist Karl Menninger wisely labelled "the crime of punishment."

St. Louis Globe-Democrat
St. Louis, Mo., September 22, 1971

What are the causes of the prison turmoil that produced the bloody tragedy at Attica, N.Y.?

There is no single answer though extremists on both sides are trying to say they have THE answer—usually one that agrees with an individual's philosophy.

From what those closest to the problem say, three principal reasons caused these outbreaks:

(1) Younger, violence-oriented prisoners carrying on the same rebellion in prison that they were waging before being sent to prison.

(2) Revolutionaries from the outside who encourage convicts to rebel.

(3) Poor rehabilitation programs and other sub-standard conditions.

It is no accident that we listed the causes in this order. Gov. Ronald Reagan in California and Gov. Nelson Rockefeller in New York, where the last two bloodiest riots have taken place, both blamed "organized revolutionaries" and "outside forces" for these explosions.

☆ ☆ ☆

Fred T. Wilkinson, director of the Missouri Department of Corrections, says "We're reaping a harvest of the cult of permissiveness." He declared disciplines and controls in communities have been destroyed.

This permissiveness now is having its impact on prisons as many militants have been sentenced to prison terms. With the aid of other radicals on the outside they are attempting to carry on the revolution inside prison walls.

Some black prisoners and members of other minority groups refuse to accept any responsibility for their crimes, claiming they are "political prisoners" of an oppressive, "white racist" system even though they were sent to prison for murder and other violent crimes.

☆ ☆ ☆

Thus, at Attica, we saw how the militants who led the revolt continued to escalate their demands until they finally held out for complete amnesty from criminal prosecution and transportation out of the United States to a "non-imperialist country."

New York Commissioner of Corrections Russell G. Oswald had already granted 28 of their 30 demands that included better food, improved education and recreational programs, better medical treatment and "complete religious freedom."

Prison authorities couldn't grant amnesty or transportation to a foreign country. Only blind revolutionaries would have failed to recognize this. Or they intended to foment a bloody crisis.

The prisoners were encouraged to persist in these impossible demands by Atty. William Kunstler and Black Panther leader Bobby Seale.

One of the black leaders brought in to try to negotiate a peaceful end to the rebellion, David Anderson, told the U.S. News & World Report that the talks deteriorated after the arrival of Kunstler on the scene, because he raised the convicts' hopes of amnesty.

Governor Rockefeller criticized both Kunstler and Seale. He said Seale "made a very impassioned speech to the prisoners that they should not agree, but hold out for amnesty."

To allow Kunstler or Seale or anyone from outside to enter into these negotiations was a mistake. It is never proper to negotiate with mutineers because their act of mutiny is in itself a crime, one that can't be tolerated.

☆ ☆ ☆

Authorities in the field say the best procedure is to move at once with the necessary force to put down any rebellion. Valid grievances and complaints should be corrected only after the rebellion is put down.

We should not, however, ignore the fact that major reforms are still needed in prisons all over the nation, including those in Missouri. A recent Globe-Democrat series pinpointed glaring deficiencies in the state's job training and rehabilitation program.

The Missouri Law Enforcement Assistance Council has just released a report also critical of the poor rehabilitation and job-training efforts in Missouri prisons.

Missouri must upgrade its prison rehabilitation programs and expand efforts to help inmates make a successful return to society. But it should never take action under threat of violence and revolt.

The lesson of Attica, San Quentin and other prisons is that discipline and control must be maintained. There can be no "deals" when convicts hold knives to the throats of hostages.

ST. LOUIS POST-DISPATCH
St. Louis, Mo., September 26, 1971

"To oppressed people all over the world. We got the solution. The solution is unity." —Attica prisoner.

"There's a stigma attached to Attica now because we blew off some niggers' heads, to be perfectly blunt about it."—Attica corrections counselor.

The outer limits of a prevalent fantasy among prison revolutionaries—their solidarity with a global uprising of the oppressed—is contained in the first quotation, words uttered during the height of the Attica rebellion. The brutal insensitivity of some prison authorities, which contributes to a growing sense of militancy in the nation's prisons, is characterized by the second. As Berkeley, Columbia and Kent State became bywords for excesses in student radicalism and official overreaction to protest, now the names of Attica, San Quentin and Soledad stand for a new mood among many of the nearly 00,000 Americans incarcerated in state and federal penitentiaries. The mood is often referred to as the politicalization of convicts, which carries a certain irony inasmuch as felons are legally disenfranchised. Most authorities fear it, since any unifying force among convicts is a threat to prison order; many prisoners find in it a deeply satisfying sense of self-respect and membership in a movement that transcends prison walls.

Here the causes of prisoner radicalism are easy enough to identify: as a group, inmates now are younger, more predominantly nonwhite (at Attica, 85 per cent are black or Puerto Rican) and more likely to have been exposed to militant ideologies. A significant number of prisoners are those serving time for draft evasion, violent antiwar protests and drug offenses, which they consider not offenses against society but political or moral acts.

But while prison populations have changed, the prisons themselves have not. They remain cattlepens with stone walls, superintended by a poorly paid and poorly educated guard force that is at least 98 per cent white. Despite increasing rehabilitative programs, the principal emphasis is still upon confinement and punishment. To be sure, prison radicalism is often a cruel and dangerous hoax. A black convicted of robbing another black is not exactly a classic political prisoner — although attempts may be made to convince him he is. He may indeed be oppressed but that oppression is legally sanctioned and society will use overwhelming and even unnecessary force to subdue him if he rebels against his condition.

But a political awareness among prisoners need not result in bloody confrontations if prison authorities are willing to cut through the rhetoric, the very excesses of which are desperate pleas to be heard, and concentrate on the substance. The final demand at Attica was amnesty but that was not what the insurrection was about. As they said over and over again, the prisoners wanted to be treated as men—to be able to communicate with friends and families, to be supervised by more members of their own race, to have a healthy diet, to enjoy religious freedom. Corrections Commissioner Oswald granted these demands, as he should have. They are not beyond the capacity of a civilized society to bestow, even on those who must be imprisoned.

The challenge is to channel the politicalization of prisoners into constructive and legitimate avenues, and not to attack it wherever it apears, for the latter can only add to the sense of hopelessness which more than anything destroys the lives of prisoners. There is no point to denying prisoners' grievances if to act on them would improve the penitentiary; action is evidence of wisdom, not of weakness. Widespread penal reform, of course, is imperative, and this might well include the establishment of an independent ombudsman for prisons, through which complaints could be acted upon or made public.

Most important, it is senseless, we think, to forever deprive a prisoner of his citizenship. When a prisoner has fulfilled his sentence—when his debt to society, if you will, has been paid in full—his right to vote should be restored. Perhaps more than anything this might persuade convicts that their interest in political affairs could ultimately find expression within the mainstream of society.

STATES REQUIRED TO AID PRISONERS IN PREPARING, FILING LEGAL BRIEFS

The Supreme Court April 27, 1977 ruled that states were required to provide their prison inmates with adequate legal assistance. The 6–3 decision was the result of a suit brought in federal court by three state prisoners in North Carolina. Justice Thurgood Marshall, author of the majority opinion, held that "the fundamental constitutional right of access to the courts requires prison authorities to assist inmates in the preparation and filing of meaningful legal papers." Chief Justice Warren E. Burger, who was joined in dissent by Justices William H. Rehnquist and Potter Stewart, said he could find no legal basis for requiring states to "fund costly law libraries for prison inmates" nor "the source of the 'right of access to the courts.'"

In a related development, a committee of the American Bar Association April 26 issued a 293-page report on the legal rights of prisoners. The report, published in the *American Criminal Law Review*, proposed that inmates should have the same legal rights as free citizens except where restrictions were needed to insure orderly incarceration or to protect the rights and safety of the prison community. Among the most controversial recommendations in the study was one to provide standard wages and employment benefits to working prisoners. However, the report also said that those same inmates should be made to pay taxes and to reimburse the state for room, board and other expenses. The committee was chaired by Prof. Herbert S. Miller of Georgetown University Law Center. The report was the result of 2-1/2 years of research. The ABA House of Delegates was not expected to consider the report until 1978.

AKRON BEACON JOURNAL
Akron, Ohio, May 2, 1977

THE U. S. SUPREME Court ruling that prisons must provide inmates with law libraries or legal assistance is so obviously just that Ohio has been doing it for nearly five years.

The University of Akron School of Law last year won an award from the National Student Bar Association for its Inmate Assistance Program — judged the best of its kind in the country. In the program, Akron U law students, closely supervised by faculty, visit inmates to help them with legal problems.

Even if the inmates at Mansfield, Marysville, Lucasville, Chillicothe, Marion and London didn't get the student assistance, they would have access to legal library resources through a decision made by the Department of Rehabilitation and Corrections under former Gov. Gilligan.

It's such a natural in the area of student motivation, it's a wonder the Supreme Court ever had to consider the issue. If study and learning are a form of rehabilitation of criminals, what better field to study than law — where such students already have had the benefit (in most cases, anyway) of experience, often the best teacher?

If they want to learn how to escape punishment, reduce the penalty or win a new trial, what more likely course would they pursue?

Then, finally, there's always the possibility that they'll come in contact with some of the field's experts. After all, Judge Otto Kerner, once governor of Illinois, spent some time in the barred classrooms, John Dean's been there, John Ehrlichman's in residence now, and there's still the possibility that John Mitchell will have a chance to conduct prison classes.

There have been cases where criminals with access to legal references have studied law so diligently they have brought about their own release in new trials.

With the incentive added by the Supreme Court to open wider this avenue of learning, it's conceivable that someday we'll find ourselves with a Lewisburg or Leavenworth School of Law whose graduates may give the Hahvawd law alumni a run for their money.

You can't beat that for rehabilitation.

The Cincinnati Post
Cincinnati, Ohio, May 13, 1977

A new Supreme Court ruling on the legal rights of prison inmates will make it harder than ever for federal judges to keep up with their caseloads.

The court ruled, 6 to 3, that prisons in North Carolina (and elsewhere) must provide inmates with law libraries or other legal aid so they can ask to have their convictions reviewed by a federal judge.

In addition to law libraries, Justice Thurgood Marshall suggested that some inmates be trained as paralegal assistants, that law students counsel the inmates or that lawyers and public defenders be made available on a full-time or part-time basis.

All of this may be constitutionally correct. In fact, it closely parallels the court's ruling in a California case six years ago. It even may be true—as one survey seemed to show—that prison law libraries are a good safety valve for inmate grievances.

But it's hard to be elated about a ruling that encourages jailhouse lawyers to further bombard the courts with mostly meaningless pleas and petitions.

Justice Potter Stewart of Cincinnati predicts—and he may be right—that most of the petitions will be "heavily larded with irrelevant legalisms" that look professional but really aren't.

In any event, the ruling is another reason why Congress should stop stalling and approve the 50 to 100 new federal judges we've been needing for the past five years. There's no doubt now they'll have plenty of work to do.

The Hartford Courant

Hartford, Conn., May 7, 1977

Those who are incensed at any show of leniency toward people behind bars are sure to dislike a decision by the Supreme Court of the United States. The high bench held the other day that prison officials must make available law libraries or adequate legal help to all inmates seeking freedom.

It is easy to view that ruling as but another avenue for the guilty to find release. Further reflection would show, however, the opinion provides a fair recourse for the innocent.

Recognizing the imperfections of any legal framework, six of the nine justices decided that prisoners' fundamental constitutional rights of admittance to the courts require "meaningful access" at government expense. While the case involved a state prison system, the ruling on a constitutional right applies to federal prisons, too.

Characteristically, there are reservations and dissent. The ruling does not mean that every prison must have a law library. But it tells authorities that every prisoner seeking a new trial must be allowed to use a prison-system library or, as an alternative, be given the help of a lawyer or a lawyer's aide. Though agreeing with the majority, Justice Lewis F. Powell Jr. emphasized the court was not deciding what kinds of prisoner claims the Constitution requires state or federal courts to hear. Chief Justice Burger, in speaking for the negative, questioned the consequences of forcing states to "foot the bill."

Those doubts and limitations are definitely valid. They do not destroy the argument, however, that justice sometimes fails the first time it's meted.

Richmond Times-Dispatch

Richmond, Va., July 5, 1977

Justifiably concerned over excessively harsh treatment of prisoners in some penal institutions, some "reformers" would like to see prison inmates enjoy most of the rights available to society on the other side of the prison walls. Fortunately, a majority of the members of the U.S. Supreme Court recognize the fallacy in that position.

Recently, in a 7-to-2 decision, the court upheld restrictions the North Carolina Department of Corrections had imposed on a prisoners' labor union. The department had prohibited prisoners from soliciting other inmates to join the union and had barred union meetings and also bulk mailings to prisoners concerning the union from outside sources.

A three-judge federal District Court had ruled for the union, but the Supreme Court majority, in an opinion by Justice William H. Rehnquist, declared that "the District Court, we believe, got off on the wrong foot in this case by not giving appropriate deference to the decisions of prison administrators and appropriate recognition to the peculiar and restrictive circumstances of penal confinement." Justice Rehnquist quoted from an earlier Supreme Court opinion which said that "lawful incarceration brings about the necessary withdrawal or limitation of many privileges and rights, a retraction justified by the considerations underlying our penal system."

The majority said that prison officials must be permitted to take reasonable steps to forestall trouble in prisons and that "the case of a prisoners' union, where the focus is on the presentation of grievances to, and encouragement of adversary relations with, institution officials surely would rank high on anyone's list of potential trouble spots."

Not surprisingly, the two most liberal members of the court, Justices Thurgood Marshall and William J. Brennan Jr., dissented, charging the majority with "wholesale abandonment of traditional principles of First Amendment analysis." They said even if the union did pose some threat, "the Constitution requires the state to bear certain risks to preserve our liberty."

That warped reasoning, as applied to the labor union issue, was effectively answered by Chief Justice Warren Burger in a separate concurring opinion:

"Prisons, by definition, are closed societies populated by individuals who have demonstrated their inability, or refusal, to conform their conduct to the norms demanded by a civilized society. Of necessity, rules far different than those imposed on society at large must prevail within prison walls. The federal courts, as we have often noted, are not equipped by experience or otherwise to 'second guess' the decisions of state legislatures and administrators in this sensitive area except in the most extraordinary circumstances."

The significance of the majority opinion in this case is not limited to the labor union issue, of course. Rather, the decision sets forth basic principles as to the limitation of prisoners' constitutional rights and as to the authority of penal officials to take reasonable action as a precaution against serious inmate-induced troubles. For those reasons, the decision should be welcomed by law-abiding society.

The Topeka Daily Capital

Topeka, Kans., April 30, 1977

The United States Supreme Court has ruled, 6-3, that prison officials must provide, at public expense, law libraries or adequate legal help to all inmates who plan appeals.

Justices who dissented from Thurgood Marshall's opinion, offered good arguments.

Justice Potter Stewart said placing lawbooks at the disposal of prisoners untrained in their use would "simply result in filing of pleadings heavily larded with irrelevant legalisms."

Chief Justice Warren Burger said requiring states to foot the bill for assuring access to court for prisoners "has far-reaching implications" which have not been thoroughly analyzed. It will add to state costs for libraries as well as for court expense.

Atty. Gen. Rufus Edmisten of North Carolina, where the case originated, said his state doesn't even provide libraries for its judges and prosecutors, and it is ironic it must now provide them for convicts. The ruling will merely stir up litigation when courts are overburdened with frivolous cases, he believes.

Most of those convicted deserve punishment because they are guilty. But a few may have been convicted unjustly, so the court majority believes aid should be given them in bringing appeals.

Certainly inmates have rights. So do crime's victims — those who are robbed or raped or swindled — or whose relatives have been murdered.

Let the courts be as solicitous of the rights of the law-abiding as they are of inmates. They should not put roadblocks in the way of speedy, fair trials. These are necessary to deter crime and protect the innocent.

The Kansas City Times

Kansas City, Mo., June 22, 1977

A basic constitutional right has been upheld by the U. S. Supreme Court in its decision on law libraries for prison inmates. Access to courts for appeals and other litigation can be assured, the court ruled, only if prisoners have adequate legal materials or assistance of persons trained in the law. In essence the court is saying that inmates, regardless of their citizenship status, should have an entrance to the justice system.

This ruling will not make life simpler for the administrations and staffs of state and federal correctional facilities. It is always possible that the jailhouse lawyers, inmates who specialize in writing petitions for themselves and other inmates, will have undue powers—and large supplies of cigarettes for their time and knowledge—over other inmates. Purchasing a law library and maintaining it can be an expensive and tedious task. If legal assistance is provided, a program must be developed to carry out the mission.

In Kansas the emphasis is on legal assistance and has been for five years. An organization called Legal Services for Prisoners, Inc., administers a program in which four lawyers work full time and another spends half his time on legal matters of prisoners. In the penitentiary at Lansing one of the lawyers supervises the work of 15 to 20 law students from the University of Kansas. A legal clinic at Washburn University and law students are involved with a project at state correctional facilities in the Topeka area. Other institutions also have similar programs.

The Kansas venture, started in 1972 with a grant from the Law Enforcement Assistance Administration, is funded with an appropriation through the state Supreme Court's aid-to-indigent defender program. In addition to supplying legal aid, the effort helps to cut down on the number of frivolous cases that have been filed in the past. In some instances legal agents for the inmates can take a complaint directly to the prison administration. If it can be resolved, the courts are spared the filing of a case. Because all inmates are not capable of effectively using a law library, the legal assistance is considered a more equitable approach.

Missouri's program lags behind. Although there are some law books at all institutions, only the penitentiary at Jefferson City and the medium-security facility at Moberly have collections that are considered to be sufficient. There is no formal legal assistance program for the entire system.

One state, Kansas, has proceeded on its own to provide legal assistance. Now Missouri will be forced to by this decision. It is another example of Missouri being prodded into doing something that should have been done because it was the right thing to do.

WINSTON-SALEM JOURNAL
Winston-Salem, N.C., April 30, 1977

The recent ruling by the U.S. Supreme Court in a North Carolina case that prison inmates have a constitutional right to "meaningful access" to the courts is one thing as a principle, but quite another as a practicality. It is possible to applaud the decision on the first score, and at the same time to be appalled at the implications of the second.

The court held by a 6-3 margin that states must make available legal assistance, through law libraries, lawyer services or other means, for prisoners seeking to overturn their convictions or to complain of prison conditions. What impact the decision will have for North Carolina is not yet clear, but it seems certain to add a burden of new costs to the underbudgeted prison system and to invite a further tide of litigation on flooded court dockets.

The proposition that the state should not by action or inaction, make it hard for prisoners to get into court is reasonable enough. How far the state is obligated to go in making it easy is the disturbing question. Correction Secretary Amos Reed raised the point in his reaction to the ruling. As a penologist, he said, he had no quarrel with the principle it laid down. Setting up a law library, he said, poses no serious problem. "My concern would be with how many, where and to what degree," Reed said. "If we're talking about a mobile library or a central location where prisoners could check out books or write to have questions answered, that's one thing. If we're required to establish legal libraries in 77 locations, then it would be unreasonable and prohibitive."

The court gave no certain guidance, but left states to work out their own legal access plans — which, naturally, would be subject to attack in court by dissatisfied prisoners. Justice Thurgood Marshall, author of the majority opinion, suggested several alternatives. They included law libraries in prisons, training inmates as para-legal assistants to work under the supervision of lawyers, volunteer programs using law students and lawyers, and hiring lawyers on a consulting or staff basis. "A legal access program need not include any particular element we have discussed, and we encourage local experimentation," Marshall wrote. However, he added that any plan would have to be "evaluated as a whole to ascertain its compliance with constitutional standards."

The case came to the Supreme Court on the appeal by the State of North Carolina from a district court decision in 1975 which required the establishment of seven law libraries within the prison system. That same year, the legislature refused the request of the Department of Correction for $60,000 to comply with the court order.

In disposing of the appeal, the Supreme Court affirmed and reinforced a 1971 ruling in a California case, which North Carolina had asked it to overturn. Separate dissents were filed by Chief Justice Warren E. Burger and Justices Potter Stewart and William H. Rehnquist. Warren said the only burden placed on a state should be negative; that is, to refrain from actions inhibiting prisoners from the exercise of their rights.

Atty. Gen. Rufus Edmisten said the decision threatens to clog courts with frivolous cases and to cost the states millions of dollars. "North Carolina does not provide state-supported libraries even for its judges and prosecutors," he said. "I find it a bit ironic that now North Carolina has to provide such libraries for convicted criminals."

Many Tar Heels will share the puzzlement. Legal access for prisoners is a fine principle. It should not be followed to the blind extreme of requiring the state to give more assistance to persons convicted and sent to prison than it provides for law-abiding citizens on the outside.

ARKANSAS DEMOCRAT
Little Rock, Ark., May 3, 1977

The Supreme Court has ruled and ruled rightly that a prisoner who wants to challenge his conviction from his cell must not be denied law books or voluntary help from lawyers in preparing his appeal. "Access to the courts" is the reasoning behind the ruling that affirms this constitutional right.

It's a way of saying that the law is not infallible, that justice can err — and that no one should be shut off from proving it erred by rulings that his appeal comes too late. We have seen too many cases of injustice — men cleared after years in prison — to believe that trials and appeals say the last word for justice.

The states, of course, don't like the cost of providing prisoners legal study materials and lawbooks. And prison administrators aren't fond of "jailhouse" lawyers, who give them disciplinary problems. But the possibility of justice denied overrides such objections.

True, there are a great many prison appeals. Chief Justice Warren Earl Burger says they burden the courts, which are not in need of any new business. We hear, moreover, that too many pleas for habeas corpus are granted on light grounds and that most prisoners who win another round in court by such means merely return to their cells. Former Atty. Gen. John Mitchell even once argued that writs should be shut off because justice should have a final stopping point. He might not argue that now.

But the poorest argument offered by any of the dissenters against the new ruling came from Justice Potter Stewart, who said that letting prisoners work up their own appeals would result in "the filing of pleadings heavily larded with irrelevant legalisms."

No doubt. It is good that the judge recognizes that there are such things. But many briefs filed by lawyers and quite a few decisions handed down by courts are open to the same charge. The public feeling is that the law itself is burdened with too much of the same. So it is hardly surprising that a "jailhouse lawyer," taking lawbooks for his text, might try to follow what he thinks is the proper form in such matters.

But however he phrases his appeal, the right to make it is more important than any of the objections brought against his doing so. Justice shouldn't be a matter of a final shutting of both prison and courtroom doors once regular court process is carried out.

The Virginian-Pilot
Norfolk, Va., April 29, 1977

Jailhouse lawyers are a different breed from Gary Mark Gilmore, who pleaded for a chance to stand in front of a Utah firing squad. Or Wayne Ritter and John Evans III, who insisted on being sentenced to the electric chair for killing a pawnbroker and were accommodated this week by an Alabama jury. Escape from prison by legal means is a more usual—and understandable—urge for them.

There must be some behind bars who are innocent. They are outnumbered by thousands who did it but don't want to pay, if a fiddle can be found to get them out of their fix. The U.S. Supreme Court brought such dreams of freedom closer to reality this week with a 6-3 decision that will require state and Federal penal systems to provide access to legal research, or to trained legal help, for convicts hoping to law their way out.

Justice Thurgood Marshall, writing for the majority, said that "the fundamental constitutional right of access to the courts requires prison authorities to assist inmates in the preparation and filing of meaningful legal papers." If it borders on incompetence for a lawyer to file pleadings without research, he reasoned, then it is incumbent on jailhouse lawyers helping themselves or fellow inmates to have some expertise in law. That would require access to a legal library, or the equivalent in licensed lawyer help. While the expense of such services to the states may be great, Justice Marshall insisted there is no way to reckon the cost of protecting a constitutional right. He got concurrence from Justices Harry A. Blackmun, William J. Brennan Jr., Lewis F. Powell Jr., John Paul Stevens, and Byron R. White.

The dissenters—Chief Justice Warren E. Burger, Justice William H. Rehnquist, who wrote the minority opinion, and Justice Potter Stewart—feared the high cost of the new requirement and other unanticipated consequences. Certainly a presumable flood of pleadings would mean a lot more pseudolegal detritus for courts to winnow. It also could—and likely will—mean a rising tide of paperwork from prisoners for the courts to cope with. That is a prospect to unsettle Chief Justice Burger, who has complained often of the judiciary's mounting workload.

The majority ruling mingled liberals and strict constructionists in one of a series of decisions solicitous of prisoners' rights. Federal courts of late have been cracking down on state prisons, largely in the South, to require them to provide humane living conditions. And if distinctions between privileges accorded felons and citizens seem to be dimming now, the possibilities of further erosion have hardly been exhausted: a study committee of the conservative American Bar Association has concluded that convicts ought to have the same rights as free citizens, except as regards confinement and the demands of public safety.

North Carolina, where the case originated on three convicts' complaint of inadequate research material to nourish their appeals, may be saddled by the decision with what its prisons director fears will be an "unreasonable and prohibitive" cost of compliance. The state has 13,000 inmates scattered among 77 prisons in 67 counties but only one prison law library and no prison legal-aid system. North Carolina has proposed to set up seven major libraries plus branches, transporting prisoners to them for research. Whether that solution will be adequate is uncertain.

More calculable is the benefit of the new ruling to convicts. Many may be able to sift the nugget of reversal from tons of legal tailings to which they now will have access. But others may mine for years and miss paydirt. Caryl Chessman, with his handhewn writs and books about his legal fight, managed to stave off California's electric chair for 13 years. Eventually, though, he exhausted the bag of tricks and the executioner had his day. That's the sobering thought for jailhouse lawyers: the paper chase doesn't invariably lead over the wall.

Rehabilitation and Parole: Reform or reinforcement?

Interconnected with the issue of prison overcrowding is parole. Without the use of parole, prisons would be even more overcrowded because long sentences would have to be completely served before release. Parole systems vary throughout the country. In New Hampshire and Washington practically every convict leaves prison before completing his sentence; in Oklahoma, Wyoming and South Dakota only 20% do.[1]

Parole has been extensively used in this country since the 1930s. Its origins date back to the 1830s, when Alexander Maconochie, the English administrator of a prison on Norfolk Island (off Australia), established the principle of tickets-of-leave.[2] Tickets-of-leave, the first attempt to use stages of prison discipline to introduce periods of freedom, allowed convicts to leave the prison walls prior to their release. However, since Manochie believed that once a convict had finally completed his sentence he should not be subject to any special restraints, it is likely he would take exception to parole as we know it today.[3]

When a prisoner is paroled, he is subject to a wide range of intrusions on his personal life. Parole is considered to be an extension of prison: a prison without walls. Parolees must report regularly to a parole officer and must consent to the right of the officer to visit and search him at anytime. The parole officer often must be consulted if the parolee wishes to move, change his job or even obtain a drivers license. Parolees are frequently prohibited from patronizing bars, socializing with people who have criminal records or engaging in any activity that may lead the parolee "to lapse into criminal ways."[4]

The parole officer's police function, necessary to enforce the plethora of behavioral rules, must also be shared with his role as a social worker. But for understandable reasons, the officer's duty to report infractions to the parole board makes it difficult for parolees to confide in him.

The parolee receives few social benefits upon release, apart from having a parole officer. In New York, upon release from prison, an inmate receives only $40, a suit and the name and address of a parole officer to whom he must report within 24 hours. Parolees are not eligible for unemployment, public housing or any special loans. Parole officers discourage parolees from applying for public relief benefits, since parole is not a form of self-support.[5]

A substantial number of parolees are returned to prison before their parole period is completed. In Sweden, when a parolee violates the rules he is given three or four reprieves before being returned to jail.[6] In the United States, however, a single violation of the regulations usually results in a revocation of parole status. Until recently, parole officers and boards had wide latitude in deciding when to revoke parole.

Now, pursuant to the Supreme Court decision of *Morrissey v. Brewer,* parole boards are constitutionally obligated to operate within limited due process guidelines in reaching their determination to return the parolee to custody.[7] No longer can a parole officer who made the decision to re-arrest the parolee preside as the hearing officer. Though a hearing body need not be composed of judicial officers or lawyers, it must be "neutral and detached." The hearing must be held within a reasonable time after the parolee is deprived of his freedom. The hearing officer must find good cause if he denies the right to confront and cross-examine witnesses. Finally, a written statement must be submitted reciting the factual conclusions and the reasons for denying parole.

The failure of the Court to specify if the right to counsel attaches in a parole revocation hearing was remedied the following year in *Gagnon v. Scarpelli.*[8] The Court held that the right to counsel must be determined on a case by case basis. The right to counsel would be triggered if the probationer or parolee had difficulty in presenting his version of the disputed facts without confrontation of witnesses or the presentation of complicated documentary evidence; or if counsel was requested and there were a timely claim of innocence; or, if the facts were clear or uncontested, there were substantial grounds for justification or mitigation. If the hearing body does deny counsel, the grounds must be stated for the record.

The recognition of certain due process rights in parole revocation hearings has not been extended to the hearing which determines the right to parole in the first place. The courts, however, have ordered that a meaningful hearing should be held prior to the expiration of that portion of the sentence required for parole eligibility.[9] This period is usually a third of the sentence, and two-thirds of the sentence in serious crimes.

The absence of any standards or criteria in parole hearings was a cause of the prison uprising at Attica State Prison in New York.

"Inmates' criticisms were echoed by many parole officers and corrections personnel, who agreed that the operation of the parole system was a primary source of tension and bitterness within the walls."[10]

Because of the sentencing structure, parole is viewed as an integral part of the prison sentence. Most sentences today are not fixed as to an exact period of incarceration. They are indeterminate sentences that allow great flexibility to prison and parole authorities in determining the length of imprisonment within the set maximum and minimum terms prescribed by the sentencing judge. Though a general rule is hard to establish because of arbitrary procedures and differences from state to state, it is not uncommon for a prisoner to be released after a third of the maximum term is served. A defendant's decision to plead guilty is often based upon this expectation. Prosecutors, in turn, take early parole release into consideration when deciding what crime to charge the defendant with, in order to assure that the defendant will spend the desired period in prison.

The indeterminate sentence permits the parole board to determine when the prisoner is prepared for release, based upon his rehabilitation in prison rather than upon the expiration of a fixed and definite sentence. The logic of the indeterminate sentence is the philosophy of a prison as a place for treatment and cure, not punishment.

However, prisons often do not provide a method of rehabilitation. This was recognized at Attica State Prison.

"There was no meaningful programming, employment training, psychological help or drug rehabilitation; and there were no real efforts to prepare inmates for society. If inmates were rehabilitated it was not because of Attica but in spite of it."

Even the decision to grant parole suffers from the absence of a determined commitment of resources. A study of parole in New York state revealed that the average parole interview lasted 12 minutes, but none was more than 25 minutes long.[12] In this time period the parole board has to decide if there is a "reasonable probability that he [the prisoner] will live and remain at liberty without violating the law and that his release is not incompatible with the welfare of society."[13]

The parole board is supposed to base its finding upon the following criteria: the inmate's psychological condition; his past record and present offense; his adjustment in prison; his past parole record; and his plans for the future in terms of family, a job and housing. The report on New York parole found that there was no empirical evidence that any of these criteria are reliable indications of whether an inmate will commit another crime or how serious a crime he might commit.[14] In fact, a comparison of those inmates released on parole and those released on conditional release (reduced sentences for good time, usually two-thirds of the maximum) shows no significant difference in return rates.[15] But the present dilemma of devising an adequate risk assessment device for parole applicants pales before the fundamental dilemma of whether the concept of rehabilitation has any basis in fact.

Though a small minority hold otherwise,[16] a majority of analysts believe that there is no evidence that any programs sponsored in prison effect behavior after release.[17] A survey of all the studies of rehabilitation programs undertaken in the United States between 1945 and 1967 revealed that "the present array of correctional treatment has no appreciable effect, positive or negative, on the rates of recidivism of convicted offenders."[18]

If prison does not contribute to reform it is not surprising that a study of the California Correctional System, considered to be the most advanced in penology, revealed that the longer a person is imprisoned, the more he will deteriorate and the greater the likelihood of recidivism.[19]

The reaction of politicians to the growing consensus has been uneven. There has been a steady movement toward abolishing parole and instead allow judges to reconsider sentences. Maine accomplished this in the 1977 legislative term. Attorney General Griffin Bell is also in favor of eventually abolishing parole. The proposed federal criminal codification law reduces the scope of parole considerably. Prison administrators, however, warn that without the promise of parole there will be fewer methods to maintain order among prisoners. They also fear even more over-crowding.[20]

Halfway Houses

Halfway houses, which date back to the 1830's with two residences for female ex-inmates, have been regarded as an alternative to prison and an improvement upon parole. They are also widely used in juvenile delinquency programs to enable the offending youth to remain in his neighborhood in a supervised setting. Federal support for the concept first occurred in 1962 with a grant from the National Institute of Mental Health, providing for the creation of ex-offender houses. Halfway houses can be residential programs, either 24-hours or just daytime, where people released on parole may attend. Halfway houses are also employed as alternatives to prisons and court process; prosecutions are dropped in return for entering a program.

The theory, as outlined in the United States President's Commission on Law Enforcement and the Administration of Justice, is that it should minimize the disruption of ties between the offender and the community or structure a return process to recultivate such ties.[21] This formulation would be achieved by providing employment, education and nourishing family connections. Certain parole boards have mandated that parolees enroll in these programs.

The two criteria in evaluating correctional programs have been cost and recidivism rates. On both counts the results are unclear. Several researchers insist that it is 30% less costly than prison.[22] Other studies indicate that a well-funded halfway house may be cheaper than maximum security but not normal penitentiaries.[23] As to recidivism, the results are subject to interpretation. Studies usually demonstrate lower recidivism rates, but this may be attributed to the fact that those who volunteer or are selected for halfway houses are just better risks in the first place.[24]

But those who view alternatives to prison as a goal in itself and are less concerned by cost-effectiveness arguments believe halfway houses are an important step forward.

"It appears that their more civilized and humane atmosphere and programs must be less destructive of the personalities sent there than the institutional experience, however difficult it may be to measure the difference."[25]

1. David J. Rothman, "History of Prisons, Asylums and Other Decaying Institutions," in *Prisoners' Rights Sourcebook,* ed. by Marilyn G. Haft & Michelle G. Hermann (New York: Clark Boardman, 1973) p. 11.
2. Alexander Maconochie, *General Views Regarding the Social System of Convict Management* (1839).
3. Stephen White, "Alexander Maconochie and the Development of Parole," 67 *Journal of Criminal Law & Criminology* 72, 88 (1976).
4. New York State Corrections Law S216.
5. "Report on N.Y. Parole: A Summary," 11 *Criminal Law Bulletin* 273, 289 (1975). For a full explication of the study see, *Prison Without Walls: Report on N.Y. Parole* (New York: Praeger, 1975).
6. David J. Rothman, *supra* at p. 18.
7. *Morrisey v. Brewer,* 408 U.S. 471 (1972).
8. *Gagnon v. Scarpelli,* 411 U.S. 778 (1973).
9. *Garafola v. Benson,* 505 F.2d 1212 (7th Cir. 1971).
10. *Attica: The Official Report of the N.Y.S. Special Commission on Attica* (New York: Bantam, 1972). p. 93.
11. *Attica, supra,* p. 21.
12. "Report on New York Parole," *supra,* p. 285.
13. New York State Correction Law S213.
14. "Report on New York Parole," *supra,* p. 287.
15. *Ibid.,* p. 288.
16. Daniel Glaser, *The Effectiveness of a Prison and Parole System* (Indianapolis: Bobbs-Merrill, 1969).
17. Robert Martinson, "What Works: Questions and Answers About Prison Reform," 35 *The Public Interest* 22 (1974).
18. Robert Martinson, "The Paradox of Prison Reform," *The New Republic,* April 8, 1972 p. 14.
19. James Robinson & Gerald Smith, "The Effectiveness of Correctional Programs," 17 *Crime & Delinquency* 67 (1971).
20. Edgar May, "Official Fear Long Flat Terms," *Corrections Magazine,* September, 1977 p. 43.
21. *Task Force Report: Corrections. U.S. Presidents Commission on Law Enforcement & the Administration of Justice* (Washington, D.C.: Gov't Printing Office, 1967) p. 105.
22. Ronald Goldfarb & Linda Singer, *After Conviction* (New York: Simon & Schuster, 1973).
23. T. Grygier, B. Nease & C. Anderson, "An Exploratory Study of Halfway Houses," 16 *Crime & Delinquency* 280 (1970).
24. James A. Beha, "Halfway Houses in Adult Corrections," 11 *Criminal Law Bulletin* 434, 465 (1975).
25. Ronald Goldfarb, *supra* at p. 587.

THE MILWAUKEE JOURNAL
Milwaukee, Wisc., December 18, 1977

Behind Bars — Why and How Long?

There is deep discontent over the American way of sentencing people to prison, and of returning them to society again on parole. Four states already have sharply changed their sentencing systems. Wisconsin is contemplating a similar change. So is Congress, at the federal level.

We see flaws in the present system, and merit to some of the changes. We also see a danger of the penal pendulum swinging too fast, too far — away from the ideal of prisoner rehabilitation and toward pure punishment.

Under attack is "indeterminate" sentencing, introduced early in this century on the theory that offenders can be rehabilitated in prison. Judges have wide discretion in setting sentences. (In Wisconsin, for instance, a judge may sentence a burglar to "not more than 10 years.") But the time actually *served* in prison is determined by a parole board that (in theory) releases the prisoner once it feels his rehabilitation is achieved.

What happens, in fact, is that sentencing responsibility is raggedly divided between judge and parole board. As one critic put it, "Offenders are sentenced by a chaotically irrational decision making system (if it is a system) and the sentences then are reduced (or not reduced) by another equally erratic process, parole release."

Liberals point with horror to people locked up for years on minor offenses (such as possession of marijuana). Conservatives are outraged by cases of murderers or armed robbers turned loose after short sentences. Both concerns are valid.

Maine, California, Indiana and Illinois now have moved toward variations of "determinate" sentences, in which judges set prison terms — within certain legislated guidelines that consider the type of offense and the defendant's record. Parole is eliminated. When the judge says 10 years, that's what you get, minus time off for good behavior.

Similarly, a bill in the Wisconsin Legislature proposes setting "base sentences" for different crimes. Judges could adjust the term up or down, within limits, depending on circumstances. Again, parole would be eliminated, although the judge in most cases could put the defendant on probation.

There is merit in letting criminals know that sentences largely mean what they say. Yet there is also value in retaining some flexibility, in remembering that criminals may be capable of turning themselves around. Thus we're more comfortable with the approaches of the federal proposal, part of the criminal code reform bill now in the US Senate.

Instead of setting arbitrary sentencing parameters, the measure would form a federal commission to establish rather tight guidelines for sentencing. A judge could ignore these limits, but if he gave less than the recommended minimum, the prosecution could appeal to a higher court. If he exceeded the limit, the defense could appeal.

The Senate bill puts new limits on parole but, happily, doesn't scrap it. This gives at least a slight nod to that elusive goal, rehabilitation. And why not try once again to improve and refine rehabilitation in prison, and parole afterwards?

Without the parole option, prisoners would have even less incentive to straighten themselves out — and, surely, some are capable of pulling themselves out of the muck. Why prolong imprisonment if they no longer endanger society? That's expensive vengeance.

States, Wisconsin included, might copy the carefully structured point system designed by the US Parole Commission in 1974. Based on details of the prisoner's offense and background, it makes parole decisions far more rational and predictable.

But where the present parole system really stumbles is back home, in the community, after the prisoner's release. Consider one federal study. During a recent year, it found, federal parole officers devoted an average of 6.4 hours a year, or 32 minutes a month, or 7 minutes a week to *each* offender in their charge.

The parole supervision system is overwhelmed, undermanned and badly designed. The typical parole officer, federal or state, is forced to serve in the impossible dual role of policeman and social worker. Rubbed raw by prison, resentful, disoriented, the released offender needs help — crisis counseling, job finding, emergency credit, temporary housing, psychiatric therapy. Whatever is done about the parole officer system, more federal and state funds should be channeled into postrelease assistance.

This approach, along with more firmly guided sentencing and parole releases, might restore many more ex-cons to a productive place in society.

OKLAHOMA CITY TIMES
Oklahoma City, Okla., June 21, 1977

A blow to deterrence

EARLY efforts to move the state toward compliance with a federal court order to reduce prison populations show the depth of the treacherous quagmire it has produced.

Last week the legislature was urged to bar the imprisonment of "nonviolent" criminals and those sentenced to serve two years or less. Now the state Pardon and Parole Board has adopted a more liberal stance on releases. It will recommend paroles two to four months early for first termers and nonviolent offenders with short criminal backgrounds.

Ironically, in a monumental act of poor timing, the board included in the 81 inmates recommended for clemency Sunday two convicted slayers and four armed robbers serving lengthy sentences.

Dist. Atty. Andrew M. Coats of Oklahoma County is understandably alarmed by the loosening of the parole board's attitude. He fears a rise in burglaries, rapes and car thefts and predicts most of the convicts released early will be back in prison in three to five years.

The point the prosecutor correctly makes is that a climate is being developed that will almost entirely eliminate the crime-deterrence factor. It has already been seriously weakened in recent years by court rulings tying the hands of law enforcement officers.

If criminals know they are likely —at worst—to serve only a short time before they are paroled, they'll consider their ill-gotten gain from unlawful activities worth the risk of getting caught. Punishment is—or should be—just as much a part of the criminal justice system as is rehabilitation of the offender. And punishment without doing time behind bars is not much punishment at all in a majority of cases.

Perpetrators of so-called nonviolent crimes deserve punishment just as surely as do those whose offenses involve bodily injury. Their victims often suffer monetary losses and mental anguish for which there can never be adequate compensation.

It's important to note, too, that the "first termer" label applies to those who have been convicted for the first time. Many of them have been arrested and charged on previous occasions but, for various reasons, a conviction could never be obtained.

Despite the ruling of U. S. Dist. Judge Luther Bohanon, state prosecutors will continue trying criminal cases and getting convictions and the courts will keep sentencing convicts to prison. Each district attorney will think the convicts in his cases deserve incarceration and will resent attempts to keep them out of prison. By the same token, the DAs who obtained the convictions of the people already in prison will think it's important they serve their time.

Carefully supervised probation may be a preferred and logical alternative to imprisonment in certain criminal cases. But it's sheer folly to set it in statutory concrete. It's just as damaging to the deterrence of crime to let offenders know they can expect early release on their prison sentences.

Herald ✦ News
Fall River, Mass., June 9, 1977

Parole System

Senator Kennedy has proposed that the parole system be eliminated in terms of federal offenses in favor of a fixed sentence. The Massachusetts senator points out that the present parole system inevitably creates sentence disparity, and that the effect of this disparity "on our criminal justice system is devastating. Certainty of punishment is a joke."

The senator is right, and it is likely that the new criminal code bill will incorporate his proposal. Once the parole system is eliminated in terms of federal offenses, it is almost certain to be eliminated in state prisons as well. This is all part of the process of stiffening and strengthening the criminal code in an effort to cope with the spread of crime throughout the country.

The parole system was not bad in concept, but as it has turned out, it has far too often become a means for criminals to avoid the consequences of their misdeeds. In operation it has, as Senator Kennedy indicates, become a means of creating real injustices. Often, too, persons are paroled who should not be, and who abuse the confidence the state has placed in them by committing fresh crimes.

Perhaps the parole system, under some other form, will be more usable in the future than it is at present. Right now there seems to be no way of eliminating disparities in sentencing except by phasing it out.

Arkansas Gazette.
Little Rock, Ark., February 7, 1977

Prison and Parole: The Price

This General Assembly, with the backing of Governor Pryor, seems determined to greatly aggravate the conditions of overcrowding in the state prisons that the federal courts say they just won't allow.

Earlier in the session, the legislature passed, and Mr. Pryor signed, a measure that becomes Act 93 of 1977. It is worded to keep offenders in prison longer than is usually the case under the existing parole laws. Another measure of the same genre (HB 14) is still under consideration. It would extend the time until perpetrators of certain crimes would be eligible for parole.

State Correction Department officials have made some projections about the prison population that are not in the least reassuring, but the figures should be emphasized for the Assembly and the governor. With both Act 93 and HB 14 in the statutes, projections indicate that the male inmate population would increase from 2,485 in 1977 to 4,088 in 1980. The estimated cost of construction for housing this prison population increase, using costs not adjusted to likely inflation, would be $37 million, to be spent over the next four years. Mr. Pryor, apparently by way of playing down the harsh dollar numbers, says the figure is based on doing the work "all at one time." His concern for the federal court requirements sound precariously self-assured.

It is true that the legislature has not yet taken up the hard questions of financing, but when it does there is strong likelihood that somebody is going to have to find more money than the governor and Assembly have been expecting. Indeed, we already know that even without Act 93 and HB 14, using provisions of the existing laws, the prison system is likely to meet its inmate population limit in August. The limit is the level that is acceptable to the federal courts, which have the Correction Department under order not to allow the institutions to become overcrowded.

Money. This is what Arkansas's prison situation usually gets back around to. This is what adequate support for the entire sweep of state services always engages first and foremost. All this, alas, right at a time when Governor Pryor is trying to get enacted various provisions of his heralded "home rule" plan that in part would *reduce* the state income tax and make a shambles of the existing orderly system of state finance. There is one sensitive and sensible way to address such problems as those posed by the critical space needs in the prisons and that could be found in the imposition of a fourth cent of sales tax at the state level, where such taxation belongs.

If we in Arkansas are going to reshape our parole laws to keep more inmates in prison for longer periods—a concept that may not necessarily be bad in itself—then we have to be willing to pay the price in terms of revenue and taxation. It means, immediately, an additional $10 million to $12 million, at least, just to build and staff a new prison at Tucker Intermediate Reformatory over the next two years. And it means, all told over the next four years, an expenditure of at least $37 million.

Legislators have the choice of taking the money from the schools and colleges and other worthy wards of the state coffers—a wholly unacceptable alternative—or finding additional revenues to build housing at the prisons. Or, we suppose, Arkansas can simply start turning convicted felons loose or storing them temporarily in the county jails. The governor and the legislature have clear choices and their responsibilities are unavoidable.

ARKANSAS DEMOCRAT
Little Rock, Ark., January 23, 1977

Crime consensus

The Arkansas House has voted "ninety to nothing" to toughen state parole laws. A vote like that can only mean that the voice of the people was echoing in the legislative chamber Wednesday.

Last year's long debate on crime and punishment seems to have crystallized both the public and legislative determination to crack down on repeat offenders.

We'd date the consensus back to last June when Rep. Bobby Glover of Carlisle took this identical bill before the Legislative Council. Let the first offender serve his usual one-third-of-sentence, Glover said, but after that — zap: half time for second offenders, three-fourths time for three timers and no parole at all for four-time losers, meaning full time served.

Glover had wanted something even tougher — no prisoner "good time" at all; full sentences for everybody. Pulaski Prosecutor Lee A. Munson backed Glover. But Glover gave up on elimination of good time when prison administrators declared that eliminating all early release meant disciplinary ruin. It was also plain that such a policy would run the cost in new prison space off the graph.

The Council's reaction to the revised Glover plan amounted to a love feast. Sen. Max Howell, Munson, then Corrections Commissioner Terrell Don Hutto, and last but not least Governor Pryor all gave their assent.

Glover now puts Hutto's price-tag on the new space needed to keep repeat offenders in prison longer — $9 million. That doesn't include the $750,000 a year that Hutto said would be needed for operation and maintenance, nor does it take in the $8 million in new space he said we'd need by 1980 to absorb the normal growth in the prison population. So the prison bill is bigger than it looks.

Hopefully, of course, tougher prison-time policies could reduce that growth figure through deterrence; almost half our criminals are repeaters. But taken together, tightened parole laws and rising inmate counts could in the next few years run the cost of new prison space close to $20 million. And that doesn't take in the $25 million Pryor thinks may be needed to satisfy federal demands for upgraded prison facilities.

Looked at that way, the costs of building new and upgrading old prison space are daunting enough, but we can think about the added millions after we've tended to the first priority — getting the repeaters off the parole list and behind bars...

The Salt Lake Tribune
Salt Lake City, Utah, November 7, 1977
Swing Away From Parole

If the first comprehensive revision of the federal criminal code finally occurs next year the practice of paroling prisoners could become a thing of the past.

Maine and California have already abolished parole and the federal criminal code revision bill approved by the Senate Judiciary Committee Thursday would do the same except in a few special circumstances.

The bill would create a sentencing commission to establish narrow guidelines of prospective sentences, for example four to five years for certain crimes. The length of a prison term could, however, be increased or decreased in accordance with carefully defined factors such as whether it was a first offense or whether violence was used in commission of the crime.

Once sentenced there would be no possibility of parole as it is now used. The only reduction in sentence would be a 10 percent good behavior credit earned in prison.

In Utah, where the extensive power of the Board of Pardons is set forth in the state Constitution, parole is not likely to be abolished until experience elsewhere demonstrates impressive benefits from such action. But Utah would be affected where federal offenses are involved.

Although the fixed sentence-no parole approach is gaining favor in modern corrections thinking, the end result as far as the public is concerned will be little changed. Prisoners serving fixed but generally shorter terms will do about the same time as those sentenced to longer indeterminent terms but paroled when a minimum portion of the term has been served.

There is a difference, however. Advocates of the shorter, fixed sentence believe it promises more certain punishment for more criminals. Further, it would remove the flagrant disparity that now exists in sentencing even within the same judicial district. From the inmate's standpoint, it affords a definite release date in place of a probable date set in the future by a pardons or parole board.

In moving toward the fixed sentence-no parole concept the federal government and states which do likewise are taking a calculated risk. Mandatory sentences traditionally make it more difficult to obtain convictions. They virtually rule out consideration of most mitigating circumstances that normally are weighted by a sentencing judge.

Ideally, parole provides added protection to society by making it possible to phase an inmate back into the real world and supervise him or her for a period after release. It hasn't always worked out that way which is one reason for the swing back to fixed sentences.

Democrat Chronicle
Rochester, N.Y., June 1, 1977
Tossing people in prison isn't enough

AN EYE for an eye and a tooth for a tooth is the natural reaction of people hurt and harassed by violent crime. A man who takes a life should forfeit his own. So the thinking goes.

But even if it could be demonstrated that it would help, and we don't think it could be, the death penalty touches only the punitive aspects of the justice system.

Even shorter, sharper, faster sentencing, surely part of the solution, is apt to miss the boat if it is not accompanied by strong, equitable, efficient prison parole services.

Today, alas, the state Parole Board and the Division of Parole are appendages of the Department of Correctional Services. Their functions are too often either overlooked or relegated to a backwater.

Gov. Carey, in the program he has proposed to the legislature, would change this undesirable situation by setting up a separate Division of Parole in the executive department.

In addition, his bill would establish qualification standards for membership on the Parole Board, authorize the use of hearing officers for certain Parole Board functions and require written criteria for making parole determinations.

"This bill," Carey has said, "would abolish a system that is archaic and needlessly complex and rigid. The parole process must be modernized to enable it to work."

AT THE MOMENT, Parole Board members are too heavily burdened. With an increasing number of smaller, community-based correctional facilities being added to the existing big institutions, 12 board members must make most of the determinations on minimum periods of imprisonment, release and revocation.

"The establishment of the position of hearing officer," says Carey's message, "would relieve board members of their current hectic schedule, which all too often has resulted in inordinately brief parole interviews upon which parole decisions are based."

The use of professional hearing officers would, it's felt, permit a more complete study of inmates and would also free the Parole Board for a true policy-making role.

Clearly the parole system needs this kind of reform. Clearly it's going to call for more staff and more money.

For example, one of the bill's provisions would require that minimum periods of imprisonment be set within 120 days from the time a prisoner goes into an institution, instead of the present 10 months. Such a mandate could only be met by more staff.

IF THE LEGISLATURE is to act favorably, it must have the support of the public, and the public in turn must understand that it's not enough to put criminals in prison. Most of them will sooner or later go back into the community and it's important that they not be released prematurely to prey again or held so long that bitterness twists them hopelessly.

The kind of judgment needed to do the job well can't be as widely exercised as it should be under the present system. Hence the call for reform.

And it should be noted in conclusion that the existing system, outdated and inefficient though it is, has been given a boost in morale by the appointment of Edward R. Hammock as Parole Board chairman.

Hammock has been making a good impression as a straightshooter.

And as he pointed out on a visit to Rochester last week, it's vital that parole get out of the position of forever reacting to problems and establish a position of leadership.

Prisoner rights, as he noted, shouldn't have to be defined by the courts. They should be inherent in a well-functioning parole system.

The News and Courier
Charleston, S.C., December 6, 1977
Chances For Parole

Sentenced to life in prison, Milton Archie Harriott was advised by a circuit court judge at Manning of his right to appeal to the South Carolina Supreme Court. "No thanks, that's okay," Harriott was quoted as replying. "Everything's cool."

What precisely was defendant Harriott's crime, and why did he consider the situation "cool"?

Defendant Herriott, 28, was convicted of beating a 68-year-old man to death with a tire iron at a rest stop on Interstate 95 after their cars were involved in a minor accident. Police allege that after the fatal attack, Harriott smashed the window of another car, struck a 15-year-old girl, beat two other men, and rammed a state highway patrol car before he was shot by a Georgia sheriff who had gone to the aid of the victims.

It is safe to presume that Harriott figured things were "cool" because he was aware that he will be eligible for parole in 10 years.

Defendant Harriott was tried on but one charge. He must be presumed innocent until proven guilty of the other charges pending against him. His unruffled response, however, should convey to legislators the clear message that it is time again to think about rewriting the laws prescribing eligibility for parole of those convicted of callously taking the lives of others.

THE SUN
Baltimore, Md., July 2, 1977
Why Have Parole?

When the American Correctional Association sharply criticized the operation of Maryland's Division of Parole and Probation, Robert J. Lally, secretary of corrections, moved to reform the administration of the division. But, administrative chaos aside, there is a second approach to parole that state legislators might consider. That is its abolition.

There is growing support for that idea. Several U.S. senators have proposed legislation to do away with parole in the federal justice system. Recently Attorney General Griffin Bell endorsed abolition. Perhaps the most extensive of recent studies of federal sentencing, parole and corrections is one just concluded at Yale University. It says parole is no longer needed.

The arguments most often heard in favor of parole are (1) that it provides an incentive for the prisoner's rehabilitation, (2) that it facilitates prison discipline, (3) that it controls the size of prison populations and (4) that it rectifies unjust disparities in sentencing. But, many critics, including Dean Norval Morris of the University of Chicago Law School in a lecture at the University of Maryland Law School last fall, claim parole doesn't live up to its billing. They say, for example, that:

(1) Prisoners who volunteer for rehabilitative programs in order to be rehabilitated are more likely to benefit than those who volunteer just to get out of prison earlier; (2) time off a sentence for good behavior may be a good disciplinary device, but it is irrelevant to parole decision-making; (3) deciding when a prisoner has "paid his debt" on the basis of how many other individuals have committed crimes and been jailed is clearly unjust and illogical. As to (4), many parole boards do very well in minimizing the wide variations in sentences for the same crime. But there is a better way to do this—establishing inflexible standards for sentences and/or creating a commission to fix the sentence at the time of conviction.

The federal abolition proposal is part of a huge, complicated crime bill and may or may not become law soon. Regardless of what Congress does, the states, including Maryland, could be examining the question. Alternatives to parole are worth exploring. The idea of stiff sentences without possibility of parole appeals to many people. But any state legislature that abolishes parole in favor of a system requiring longer imprisonment for inmates must also provide sufficient prison facilities.

Roanoke Times & World-News
Roanoke, Va., June 22, 1977
Abolish Parole System

Serious proposals now made to abolish parole in the federal prison system should be taken seriously in Virginia. The reasoning is as good in one place as in another. Shorter sentences served certainly are a more equitable treatment and just as likely to produce rehabilitation as anything else.

James Q. Wilson, of Harvard, took note of a 1974 New York State study in his book, *Thinking About Crime* (Basic Books), writing: "For a four-year period, the percentage of prisoners returned to prison within one year was calculated for those who were granted parole and those who, by being denied parole, were required to serve their full sentence. Overall, there was no statistically significant difference...Clearly, the parole board was unable to guess who had been rehabilitated and who had not."

Common sense will serve as well as statistics. The really smart convict—the sex offender is a likely prospect for this—makes himself a model prisoner as soon as possible to get himself out as soon as possible. Some 1972 California studies (Wenk and Associates) found a tendency by authorities to *over-predict* violence by ex-offenders. The results "should give pause to any member of a parole board who has confidence in his capacities as a seer of future violent crime"—so wrote Norval Morris, of the University of Chicago, in his book, *the future of imprisonment* (Basic Books).

Dr. Morris' suggestion, made in 1974, was for prison authorities to fix the parole date when the prisoner arrives in prison. A better solution would be to junk the parole system completely and divert all the resources used to other purposes within the correctional system.

Abolition of parole would *not* mean abolition of educational and vocational programs within the prison, to be taken if the prisoner wants them. I would *not* mean firing the host of conscientious workers in parole frustrated by the size as well as the nature of the job. Their services are needed within the system and for those emerging from the institutions. Abolition of parole would *not* mean life without hope or incentive in a prison; time for good behavior would still be possible. Under the no-parole policy, sentences would be shorter and more uniform as prescribed by law.

Abolition of parole would mean the abolition of a system which prisoners view as capricious and unfair, which calls upon parole board members to exercise a capacity possessed by no people on earth, including priests and psychiatrists. It would release people and funds badly needed for educational programs and assistance to ex-convicts on the outside. It is time to get rid of what has proved to be an experimental and expensive dream.

HERALD-JOURNAL
Syracuse, N.Y., June 30, 1977
Parole is a failure

The concept of parole is outdated. It's a failure.

In a recent interview, U.S. Attorney General Griffin Bell said there have to be alternatives to the parole system.

New York State Correctional Services Commissioner Benjamin Ward testified at a U.S. Senate hearing in Washington that the parole system is a failure which should be abolished.

Not just in New York City, Chicago and Detroit — the big cities where crime runs rampant. The system has failed even in Upstate New York, where criminal activity is considerably less.

There are not enough parole officers to oversee the activities of the hundreds of parolees they are supposed to account for. The caseload is so heavy that literally thousands of parolees are unchecked.

And consider the problems of the 12-member Board of Parole, which has the responsibility of holding hearings and deciding who among the thousands of the state's prison inmates will become eligible for parole

— and when, and why.
* * *
In his Washington testimony, Commissioner Ward said:

"Parole was created on the twin theories that prisons could rehabilitate prisoners and that penal authorities could predict human behavior. Experience has demonstrated the fallibility of both theories.

"The combination of sentences doled out for similar offenses and the quixotic and often arbitrary character of parole decisions has undermined the rationality of the criminal justice system and greatly contributed to prison tensions."

Bell, Ward and others who know and understand the shortcomings of our present system have called for a new system of sentencing that would assure equal sentences for equal crimes, with early release based solely on good behavior in prison.

A program of rehabilitation for prisoners who want it would be made available.

This, too, is an idea whose time has come.

The Detroit News

Detroit, Mich., February 4, 1977

'Good-time' law needs revision

The Michigan Parole Board has been criticized so severely for alleged leniency toward criminals that it was properly labeled "a beleaguered body of decision makers" in the 1976 report of the Department of Corrections.

Fact: The parole board is merely following the law.

State law enacted in 1953 requires the parole board to reduce prison terms for "good time" and "special good time" ("warden's good time").

A prisoner, sentenced to a minimum five-year term, can be paroled after three years, six months and 18 days because of good time.

The problem that has led to the outcry against the parole board is serious: parolees committing felonies, including murder.

This has caused Brooks Patterson, Oakland County prosecutor, to open a petition drive get a constitutional amendment on the ballot in 1978. The amendment would require a convicted felon to serve at least "his minimum sentence" before becoming eligible for parole.

Patterson has an unfortunate penchant for going for "the gut," for relying more on emotion than reason. He has been attacking the parole board for "reckless policies" and callousness about releasing "dangerous felons."

The truth is that the parole board is made up of professionals, most of whom have 20 years in the corrections system. Board members take their jobs seriously. They are grieved when a parolee returns to violent crime.

We agree that the state board should toughen its parole decisions. It must be more exacting about its standards. But Patterson's proposal goes too far. It would deny the board the discretion and flexibility it must have.

Parole is essential. It is humane. It serves no good to keep people in jail after they have proved themselves ready for release. Besides, keeping prisoners unnecessarily is costly.

The law is wrong in forcing the parole board to rely more on "good time" rather than criminal records. Prisoners do their best to earn good time.

State law should be amended to consider the career-criminal aspect of parole. Prisoners with two or three felony convictions — obviously career criminals — should not be credited with good time.

Good-time provisions also put the parole board in a dilemma. If it follows the law, it is threatened with a suit from people like Patterson.

If it doesn't follow the good-time law because it feels that some prisoners are a bad risk to society, such prisoners sue because the board isn't following the law.

The parole board's new reliance on more "scientific predictive tools," enabling it better to determine high and low risks, should help.

But the best thing would be for the Legislature to rewrite the good-time law so that career criminals can't return to crime so speedily.

The Chattanooga Times

Chattanooga, Tenn., June 12, 1977

Phasing Out Parole

Atty. Gen. Griffin Bell made a good argument the other day in outlining the Carter Administration's proposal for abolition of parole for convicts as one of several major changes in federal criminal justice policy.

Releasing prisoners on parole does not rehabilitate them, the attorney general testified. Instead, he said, fixed sentences, altered after imposition only by time off for good behavior, would do more to deter crime and "make the system more rational in the eyes of the public."

Mr. Bell was testifying in support of Senate Bill 1437, the proposed recodification of federal criminal laws that has been introduced by an unlikely pair of senators, Edward Kennedy of Massachusetts and John McClellan of Arkansas. The bill is supported by a substantial number of liberal and conservative senators.

Significantly, these senators also support the administration's proposal for parole reform. The parole system has "lost respect," said one senator, and has "served its purpose," according to another.

That reform would fit in nicely with the Senate bill's proposal of firm sentencing guidelines for crimes to eliminate or greatly reduce dispairities in the punishment of prisoners convicted of similar offenses but in different parts of the country.

A key defect of the existing parole system is that it is subject to great abuse, primarily because most parole boards have shown they are unable to judge rehabilitation and to predict how a released prisoner will behave in society.

All of this is tied to the idea of replacing the present system of indeterminate sentences with determinate ones. The latter concept—now being implemented in criminal justice systems in Illinois, Maine and California—aims at reinforcing a prisoner's determination to exhibit good behavior during his stay behind bars in return for partial reduction in his sentence. The higher hope is that such good behavior will continue after the prisoner is released.

The goal is a worthy one. If abolishment of parole and the institution of determinate sentencing can bring it closer (it's understood there can be no guarantees), then affirmative Senate action is necessary.

THE SUN

Baltimore, Md., May 16, 1977

Incorrigibles: a Waste of Effort

New to the bench but not to criminal law proceedings, Judge Joseph H. H. Kaplan has given the new Baltimore grand jury more of a challenge than a charge: to find out how the rehabilitative programs in Maryland's correctional system might better be utilized. The Supreme Bench judge has said bluntly what others have soft-pedaled; namely, that some criminals are beyond social redemption and should be put away without having precious rehabilitation efforts wasted on them. He wants the retraining programs aimed at young, nonviolent prisoners who offer hope of being turned around.

Without necessarily disagreeing with Judge Kaplan, we wonder if criminal psychology is refined enough to separate the hopeless from the salvable, although in fact this is what the state Division of Correction tries to do with its overburdened classification system. Sometimes, contrary to past record, a prisoner becomes inspired and blossoms as an artist, accountant, novelist, even a White House nursemaid. And sometimes the seemingly model prisoner, once released, turns unexpectedly violent.

Yet Judge Kaplan in general terms has a valid point. With rehabilitation programs so scarce, it is a shame to have correctional efforts lost on those he brands as "factually outlaws, the enemies of society." For such persons, if they are clearly distinguishable, a penal warehouse could be appropriate, since the main purpose would be to safeguard society from their presence, not to expect miracles.

Maryland's greater shame, though, is that all of its penal institutions have become warehouses, so far behind needs has the correctional system fallen. Those prisoners who might benefit most from a well-directed correctional program are warehoused with the rest and hardened in their anti-social attitudes.

The kind of penal system Judge Kaplan seeks would be one with the physical capacity as well as the enlightenment to steer tractable offenders into training programs and community centers, and the incorrigibles into secure, long-term custody. A grand jury cannot bring this about, but in addressing the jury Judge Kaplan in effect addresses a wider audience of Marylanders who can influence state legislation and budgets. We hope they are listening.

The Salt Lake Tribune

Salt Lake City, Utah, June 17, 1977

Prisoner Rehabilitation Faulted But It Can't Be Abandoned

As with most other facets of the American lifestyle, fashions in care and treatment of prisoners change from time to time.

Earnest Dean Wright, veteran director of Utah's Division of Corrections, confirmed that prisoner rehabilitation is passe and that protection of society for protection's sake, is the latest mode.

Addressing a convention of assistant prison wardens, Mr. Wright said that corrections officials should discard the role of "rehabilitator" and become "protectors of society." Just 10 years ago the corrections task force of the President's Commission on Law Enforcement and the Administration of Justice endorsed rehabilitation of convicts as a major means of easing the nation's growing crime burden.

Rehabilitation's failure has been documented by numerous professional studies. But as late as 1973 a cabinet level federal commission's report once again roundly endorsed the rehabilitation concept, at least by implication. Belief in the possibility of reforming wayward individuals through isolation and religious instruction was what started prison construction in the early 19th Century.

Rehabilitation failed then. With some exceptions, it has failed since.

Some say rehabilitation never got a fair chance to show its stuff because the public was ever reluctant to spend tax money on lawbreakers. Others argue that it is simply unlikely that a felon, deep into criminal behavior and well past his or her formative years, can be turned about during confinement no matter how lavish the facilities.

Although it has failed generally, rehabilitation cannot be written off and abandoned. Even the most critical studies must concede that at least some criminals have been reclaimed for law-abiding society by positive efforts of enlightened penal institutions.

Rehabilitation has proven to be a false god. But that doesn't mean all its idols must be smashed forthwith.

Those relative few who seek to rebuild their lives behind prison walls should not be denied the opportunity just because most of their fellow inmates cannot or will not be helped.

As for the unmalleable mass of convicts society might as well face the disappointing fact that they will leave prison some day not much better, and probably worse, than when they entered.

Democrat and Chronicle

Rochester, N.Y., November 23, 1977

Give that second chance to ex-inmates

YES, the weather was bleak. And yes, the matter at hand wasn't particularly appealing.

All the same, a turnout of barely a score of people was a disappointing response to the 500 invitations that had been sent out.

But that's precisely the problem when it comes time to rehabilitate ex prison inmates — not many people are much interested.

What we're talking about here is the community-wide meeting that was called for the night of Nov. 16 at the Criminal Justice Center in old First Presbyterian Church on S. Plymouth Ave. to ease the way back for criminals who enter the community after serving their time.

In their newsletter announcing the meeting and in their comments at the meeting itself, John Ives, community coordinator for the Judicial Process Commission of Genesee Ecumenical Ministries, and John Walker, director of the Baden Street Drug Counseling Program, made these principal points:

• Of the 340 or so men and women who come into the community each year from the state prison system, at least 50 desperately need help.

• After years of making no decisions for themselves, they are released into the community "with $40, a new suit, and the cards all stacked against them."

• If these ex-offenders can't get help quickly, particularly a job, chances are that they'll go back to their old criminal ways within in a matter of days.

• Though it's tough to find jobs when there aren't enough even for those who aren't felons, the fact remains that it costs $15,000 a year to keep a person in prison.

• Because they can't get assurances of work or of places to stay, many prisoners are kept in prison up to four months beyond the time they might have been released.

• The most urgent need in Rochester is for a halfway house that could ultimately erect an umbrella of services for ex-offenders.

THOUGH the situation is not a good one, it's by no means without hope.

There's at least a possibility that a halfway house might be established in Hanover Houses.

Baden Street Settlement is anxious to give support.

The parole department is giving strong counsel and encouragement.

But beyond this, as John Walker emphasized at the meeting, there's a need for community sanction.

In other words, Rochester must make up its mind that giving ex-offenders a chance to go straight is worth the effort.

Is there really any alternative?

THE COMMERCIAL APPEAL
Memphis, Tenn., November 26, 1977
Give It A Chance

CONGRESS' EFFORT to codify federal criminal laws should help provide fairer sentencing of prisoners than the current statutes allow. But why should pending legislation give such low priority to rehabilitating those convicted of crimes when rehabilitation has yet to receive a fair try?

How can prisoners expect any kind of rehabilitation in mammoth and impersonal federal facilities such as San Quentin, Leavenworth or Lewisburg? They are crime schools for the untutored, not classrooms for correction. How can individuals be reclaimed when the prisoners themselves run our prisons through force, drugs and the authorities' abdication? How can teaching criminals to make license plates or to repair manual typewriters hope to prepare them to be useful, productive citizens upon release?

"Rehabilitation simply has not been working," according to Memphis' U.S. attorney, Mike Cody. "About all we can do is try to deter others from committing the same crime, take that person convicted off the streets and try to keep conditions in prisons as humane as possible."

Cody is merely echoing the Justice Department's position, which also is reflected in the recodifying bill, S. 1437. Justice Department officials contend that "our behavioral scientists do not yet know of any reliable means of inducing rehabilitation of prisoners, nor can they provide a means of identifying an individual who has become rehabilitated." Even if this is so, is it adequate reason to push aside what hasn't really been tried? And shouldn't rehabilitation — if given a chance to work — help save the public more than tax dollars by helping keep down the number of repeat offenders?

THE SENATE bill is right to aim at ending disparities in sentencing, caused primarily by the piecemeal passage of criminal laws. Persons convicted of similar crimes currently may be sentenced under different statutes with varying penalties, and federal judges have no adequate guidelines to determine what is or isn't fair. The result too often is indeterminate sentences, imposed with prisoners knowing only the maximum time they are to serve until parole official are satisfied of their rehabilitation. The byproduct is uncertainty and bitterness for prisoners, who have little chance for rehabilitation under a sentencing system they see as unjust.

The bill also would specify fine levels, substantially higher than those in current law, and would allow judges to consider ability to pay before levying them. Included are provisions to increase corporate fines, now primarily wrist-slaps for those convicted of illegal campaign contributions, price fixing and so forth. Finally, it would establish a needed program to compensate the victims of violent federal crimes.

But regardless of its merits, the Senate bill is wrong to rank rehabilitation as our prisons' last priority. Rehabilitation hasn't been happening because it hasn't been given a chance. It's time it got one.

The Times-Picayune
New Orleans, La., April 8, 1977
Release To Work

Most of the inmates of penal institutions some day will be returned to society for the simple reason that a vast majority of them will not be confined for the balance of their lives.

If this fact is kept in mind, some of the recommendations made by visitors who will be attending today's symposium in New Orleans on "Progress in Criminal Justice — By Whose Standards" appear to make good sense.

The suggestions are from Keith Mossman, a member of the committee on corrections and correctional facilities of the American Correctional Association, William Leake, president of the American Correctional Association, and U.S. Rep. Tom Railsback, an Illinois Republican.

Fundamentally all three believe that some prisoners, with the accent on "some," should be released from incarceration on a probationary basis and permitted to enter the labor market, thus shifting the burden of paying for their room and board from the taxpayers to themselves.

While conceding that "there are dangerous people who should be and have to be confined," Mr. Mossman is of the belief that a large percentage of the prison population could be placed on probation or in "restitution homes."

Mr. Leake, who is a commissioner in the South Carolina Department of Corrections, reports that more and more corrections officials are leaning toward restitution programs under which prisoners work and reimburse the victims of their crimes. Such programs appear to be working in Georgia and Minnesota, he says.

Granting that there are those offenders for whom the only solution is to lock them up and throw away the key, there is another just as reasonable solution for the rest.

That is to return them as soon as prudently possible to the free society of law abiding citizens.

Newsday
Garden City, N.Y., July 10, 1977
Is Criminal Rehabilitation an Unrealistic Goal?

A rehabilitated criminal behaves in accordance with society's rules not because he *has to* in order to get out of prison but because he *wants to*. The carrot and stick approach—early release in return for good behavior and a satisfactory prison work or study record—gives the appearance of rehabilitation according to the first definition. Unfortunately, today's prisons do a poor job with true rehabilitation in the second mode.

This, in part, accounts for the high degree of recidivism. It also accounts for a time-serving system that seems totally unfair and arbitrary whether viewed from the inside or the outside. And that's why an increasing number of liberals are coming around to the conservative view that incarceration primarily should be punishment. Among them is Senator Edward Kennedy (D-Mass.), who in today's Ideas section makes a strong case for changes in parole and sentencing policies as part of revisions of the federal criminal code.

But if punishment is to serve as a deterrent, it must be administered swiftly and fairly. The present procedure is ill suited for either. Study upon study has shown vast differences in the punishment meted out to different individuals with similar backgrounds committing similar crimes under similar circumstances. Within the minimum and maximum ranges declared by the court, a parole board usually has wide latitude in actually determining the length of the sentence. That determination is usually based on the degree of "rehabilitation" exhibited by a prisoner. Small wonder they try to make the parole board believe the lesson has stuck.

We're not arguing, of course, against providing the opportunities for social and vocational or educational rehabilitation within the prison system. If anything, they should be broadened. But they should not be mandatory, nor should release be conditioned upon participation. That means, in essence, an end to indeterminate sentencing.

That concept lies at the heart of a simplified reform of the federal criminal code introduced by Kennedy and John McClellan, a conservative senator from Arkansas. They have excised many of the most controversial features from the original bill, the so-called S.1, an enormously complicated and lengthy attempt to rewrite, codify and add to the loose collection of statutes that now passes for a federal criminal code.

Eventually, Congress will have to deal with the issues the Kennedy-McClellan bill omits. Meanwhile, it's a sensible approach to dealing with crime and criminals as fairly and realistically as possible. We urge Congress to get on with a reform job that's been in the making for more than a decade.

The Chattanooga Times

Chattanooga, Tenn., June 11, 1977

Cutting the Prison Load

At a time when the nation's prisons are literally bursting at the bars, programs to reduce the crush are coming into increasing disfavor. Legislators as well as local residents are showing less and less willingness to push the decentralization of inmate populations through regional prisons. Parole and work-release projects are under fire because the rate of recidivism is high under inadequate supervision and poor planning.

The need to relieve overcrowded prisons is great. Figures gathered by the Law Enforcement Assistance Administration show a record number of 283,145 in state and federal custody at the end of last year. The total was an increase of 29,329 in a single year, and included 7,738 prisoners held in local jails because state institutions were too full to house them.

The LEAA insists, however, there is hope in a properly conducted program for supervision of prisoners, some on early release, who have good prospects for steady jobs before they leave the prison gates.

A pilot project in San Francisco, involving prison rehabilitation departments, probation personnel, local enforcement officers and representatives of private business, has shown a marked degree of success in establishing released prisoners as productive members of society. Only 1.1 per cent of ex-offenders enrolled in the program have committed a crime and returned to prison.

The essential ingredient is the assurance of help in finding full-time work in advance of release. "An ex-offender who gets a job shortly after release from prison is five times more likely to complete parole than an ex-offender who has not had assistance in locating a job," officials say.

The process starts with work training in prison, opportunity for interviews with prospective employers, medical or dental work to increase the chances for acceptance, and help with minor expenses if necessary until the first post-prison paycheck is received.

The cost has not been excessive. A LEAA grant of $89,000 for 18 months has financed a program serving 1,500 ex-prisoners a year. The investment could pay off beyond measure if the tentative results prove a reliable index.

The Birmingham News

Birmingham, Ala., July 14, 1977

Corrections Quandary

A few years ago a consensus existed in enlightened circles that given enough money and the proper facilities, America could solve its immense crime problem by rehabilitating criminals.

Alabama is certainly not one of those states which has given rehabilitation its best effort. While other states were innovating and upgrading their corrections policy, Alabama was putting barely enough money into its system to warehouse its offenders. Yet, in the states which have spent the most on facilities and programs, recidivism rates are not any better than those here.

Exceptions can be cited, of course. If you screen the entire prison population for those most likely to be rehabilitated and put this "cream" of the system into one program, that program will have greatly reduced recidivism statistics. But that doesn't really help anything but the egoes of those who direct the special programs. The percentage of those in the system as a whole who will repeat criminal offenses after getting out of prison remains high.

Problems are also being seen in probation and parole. A story recently by a Chicago Daily News wire service reported the frustrations of a probation officer. That officer told of case after case in which persons had committed serious offenses but who were put on probation. The officer said he had 300 such cases to monitor, an impossible assignment. He said that if he knows that a probationer has violated his probation, it takes four months to get the offender off the street and into prison. Four months, that is, under ideal conditions. The red tape is such, however, that even longer delays are frequent.

Recent thinking in criminology has favored probation as one of numerous ways to divert offenders from the prison system. According to this line of thinking, prison is so destructive that it is best to try to rehabilitate the offender without incarcerating him. But probation and other means of diversion, even special centers emphasizing counseling and training, don't always work.

Parole is also under scrutiny. Senate hearings on the revision of the federal criminal code have questioned procedures under which offenders are given indeterminate sentences subject to parole. Opponents of parole range from Atty. Gen. Griffin Bell to the American Civil Liberties Union, from liberal Sen. Edward M. Kennedy to conservative Sen. Roman L. Hruska. These opponents have come to believe that penology has not developed reliable means either of rehabilitating criminals or judging when they are rehabilitated.

Benjamin Ward, New York Corrections Commissioner, called parole "a noble experiment that failed."

The alternative to parole is fixed sentences uniformly applied. No one expects fixed sentences to be a panacea, but it is felt that frictions in prisons among inmates and administrators would be reduced if everyone serves the same time for a given offense.

★★★

ONE PRINCIPLE of corrections seems to hold up best under scrutiny: The certainty of punishment is the best deterrent to crime.

Unfortunately, we have so much crime in this country that the criminal justice system often cannot cope with the volume of cases.

The police are often criticized for not being effective enough in apprehending criminals, but of the entire system, policemen are probably doing the best job.

The courts are so clogged with cases that most never come to trial. The typical case involves plea bargaining, in which a defense attorney pleads his client guilty in exchange for a conviction on a lesser charge. The criminal gets a break right there, and is given another indication that the criminal justice system is soft on crime.

If given probation, the offender is practically encouraged to go out and commit other crimes. Even if sentenced, the criminal can look forward to time off for good behavior and an award-winning performance before a parole committee. With the prison system, especially in Alabama, filled to permissible capacity, the pressure is on the system not to punish the criminal according to the crime he has committed but to hustle him along in the briefest time possible and get rid of him so space will be made available for another inmate waiting in a county jail to get into a state prison.

The weak link in the criminal justice system is in prison capacity. Alabama prisons, especially, are severely limited in space. If the system cannot incarcerate all those who have been convicted of offenses, then there is no certainty of punishment.

If there were enough space in prisons, the next step would be to put more resources into the courts so that more cases could be prosecuted vigorously instead of plea-bargained.

As long as the public actively opposes the construction of new prisons, it is only adding to the problem. And crime is the worst domestic problem that we have.

THE PLAIN DEALER
Cleveland, Ohio, April 4, 1977
Her dream came true

Every month, four minibuses visit Ohio's prisons and deposit reassurance and hope, in the form of inmates' families and friends. An East Cleveland black woman, whose legal name is only Azadi, has made the visits possible for five years.

She has been the driving force supplying hope as rehabilitation incentive to hundreds of inmates in Ohio prisons. She supplements the state's rehabilitation efforts with essential intangibles in the form of people who care. Her concern also extends to the families and friends whom she feels are being penalized if they are unable to visit.

The People's Busing Program Inc. was begun by the Black Panthers, but as their movement declined, a determined Azadi, often confined to a wheelchair by rheumatoid arthritis, took over and built the program from almost nothing.

Although she had no one in prison herself, she recognized the value of a visit from home, especially to blacks isolated in predominantly white locations of some state prisons.

With the motto, "Keeping Families Together," she launched the busing program with volunteers, donations and a lot of spunk. She was undeterred by harassment from prison guards and officials who had never seen such a project, probably did not understand its purpose and undoubtedly saw it as threatening.

In 1974, Azadi expanded the visits to juvenile detention centers. Prison trips began to include tours for persons 16 and older to give them a firsthand look at what it means to be locked up away from society, family and friends.

Today, People's Busing has two offices in Cleveland, one in Columbus and another under way in Cincinnati. The program is a national model. Azadi believes her emphasis on the family gives inmates a reason for working to stay out of prison once they are released.

"Crime," she once explained, "affects everybody — businessmen, housewives, kids at school. We can't afford crime, and we can't afford to pay tax dollars for a system that doesn't work." Our wishes for continued success to Azadi and her associates for advancing a system that does.

THE KANSAS CITY STAR
Kansas City, Mo., May 20, 1977
New View on Halfway Houses

The curtain has been drawn on hopes for legislation on halfway houses in the 1977 session of the Missouri Legislature.

Even though the sponsors were not successful this time, the effort paid some dividends. The discussions and hearings have stimulated governmental officials and halfway house managers to examine the objectives of these enterprises and how they might be improved.

Halfway houses are considered to be useful in the rehabilitation of criminals. Individuals on probation or parole and persons soon to be released from prison live in them under supervision. It is generally considered a transition period between incarceration and freedom. The idea is to help the ex-offender adjust to the return to society. Those who can find employment work in the day and return to the house at night. If the income is sufficient, the residents contribute toward their food and lodging expenses.

A proliferation of privately operated halfway houses has occurred in Missouri in recent years, especially in the urban areas. The state has contracted with some of them to house prisoners or former prisoners. Some of the houses are considered better than others in physical facilities and programs.

The over-all goal of the legislation was to set standards that would lead to greater uniformity for the halfway operations. One bill would have set up a new agency to co-ordinate the placement of offenders in the houses.

While there is merit in these proposed changes, some of the halfway house supporters and directors did not relish the legislation. They contended it would be a step toward an institutionalized setting, the very thing that halfway houses are designed to avoid. Advocates of the legislation pointed out that the standards could help to upgrade the houses.

The issue of halfway houses is important to the rehabilitation of prisoners. It will also become increasingly vital as the prison population, which is growing rapidly, overcrowds the facilities. It will become imperative in the years ahead, even with the buildings now planned, to have additional space for inmates. Halfway residences could be a factor in relieving pressure.

Thus the 1977 legislation has brought this matter to public attention. If halfway houses are to have a larger role in corrections, as it appears they will, it will be necessary to develop a state policy that will put them to the most effective use.

The Wichita Eagle
Wichita, Kans., April 12, 1977
Corporate Incarceration

We human beings are gung-ho for having the offenders in our midst punished, preferably by being locked up and out of our sight. During the months or years of incarceration, we assume, they will meditate and see the error of their ways, then return to us better citizens.

The only trouble — it's a problem knowing what to do with them while they're locked in. They need to be fed. If they get sick, they need to be given medical attention. They need to be given something to occupy their time — because haven't we always been taught that idle hands do mischief?

Modern penologists understand and accept all this and consider it part of their responsibility not only to look after the health of their prisoners but to try to rehabilitate them. One of the reasons a medium security prison has been advocated for Kansas is that it would provide a better environment for retraining programs than is possible in the penitentiary at Lansing.

Rehabilitation also is a major goal of the regional corrections center Judge Sam Mason has helped set up at Fort Scott.

But now an organization called Kansas Corrections Inc. wants to take over contract operation of Wichita's former Detention and Rehabilitation Center — also once known as the "P Farm."

Educational corporations sometimes administer teaching programs. A private contractor now operates Wichita's dog pound. School lunches are provided by a large catering company. . . .

But are we ready for corporate incarceration? It might work, but somehow the idea evokes memory of stories about old time bounty hunters who made their living chasing fugitives.

The organizers of Kansas Corrections Inc. undoubtedly are sincere in wanting to help both local government and whatever prisoners may be entrusted to their care.

But shouldn't prisoners continue to be the responsibility of the courts which mandated their punishment and corrections professionals? Would assignment to a contract jailer weaken a prisoner's legal rights? In case of a jail disturbance, would the corrections corporation accept responsibility for restoring control?

THE TENNESSEAN
Nashville, Tenn., October 23, 1977

'Comeback' Provides Link

A NEW non-profit organization is attempting to help ex-prisoners begin new lives for themselves in the Nashville area.

Appropriately called "Operation Comeback," the group has as one of its main goals finding jobs for the ex-convicts. Since May, when the organization began its work, it has placed almost 150 ex-inmates.

Ms. Theresa Cook, director of "Operation Comeback," said this part of the program has been so successful that several businesses have requested that more ex-prisoners be sent for job interviews.

Jobs are especially important if an ex-convict is to have a chance after getting out of prison. A job gives a former prisoner both a responsibility to shoulder and an opportunity to prove his or her worth.

"Equally important is having someone who will take a humane, active interest. Many former prisoners come from broken homes," Ms. Cook said. "They have no relatives, no parents and no spouse. They need someone they can relate to and rely on."

To meet these needs of the ex-inmates, "Operation Comeback" has a professional staff that offers counseling and also help in coping with minor crises, such as emergency housing.

The organization also trains volunteers from the community to work with some ex-convicts on a one-to-one basis. Although there are state probation and parole officers, many of these are carrying caseloads of 70 to 80 former prisoners and simply cannot spend the time that volunteers can.

"Operation Comeback" is a program that provides a link between the ex-convict and society. It is a link that is often missing, and the Nashville community should welcome and support this organization's efforts.

THE ATLANTA CONSTITUTION
Atlanta, Ga., April 12, 1977

Helping Ex-Offenders

The argument continues over how to deal with criminals in our society. On the one side are those pushing the hard line. Lock 'em up and throw away the key, they say. Others stress rehabilitation, training.

The latter approach must be the better way to go. Common sense shows that society benefits more when ex-offenders have job skills than when they don't. If an ex-offender has a skill, he has a chance to get a job. That means there is less chance of his committing a crime to get money.

Georgia Industrial Institute is one way for prisoners to acquire job skills. The institute has a training program that comes through a four-way effort. Participating are the state Department of Offender Rehabilitation, state Department of Human Resources, state Board of Education and state Labor Department. Together these organizations work at upgrading prisoners' educational levels and giving them skills to take outside.

The big question is does it work? According to a study by DHR, of the 80 prisoners who had vocational training at the institute five years ago, 68 of them are still on the job. That's 84 per cent, a great success rate in anyone's book.

It seems impossible to argue with success like that, but still the argument comes. It comes through our financially deprived prison systems. It comes also through the stigma that plagues ex-offenders (even first offenders) when hiring time comes.

A program like Georgia Industrial Institute is successful because it is the result of several groups pulling together. If rehabilitation of offenders is to be truly successful, generally, the same concerted effort must spread to the rest of society.

Roanoke Times & World-News
Roanoke Va., April 7, 1977

Giving Felons a Shock

Prisons usually fail to rehabilitate felons, and there is doubt anyway whether that should be a prime purpose of incarceration. On the other hand, locking people up for long periods can be very expensive: It can cost taxpayers $25,000 or more to provide one cell-space, and up to $5,000 to maintain a man or woman there for a year. And after the prisoner gets out, he or she may have become thoroughly acclimated to criminal thinking and habits.

Is there no middle way, no method that can turn imprisonment to better use for prisoner and society? Ohio thinks there is, and recently Indiana and Kentucky have followed its lead. Since 1965, Ohio has utilized "shock treatment" for certain felons, under which first offenders convicted of serious crimes can be released from prison within months. "The rationale," recently wrote John W. Shoemaker, chief of the Ohio Adult Parole Authority, "is that a short dose of harsh prison life is enough to deter most people from future criminal activity."

In the winter issue of *State Government*, publication of the Council of State Governments, Mr. Shoemaker explained how the program works. Since 1965, judges have been allowed to release offenders within 130 days: "shock probation." Since 1974, the state's parole board has been allowed to grant release after six months: "shock parole."

The success rate of shock probation in Ohio is claimed to be 85 per cent; that is, only 15 per cent of some 7,000 prisoners given this early release have been returned to prison because of further criminality or for a parole violation. With shock parole, granted so far to 1,550 prisoners, the success rate is close to 90 per cent.

Mr. Shoemaker says the method saves many millions of dollars on prison costs and on welfare expenses for families of prisoners the state would have to support. He adds:

In the United States today, there are 250,000 prisoners in state and federal penal institutions. Typically, in the course of a year, about 96,000 will be released. The question then is not whether to release or not, but to release at the right time . . . . Another argument for shock treatment is that it decreases the chances of prisoners becoming hardened and embittered. By early release, the prisoner avoids the typical contamination by seasoned criminals and is released before he becomes part of the inmate subculture. . . .

The system has had hitches. Although Ohio law is supposed to deny shock treatment to a murderer, dangerous offender or a repeater, in 1974 it allowed parole to be granted to 279 armed robbers, 91 burglars and two rapists who had served less than nine months of their sentences. Public outcry against loose use of the method led to a cutback by state officials—reminiscent of the reaction in Virginia a few years ago against over-utilization of work-release for criminals.

No infallible way of dealing with human beings who have shown antisocial behavior has been developed. Shock treatment as employed in Ohio is only one method. But it is reasonable to expect that many non-dangerous first offenders who have had no idea of the consequences of crime would be permanently deterred from a brief brush with the harsh reality of prison. Virginia and other states might consider adding some form of this method to their correctional tool chests.

Honolulu Star-Bulletin

Honolulu, Hawaii, November 28, 1977

Prison Furloughs Mustn't Be Abused

The public probably will back the State Corrections Division in the decision to continue the prison furlough program despite a Thanksgiving Day shooting incident involving a furloughed prisoner.

But support for humanitarian programs, such as the prison furlough program, erodes every time something goes wrong, and that is only natural.

The Corrections Division is on a spot. Too many wrong calls in judging which prisoners are safe for furlough, or even one serious one, will bring demands that the releases stop entirely.

Furloughs are not a "right" for prisoners to claim. They are a special privilege. They are justified only if they help in rehabilitation and readjustment to life outside prison.

The public will not and should not tolerate them if they lead to innocent people being victimized. That is a message that needs to get home to the prisoners who benefit from the program as well as to the corrections administrators.

The Providence Journal

Providence, R.I., December 22, 1977

Furloughs and public safety

Recent publicity given the prisoner furlough program at the Adult Correctional Institutions has stirred anger across the state. Feelings are running high, and everyone concerned might try to see this situation in perspective, so that things aren't made worse.

Furloughs — short periods of time away from prison for selected inmates — are now widely accepted as a valuable penological device. The chance for a furlough works as an incentive for an inmate's good behavior within the prison, as former Gov. Philip W. Noel (himself hardly a softie on these matters) has said. Furloughs also can be useful as a guide to those inmates who someday may be able to return to society.

The ACI's furlough program has been working since July of 1975 with few problems and virtually no public outcry. During that period, 4,202 leaves were granted; only 13 furloughed inmates failed to return voluntarily (all of these were recaptured); and only four of all those on furlough were known to have committed crimes while on release. As Corrections Director Bradford E. Southworth noted the other day, these figures reflect "a pretty damned good percentage of success."

The ACI program also has drawn praise from outside experts. Last year, a study of prison furlough programs across the country, made for the U.S. Law Enforcement Assistance Administration, concluded: "If all the states ran their programs as Rhode Island does, there would be no need for us to be doing this research project on furloughs. It will be my recommendation that the other states use your program as a model by which to operate."

Despite all this, publicity of the program's details has stirred wide public opposition, and the reason is clear: At least a few among the 62 inmates approved for Christmas furloughs are known vicious criminals whose freedom might endanger the public's safety. This fact has raised questions (from Governor Garrahy and others) about how inmates are evaluated before furloughs are approved.

This question — how wisely do prison officials use their discretion in approving furlough requests? — is the core of the current problem. In all likelihood, the potentially dangerous inmates (those whose names stir immediate public clamor) are only a small fraction of the group of 62. Yet the truly dangerous inmates in this group, however few, may represent a risk to peace and calm in the outside community. This is why police departments have been uneasy, and it is why the furlough-evaluation process deserves prompt and critical scrutiny. In their enthusiasm for rehabilitation, prison officials may forget that incarceration is for the protection of society as well as for punishment of crimes committed.

It would be useful if Allen F. Breed, the court-appointed special master now studying the ACI, could give his assessment of how well (or badly) the prison's classifications board uses its discretion in deciding who will get furloughs and who won't. It would helpful if prison officials would subject each furlough applicant to a psychological screening program (if this is not now being done), since an inmate's behavior record may not always reveal stresses built up since his incarceration.

In the reappraisals now under way, however, officials need to guard against throwing the baby out with the bath. Concerns over furloughs for a few clearly dangerous felons cannot be allowed to wreck what has been proven to be a generally solid program. In his understandable concern for allaying the public's fears, Governor Garrahy, as he studies the program, would do well to reflect on this past success.

Index

A

AGNEW, V.P. Spiro 271
ALABAMA
  Crime compensation 256
  Prisons 261
AMERICAN Bar Association
  Crime compensation 253
  Federal criminal code codification
    173, 176
  Grand juries 115, 117–118
  Marijuana decriminalization 60,
    87–88
  Prisoner rights 261
AMERICAN Civil Liberties Union
  Capital punishment 230, 232–233,
    237
  Criticisms of 164–165
  Prisons 265
AMERICAN Medical Association
  Marijuana laws 60, 87–88
ARIZONA
  Sentencing 199
ARKANSAS
  Parole 282
  Prisons 267
ATTICA State Prison
  Causes for rebellion 261, 268
  Compared to My Lai & Kent State
    270
  Generally 268–273
  Parole 278
  Population 262
  Rehabilitation 278

B

BAIL
  Bail bondsmen 114
  Effects of bail denial 91
  Generally 91, 113–114
  Pre–trial release 113
  Reason for 91
BATES v. State Bar of Arizona see
  Supreme Court
BAXTER v. Palmigiano see Supreme
  Court
BAYH, Sen. Birch 42–43, 46–47
BAZELON, Judge David L.
  On roots of crime 12
  On mandatory sentencing 182
BECCARIA, Cesare 182, 205
BELL, Attorney General Griffin B.
  Crime rate 19
  Crime statistics 22
  Federal court judges 131, 133–135
  Grand jury reform 115, 117
  LEAA 35–38
  Parole 279, 284–285
BENTHAM, Jeremy 259
BERGMAN, Bernard 179
BETO, George 218
BLACKMUN, Justice Harry
  148–149, 213
BOUNDS v. Smith see Supreme
  Court
BOURNE, Peter 60, 78–82, 87
BRADFORD, William 205
BRADY v. United States see
  Supreme Court

BRENNAN, Justice William J.
  95–95, 100–102, 104, 210
BREWER v. Williams see Supreme
  Court
BUCK, Martha 245
BURGER, Chief Justice Warren
  89–90, 96-98, 100, 102, 104–112,
  119, 123–131, 134, 140,
  159–160, 210, 213–215, 217
BURKE, Edmund 207

C

CALIFORNIA
  Crime compensation 25, 255, 257
  Lawyers 150
  Parole 194, 283
  Plea bargaining 141
  San Francisco, schools 46
  San Jose 21
  Sentencing 194–195
CALLISTER, Judge E. Talbot
  202–204
CAMUS, Albert 211, 235, 245
CAPITAL Punishment
  Aggravating factors 219
  Arbitrary & capricious 219–220,
    223, 235
  As deterrent 206
  Canadian view 235, 37
  Certainty of punishment 243–246
  Death row count 222–223
  Discriminatory nature 207, 212,
    236–237, 243–244
  Effect on juries 243–244
  England 205, 207–208, 228–229
  Equal protection 240
  Generally 205–246
  History of 205, 231
  Homocide statistics 234
  International perspective 208
  Mandatory death sentences 207
  Mandatory death penalty 238–242
  Opinion polls 205, 221
  Public executions 208, 225–237
  Rape 206, 243–246
  Recidivism among murderers 206
  Resumption of in U.S. 230–237
  Retribution 237
CAREY, Gov. Hugh 283
CARTER, Pres. Jimmy 60, 78–88,
  119, 131, 133–134
CAUSES of Crime
  Alcohol 9
  Biological 8
  Child abuse 9
  Guns 9
  Media influence 12
  Narcotic addiction 9
  Poverty 14
  Psychological 8–9
  Rand study 11, 20, 57
  Samenow, Stanton & Yochelson,
    Samuel study 11
  Social 8
  Unemployment 9
CLARK, Att. Gen. Ramsay 271
CLEAVER, Eldridge 271
CLUTCHETTE v. Procunier see
  Supreme Court

COHEN, Rep. William S. 24
COKER v. Georgia see Supreme
  Court
COKER, Ehrlich Anthony 243
COLORADO
  Prisons 264
CONNECTICUT
  Crime compensation 256
CONYERS, Rep. John 24
CORNUELLE, Herbert
  Discussion of Honolulu crime 13
CORRUPTION,
  Swiss view of U.S. 12
COURTS
  Access 119–120, 124–125,
    140, 274–276
  Caseload 119, 123–128, 138,
    186–187
  Diversity jurisdiction 120, 124–125
  Enforcement of narcotic laws 71–73
  Federal judges 119, 123–128
  Integration orders 140
  Sentencing disparity 195–196
  Speedy Trial 123, 138–139
CRIME
  Apprehension 7
  Causes of 8, 191, 194, 242
  Definition of 7
  Foreign 12, 28
  Monetary costs 8
  Psychological harm 258
  Racial factors 7
  Rural 8, 13
  Study of international crime by Leon
    Radzinowicz & Joan King 12
  Surburban 21
  Turkey 12
  White-collar 7–8
CRIME Compensation
  Congressional proposal 189–190,
    248–253
  Generally 243–258
CRIME Prevention
  Career criminals' program 38
  Community organizations 14–17, 38
  Elderly 17
  Identification program 15
  READ program for juveniles 55
CRIME Statistics
  FBI 7, 20–22
  Gallup Poll 7
  Juvenile Delinquency 39
  LEAA 7
  Reliability of 7, 19, 22
  School crime 42–47
  Unreported crimes 7
CRIMINAL Defendants,
  Rights of 96–112, 115–118
  Right to counsel 89
  Self-incrimination 89–90
  Supreme Court review 119
CRUEL and Unusual Punishment see
  also Capital Punishment
  Definition of 205–206

D

DERSHOWITZ, Alan 181
DETERRENCE
  Capital punishment 206, 230-237

Drug laws 62, 63–73
Effect of sentencing 180–181
Marijuana laws 78–88
Public executions 225–229
Solution to crime 14
Study of N.Y. mandatory drug
   sentence law 71–73
DICKENS, Charles 208, 259
DOSTOEVSKY, Fyodor 235
DOUGLAS, Justice William O. 212
DUPONT, Robert L. 60

E

EDDY, Thomas 39
EILBERG, Rep. Joshua 118
ELLSBERG, Daniel 161, 174
EXCLUSIONARY Rule 89, 92–93,
   95–96

F

FEDERAL Criminal Law Codification
   Administration cover-ups 175
   Generally 161–178
   Labor union activity 165
   Limitations on political protest
      172–178
   Logan Act 165, 167, 170
   Marijuana revision 164–165, 167
   Nuremburg defense 161
   Official Secrets Act 161
   Parole 287
   Pornography 170
   Press freedom 171–172, 177
   S-1, generally 161–172
   Sentencing provisions 162–164,
      169
   Smith Act 161, 165, 170
FINES 247
FLORIDA
   Grand Juries 116
   Prisons 267
   Sentencing 200
FOOTE, Caleb 182
FORD, Pres. Gerald 74–77, 184–191
FOURTH Amendment 95–100
FOX, James A. 20
FRANKEL, Judge Marvin 197
FREUD, Sigmund 8
FURMAN v. Georgia see Supreme
   Court

G

GAGNON v. Scarpelli see Supreme
   Court
GEORGIA
   Atlanta, school crime 45
GILMORE, Gary
   Generally 230–237
   Literary rights 237
GOLDFARB v. Va. State Bar see
   Supreme Court
GRAND Juries
   Abuse 92–93, 115–118
   Bill of Rights 92–93
   Generally 91–93, 115–118
   History 91
   Racial prejudice 92
   Reform 92–93, 115–116
GREGG v. Georgia see Supreme
   Court
GREGG, James M. H. 22, 38
GRIFFIN v. Illinois see Supreme
   Court
GUNS
   Gun control 188–191
   Gun lobby 23–27
   House bill 23–27
   Massachusetts mandatory sentence
      9
   National Rifle Association 23–28
   Role in crime 23–28
   Saturday-night specials 24–27

H

HALFWAY Houses
   Cost 279
   Generally 279–280
   History 279
   Purposes 279–280
   Rehabilitation 289
   Success 279–280
HARRISON Act 59
HARRISON, Thomas R. 12
HAWAII
   Crime proposals & solutions 13
   Crime statistics 13
   Lawyers 151
   Marijuana 83
HAWKINS, Gordon 8
HEARST, Patricia 179, 202–204
HELMS, Sen. Jesse 154
HURTADO v. California see
   Supreme Court

I

IDAHO
   Juvenile delinquency 53
ILLINOIS
   Bail 114
   Capital Punishment 214, 239
   Chicago, school crime 43
   Crime compensation 255
   Prisons 263
   Sentencing 192
IN re Gault see Supreme Court
INDIANA
   Prisons 263
IOWA,
   Crime in 13
   Juvenile delinquency 51
   Plea bargaining 141

J

JOHNSON v. Avery see Supreme
   Court
JOHNSON, Judge Frank M. 261
JOHNSON, Dr. Samuel 228
JUDGES
   Merit selection 131–137
JUREK v. Texas see Supreme Court
JUREK, Jerry Lane 225, 236
JUVENILE Courts
   Chicago Reform Movement 39
   Confidentiality of criminal records
      53–54, 113
   Houses of Refuge 39
   Origins 39
   Parens patriae doctrine 39, 49
   Pre-trial adjudication 39
JUVENILE Delinquency
   Attacks on the elderly 57
   Causes of 55
   Congressional bill 43
   Curfews 57
   Demographic patterns 18–20, 57
   Effects of peer pressure 52
   Future outlook 18–20
   Illinois Dept. of Mental Health study
      52
   Rehabilitation 40
   Rights of juveniles 50
   School crime 42–47, 56
   Sex bias in prosecution 55
   Status offenders 51, 54, 57
   Treatment 40
   Youth gangs 54, 56, 58

K

KAMISAR, Yale 103
KANSAS
   Capital Punishment 210, 215
   Prison legal services 275
   Prisons 263

KENNEDY, Sen. Edward P.
   Federal court judges 133
   Federal criminal code codification
      161, 163–172
   Parole 282, 285
   Sentencing reform 198
KERNER Commission 7
KING, Joan 12
Krendel, Ezra S.
   Philadelphia crime study 16
KUNSTLER, William 273

L

LAW Enforcement Assistance
   Administration Center
   Center for National Securities
      Studies recommendation 30–33
   Closing offices 35, 38
   Crime statistics 22
   Criticisms of 29–38
   Criticisms of 29, 30–38
   Department of Justice 9
   Future outlook 9
   History 9–10
   Restructuring 35–38
   Senate position on 31
   Twentieth Century report 29–34, 38
LAWYERS
   Abundance of 144
   Access to 143
   Advertising 143, 147–151
   Alternatives 158–159
   Generally 143–160
   Legal Clinics 144
   Minimum-fee schedules 143,
      145–147
LEGAL Services Corporation
   Back-up Centers 156–157
   Generally 143, 152–157
LEVI, Att. Gen. Edward H. 191
LEVIN, Joseph J. 133
LOMBROSO, Cesare 8
LOUISIANA
   Prisons 261

M

McKAY, Robert B. 62, 195
MCKEIVER v. Pennsylvania see
   Supreme Court
Mc CLELLAN, Sen. John L. 163–172
MACONOCHIE, Alexander 277
MAINE
   Capital punishment 223
   Orrington, crime prevention 15
   Parole 283
MAPP v. Ohio, see Supreme Court
MARIJUANA see also Narcotics
   Arrests 60
   Criminal sanctions 59–60
   Decriminalization effort 60, 73,
      78–88
   Generally 78–88
   Health effects 81–82
   Moral effects 85
   N.Y. Mandatory Drug Sentence law
      70
MARSHALL, Justice Thurgood 90,
   95–96, 100–101, 104, 108, 205,
   210
MARYLAND
   Parole 286
MASSACHUSETTS
   Capital punishment 224
   Mandatory gun sentencing law 9
   Prisons 265
MENNINGER, Karl 8
MICHIGAN v. TUCKER, see
   Supreme Court
MICHIGAN
   Ann Arbor, schools 46
   Bail 114
   Detroit 16, 22
   Juvenile delinquency 50
   Juvenile justice system 48–49

Parole 285
Sentencing 199
MILLER, Herbert S. 274
MINNESOTA
Prisons 271
MIRANDA v. Arizona, see Supreme Court
MISSISSIPPI
Federal courts 135
MISSOURI
Halfway houses 289
Prison legal services 275
Prisons 263, 266
St. Louis 17
MITFORD, Jessica 180
MORRIS v. Schoonfield see Supreme Court
MORRIS, Norval 8, 191, 284
MORRISSEY, v. Brewer see Supreme Court
MUSKIE, Sen. Edmund 272

N

NARCOTICS *see also Marijuana*
Federal regulation 74–77
Harm of 74–77
History 59
Law enforcement problems 59, 61
New York State 59, 61–73
Study of N.Y. mandatory drug sentence law 71–73
NEW Left 271
NEW Mexico
Prisons 264
NEW YORK STATE
Crime compensation 248
Mandatory drug sentence law 59, 62–73
New York City,
Harlem 13
school 45–46
subway & bus crime 17
Parole 277, 283
Sentencing 57, 197
NIXON, Pres. Richard 102, 152–157
NORTH Carolina
Prison legal services 276

O

OHIO
Akron 17
Cincinnati 21
Juvenile delinquency 50
Legal Services Corporation 156
Prisoners' right to counsel 274
Prisons 266
Sentencing 200
Toledo, myth of downtown crime explosion 14
OKLAHOMA
Juvenile delinquency 53
Oklahoma City 19
Parole 281
Prisons 263
OREGON v. Mathieson see Supreme Court
OREGON
Lawyers 150
Marijuana decriminalization 60
Portland 21
OSWALD, Russell 270–271, 273

P

PAROLE
Conditions of 277
Experimental programs 290
Federal law 198
Furloughs 291
Generally 277–291
History 277
Indeterminate sentences 278

New York study, 278–279
Parole officers 278–279, 281
Pleading guilty 278
Prisoner objections to 194
Recidivism rates 279
Rehabilitation 286–289
Revocation 277–278
Right to counsel 278
Sentencing determination 179–180
Work-release 287–288
PENNSYLVANIA
Bail 114
Marijuana decriminalization 73–81
Philadelphia 16
Pittsburgh 16
Sentencing 196–197, 201
PLEA Bargaining
Constitutionality 120–121
Generally 120–21, 141–142
Georgetown University study 141
POLICE
Apprehension of offenders 179
Brutality 7
Capital punishment 238–242
Community relations 16
Deterrent value 16
Discretionary powers 7, 181
Racial prejudice 7
POST-Conviction Relief
Supreme Court review 95
POWELL, Justice Lewis F. 95–96, 100, 112
PRESIDENT'S Commission on Law Enforcement and the Administration of Justice 7
PRISONS *see also individual states, Parole, Sentencing*
Access to courts 124–125
Alternatives to 11, 247, 251, 265–267, 279–280
As punishment 269
Assistance to ex-convicts 286
Community ties 289
Conditions 259–267, 272, 274–276
Construction costs 261
Corporate take-over 289
Cost of 180
Disciplinary hearings 260
Emphasis on custody 271
Foreign statistics 261
Generally 259–276
Guards 272–273
History 259, 272
Indeterminate sentences 180
Inmate grievances 260
Jail-house lawyers 274–276
Labor unions 275
Legal services 260, 274–276
Mandatory sentences 188
Maintenance costs 261
Overcrowding 33, 261–267
Population statistics 261
Purpose 259
Racial composition 271, 273
Rehabilitation 259–267
Work programs 290
PROFITT v. Florida see Supreme Court
PUGSLEY, Robert A. 236
PURSER, Police Chief I.G. 186

Q

QUAKERS
Capital punishment 205
Prison reform 259

R

RADZINOWICZ, Leon 12
RESTITUTION
Generally 243–258
RHODE ISLAND
Bail 113

Crime compensation 258
Prison furloughs 291
RITTER, Judge Willis 230
ROBERTS, Harry 238, 240
ROBERTS v. Louisiana see Supreme Court
ROCKEFELLER, Gov. Nelson
Attica role 268
Mandatory drug sentence law 59, 62–73
RODINO, Rep Peter 135
RUSSO, Rep. Martin A. 27

S

S-1 *see Federal Criminal Law Codification*
S-1437 *see Federal Criminal Law Codification*
SCOTT, Judge Charles R. 267
SEALE, Bobby 273
SEARCH and Seizures 89
SENTENCING *see also Parole*
Appeal of 127, 129–130
As cause of crime 200
Basis for determining 181, 196
Certainty of punishment 181
Cost of mandatory sentencing 201
Discretionary act 179
Disparity of sentences 202–204
Generally 179–204
History of 182
Indeterminate sentences 179–180
Mandatory gun sentence law 200
Mandatory sentences 129–130, 184, 186
Prison population 261
President's Crime Commission 186
Prosecutors role 181
Purposes of 179
Rehabilitation 187
White-collar criminals 179, 198–199
SOUTH Dakota
Crime compensation 253
STANLEY, Justin 254
STEWART, Justice Potter 15, 107–109, 111, 210, 216
SUPREME Court
Bates v. State Bar of Arizona 143
Baxter v. Palmigiano 261
Bounds v. Smith 260, 274
Brady v. U.S. 120
Brewer v. Williams 90, 105–112
Clutchette v. Procunier 61
Coker v. Georgis 243
Furman v. Georgia 205, 207
Gagnon v. Scarpelli 278
Goldfarb v. Virginia State Bar 143
Gregg v. Georgia 206, 219
Griffin v. Illinois 260
Hurtado v. California 92
In re Gault 40
Johnson v. Avery 260
Judicial review 212
Jurek v. Texas 219
McKeiver v. Pennsylvania 40
Mapp v. Ohio 89
Michigan v. Tucker 90
Miranda v. Arizona 89, 101–112
Morris v. Schoonfield 247
Morrissey v. Brewer 278
Oregon v. Mathieson 90
Profitt v. Florida 219
Roberts v. Louisiana 219, 238
Stone v. Powell 95
Tate v. Short 248
United States v. Calandra 93
United States v. Mandujano 93
United States v. Washington 93, 115
United States v. Wong 115
Williams v. Illinois 247
Wolff v. McDonnell 260
Wolff v. Rice 95
Woodson v. North Carolina 219
Younger v. Gilmore 260
Younger v. Harris 119

SWEDEN 277
SYMBIONESE Liberation Army 202
SZASZ, Thomas S. 9, 40

T

TAFT, Donald 7
TATE v. Short see Supreme Court
TAYLOR, Judge William 225–229
TELEVISION Media
  Effect on violence 225–229
TENNESSEE
  Crime compensation 249
  Nashville 17–18
  Prisons 264
TEXAS
  Crime compensation 254
  Fort Worth,
  crime prevention 15
  crime rate 19
  Public executions 225–229
  Sentencing 189
THOMPSON, Gov. James 192–193
TUCKER, Donald 116
TYDINGS, Joseph D. 135

U

U.S. v. Calandra, see Supreme Court
U.S. v. Mandujano see Supreme Court

U.S. v. Washington see Supreme Court
U.S. v. Wong, see Supreme Court
U.S. Attorneys
  Merit selection 127–128
UTAH
  Capital punishment 230–237
  Cause of crime 12
  Parole 283
  Prisons 266
  Sentencing 201
  Survey of inmates 12

V

VAN den Haag, Ernest 14, 57
VELDE, Richard W. 29, 31
VERMONT
  Crime rate 21
  Juvenile Delinquency 53
  Prisons 264
VICTIMS of Crime
  139, 190–191, 252, 256
VIRGINIA
  Capital punishment 230
  Juvenile delinquency 51
  Prisons 33
  Study of criminal justice system 11

W

WARD, Benjamin 130, 197, 284
WARREN, Chief Justice Earl 89,
  96–99, 101, 104, 106, 109, 236

WHITE, Justice Byron 95, 205, 243
WICKER, Tom 271
WIGGINS, Rep. Charles E. 252
WILLIAMS v. Illinois see Supreme Court
WILSON, James Q. 18, 20, 188, 284
WISCONSIN
  Capital punishment 236
  Parole 281
WOLFF v. McDonnell see Supreme Court
WOLFGANG, Marvin E.
  Philadelphia homicide study 9
WOMEN'S Groups 243–246
WOODSON v. North Carolina see Supreme Court
WYOMING
  Casper,
  crime prevention 15

Y

YOUNG, Mayor Coleman 16
YOUNGER v. Gilmore see Supreme Court
YOUNGER v. Harris see Supreme Court

Z

ZIRPOLI, Judge Alphonzo J. 121